Revit Architecture 2026 for Electrical Workers

Elise Moss

SDC PUBLICATIONS

SDC Publications
P.O. Box 1334
Mission, KS 66222
913-262-2664
www.SDCpublications.com
Publisher: Stephen Schroff

ISBN-13: 978-1-63057-794-0
ISBN-10: 1-63057-794-4

Printed and bound in the United States of America.

Preface

This book began with a call to Nancy Tremblay at Autodesk's Training Program. I am an Autodesk Certified Instructor. This means I am "on call" to provide training at Autodesk Training Centers and also to provide in-house corporate training on Autodesk software. Susan Bowron is an instructor for the IBEW Local 35 in San Leandro, CA. The union provides training to local electricians to provide them with the necessary skills to remain competitive in the job market. Susan wanted to provide a training class in Revit specific to electricians, so they could provide the necessary construction documentation to their clients. She needed an instructor and Nancy recommended me.

I was intrigued by the idea for a lot of reasons. Firstly, I am an avid Revit user. I started using Revit before it was an Autodesk software. I advocated Autodesk to acquire Revit to add to their offerings because I felt strongly that it was a major player in the BIM market. Secondly, I am a strong advocate for users and training. Knowledge is power. Learning the right skills is so very important in today's job market. It can make the difference between being able to feed your family and being homeless. I have seen the results in my own classrooms. Thirdly, I have always felt that the existing MEP training books are insufficient for many students like the members of the IBEW. They need step by step instructions and explanations behind why they are doing each step. This method has been the foundation for the types of books I write. Trying to make complex software and ideas accessible to users has been my primary goal.

Susan and some of her colleagues have reviewed the content in the text and provided valuable feedback.

I also am struck that in an era where people are calling for more women in STEM: Nancy, Susan, and I are all female. There are plenty of women in STEM, we just tend to work quietly to make things happen…like this textbook.

Acknowledgements

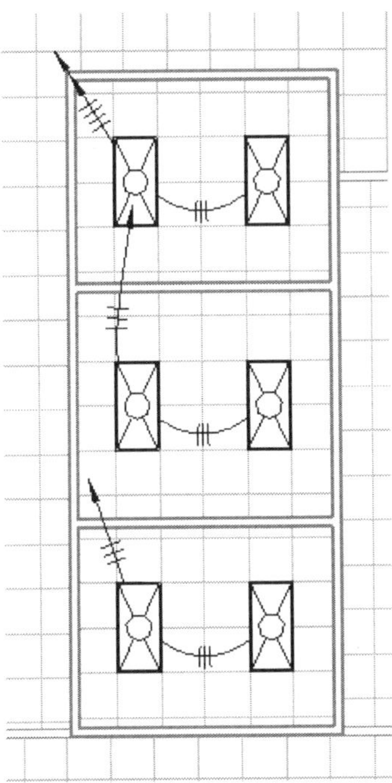

Feel free to email me if you have any questions, comments, or problems with any of the exercises in this text. I get email from all over the world and usually respond within twenty-four hours. My email address is elise_moss@mossdesigns.com.

I have been teaching for more than a decade. I started using AutoCAD in 1982 while I was still attending college. Even then, there was no doubt in my mind that Computer Aided Drafting, as it was called then, was the future of design. Revit continues to evolve, and its power continues to grow in the marketplace. My students amaze and inspire me every day. When I write my textbooks, I imagine one of my students sitting in front of me struggling, trying to figure out how to use a mouse, how to locate the right icon, and feeling frustrated with the effort, but not giving up. This text is intended for classroom use and for beginner learners.

This is the third edition of the text. The content has been expanded and adjusted based on feedback from electricians who attended training at the JATC in San Leandro, CA. Thanks to Kevin Meyer, Doug Rose, Tom Shimabukuro, Brett Hoffman, Christine Sigel, Anthony Barrera, Jack Waller, Emily Chen, Jeffrey Basque, and Susan Bowron. This text has improved thanks to these students. Revit 2026 has brought several improvements to the electrical tools and I have tried to adjust the exercises to include those new features.

Infinite thanks to Ari for his encouragement and his faith.

Elise Moss
San Jose, CA

Table of Contents

The Revit Interface

Go to Start→Programs→Autodesk → Revit 2026.

You can also type Revit in the search field under Programs and it will be listed.

When you first start Revit, you will see this screen. It is called the Revit Home page:

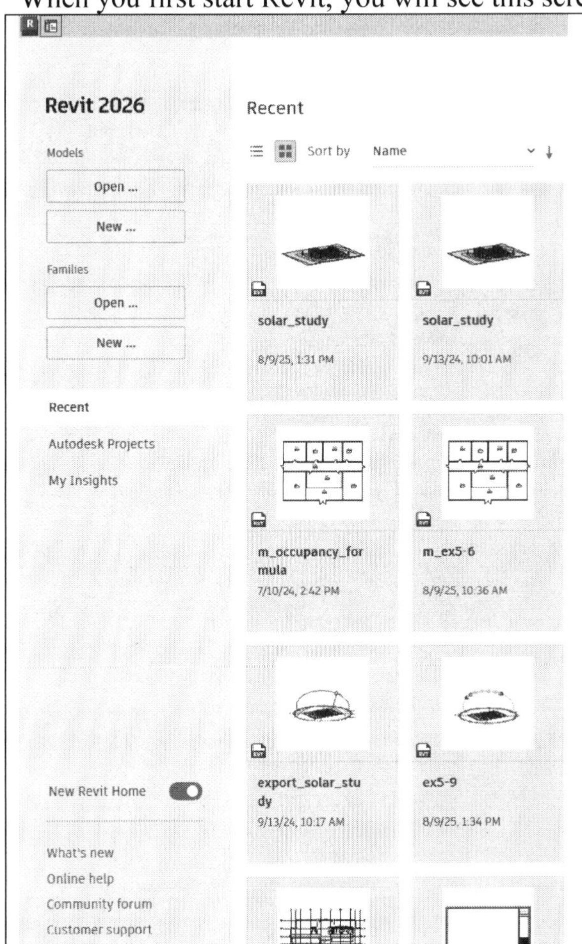

It is divided into three sections:

The Left section has two panels. The top panel is to Open or Start a new project. Revit calls the 3D building model a project. Some students find this confusing.

The bottom panel in the left section is used to open, create, or manage Revit families. Revit buildings are created using Revit families. Doors, windows, walls, floors, etc., are all families.

Recent Files show recent files which have been opened or modified as well as sample files.

There are Links to Autodesk Projects and My Insights.

Autodesk Projects is a cloud-based storage area provided by Autodesk. You can use this to collaborate with other team members, including outside vendors. Autodesk Projects leverages the Autodesk Construction Cloud application.

Autodesk Insights uses Autodesk AI to monitor your use of Revit and suggest commands and tools which may make your work more productive.

At the lower left, there are links for Online help and to connect to the Community forum, where you can post questions to other users.

You should be able to identify the different areas of the user interface in order to easily navigate around the software.

You have the ability to toggle access of the Revit Home or launching page on or off.

In the upper right of the Revit Home page, there is a search and filter tool that allows you to quickly locate files.

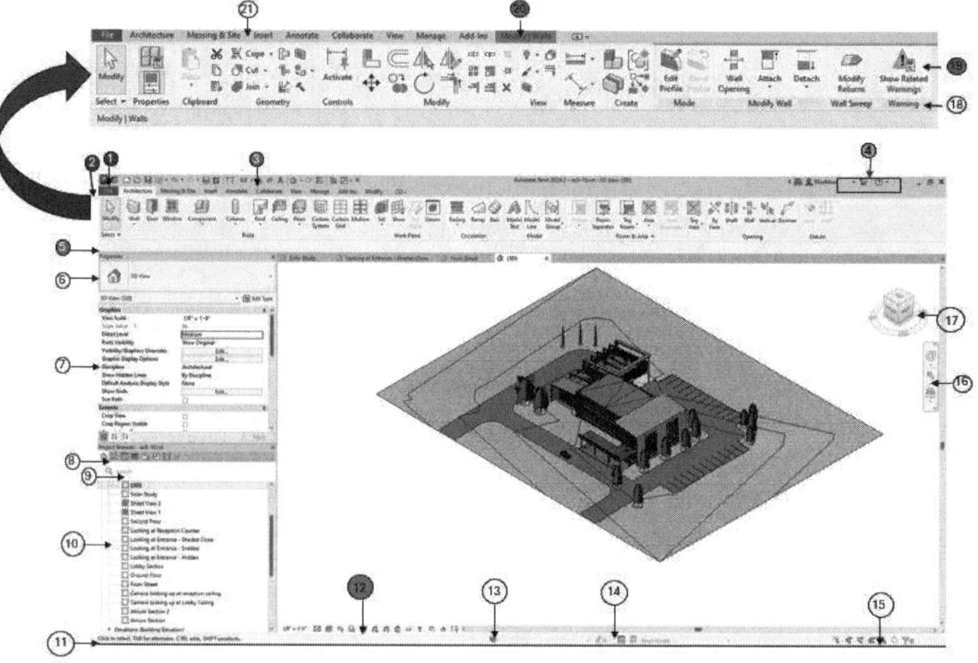

1	Revit Home	12	View Control Bar
2	File tab	13	Worksets
3	Quick Access Toolbar	14	Design Options
4	Search/Help	15	Selection tools
5	Options Bar	16	Navigation Bar
6	Type Selector	17	Viewcube
7	Properties Palette	18	Ribbon Panels
8	Project Browser Filters	19	Contextual Ribbon
9	Project Browser Search	20	Tools on the current tab of the ribbon
10	Project Browser	21	Ribbon Tabs
11	Status Bar		

The Revit Ribbon

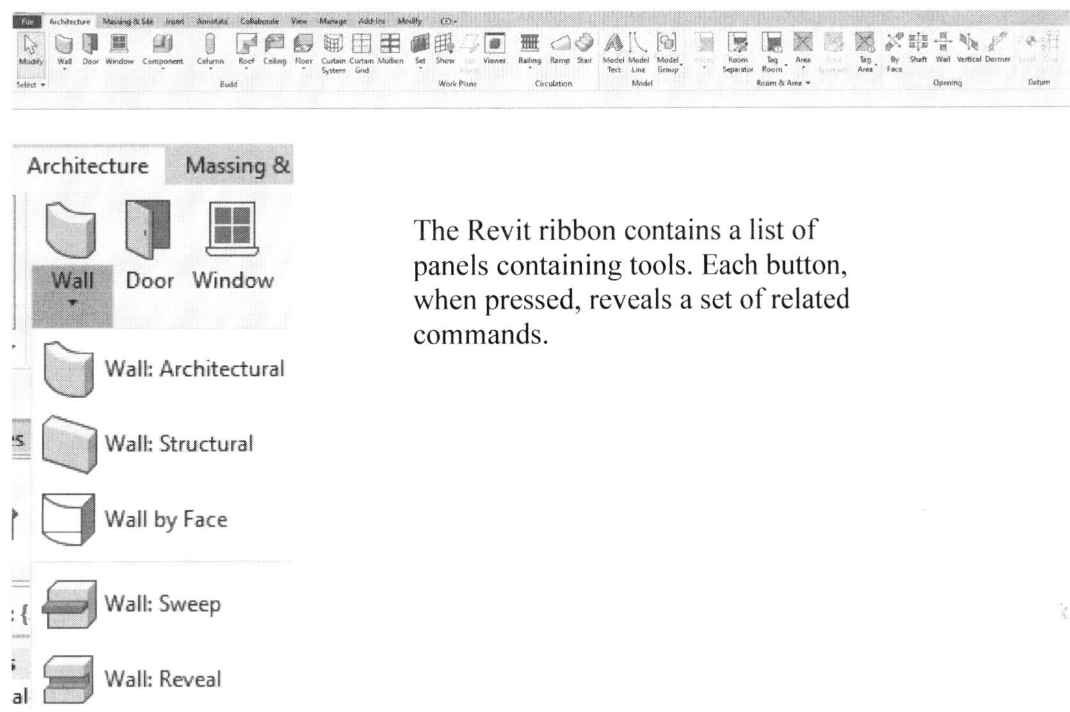

The Revit ribbon contains a list of panels containing tools. Each button, when pressed, reveals a set of related commands.

The Quick Access Toolbar (QAT)

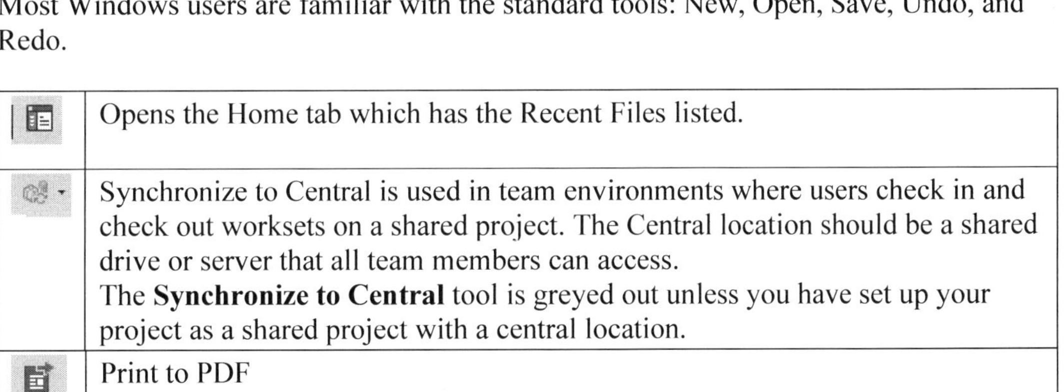

Most Windows users are familiar with the standard tools: New, Open, Save, Undo, and Redo.

	Opens the Home tab which has the Recent Files listed.
	Synchronize to Central is used in team environments where users check in and check out worksets on a shared project. The Central location should be a shared drive or server that all team members can access. The **Synchronize to Central** tool is greyed out unless you have set up your project as a shared project with a central location.
	Print to PDF
	Toggles the display of constraints, such as pins.
	Measure is used to measure distances.

	Places a permanent linear dimension.
	Tag by Category adds a label or symbol on doors, windows, equipment, etc.
	Adds annotation text to the current view.
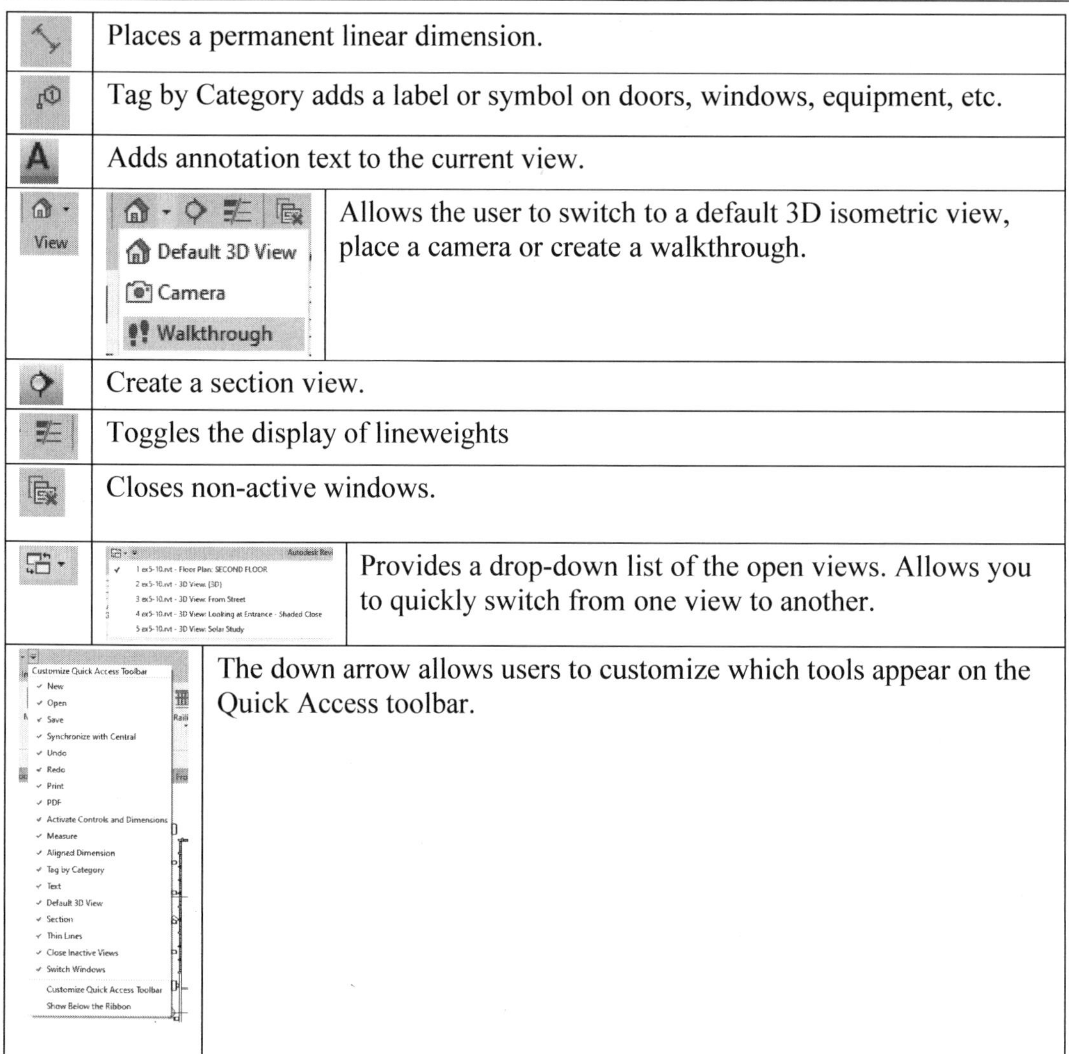	Allows the user to switch to a default 3D isometric view, place a camera or create a walkthrough.
	Create a section view.
	Toggles the display of lineweights
	Closes non-active windows.
	Provides a drop-down list of the open views. Allows you to quickly switch from one view to another.
	The down arrow allows users to customize which tools appear on the Quick Access toolbar.

Printing

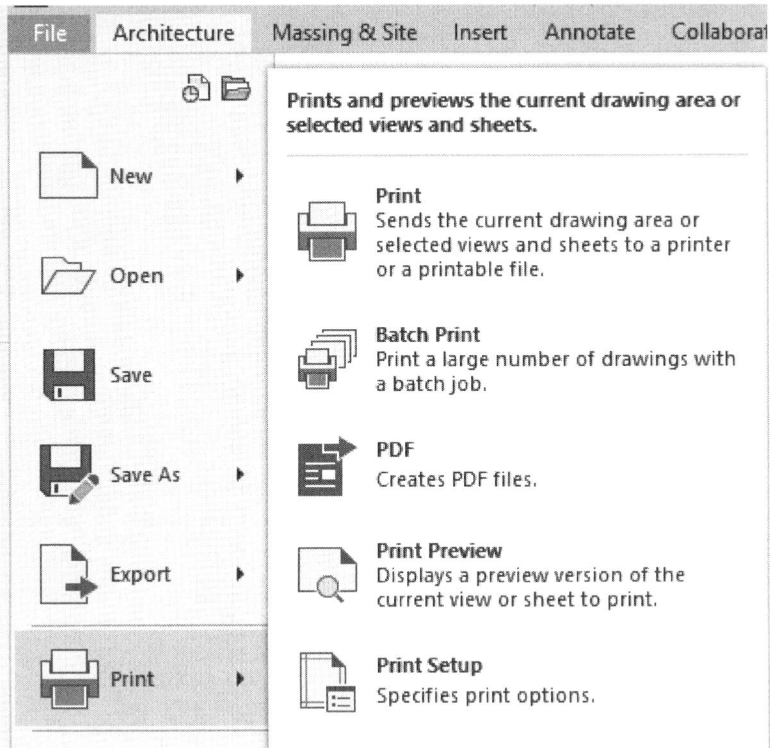

Print is located in the Application Menu as well as the Quick Access Toolbar.

The Print dialog is fairly straightforward.
Select the desired printer from the drop-down list, which shows installed printers.

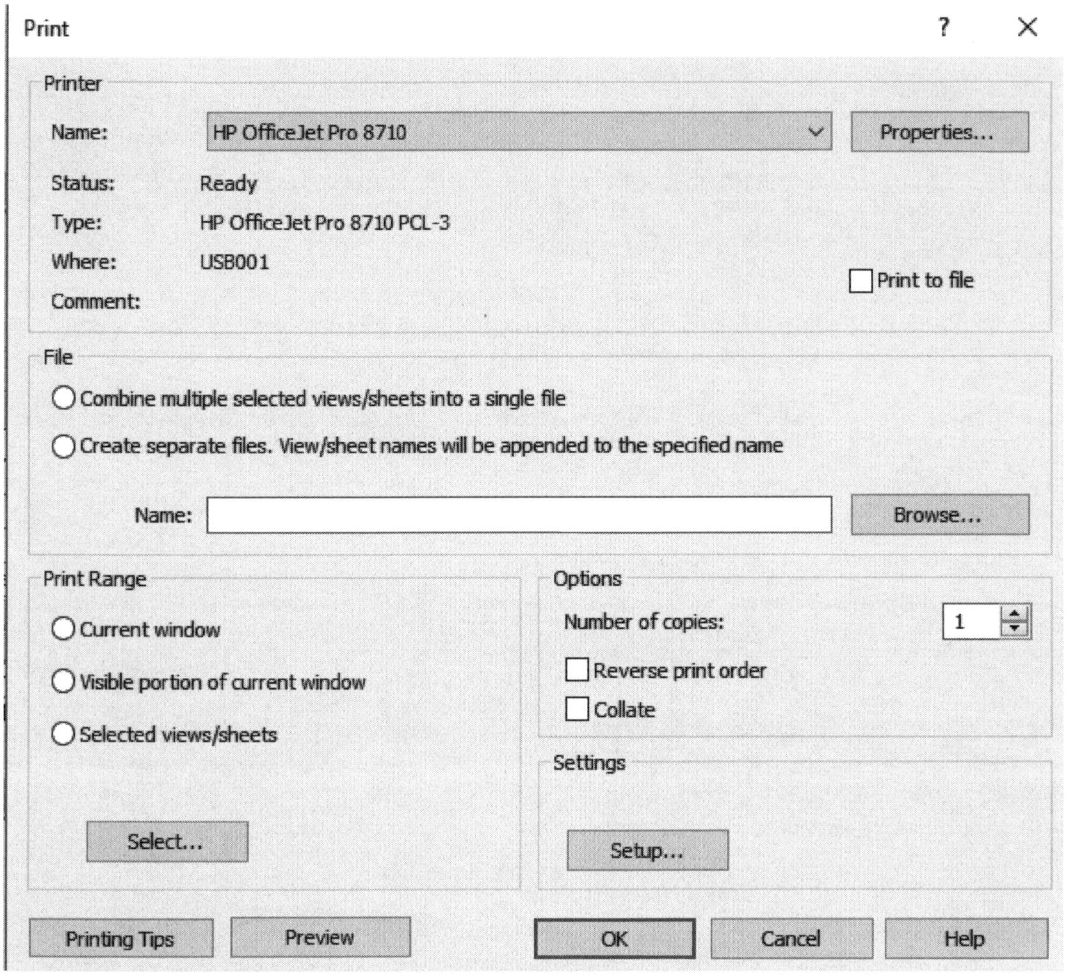

You can set to 'Print to File' by enabling the check box next to Print to File.
The Print Range area of the dialog allows you to print the current window, a zoomed in portion of the window, and selected views/sheets.

Undo

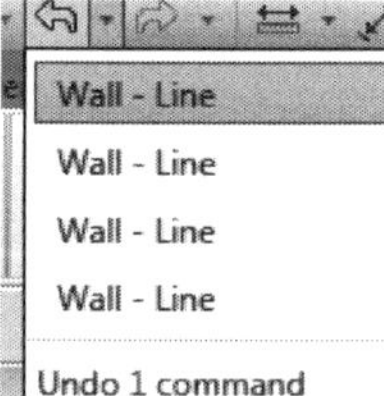

The Undo tool allows the user to select multiple actions to undo.
To do this, use the drop down arrow next to the Undo button; you can select which recent action you want to undo. You cannot skip over actions (for example, you cannot undo 'Note' without undoing the two walls on top of it).
Ctrl-Z also acts as UNDO.

Redo

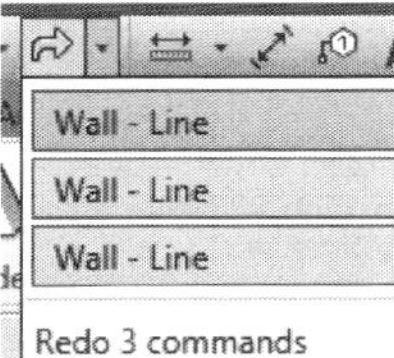

The Redo button also gives you a list of actions which have recently been undone. Redo is only available immediately after an UNDO. For example, if you perform UNDO, then WALL, REDO will not be active.

Ctrl-Y is the shortcut for REDO.

Viewing Tools

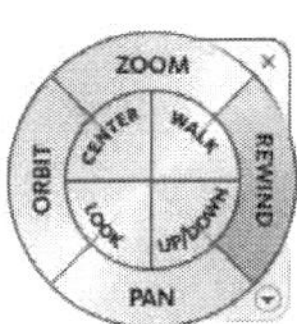

A scroll wheel mouse can replace the use of the steering wheel. Press down on the scroll wheel to pan. Rotate the scroll wheel to zoom in and out.

The Rewind button on the steering wheel takes the user back to the previous view.

Different steering wheels are available depending on whether or not you are working in a Plan or 3D view.

The second tool has a flyout menu that allows the user to zoom to a selected window/region or zoom to fit (extents).

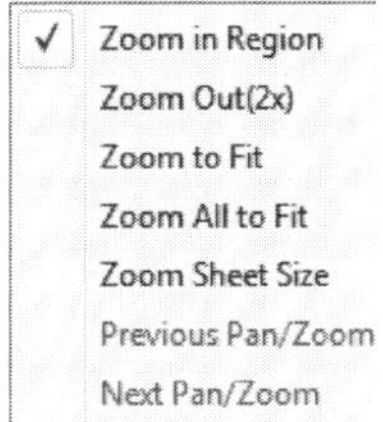

> Orient to a view allows the user to render an elevation straight on without perspective. Orient to a plane allows the user to create sweeps along non-orthogonal paths.

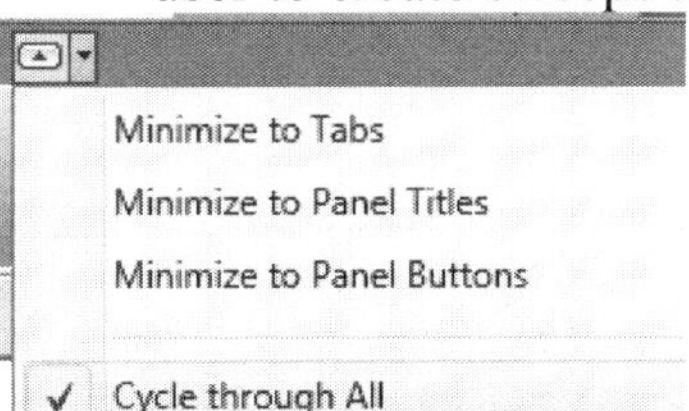

> If you right click on the Revit Ribbon, you can minimize the ribbon to gain a larger display window.

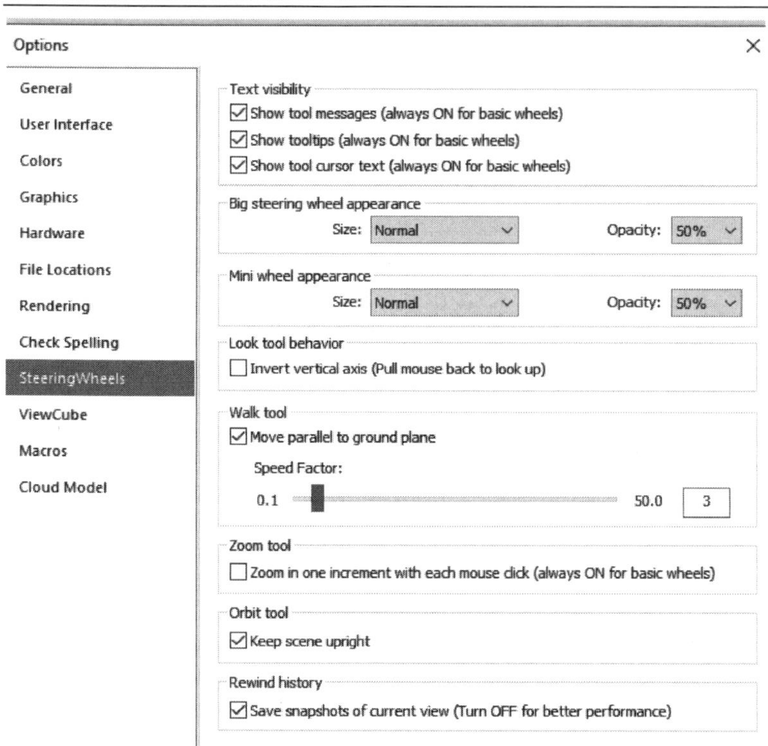

You can control the appearance of the steering wheels by right clicking on the steering wheel and selecting Options.

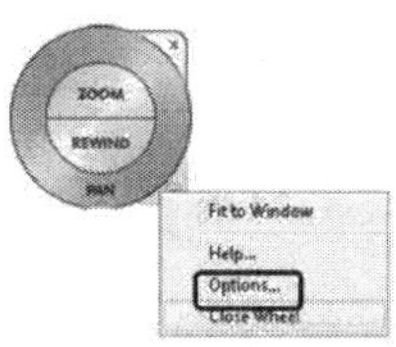

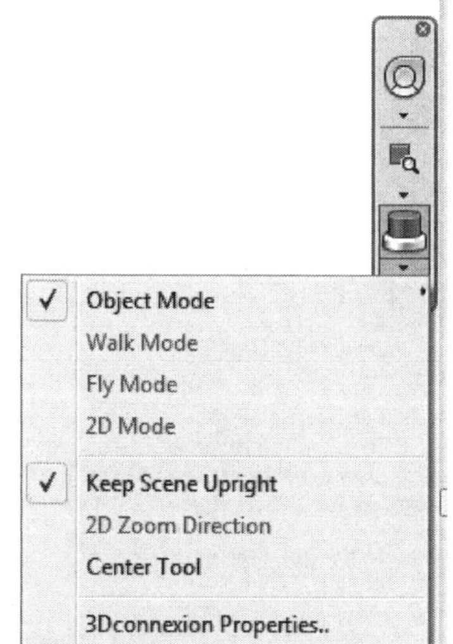

Some users have a 3D Connexion device – this is a mouse that is used by the left hand to zoom/pan/orbit while the right hand selects and edits.

Revit will detect if a 3D Connexion device is installed and add an interface to support the device.

It takes some practice to get used to using a 3D mouse, but it does boost your speed.

For more information on the 3D mouse, go to 3dconnexion.com.

Exercise 1-1:

Using the Steering Wheel & ViewCube

Drawing Name: *rac_basic_project.rvt*
Estimated Time: 30 minutes

Before learning how to start a project from scratch, we will be using practice files to help you understand Revit's interface and get comfortable with the tools available inside of Revit.

This exercise reinforces the following skills:

- ❑ ViewCube
- ❑ 2D Steering Wheel
- ❑ 3D Steering Wheel
- ❑ Project Browser
- ❑ Shortcut Menus
- ❑ Mouse

1.   Select Home from the QAT or press **Ctl+D**.

2. 

  Click **Open**.

3. Select the Sample Architectural Project file. The file name is *rac_basic_project.rvt*. *The file rac_basic_project is included with the Class Files available for download from the publisher's website. To download the Class Files, type the following in the address bar of your web browser:*
   SDCpublications.com/downloads/978-1-63057-794-0

4. 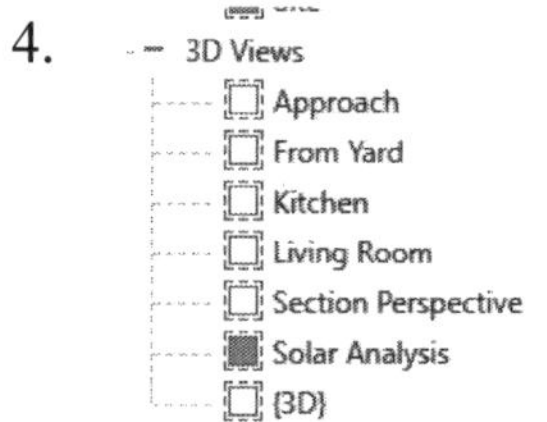
   In the Project Browser:
   Expand the 3D Views.
   Double left click on the {3D} view.
   This activates the view.
   The active view is already in BOLD.

5. 
   If you have a mouse with a scroll wheel, experiment with the following motions:
   If you roll the wheel up and down, you can zoom in and out.
   Hold down the SHIFT key and press down the scroll wheel at the same time. This will rotate or orbit the model.
   Release the SHIFT key. Press down the scroll wheel. This will pan the model.

6. 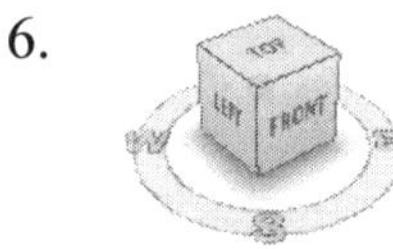
   When you are in a 3D view, a tool called the ViewCube is visible in the upper right corner of the screen.

   The Viewcube orientation mirrors the model orientation.

7. 
   Click on the top of the cube as shown.

   The display changes to a top or plan view.

8. 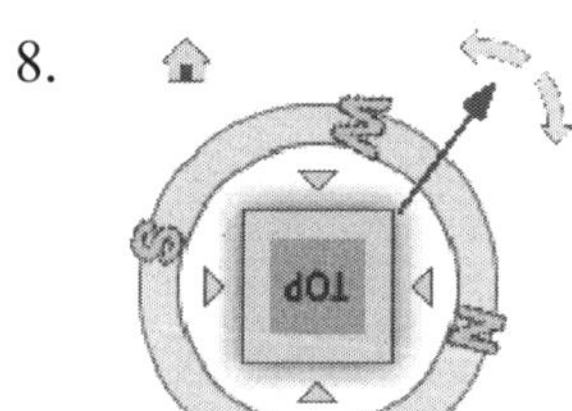
   Use the rotate arrows to rotate the view.

9. 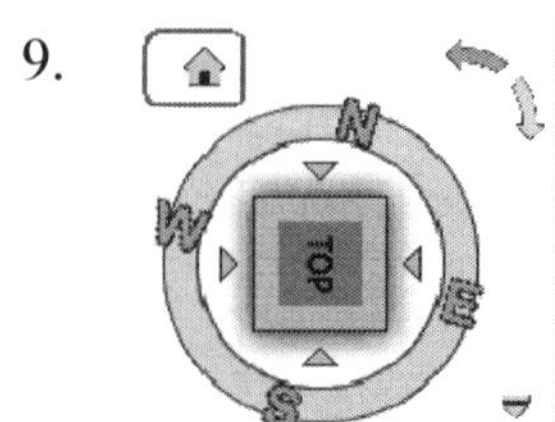
   Click on the little house (home/default view tool) to return to the default view.

   The little house disappears and reappears when your mouse approaches the cube.

10. 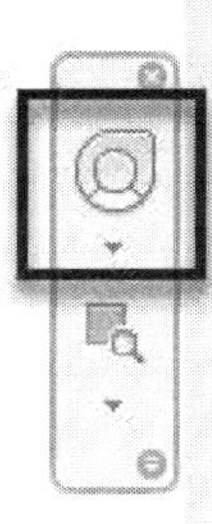 Select the Steering Wheel tool located on the View Control toolbar.

11. A steering wheel pops up.

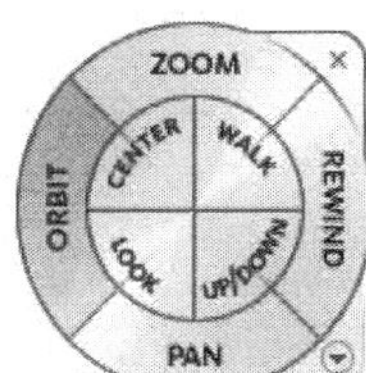

Notice that as you mouse over sections of the steering wheel they highlight.

Mouse over the Zoom section and hold down the left mouse button. The display should zoom in and out.

Mouse over the Orbit section and hold down the left mouse button. The display should orbit.

Mouse over the Pan section and hold down the left mouse button. The display should pan.

12.

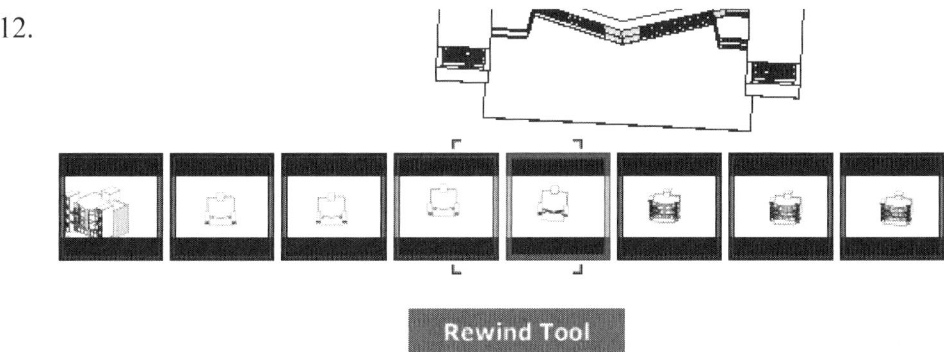

Select the Rewind tool and hold down the left mouse button.

A selection of previous views is displayed.

You no longer have to back through previous views. You can skip to the previous view you want.

Select a previous view to activate.

Close the steering wheel by selecting the X in the top right corner.

13.
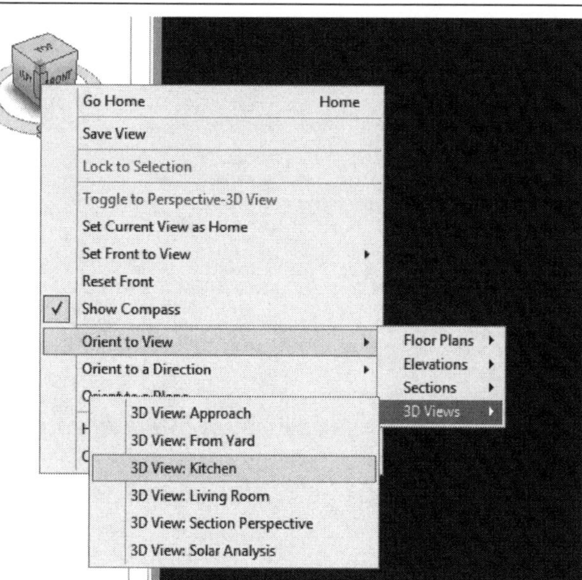

Place the mouse cursor over the View Cube. Right click and a shortcut menu appears.

Select **Orient to View→ 3d Views→3D View: Kitchen**.

14.
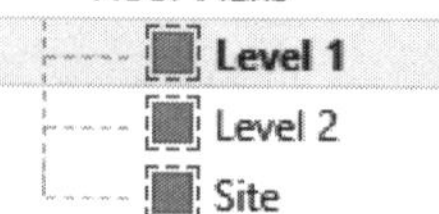

Double click on **Level 1** in the Project Browser. This will open the Level 1 floor plan view.

Be careful not to select the ceiling plan instead of the floor plan.

15.
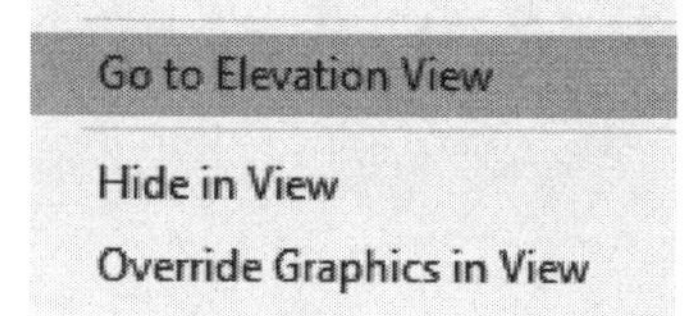

This is an elevation marker. It defines an elevation view.

16.

If you right click on the triangle portion of the elevation view, you can select **Go to Elevation View** to see the view associated with the elevation marker.

17.
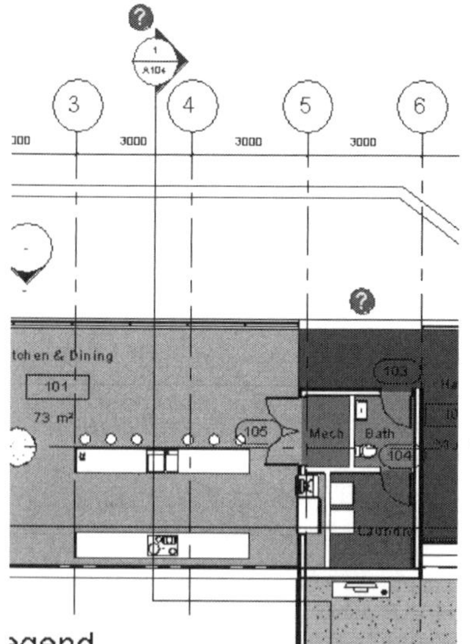

Select the Level 1 tab.

Locate the section line on Level 1 labeled A104.

18. The question mark symbols in the drawing link to help html pages. Click on one of the question marks.

19. 

Look in the Properties palette.
In the Learning Links field, a link to a webpage is shown. Click in that field to launch the webpage.

20. A browser will open to the page pertaining to the question mark symbol.

21. Return to the Level 1 view in Revit.

Double left click on the arrow portion of the section line A104.

22. This view has a callout.

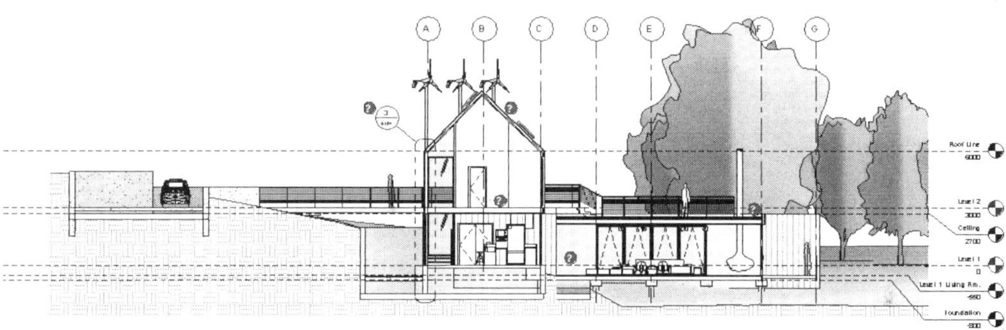

Double left click on the callout bubble.

The bubble is located on the left.

23.

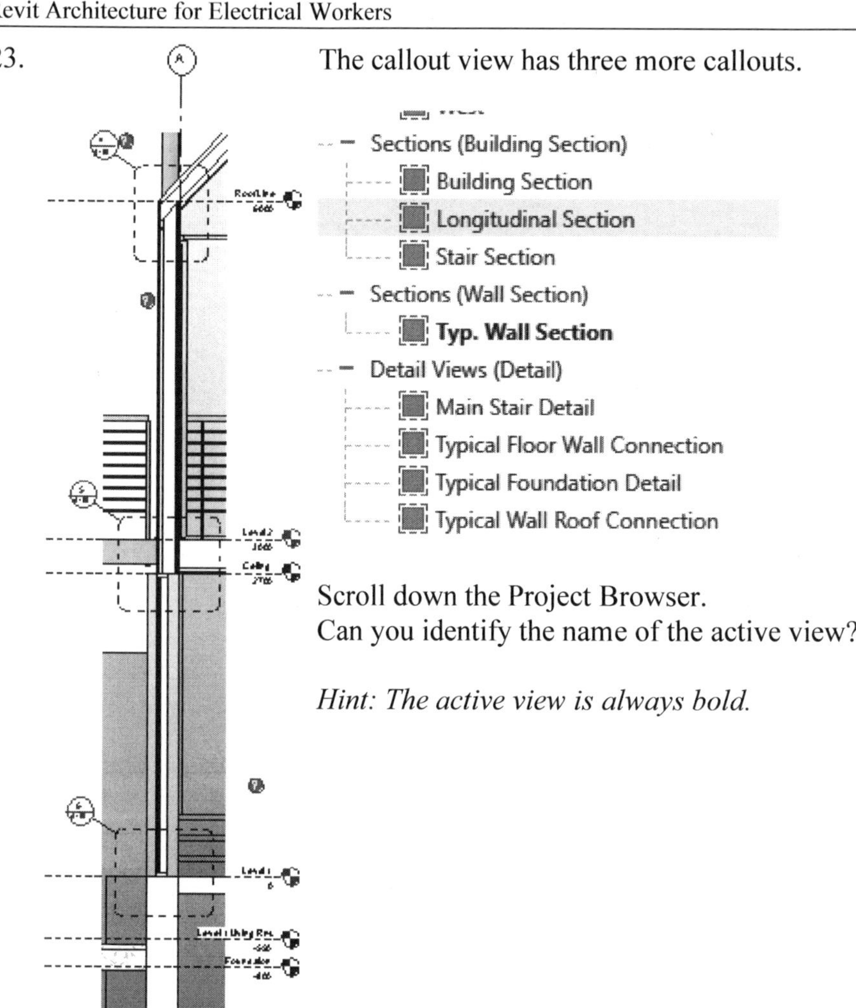

The callout view has three more callouts.

- ─ Sections (Building Section)
  - Building Section
  - Longitudinal Section
  - Stair Section
- ─ Sections (Wall Section)
  - **Typ. Wall Section**
- ─ Detail Views (Detail)
  - Main Stair Detail
  - Typical Floor Wall Connection
  - Typical Foundation Detail
  - Typical Wall Roof Connection

Scroll down the Project Browser.
Can you identify the name of the active view?

Hint: The active view is always bold.

24.

To the right of the view, there are levels. Some of the levels are blue, and some of them are black.

The blue levels (like Level 1) are story levels; they have views associated with them.

The black levels (like Foundation) are reference levels; they do not have views associated with them.

Double left click on the Level 1 bubble.

25. The Level 1 floor plan is opened. *We are back where we started!*

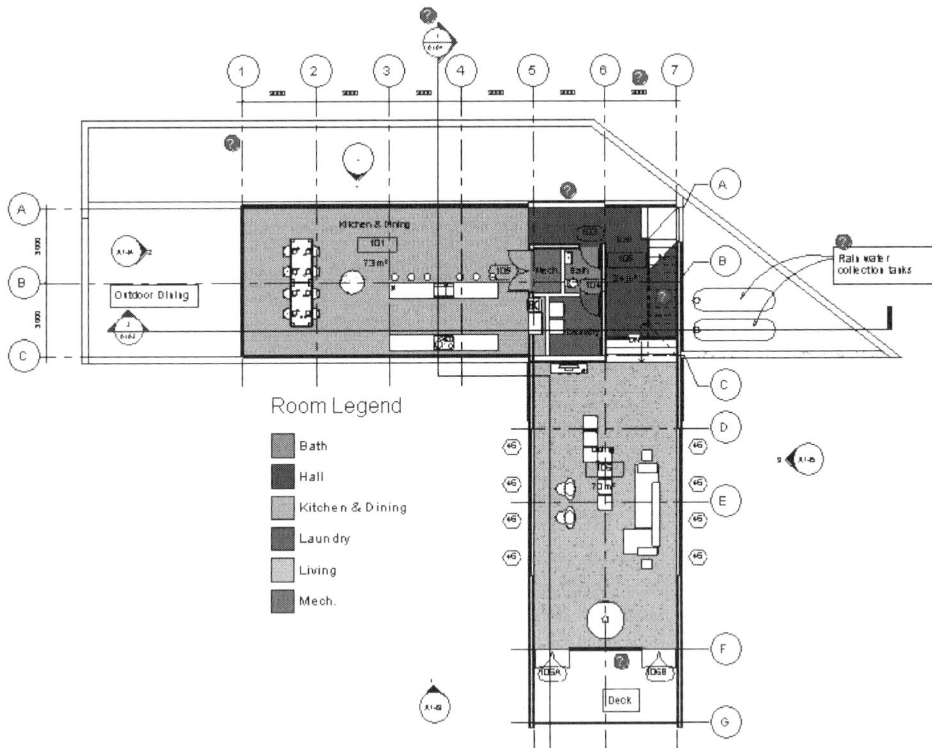

Level 1 is also in BOLD in the project browser.

26.

Right click in the window.
On the shortcut menu:
Select **Zoom In Region**.

This is the same as the Zoom Window tool in AutoCAD.

27. 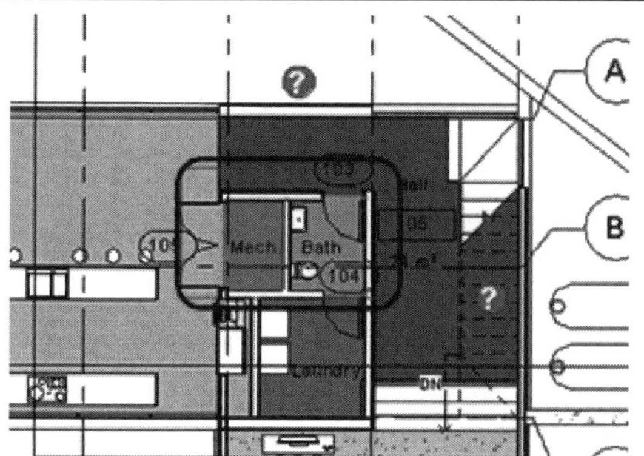 Place a rectangle with your mouse to zoom into the bathroom area.

28. 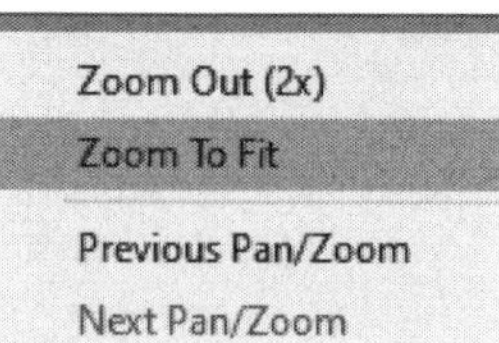 Right click in the window.
On the shortcut menu:
Select **Zoom To Fit**.
This is the same as the Zoom Extents tool in AutoCAD.
You can also double click on the scroll wheel to zoom to fit.

29. Close the file without saving.
Close by pressing **Ctl+W** or using **File→Close**.

Exercise 1-2:

Changing the View Background

Drawing Name: *rac_basic_project.rvt*
Estimated Time: 5 minutes

This exercise reinforces the following skills:
- ❏ Graphics mode
- ❏ Options

Many of my students come from an AutoCAD background and they want to change their background display to black.

1. 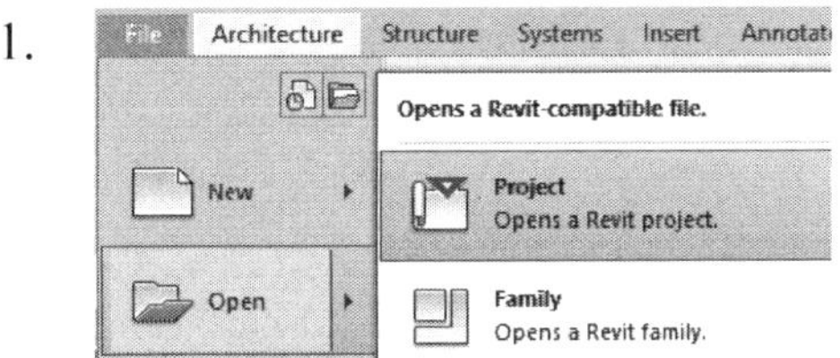

Go to **File→Open→Project**.

2. `rac_basic_project.rvt`

    Locate the file called *rac_basic_project.rvt*.
    This is included with the Class Files you downloaded from the publisher's website.

3.

Select the drop-down on the Application Menu.
Select **Options**.

Options manages all the system options for your projects and files.

4. 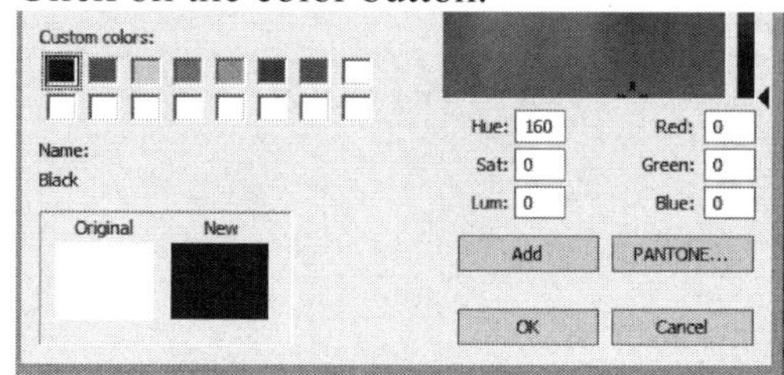

Select **Colors**.
Locate the color tab next to Background.
Click on the color button.

Select the Black color.
Press **OK** twice.

5. Close the file without saving.

Revit's Project Browser

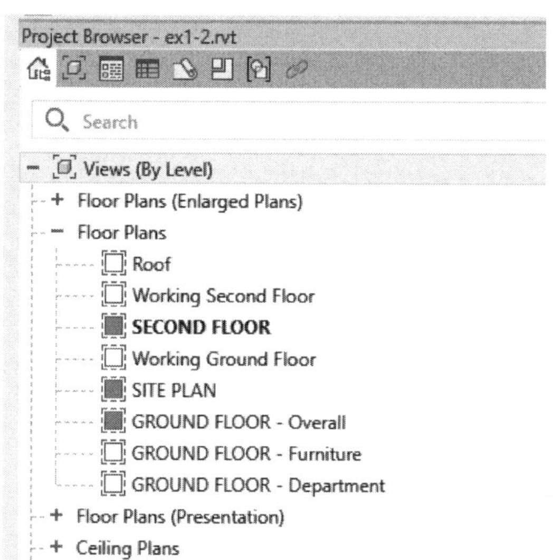

The Project Browser displays a hierarchy for all views, schedules, sheets, families and elements used in the current project. It has an interface similar to the Windows file explorer, which allows you to expand and collapse each branch as well as organize the different categories.

You can change the location of the Project Browser by dragging the title bar to the desired location. Changes to the size and the location are saved and restored when Revit is launched.

You can search for entries in the Project Browser by right-clicking inside the browser and selecting Search from the right-click menu to open a dialog.

The Project Browser is used to navigate around your project by opening different views. You can also drag and drop views onto sheets or families into views.

Exercise 1-3:

The Project Browser Interface

Drawing Name: *rac_basic_project.rvt*
Estimated Time: 20 minutes

This exercise reinforces the following skills:
- Project Browser
- Views
- Zoom to Region
- Groups
- Create Instance
- Move

1. 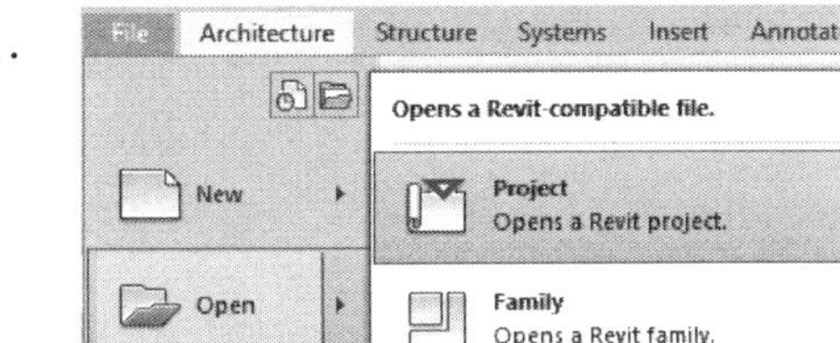 Go to **File→Open→Project**.

2. rac_basic_project.rvt

    Locate the file called *rac_basic_project.rvt*.
    This is included with the Class Files you downloaded from the publisher's website.

3. Place your mouse over Views.

    Right click and select **Collapse All.**

4. The Project Browser is organized by different categories:
   - Views
   - Legends
   - Schedules
   - Sheets
   - Families
   - Groups
   - Revit Links

    If a + is next to the category, it can be expanded.

    Which category is empty?

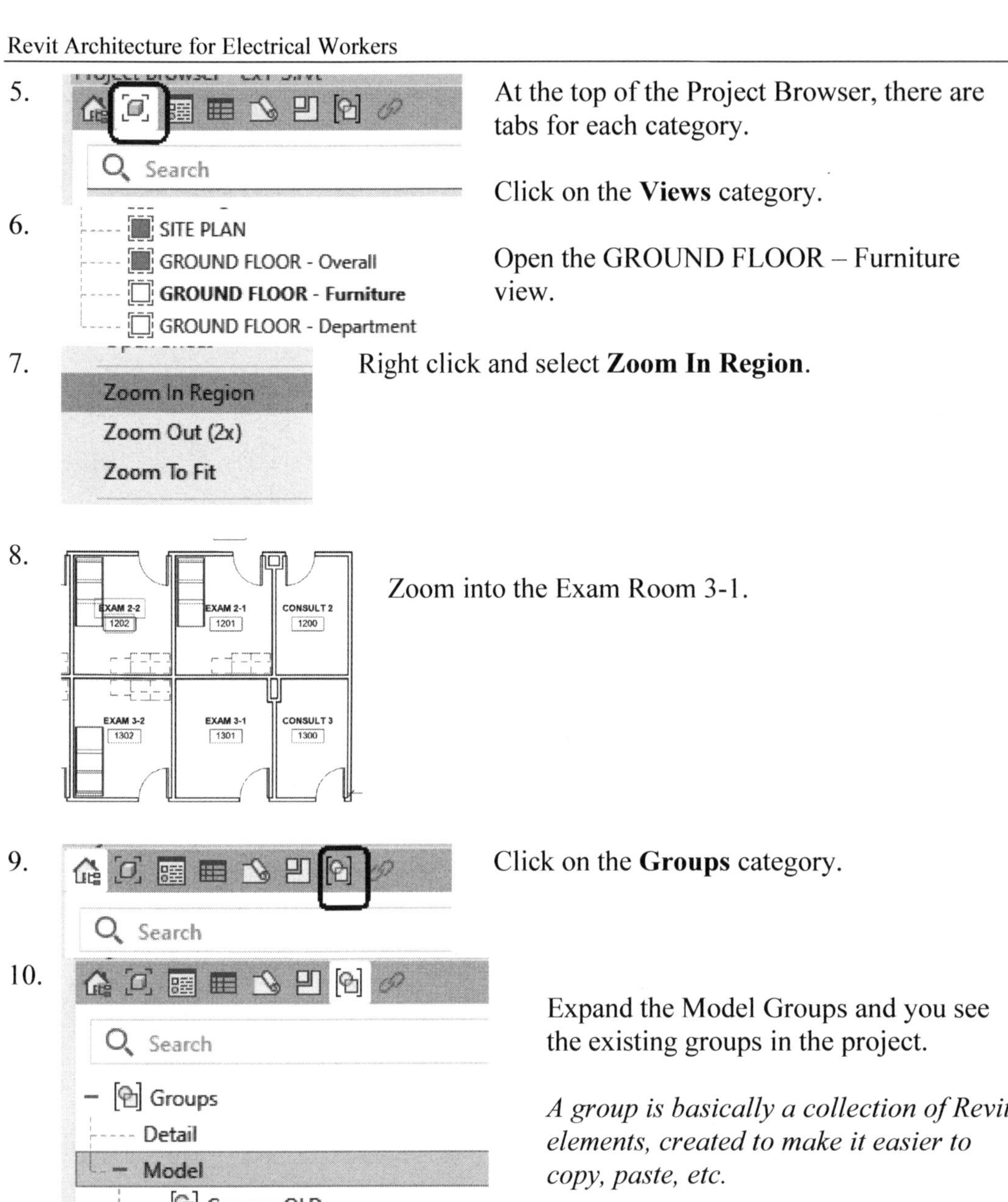

5. At the top of the Project Browser, there are tabs for each category.

Click on the **Views** category.

6. Open the GROUND FLOOR – Furniture view.

7. Right click and select **Zoom In Region**.

8. Zoom into the Exam Room 3-1.

9. Click on the **Groups** category.

10. Expand the Model Groups and you see the existing groups in the project.

A group is basically a collection of Revit elements, created to make it easier to copy, paste, etc.

11. Highlight **Exam Room**.

Right click and **Create Instance.**

12. Place the group in Exam Room 3-1.

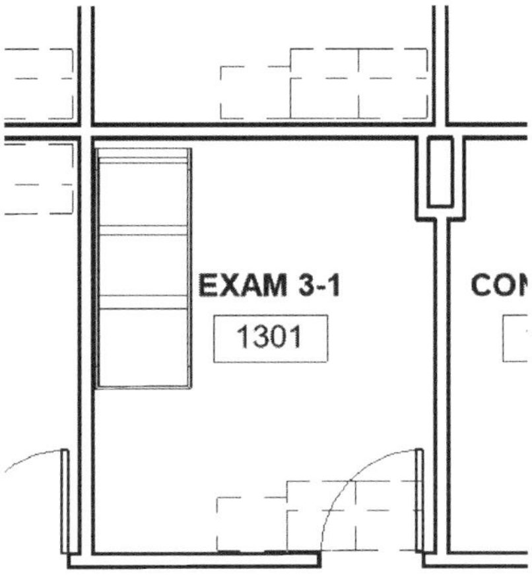

13. Select the group that was placed.

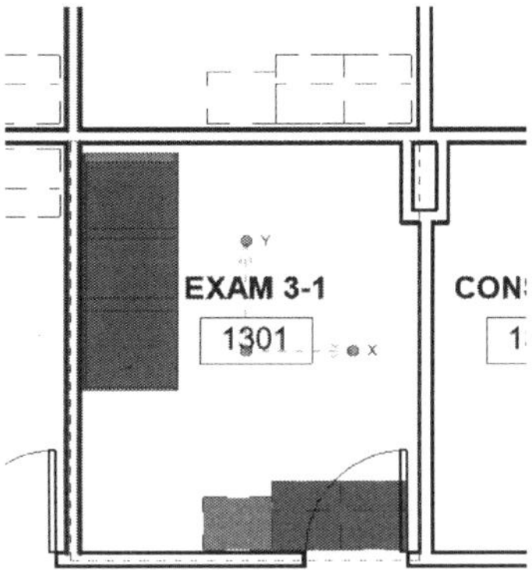

Click **ROTATE** on the Modify panel on the ribbon.

14. On the ribbon:

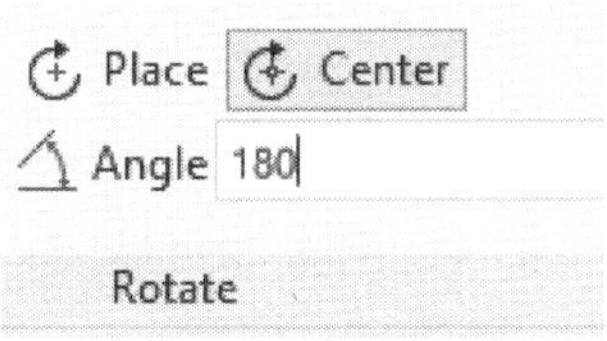

Enable **Center**.

Set the Angle to **180**.

15. The exam bed is now blocking the door.

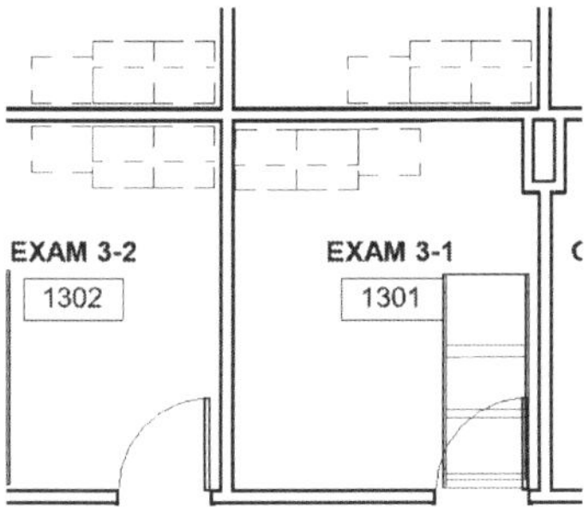

Click to select the group.

16. 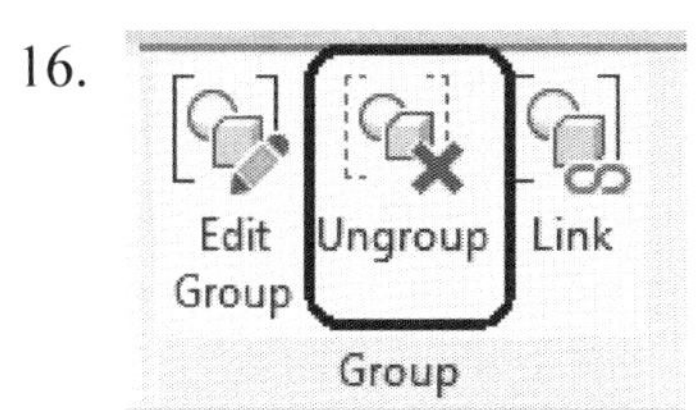

Click **Ungroup** on the ribbon.

You don't want to edit the group because that would update all the group placements.

17.

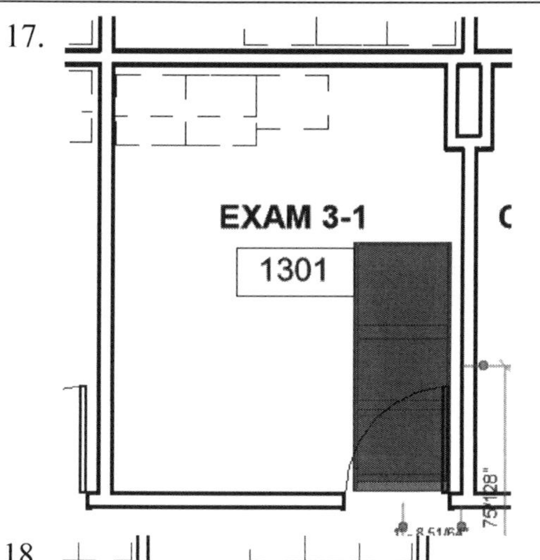

Select the bed.

Select the **MOVE** tool on the ribbon.

18.

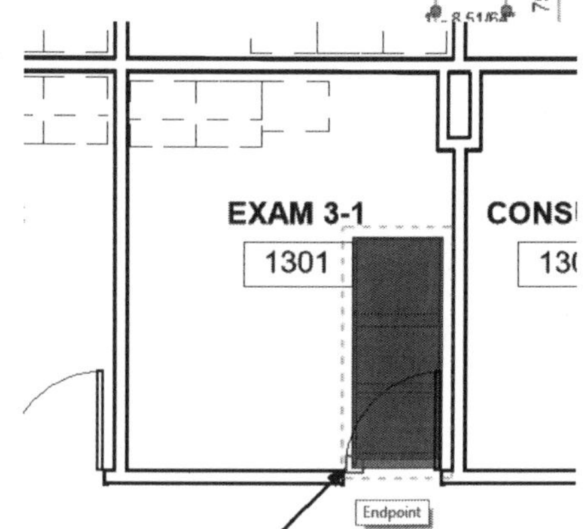

Look in the lower left corner of the window for the prompt.

Click to enter move start point.

Select the lower left corner of the bed as the base point.

19.

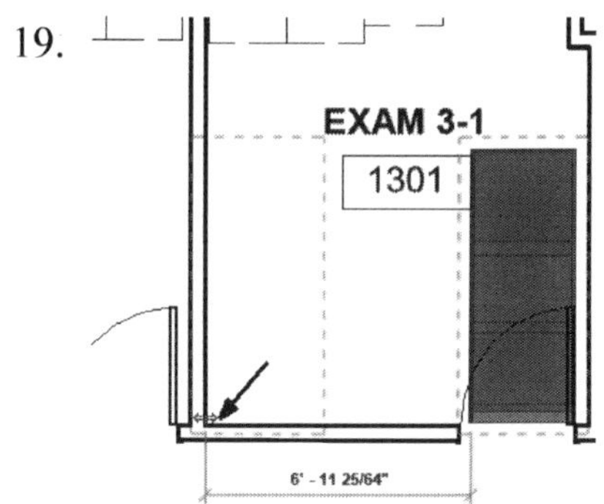

Select the lower left corner of the room as the destination point.

Left click to release the selection.

20.

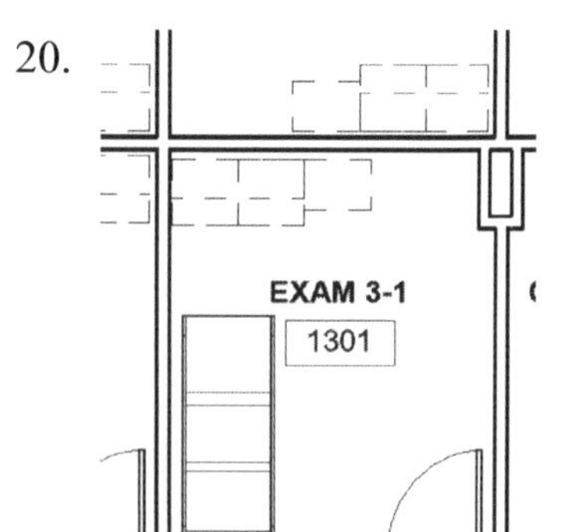

Save as *ex1-3.rvt*.

Revit's Properties Palette

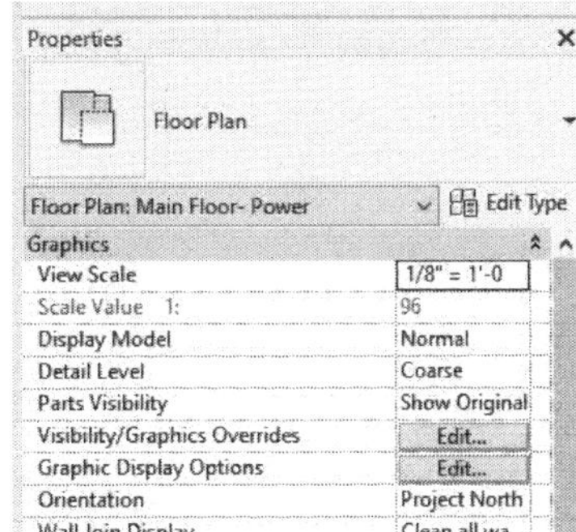

The Properties Palette is a contextually based dialog. If nothing is selected, it will display the properties of the active view. If something is selected, the properties of the selected item(s) will be displayed.

By default, the Properties Palette is docked on the left side of the drawing area. You can modify the location of this palette by dragging the title bar to the desired location.

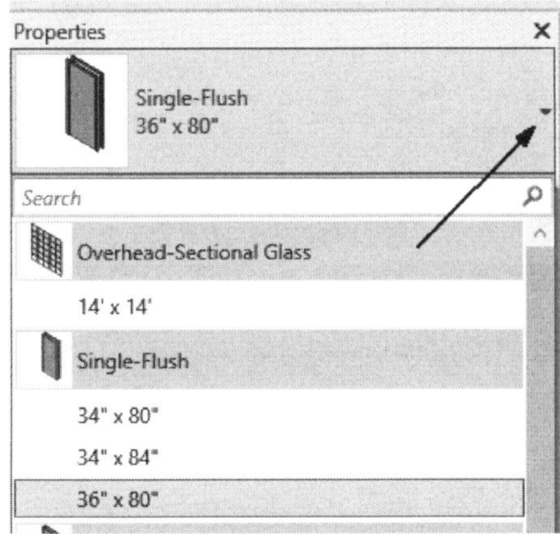

The Type Selector is a tool that identifies the selected family and provides a drop-down from which you can select a different type. You can use the type selector to change Revit family types. For example, if you placed a PVC conduit, you can select it in the model and then use the Type Selector to change the PVC conduit to an EMT conduit. However, you cannot change a conduit to a wire or a door to window as these are considered different families.

To make the Type Selector available when the Properties palette is closed, right-click within the Type Selector, and click Add to Quick Access Toolbar. To make the Type Selector available on the Modify tab, right-click within the Properties palette, and click Add to Ribbon Modify Tab. Each time you select an element, it will be reflected on the Modify tab.

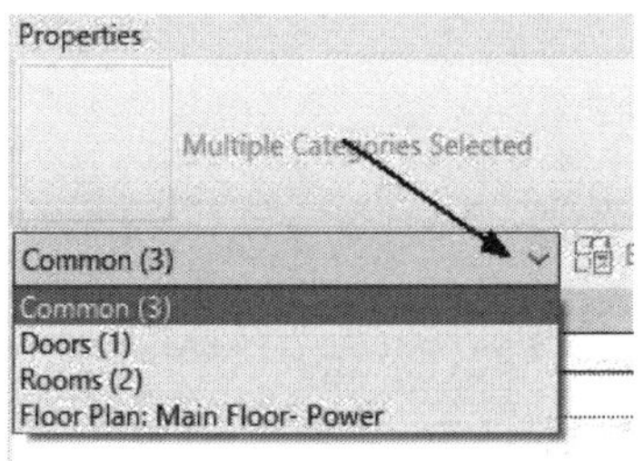

Immediately below the Type Selector is the Properties filter; this may be used when more than one element is selected. When different types of elements are selected, such as walls and doors, only the instance properties common to the elements selected will display on the palette.

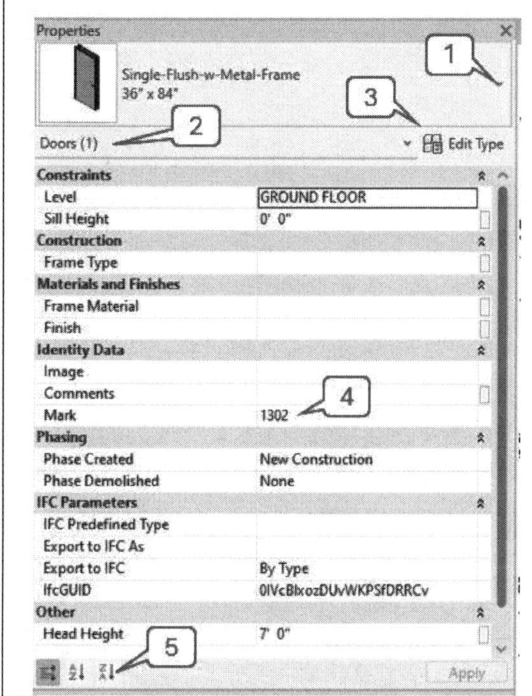

1. Type Selector

2. Properties filter

3. Edit Type button

4. Instance properties

5. Sort Parameters

The Edit Type button is used to modify or duplicate the element family type. The parameters can be sorted by default or alphabetically.

Revit uses three different family classes to create a building model:
- system
- loadable
- in-place masses

System families are walls, floors, roofs, conduits, wires, and ceilings. Loadable families are doors, windows, columns, receptacles, appliance panels, and furniture.

In-place masses are basic shapes which can be used to define volumetric objects and are project-specific.

Revit uses three types of elements in projects:

- Model
- Datum
- View-Specific

Model elements represent physical components in a building, such as equipment panels and lighting fixtures.

Datum elements help to define the project context. Examples are grids, levels, and reference planes.

View-specific elements only display in the views in which they are placed. Most annotations fall into this category. Examples are dimensions, text, or tags.

When you place an element into a building project, such as a strut rack, it has two types of properties: Type Properties and Instance Properties. Type Properties do not change regardless of where the rack is placed. Type Properties are values like material, size, and electrical ratings. The Instance Properties are unique to that element, such as the location of the strut rack and the rack ID.

Exercise 1-4:

Closing and Opening the Project Browser and Properties Palette

Drawing Name: *rac_basic_project.rvt*
Estimated Time: 5 minutes

This exercise reinforces the following skills:
- User Interface
- Ribbon
- Project Browser
- Properties panel

Many of my students will accidentally close the project browser and/or the properties palette and want to bring them back. Other students prefer to keep these items closed most of the time so they have a larger working area.

1. 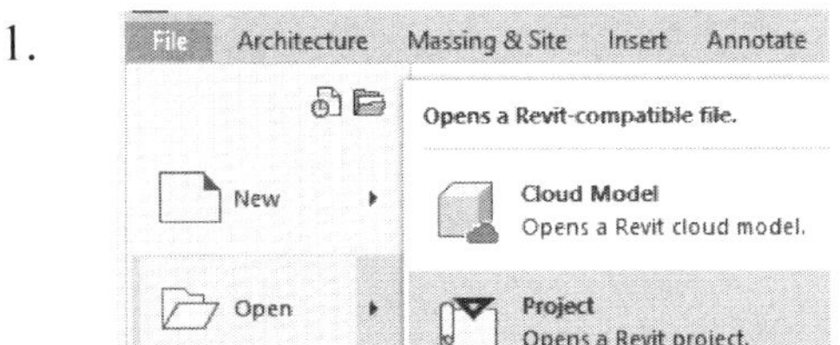

Go to **File→Open→Project**.

2. 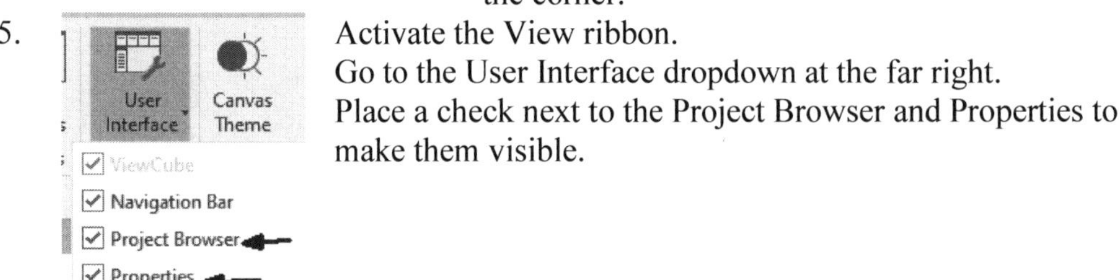 Locate the file called *rac_basic_project.rvt*.
This is included with the Class Files you downloaded from the publisher's website.

3. Close the Properties palette by clicking on the x in the corner.

4. Close the Project Browser by clicking on the x in the corner.

5. Activate the View ribbon.
Go to the User Interface dropdown at the far right.
Place a check next to the Project Browser and Properties to make them visible.

6. Close without saving.

Revit's Ribbon

The ribbon displays when you create or open a project file. It provides all the tools necessary to create a project or family.

An arrow next to a panel title indicates that you can expand the panel to display related tools and controls.

By default, an expanded panel closes automatically when you click outside the panel. To keep a panel expanded while its ribbon tab is displayed, click the push pin icon in the bottom-left corner of the expanded panel.

Exercise 1-5:

Changing the Ribbon Display

Drawing Name: *rac_basic_project.rvt*
Estimated Time: 15 minutes

This exercise reinforces the following skills:
- User Interface
- Ribbon

Many of my students will accidentally collapse the ribbon and want to bring it back. Other students prefer to keep the ribbon collapsed most of the time so they have a larger working area.

1. 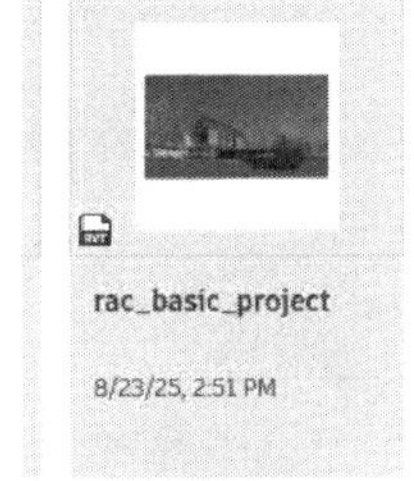 Select **rac_basic_project** from the Home window.

2. Activate **Level 1** in the Project Browser.

3. On the ribbon: Locate the two small up and down arrows.

4. Left click on the white button twice.

5. 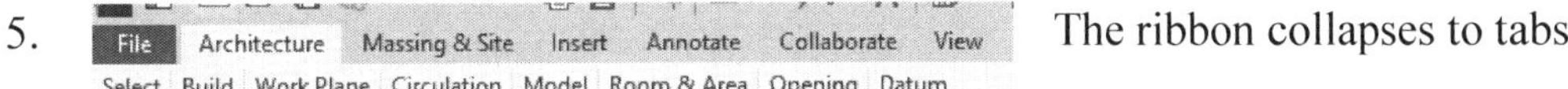 The ribbon collapses to tabs.

6. 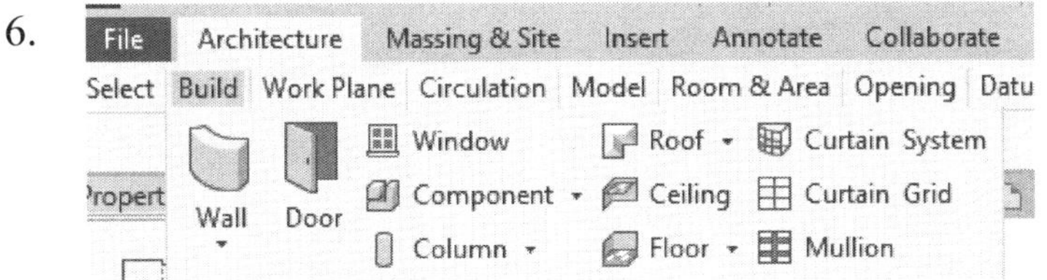 Left click on the word **Architecture**.
Hover the mouse over the word **Build** and the Build tools panel will appear. *The build tools will be grayed out in a 3D view.*

7. Click on the white button until the ribbon is restored.

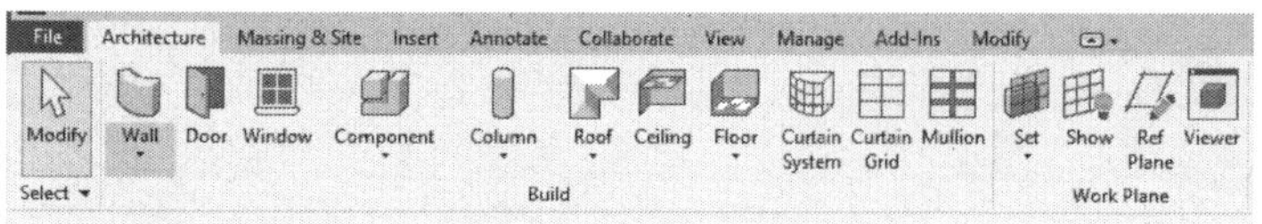

The ribbon is full-size again.

8. Click on the black arrow.

9. Click on **Minimize to Panel Buttons**.

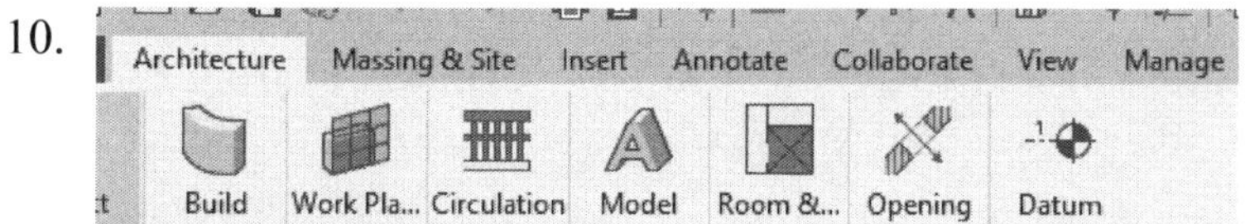

10. The ribbon changes to panel buttons.

11. Left click on a panel button and the tools for the button will display.
Some buttons are grayed out depending on what view is active.

12. Click on the white button to display the full ribbon.

13. Close without saving.

The Modify Ribbon

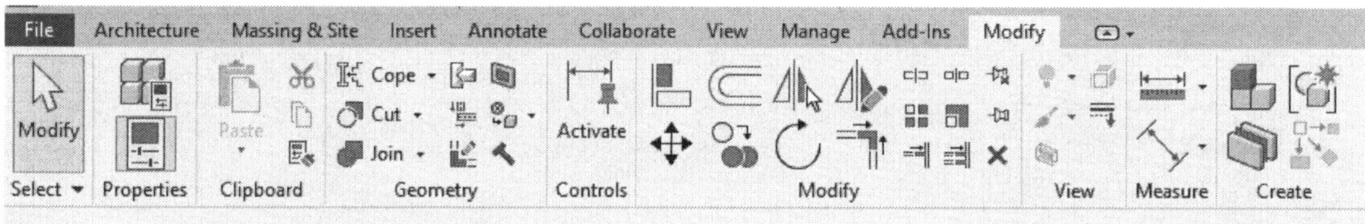

When you select an entity, you automatically switch to Modify mode. A Modify ribbon will appear with different options.

Select a wall in the view. Note how the ribbon changes.

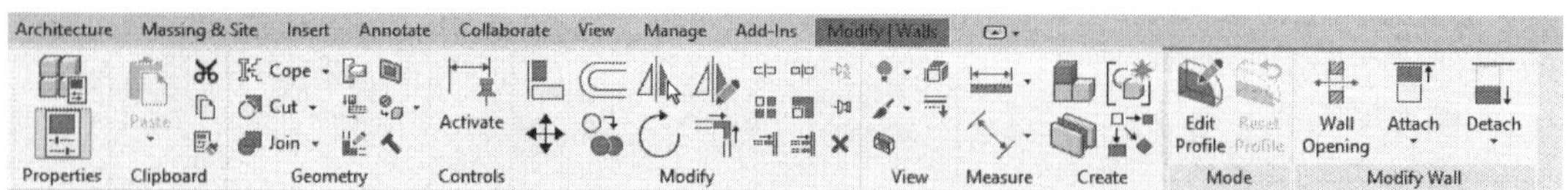

Revit uses three types of dimensions: Listening, Temporary, and Permanent. Dimensions are placed using the relative positions of elements to each other. Permanent dimensions are driven by the value of the temporary dimension. Listening dimensions are displayed as you draw or place an element.

Exercise 1-6:

Temporary, Permanent and Listening Dimensions

Drawing Name: dimensions.rvt
Estimated Time: 30 minutes

This exercise reinforces the following skills:
- Project Browser
- Scale
- Graphical Scale
- Numerical Scale
- Temporary Dimensions
- Permanent Dimensions
- Listening Dimensions
- Type Selector

1. Browse to *dimensions.rvt* in the Class Files you downloaded from the publisher's website. Save the file to a folder. Open the file.

    The file has four walls.
    The horizontal walls are 80′ in length.
    The vertical walls are 52′ in length.

    We want to change the vertical walls so that they are 60′ in length.

2. 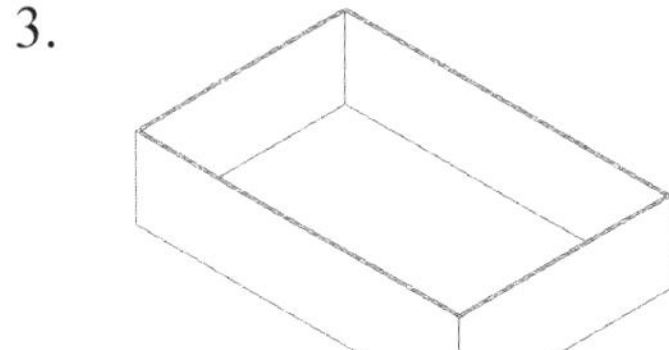   Left click the House icon on the Quick Access toolbar.

3. *This switches the display to a default 3D view.*

    You see that the displayed elements are walls.

4. 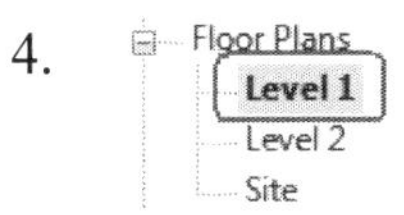   Double left click on Level 1 under Floor Plans in the Project Browser.

    The view display changes to the Level 1 floor plan.

5. 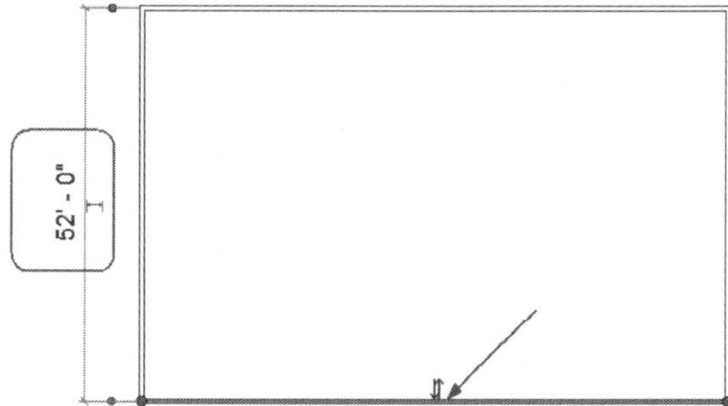 Select the bottom horizontal wall.

A temporary dimension appears showing the vertical distance between the selected wall and the wall above it.

6. A small dimension icon is next to the temporary dimension.

Left click on this icon to place a permanent dimension.

Left click anywhere in the window to release the selection.

7. Select the permanent dimension extension line, not the text.

A lock appears. If you left click on the lock, it would prevent you from modifying the dimension.

If you select the permanent dimension, you cannot edit the dimension value, only the dimension style.

8. The Properties palette shows the dimension style for the dimension selected.

Select the small down arrow.
This is the Type Selector.

The Type Selector shows the dimension styles available in the project.
If you do not see the drop-down arrow on the right, expand the properties palette and it should become visible.

9. Left click on the Linear - 1/4″ Arial dimension style to select this dimension style.

Left click anywhere in the drawing area to release the selection and change the dimension style.

10. The dimension updates to the new dimension style.

11.  Select the right vertical wall.

12. 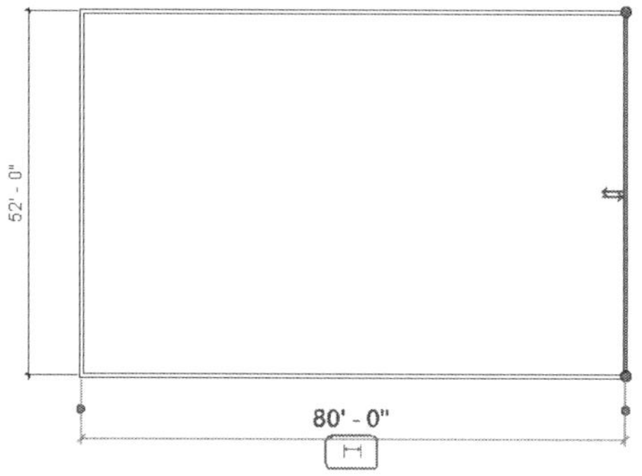 A temporary dimension appears showing the distance between the selected wall and the closest vertical wall.

    Left click on the permanent dimension icon to place a permanent dimension.

13. 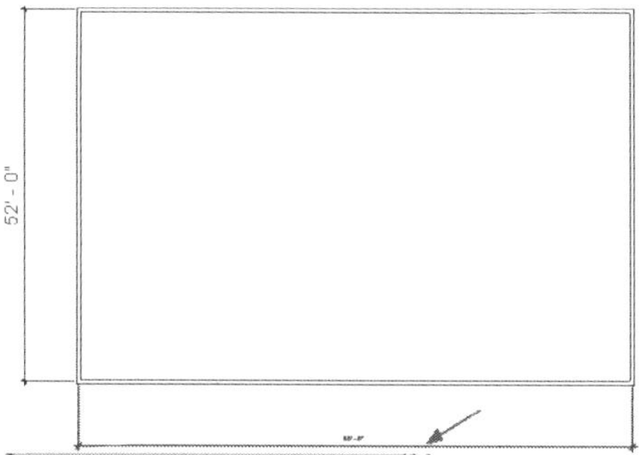 A permanent dimension is placed.

    Select the horizontal permanent dimension extension line, not the text.

14. 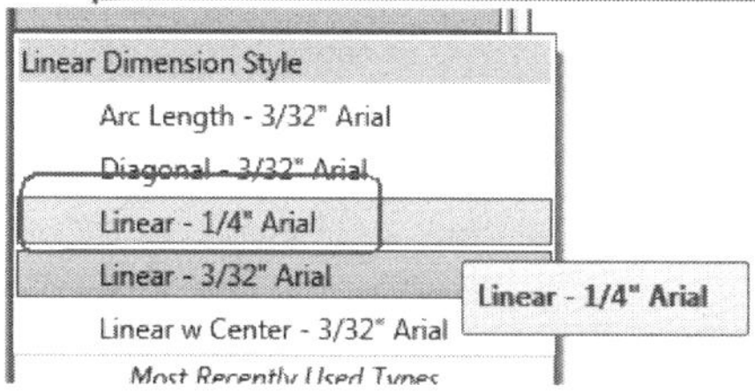 Use the Type Selector to change the dimension style of the horizontal dimension to the Linear - 1/4″ Arial dimension style.

    Left click anywhere in the drawing area to release the selection and change the dimension style.

15. 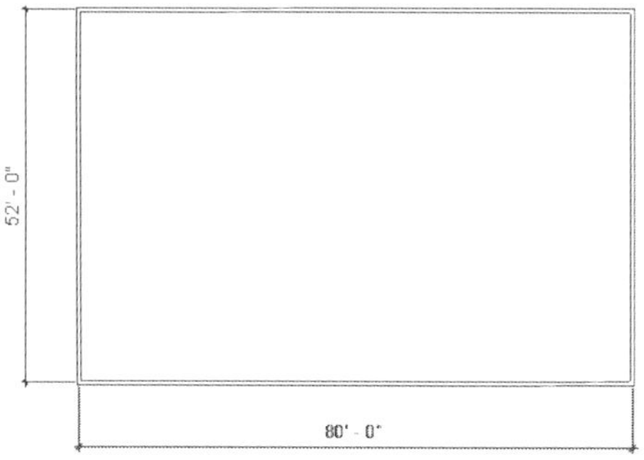 You have placed two *permanent* dimensions and assigned them a new dimension type.

16. Hold down the Control key and select both **horizontal** (top and bottom side) walls so that they highlight.

NOTE: *We select the horizontal walls to change the vertical wall length, and we select the vertical walls to change the horizontal wall length.*

17. 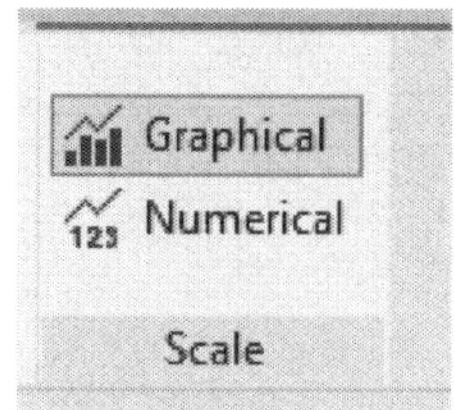 Select the **Scale** tool located on the Modify Walls ribbon.

On the ribbon, you may select Graphical or Numerical methods for resizing the selected objects.

18. 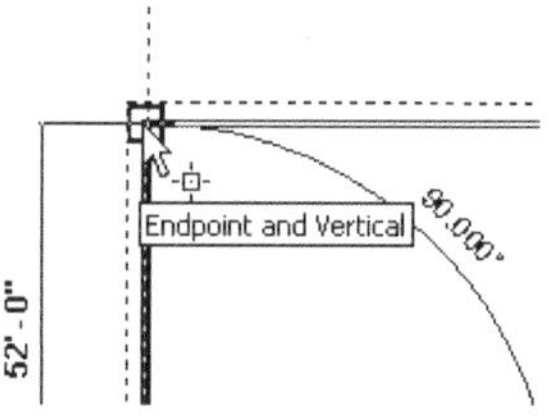 Enable **Graphical**.

The Graphical option requires three inputs.
    Input 1: Origin or Base Point
    Input 2: Original or Reference Length
    Input 3: Desired Length

19. 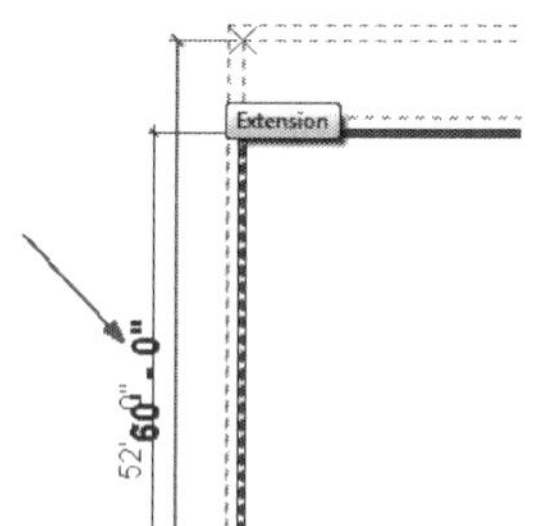 Select the left lower endpoint for the first input – the origin.

20. Select the left upper endpoint for the second input – the reference length.

21. Extend your cursor until you see a dimension of 60′.

The dimension you see as you move the cursor is a *listening dimension.*

You can also type 60' and press ENTER.

22. 
Left click for the third input – the desired length.

Left click anywhere in the window to release the selection and exit the scale command.

Note that the permanent dimension updates.

23. 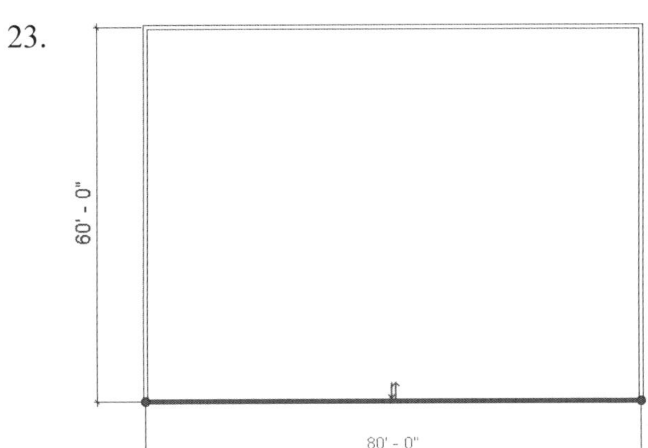
Select the bottom horizontal wall to display the temporary dimension.

24. 
Left click on the vertical temporary dimension.
An edit box will open. Type **50 0**.
Revit does not require you to enter units.
Left click to enter and release the selection.

25. The permanent dimension updates.

Note if you select the permanent dimension, you cannot edit the dimension value, only the dimension style.

26. Now, we will change the horizontal walls using the Numerical option of the Resize tool.
Hold down the Control key and select the left and right vertical walls.

27. 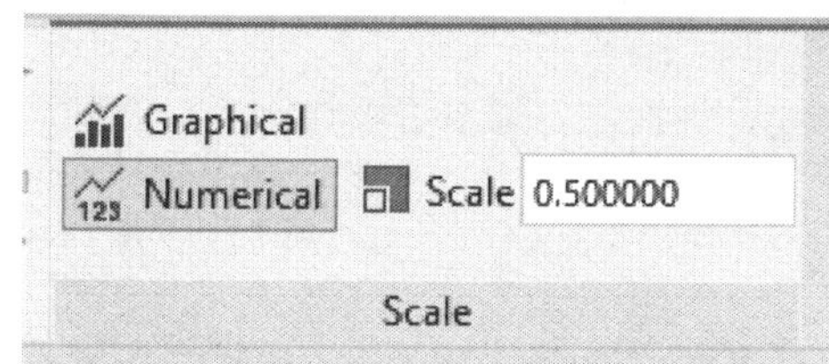 Select the **Scale** tool.

28. 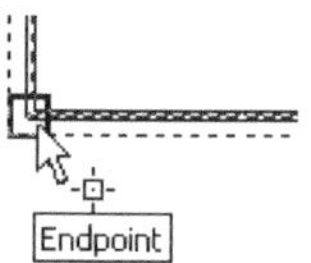 Enable **Numerical**.
Set the Scale to **0.5**.

This will change the wall length from **80′** to **40′**.

The Numerical option requires only one input for the Origin or Base Point.

29. Select the left lower endpoint for the first input – the origin.

30. The walls immediately adjust. Left click in the drawing area to release the selection.
Note that the permanent dimension automatically updates.

31. Close without saving.

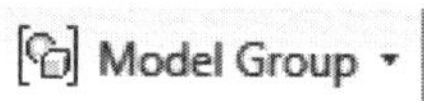

The Group tool works in a similar way as the AutoCAD GROUP. Basically, you are creating a selection set of similar or dissimilar objects, which can then be selected as a single unit. Once selected, you can move, copy, rotate, mirror, or delete them. Once you create a Group, you can add or remove members of that group. Existing groups are listed in your browser panel and can be dragged and dropped into views as required. Typical details, office layouts, bathroom layouts, etc. can be grouped, and then saved out of the project for use on other projects.

 If you hold down the Control key as you drag a selected object or group, Revit will automatically create a copy of the selected object or group.

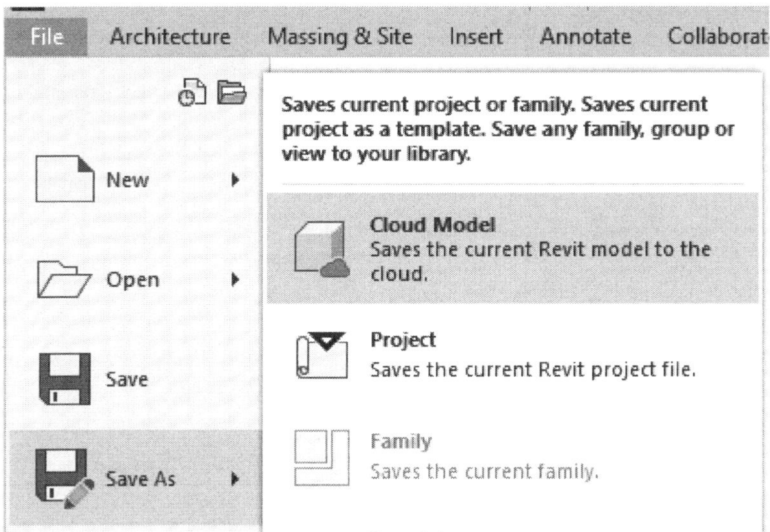

Revit has an option to save projects to the Cloud. In order to save to the cloud, the user needs to have a subscription for their software or you need to set up a free Autodesk Construction Cloud account.

This option allows you to store your projects to a secure Autodesk server, so you can access your files regardless of your location. Users can share their project with each other and even view and comment on projects without using Revit. Instead, you use a browser interface.

Autodesk hopes that if you like this interface you will opt for their more expensive option – BIM360, which is used by many AEC firms to collaborate on large projects.

The Collaborate Ribbon

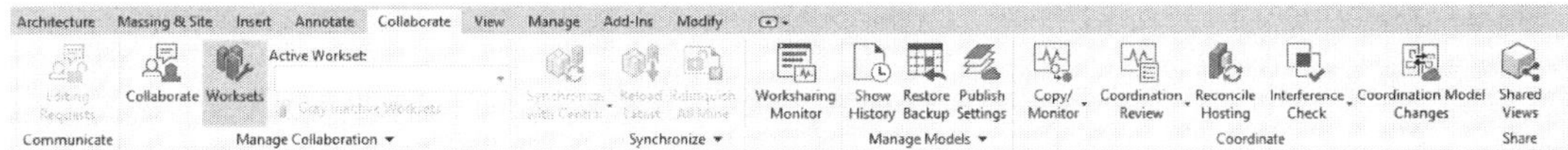

Collaborate tools are used if more than one user is working on the same project. The tools can also be used to check data sets coming in from other sources.

> If you plan to export to .dwg or import existing .dwg details, it is important to set your import/export setting. This allows you to control the layers that Revit will export to and the appearance of imported .dwg files.

> Pressing the ESC Key twice will always take you to the Modify command.

> As you get more proficient with Revit, you may want to create your own templates based on your favorite settings. A custom template based on your office standards (including line styles, rendering materials, common details, door, window and room schedules, commonly used wall types, door types and window types and typical sheets) will increase project production.

Revit's Menu

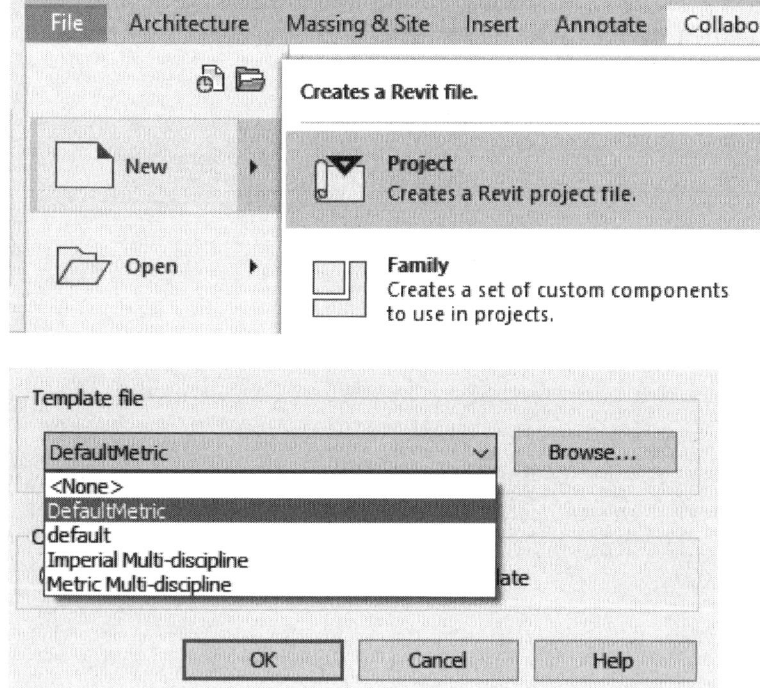

When you want to start a new project/building, you go to File→New→Project or use the hot key by pressing Control and 'N' at the same time.

When you start a new project, you use a default template (default.rte). This template creates two Levels (default floor heights) and sets the View Window to the Floor Plan view of Level 1.

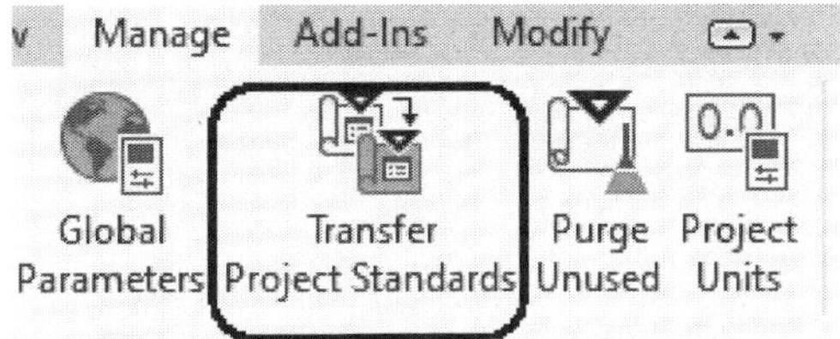

You can transfer the Project settings of an old project to a new one by opening both projects in one session of Revit, then with your new project active, select **Manage→Settings→Transfer Project Standards**.
Check the items you wish to transfer, and then click 'OK'.

Transfer Project Settings is useful if you have created a custom system family, such as a wall, floor, or ceiling, and want to use it in a different project.

The View Ribbon

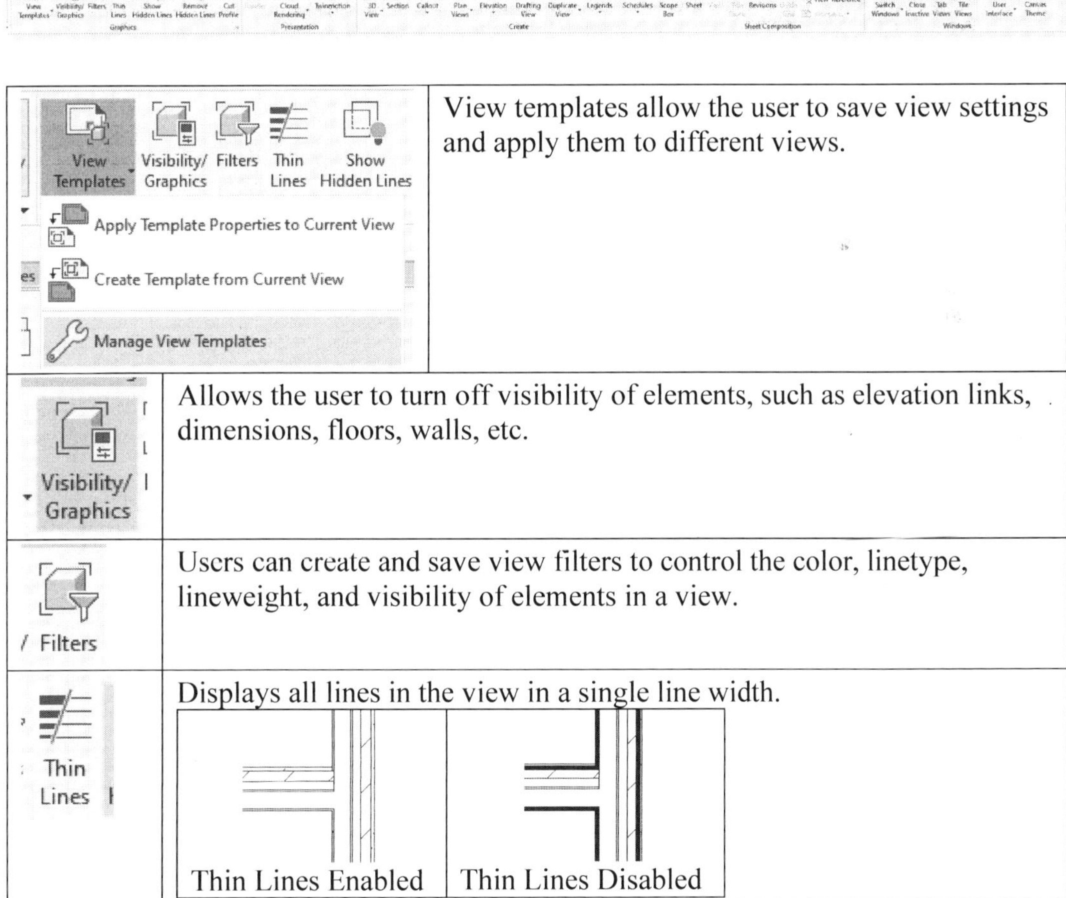

View Templates / Visibility/ Graphics / Filters / Thin Lines / Show Hidden Lines — Apply Template Properties to Current View — Create Template from Current View — Manage View Templates	View templates allow the user to save view settings and apply them to different views.
Visibility/ Graphics	Allows the user to turn off visibility of elements, such as elevation links, dimensions, floors, walls, etc.
Filters	Users can create and save view filters to control the color, linetype, lineweight, and visibility of elements in a view.
Thin Lines	Displays all lines in the view in a single line width. Thin Lines Enabled Thin Lines Disabled

Show Hidden Lines	Changes the display of elements in a view to display as Hidden Lines. *This is used primarily for drafting views.*
Remove Hidden Lines	Changes the display of elements in a view to remove Hidden Lines. *This is used primarily for drafting views.*
Cut Profile	Use the Cut Profile tool to change the shape of elements that are cut in a view, such as roofs, floors, walls, and the layers of compound structures. *This is used primarily for structural plans.*
Render Cloud Rendering Twinmotion Presentation	
Render	Render is used to create photo-realistic images to use in drawings and presentations.
Cloud Rendering Twinmotio Render in Cloud Render Gallery	Cloud Rendering uses Autodesk's servers to create the rendering. This is useful as rendering can be very time-consuming. You can use cloud rendering as a background process, so that the image is created while you continue to work. The Render Gallery is an on-line storage area where your images are stored and available for viewing and download.

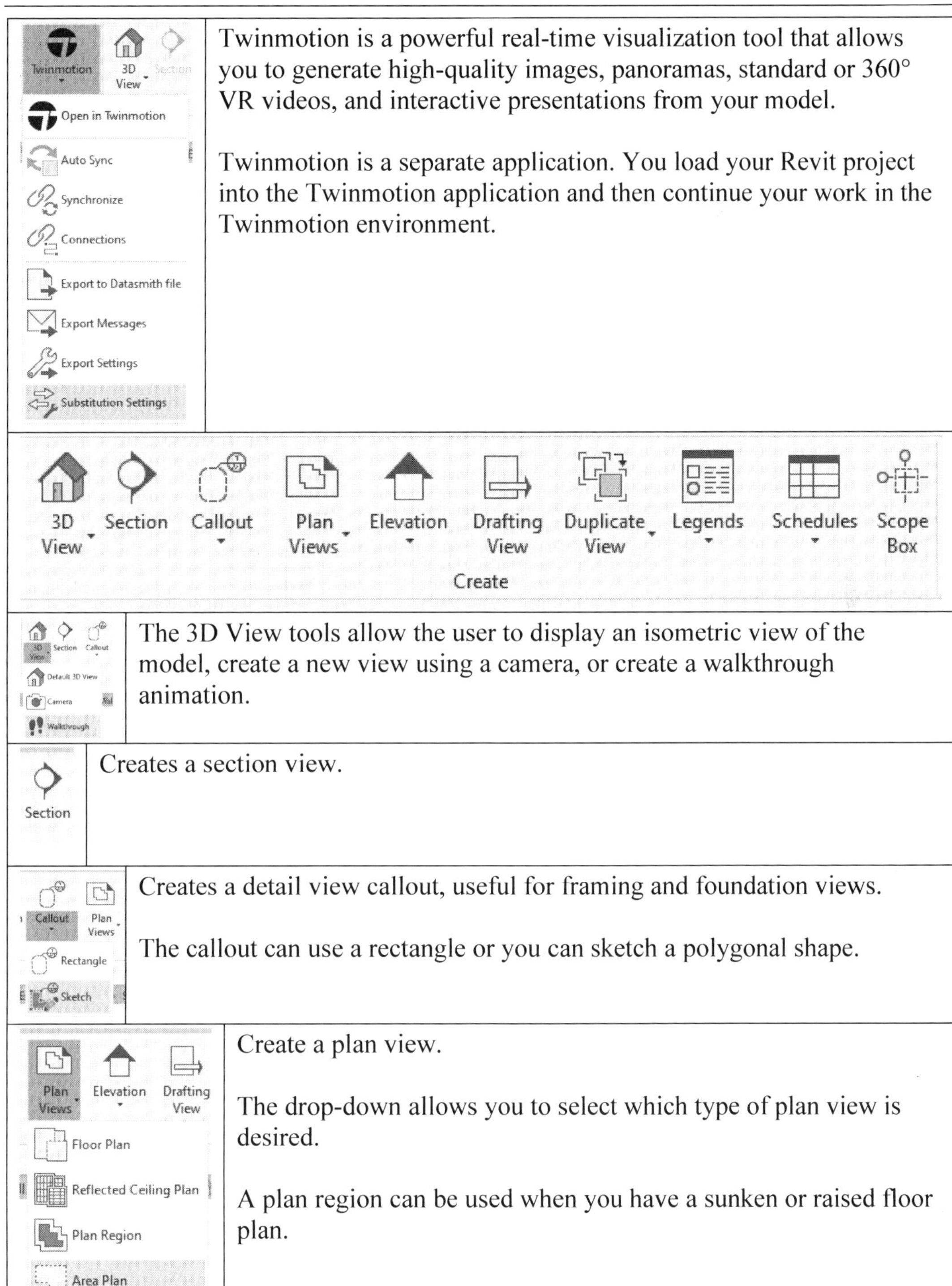

	Twinmotion is a powerful real-time visualization tool that allows you to generate high-quality images, panoramas, standard or 360° VR videos, and interactive presentations from your model. Twinmotion is a separate application. You load your Revit project into the Twinmotion application and then continue your work in the Twinmotion environment.
	The 3D View tools allow the user to display an isometric view of the model, create a new view using a camera, or create a walkthrough animation.
	Creates a section view.
	Creates a detail view callout, useful for framing and foundation views. The callout can use a rectangle or you can sketch a polygonal shape.
	Create a plan view. The drop-down allows you to select which type of plan view is desired. A plan region can be used when you have a sunken or raised floor plan.

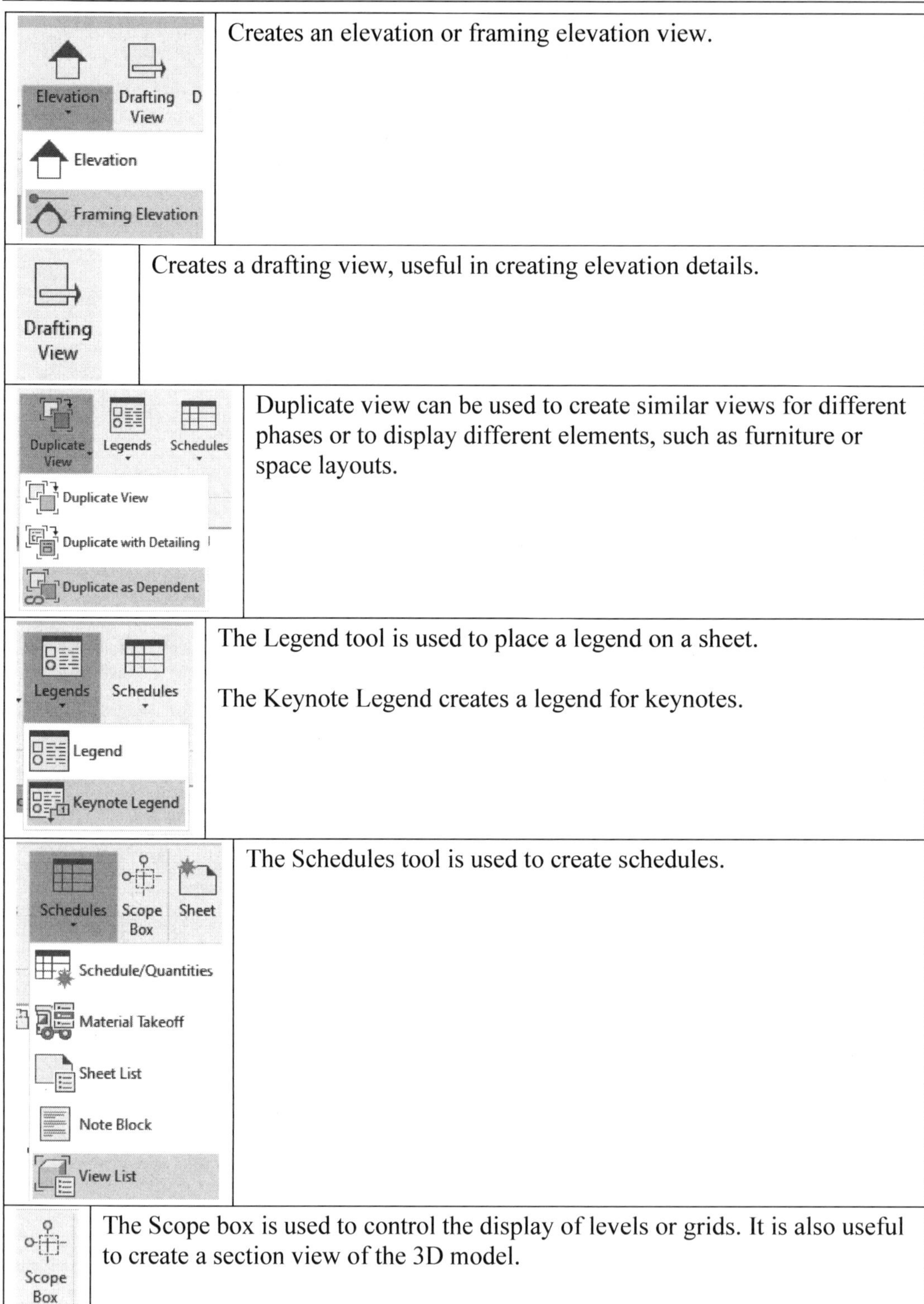

	Creates an elevation or framing elevation view.
	Creates a drafting view, useful in creating elevation details.
	Duplicate view can be used to create similar views for different phases or to display different elements, such as furniture or space layouts.
	The Legend tool is used to place a legend on a sheet. The Keynote Legend creates a legend for keynotes.
	The Schedules tool is used to create schedules.
	The Scope box is used to control the display of levels or grids. It is also useful to create a section view of the 3D model.

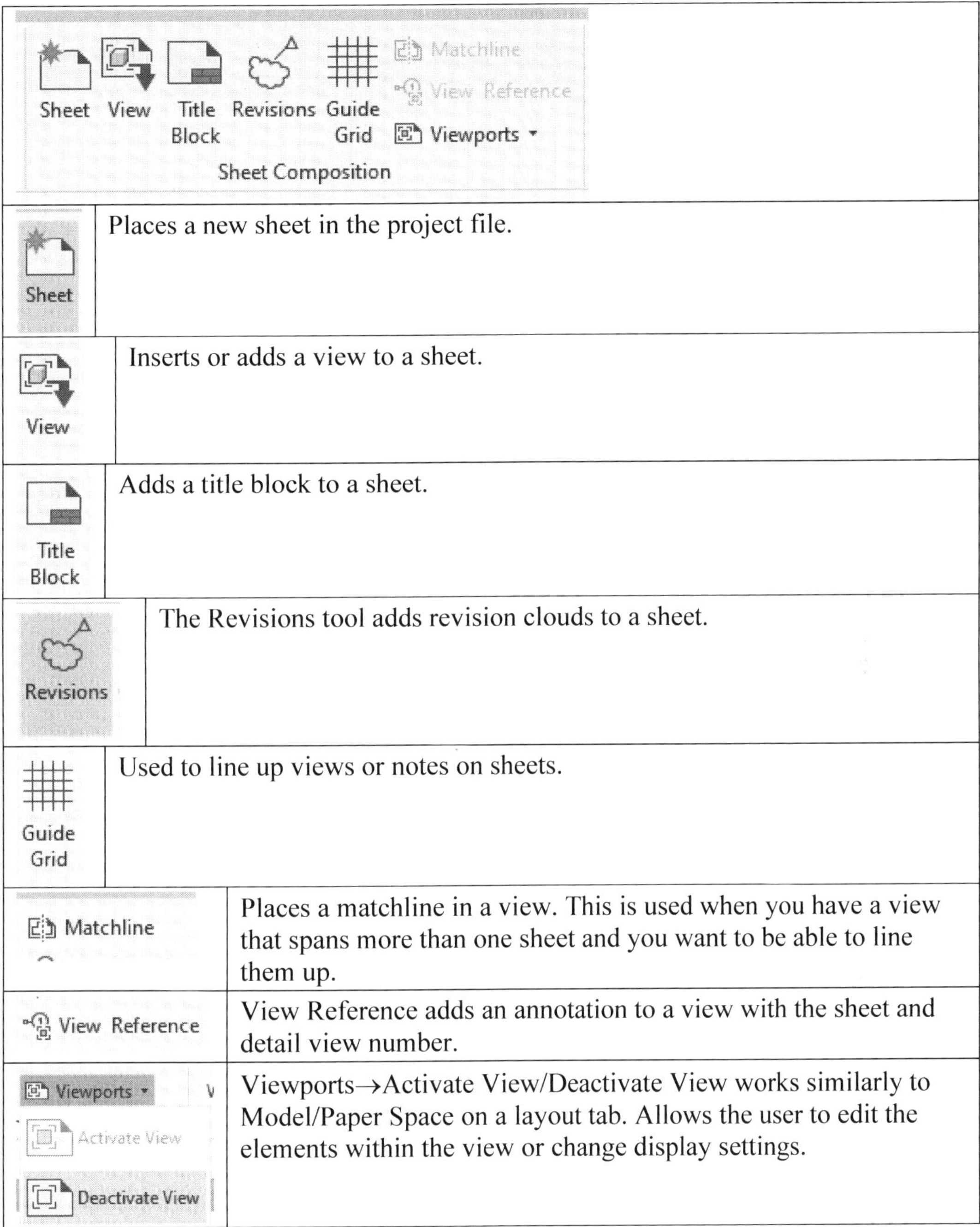

Sheet	Places a new sheet in the project file.
View	Inserts or adds a view to a sheet.
Title Block	Adds a title block to a sheet.
Revisions	The Revisions tool adds revision clouds to a sheet.
Guide Grid	Used to line up views or notes on sheets.
Matchline	Places a matchline in a view. This is used when you have a view that spans more than one sheet and you want to be able to line them up.
View Reference	View Reference adds an annotation to a view with the sheet and detail view number.
Viewports (Activate View / Deactivate View)	Viewports→Activate View/Deactivate View works similarly to Model/Paper Space on a layout tab. Allows the user to edit the elements within the view or change display settings.

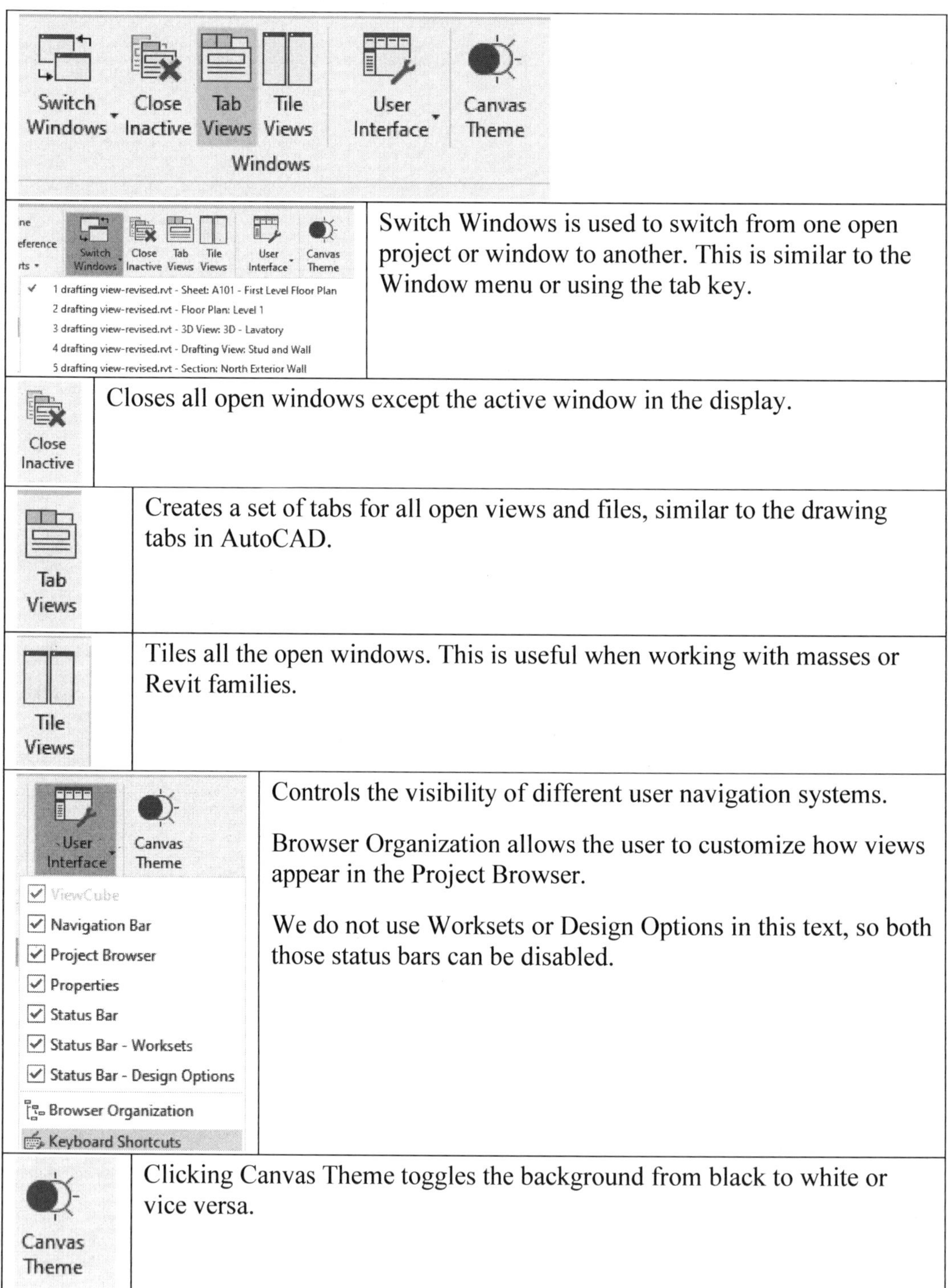

Switch Windows is used to switch from one open project or window to another. This is similar to the Window menu or using the tab key.	
Closes all open windows except the active window in the display.	
Creates a set of tabs for all open views and files, similar to the drawing tabs in AutoCAD.	
Tiles all the open windows. This is useful when working with masses or Revit families.	
Controls the visibility of different user navigation systems. Browser Organization allows the user to customize how views appear in the Project Browser. We do not use Worksets or Design Options in this text, so both those status bars can be disabled.	
Clicking Canvas Theme toggles the background from black to white or vice versa.	

Creating standard view templates (exterior elevations, enlarged floor plans, etc.) in your project template or at the beginning of a project will save lots of time down the road.

The Manage Ribbon

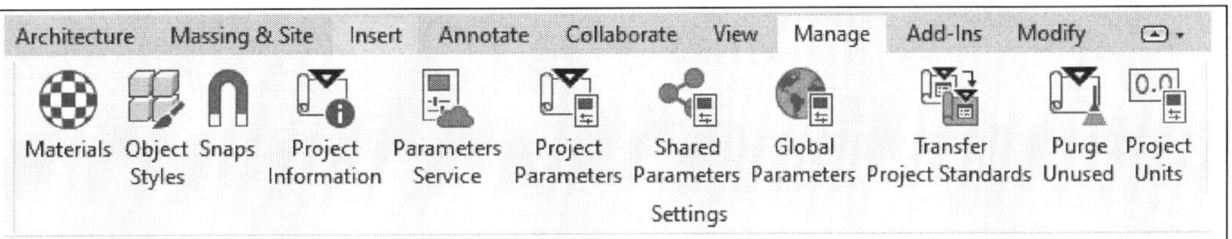

Revit comes with a library of materials, which can be applied to walls, windows, doors, etc. You can also edit and create your own custom materials.

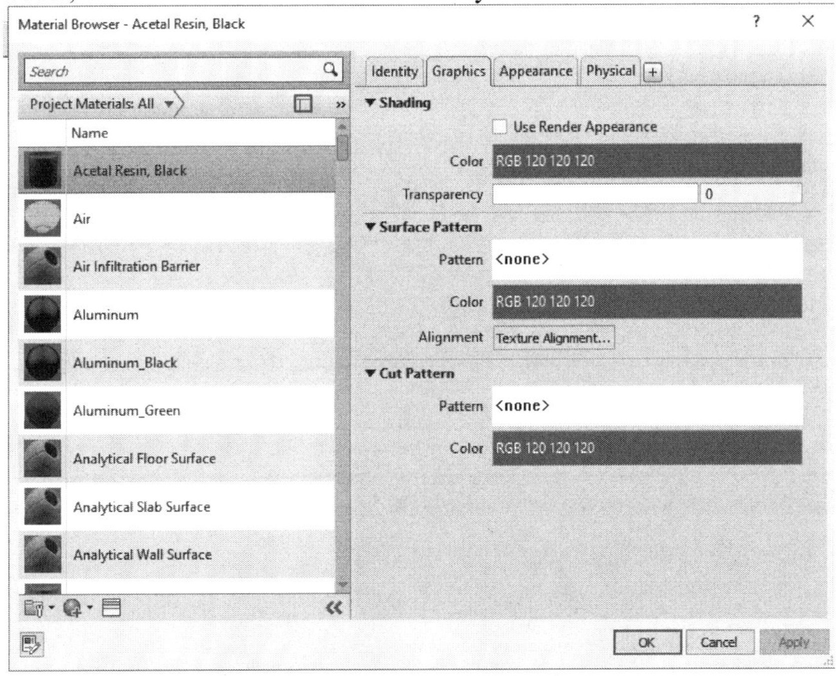

Any image file can be used to create a material.

My favorite sources for materials are fabric and paint websites.

Object Styles is used to control the line color, line weight, and line style applied to different Revit elements. It works similarly to layers in AutoCAD, except it ensures that all the similar elements, like doors, look the same.

Object Styles

Model Objects | Annotation Objects | Analytical Model Objects | Imported Objects

Filter list: <show all>

Category	Line Weight Projection	Cut	Line Color	Line Pattern	Material
Air Terminals	1		Black	Solid	
Cable Tray Fittings	1		Black	Solid	
Cable Trays	1		Black	Solid	
Casework	1	3	Black	Solid	
Ceilings	1	3	Black	Solid	
Columns	1	3	Black	Solid	
Communication Devices	1		Black		
Conduit Fittings	1		Black	Solid	
Conduits	1		Black	Solid	
Curtain Panels	1	2	Black	Solid	
Curtain Systems	2	2	RGB 000-127-000	Solid	
Curtain Wall Mullions	1	3	Black	Solid	
Data Devices	1		Black		
Detail Items	1		Black	Solid	
Doors	1	2	Black	Solid	
Duct Accessories	1		Black	Solid	
Duct Fittings	1		Black	Solid	

Select All   Select None   Invert

Modify Subcategories

New   Delete   Rename

Snaps in Revit are similar to object snaps in AutoCAD. You can set how your length and dimensions snap as well as which object types your cursor will snap to when making a selection.

Like AutoCAD, it is best not to make your snaps all-encompassing so that you snap to everything as that defeats the purpose and usefulness of snaps.

☐ Snaps Off   (SO)

Dimension Snaps

Snaps adjust as views are zoomed.
The largest value that represents less than 2mm on screen is used.

☑ Length dimension snap increments

4' ; 0' 6" ; 0' 1" ; 0' 0 1/4" ;

☑ Angular dimension snap increments

90.00° ; 45.00° ; 15.00° ; 5.00° ; 1.00° ;

Object Snaps

☑ Endpoints	(SE)	☑ Intersections	(SI)
☑ Midpoints	(SM)	☑ Centers	(SC)
☑ Nearest	(SN)	☑ Perpendicular	(SP)
☑ Work Plane Grid	(SW)	☑ Tangents	(ST)
☑ Quadrants	(SQ)	☑ Points	(SX)

Check All   Check None

☑ Snap to Remote Objects	(SR)	☑ Snap to Point Clouds	(PC)
☑ Snap to Coordination Models	(LM)		

Temporary Overrides

While using an interactive tool, keyboard shortcuts (shown in parentheses) can be used to specify a snap type for a single pick.

Object snaps	Use shortcuts listed above
Close	(SZ)
Turn Override Off	(SS)
Cycle through snaps	(TAB)
Force horizontal and vertical	(SHIFT)
Snap Mid Between 2 Points	(SZ)
Force Perpendicular (Measure 3D)	(CTRL)

Restore Defaults

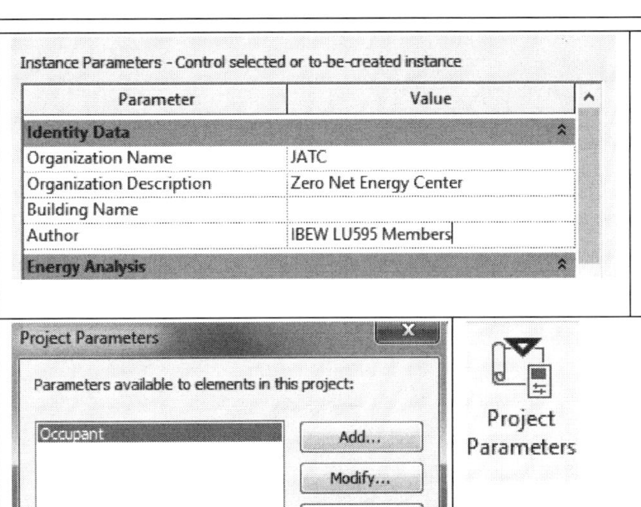

Project
Information

Project Information will automatically fill in on the title blocks for each sheet.

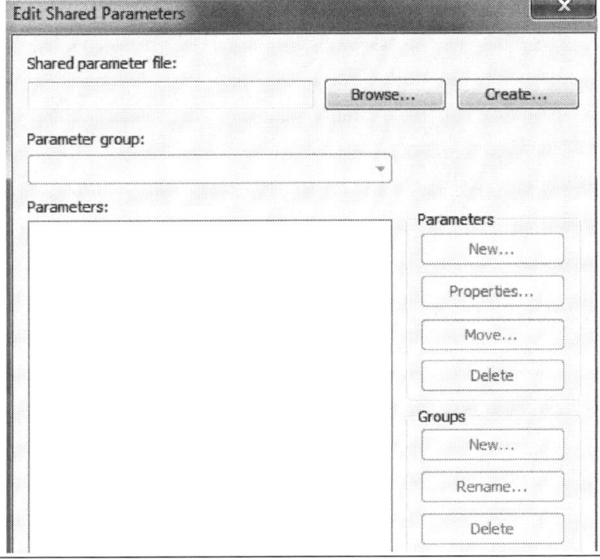

Project
Parameters

Project parameters may be used to create custom parameters to be added to a title block or to organize your project browser, families or views.

Shared
Parameters

Shared Parameters are used to create labels for Revit families and for use in schedules.

This dialog allows you to set up parameters that can be shared across family categories for use in schedules.

For example, a window assembly and a window both have width, height, glass type, etc.

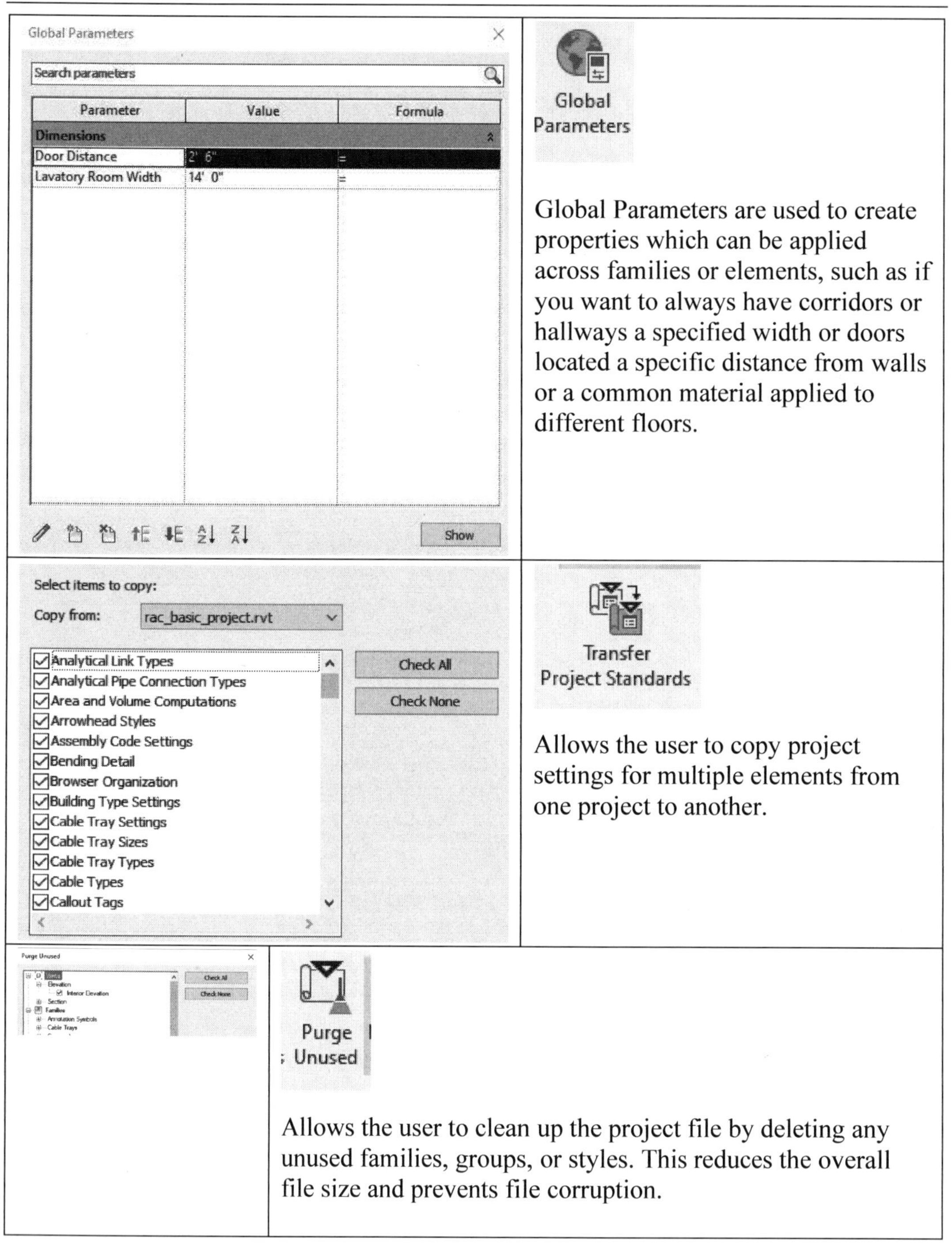

Global Parameters

Global Parameters are used to create properties which can be applied across families or elements, such as if you want to always have corridors or hallways a specified width or doors located a specific distance from walls or a common material applied to different floors.

Transfer Project Standards

Allows the user to copy project settings for multiple elements from one project to another.

Purge Unused

Allows the user to clean up the project file by deleting any unused families, groups, or styles. This reduces the overall file size and prevents file corruption.

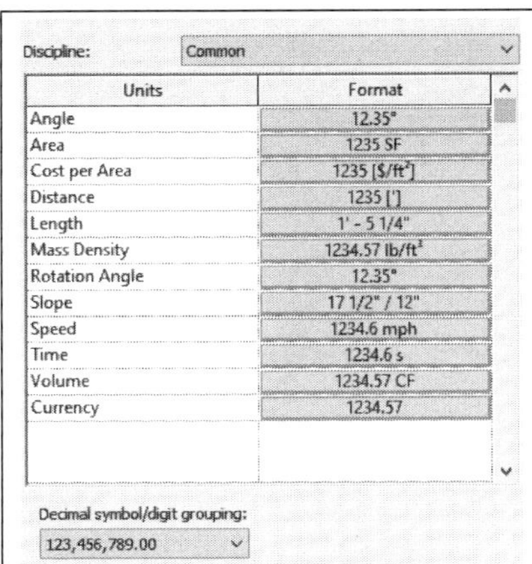

Project Units

Project Units allow you to set the units in the project. Unfortunately, any dimensions that are placed do not automatically update to the new units. If you change the units after dimension annotations have been placed, you have to place new dimension annotations.

The Additional Settings menu allows the user to customize the interface.

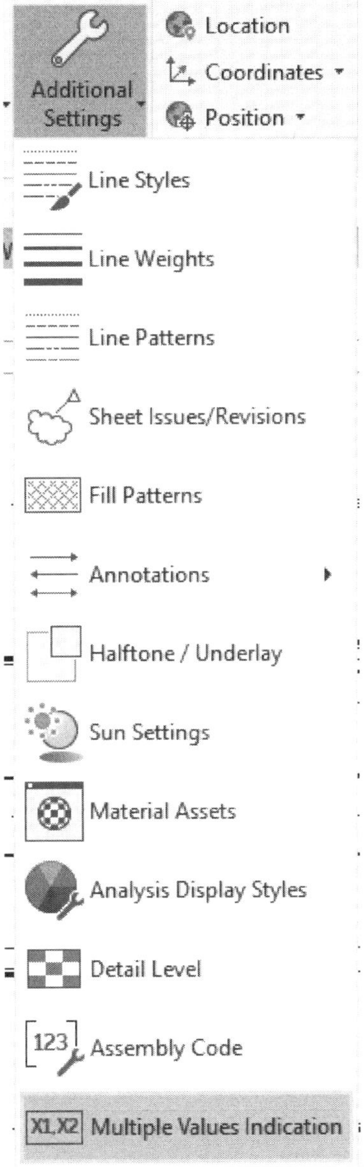

- Location
- Coordinates ▾
- Position ▾
- Line Styles
- Line Weights
- Line Patterns
- Sheet Issues/Revisions
- Fill Patterns
- Annotations ▸
- Halftone / Underlay
- Sun Settings
- Material Assets
- Analysis Display Styles
- Detail Level
- Assembly Code
- Multiple Values Indication

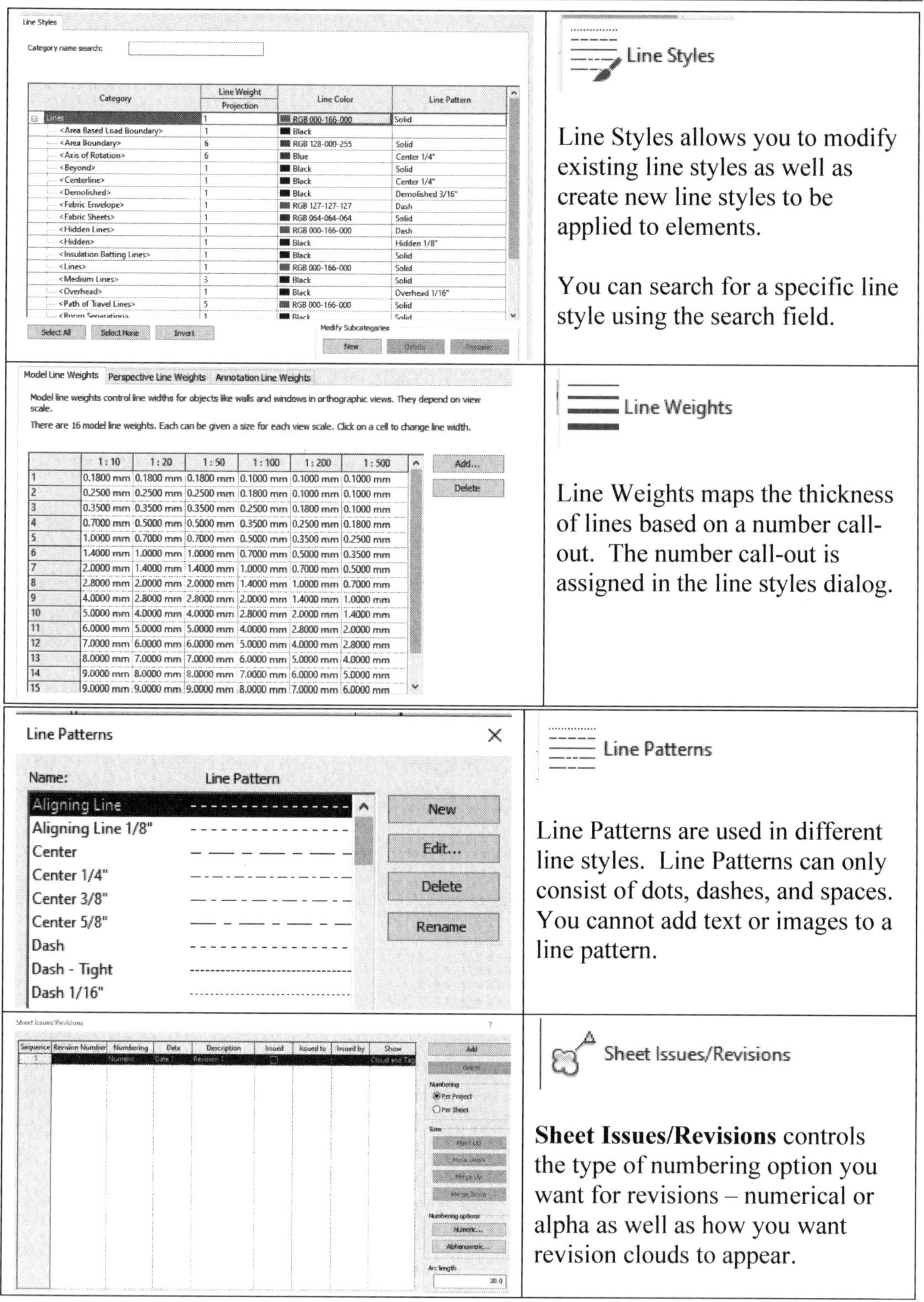

Line Styles

Line Styles allows you to modify existing line styles as well as create new line styles to be applied to elements.

You can search for a specific line style using the search field.

Line Weights

Line Weights maps the thickness of lines based on a number call-out. The number call-out is assigned in the line styles dialog.

Line Patterns

Line Patterns are used in different line styles. Line Patterns can only consist of dots, dashes, and spaces. You cannot add text or images to a line pattern.

Sheet Issues/Revisions

Sheet Issues/Revisions controls the type of numbering option you want for revisions – numerical or alpha as well as how you want revision clouds to appear.

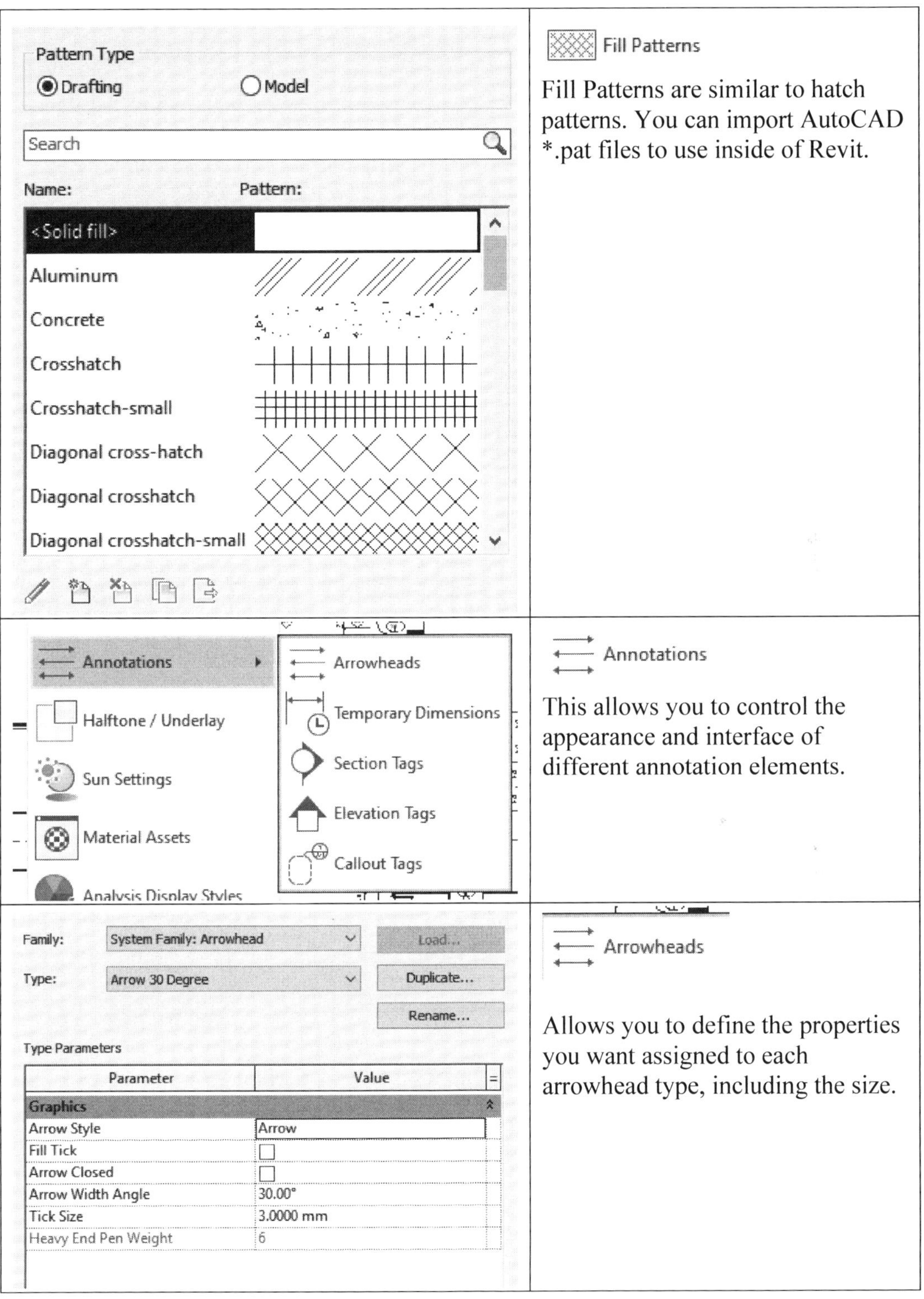

Fill Patterns

Fill Patterns are similar to hatch patterns. You can import AutoCAD *.pat files to use inside of Revit.

Annotations

This allows you to control the appearance and interface of different annotation elements.

Arrowheads

Allows you to define the properties you want assigned to each arrowhead type, including the size.

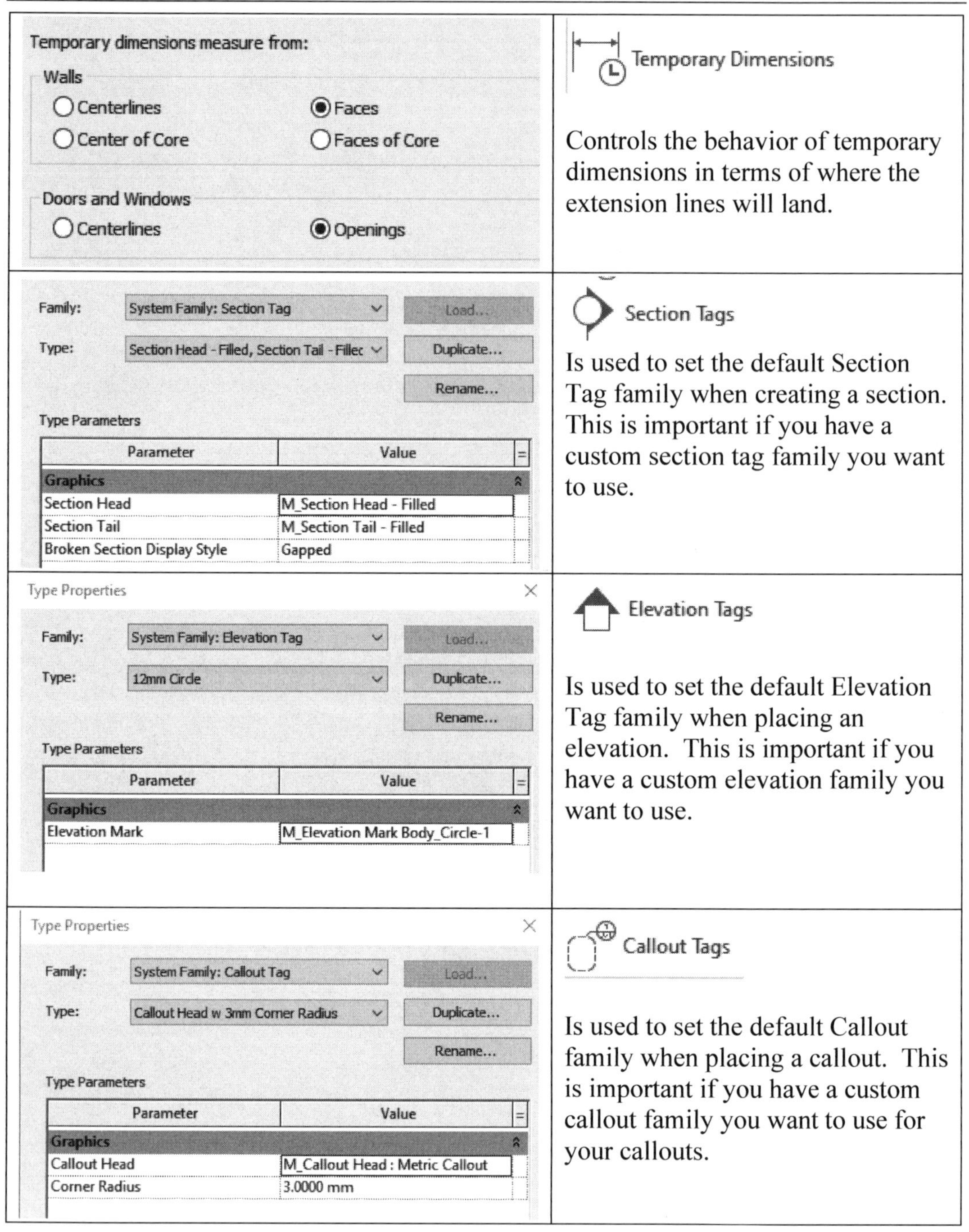

Temporary Dimensions

Controls the behavior of temporary dimensions in terms of where the extension lines will land.

Section Tags

Is used to set the default Section Tag family when creating a section. This is important if you have a custom section tag family you want to use.

Elevation Tags

Is used to set the default Elevation Tag family when placing an elevation. This is important if you have a custom elevation family you want to use.

Callout Tags

Is used to set the default Callout family when placing a callout. This is important if you have a custom callout family you want to use for your callouts.

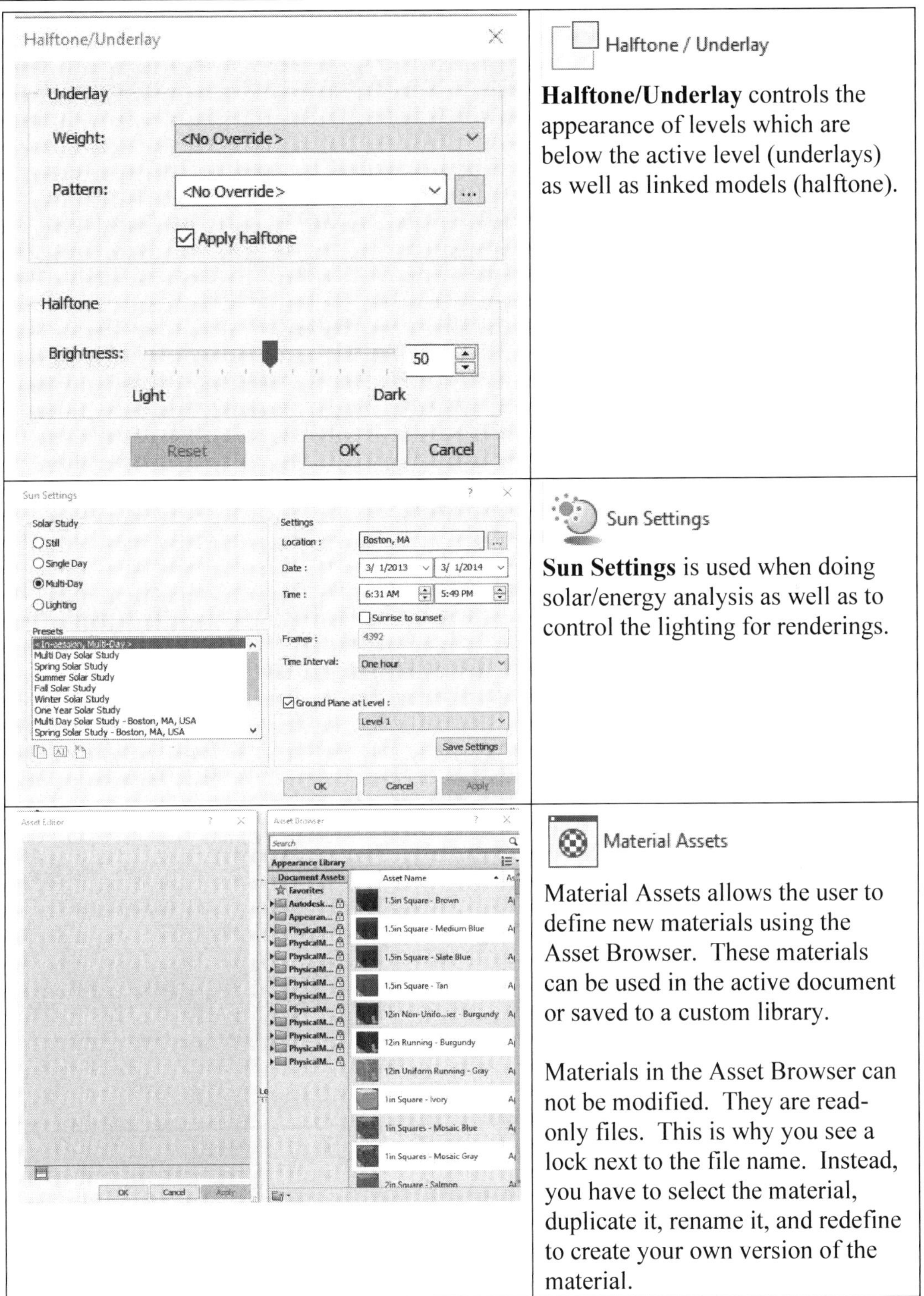

Halftone/Underlay controls the appearance of levels which are below the active level (underlays) as well as linked models (halftone).

Sun Settings is used when doing solar/energy analysis as well as to control the lighting for renderings.

Material Assets allows the user to define new materials using the Asset Browser. These materials can be used in the active document or saved to a custom library.

Materials in the Asset Browser can not be modified. They are read-only files. This is why you see a lock next to the file name. Instead, you have to select the material, duplicate it, rename it, and redefine to create your own version of the material.

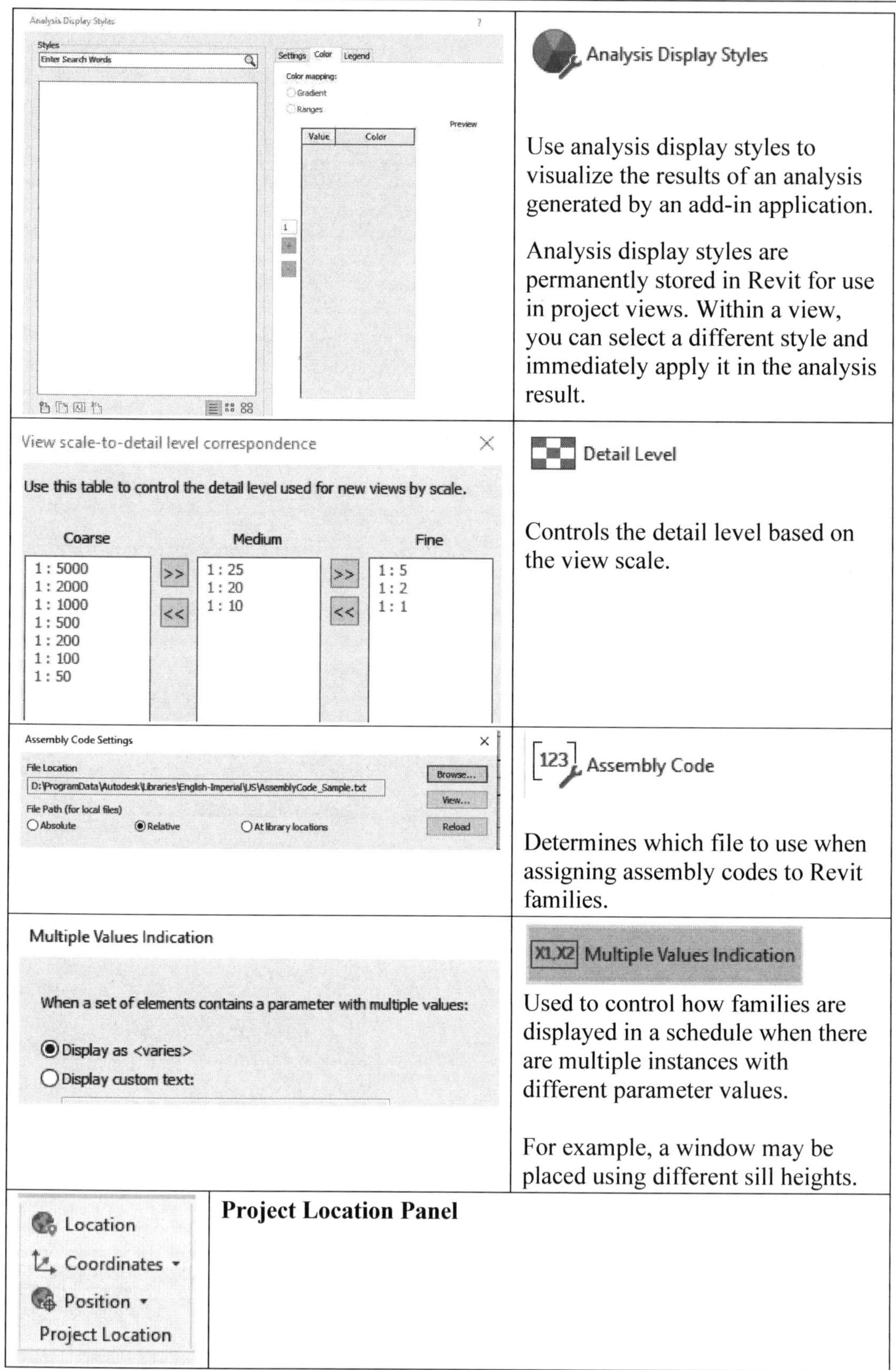

Analysis Display Styles

Use analysis display styles to visualize the results of an analysis generated by an add-in application.

Analysis display styles are permanently stored in Revit for use in project views. Within a view, you can select a different style and immediately apply it in the analysis result.

Detail Level

Controls the detail level based on the view scale.

Assembly Code

Determines which file to use when assigning assembly codes to Revit families.

Multiple Values Indication

Used to control how families are displayed in a schedule when there are multiple instances with different parameter values.

For example, a window may be placed using different sill heights.

Project Location Panel

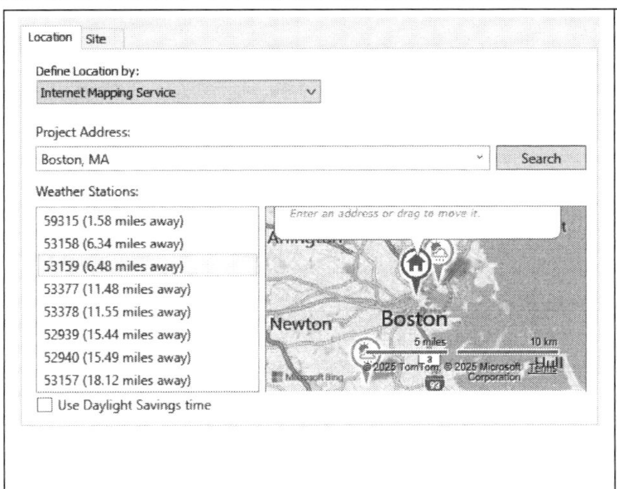

 Location

Use the Location setting to place the project in the correct geographic location. This is relevant for solar studies.

Revit interfaces with Google maps. You must have an internet connection to use Google maps. Otherwise, you can just select a location using a drop-down list of standard cities around the world on the Site tab.

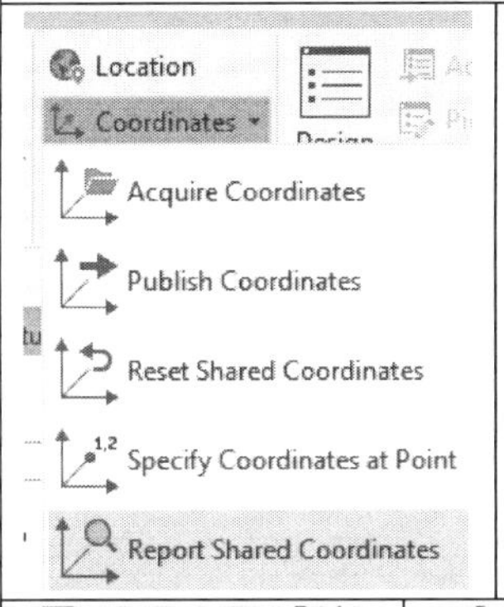

Coordinates ▾

The Coordinates tools are used when you have placed a linked CAD file into a project and allow the user to acquire coordinates from the linked file or transfer (publish) the Revit coordinates.
Shared coordinates are used to recognize the position of multiple linked files.

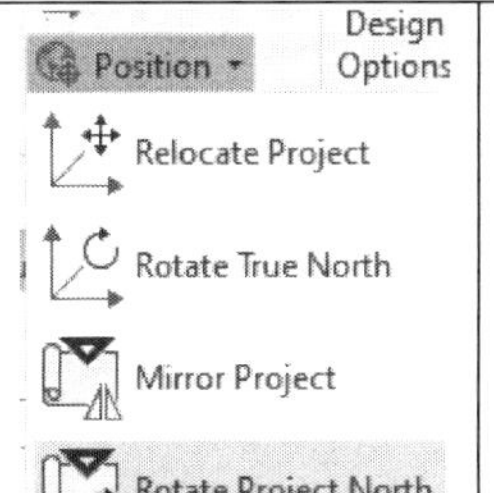

Position ▾

The position tools are used to position the model to reflect the correct geographical location and position relative to the sun.

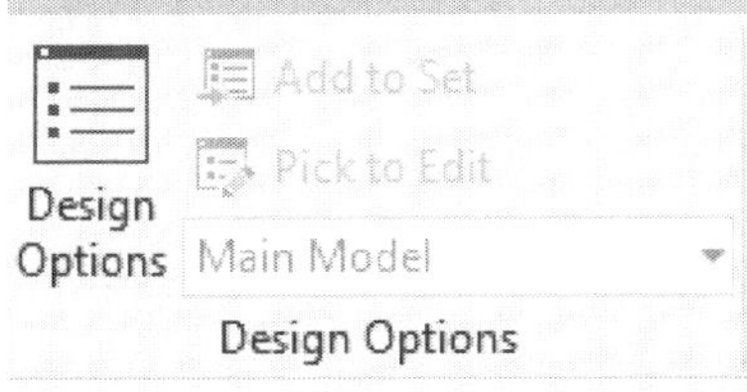

Design Options are used to design different options for a building model. This allows the user to create different versions of the same building to present to a client.
Elements may be added to different option sets and then displayed.
This is similar to a Configuration Manager.

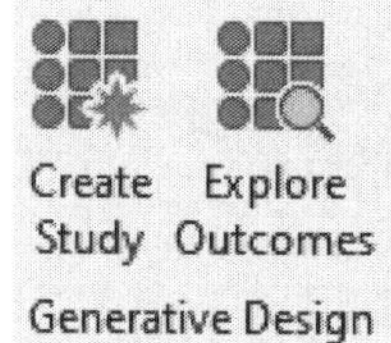

Generative Design in Revit allows you to leverage Dynamo graphs to explore outcome-based solutions for your designs. You define criteria and constraints for the design problem. Then Generative Design uses this information to iterate many possible solutions, presenting them to you for further evaluation. When you decide on the optimal solution, click a button to integrate it into the model for further development.

For example, it could be used to explore different wiring layouts.

Use Create Study to select a study type and define the goals and study criteria. Then click a button to start the study and generate design alternatives. While the process is running, you can continue to work on your model.

Use the Explore Outcomes dialog to examine the design alternatives created by the study. You can filter the outcomes for specific criteria and narrow down the possible choices. Select the optimal solution, and click a button to integrate it into the model.

The Manage Project panel is used to manage different file types as well as set the starting/default view when you open a project file.

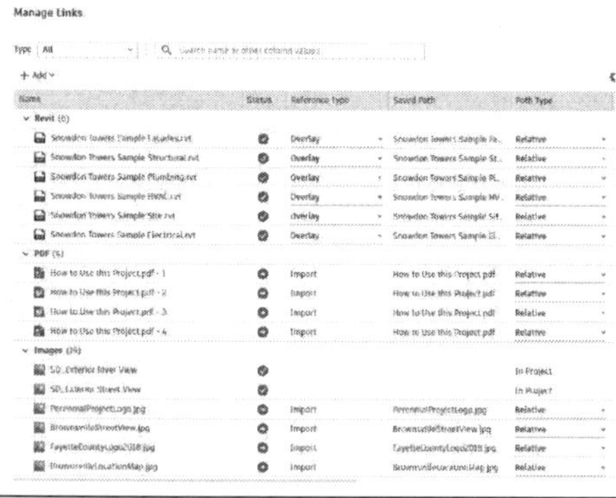

The Manage Links dialog is similar to the External References dialog in AutoCAD. You can manage any external files, unload, reload, and remove them.

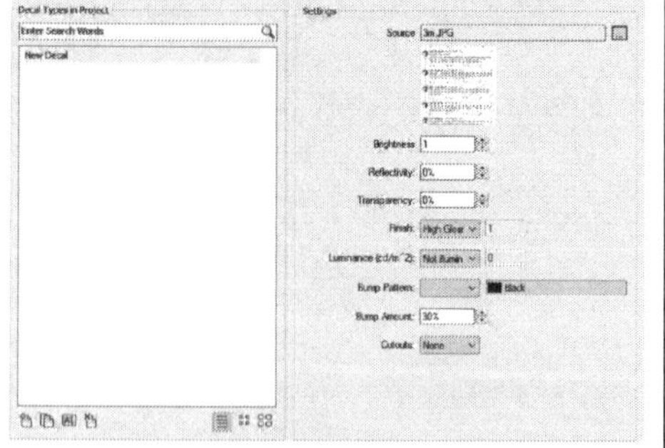

Decals are used to place images inside the building model. I use decals for signage, paintings, etc. This dialog allows you to create new decals and modify existing decals.

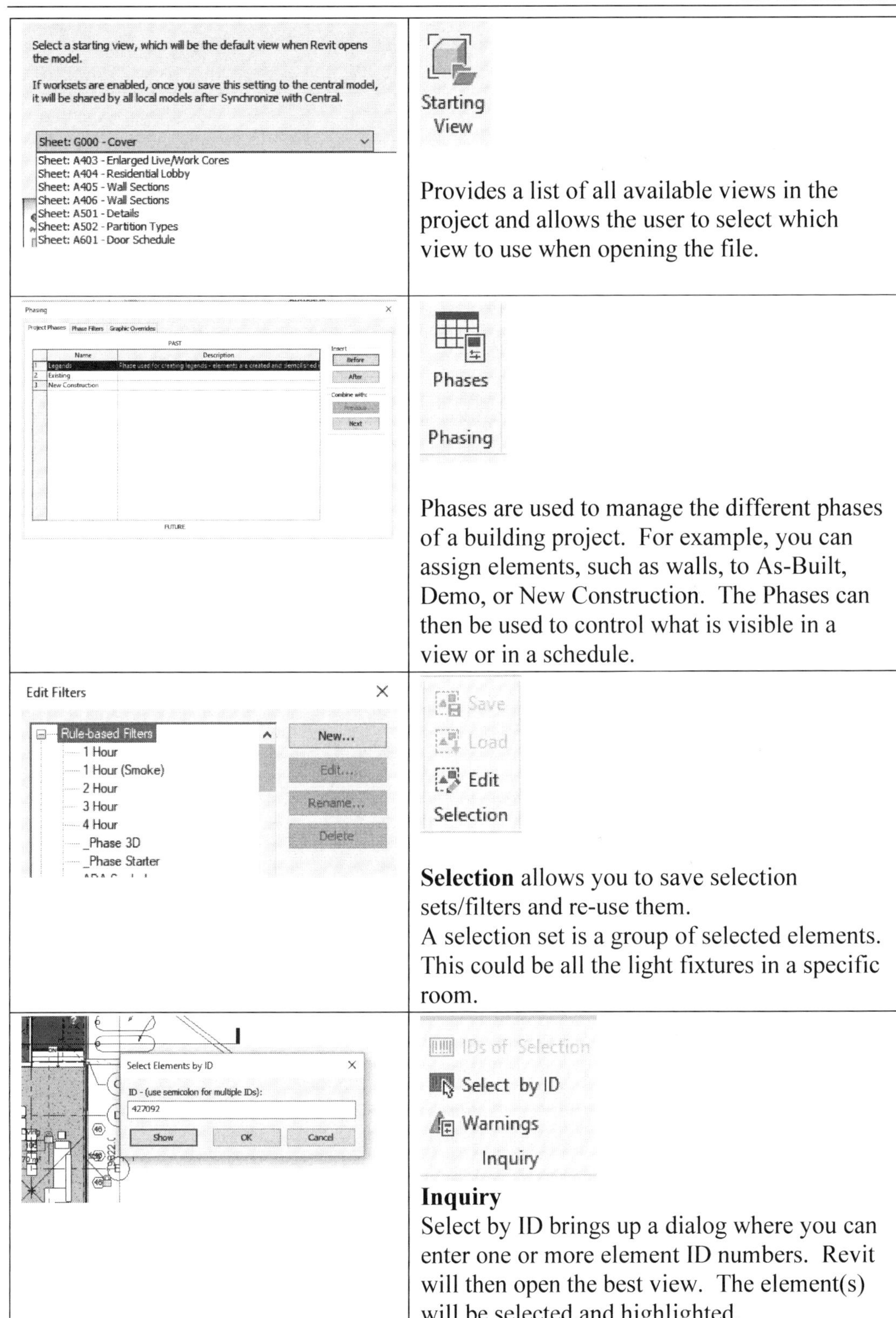

Select a starting view, which will be the default view when Revit opens the model. If worksets are enabled, once you save this setting to the central model, it will be shared by all local models after Synchronize with Central. Sheet: G000 - Cover Sheet: A403 - Enlarged Live/Work Cores Sheet: A404 - Residential Lobby Sheet: A405 - Wall Sections Sheet: A406 - Wall Sections Sheet: A501 - Details Sheet: A502 - Partition Types Sheet: A601 - Door Schedule	**Starting View** Provides a list of all available views in the project and allows the user to select which view to use when opening the file.
Phasing dialog: Project Phases, Phase Filters, Graphic Overrides tabs. PAST. Name / Description columns with rows: 1 Legends — Phase used for creating legends - elements are created and demolished; 2 Existing; 3 New Construction. Insert: Before, After. Combine with: Previous, Next. FUTURE.	**Phases** *Phasing* Phases are used to manage the different phases of a building project. For example, you can assign elements, such as walls, to As-Built, Demo, or New Construction. The Phases can then be used to control what is visible in a view or in a schedule.
Edit Filters dialog: Rule-based Filters — 1 Hour, 1 Hour (Smoke), 2 Hour, 3 Hour, 4 Hour, _Phase 3D, _Phase Starter. Buttons: New..., Edit..., Rename..., Delete.	Save Load Edit **Selection** **Selection** allows you to save selection sets/filters and re-use them. A selection set is a group of selected elements. This could be all the light fixtures in a specific room.
Select Elements by ID dialog: ID - (use semicolon for multiple IDs): 427092. Buttons: Show, OK, Cancel.	IDs of Selection Select by ID Warnings Inquiry **Inquiry** Select by ID brings up a dialog where you can enter one or more element ID numbers. Revit will then open the best view. The element(s) will be selected and highlighted.

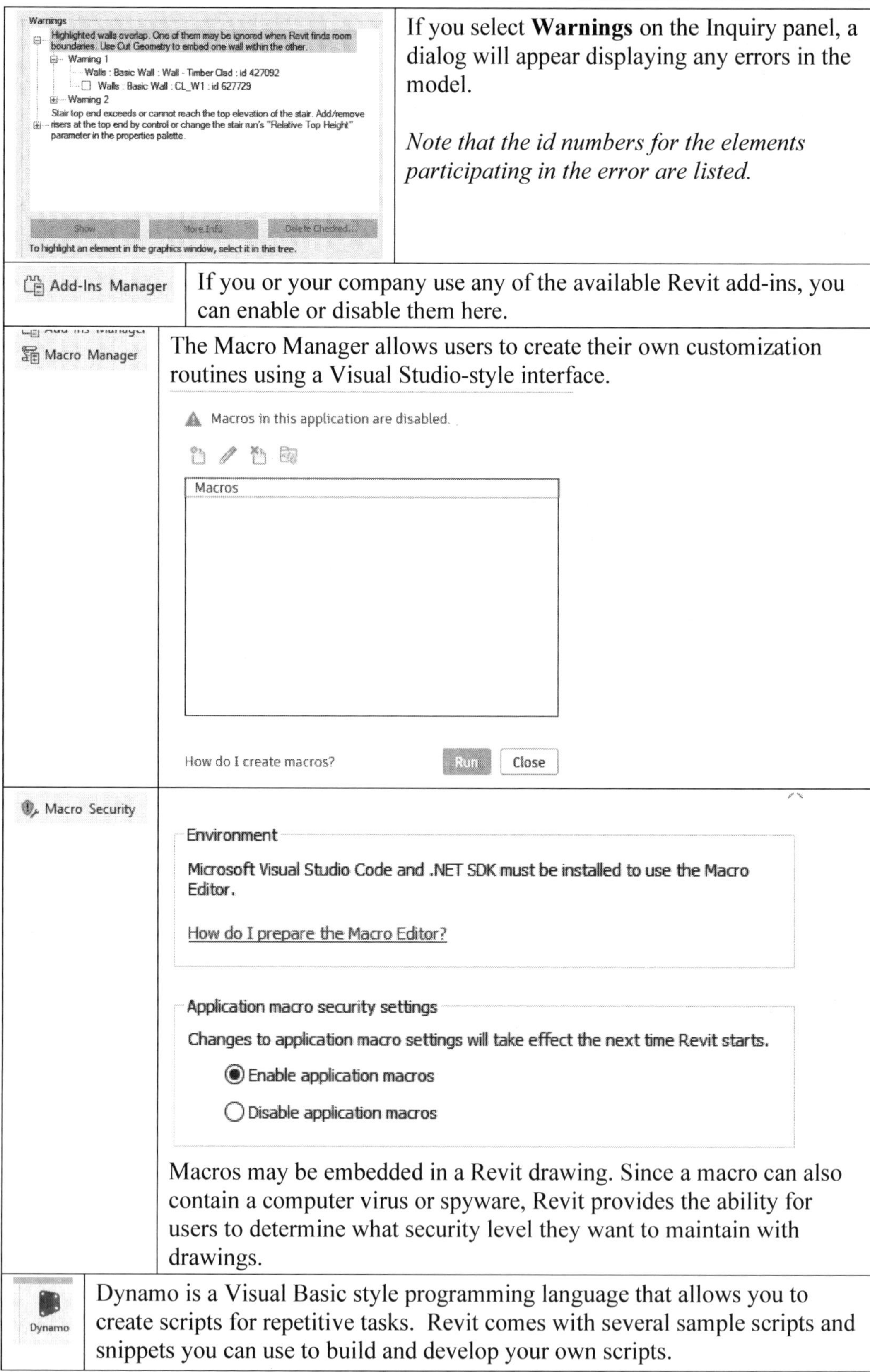

If you select **Warnings** on the Inquiry panel, a dialog will appear displaying any errors in the model.

Note that the id numbers for the elements participating in the error are listed.

Add-Ins Manager

If you or your company use any of the available Revit add-ins, you can enable or disable them here.

Macro Manager

The Macro Manager allows users to create their own customization routines using a Visual Studio-style interface.

Macro Security

Macros may be embedded in a Revit drawing. Since a macro can also contain a computer virus or spyware, Revit provides the ability for users to determine what security level they want to maintain with drawings.

Dynamo

Dynamo is a Visual Basic style programming language that allows you to create scripts for repetitive tasks. Revit comes with several sample scripts and snippets you can use to build and develop your own scripts.

	Dynamo Player allows you to run Dynamo routines.

> ➤ By default, the Browser lists all sheets and all views.
> ➤ If you have multiple users of Revit in your office, place your family libraries and rendering libraries on a server and designate the path under the File Locations tab under Options; this allows multiple users to access the same libraries and materials.

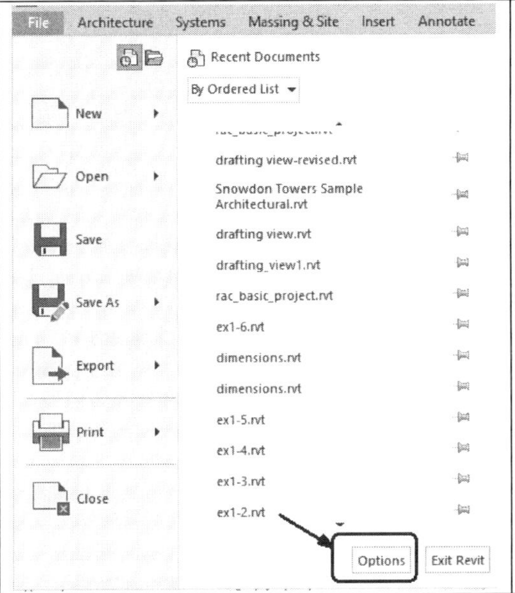

To access the System Options:

Go to the Revit menu and select the Options button located at the bottom of the dialog.

Save Reminder interval:

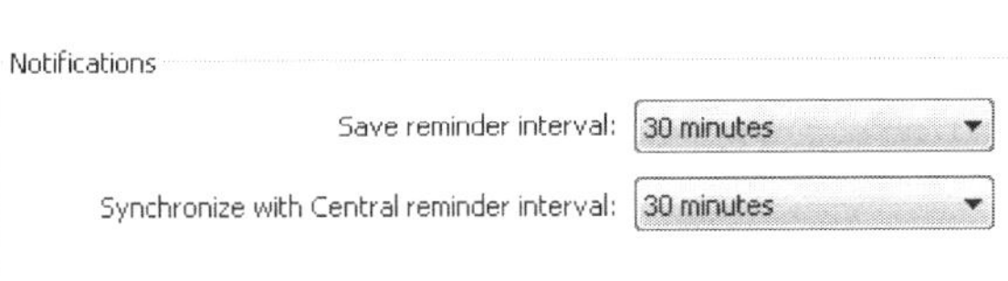

Notifications

You can select any option from the drop-down. This is not an auto-save feature. Your file will not be saved unless you select the 'Save' button. All this does is bring up a reminder dialog at the selected interval.

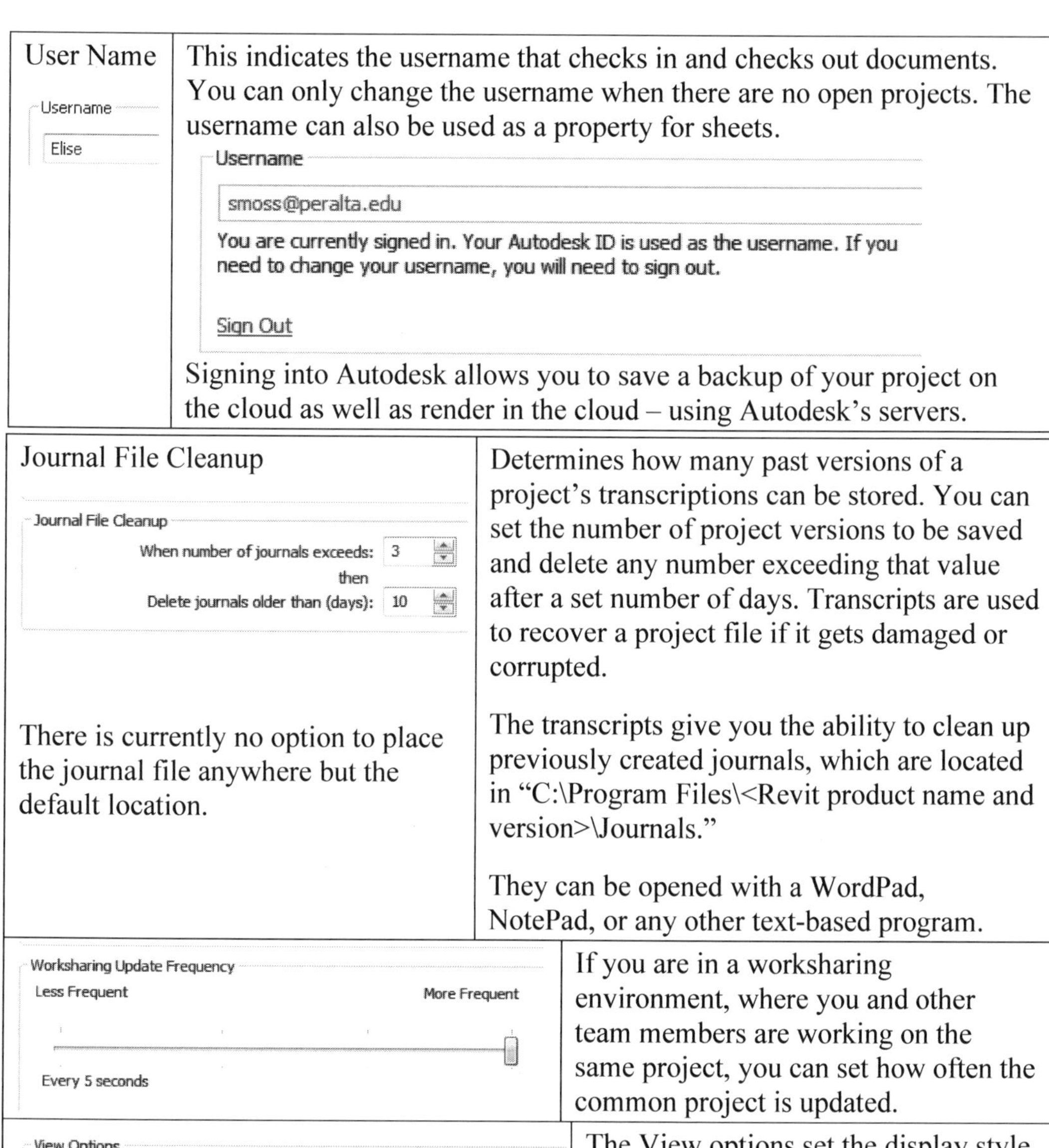

User Name	This indicates the username that checks in and checks out documents. You can only change the username when there are no open projects. The username can also be used as a property for sheets.

Signing into Autodesk allows you to save a backup of your project on the cloud as well as render in the cloud – using Autodesk's servers.

Journal File Cleanup	Determines how many past versions of a project's transcriptions can be stored. You can set the number of project versions to be saved and delete any number exceeding that value after a set number of days. Transcripts are used to recover a project file if it gets damaged or corrupted.

There is currently no option to place the journal file anywhere but the default location.

The transcripts give you the ability to clean up previously created journals, which are located in "C:\Program Files\<Revit product name and version>\Journals."

They can be opened with a WordPad, NotePad, or any other text-based program.

If you are in a worksharing environment, where you and other team members are working on the same project, you can set how often the common project is updated.

The View options set the display style for views depending on discipline.

The User Interface Options

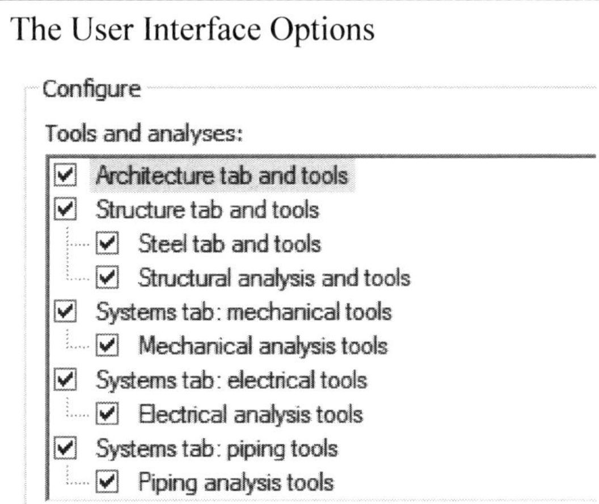

Enabling the Tools and analyses controls the visibility of the ribbons. You can hide the ribbons for those tools which you don't need or use by unchecking those ribbons.

In order to access the Systems Browser, the MEP Fabrication parts, and the P&ID Modeler, the Systems tab tools need to be enabled.

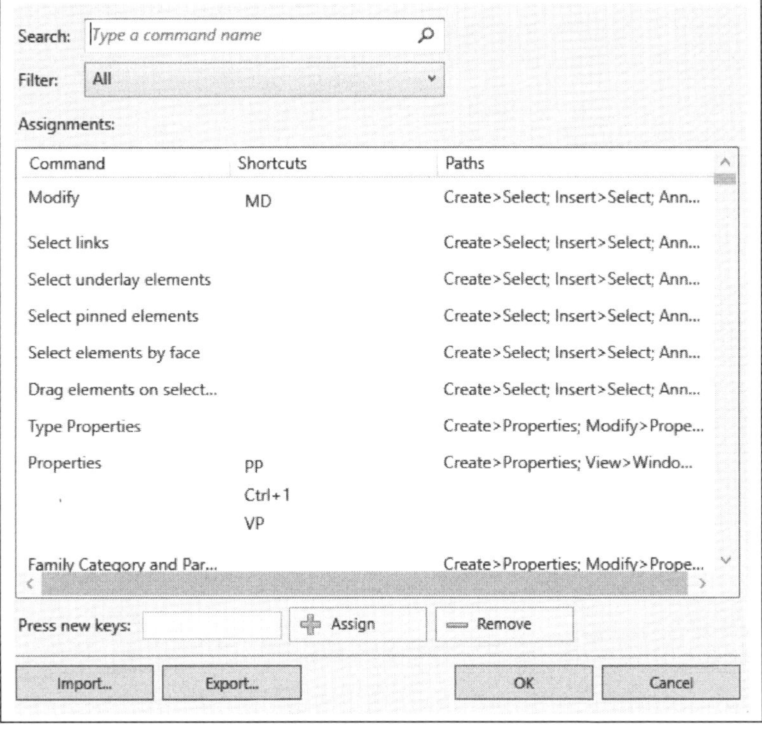

Keyboard Shortcuts (also located under User Interface on the View ribbon) allow you to assign keyboard shortcuts to your favorite commands.

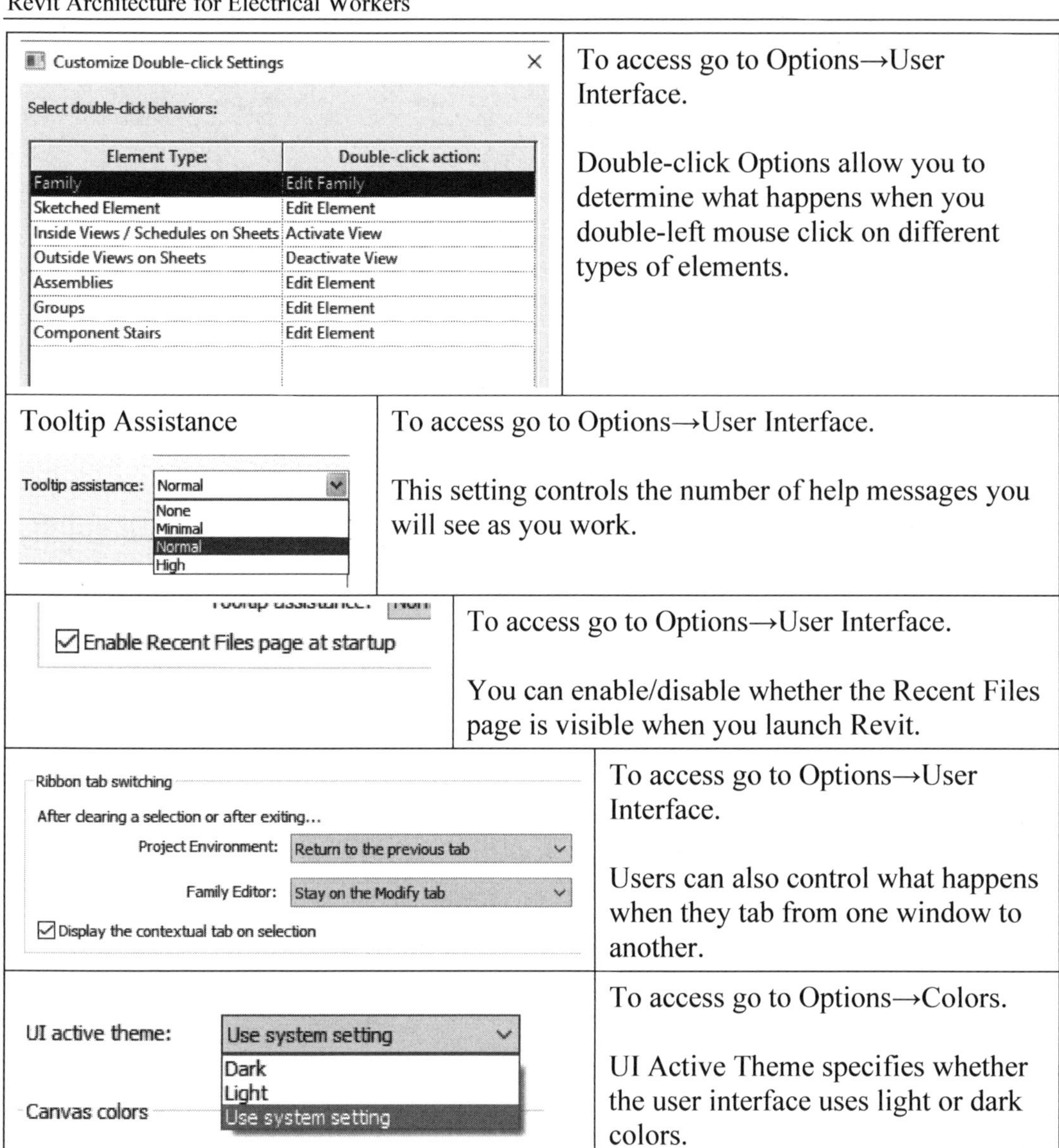

To access go to Options→User Interface.

Double-click Options allow you to determine what happens when you double-left mouse click on different types of elements.

Tooltip Assistance

To access go to Options→User Interface.

This setting controls the number of help messages you will see as you work.

To access go to Options→User Interface.

You can enable/disable whether the Recent Files page is visible when you launch Revit.

To access go to Options→User Interface.

Users can also control what happens when they tab from one window to another.

To access go to Options→Colors.

UI Active Theme specifies whether the user interface uses light or dark colors.

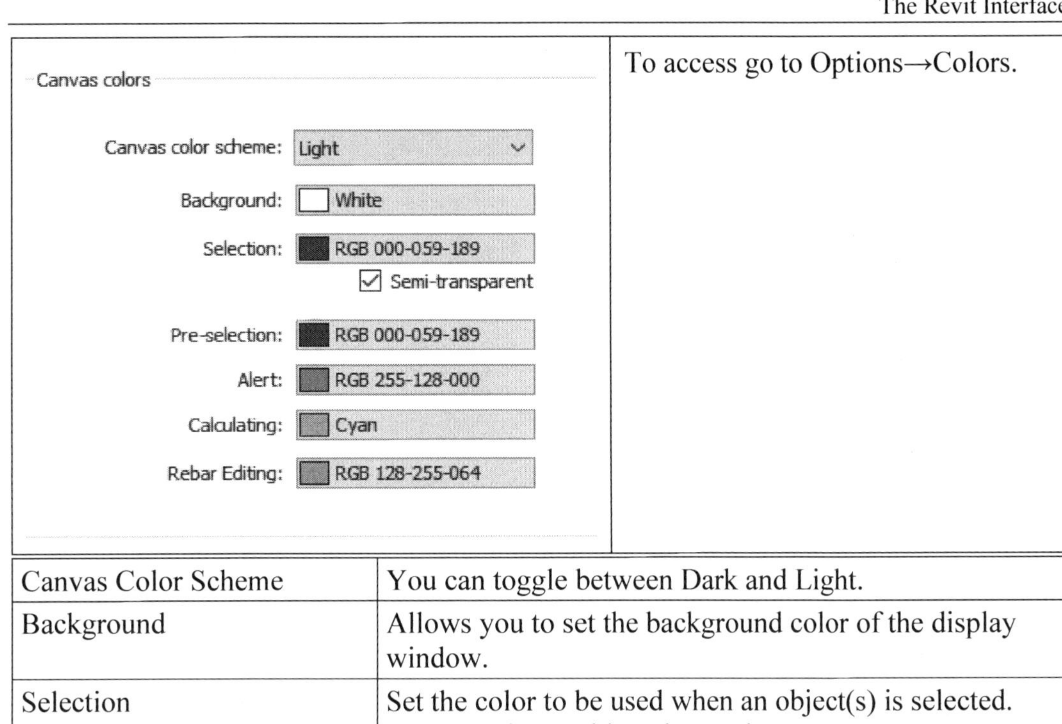

To access go to Options→Colors.

Canvas Color Scheme	You can toggle between Dark and Light.
Background	Allows you to set the background color of the display window.
Selection	Set the color to be used when an object(s) is selected. You can also enable to be semi-transparent.
Semi-transparent	If this is enabled, you can see elements that are located behind the selected element(s).
Pre-selection	Set the color to be used when the cursor hovers over an object.
Alert	Sets the color for elements that are selected when an error occurs.
Calculating	This sets the colors used for background calculations.
Rebar Editing	This changes the highlight color when rebars are selected.

The Graphics tab

View navigation performance

☑ **Allow navigation during redraw**

Interrupts the drawing of model elements to allow view navigation (pan, orbit, and zoom). Use this option to improve performance when you are navigating views in large models.

☑ **Simplify display during view navigation**

Suspends certain graphic effects and reduces detail during camera manipulation: Fill and Line, Shadows, Hidden Lines, Underlays, Small Objects (LOD).

Graphics mode

☑ **Smooth lines with anti-aliasing**

Improves the quality of lines in views.

⦿ Allow control for each view in the Graphic Display Options dialog

◯ Use for all views (control for each view is disabled)

Temporary dimension text appearance

Note: Includes appearance of dimensions when using the Measure tool.

Size: 8

Background: Transparent

Accelerated Graphics

☑ **Enable the Accelerated Graphics Tech Preview**

Temporarily accelerate graphics performance by turning on per view.

◯ Show onscreen toolbar and toggle with right click menu

⦿ Toggle with right click menu only

Activation requirements include hardware acceleration.

Tech Preview Terms of Use.

Learn more about Accelerated Graphics - Tech Preview.

Allow navigation during redraw	Enable this option to improve performance when you are zooming/orbiting/panning in a large model.
Simplify display during view navigation	Improve performance when you are zooming/orbiting/panning in a large model by reducing the amount of detail displayed and suspending some graphic effects.
Smooth lines with anti-aliasing	Improves the quality of lines, smoothing edges.

Temporary dimension text appearance	You can increase the font size of the temporary dimension to make it easier to read. You can set the background to be transparent or opaque.
Accelerated Graphics	The Accelerated Graphics Tech Preview offers an increase in speed for both 2D and 3D views, as well as an enhanced visual appearance. Some elements, such as duct work, slabs, and railings, may not appear properly when this mode is enabled.

Hardware Hardware setup Video Card: Intel(R) HD Graphics 530 Driver Version: 31.0.101.2112 Status: **Your hardware configuration meets the hardware acceleration requirements.** DirectX 11 Shader Model 5.0 GPU Memory 4 GB Learn more about system requirements. Disable hardware acceleration only if you are experiencing graphics issues or have an incompatible video card. ☑ **Use hardware acceleration** 　☑ **Draw visible elements only** 　　Improves performance when you navigate the model. Hidden elements in the view are ignored during navigation.	Displays the video card in use and provided driver status. If your graphics quality is low, use this option to see if your video/graphics card is sufficient.

File Locations

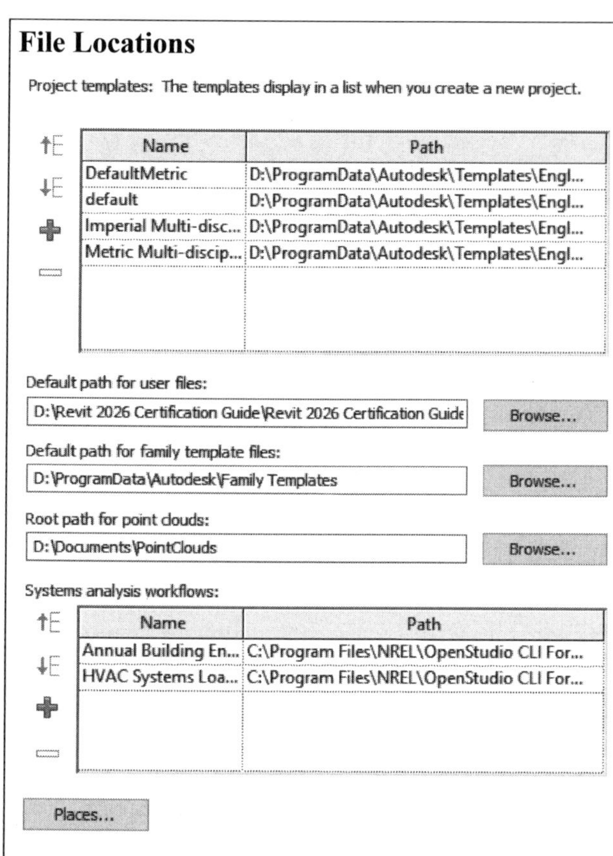

File Locations is used to set the default search locations for templates and families.

You can set the folder to automatically save project files.

Rendering

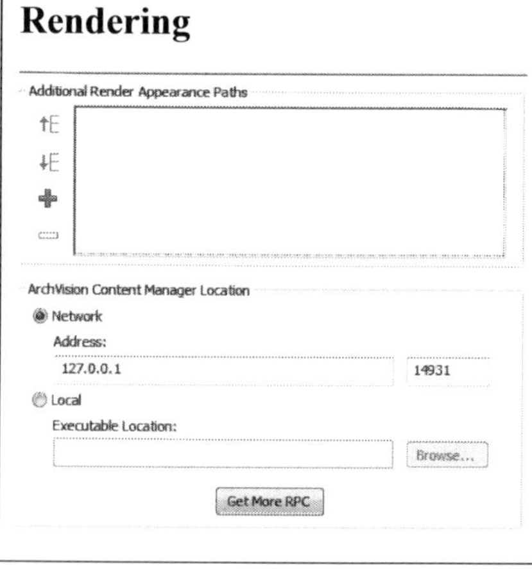

Rendering controls where you are storing your AccuRender files and directories where you are storing your materials.

This allows you to set your paths so Revit can locate materials and files easily.

If you press the Get More RPC button, your browser will launch to the Archvision website. You must download and install a plug-in to manage your RPC downloads. There is a free exchange service for content, but you have to create a login account.

Check Spelling

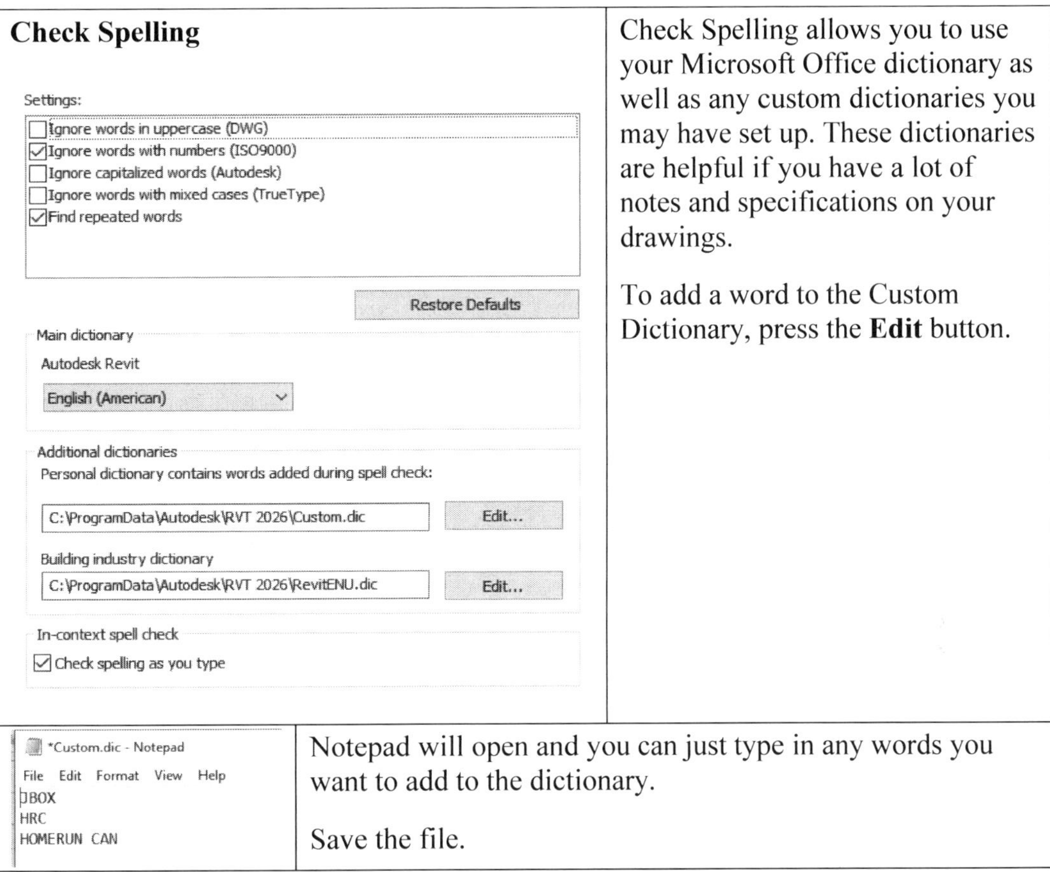

Check Spelling allows you to use your Microsoft Office dictionary as well as any custom dictionaries you may have set up. These dictionaries are helpful if you have a lot of notes and specifications on your drawings.

To add a word to the Custom Dictionary, press the **Edit** button.

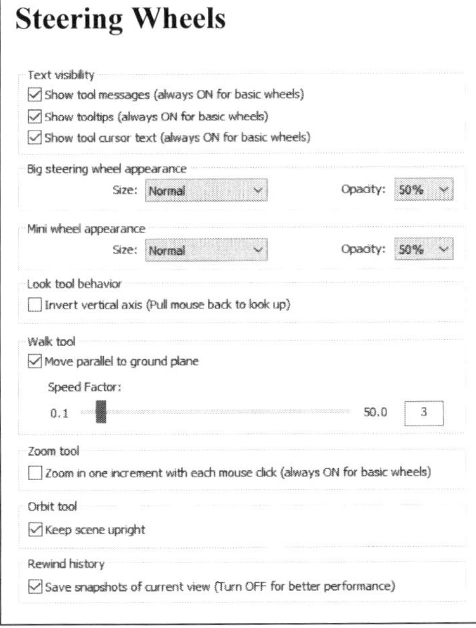

Notepad will open and you can just type in any words you want to add to the dictionary.

Save the file.

Steering Wheels

Steering Wheels control the appearance and functionality of the steering wheels.

Steering Wheels are used to change the display.

ViewCube

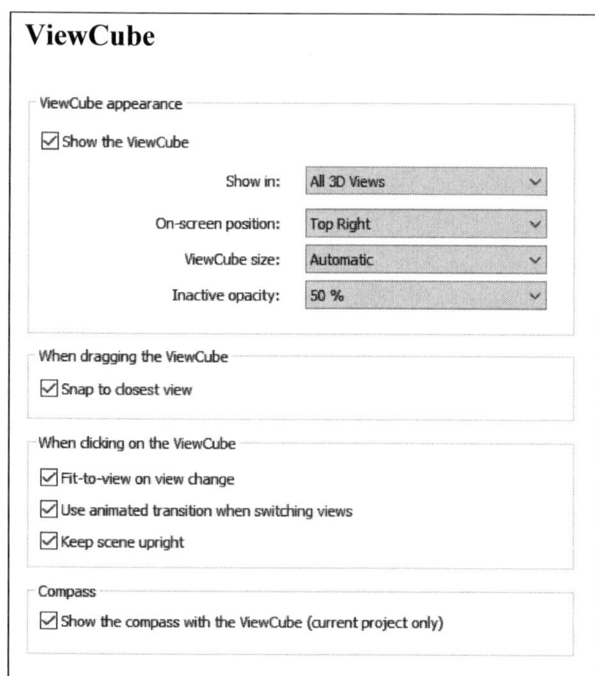

ViewCube controls the appearance and location of the ViewCube.

The user can also determine how the display changes when the ViewCube is selected.

Macros

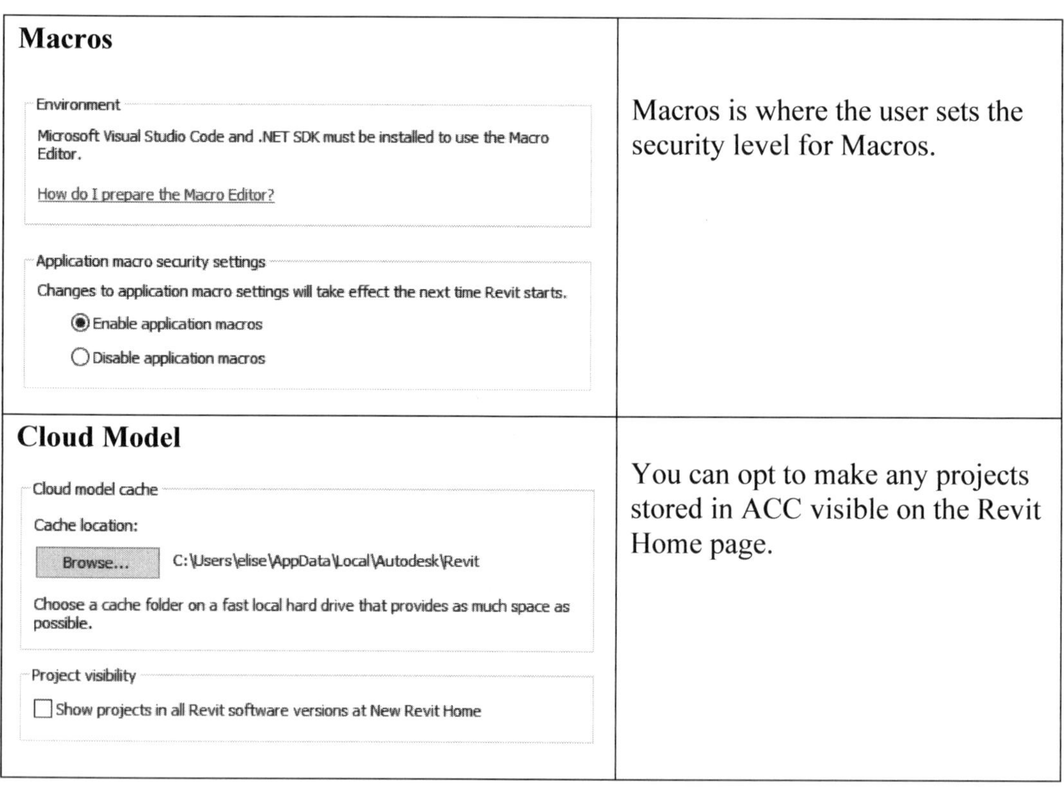

Macros is where the user sets the security level for Macros.

Cloud Model

You can opt to make any projects stored in ACC visible on the Revit Home page.

To boost productivity, store all your custom templates on the network for easy access and set the pointer to the correct folder.

The Help Menu

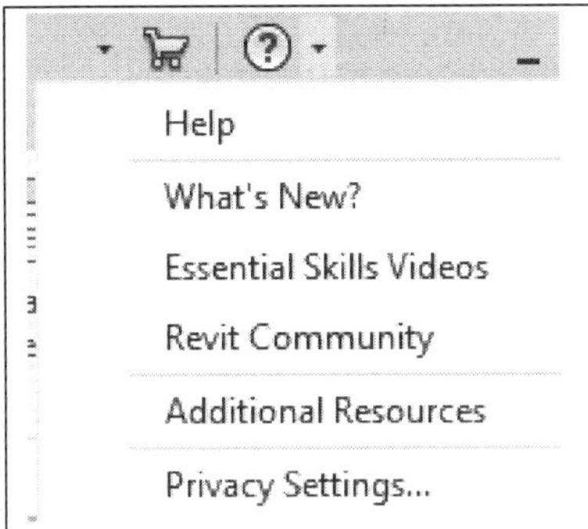

Revit Help (also reached by function key F1) brings up the Help dialog.

What's New allows veteran users to quickly come up to speed on the latest release.

Essential Skills Videos is a small set of videos to help get you started. They are worth watching, especially if your computer skills are rusty.

Revit Community is an internet-based website with customer forums where you can search for solutions to your questions or post your questions. Most of the forums are monitored by Autodesk employees who are friendly and knowledgeable.

Additional Resources launches your browser and opens to a link on Autodesk's site. Autodesk Building Solutions take you to a YouTube channel where you can watch video tutorials.

Support Knowledge Base

3rd Party Learning Content

Autodesk.com/revit

Autodesk Building Solutions

About Revit Architecture reaches a splash screen with information about the version and build of the copy of Revit you are working with. If you are unsure about which Service Pack you have installed, this is where you will find that information.

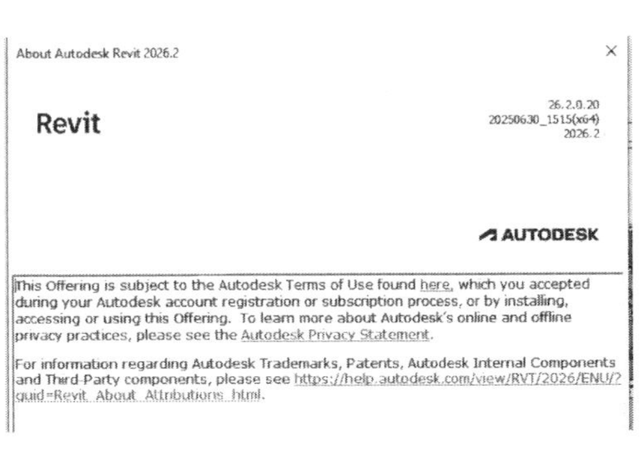

Exercise 1-7:

Setting File Locations

Drawing Name: Close all open files
Estimated Time: 5 minutes

This exercise reinforces the following skills:
- Options
- File Locations

1. Close all open files or projects.

2. 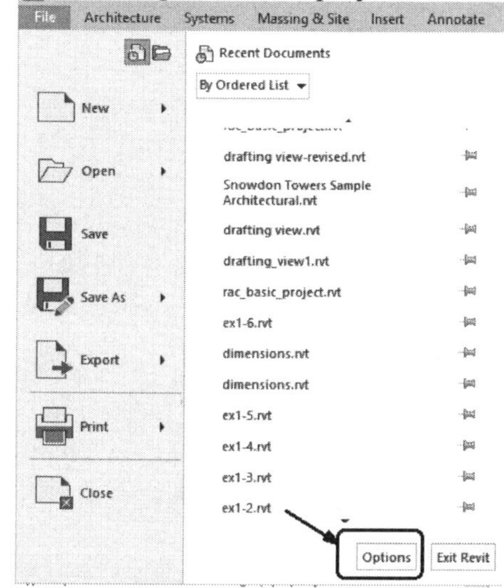 Go to the **File Menu**.

   Select the **Options** button at the bottom of the window.

3. Select the **File Locations** tab.

4. Default path for user files:

   C:\Users\Elise\Documents

   In the **Default path for users** section, pick the **Browse** button.

5. Default path for user files:

   C:\IBEW LU 595 Class\

   Navigate to the local or network folder where you will save your files. When the correct folder is highlighted, pick **Open**. Your instructor or CAD manager can provide you with this file information.

I recommend to my students to bring a flash drive to class and back up each day's work onto the flash drive. That way you will never lose your valuable work. Some students forget their flash drive. For those students, make a habit of uploading your file to Google Drive, Dropbox, Autodesk 360, or email your file to yourself.

Exercise 1-8:

Adding a Template to the Template list

Drawing Name: Close all open files
Estimated Time: 5 minutes

This exercise reinforces the following skills:
- Options
- File Locations
- Project Templates
- Recent Files

1. 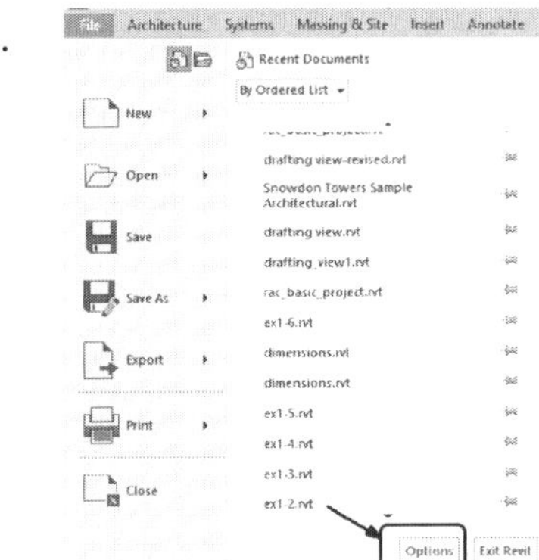

   Select **Options** on the File Menu.

2. Activate File Locations.

   Press the **Plus** icon to add a project template.

3.

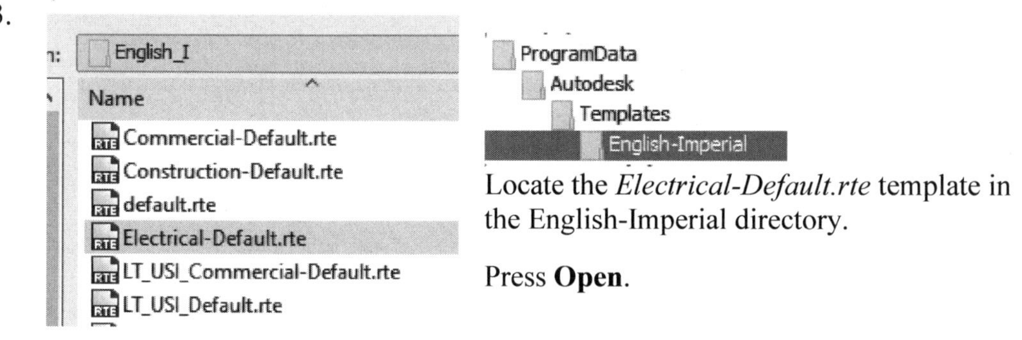

Locate the *Electrical-Default.rte* template in the English-Imperial directory.

Press **Open**.

4.

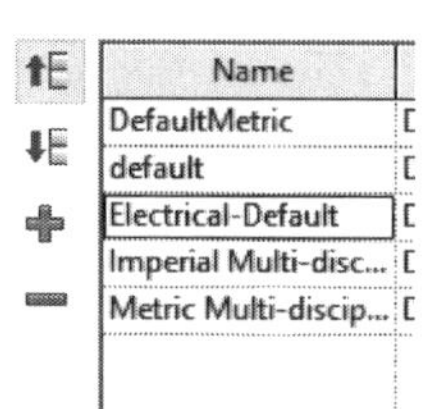

Note the file is now listed.
Select the Up arrow to move it to the top of the list.

Click **OK**.

Exercise 1-9:

Turning Off the Visibility of Ribbons

Drawing Name: Close all open files
Estimated Time: 5 minutes

This exercise reinforces the following skills:
- Options
- User Interface
- Ribbon Tools

1.

Select **Options** on the Application Menu.

2. 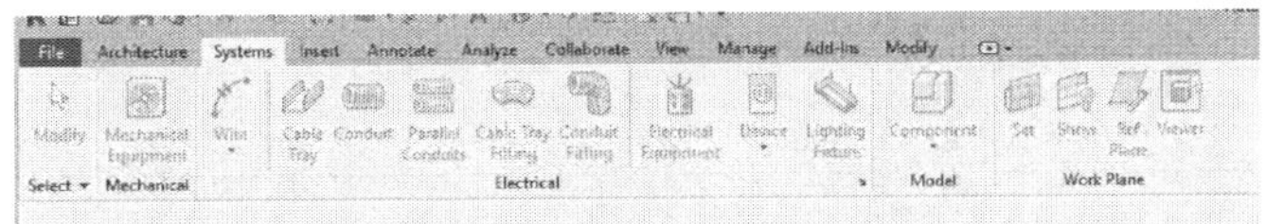 Highlight **User Interface**.

Uncheck/disable Structure and tab tools, System tab: mechanical tools.

Verify that the System tab: electrical tools are enabled.

Press **OK**.

3. Notice that the Systems ribbon updates to only display the tools that are enabled.

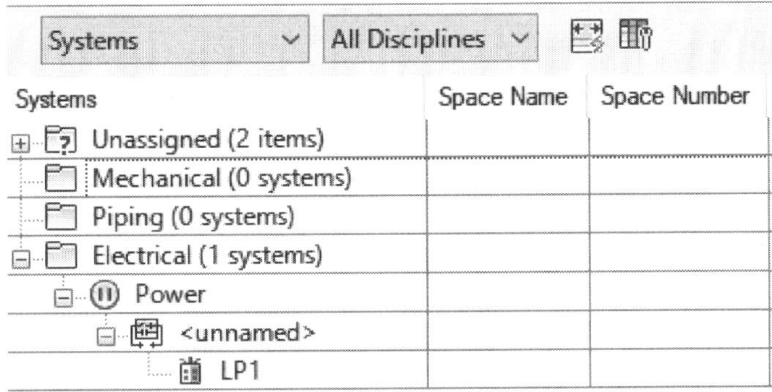

Revit's System Browser

Systems ∨	All Disciplines ∨		
Systems		Space Name	Space Number
⊞ ? Unassigned (2 items)			
Mechanical (0 systems)			
Piping (0 systems)			
⊟ Electrical (1 systems)			
⊟ ⓘ Power			
⊟ <unnamed>			
LP1			

The System Browser opens a separate window that displays a hierarchical list of all the components in each discipline in a project, either by the system type or by ones.

The System Browser contains a list of all electrical components in a project and the systems to which they are assigned. Any electrical elements that are not assigned to a system appear in the Unassigned category. Using the system browser allows you to quickly locate any unassigned electrical components and assign them to the correct system.

Customizing the View of the System Browser

The options in the View bar allow you to sort and customize the display of systems in the System Browser.

- **Systems**: displays components by major and minor systems created for each discipline.

- **Zones**: displays zones and spaces. Expand each zone to display the spaces assigned to the zone.

- **All Disciplines**: displays components in separate folders for each discipline (mechanical, piping, and electrical). Piping includes plumbing and fire protection.

- **Mechanical**: displays only components for the Mechanical discipline.

- **Piping**: displays only components for the Piping disciplines (Piping, Plumbing, and Fire Protection).

- **Electrical**: displays only components for the Electrical discipline.

- **AutoFit All Columns**: adjusts the width of all columns to fit the text in the headings.

  Note: You can also double-click a column heading to automatically adjust the width of a column.

- **Column Settings**: opens the Column Settings dialog where you specify the columnar information displayed for each discipline. Expand individual categories (General, Mechanical, Piping, Electrical) as desired, and select the properties that you want to appear as column headings. You can also select columns, and click Hide or Show to select column headings that display in the table.

Exercise 1-10:

Using the System Browser

Drawing Name: *system_browser.rvt*
Estimated Time: 10 minutes

This exercise reinforces the following skills:
- User Interface
- Ribbon
- System Browser

This browser allows the user to locate and identify different elements used in lighting, mechanical, and plumbing inside the project.

1. Activate the **View** ribbon.

2. 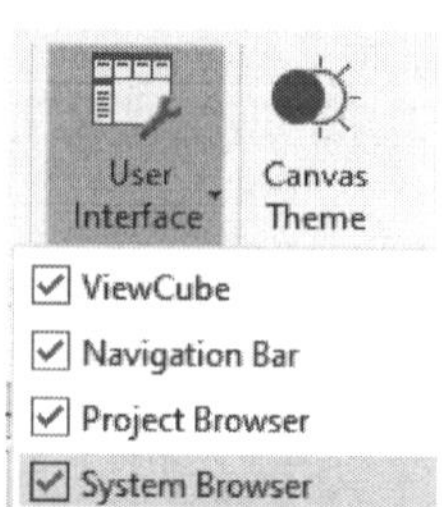 Go to the User Interface drop-down list.
   Place a check next to **System Browser**.

3. 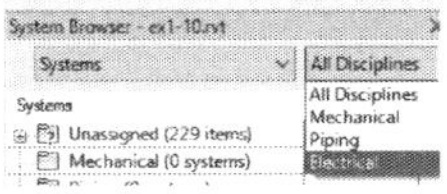 At the top of the Browser, use the Filters to show only the Electrical elements.
Enable **Systems**.
Enable **Electrical.**

4. 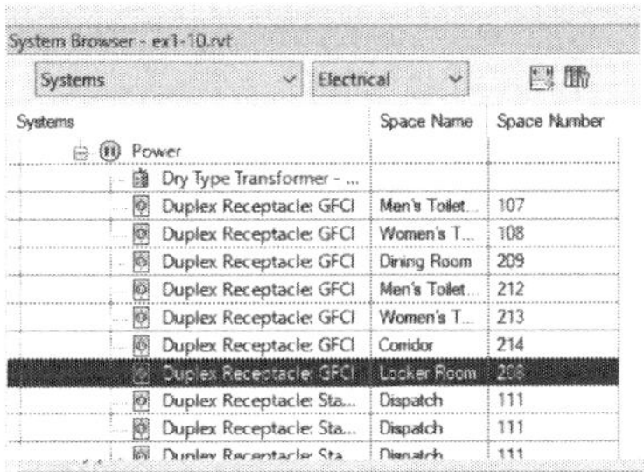 Expand the **Unassigned** category.
Expand the **Electrical** category.
Expand the **Power** category.
Locate the **Duplex Receptacle** in the Locker Room and highlight.

5. 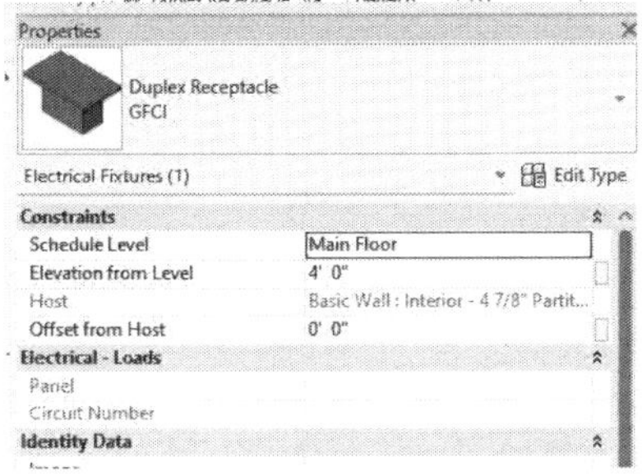 Look in the Properties panel. This receptacle has not been assigned to an electrical panel, and it doesn't have a circuit number.

6. 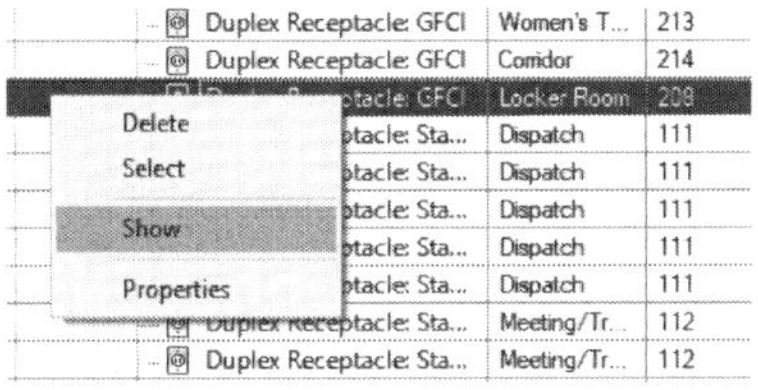 Right click on the **Duplex Receptacle** in the Locker Room.
Select **Show**.

7. 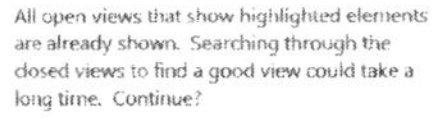 Press **OK**.

8. 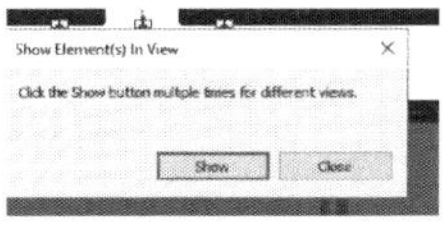 Select the **Show** button.

9. 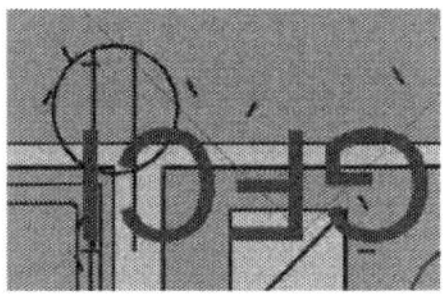 Press the **Show** button until you see this view.

Press **Close**.

10. 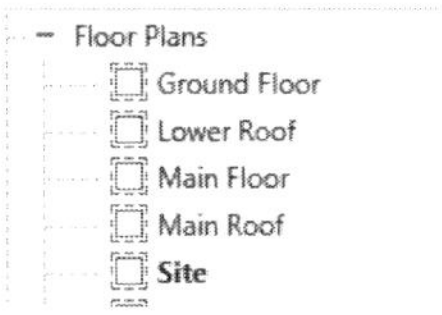 Verify in the Project Browser that you are in the Site floor plan.

This is bold in the Project Browser.

11. 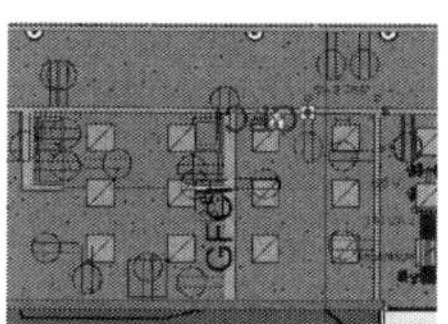 Zoom out to see the Locker Room.

To close the System Browser, select the x button in the upper right corner of the dialog.

12. Close the file without saving.

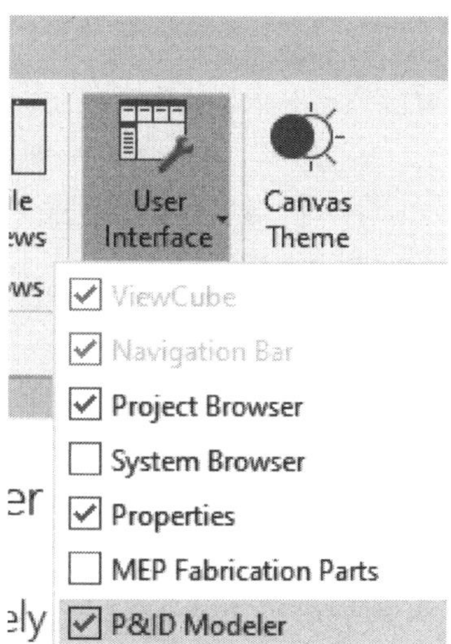

The P&ID Modeler is only available for paid subscribers, so I won't cover it in this textbook.

Lesson
02

Revit Families

Revit projects use Revit families.

There are three types of families:

- System
- In-Place
- Loadable

System families are specific to a project. You can copy system families from one project to another, but they are not stand-alone files, like loadable/model families. Examples of system families are walls, conduits, wires, and ceilings.

In-Place families are elements which are created "on the fly" using massing tools. Users often create an in-place family for a feature that is unique to a project. A generator or electrical equipment that is specialized may be created using massing tools, so that users can see the amount of space it takes up in a project.

Loadable families are the most common type of family. Examples include cable trays, power devices, and electrical equipment. These are external files which are inserted/loaded into a project and placed in the desired location. These families can be counted, and their properties can be organized in schedules. These elements can be created from scratch using the Family Editor using family templates. They can be created and loaded into a project, as well as deleted or saved from a project.

Revit families are defined using parameters. There are two types of parameters: Type and Instance.

Revit elements are defined by a hierarchy.

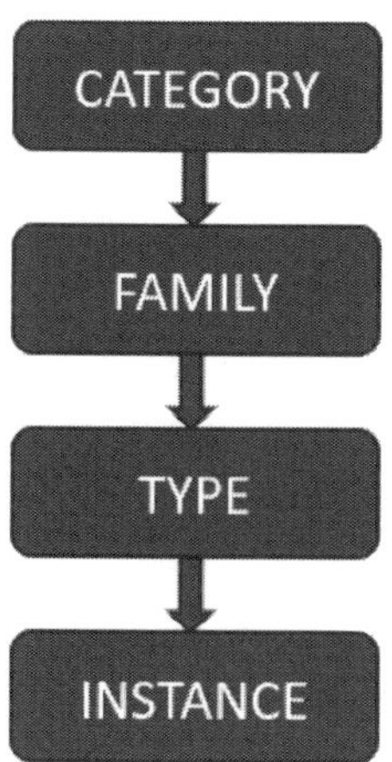

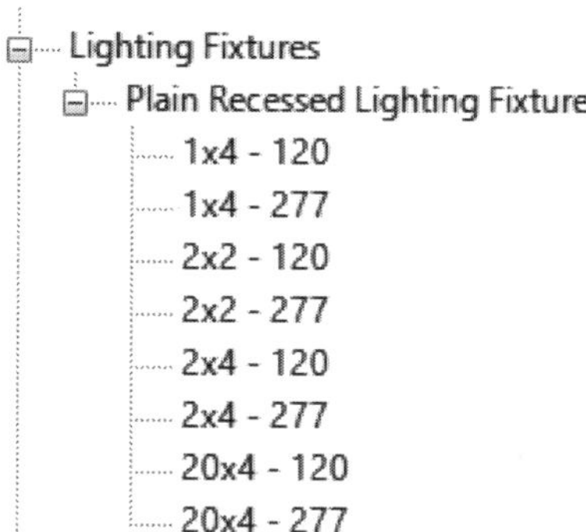

In the Revit Project Browser under the Families folder, you see the families organized into categories. Lighting Fixtures is a Category. The Plain Recessed Lighting Fixture is a Family. A family is an element that represents a specific component used in a project. Each Family can have several different types. This lighting fixture has different types which are defined by size and voltage. The family type doesn't change regardless of where it is placed in the project. If you place a 1x4 lighting fixture in the living room or the bedroom, it is still a 1x4 lighting fixture.

Every time you place or define a family in a project, you are creating an "instance" of that family. Location is an instance parameter. Hardware or finish can be unique to each family places, so these can also be instance properties. Type properties are properties that are common to all elements of that type. Instance properties are properties that are unique to each individual element.

Throughout the rest of the text, we will be creating new types of families.
Here are the basic steps to creating a new family.

1. Select the element you want to define (switch gear, receptacle, panel, etc.).
2. Select **Edit Type** from the Properties pane.
3. Select **Duplicate**.
4. Rename: Enter a new name for your family type.
5. Redefine: Edit the structure, assign new materials, and change the dimensions.
6. Reload or Reassign: Assign the new type to the element.

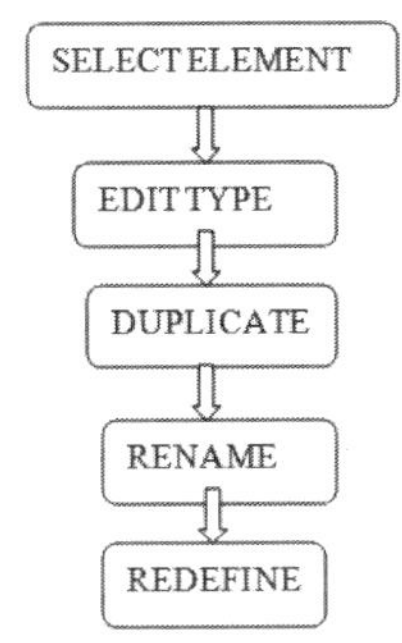

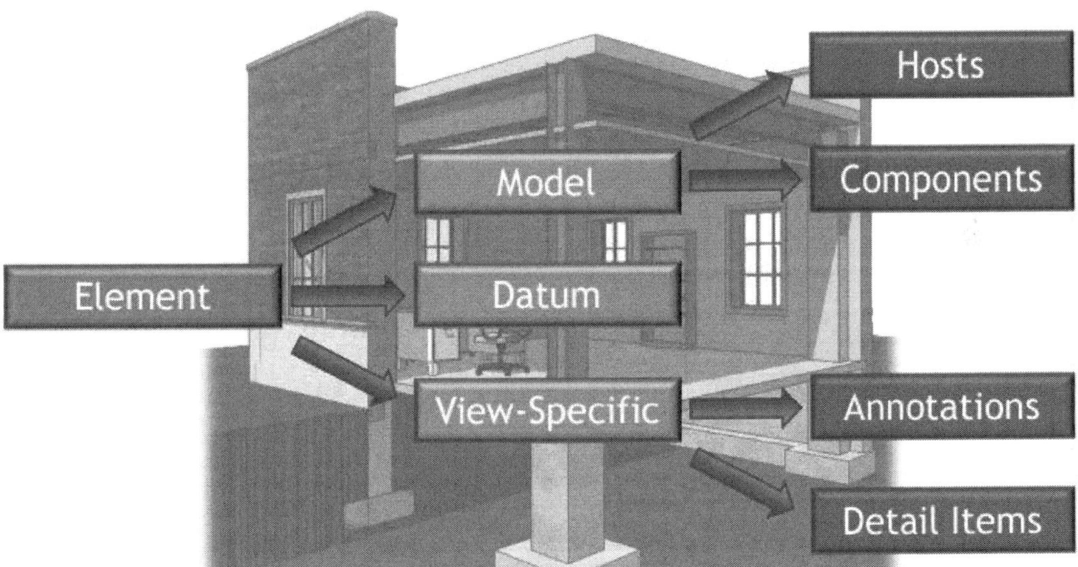

Elements are the building blocks of any Revit Project. Everything used in a Revit project is
considered an element.

There are three classes of Revit families:

- Model
- Datum
- View-Specific.

Model families are families which you can physically touch if you were walking through a building, such as walls or electrical panels. A host model family is an element which can be used to hold or place other components. For example, a wall can host a door, window, or electrical panel. An element which is placed on a host is considered a component. Datums are levels, grids, and survey points. They are used to constrain the project. View-specific families are annotations, like dimensions or text, and detail items, like filled regions

Non-hosted families can be placed anywhere in the view. They are typically placed aligned to the elevation of the view. If you need to offset them from the elevation, place the element in the view, then select it, then change the offset from elevation value in the Properties palette to the desired location.

Hosted families must be placed on a surface or work plane and the surface must be visible in the view. If a fixture needs to be placed on a ceiling, the view needs to be a ceiling plan. Check on the ribbon to specify the type of face to be used for placement. If the placement face is deleted, any elements hosted by the face will also be deleted. If the placement face is moved, then the elements will also move.

Electrical Devices

The workflow to add electrical devices.

1. Select a category of family to add to the model on the ribbon.
2. Use the Type selector to choose the exact type in the category.
3. Place it as required on a vertical, horizontal, or work plane face.
4. Adjust the instance properties of the family in the Properties palette.
5. Tag if needed.

Some guidelines when working with Revit families to help you work efficiently:

- Familiarize yourself with the content libraries which come with the software as well as the libraries used within your company. Then, when you are looking for a specific family, you might be able to use or modify an existing family.
- When you modify a Revit family or element, save the family under a new name and save it to a custom library location, preferably on your company's server. This will make the family type available across projects as well as to other users in your company.
- Avoid accidentally selecting elements in a view so they don't get modified.
- If you hover your cursor over an element, a small dialog will appear informing you of the family and type.

Lighting Fixtures

Lighting fixtures follow the same workflow as other electrical devices and are powered the same way. They also have the ability to calculate an average estimated illumination level for spaces.

When loading light fixture families, make sure to pull them from the MEP folder, not the Architectural folder.

Exercise 2-1:

Working with Revit Families and Elements

Drawing Name: *elements.rvt*
Estimated Time: 20 minutes

This exercise reinforces the following skills:

- ❑   Identifying elements and their families in a project
- ❑   Place a Component

1. 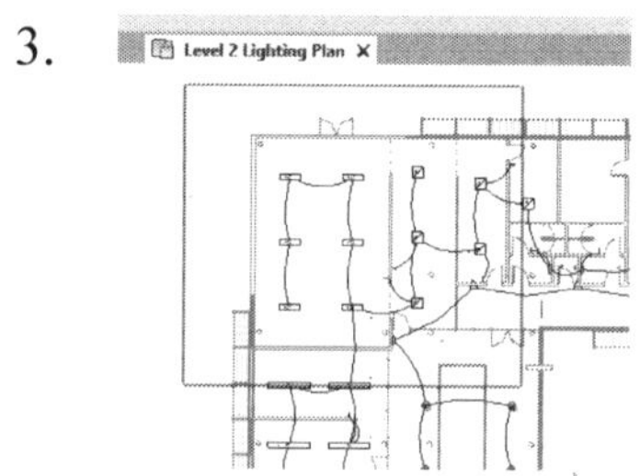   Open the Level 2 Lighting Plan.

2.   Right click and select **Zoom In Region**.

3.   Draw a rectangle/region in the upper left corner of the building.

4.   Hover the cursor over one of the lighting fixtures labeled 'C'.
Note that the family and type are displayed.

5.   Pan down.
Hover the cursor over one of the lighting fixtures labeled 'B'.
Note that the family and type are displayed.
The 'B' and 'C' lighting fixtures are the same family, but different types.

6.   Select the 'C' lighting fixture that is located on the upper left.

7. 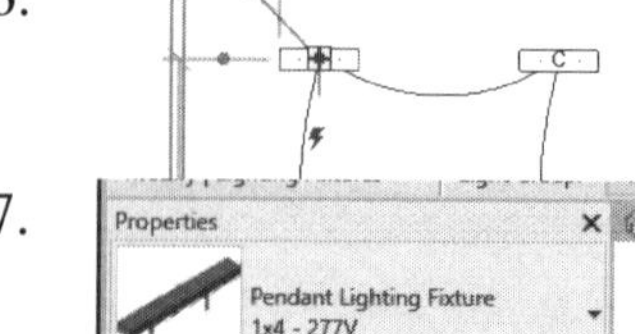   *Note that the Family and Type are displayed in the Properties panel.*

8. 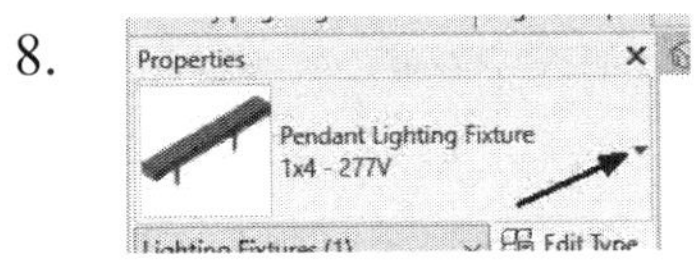 Select the small down arrow located at the top of the Properties panel.

This is called the Type Selector.

9. 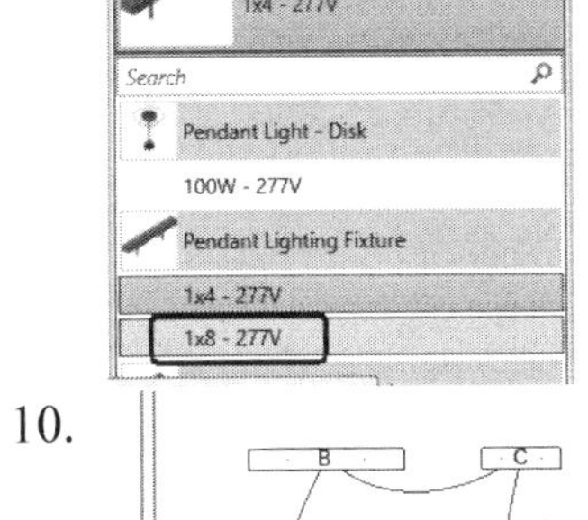 Select the **1x8-277v** from the Type Selector list.

Press **ESC** to release the selection.

10. 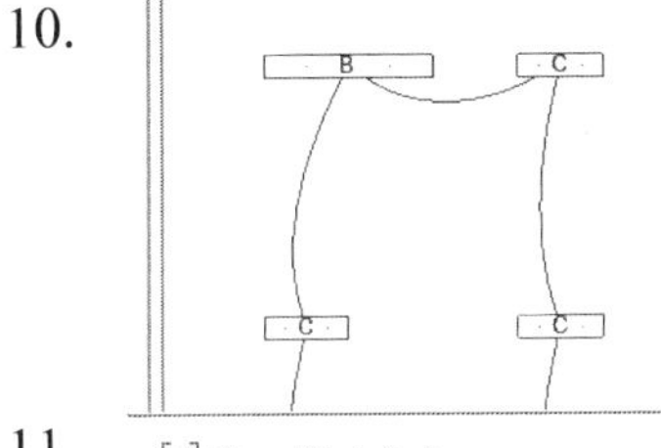 *Notice that the element is updated to the new type which you selected.*

11. 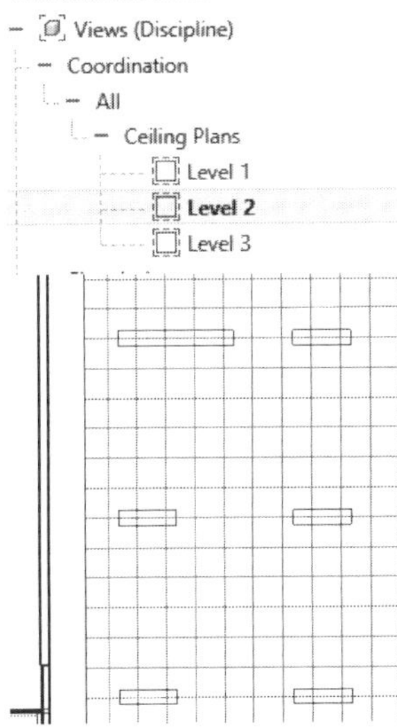 Open the **Level 2** view under Ceiling Plans.

Look in the Coordination category.

Note that the lighting fixture which was changed in the previous view updated in this view.

Revit has bi-directional associativity. This means that if you make a change to a model element in one view, the change is propagated throughout the model. All the views update.

This only applies to model elements – NOT to annotation elements. Annotation elements, like dimensions and notes, are view-specific.

12. 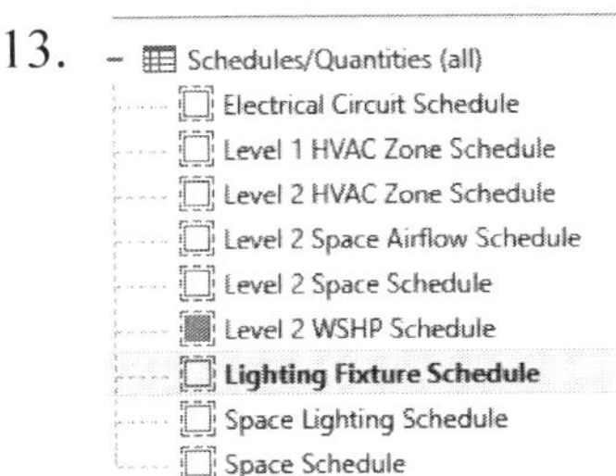 Enable the Schedules tab at the top of the browser.

This changes the display to show only schedules.

13. Open the Lighting Fixture Schedule view.

The schedule is a view-element. The light fixtures are a component/model element.

Notice the quantities for Type Mark A and Type Mark B. These quantities updated when the fixture was changed.

14. Enable the Views tab at the top of the Project Browser.

Type **Section** in the search field.

15. Open the **Section 18** view under Sections (Building Section).

16. Hover your cursor over one of the electrical panels. *Note that the family and type are displayed.*

17. Select the **View** ribbon.

18. Select **Tile Views**.

19. 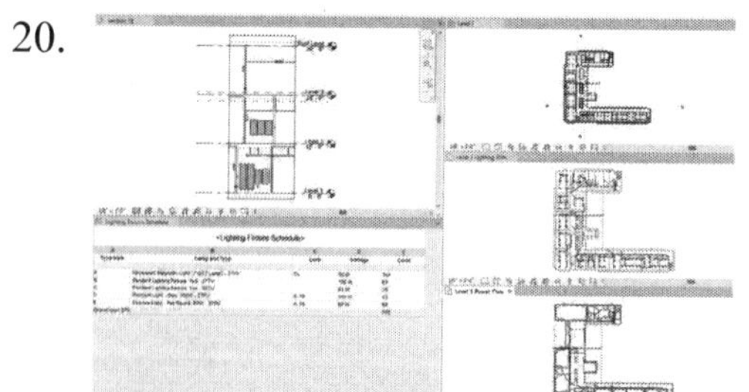
The open views are tiled.

20. Click in the upper left window to activate it. Double click on the mouse wheel to Zoom All.
Repeat for the other windows.

21. 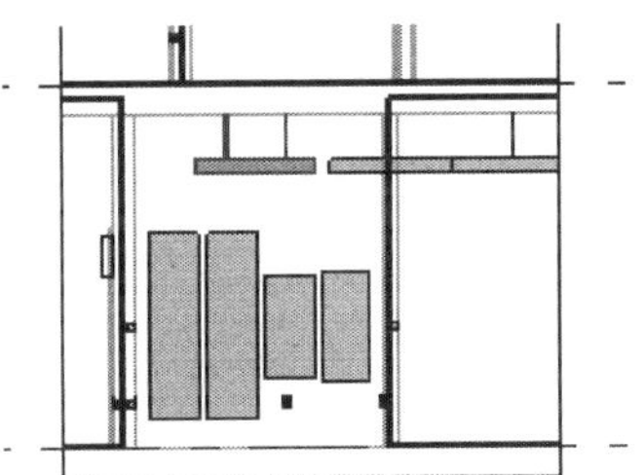

In the window with the schedule:

Put your mouse in the field for Family and Type for the 'C' type mark fixture.

Notice how the lighting fixture is highlighted in the other windows.

22. Close without saving.

Many electricians need to determine the location of the stud framing in a wall as they are routing their wiring between the studs. Most Revit projects created by electrical workers are defined by using a host project which links to the files provided by the architect and the other sub-contractors. It is helpful to be able to select elements that reside in the linked file, so you can identify them and determine how they are defined.

Exercise 2-2:

Identifying a Wall in a Linked File

Drawing Name: *Simple-Building.rvt*
Estimated Time: 10 minutes

This exercise reinforces the following skills:

- ❑ System Families
- ❑ Revit Links
- ❑ Walls

1. 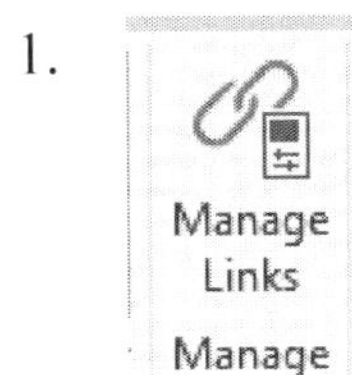

This project uses a Linked Revit project.
Open the **Insert** tab on the ribbon.

Select **Manage Links**.

2.

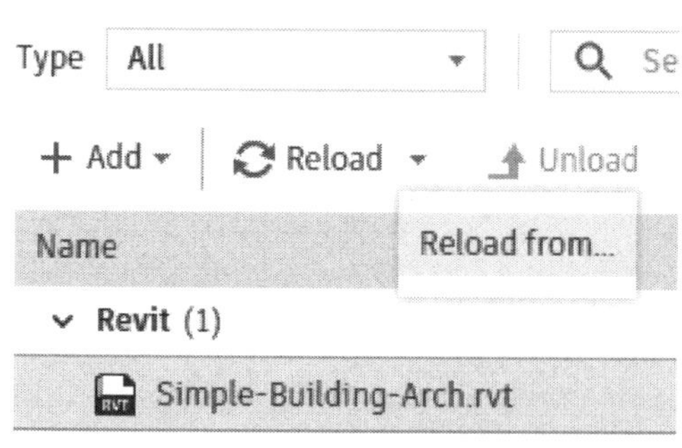

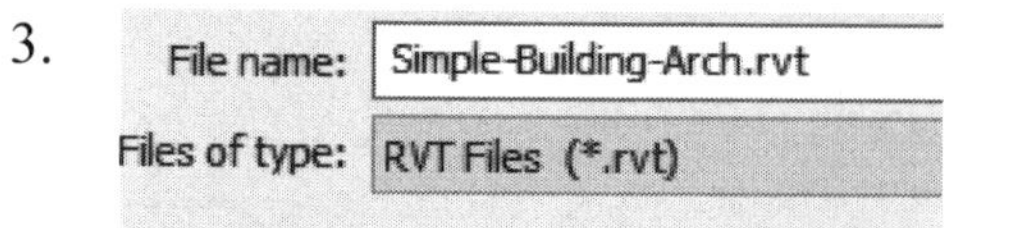

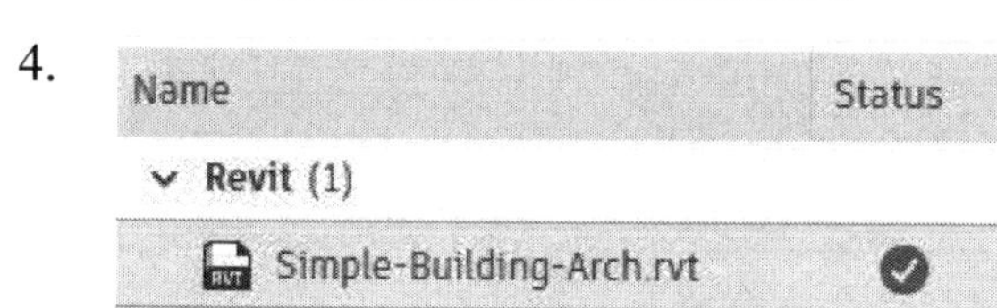

The linked file is named *Simple-Building-Arch.rvt.*

Because the files are now in a new location, the link has to be re-established.

Select **Reload From.**

3.

Locate the file in the downloaded files from the publisher's website.

Select **Open**.

4.

The file now shows as loaded.

Close the dialog.

5.

In the lower right hand corner of the display are selection tools.

The link tool allows you to select elements which are linked to the host file.

The select underlay tool allows you to select elements which are part of the linked file.

6.

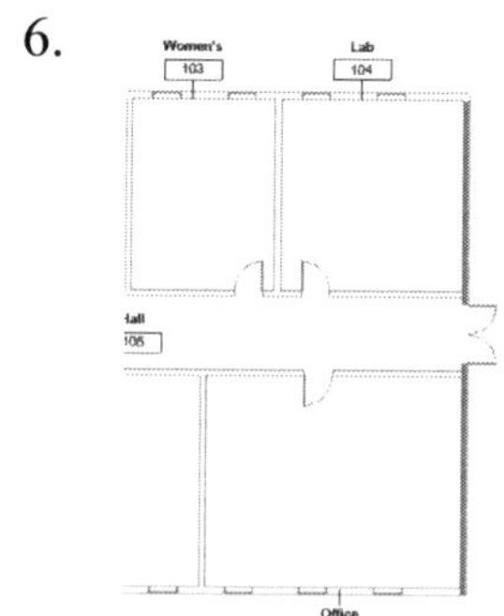

See if you can select the right vertical wall using the TAB key.

Left click on the linked file.
Click TAB until the right vertical wall highlights.

7. 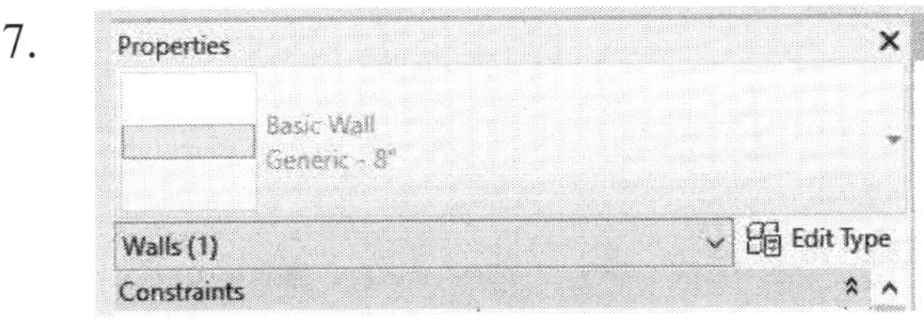 On the Properties palette, select **Edit Type**.

8. 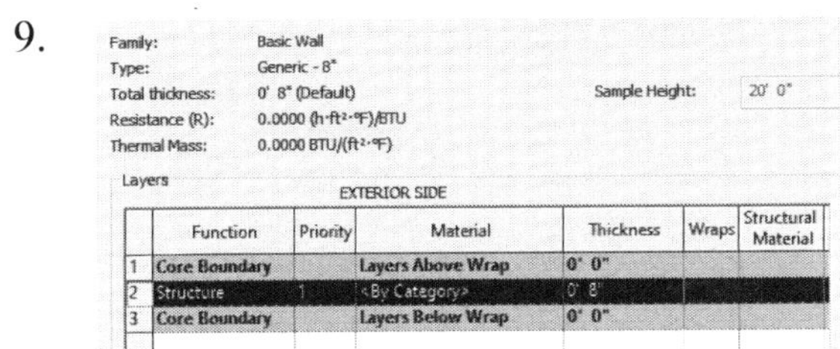 Select **Edit** next to Structure.

9. You see how the wall has been defined by the architect.

   Notice that it has an exterior side and an interior side.

   The Core boundary is the boundary around the stud or framing. Anything outside of the core boundary is considered a wrapped layer and is usually a finish, like gypsum board or siding.

10. Press **OK** twice to close the dialogs.
11. Left click in the window to release the selection.
12. Close the file without saving.

Exercise 2-3:

Place a Lighting Fixture and a Switch

Drawing Name: *Simple-Building.rvt*
Estimated Time: 10 minutes

This exercise reinforces the following skills:

- System Families
- Revit Links
- Walls

1. 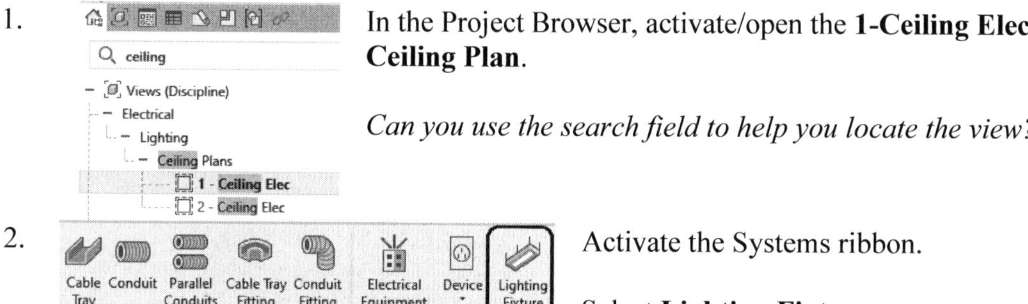 In the Project Browser, activate/open the **1-Ceiling Elec Ceiling Plan**.

    Can you use the search field to help you locate the view?

2. 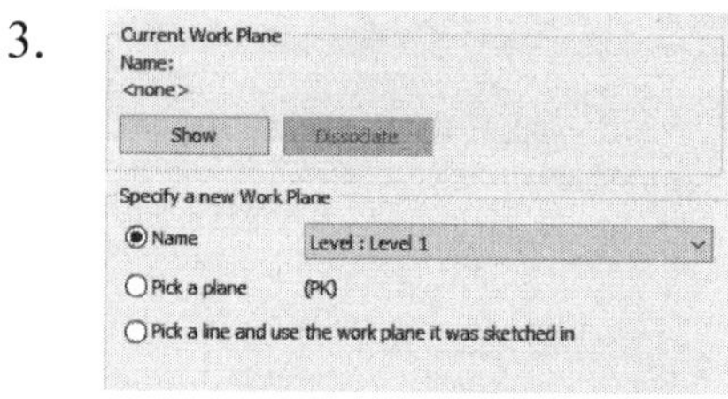 Activate the Systems ribbon.

    Select **Lighting Fixture**.

3. 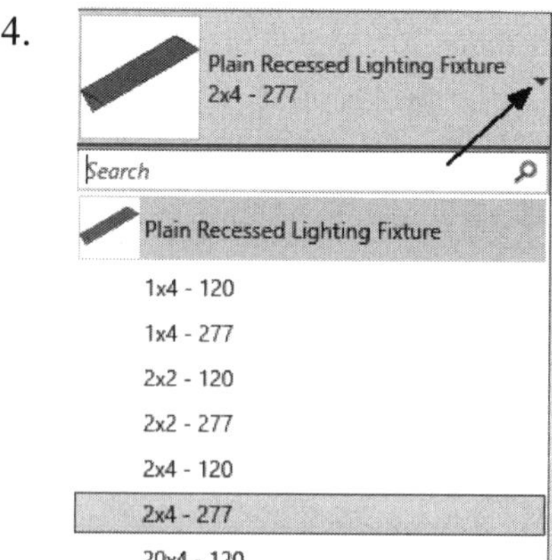 Enable **Name**.
    Set the Work Plane to **Level 1**.
    Click **OK**.

4. Use the Type Selector to select **Plain Recessed Lighting Fixture:2x4 – 277**.

    The Type Selector is the small down arrow located to the right of the family name. The Type Selector is used when a family has more than one version available.

5.

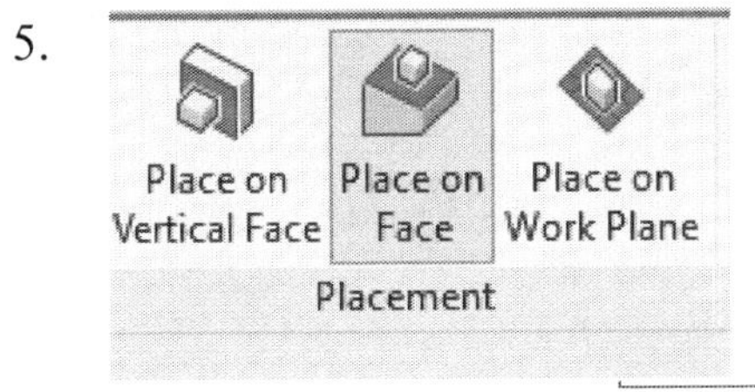

The ribbon has changed to a contextual style.
Enable **Place on Face.**

This means the fixture will be hosted by a ceiling grid or selected face.

6.

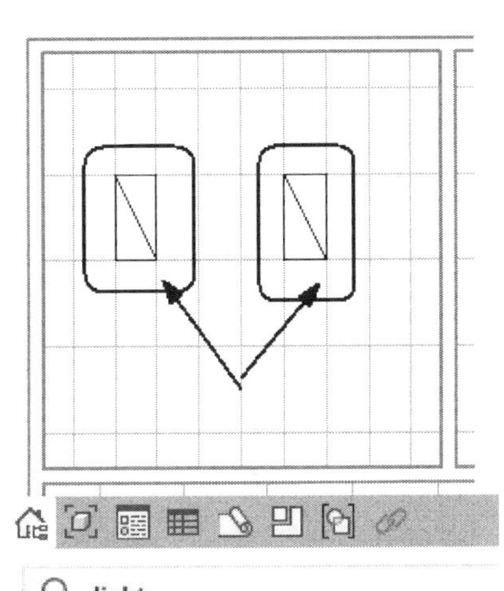

Use the SPACEBAR to rotate the light fixture.

Place two lighting fixtures in the upper left room.

Click ESC or right click and select CANCEL to exit the command.

7.

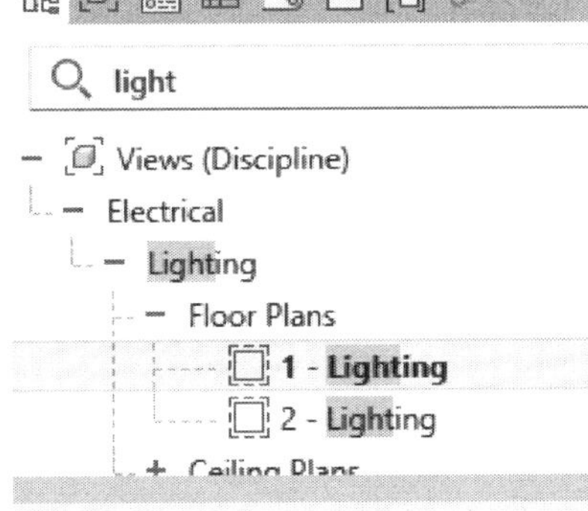

In the Project Browser, activate/open the **1-Lighting** floor plan.

Notice you see the lighting fixtures you placed in the ceiling plan. This is because Revit is a BIM software. If you make a change to the model, any relevant views will update.

8.

Select **Lighting** under the **Device** drop-down list.

9.

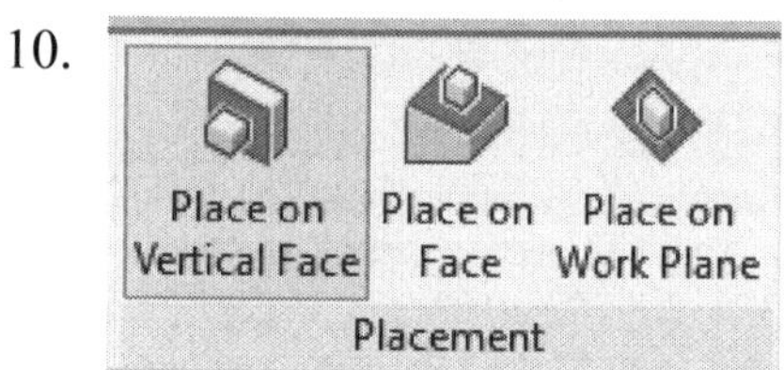

Use the Type Selector to select **Lighting Switches – Single Pole**.

10.

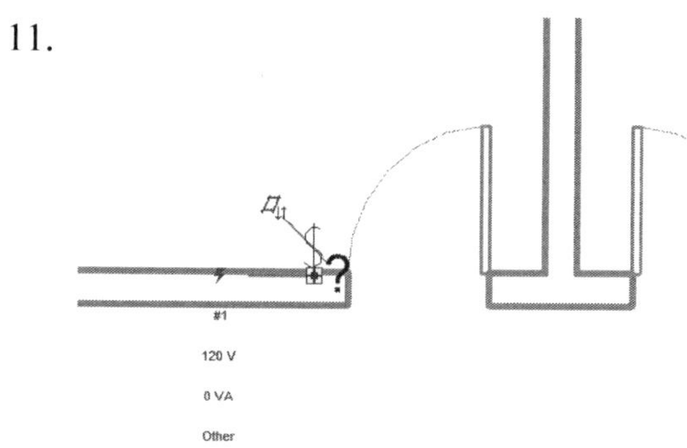

Enable **Place on Vertical Face** on the ribbon.

We are placing the switch on a wall.

11.

Place the switch to the left of the door in the upper left room where the lighting fixtures were placed.

Right click and select CANCEL to exit the command.

12.

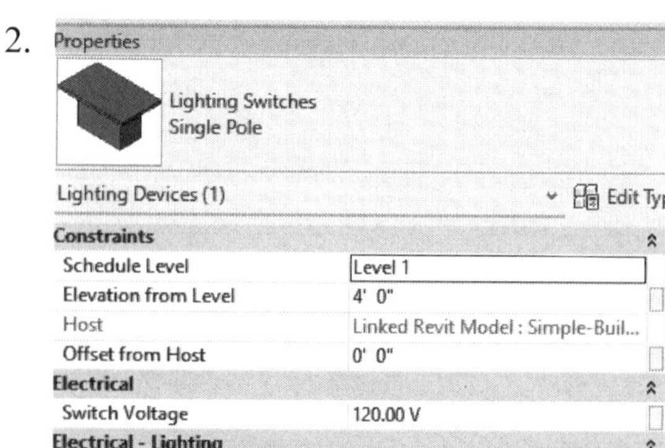

Select the switch that was placed.

Note that the Elevation from the Level is set to 4'-0".

Save the project as *ex2-3.rvt*.

Exercise 2-4:

Select and Modify a Component

Drawing Name: *modify.rvt*
Estimated Time: 5 minutes

This exercise reinforces the following skills:

- Filter
- Type Selector

1.  If you open the modify file, remember you may have to reload the linked file.

2. 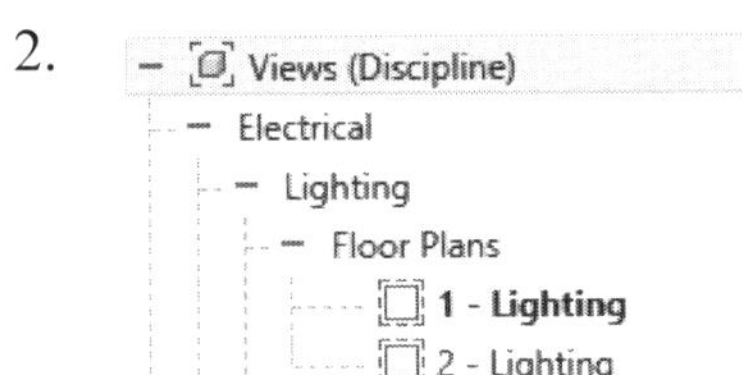 In the Project Browser, activate/open the **1-Lighting** floor plan.

3. 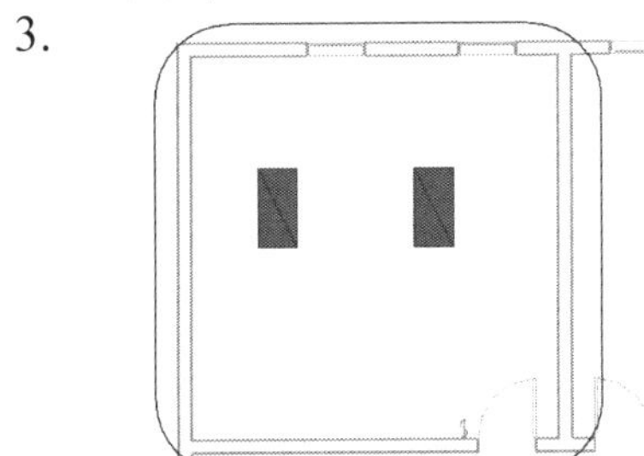 Left click at the upper left corner of the room with the lighting fixtures. Hold down the left mouse button to create a window.

   Left click at the lower right corner of the room with the lighting fixtures.

   This creates a selection group using a window.

4. 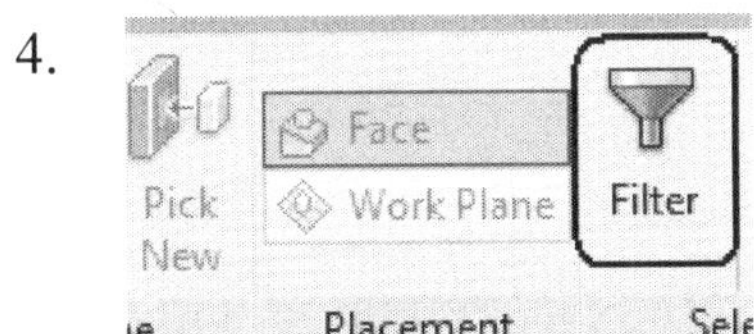 Select the **Filter** tool from the ribbon.

5. 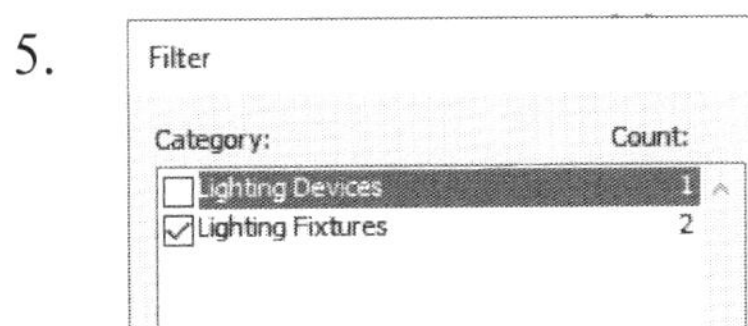 Uncheck any items in the list except for **Lighting Fixtures.**

   Press **OK.**

6. 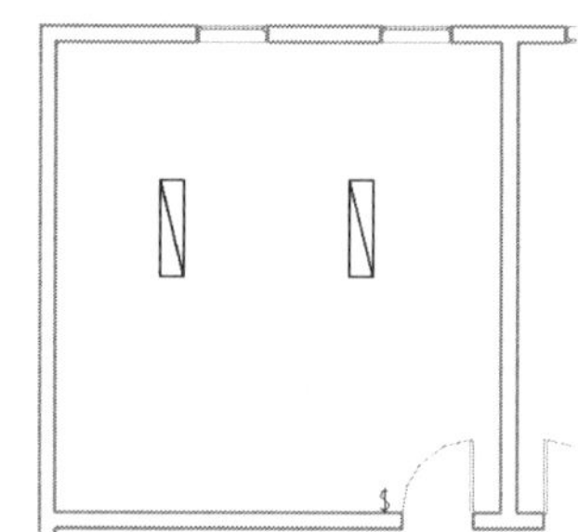

Use the Type Selector to change the lighting fixtures to **1x4 – 277**.

Press **ESC** to release the selection.

7. The lighting fixtures update.

Save the project as *ex2-4.rvt*.

Copy

The Copy tool copies one or more selected elements.

The Copy tool is different than the Copy to Clipboard tool. Use the Copy tool when you want to copy elements within the same window or view. Use the Copy to Clipboard tool to copy from one level to another or between project files.

Exercise 2-5:

Copy a Component

Drawing Name: *copy.rvt*
Estimated Time: 5 minutes

This exercise reinforces the following skills:

- ❑ Copy
- ❑ Type Selector

1. 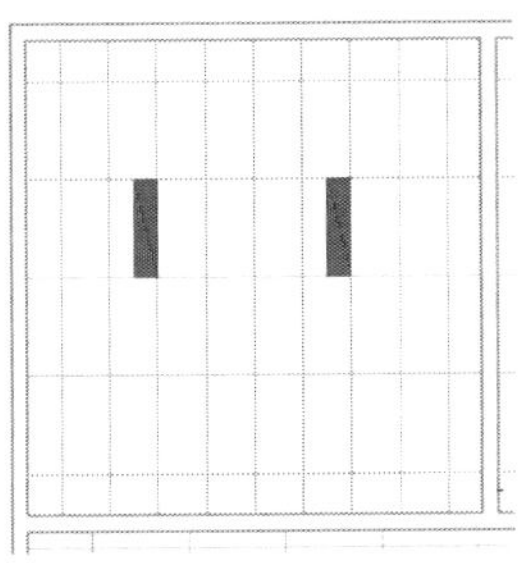   *You may need to use Manage Links to reload the linked file.*

    In the Project Browser, activate/open the **1-Ceiling Elec** Ceiling plan.

2. Window around the first room to select the two lighting fixtures.

3. 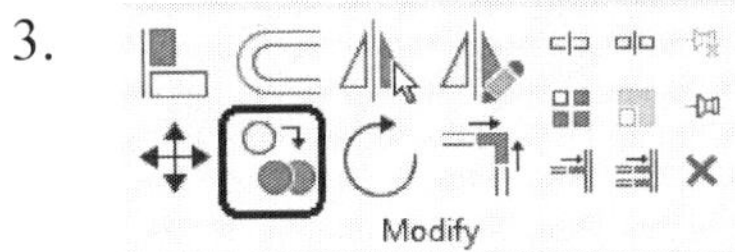   Select the **Copy** tool on the ribbon.

4. 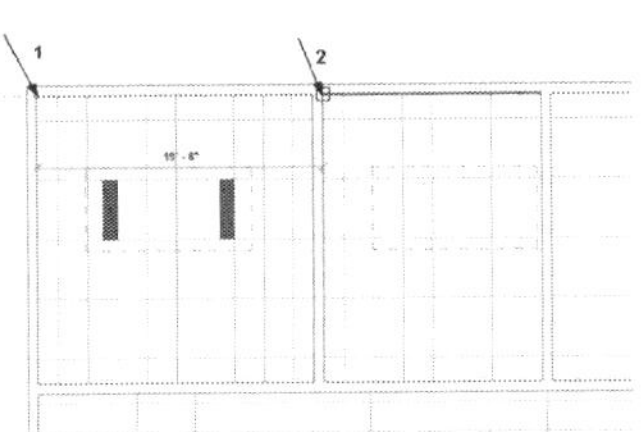   Select the top left corner of the first room as the base point.

    Select the top left corner of the second room as the target point.

5.   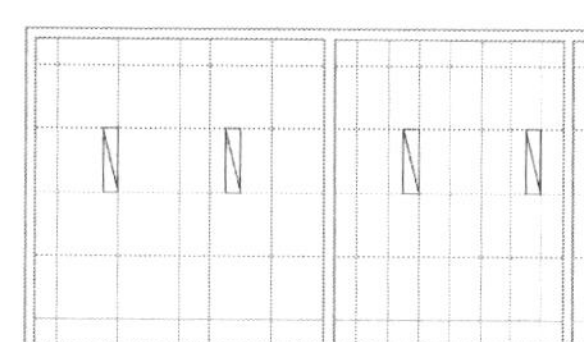   Save the file as *ex2-5.rvt*.

Mirror

The Mirror tool reverses the position of a selected model element, using a line as the mirror axis. You can pick the mirror axis or draw a temporary axis. Use the Mirror tool to flip a selected element, or to make a copy of an element and reverse its position in one step.

You can select doors or windows to mirror even though these elements are hosted by walls. As long as the mirrored elements land on a wall, the command will work with no errors.

Exercise 2-6:

Mirror a Component

Drawing Name: *mirror.rvt*
Estimated Time: 5 minutes

This exercise reinforces the following skills:

    ❑   Mirror→Draw Axis

1.   In the Project Browser, activate/open the **1-Ceiling Elec** Ceiling plan.

2.   Window around the lighting fixtures to select them.

3. 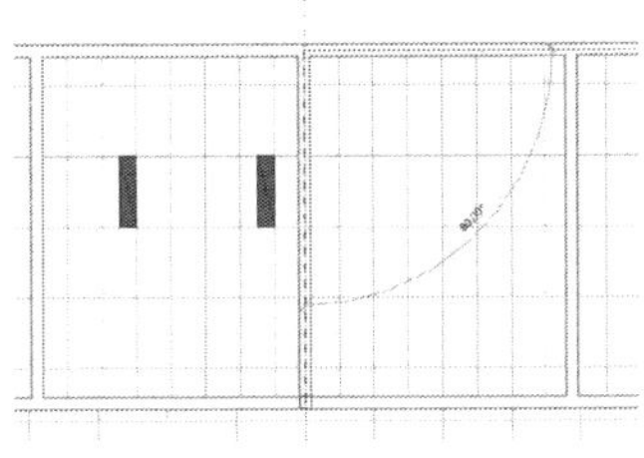

Select the **Mirror→Draw Axis** tool.

4. Select the top of the center line of the wall.

Select the bottom of the center line of the wall.

5. The light fixtures are mirrored to the other rooms.

Save as *ex2-6.rvt*.

Align

Use the Align tool to align one or more elements with a selected element.
This tool is generally used to align walls, beams, and lines, but it can be used with other types of
elements as well.

The elements to align can be of the same type, or they can be from different families. You can
align elements in a plan view (2D), 3D view, or elevation view.

For example, in 3D views you can align surface patterns of walls with other elements.

When using the command, select the source object first and then the element(s) you want to align
with the first element. You can align more than one element to the source object.

Exercise 2-7:

Align a Component

Drawing Name: *align.rvt*
Estimated Time: 5 minutes

This exercise reinforces the following skills:

❑ Align

1. 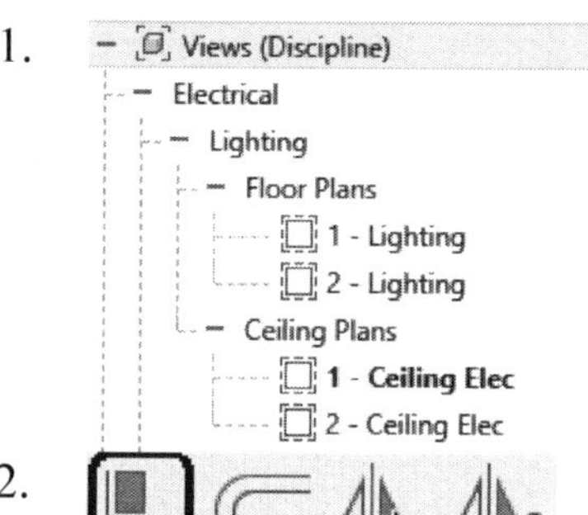
In the Project Browser, activate/open the **1-Ceiling Elec** Ceiling plan.

2. Select the **ALIGN** tool on the Modify ribbon.

3. 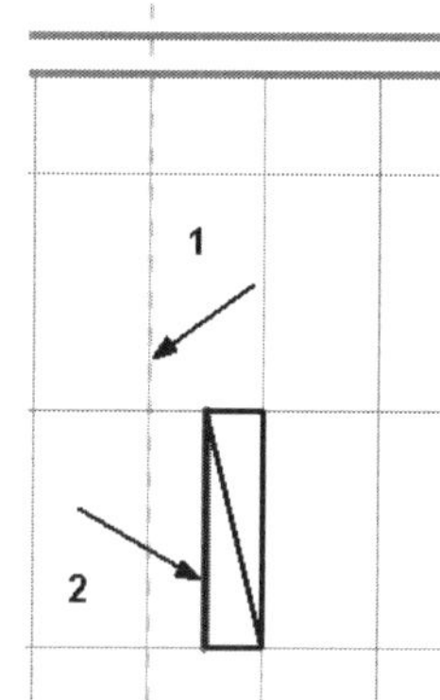
Select the ceiling grid line to the left of the lighting fixture.

This is the target or source element.

Select the left edge of the lighting fixture.

This is the element to be aligned.

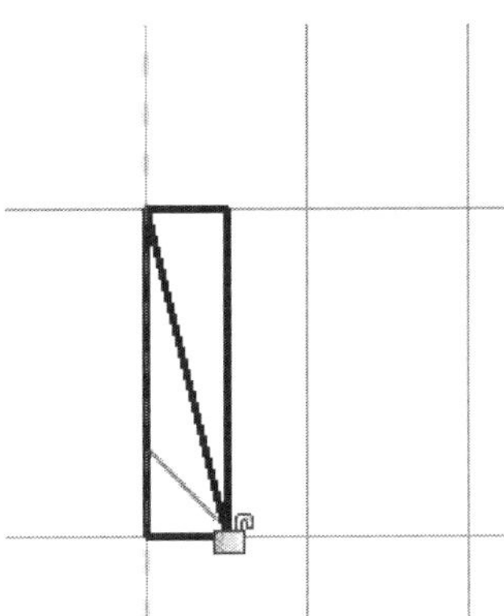

The lighting fixture's position adjusts.

The lock is used if you want to lock the element to the target element. Then, if the grid changes, the light fixture will remain aligned.

4. Use the ALIGN tool to adjust the position of the lighting fixtures so they are aligned to the ceiling grid.

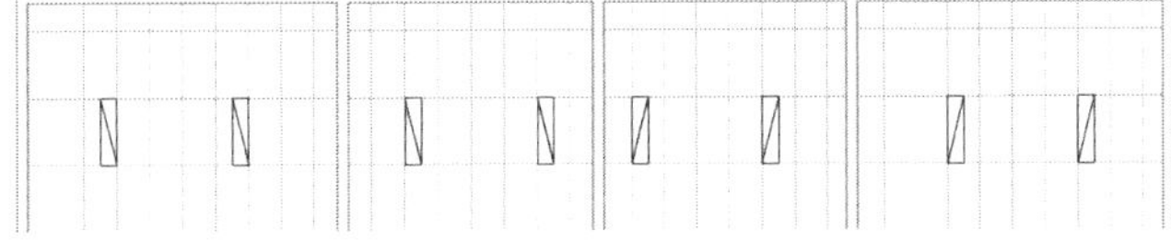

Save as *ex2-7.rvt*.

Exercise 2-8:

Draw, Modify, and Offset Cable Trays

Drawing Name: *cable_trays.rvt*
Estimated Time: 30 minutes

This exercise reinforces the following skills:

- Cable Trays
- Offset
- Trim
- Split
- Options Bar
- Properties

1. 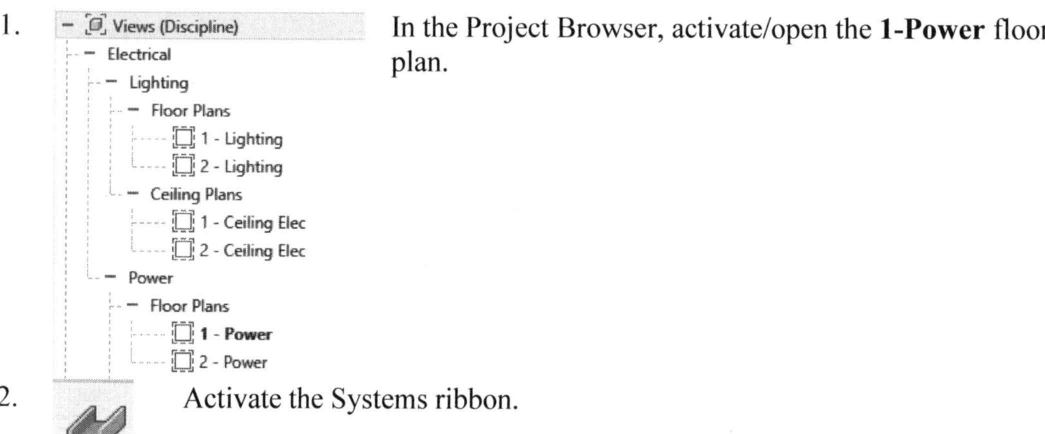 In the Project Browser, activate/open the **1-Power** floor plan.

2. Activate the Systems ribbon.

   Select the **Cable Tray** tool.

3. 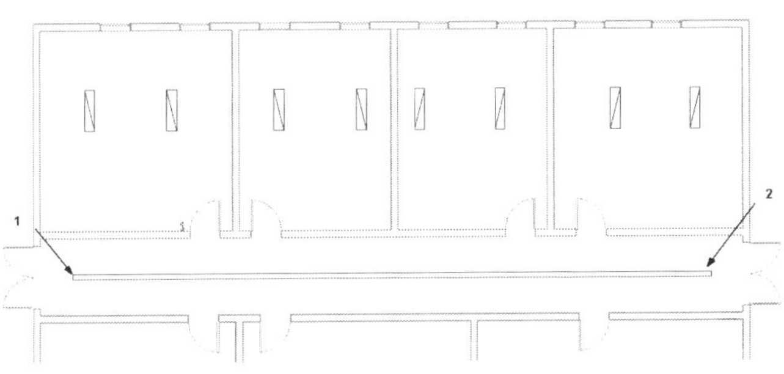 Select the **Trough Cable Tray** from the Type Selector.

4. On the Options bar:

   Set the Width to **6"**.
   Set the Height to **2"**.
   Set the Middle Elevation to **10'-0"**.

5. Left click to place the start of the cable tray at the left side of the corridor (indicated by 1).

   Left click to place the end of the cable tray at the right side of the corridor (indicated by 2).

6. Press **ESC** to complete placing the tray but remain in the Cable Tray command.

7. 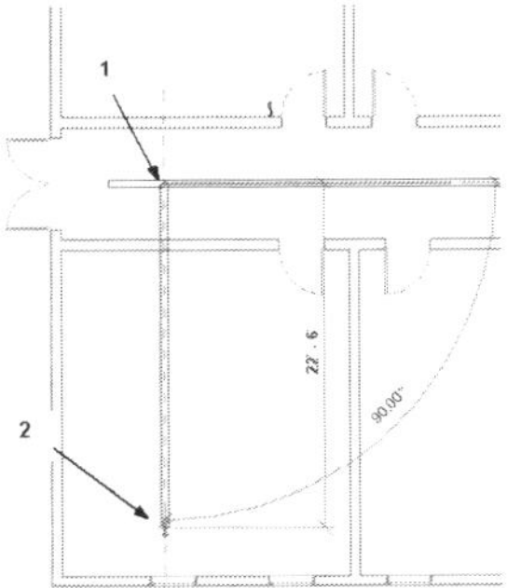 Place a second cable tray perpendicular to the first cable tray and into the Mech/Elec room (lower left).

   Right click and select **Cancel** to exit the command.

This is what the layout should look like.

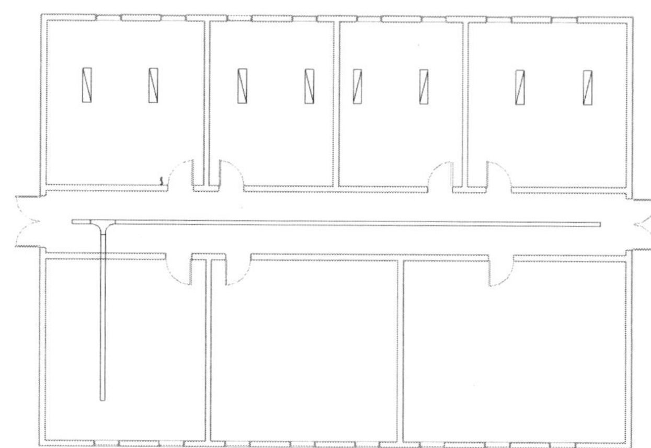

8. 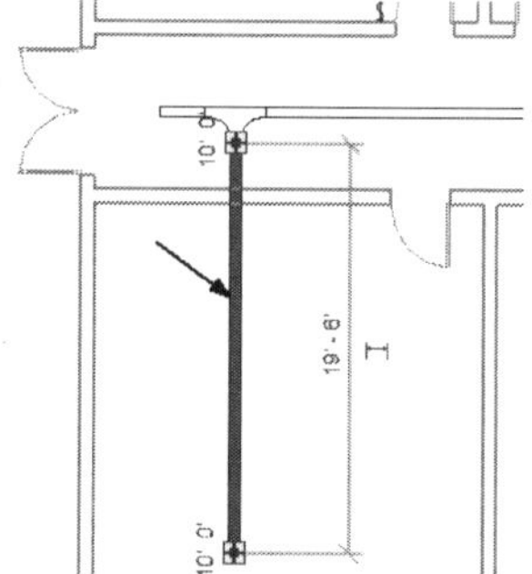 Select the vertical cable tray so it is highlighted.

9. 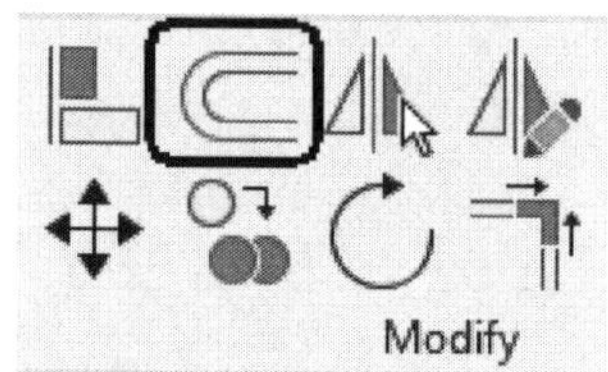 Select the **Offset** tool.

10. On the Options bar:

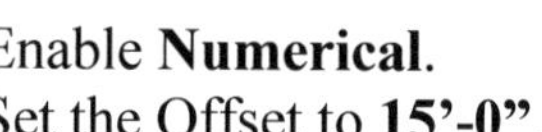

Enable **Numerical**.
Set the Offset to **15'-0"**.
Enable **Copy**.

11. 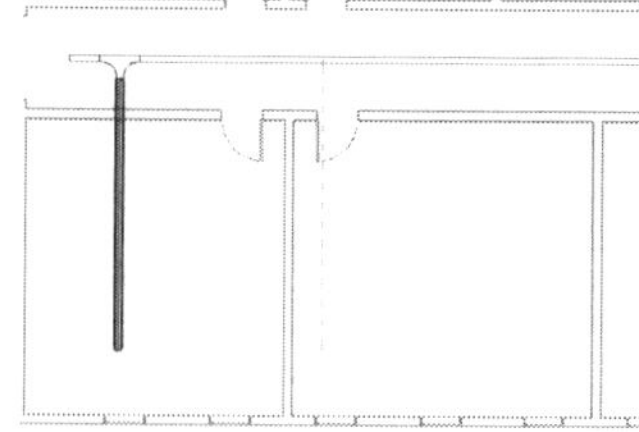 Left pick the cable tray.

Use the Preview to determine the cable tray is placed to the right.

12. Repeat the Offset to place a total of five vertical cable trays.

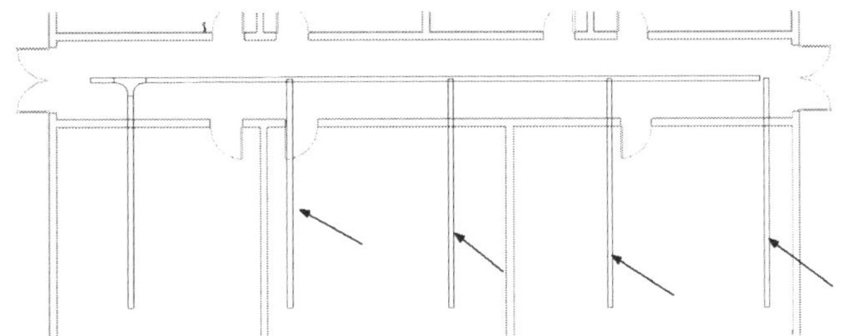

13. 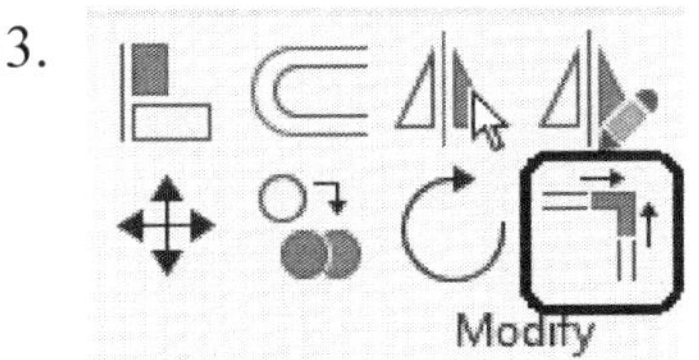 Select the **Trim to Corner** tool on the Modify ribbon.

14. 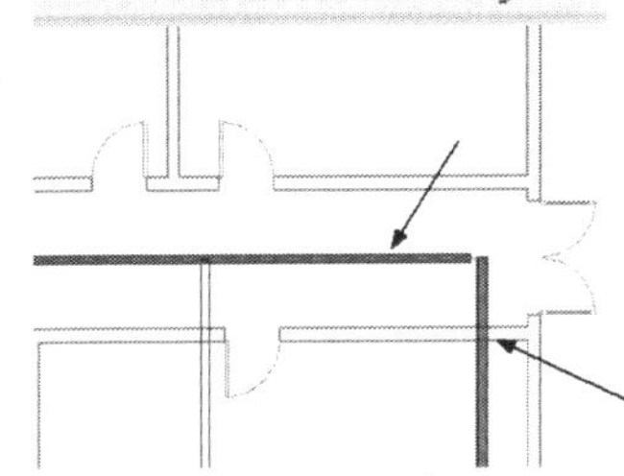 Select the horizontal cable tray and the far right cable tray.

    Click ESC to exit the command.

The two cable trays are joined.

15. On the Modify ribbon:

    Select the **Trim/Extend Multiple** tool.

16. Select the lower line of the horizontal cable tray to define the boundary of the trim.

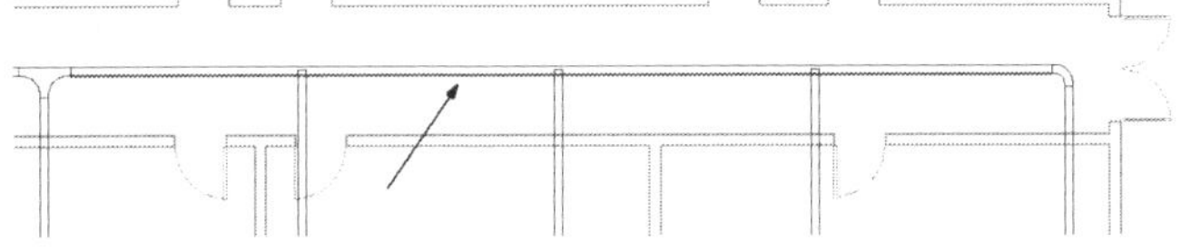

17. Left pick to the right of the fourth vertical cable tray to start the selection/crossing window.

    Left pick to the left of the second vertical cable tray to complete the selection/crossing window.

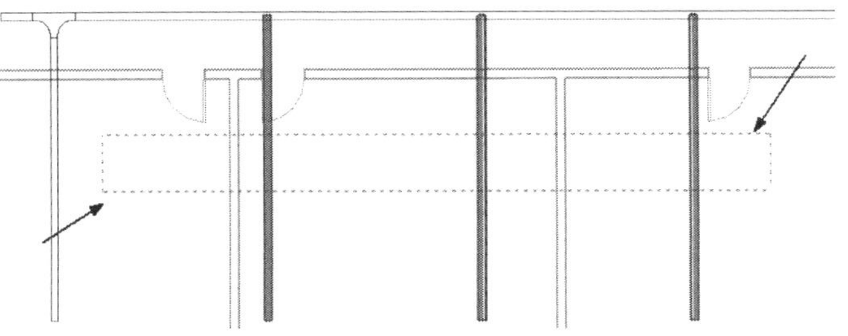

Click ESC to exit the
command.
This is the cable tray
layout so far.

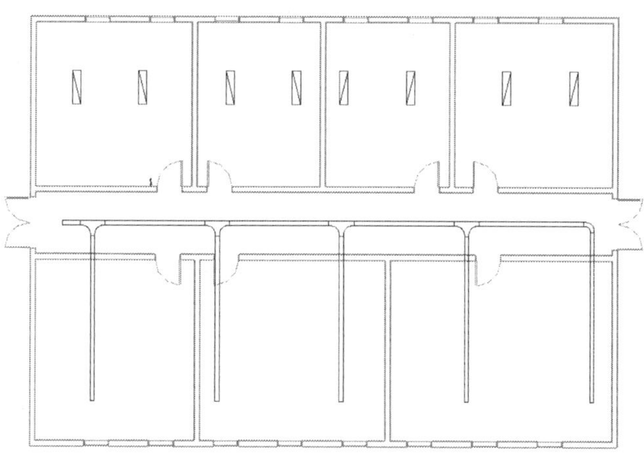

18. 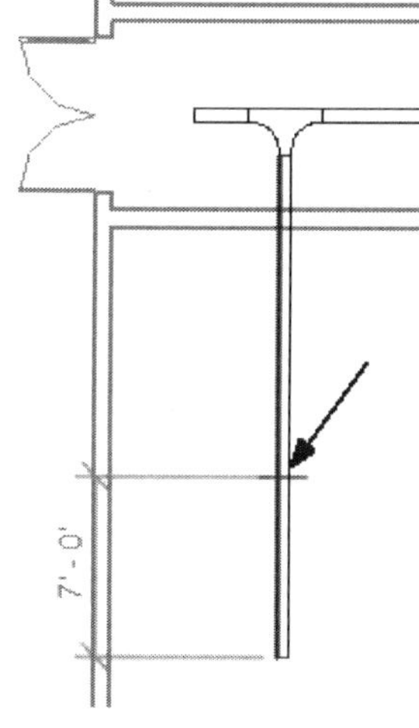   Select the **Split** tool on the Modify ribbon.

19. Use the temporary dimension to split the first cable tray
7'-0" from the end.

Right click and select Cancel twice to exit the
command.

20.

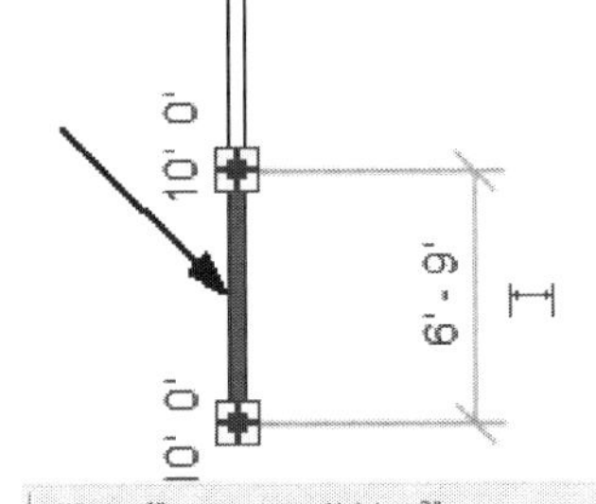

Select the lower part of the cable tray.

21. 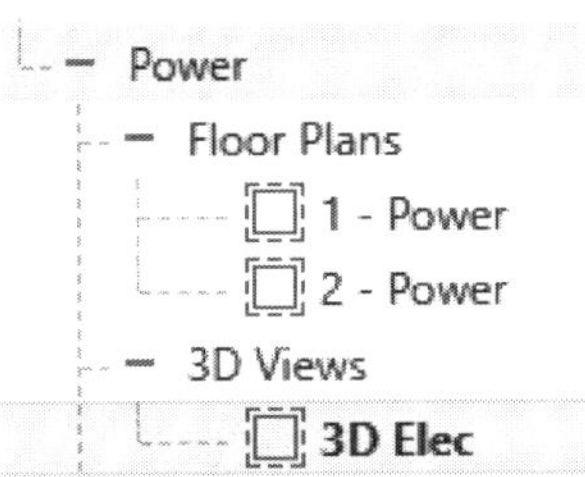

On the Options bar:

Set the Width to **4"**.

22. Switch to a 3D view to see the elements.

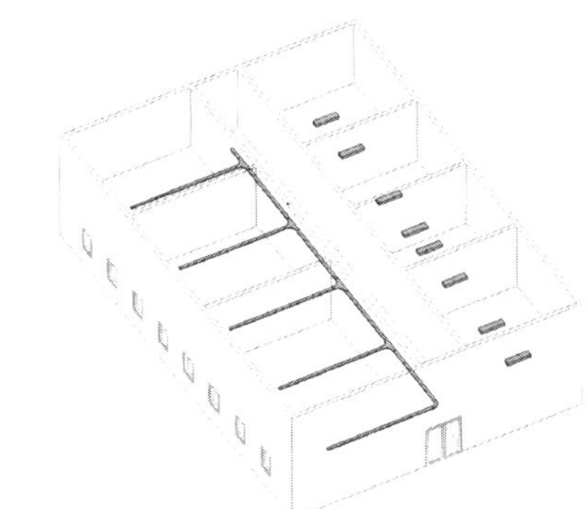

23. Save as *ex2-8.rvt*.

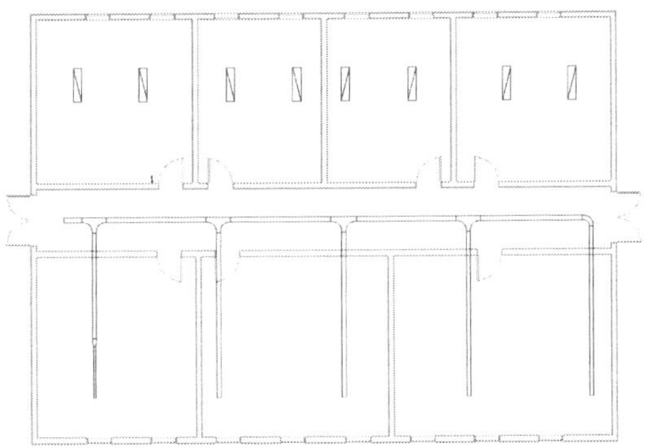

Exercise 2-9:

Place Light Fixtures and Switches (reprised)

Drawing Name: *elec_circuits.rvt*
Estimated Time: 20 minutes

This exercise reinforces the following skills:

- ❑ Place Components
- ❑ Copy

1. 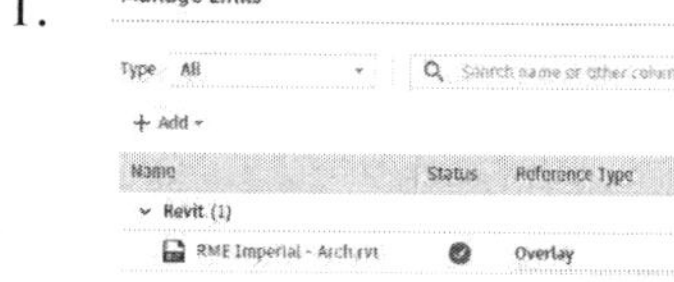
   This file uses RME Imperial-Arch as the linked file. Use the Manage Links tool on the Insert tab to reload the file, if necessary.

2. Verify that you are in the **3rd Floor Ceiling Plan** view.

3. 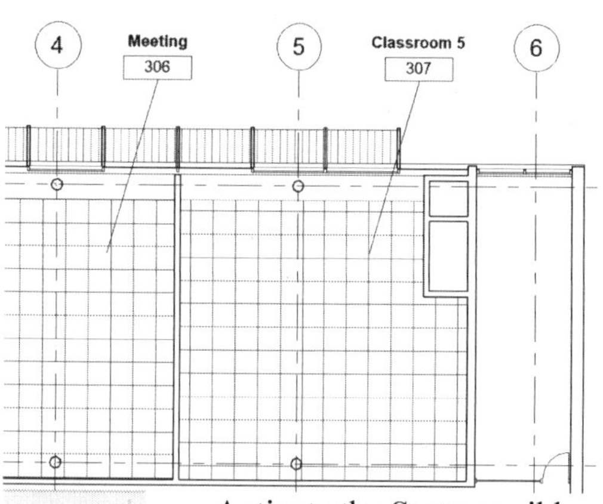
   Use **Zoom In Region** to change the display to focus on Classroom 5 Room 307 between Grids 5 and 6.

4. 
   Activate the Systems ribbon.

   Select **Lighting Fixture**.

5.

Use the Type Selector to select **Plain Recessed Lighting Fixture:2x4 – 277**.

The Type Selector is the small down arrow located to the right of the family name. The Type Selector is used when a family has more than one version available.

6.

The ribbon has changed to a contextual style.

Enable **Place on Face.**

This means the fixture will be hosted by the face of an element, such as the ceiling grid.

7.

Use the SPACE BAR to rotate the component prior to placing.

Left click to place in the upper left area of the room.

Click ESC to exit the command.

8.

Select the light fixture you just placed.

9. 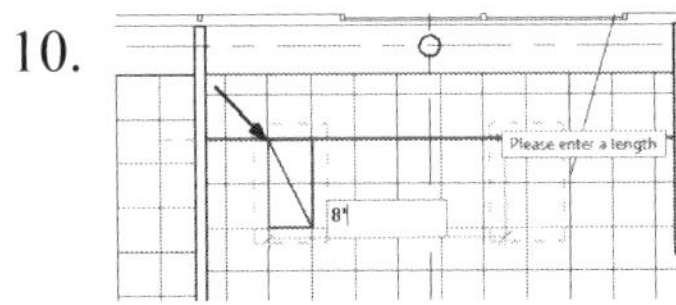

Select the **Copy** tool from the ribbon.

10.

Left click to select the upper left corner of the light fixture as the base point.
Move the cursor to the right and type **8'** for the distance.
Press ENTER or left click to complete the copy.

11.

Repeat to place a third light fixture 8' to the right of the copied/second light fixture.

Click ESC to exit the command.

12. 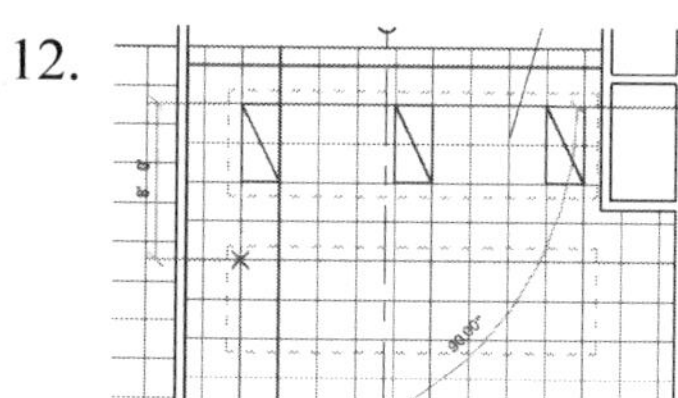 Use the CTL key to select the three light fixtures.
Use the COPY tool to place a copy of the three fixtures 8'
below them.

13. 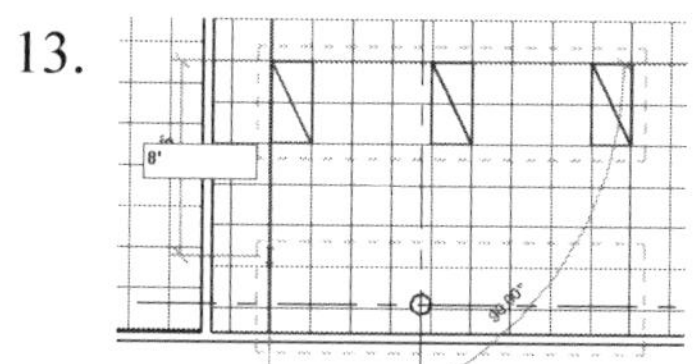 Repeat to place a third row of light fixtures 8' below the
second row.

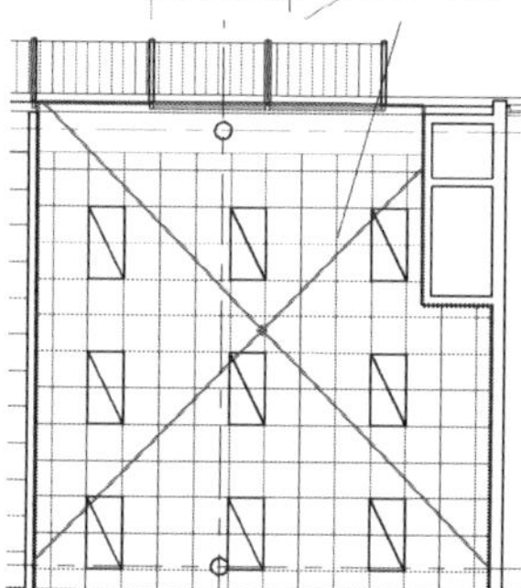

The room should show a total of nine light fixtures.

*Disable the LINEWEIGHT display on the Quick Access
toolbar to make it easier to see the light fixtures.*

14. 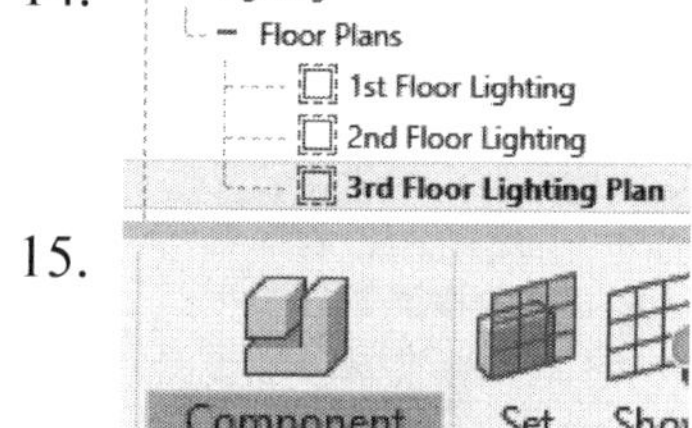 Open the **3rd Floor Lighting** floor plan.

15. 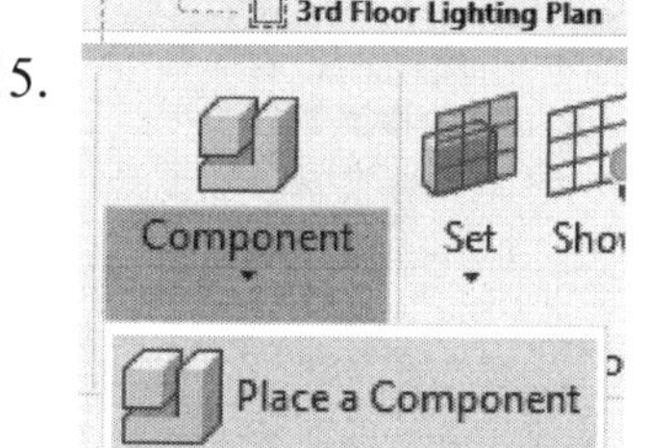 Select **Component→Place a Component**.

16. 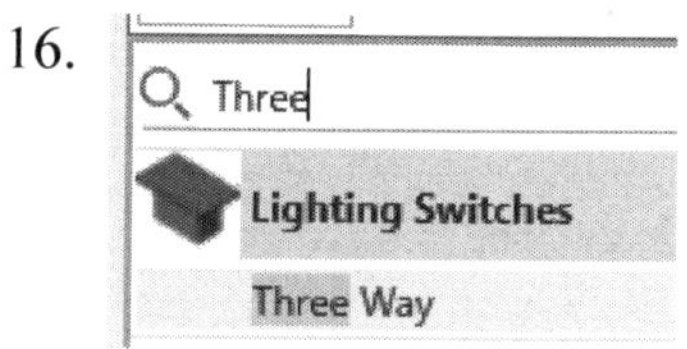 Use the Type Selector to locate the **Lighting
Switches→Three Way**.

*Type **Three** in the search field to locate the switch.*

17. 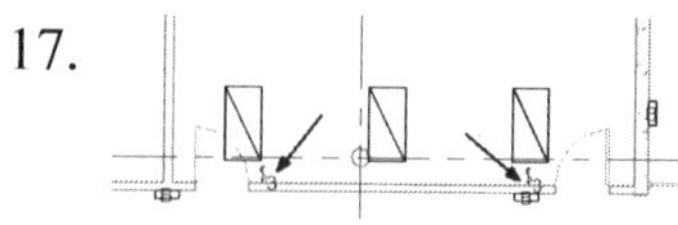 Place a light switch next to each door located at the south
wall of the room.

18. Save as *ex2-9.rvt.*

Exercise 2-10:

Adding and Modifying Equipment, Devices and Fixtures

Drawing Name: *adding_elements.rvt*
Estimated Time: 20 minutes

This exercise reinforces the following skills:

- ❑ Place Components
- ❑ Electrical Equipment
- ❑ Load Families
- ❑ Type Selector
- ❑ Naming Equipment

1. 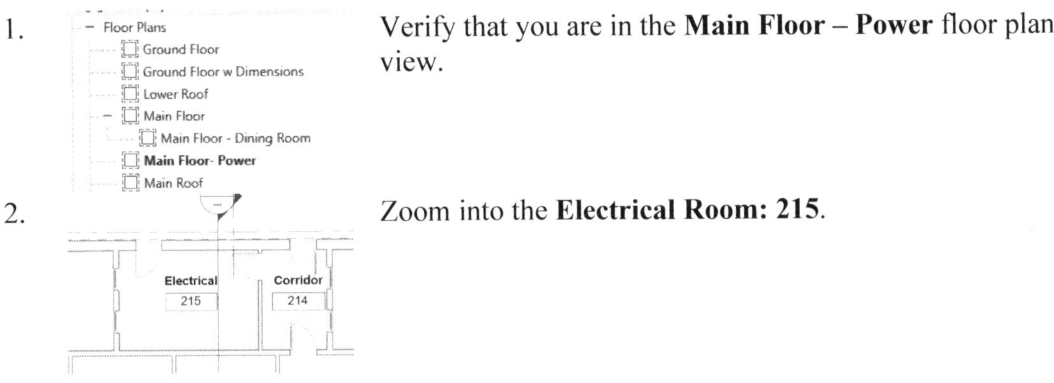

Verify that you are in the **Main Floor – Power** floor plan view.

2. Zoom into the **Electrical Room: 215**.

3. 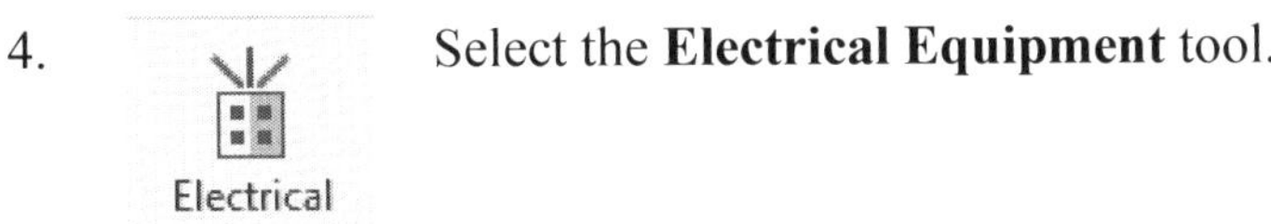

Activate the Systems ribbon.

4. 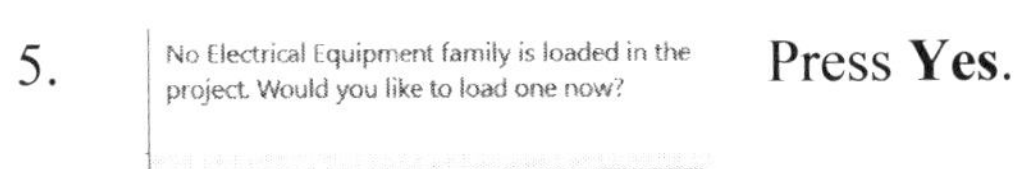

Select the **Electrical Equipment** tool.

5. No Electrical Equipment family is loaded in the project. Would you like to load one now?

   Yes   No

   Press **Yes**.

6.

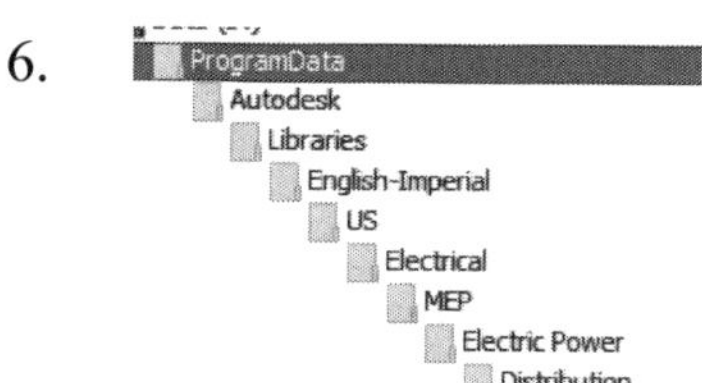

Browse to the *Distribution* folder under *US Imperial\Electrical\MEP\Electric Power.*

7.

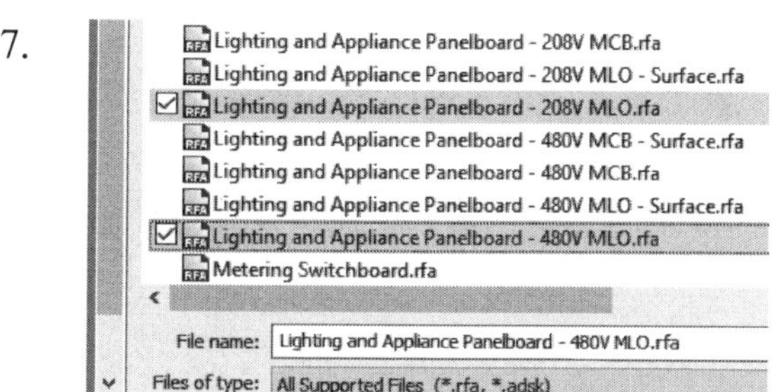

Hold down the CTL key to make a multiple selection.

Select *Lighting and Appliance Panelboard – 208V MLO* and *Lighting and Appliance Panelboard – 480V MLO.*

Press **Open**.

8.

On the Properties palette:

Verify that the *Lighting and Appliance Panelboard – 208V MLO-225A* is active.

9.

Enable **Place on Vertical Face** on the ribbon.

This is a face-based component, meaning it needs a vertical or horizontal face to be placed. Since it is a hosted component, if the wall where it is placed moves, it will also move.

10.

Place it on the east wall of Room 215.

Type ESC out of the command.

11.

Select the panel that was just placed.

On the Properties palette, note the elevation from the level.

Left click anywhere in the display window to release the selection.

12. 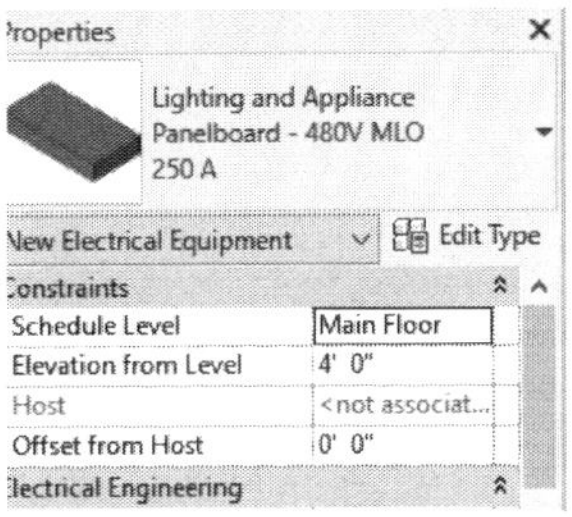 Select the **Electrical Equipment** tool.

Using the Type Selector:
Select *Lighting and Appliance Panelboard – 480V MLO 250A*.

Note that by default it is located at the same elevation as the other panelboard.

13. 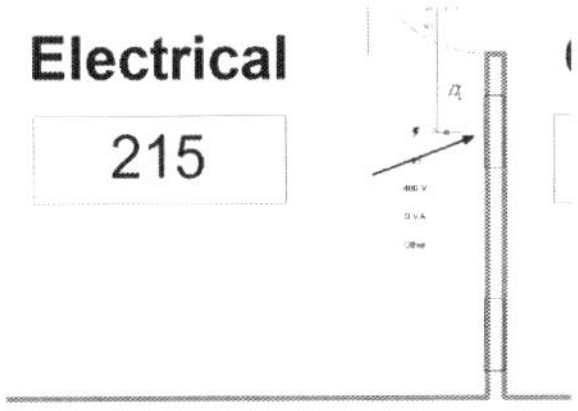 Place the *Lighting and Appliance Panelboard – 480V MLO 250A* above the other panelboard close to the door with a space between the two elements.

14.  Select the **Electrical Equipment** tool.

15.  Select **Load Family**.

16. 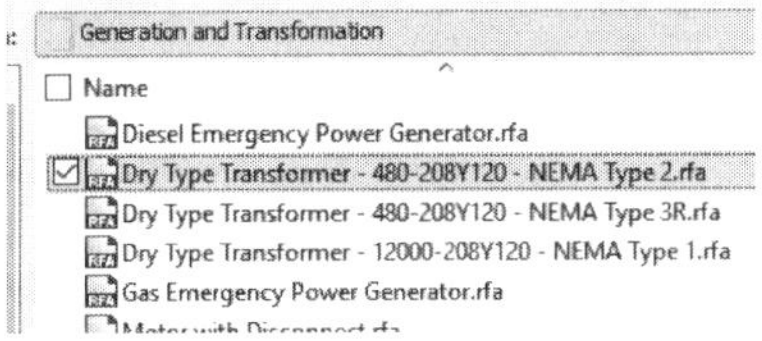 Browse to the *Generation and Transformation* folder.

Select the *Dry Type Transformer – 480-208Y120- NEMA Type 2*.

Press **Open**.

17. 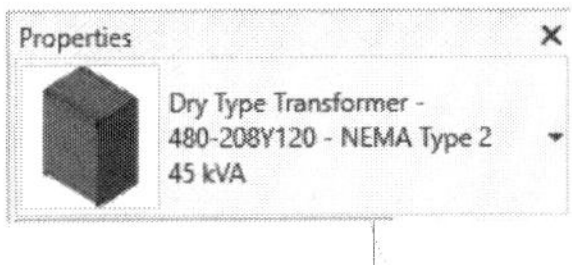 Use the Type Selector to select the **45 kVA** type.

18. 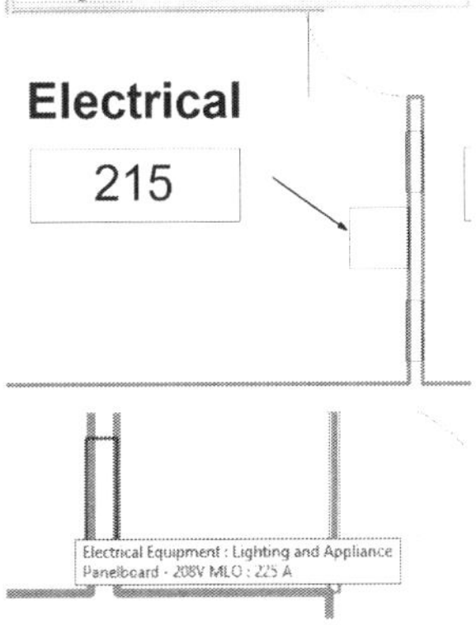 Place the transformer next to the panelboards in Room 215.

Use the SPACEBAR to rotate the element prior to placing.

Escape out of the command.
Remember that if you hover the cursor over an element a tooltip will appear showing you the element information.

19. Select the 208V MLO panelboard.

In the Properties palette:
Scroll down to the General area.
Type **LP1** in the Panel Name.

20. Select the 480V MLO panelboard.

In the Properties palette:
Scroll down to the General area.
Type **HP1** in the Panel Name.

21. Select the Transformer.

In the Properties palette:
Scroll down to the General area.
Type **T1** in the Panel Name.

22. Save as *ex2-10.rvt*.

Exercise 2-11:

Adding Receptacles

Drawing Name: *receptacles.rvt*
Estimated Time: 15 minutes

This exercise reinforces the following skills:

- ❑ Place Components
- ❑ Electrical Fixture
- ❑ Load Families
- ❑ Type Selector

1. Verify that you are in the **Main Floor – Power** view.

2. 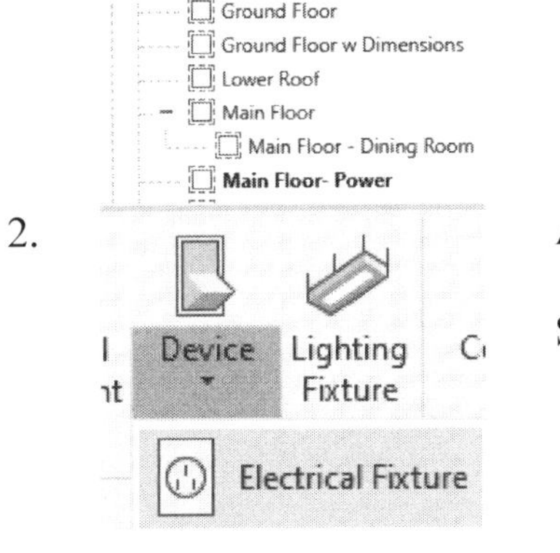

   Activate the Systems ribbon.

   Select **Device→Electrical Fixture**.

3. Press **Yes**.

4. Browse to the *Terminals* folder under *Electric Power*.

5. Select the *Duplex Receptacle*.
   Press **Open**.

6. 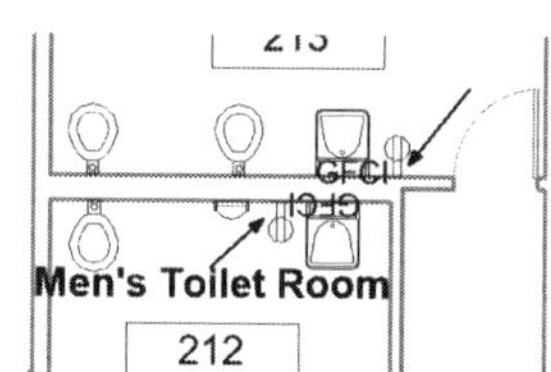 Select the **GFCI** type from the Properties palette.

7. 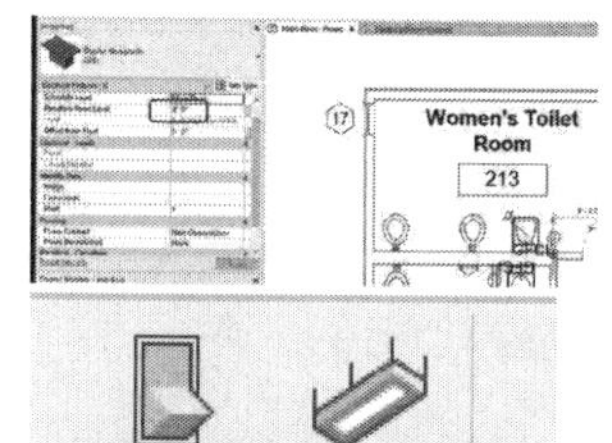 Place a GFCI receptacle next to each of the sinks in the lavatories.

Note that the receptacles are hosted by walls. You do not see the models unless you hover over a wall.

You can use the SPACE BAR to flip the orientation of the receptacle if needed.

Click ESC to exit the command.

8. 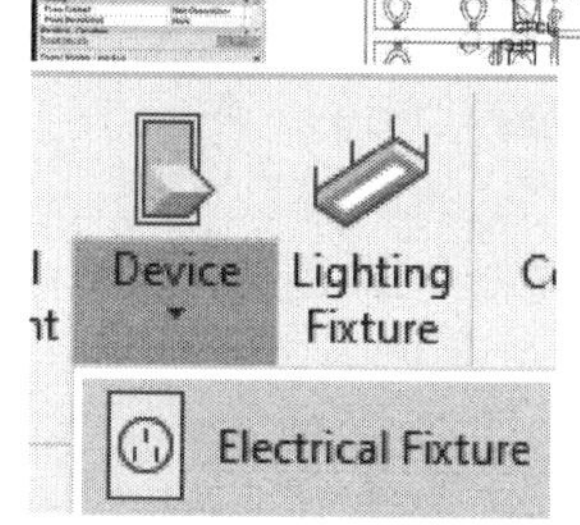 Select one of the receptacles that was placed.

Note the elevation of the receptacle in the Properties palette.

9. Select **Device→Electrical Fixture**.

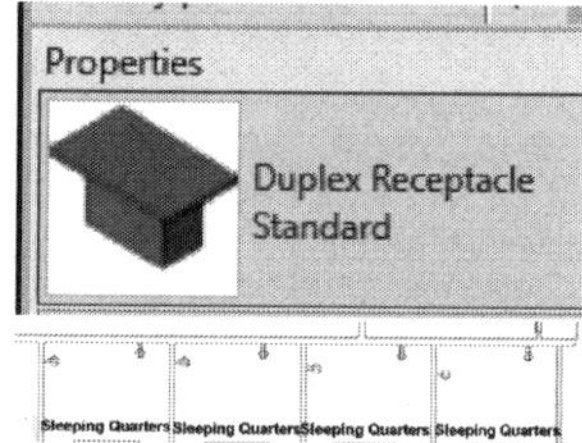

10. Select the **Standard** type from the Properties palette.

Note the elevation of the receptacle in the Properties palette.

11. Place four receptacles in each of the sleeping quarters as shown.

12. Save as *ex2-11.rvt*.

Exercise 2-12:

Create a New Family Type

Drawing Name: *receptacle_family.rvt*
Estimated Time: 20 minutes

This exercise reinforces the following skills:

- ❑ Place Components
- ❑ Electrical Fixtures
- ❑ Load Families
- ❑ Type Selector
- ❑ Type Properties
- ❑ New Type

1. 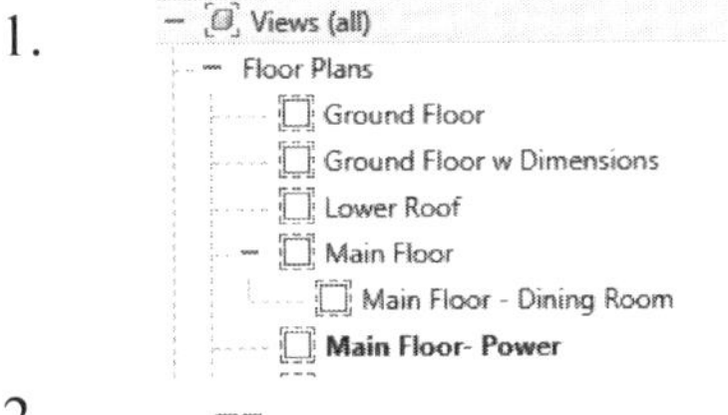 Open the **Main Floor – Power** floor plan.

2.  In the Project Browser:

Enable the Families filter.
Type **duplex** in the search field.

Scroll down to the *Families* category.
Locate the *Electrical Fixtures* folder.
Locate the **Duplex Receptacle** family.

There are currently two types:

- GFCI
- Standard

3. 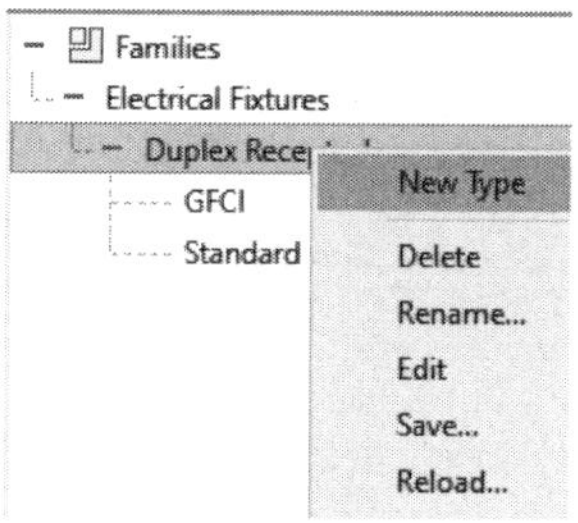   Highlight the **Duplex Receptacle** family.
     Right click and select **New Type**.

4. 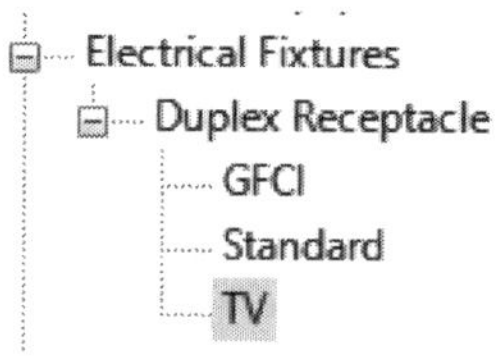   Name the new type **TV**.

5. 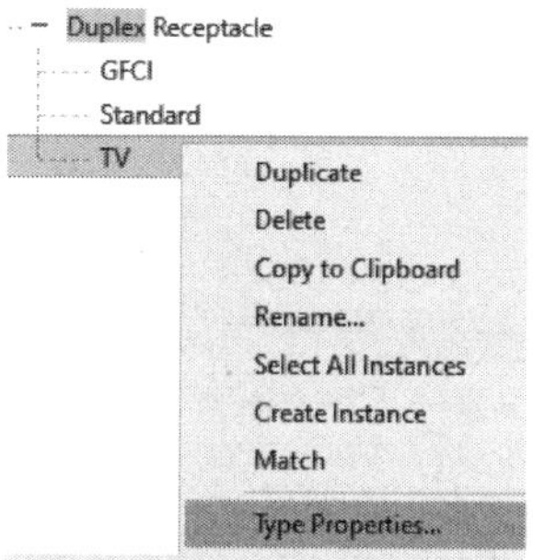   Right click on the **TV** type.

     Select **Type Properties**.

6. 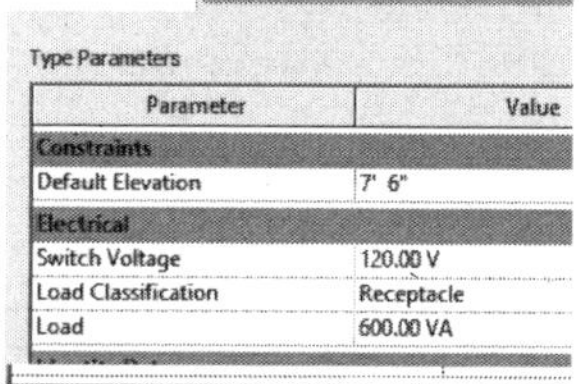   Set the Default Elevation to **7' 6"**.
     Set the Load to **600.00 VA**.

7.    Scroll down to the Other category.
     Locate the **Label** field.
     Set the Value to **TV**.
     Press **OK**.

8. 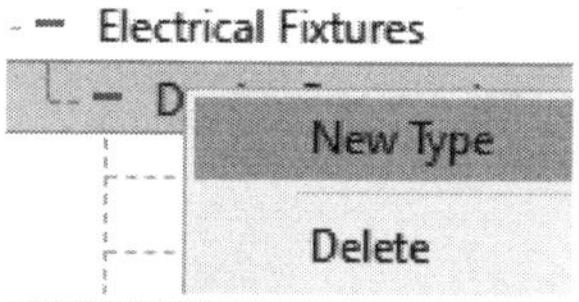   Highlight the **Duplex Receptacle** family.
     Right click and select **New Type**.

9. 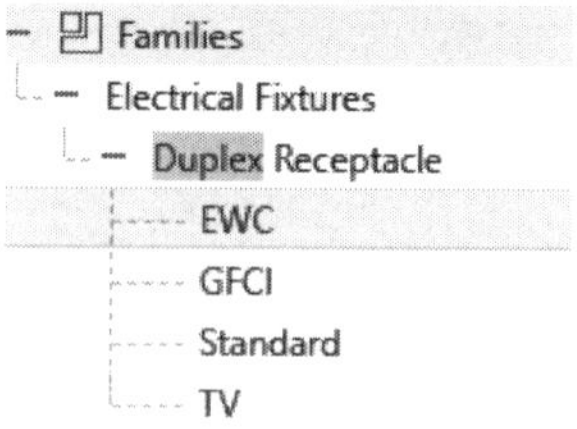   Name the new type **EWC**.

10. 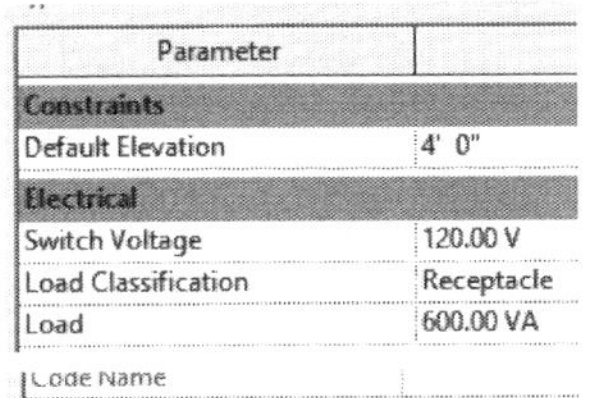 Right click on the **EWC** type.

Select **Type Properties**.

11.  Set the Default Elevation to **4' 0"**.
Set the Load to **600.00 VA**.

12. Scroll down to the Other category.
Locate the **Label** field.
Set the Value to **EWC**.
Press **OK**.

13. 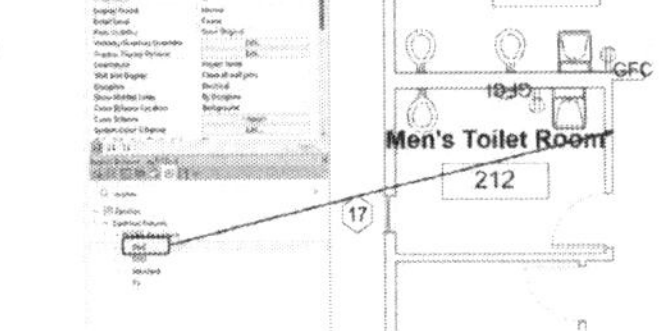 Using the left mouse button, drag and drop the EWC receptacle family to place it on the wall outside the **Room 212 - Men's Lavatory**.

14. 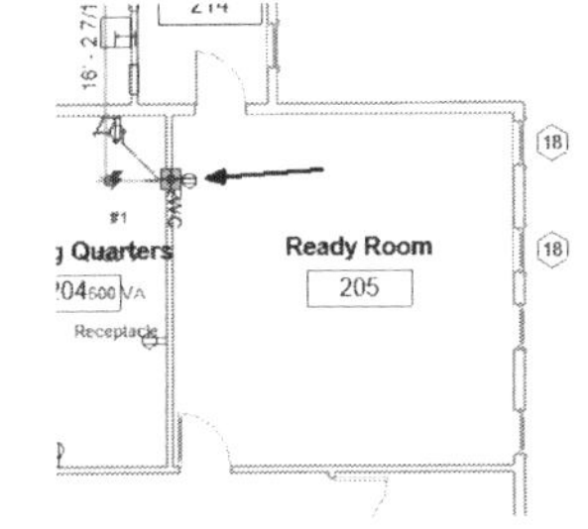 Place the EWC receptacle family to place it on the west wall in **Room 205 – Ready Room**.

15. 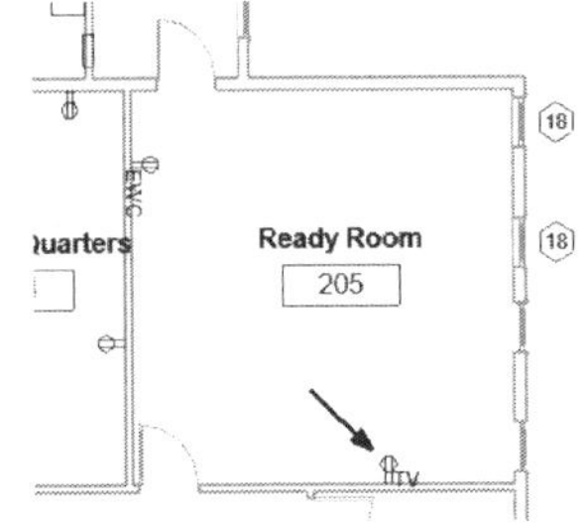 Click on the TV receptacle family in the Project Browser.

Using the left mouse button, drag and drop the TV receptacle family to place it on the south wall in **Room 205 – Ready Room**.

Click ESC to cancel out of the command.

16. Save as *ex2-12.rvt*.

Revit doesn't have a lot of MEP families which work well with creating legends. In this exercise, we create a detail component family which can be used when creating an electrical symbol legend.

Exercise 2-13:

Create a Detail Component Family

Drawing Name: none
Estimated Time: 10 minutes

This exercise reinforces the following skills:

- Families
- Detail Components
- Detail Lines
- Dimensions

1. 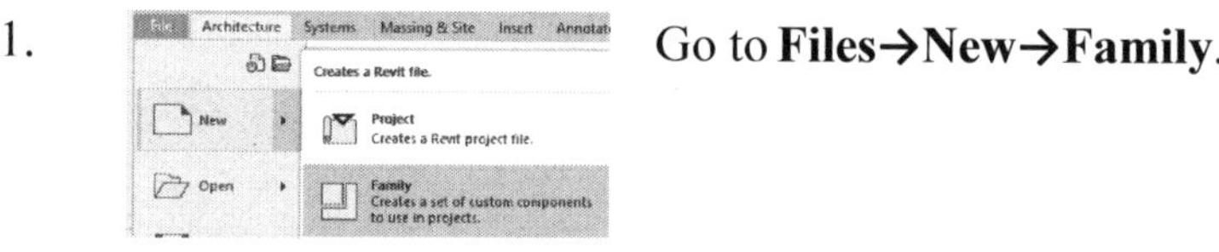 Go to **Files→New→Family**.

2. Select the *Detail Item.rft* template. Press **Open**.

3. Select **Line** from the Create ribbon.

4. On the ribbon:

   Set the line style to **Heavy Lines**.

5. 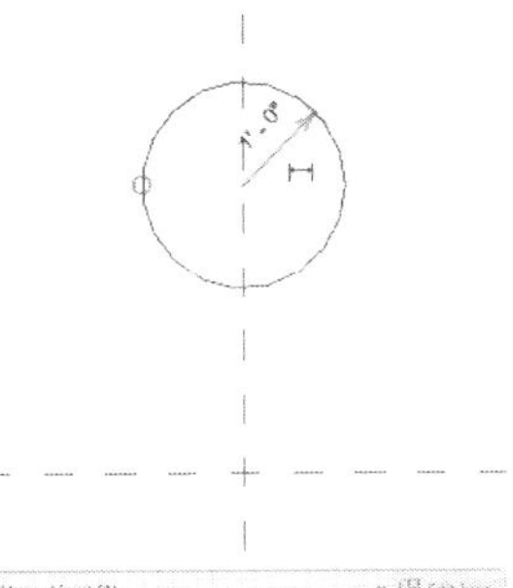 Draw a 1' radius circle above the horizontal reference plane.

Cancel out of the command.

6. 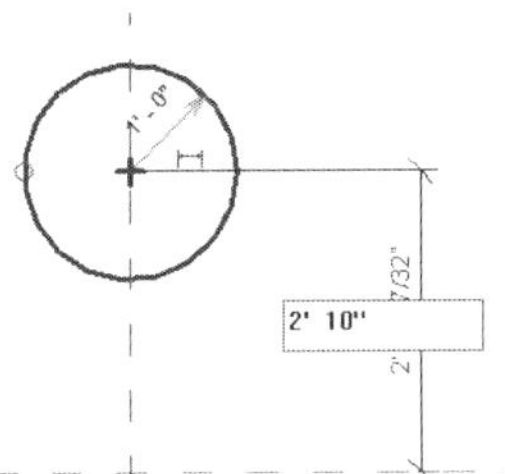 Select the Circle.
On the Properties palette:
Enable **Center Mark Visible**.

7.  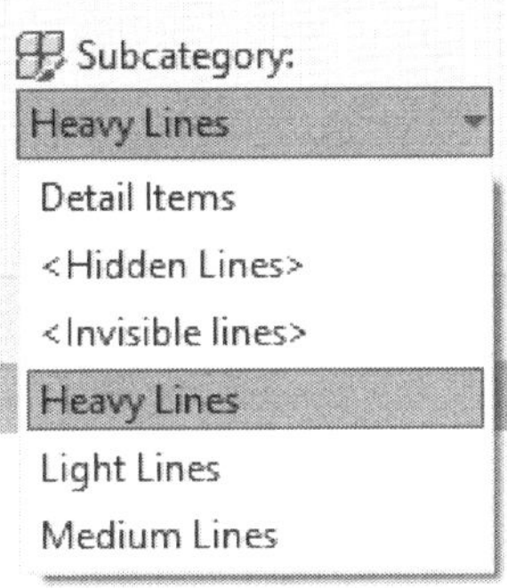 Use the **ALIGNED** dimension tool on the Create ribbon to position the circle 2' 10" above the horizontal reference plane.

8. Select **Line** from the Create ribbon.

Line

9. On the ribbon:

Set the line style to **Heavy Lines**.

Subcategory:

Heavy Lines

Detail Items
<Hidden Lines>
<Invisible lines>
Heavy Lines
Light Lines
Medium Lines

10.

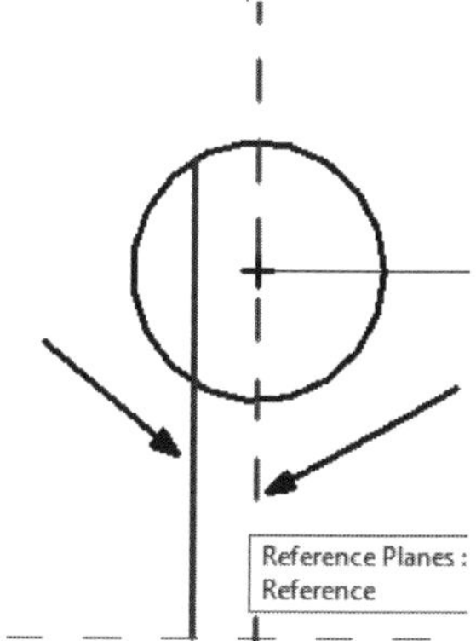

Draw a vertical line from the horizontal reference plane to intersect with the circle.

Use the temporary dimension to position the line 6" left of the circle's center.

11.

Select the vertical line.
Select Mirror →Pick Axis.
Select the vertical reference plane/dashed green line.

12.

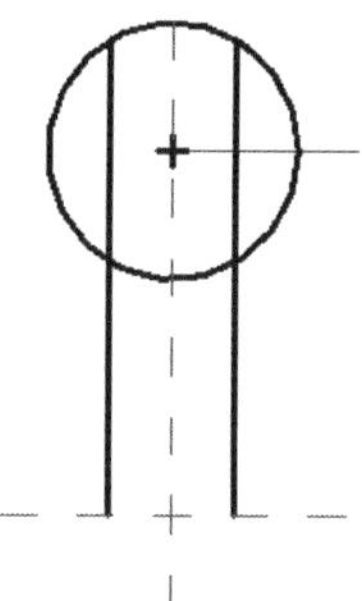

A second vertical line is placed.

13.   Save as *receptacle_symbol.rfa*.

Exercise 2-14:

Create a Detail Item Family

Drawing Name: new family
Estimated Time: 20 minutes

This exercise reinforces the following skills:
- ❑ Detail Component families

1. Go to **File→New→Family**.

2. Browse to the *English-Imperial* folder under Family Templates.

3. Select the *Detail Item* template.
Click **Open.**

4. Select **Line** on the Create tab.

5. Draw a square using the RECTANGLE tool.

Click ESC to cancel out of the command.

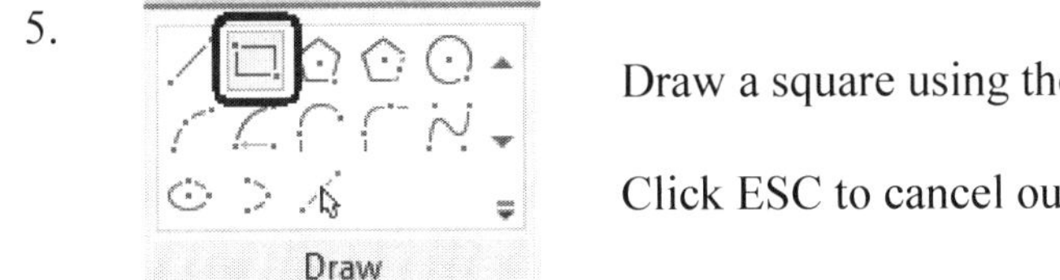

6.

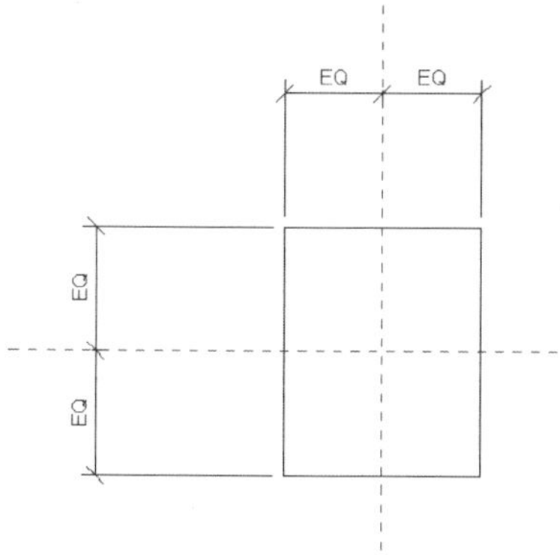

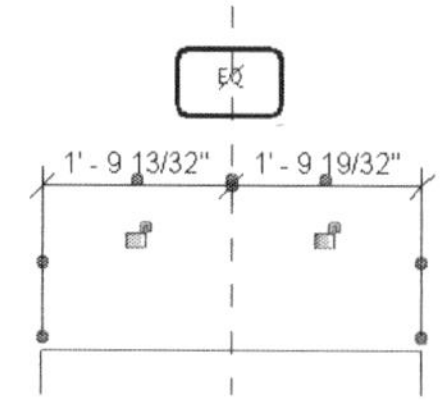

Place a continuous dimension in the vertical and horizontal direction to center the square on the insertion point.
To place the dimension, select one line, then the center reference plane, then the next line, then left click to place.

Left click on the EQ icon to set the dimension equal.

7.

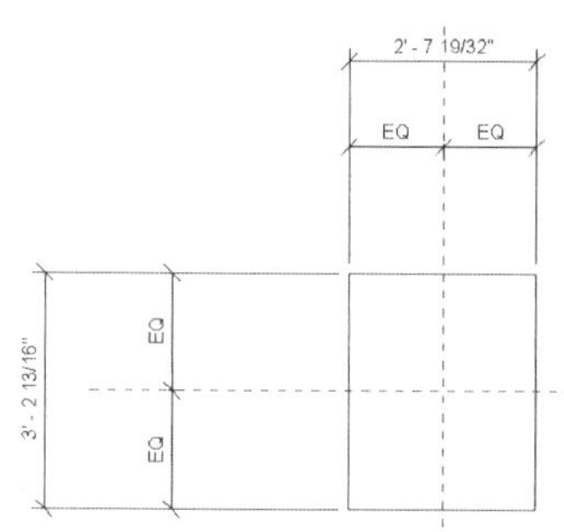

Place an overall horizontal dimension and an overall vertical dimension.
To place the dimensions, select the outside lines, then left click to add the dimension.

Cancel out of the dimension command.

8.

Select the horizontal dimension.

9.

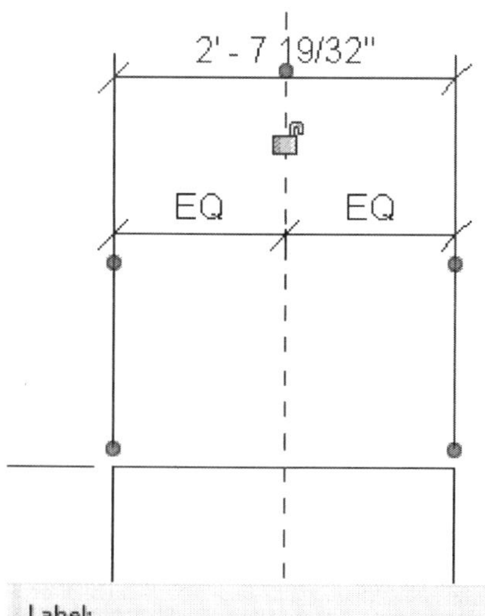

On the ribbon:
Select **New** to add a label parameter to the dimension.

10. 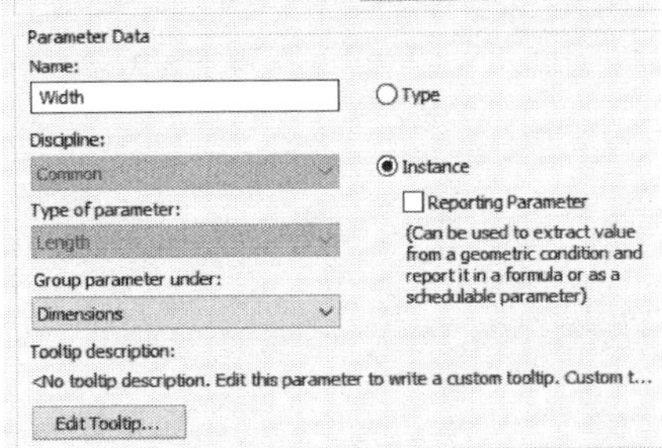   Type **Width** in the Name field.
Enable **Instance**.
Click **OK**.

11.   You should see Width in front of the dimension value now.

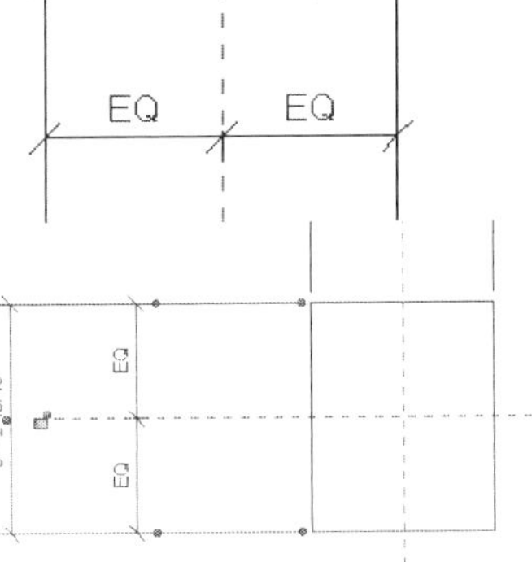

12.   Select the vertical dimension.

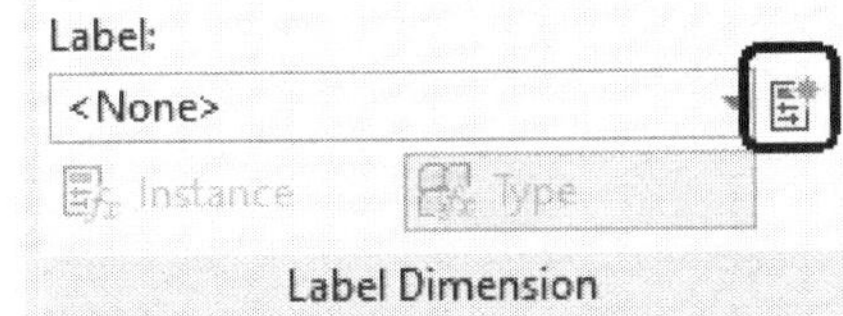

13. 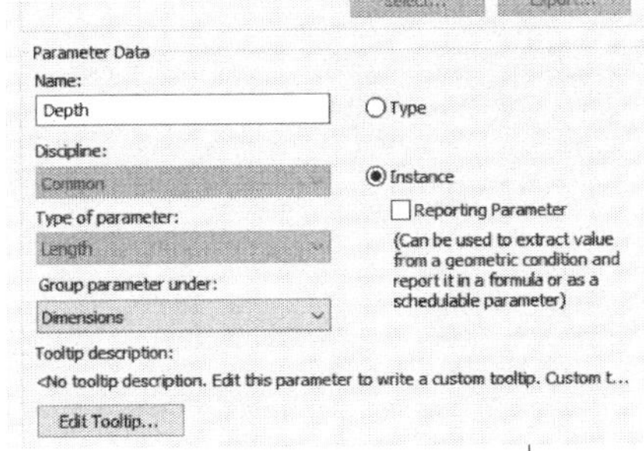   On the ribbon:
Select **New** to add a label parameter to the dimension.

14. 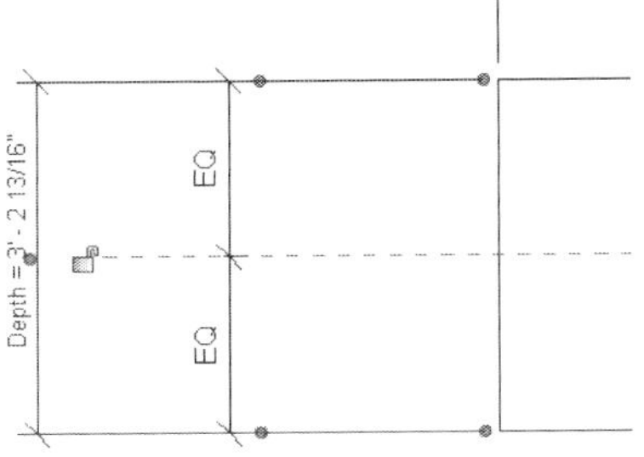   Type **Depth** in the Name field.
Enable **Instance**.
Click **OK**.

15.   You should see Depth in front of the dimension value now.

16.  Select **Family Types** from the ribbon.

17. 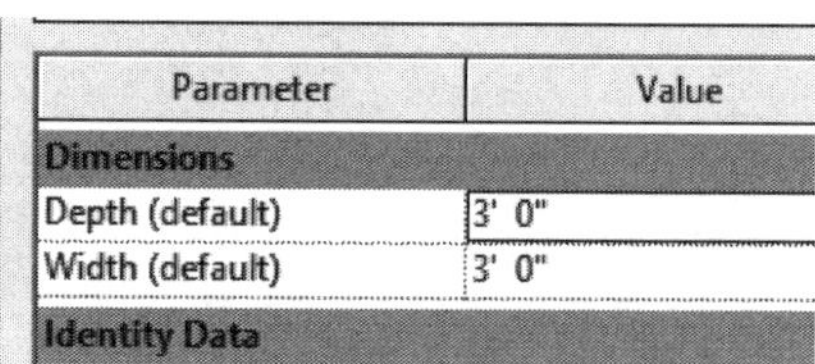 Set the Default values for the Depth and Width to **3' 0"**.
Click **Apply.**

18. 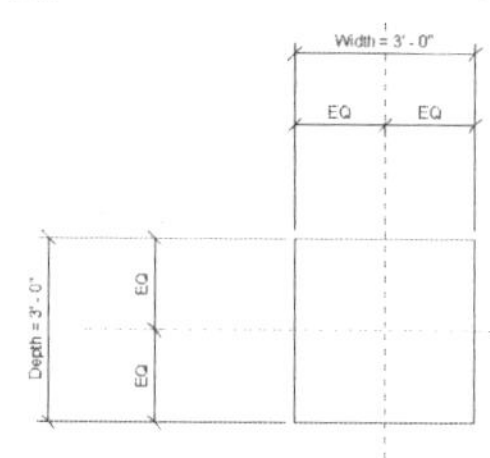 The values in the display window should update. *If the values do not update, you did not place the dimensions correctly. You will need to delete the dimensions and try again.*

Close the Family Types dialog.

19.  Select **Line** on the Create tab.

20. 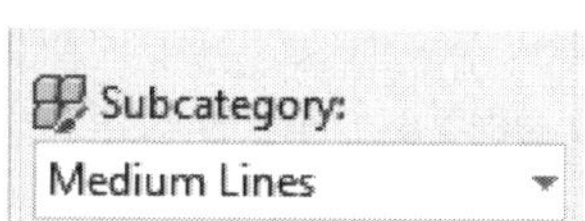 Set the line style to **Medium Lines**.

21.  Disable **Chain** on the Options bar.

22. 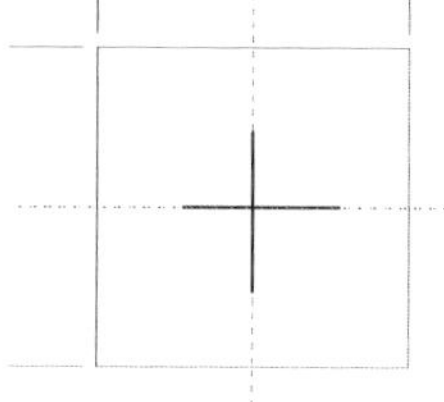 Draw two lines to indicate a center mark.

23. Save as *switchboard-section.rfa.*

This family will be used in an exercise in Lesson 9.

Lab Exercises

Create the following legend symbols:

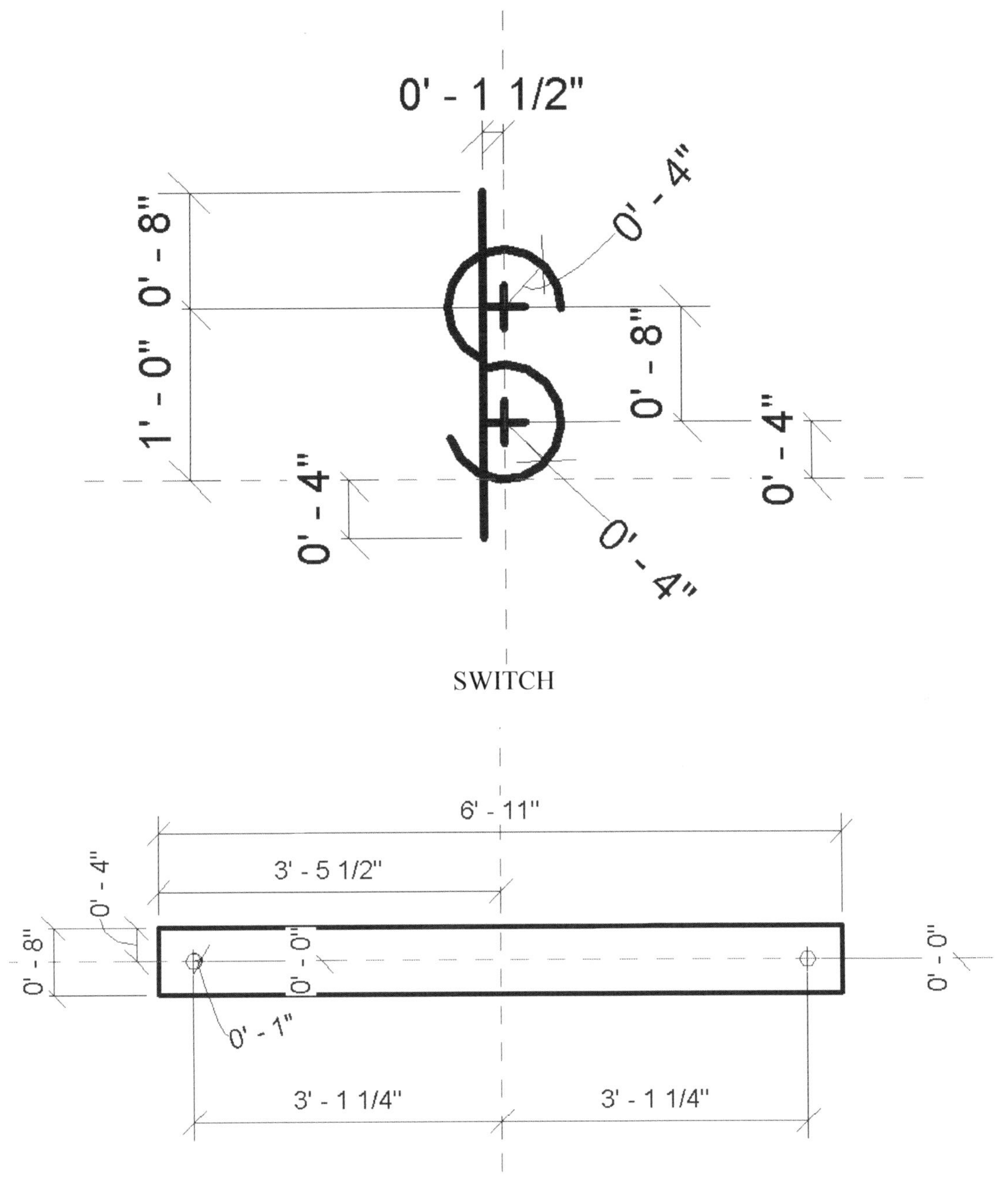

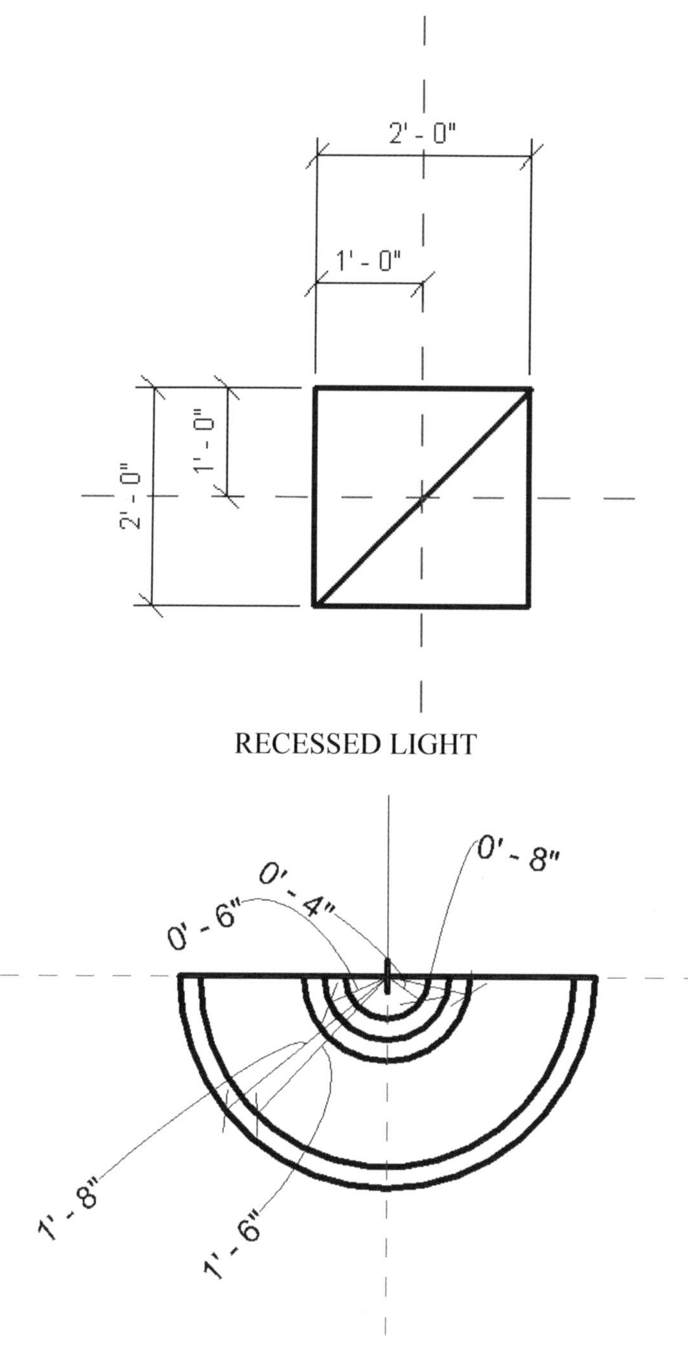

RECESSED LIGHT

SCONCE LIGHT FIXTURE

Revit Systems

Electrical Settings

The basis of electrical systems in Revit is defined in the Electrical Settings dialog. This is most easily accessed by typing the shortcut (ES). There is an icon in the Settings panel on the Manage tab of the ribbon or it can be accessed by clicking the cleverly hidden southeast pointing arrow found in the bottom right-hand corner of the Electrical panel of the Systems tab.

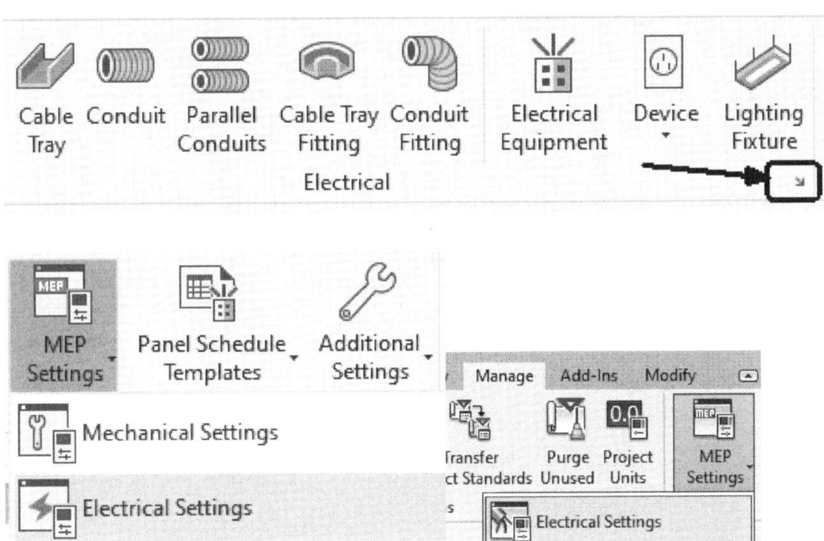

The left-hand side of the Electrical Settings dialog lets the user navigate differing settings for Wiring, Voltage Definitions, Distribution Systems, and more. Simply select the area of interest on the left and its setting will appear on the right. The out-of-the-box settings in the Electrical-Default template should suffice for beginners to the software. That being said, users should verify that the required voltages are defined and the required distribution systems are present before proceeding.

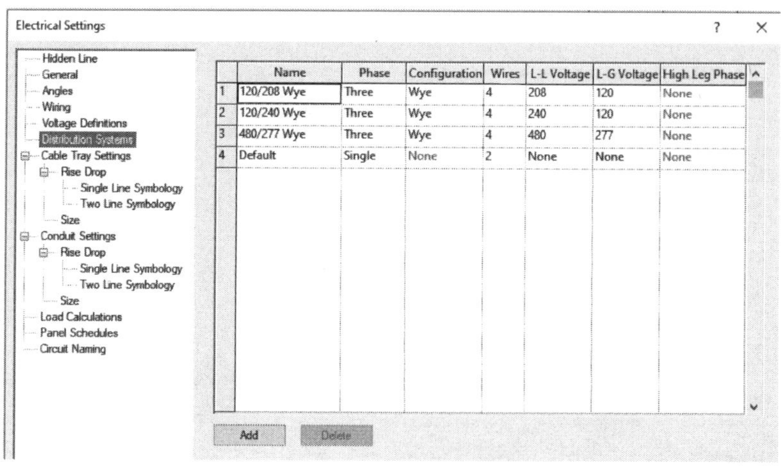

Exercise 3-1:

Space Lighting Calculations

Drawing Name: *space_lighting.rvt*
Estimated Time: 5 minutes

This exercise reinforces the following skills:

- ❏ Spaces
- ❏ Properties

1. 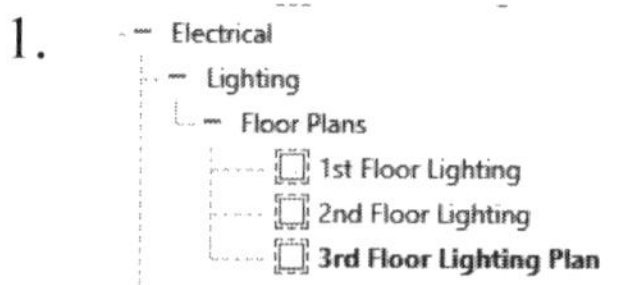

In the Project Browser, activate/open the **3ʳᵈ Floor Lighting** Plan.

2.

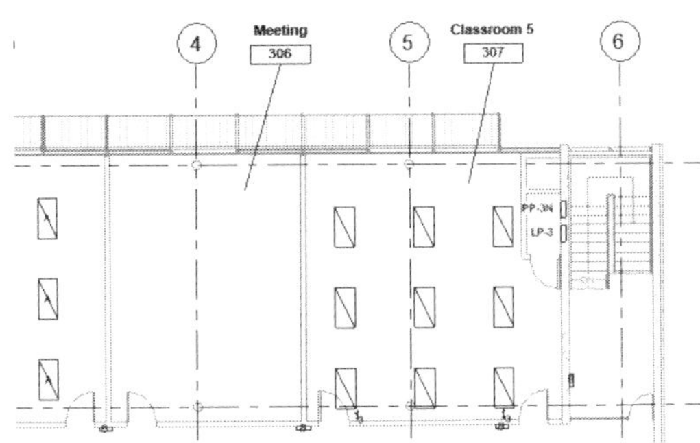

Use **Zoom In Region** to change the display to focus on Classroom 5 – Room 307 between Grids 5 and 6.

3.

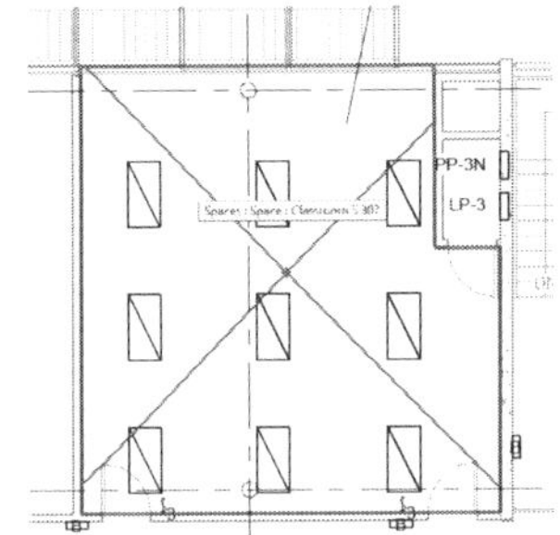

Hover your mouse in the center of Classroom 5 – Rm 307.

You should see a large blue X and the Space label.

Left click to select the space.

4.

Electrical - Lighting	
Average Estimated Illumination	67.28 fc
Room Cavity Ratio	2.231280
Lighting Calculation Workplane	2' 6"
Lighting Calculation Luminaire ...	8' 0"
Ceiling Reflectance	75.0000%
Wall Reflectance	50.0000%
Floor Reflectance	20.0000%

Look in the Properties palette.

Locate the value for the Average Estimated Illumination based on the number of light fixtures in the room.

5. Close the file without saving.

When performing lighting calculations, verify that the spaces are defined properly. If the spaces have not been set to be "room bounding", they will ignore the ceiling heights. This occurs for accurate heating and cooling loads. To ensure that lighting calculations are accurate, spaces should have an upper limit to match the ceiling heights.

Exercise 3-2:

Managing Spaces

Drawing Name: *Architecture_Model.rvt*
Estimated Time: 30 minutes

This exercise reinforces the following skills:

- Spaces
- Properties
- Linking Files

1. 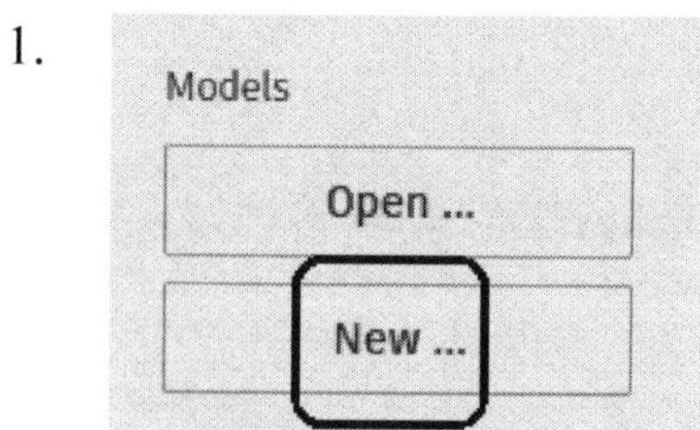   Start a **New** project.

2.   Select the *Electrical – Default* template.

Click **OK**.

3.   Activate the Insert ribbon.

Select **Manage Links**.

4.   Select the **Add →Revit**.

5. 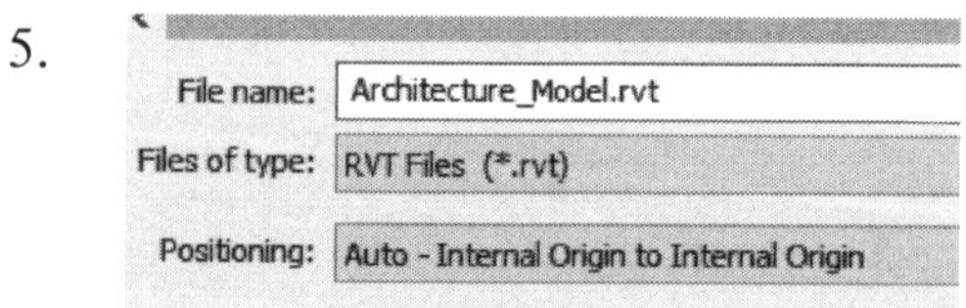   Select *Architecture_Model.rvt*.

Set the Positioning to **Auto – Internal Origin to Internal Origin**.

Click **Open**.

Close the dialog.

6. 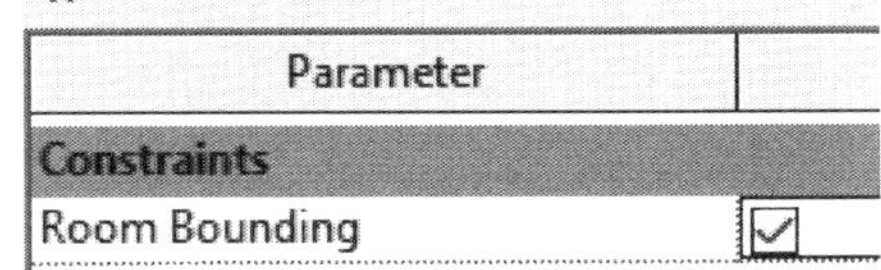

   Left click on the inserted file.

   Select **Edit Type** on the Properties palette.

7.
Type Parameters	
Parameter	
Constraints	
Room Bounding	☑

   Enable **Room Bounding**.

   This ensures any lighting calculations performed on the model are accurate.

   Click **OK** to close the dialog.

   Left click anywhere in the display window to release the selection.

8.

   Activate the Architecture ribbon.

   Expand the ribbon on the Room & Area panel.

   Select **Area and Volume Computations**.

9.

   Enable **Areas and Volumes**.

   Click **OK**.

10. 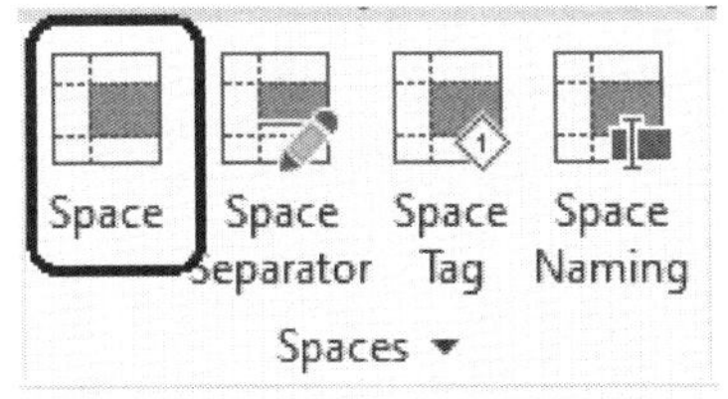

    Activate the Analyze ribbon.

    Select **Space**.

11. No Space Tags family is loaded in the project. Would you like to load one now?

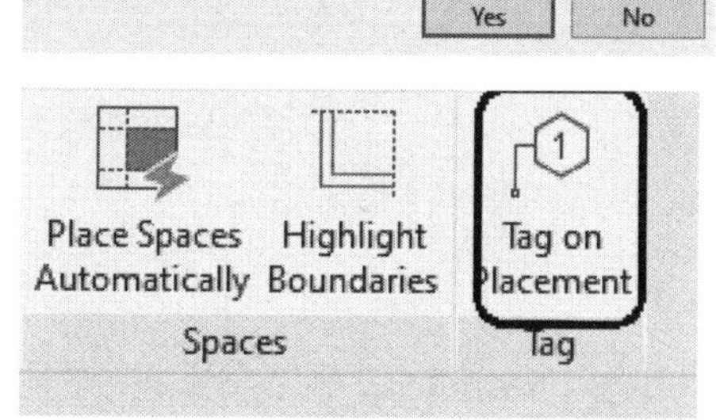

If this dialog appears:

Click **No**.

12. 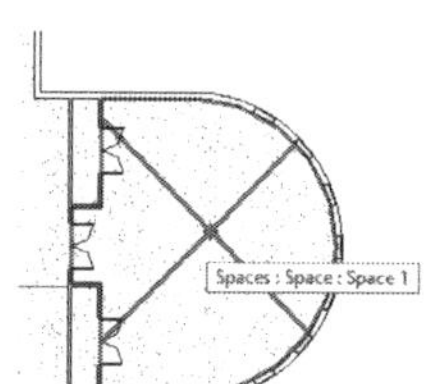

Toggle off **Tag on Placement** on the ribbon.

If this is enabled, spaces will automatically be tagged/labeled.

13. 

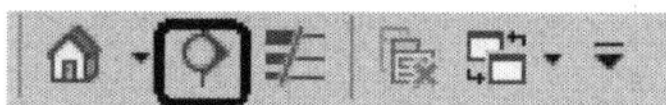

Set the Offset to **8'-0"** on the Options bar.

Left click inside the large curved room on the right side of the building.

Escape out of the command.

14. Section

Activate the View ribbon.

Select the **Section** tool.

You can also select the Section tool from the Standard toolbar at the top of the window.

15. 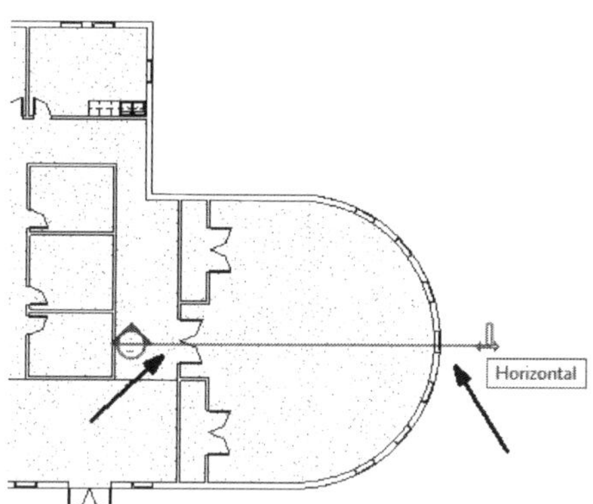

Left click to the left of the curved room with the space to start the section line.

Left click to the right and outside of the curved room to end the section line.

16.

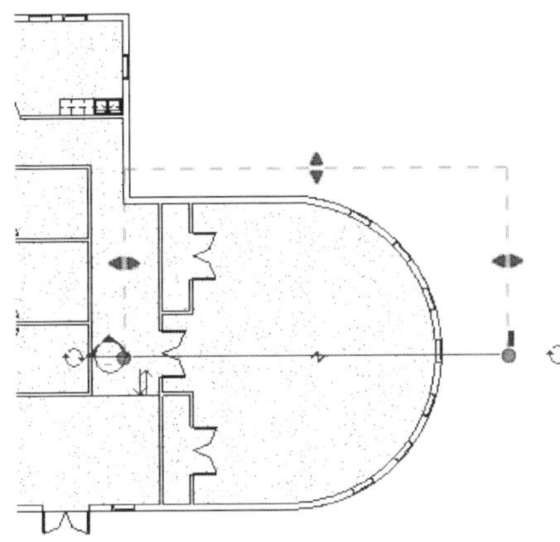

Use the arrows to extend the section above the room.

Left click anywhere in the display window to exit the command.

17.

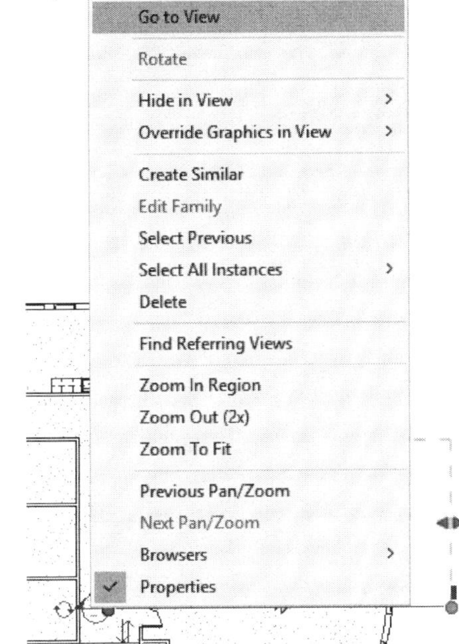

Double left click on the section bubble to open the section view.

OR

Right click on the section line and select **Go to View**.

18.

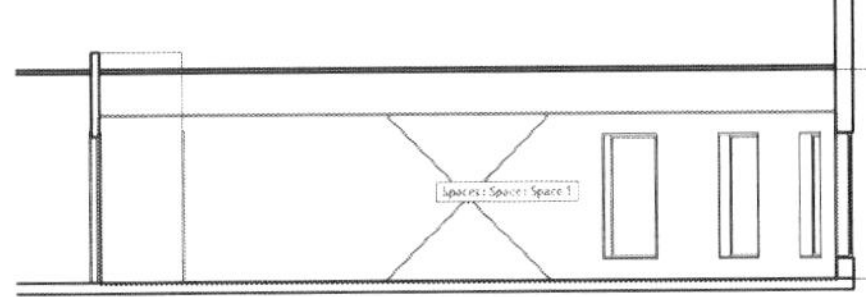

Hover your mouse over the room to "wake up" the space.

You see that the space has a height of 8' -0", but the ceiling is higher.

19.

Left click on the space to select it.

Locate the **Volume** value in the Properties palette under Dimensions.

20.

Change the Limit Offset to **10'-0"**.

Note the space now goes up to the ceiling.

21.

Scroll down to the Volume value and notice it has updated.

22.

Change the Limit Offset to **12'-0"**.

Note the space still goes up to the ceiling but shows a green dashed line to indicate the new offset.

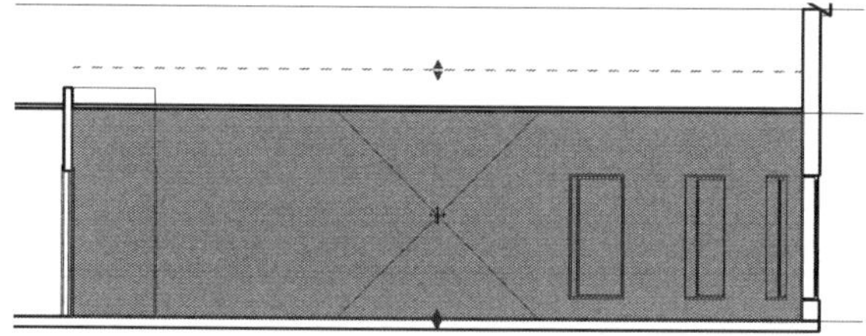

23.

Scroll down to the Volume value and notice it has remained the same value. *This confirms that the ceiling is acting as a room boundary.*

24.

Return to the **1-Lighting** floor plan.

25.	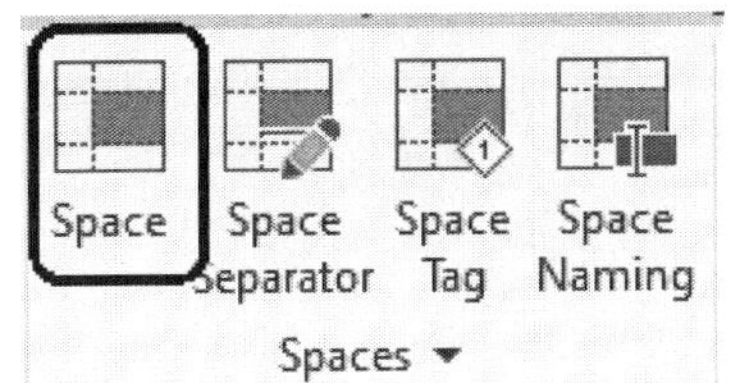	Activate the Analyze ribbon. Select **Space**.
26.	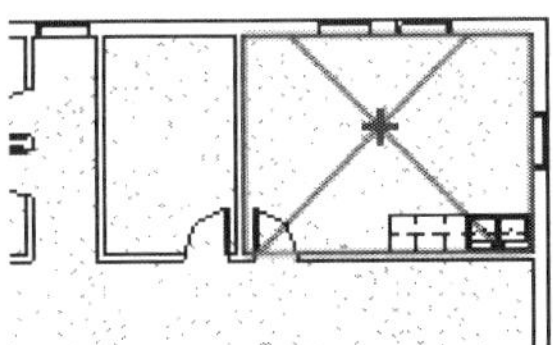	Upper Limit:　Level 1　　▾　Offset:　15' 0" Set the Offset to **15'-0"** on the Options bar. Left click inside the upper corner room on the right side of the building. Cancel out of the command.
27.		Activate the View ribbon. Select the **Section** tool.
28.	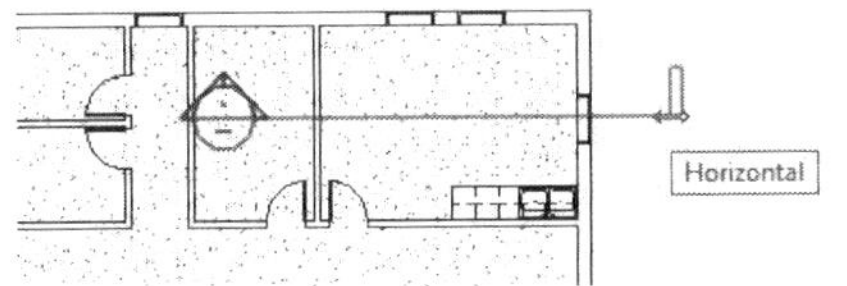	Left click to the left of the room with the space to start the section line. Left click to the right and outside of the room to end the section line.
29.	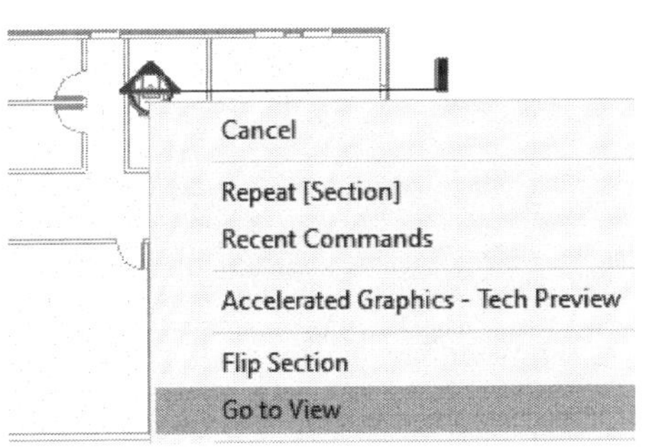	Double left click on the section bubble to open the section view. OR Right click on the section line and select **Go to View**.

30.

Hover your mouse over the room to "wake up" the space.

You see that the ceiling is still acting as a boundary for the space.

31.   Save as *ex3-2.rvt*.

Exercise 3-3:

Creating a Distribution System

Drawing Name: *systems.rvt*
Estimated Time: 15 minutes

This exercise reinforces the following skills:

- ❑   Electrical Settings
- ❑   Voltage Definitions
- ❑   Distribution Systems

1.   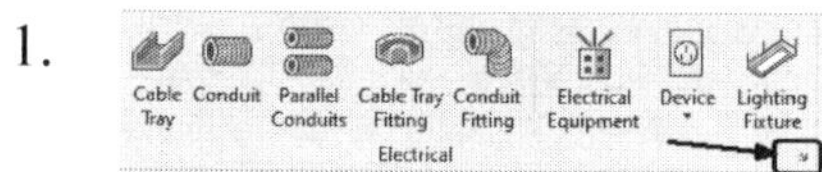

Activate the Systems ribbon.

Launch the **Electrical Settings** dialog.

2.

	Name	Value	Minimum	Maximum
1	120	120.00 V	110.00 V	130.00 V
2	208	208.00 V	200.00 V	228.00 V
3	240	240.00 V	220.00 V	250.00 V
4	277	277.00 V	260.00 V	280.00 V
5	480	480.00 V	460.00 V	490.00 V

Highlight **Voltage Definitions**.

Use the Add button to add five voltage definitions for 120V, 208V, 240V, 277V, and 480V.

The values you set in the Voltage Definitions are the values available to the Distribution Systems.

You do not need to type V – just the values.

2	120V	120.00 V	110.00 V	130.00 V
3	208V	208.00 V	200.00 V	220.00 V
4	240V	240.00 V	230.00 V	250.00 V
5	277V	277.00 V	260.00 V	280.00 V
6	480V	480.00 V	460.00 V	490.00 V

3. 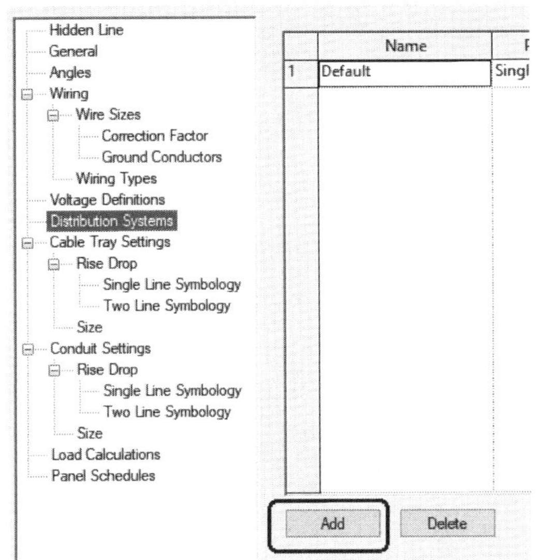   Highlight **Distribution Systems**.

   Click **Add**.

	Name	Phase	Configuration	Wires	L-L Voltage	L-G Voltage	High Leg Phase	
1	120/240 Delta	Three	Delta	4	240	120	B	

4. In the Name field: Type **120/240 Delta**.

   In Phase: Select **Three** from the drop-down list.

   In Configuration: Select **Delta** from the drop-down list.

   Set the Wires to **4**.

   Set the L-L value to **240**.

   Set the L-G value to **120**.

   Set the High Leg Phase to **B**.

   Hint: You can use the drop-down lists to select the values.

   The configuration names are case sensitive, so use sentence case or the drop-down list.

   - Two legs measure ~120 V L-N (or L-G).
   - The **high leg** measures ~**208 V L-N** (because $240 \times \sqrt{3}/2 \approx 208$ V).

   *In many setups this is labeled **Phase B** (and must be orange per code).*

	Name	Phase	Configuration	Wires	L-L Voltage	L-G Voltage	High Leg Phase
1	120/240 Delta	Three	Delta	4	240	120	B
2	120/208 Wye	Three	Wye	4	208	120	None

5. Click **Add** to add a second distribution system.

In the Name field: Type **120/208 Wye**.

In Phase: Select **Three** from the drop-down list.

In Configuration: Select **Wye** from the drop-down list.

Set the Wires to **4**.

Set the L-L value to **208**.

Set the L-G value to **120**.

Set the High Leg Phase to **None**.

*A 4-wire system with 208 V line-to-line and 120 V line-to-ground is a 120/208 V **wye** (star) system — each phase to neutral is ~120 V, so there is no elevated (≈208 V) "high leg" as in a high-leg (wild) 240 V delta.*

3	480/277 Wye	Three	Wye	4	480	277	None

6. Click **Add** to add a third distribution system.

In the Name field: Type **480/277 Wye**.

In Phase: Select **Three** from the drop-down list.

In Configuration: Select **Wye** from the drop-down list.

Set the Wires to **4**.

Set the L-L value to **480**.

Set the L-G value to **277**.

Set the High Leg Phase to **None**.

*480 V line-to-line and 277 V line-to-ground is a 277/480 V **wye** system (480/√3 ≈ 277 V), so all three phases are ~277 V to ground/neutral — there is no elevated "high" (wild) leg.*

7.

	Name	Phase	Configuration	Wires	L-L Voltage	L-G Voltage	High Leg Phase
1	120/240 Delta	Three	Delta	4	240	120	B
2	120/208 Wye	Three	Wye	4	208	120	None
3	480/277 Wye	Three	Wye	4	480	277	None

8. Click **OK** to close the Electrical Settings dialog.

9.

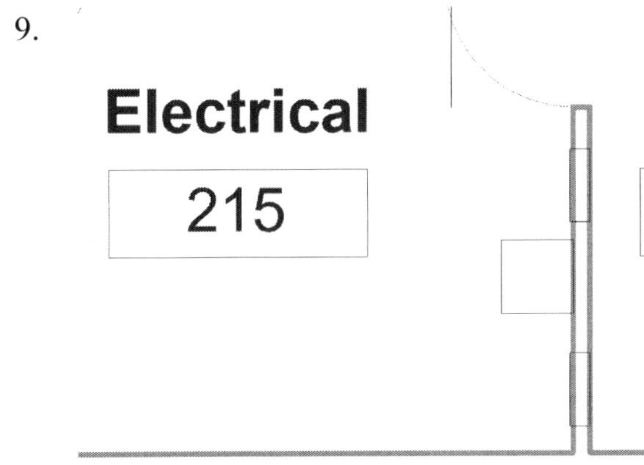

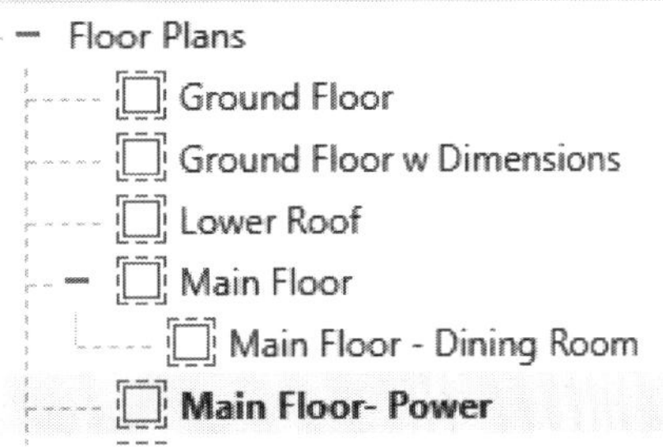

Activate the **Main Floor- Power** floor plan.

Zoom into **Room 215 - Electrical**.

10.

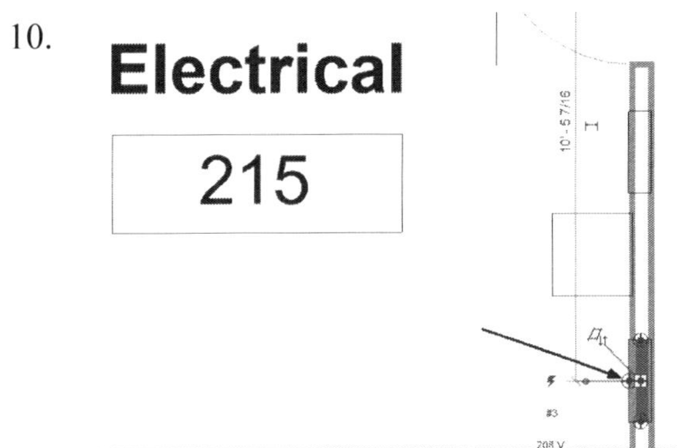

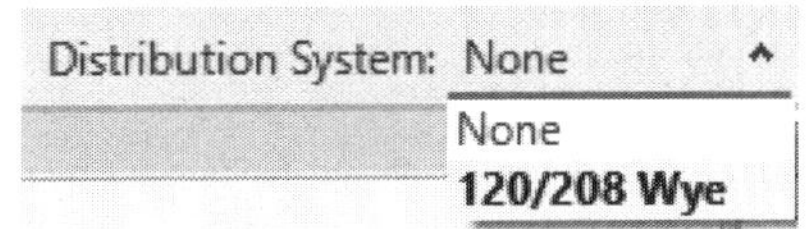

Select the lower panelboard.

On the Options bar: Assign it to the **120/208 Wye Distribution System**.

Left click in the display window to release the selection.

11.

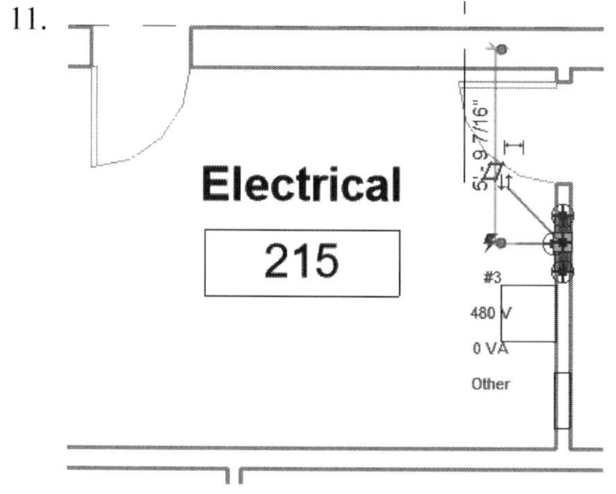

Select the high voltage panelboard.

On the Options bar: Assign it to the **480/277 Wye Distribution System**.

Left click in the display window to release the selection.

Notice that only the applicable distribution systems appear in the drop-down list.

12.

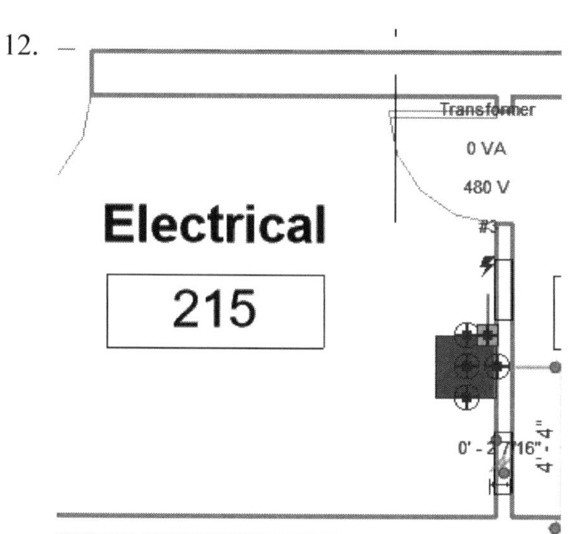

Select the transformer.

On the Options bar: Assign it to the **480/277 Wye Distribution System**.

Left click in the display window to release the selection.

13. Save as *ex3-3.rvt*.

Exercise 3-4:

Define a Power System

Drawing Name: *power_system.rvt*
Estimated Time: 30 minutes

This exercise reinforces the following skills:

- Distribution Systems
- Panels
- Power Connections
- Circuits

1. 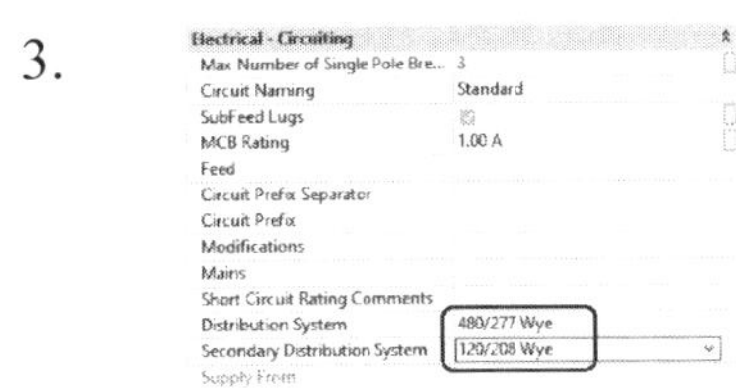

Open the **Main Floor- Power** floor plan.

2. Zoom into **Room 215- Electrical**.

   Select the transformer.

3. 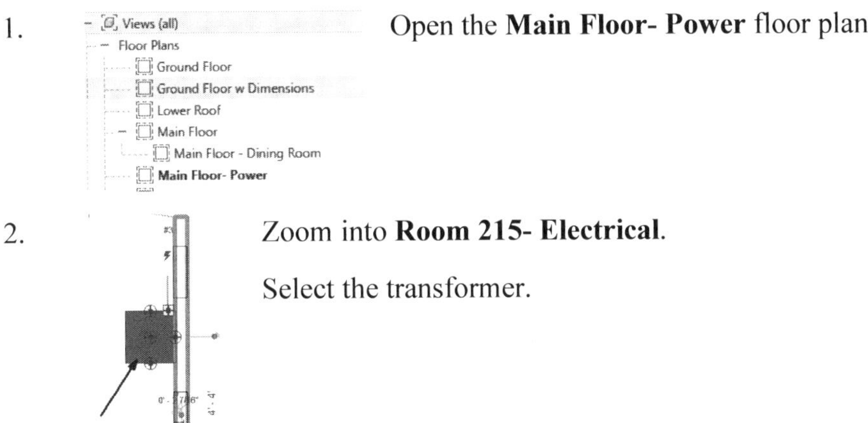

On the Properties palette:

   Under Electrical Circuiting:

   Set the Secondary Distribution System to **120/208 Wye**.

   Release the selection.

4.

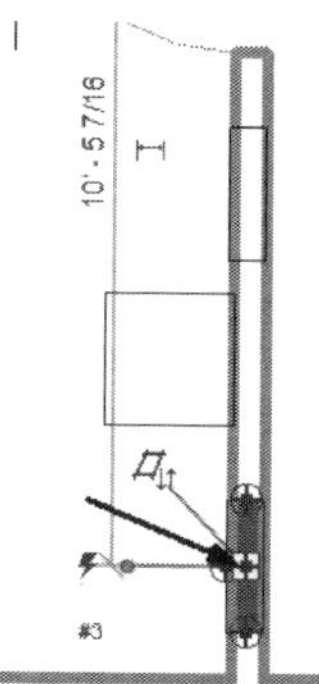

Select the low power panel board located below the transformer.

5.

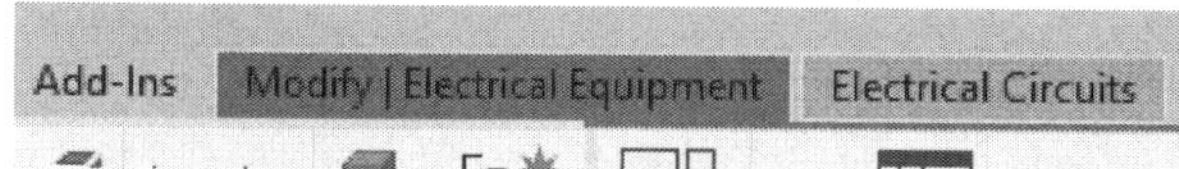

Look at the ribbon.

There are three ribbon tabs.

- The standard ribbon
- A contextual ribbon to modify the selected component
- Electrical Circuits

6.

Click the Electrical Circuits ribbon:

Select the **Select Panel** tool.

Select the transformer.

7.

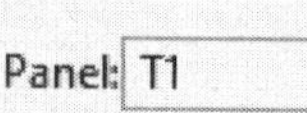

On the ribbon:

You see that T1 has been assigned to the panel.

Click to release the selection.

8.

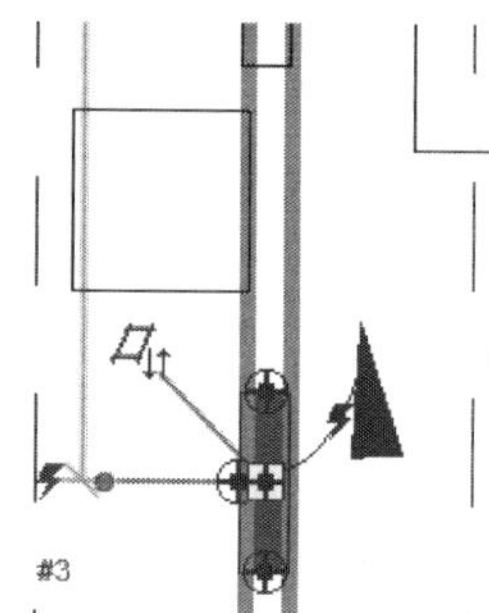

Select the low power panelboard.

Click the Electrical Circuits ribbon.

An arrow appears next to the low power panelboard representing the connection between the low voltage panel and the transformer.

Click **ESC** to release the selection.

9.

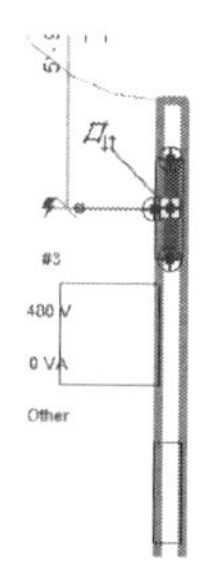

Select the high power panel board located above the transformer.

10. 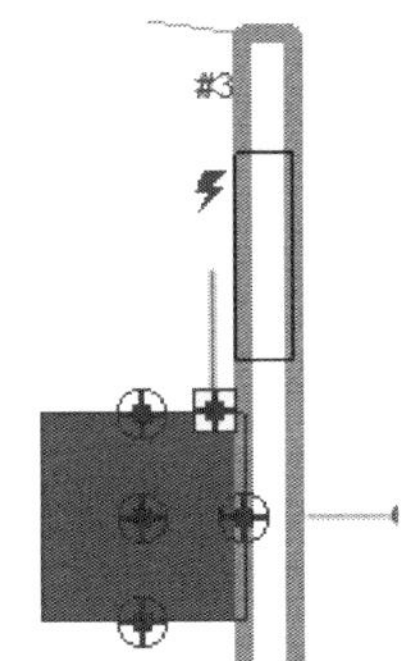 Select the **Power** tool on the ribbon.

This tool is located on the far right.

11.  Select the transformer.

A lightning bolt appears next to the high power panel to represent the connection.

Release the selection.

12.  Hold down the CTL key.

Select the four receptacles in **Room 201 – Sleeping Quarters**.

13. Select the **Power** tool on the ribbon.

14. 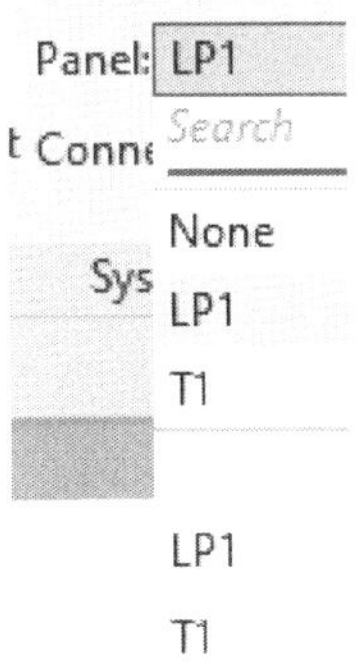 Assign to Panel **LP1** on the ribbon.

A dashed line appears showing the receptacles' connections.

15. 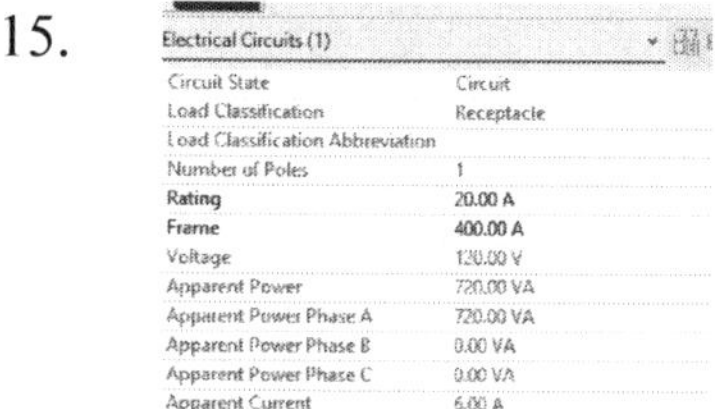

Look in the Properties palette to review the different circuit values.

16.

Select Edit Circuit on the ribbon.

Edit Circuit

17.

Verify that **Add to Circuit** is enabled on the ribbon.

Elements which are not included in the circuit are faded. Once they are selected, they are no longer faded.

18. 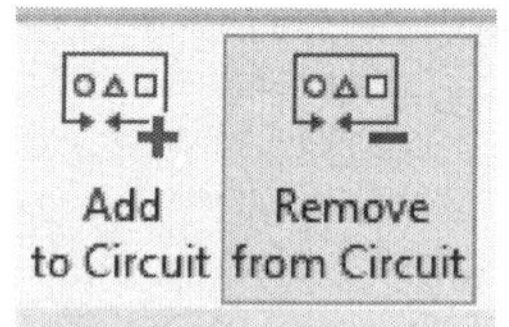

Add the duplex receptacles in Rooms 202 and 203.

You should see this dialog box.

Close the dialog.

19.

Enable **Remove From Circuit** on the ribbon.

Select the receptacles in Room 203 to remove them from the circuit.

20. 

Select **Finish Editing Circuit** on the ribbon.

Finish Editing Circuit

21. Save as *ex3-4.rvt*.

Exercise 3-5:

Define an Electrical Circuit

Drawing Name: *elec_circuit2.rvt*
Estimated Time: 10 minutes

This exercise reinforces the following skills:

- ❑ Loadable Families
- ❑ Place a Component

1. 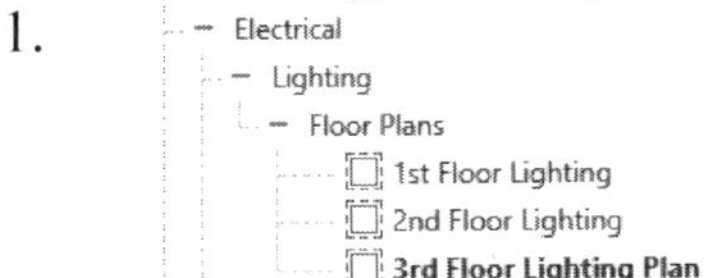 In the Project Browser, activate/open the **3rd Floor Lighting** Plan.

2. 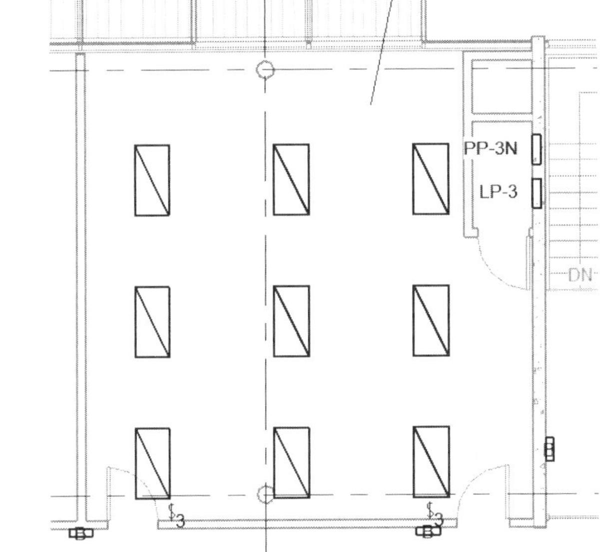 Use **Zoom In Region** to change the display to focus on Classroom 5 Room 307 between Grids 5 and 6.

3. Select the upper left light fixture.

   It doesn't really matter which light fixture you select.

4.  Select the **Power** tool on the ribbon.

5.  Select **Edit Circuit** on the ribbon.

6. 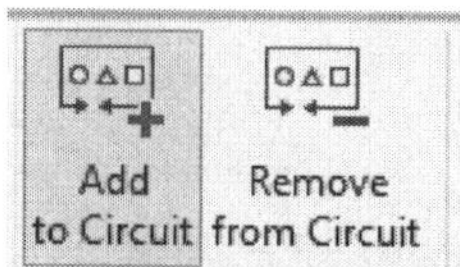 Verify that **Add to Circuit** is enabled on the ribbon.

7. 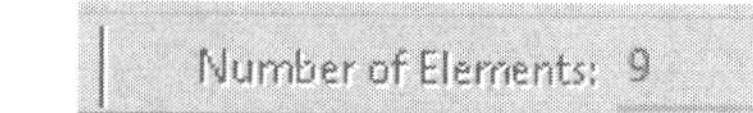 Hold down the Ctrl key and select the remaining light fixtures.

   The Options bar should display that the Number of Elements selected is **9.**

8. 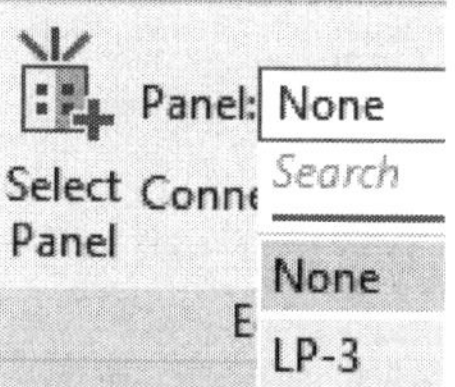 On the ribbon, select the **LP-3** panel from the panel list.

9. 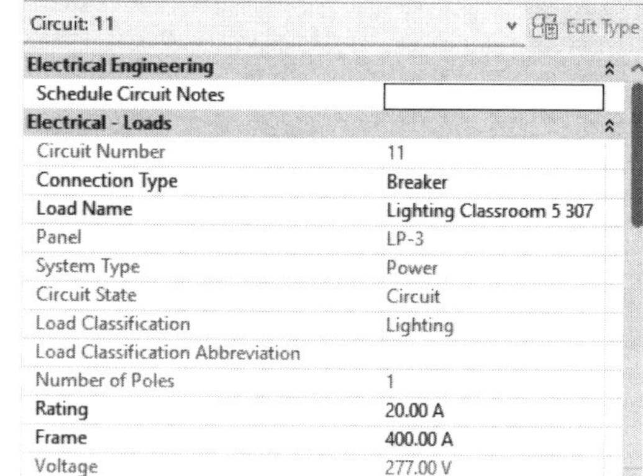 On the Properties palette:

   Note that the circuit is now assigned to LP-3 panel.

   Note the Circuit Number, the voltages and amperages.

   Notice the Load Name is set to **Lighting Classroom 5 307.**

10. 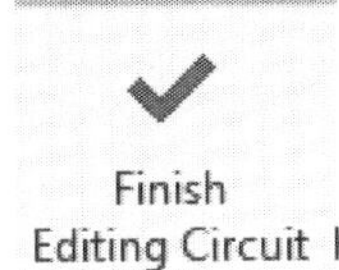 On the ribbon, select **Finish Editing Circuit**.

11. 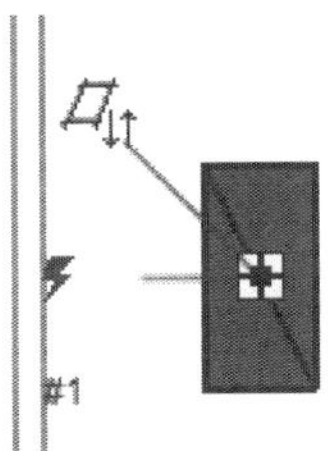 Select a lighting fixture.

12.

Electrical - Loads	
Panel	LP-3
Circuit Number	11

On the Properties palette:

Notice that the lighting fixture is assigned to Panel LP-3 and Circuit Number 11.

13. Save as *ex3-5.rvt*.

Rooms and Spaces

Rooms and spaces are independent components used for different purposes. Rooms are architectural components used to maintain information about occupied areas. Spaces are exclusively used for the MEP disciplines to analyze volume. They contain parameters that maintain information about the areas in which they have been placed. This information is used for performing a heating and cooling loads analysis.

Spaces can be placed (added) and unplaced, and deleted. Unplacing spaces is not the same as deleting spaces. Spaces are immediately assigned to the Default zone when they are initially added to a project. Spaces can be viewed in a section view. Spaces cannot be viewed or placed in elevation or 3D views.

Spaces should be placed throughout the model, including unoccupied areas such as plenums areas. Spaces that are created (manually or automatically) in an area that contains a room are created as occupied (Occupiable parameter selected).

Zones

Zones define spaces that can be controlled by environmental control systems, such as heating, cooling, and humidity control systems. This lets you perform load balancing and analysis procedures on a building model. Initially, all spaces are assigned to a single default zone until/unless more zones are defined.

Duplicating Views

Revit allows views to be duplicated in three ways:

- Duplicate
- Duplicate with Detailing
- Duplicate as Dependent

Remember there are three types of elements in Revit:

- Model
- Datum
- View-Specific

If you duplicate a view, model elements and datums will be included in that view, but view-specific elements, like dimensions and tags, will not be copied into the new view.

If you duplicate with detailing, all three element types will be copied into the new view.

If you duplicate as dependent, you link the parent and child view, so all three element types are visible in both views. If you add annotations to either the parent or the child view, it will be visible in the linked view.

Exercise 3-6:

Adding Space Tags

Drawing Name: *space_analysis.rvt*
Estimated Time: 15 minutes

This exercise reinforces the following skills:

- ❏ Visibility/Graphics Overrides
- ❏ Adding Space Tags
- ❏ Duplicate View

1. 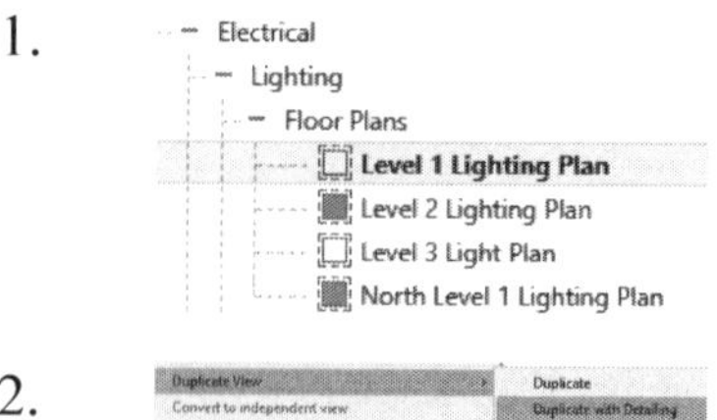

   In the Project Browser:

   Locate the **Level 1 Lighting Plan**.

2. Right click and select **Duplicate View→Duplicate with Detailing.**
   This creates a new view which includes any annotation elements, like tags or dimensions.

3.   Right click and select **Rename**.

Rename the copied view: **Level 1 Lighting Analysis**

4.   Type **VV** to open the Visibility/Graphics Overrides.

On the Model Categories tab:

Enable **Architecture** and **Electrical**.

5.   Type **wires** in the search field.

Disable **Wires**.

6.   Type **light** in the search field.

Disable **Lighting Devices.**

Disable **Lighting Fixtures**.

If you click **Apply** on the dialog, you can see a preview of what the floor plan looks like with these elements hidden.

7.   On the Annotation Categories tab:

Type **sect** in the search field.

Disable **Sections**.

Apply allows you to preview the changes you made before you commit. Click OK if you are satisfied with the new setting.

Click **OK** to close the dialog.

Notice how the view has changed.

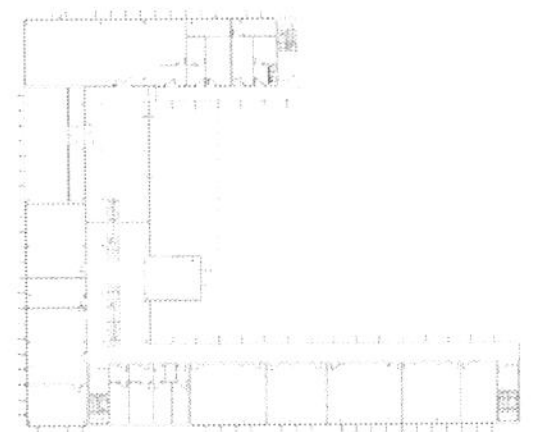

8.

If you hover over the rooms, you see that spaces have already been added to the rooms.

9.

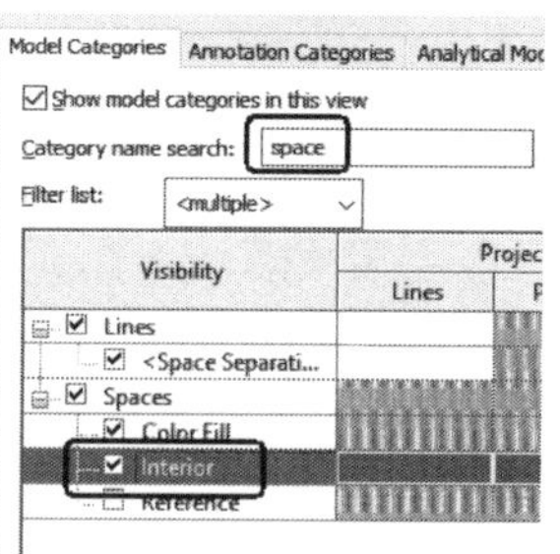

Type **VV** to open the Visibility/Graphics Overrides.

On the Model Categories tab:

Type **space** in the search field.

Enable **Interior**.

Click **OK**.

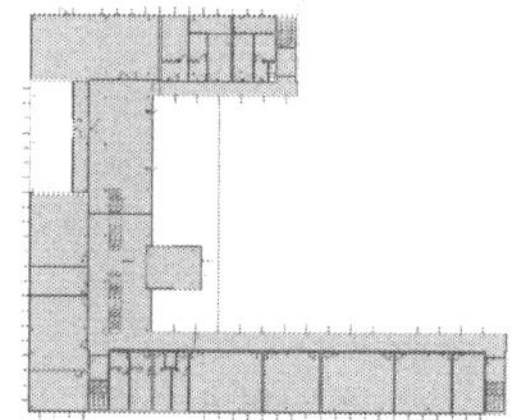

Notice that all the spaces are now indicated by a color fill.

10.

Activate the **Analyze** ribbon.

11.

Select the **Space Tag** tool from the ribbon.

12.

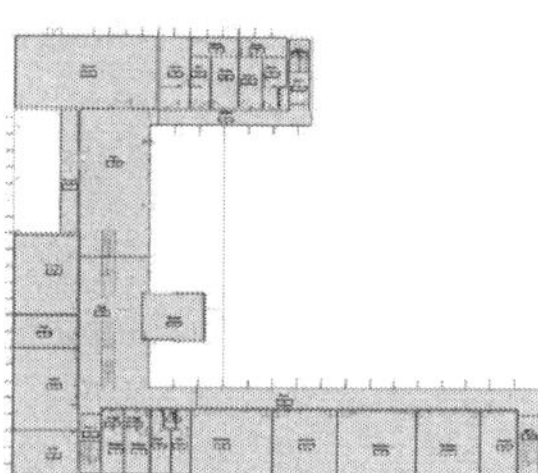

Left click in each space to place a tag.

Save as *ex3-6.rvt*.

Color Schemes

Color Schemes can be added to floor plan views and section views based on a specific value or range of values. You can apply a different color scheme to each view.

Use color schemes to color and apply fill patterns to:
- rooms
- areas
- spaces and zones
- pipes and ducts

Color Fill Legends

For views that use color schemes, color fill legends provide a key to the color representation.

Exercise 3-7:

Creating a Color Scheme For Lighting Loads

Drawing Name: *color_scheme.rvt*
Estimated Time: 15 minutes

This exercise reinforces the following skills:

- ❑ Color Schemes
- ❑ Color Scheme Definitions

1. 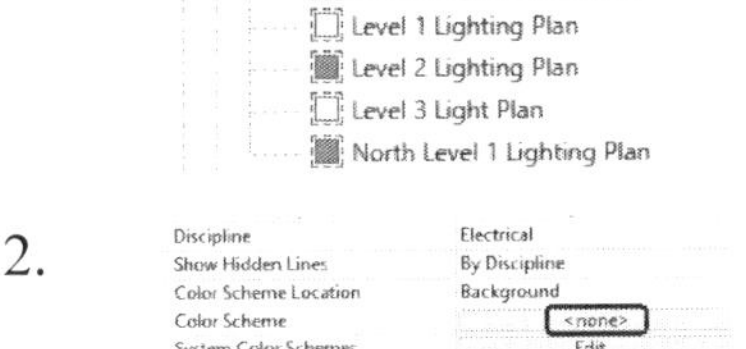

   In the Project Browser:

   Open the **Level 1 Lighting Analysis** view.

2. On the Properties palette:

   Select the button next to **Color Scheme**.

   The System Color Scheme is used for piping and ductwork.

3.

Under Category:

Select **Spaces**.

Highlight **Schema 1**.

Select **Duplicate** at the bottom left of the dialog.

4.

Name the scheme **LPD**.

Click **OK**.

5.

Change the Title to: **LPD (W/sq ft)**.

6.

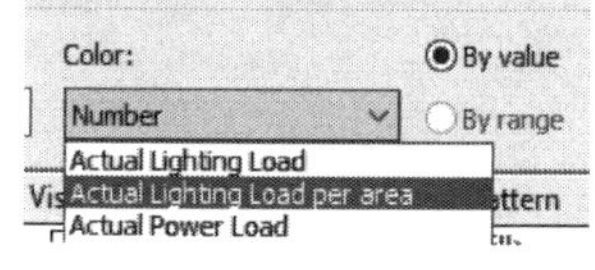

Under Color:

Select **Actual Lighting Load per area**.

7.

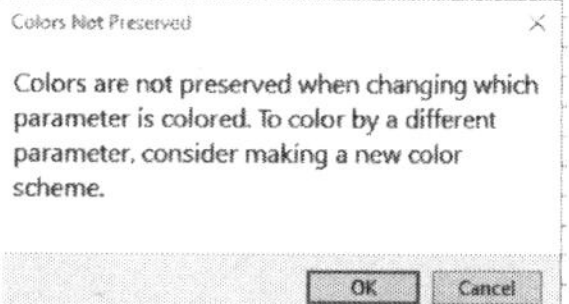

Click **OK**.

8.

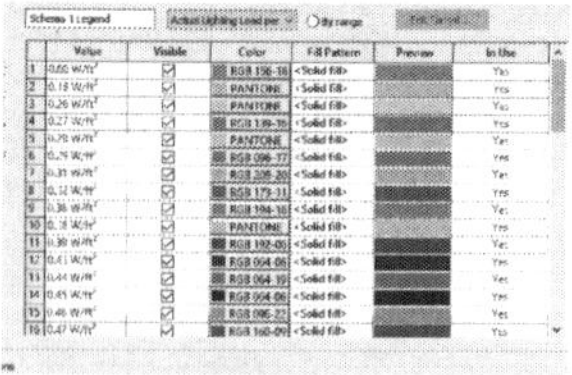

All the different values that currently exist are shown.

We can modify the table to make it a little more meaningful.

9.

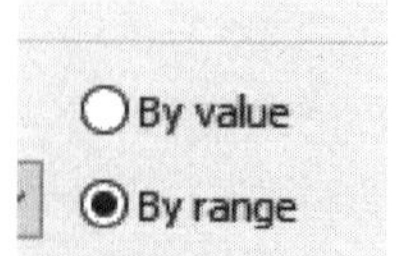

Enable **By Range**.

Now, the different colors will be sorted by minimum and maximum values.

10. 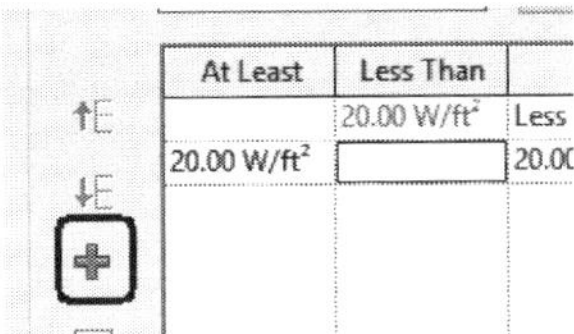   Left click in the second row.

Select the + symbol to the left of the row list to add a new value.

11. Edit the Scheme so that there are nine rows as shown.

Click **OK.**

Hint: *If you edit the At Least Column, the Caption Column will update.*

At Least	Less Than	Caption
	0.20 W/ft^2	Less than 0.20 W/ft^2
0.20 W/ft^2	0.30 W/ft^2	0.20 W/ft^2 - 0.30 W/ft^2
0.30 W/ft^2	0.35 W/ft^2	0.30 W/ft^2 - 0.35 W/ft^2
0.35 W/ft^2	0.40 W/ft^2	0.35 W/ft^2 - 0.40 W/ft^2
0.40 W/ft^2	0.45 W/ft^2	0.40 W/ft^2 - 0.45 W/ft^2
0.45 W/ft^2	0.50 W/ft^2	0.45 W/ft^2 - 0.50 W/ft^2
0.50 W/ft^2	0.80 W/ft^2	0.50 W/ft^2 - 0.80 W/ft^2
0.80 W/ft^2	1.00 W/ft^2	0.80 W/ft^2 - 1.00 W/ft^2
1.00 W/ft^2	1.25 W/ft^2	1.00 W/ft^2 - 1.25 W/ft^2
1.25 W/ft^2		1.25 W/ft^2 or more

12. Color Fill Legend   Select the **Analyze** tab on the ribbon.

Select the **Color Fill Legend** tool.

Left pick to place the legend in the view.

13.
☐ Less than 0.2 W/ft²
☐ 0.20 W/ft² - 0.3 W/ft²
☐ 0.30 W/ft² - 0.35 W/ft²
☐ 0.35 W/ft² - 0.40 W/ft²
☐ 0.40 W/ft² - 0.45 W/ft²
☐ 0.45 W/ft² - 0.50 W/ft²
☐ 0.50 W/ft² - 0.80 W/ft²
☐ 0.80 W/ft² - 1.00 W/ft²
☐ 1.00 W/ft² - 1.25 W/ft²
☐ 1.25 W/ft² or more

The legend is used to help you identify what the different colors mean.

14. Save as *ex3-7.rvt*.

Exercise 3-8:

Project Energy Settings

Drawing Name: *project_settings.rvt*
Estimated Time: 10 minutes

This exercise reinforces the following skills:

- Energy Settings
- Space Properties

1. 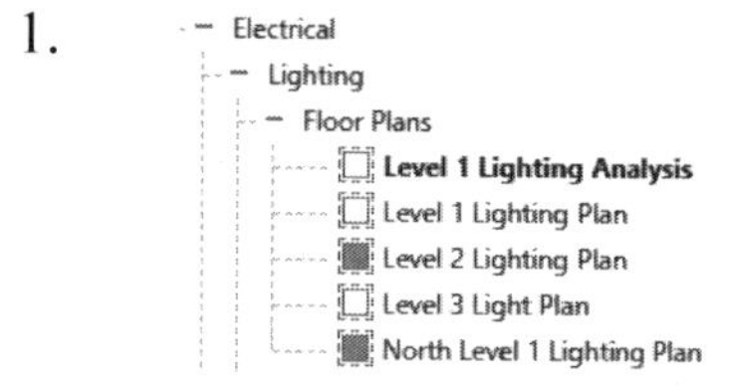
In the Project Browser:

Open the **Level 1 Lighting Analysis** view.

2. 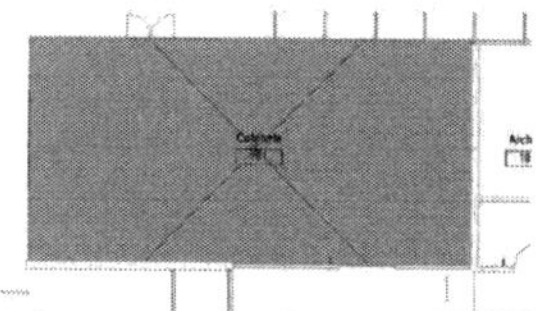
Select the Cafeteria space in the upper left corner of the building.

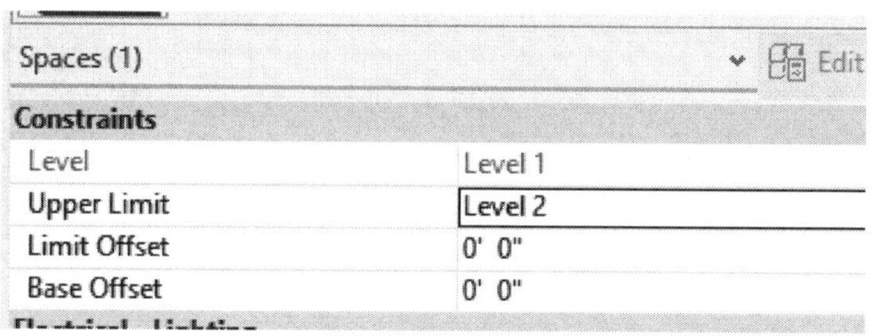

Verify that you selected the space and not the room by checking the Properties palette.

3. Note that the Actual Lighting Load and Actual Power Load is listed based on the light fixtures in the space.

4. Scroll down to the Energy Analysis category.

Locate Electrical Loads.

Click **Edit**.

5.

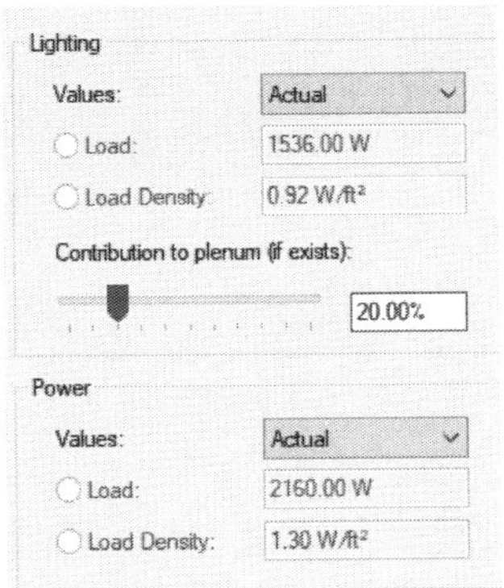

Change the Values to **Actual** for both Lighting and Power.

Click **OK**.

6.

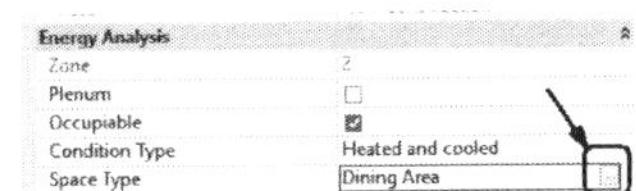

Locate the **Space Type** field under the Energy Analysis category.

Left click in the field and select the … button to the right.

7.

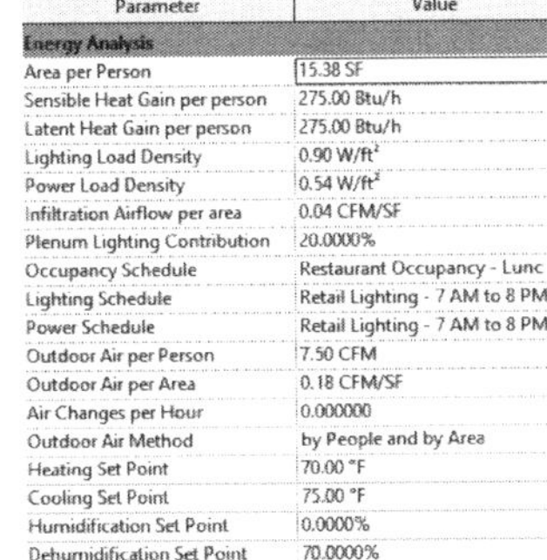

Notice the settings for this space.

8.

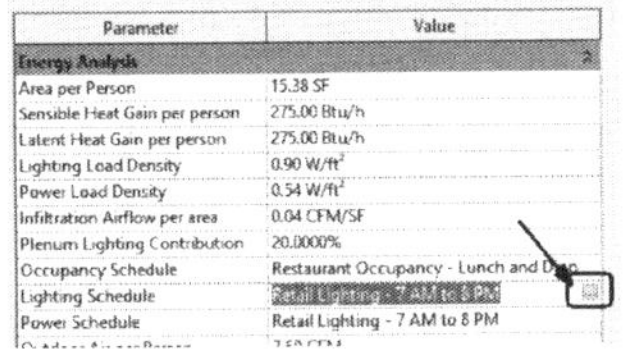

Locate the **Lighting Schedule** field.

Left click in the field and select the … button to the right.

9.   Click **OK**.

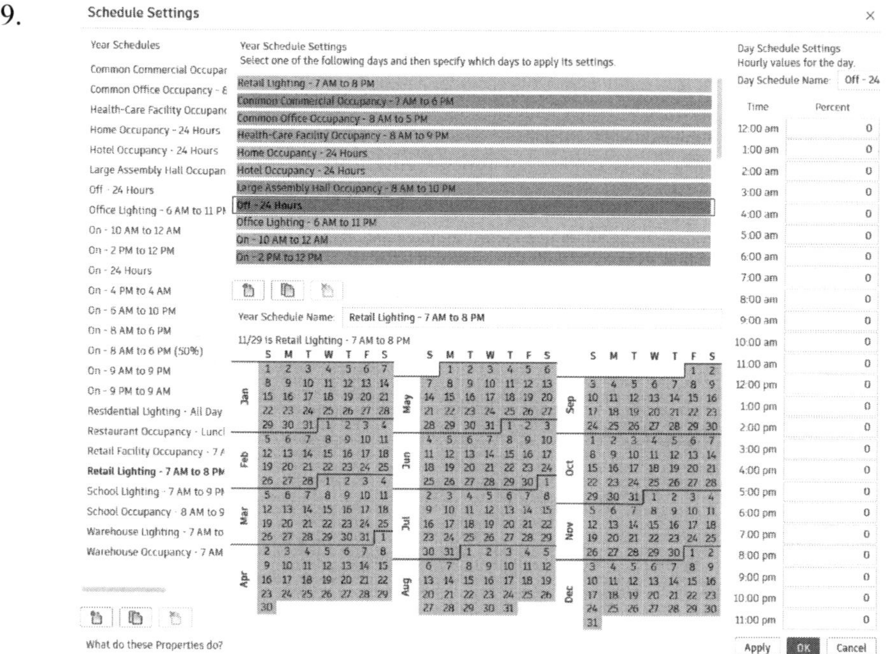

10.   Close all dialogs.

Save as *ex3-8.rvt*.

Lab Exercises

Open *distribution_lab.rvt*.

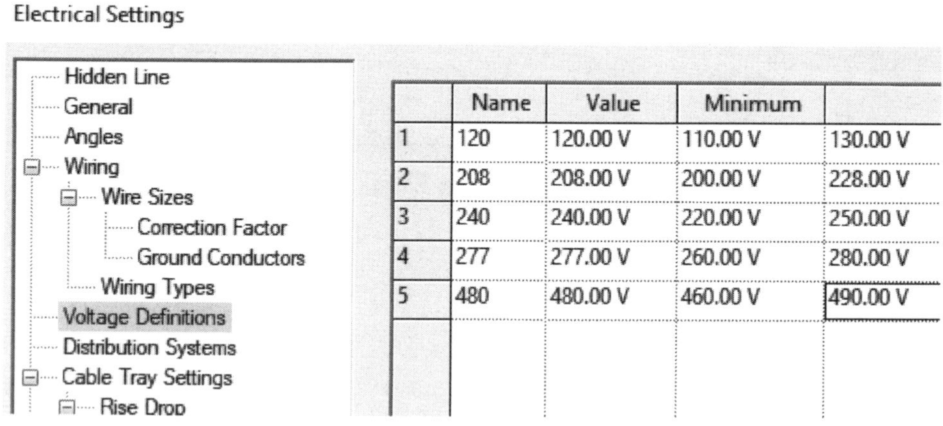

Create the Voltage Definitions shown.

Create two distribution systems: **120/208 Wye Distribution System** and **480/277 Wye Distribution System** using the Voltage definitions

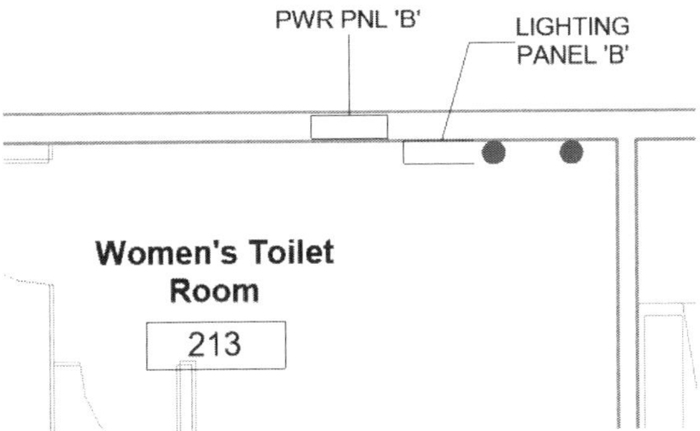

Open Main Floor Annotated under Electrical→Power.

Assign the panels in Room 213 to the correct distribution systems.

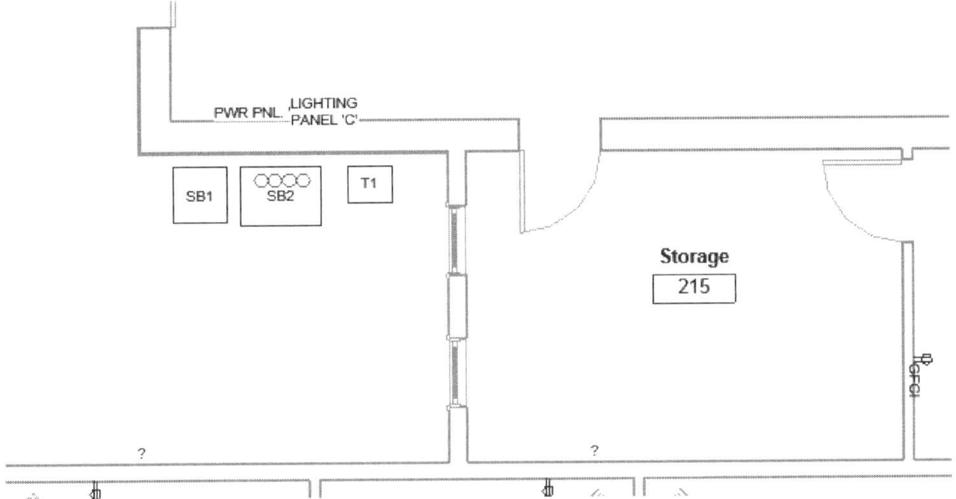

Assign the panels near STORAGE – 215 to the correct distribution systems.

Assign the T1 transformer to the correct distribution system.

Assign SB1 and SB2 to the correct distribution systems.

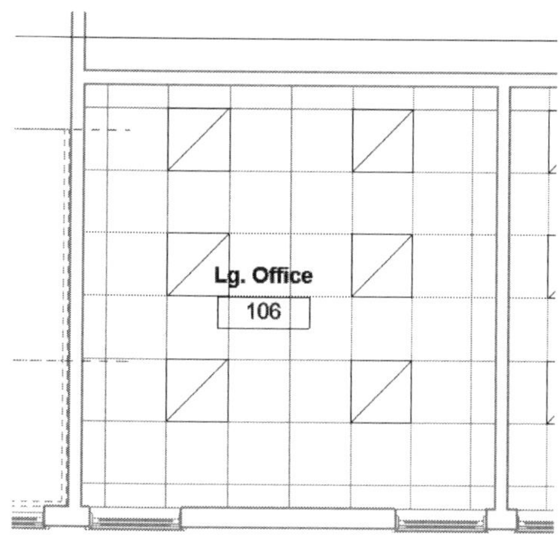

Open the **Ground Floor** ceiling plan under Electrical→Lighting.

Select the lighting fixtures in Lg Office – 106.

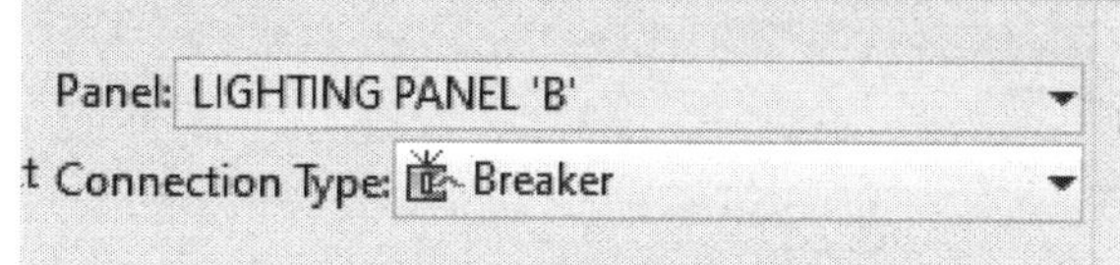

Assign them to Lighting Panel 'B'.

Lesson

04

Wiring

In this lesson, you learn the process of defining a wire type and recommended practices for creating and placing wiring.

Wiring depicts the connections between electrical components, such as lighting fixtures, switches, and panels. You can place wiring using an automatic method or a manual method. I tend to prefer the manual method simply because it provides more control.

Wiring can be displayed with or without symbols and tick marks.

A home run is the electrical cable that carries power from the main circuit breaker panel to the first electrical box, outlet, or switch in the circuit. You can designate home runs by manually drawing wires using the Wire tool. If you are using the Wire tool and have not selected an electrical component as the endpoint of a wire, Revit automatically adds a home run symbol to the wire.

Revit includes a library of standard wire sizes. Each wire size is assigned amperage and physical diameter.

Process for Creating New Wire Types

SPECIFY WIRE TYPE SETTINGS

ADD ANY NEW WIRE TYPE

DEFINE PROPERTIES FOR NEW WIRE TYPES

SAVE

Guidelines for Creating and Placing Wiring

- Specify wire settings with available wire sizes.
- Specify wire settings in project template files to save time and maintain consistency across projects.
- Transfer wire settings from one project to another using the Transfer Project Standard option on the Manage ribbon.
- Turn off wire tick marks universally to ensure consistency across all project views by selecting Never for the wiring settings in the Electrical Settings dialog box. You can also turn these settings off in a specific view by controlling the settings in the Visibility/Graphics Overrides dialog.
- Apply tags to circuit numbers.
- Manually wire devices from different circuits. This helps in creating multiple home runs.

Revit considers wires as annotation elements. This means they are view-specific. If you add wires in one view, they are not displayed in related views. If you want to display wiring in all views, then use conduits – which are model elements. Both wires and conduits are system families. This means any family types of wires or conduits you create in a project reside only in that project. To copy them to a new project, you need to use the Transfer Project Standards tool on the Manage ribbon.

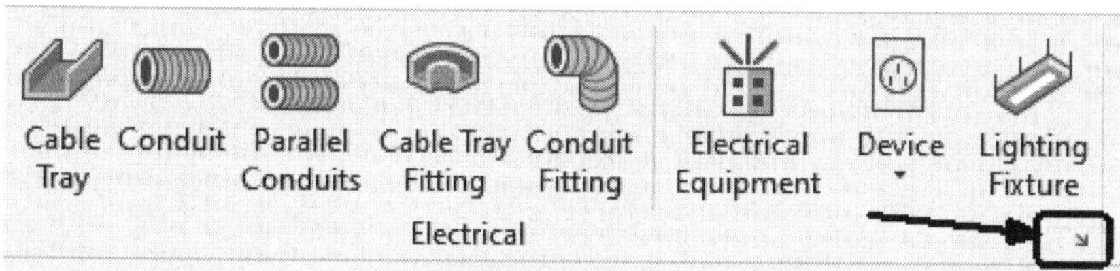

Wires are defined in the Electrical Settings dialog. You can access this dialog by typing ES or clicking in the lower right corner of the Electrical panel on the Systems ribbon.

Wiring

Electrical Settings

Hidden Line	Setting	
General	Gap of Wiring Crossing	0' - 0 1/16"
Angles	Hot Wire Tick Mark	
Wiring	Ground Wire Tick Mark	
Voltage Definitions	Neutral Wire Tick Mark	
Distribution Systems	Slanted Line across Tick Marks	No
Cable Tray Settings	Show Tick Marks	Always
Rise Drop	Arrow for Multi-Circuits Home Run	Multiple Arrows
Single Line Symbology	Home Run Arrow Style	Arrow Filled 15 Degree
Two Line Symbology		
Size		
Conduit Settings		
Rise Drop		
Single Line Symbology		
Two Line Symbology		

Gap of Wiring Crossing	Adjusts the gap when wires intersect or cross over each other.
Hot Wire Tick Mark	Specifies the style of tick mark that displays for Hot Conductor, Ground Conductor, and Neutral Conductor. Revit has four tick mark styles: Short Wire Tick Mark Circle Wire Tick Mark Hook Wire Tick Mark Long Wire Tick Mark You can assign a different tick mark style to help identify wire assignments. You can also create your own custom tick marks that can be used to identify wire types.
Ground Wire Tick Mark	Specify the wire tick mark to be used for ground wires.
Neutral Wire Tick Mark	Specify the wire tick mark to be used for ground wires.

Slanted Line across Tick Marks	Specifies whether to display the tick mark for the ground conductor as a diagonal line that crosses the tick marks for the other conductors, as shown.
Show Tick Marks	Specifies whether to always hide tick marks, always show them, or show them for home runs only.
Arrow for Multi-Circuits Home Run	Specifies whether a single arrow or multiple arrows display on all circuit wires or the end wire only.
Home Run Arrow Style	Specifies the style for the home run arrow, including the arrow angle and size.

To load a tick mark family

1. Click Insert tab→Load from Library panel→ (Load Family).
2. In the Open dialog, navigate to Annotations→Electrical→Tick Marks.
3. Select one or more tick mark family files and click Open.

You can assign a different style to each conductor.

Click the Value column, click , and select a tick mark style.

You can use the Family Editor to customize an existing tick mark or create additional tick marks.

Conductor and Cable Definitions

Revit 2026 reworked how wire types and wire sizes are managed. It has been replaced with a new system called Conductor and Cable Definitions.

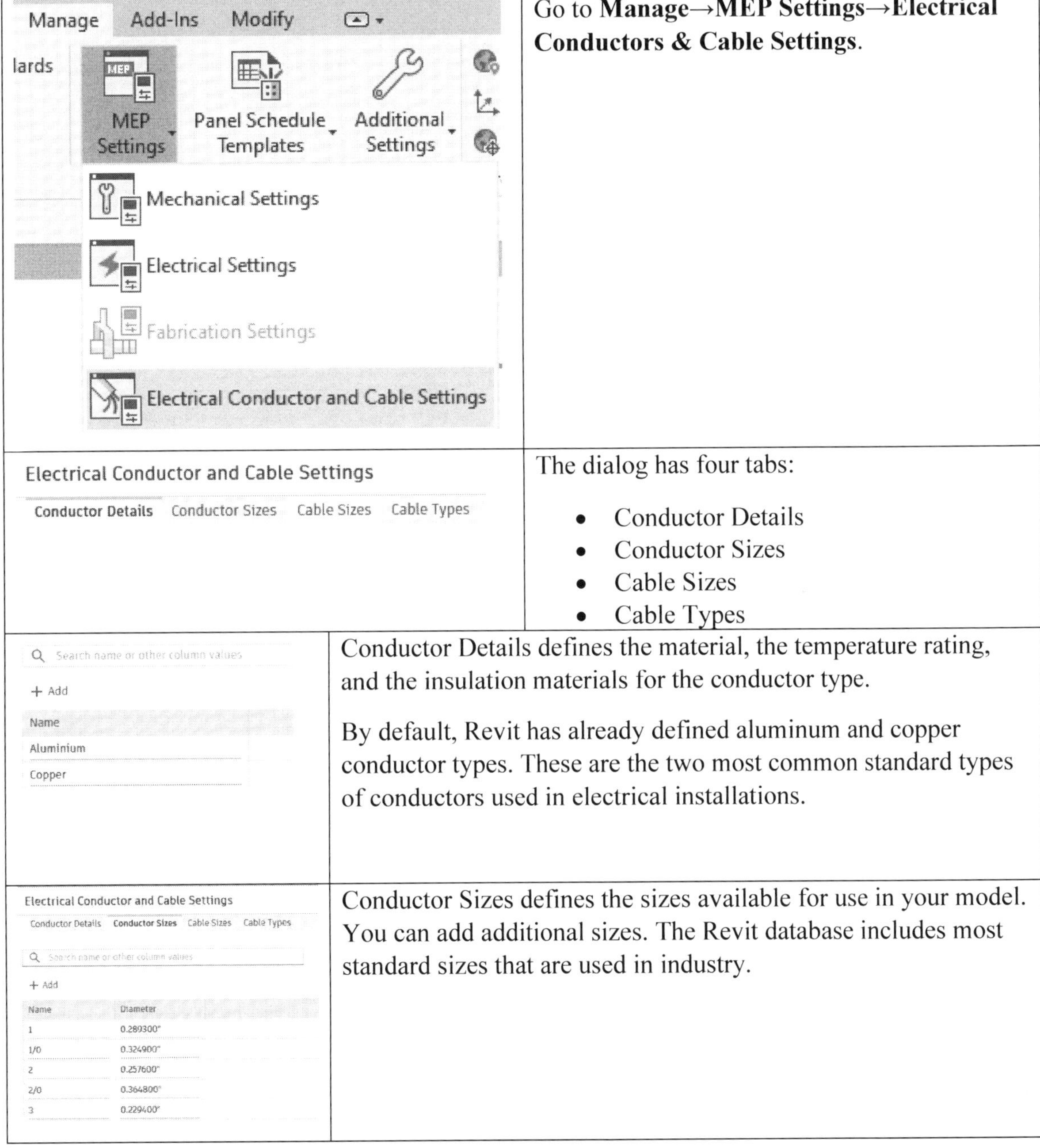

	Go to **Manage→MEP Settings→Electrical Conductors & Cable Settings**.
Electrical Conductor and Cable Settings Conductor Details · Conductor Sizes · Cable Sizes · Cable Types	The dialog has four tabs: • Conductor Details • Conductor Sizes • Cable Sizes • Cable Types
Name · Aluminium · Copper	Conductor Details defines the material, the temperature rating, and the insulation materials for the conductor type. By default, Revit has already defined aluminum and copper conductor types. These are the two most common standard types of conductors used in electrical installations.
Name / Diameter · 1 / 0.289300" · 1/0 / 0.324900" · 2 / 0.257600" · 2/0 / 0.364800" · 3 / 0.229400"	Conductor Sizes defines the sizes available for use in your model. You can add additional sizes. The Revit database includes most standard sizes that are used in industry.

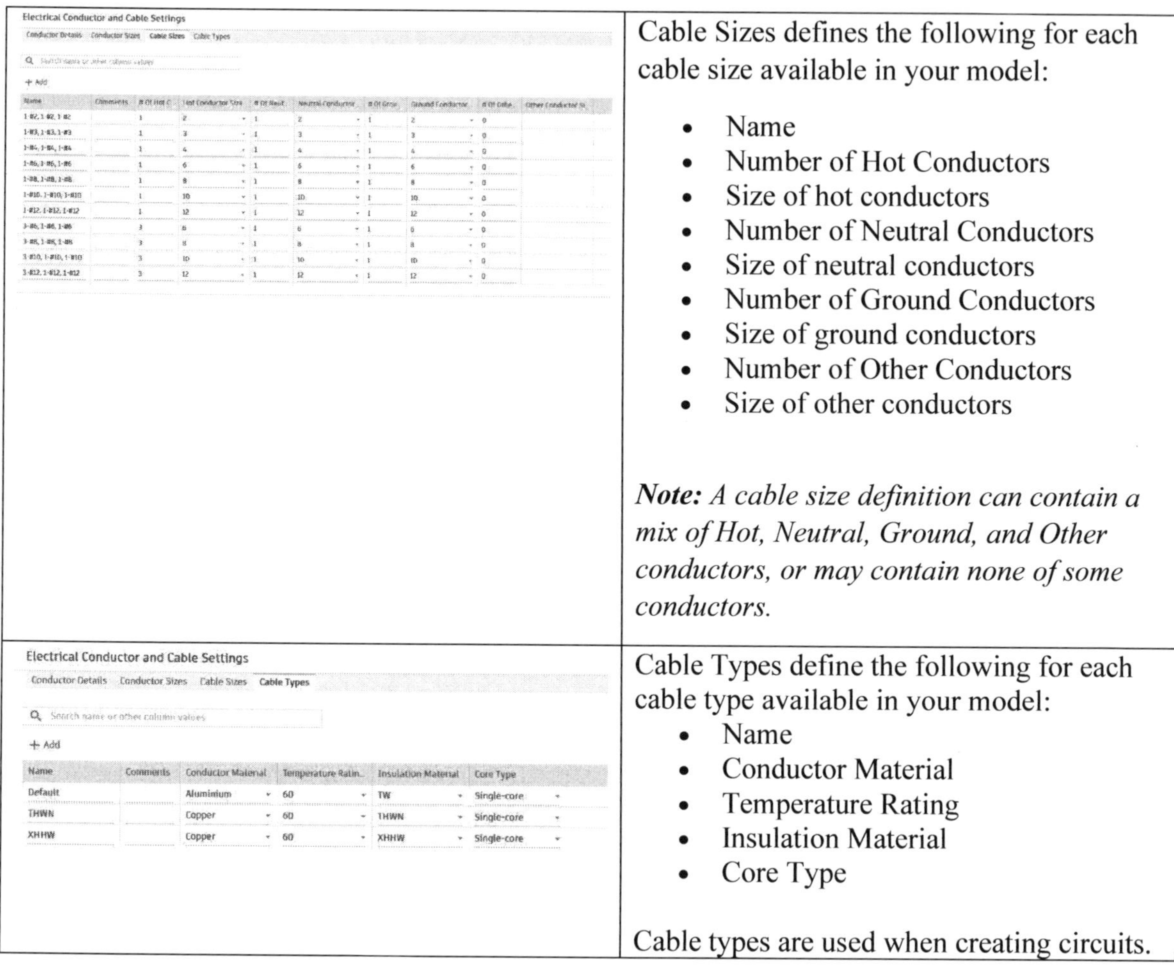

Cable Sizes defines the following for each cable size available in your model:

- Name
- Number of Hot Conductors
- Size of hot conductors
- Number of Neutral Conductors
- Size of neutral conductors
- Number of Ground Conductors
- Size of ground conductors
- Number of Other Conductors
- Size of other conductors

Note: *A cable size definition can contain a mix of Hot, Neutral, Ground, and Other conductors, or may contain none of some conductors.*

Cable Types define the following for each cable type available in your model:

- Name
- Conductor Material
- Temperature Rating
- Insulation Material
- Core Type

Cable types are used when creating circuits.

Cable Types

Name	User-defined alphanumeric string used to identify the wire type
Material	Copper or Aluminum are available by default or the user can create a custom material
Temperature Rating	30C, 60C, or 95C, or a project specific temperature rating as defined in the New Temperature dialog.
Insulation	Depending on the material selected, different insulation types can be specified, including a project specific insulation as defined in the New Insulation dialog. By default, you have three insulation types available: THWN/XHHW/TW. THWN- Thermoplastic Heat and Water-resistant Nylon-coated. XHHW -XLPE (cross-linked polyethylene) High Heat-resistant Water-resistant. TW - TW/THW is a solid or stranded, soft annealed copper conductor insulated with Polyvinylchloride (PVC).

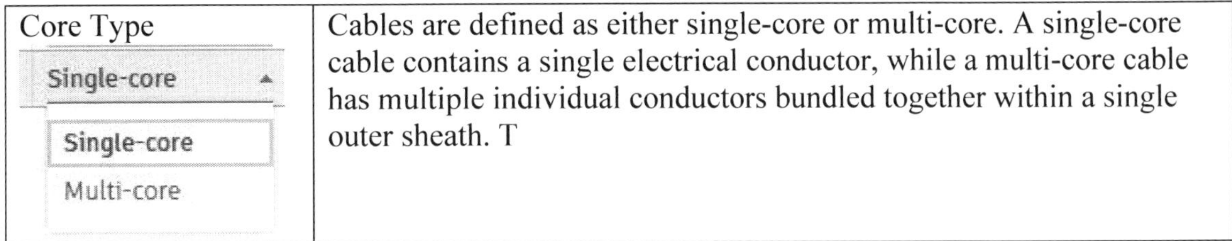

Core Type	Cables are defined as either single-core or multi-core. A single-core cable contains a single electrical conductor, while a multi-core cable has multiple individual conductors bundled together within a single outer sheath. T

Revit only allows one tick mark style *per wire type*, so if you want multiple, duplicate your wire type. Annotation families **scale with view scale**, so test at a few scales to make sure your tick mark looks good. If you want something like a **circle around the tick** or **special arrowheads**, it must be drawn in the annotation family — Revit won't generate it automatically.

Electrical Conventions

- **Hot (ungrounded conductor)** → **single diagonal slash** across the wire.

- **Neutral conductor** → often drawn without a tick, or marked separately (sometimes with a different linetype or label).

- **Grounding conductor** → typically has its own symbol (the $\perp$ ground symbol) and usually no tick.

- **Multiple conductors** (e.g., 2 hots + neutral) → you'll see **multiple slashes** to indicate how many hots are in the circuit.

The short wire tick mark that is available in Revit by default can be used to designate a hot (ungrounded conductor). The neutral conductor can be designated using the circle wire tick mark that is available in Revit. The grounding conductor will not be assigned a tick mark.

You have to set up the tick mark designations for each project or adjust the settings in your project template to your preferred designations. Your company may have its own method for designating different conductors, so it is useful to be able to create and set your own wire tick marks.

Exercise 4-1:

Define a Wire Tick Mark Family

Drawing Name: new family
Estimated Time: 15 minutes

In this exercise, we will create a custom ground wire tick mark using a triangle.

This exercise reinforces the following skills:

- Annotations
- Families

1. 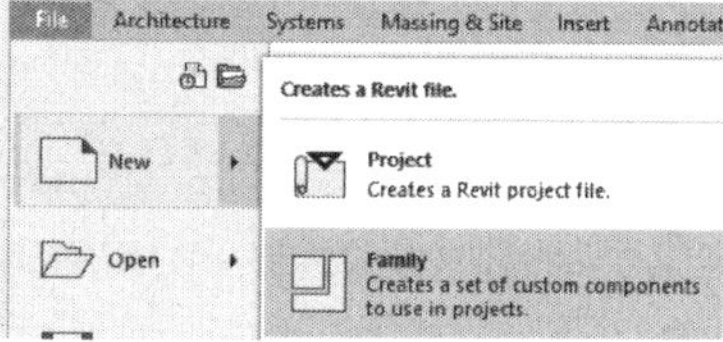   Go to **New→Family**.

2. 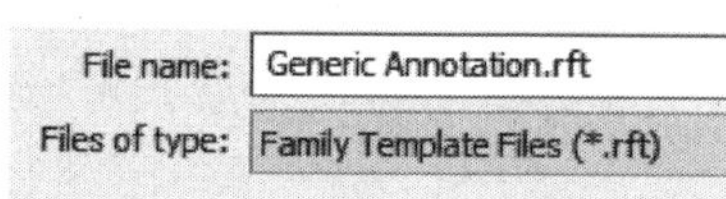   Select the *Generic Annotation.rft* template.

   Click **Open**.

3. 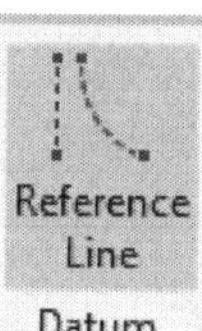   Select Reference Line from the Create ribbon.

4. 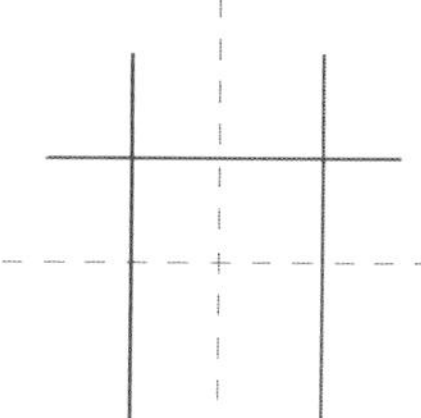   Draw two vertical lines and one horizontal line.

5. Place a continuous dimension to center the two vertical reference lines.

Toggle it equal.

6. Place an overall horizontal dimension and an overall vertical dimension.

7. Select the horizontal dimension.

Select the extension lines, not the text.

Click **New label** on the ribbon.

8. Type **Width** in the Name field.
Enable **Type**.
Click **OK**.

9. Select the vertical dimension.

Select the extension lines, not the text.

Click **New label** on the ribbon.

10. Type **Height** in the Name field.
Enable **Type**.
Click **OK**.

11.

Select **Family Types** on the ribbon.

12.

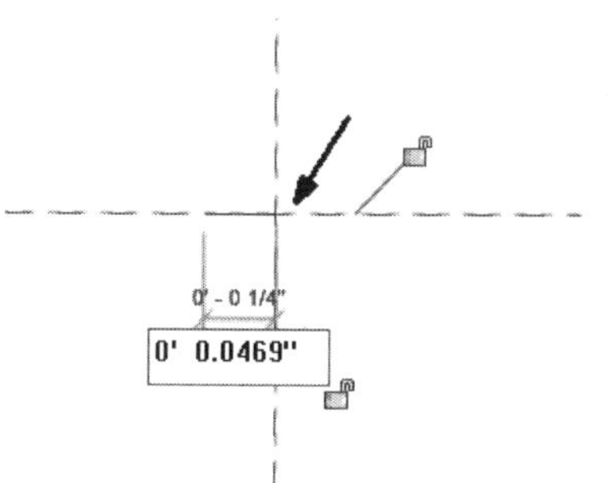

Set the Height to **5/128"**.
Set the Width to **3/64"**.

Click **OK.**

13.

Start the line at the intersection of the two reference planes. This is the origin point of the annotation.

Draw the line 0.0469" to the left.

14.

Select the **Line** tool from the Create ribbon.

15.

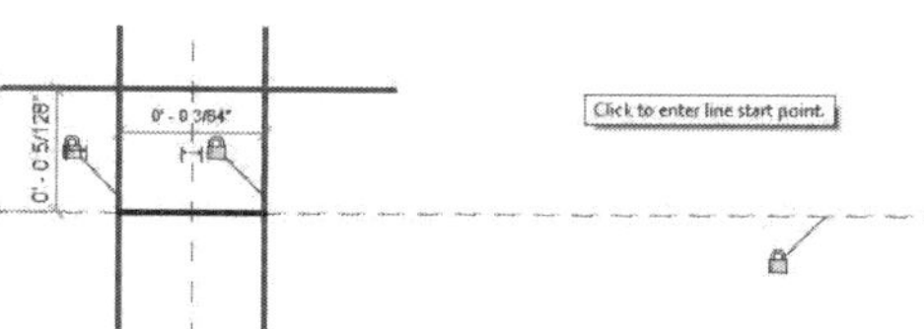

Draw a horizontal line from the left intersection of the vertical reference line and the horizontal reference plane and the right intersection of the vertical reference line and the horizontal reference plane.

Enable all the locks to constrain the line to the reference lines and plane.

16.

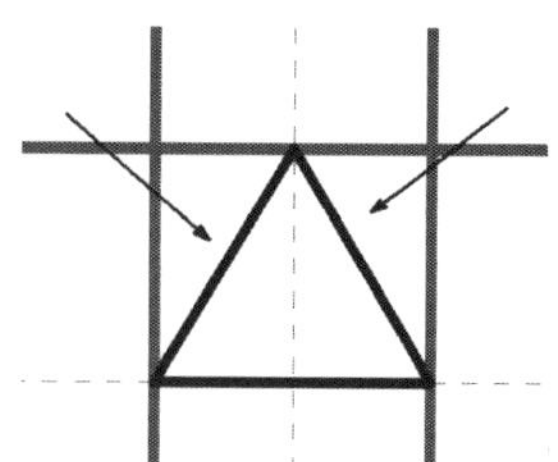

Draw two angled lines using the provided intersections to create the triangle symbol.

17. Select the note.

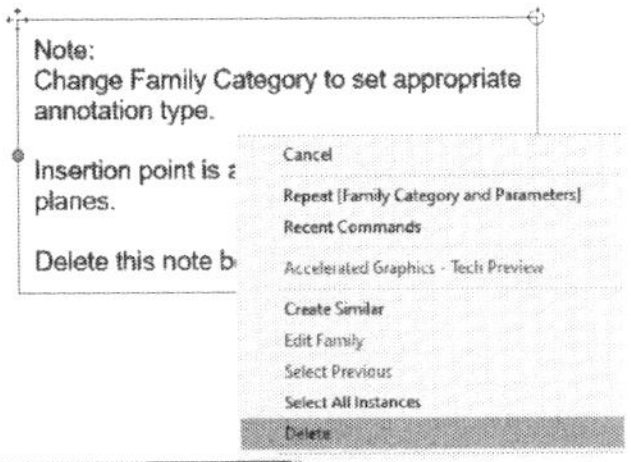

    Right click and select **Delete**.

18. Click **Family Categories**.

19. In the Category name search field:

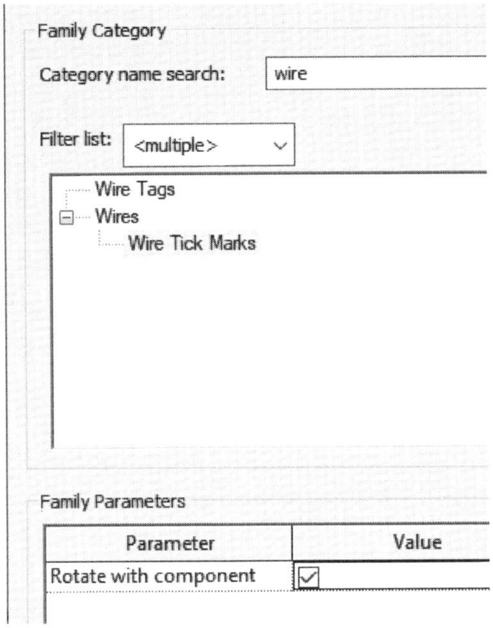

    Type **wire**.

    Highlight **Wire Tick Marks**.

    Enable **Rotate with component**.

    Click **OK**.

20. Save as *ground tick mark.rfa*.

Exercise 4-2:

Wire Tick Mark Settings

Drawing Name: wire tick marks.rvt
Estimated Time: 15 minutes

This exercise reinforces the following skills:

- Electrical Settings
- Wire Tick Marks
- Families

1.   **Insert**   Activate the **Insert** ribbon.

2. 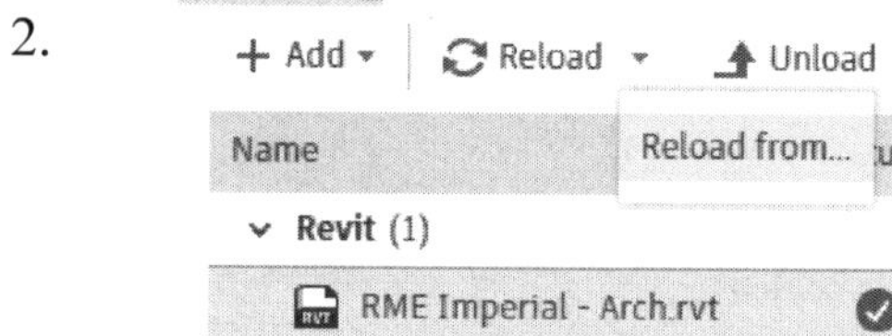 Select the **Manage Links** tool.
   Note that there is a floor plan file linked to the project.
   Highlight the file.
   Select **Reload From**.
   Browse to the downloaded exercise files and locate the file to reload.
   Click **Open.**
   Close the dialog.

3. Click **Load Family** from the Insert Ribbon.

4. 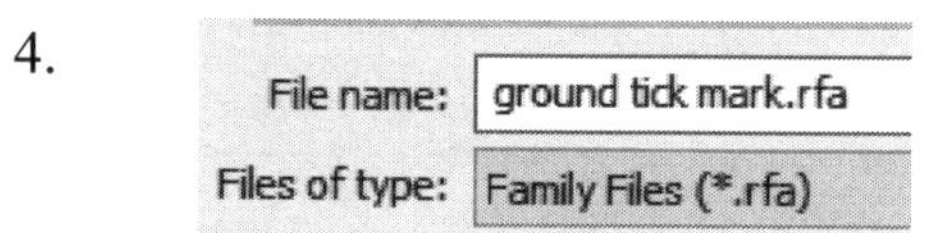 Locate the *ground tick mark.rfa* file.

   Click **Open.**

5. Click **Load Family** from the Insert Ribbon.

6. 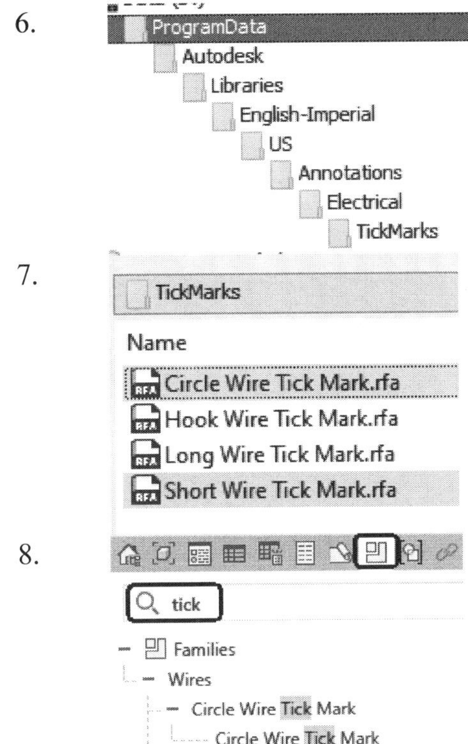 Browse to the *TickMarks* folder under *Annotations/Electrical*.

7. Hold down the **CTL** key and select the *Circle Wire Tick Mark* and the *Short Wire Tick Mark*.

Click **Open**.

8. Go to the Project Browser.
Enable the **Families** filter tab.
Type **tick** in the search field.

You should see the three tick marks you loaded. If any of the tick marks are missing, go back and use Load Family to load the missing file.

9. Open the Systems ribbon.

Launch **Electrical Settings**.

Hint: You can also type ES to launch the dialog.

10. Highlight **Wiring**.

11. 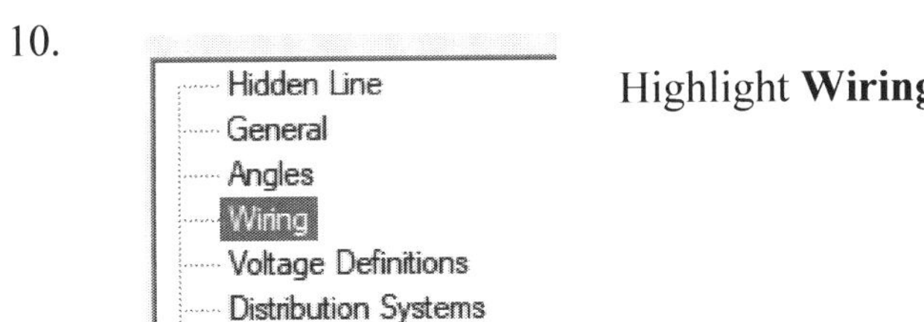

Assign the **Short Wire Tick Mark** to the Hot Wire Tick Mark.
Assign the **ground tick mark** to the Ground Wire Tick Mark.
Assign the **Circle Wire Tick Mark** to the Neutral Wire Tick Mark.
Click **OK**.

12. Save as *ex4-2.rvt*.

Exercise 4-3:

Place Wiring Manually

Drawing Name: *wiring_manual.rvt*
Estimated Time: 15 minutes

This exercise reinforces the following skills:

❑ Add Wires Manually

1. Activate the **Insert** ribbon.

2. Select the **Manage Links** tool.

Note that there is a floor plan file linked to the project.

Reload from your local files if necessary.

Click **OK**.

3. Verify that the **Level 1 Power Plan** floor plan is the active view.

4. Zoom into Room 103 – between Grids 4 &5 and Grids 19-21.

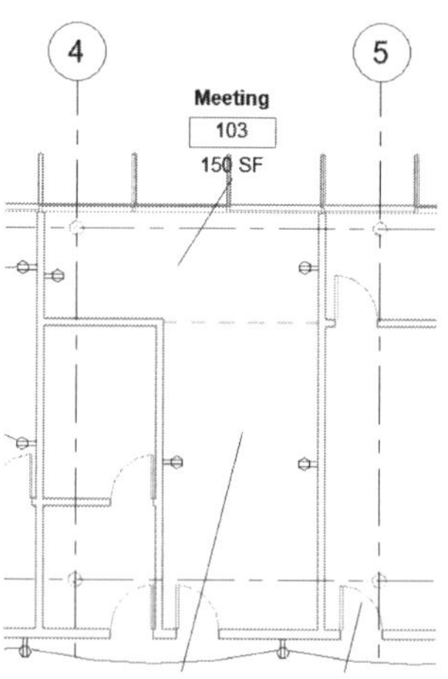

5. 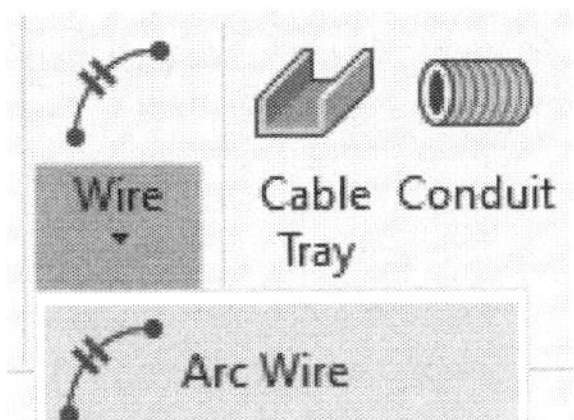 Activate the **Systems** ribbon.

    Select the **Arc Wire** tool under Wire.

6. 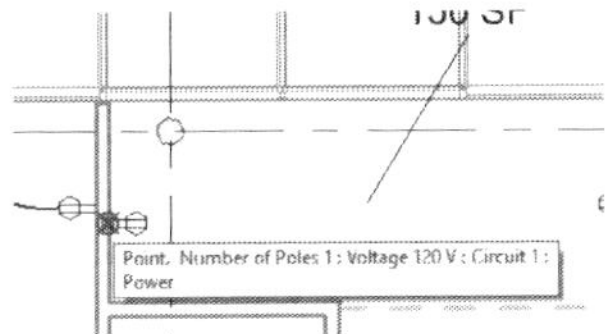 Verify that the **THWN** wire type is active in the Properties palette.

7. 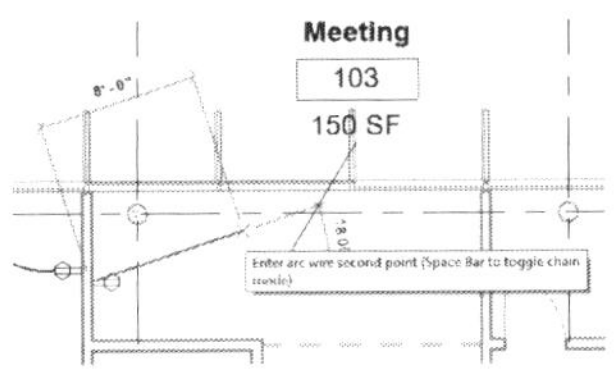 Move the cursor over the receptacle on the left wall until the wiring connection point appears.

    Left click on the connection point to set the first point for the arced wiring.

8. Left click to place a second point for the arc around the midpoint of the grid line in the room.

9. Move the cursor over the receptacle on the right wall until the wiring connection point appears.

    Left click on the connection point to set the end point for the arced wiring.

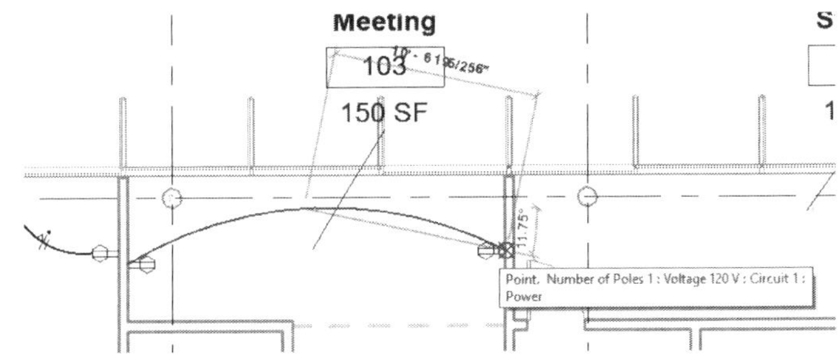

10. The wire is placed.

    Click ESC to exit the command.

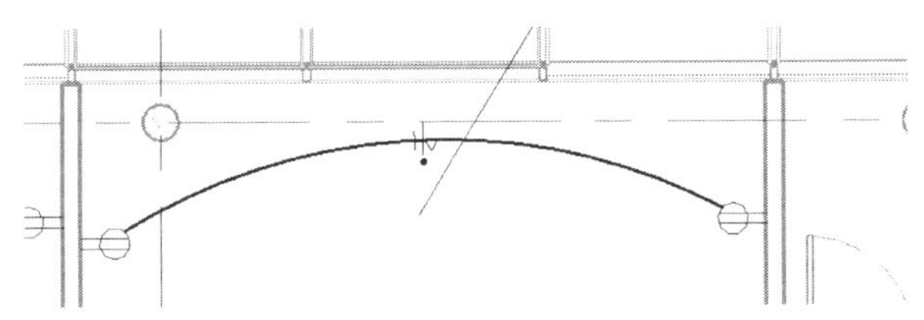

11. Zoom into the middle of the wire that was just placed.

    The tick marks for hot, neutral and ground are visible.

    Save as *4-3.rvt*.

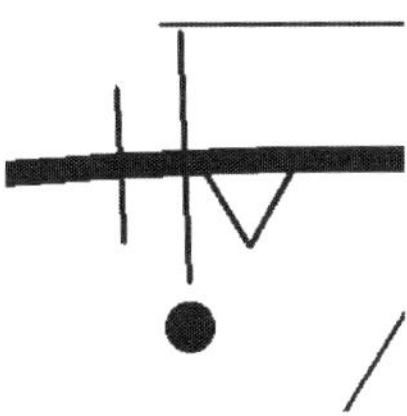

A **home run wire** is a wire (or group of wires) that runs directly from an electrical device or outlet back to the main service panel, subpanel, or junction box, without splicing or branching off to serve other devices along the way. It's called a "home run" because, like in baseball, the wire "goes all the way home" without stopping.

Exercise 4-4:

Create a Home Run Wire

Drawing Name: *wire_home_run.rvt*
Estimated Time: 5 minutes

This exercise reinforces the following skills:

- ❑ Place a home run wire
- ❑ Load Family
- ❑ Electrical Settings

1. 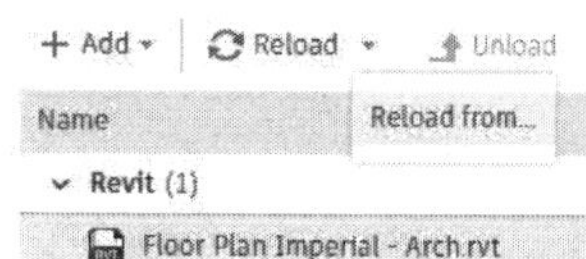
   Go to the Insert ribbon.

   Click **Manage Links**.

2. 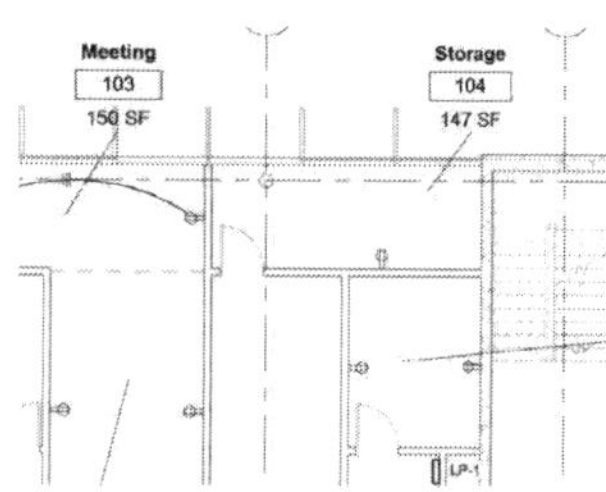
   Select **Reload From**.

   Locate *Floor Plan Imperial – Arch.rvt* and select **Open**.

   Close the dialog once the file is loaded.

3. 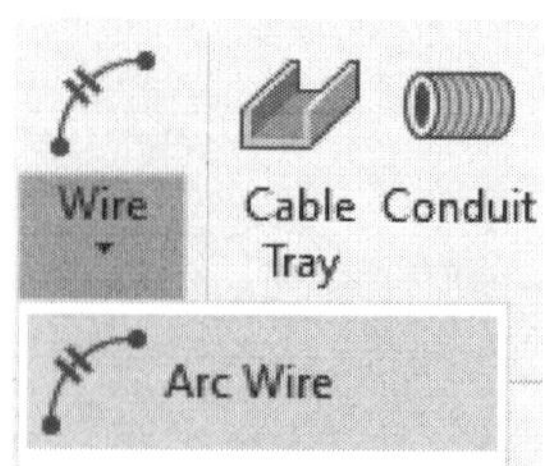
   Zoom into Room 103 & Room 104 – between Grids 4 & 6 and Grids 19-21.

4. Activate the Systems ribbon.

   Select the **Arc Wire** tool.

5. Left click on the connection point for the receptacle on the right wall in Room 103.

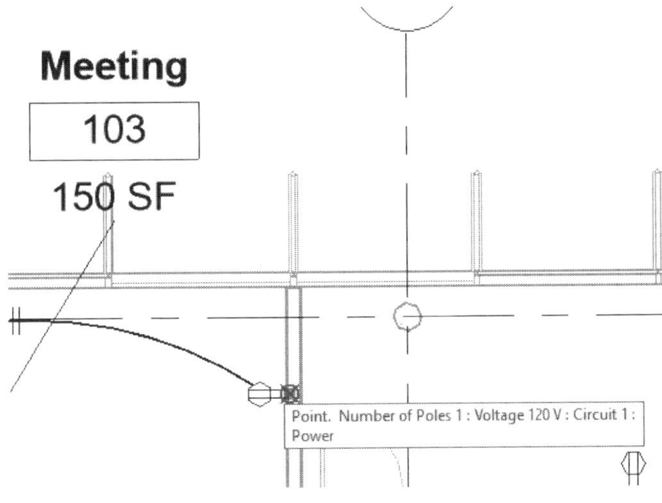

6. Left click beneath the mid-point of the grid line in Room 104 to place the second point for the arc.

    Left click slightly below and to the right of the second point to create the home run wire.

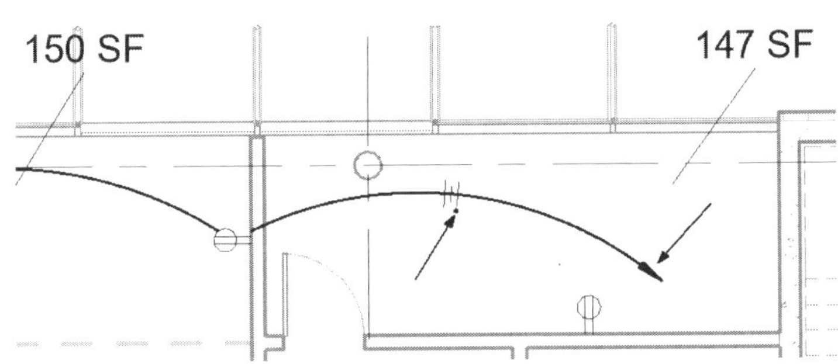

7. 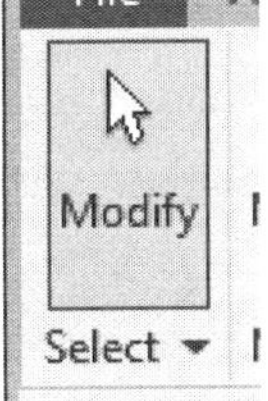

    Click the **Modify** tool on the ribbon to exit the command.

8. Save as *ex4-4.rvt*.

A **multiple circuit home run wire** (sometimes called a **multi-circuit home run**) is when more than one circuit is carried within the same cable or conduit back to the panel, instead of running a separate home run for each one. It is used because it reduces the number of cables running back to the panel.

Exercise 4-5:

Create a Multiple Circuit Home Run Wire

Drawing Name: *multiple_home_run.rvt*
Estimated Time: 10 minutes

This exercise reinforces the following skills:

- ❑ Place a home run wire
- ❑ Add wires

1. 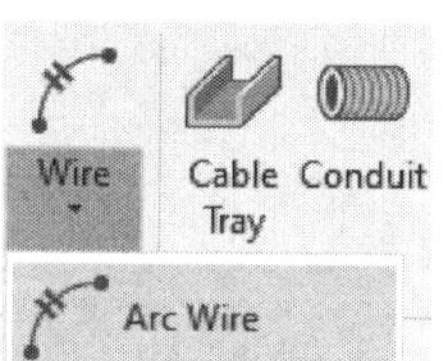
Go to the Insert ribbon.

   Click **Manage Links**.

2. Select **Reload From.**

   Locate *Floor Plan Imperial – Arch.rvt* and select **Open**.

   Close the dialog once the file is loaded.

3. Select the Home Run wire located in Room 104.

   Select the grip located at the arrowhead.

4. Drag the grip to place it at the connection point for the receptacle located on the south wall of Room 104.

5. Activate the Systems ribbon.

   Select the **Arc Wire** tool.

6. 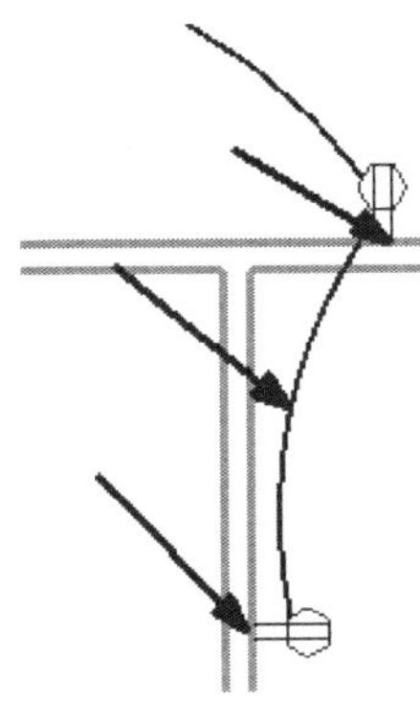

Select the south wall receptacle connection point as the start point for the wire.

Left click below and to the left of the south wall receptacle for the second arc wire point.

Left click to select the connection point on the receptacle located on the west wall of Room 107.

You are still in Place Wire mode.

7. 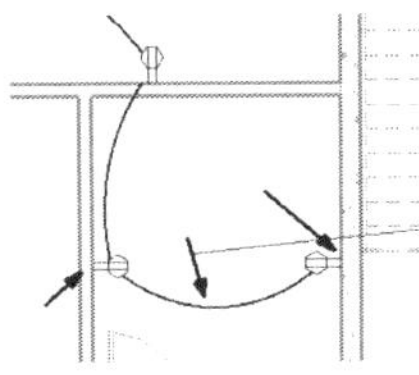

Select the west wall receptacle connection point on the west wall of Room 107 as the start point for the wire.

Left click below and to the right of the west wall receptacle for the second arc wire point.

Left click to select the connection point on the receptacle located on the east wall of Room 107.

You are still in Place Wire mode.

8. 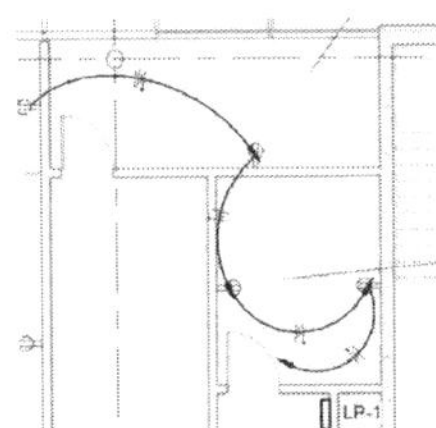

Left click to select the connection point on the receptacle located on the east wall of Room 107.

Left click below and to the left of the east wall receptacle for the second arc wire point.

Left click below and to the left of the east wall receptacle for the end arc wire point.

Click ESC to exit the command.

9. 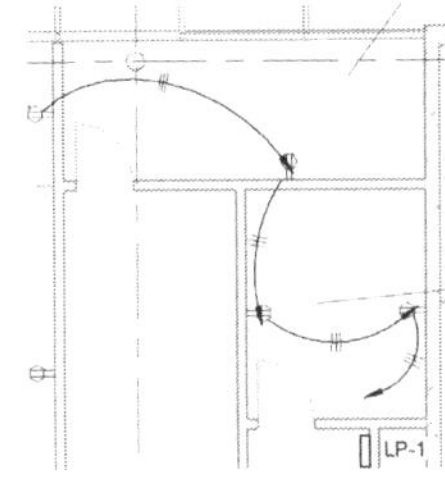

Note the home run arrows on the wires.

Save as *ex4-5.rvt.*

An **electrical circuit** is simply a path that allows electricity to flow from a power source, through conductors and devices, and back to the source.

Exercise 4-6:

Create a Circuit

Drawing Name: *circuits.rvt*
Estimated Time: 20 minutes

This exercise reinforces the following skills:

- Manage Links
- Electrical Circuits
- Arc Wires

1. 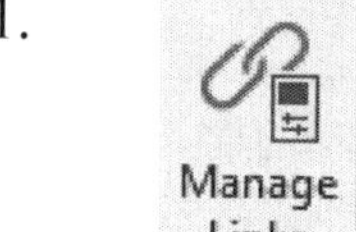
Go to the Insert ribbon.

   Click **Manage Links**.

2. 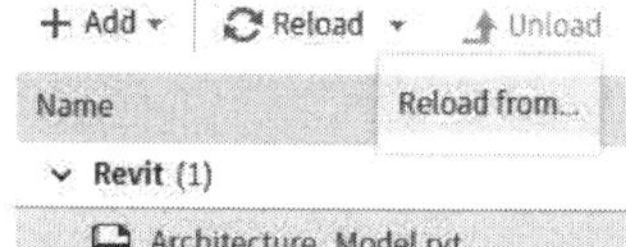
Select **Reload From**.

   Locate *Architecture_Model.rvt* and select **Open**.

   Close the dialog once the file is loaded.

3. 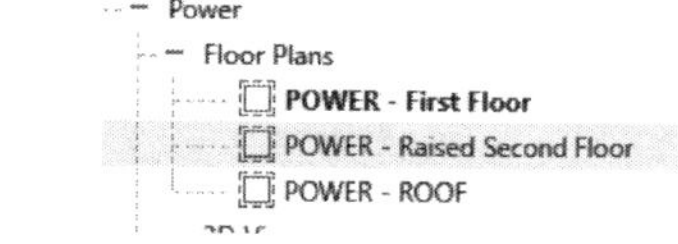
Verify that the active view is **POWER – First Floor** floor plan.

4. 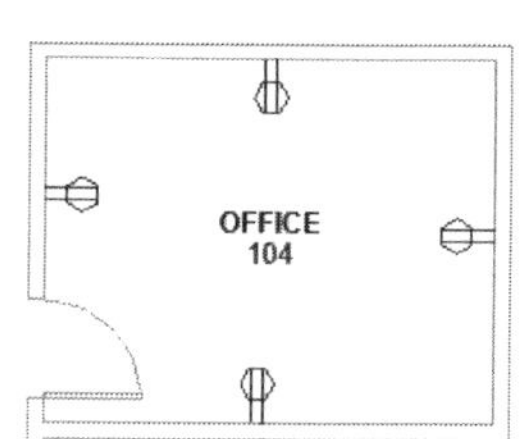
Zoom into **OFFICE 104**.

   Hold down the **CTL** key and select the four receptacles in the room.

   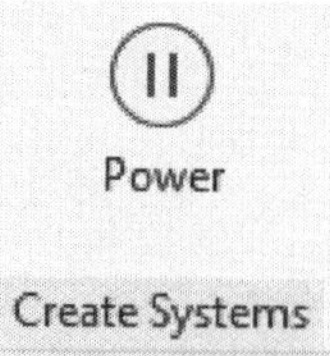

   Select the **Power** button on the ribbon.

5.

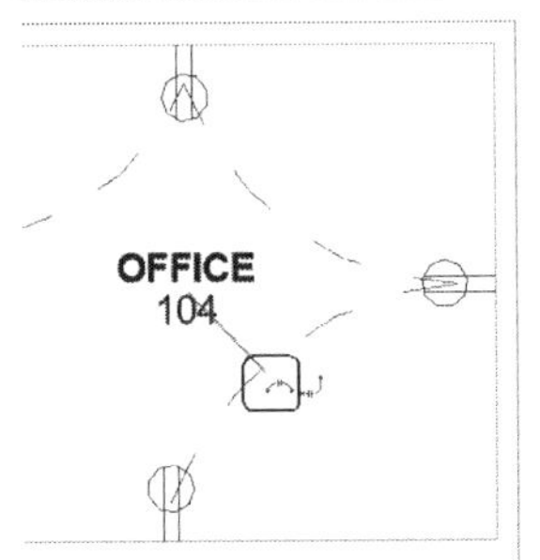

On the ribbon:
Assign the circuit to Panel **LA**.

6.

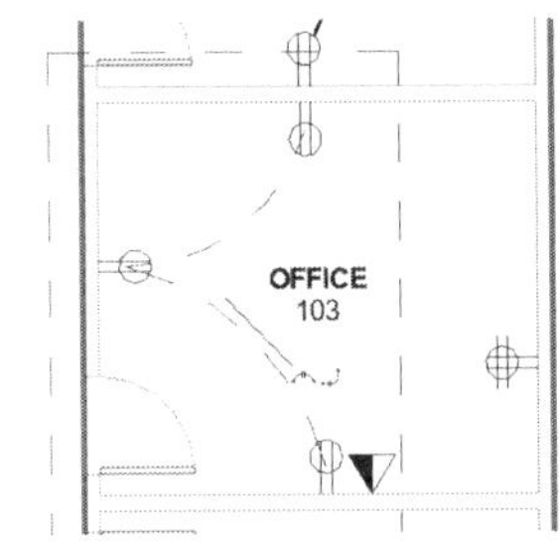

A preview of the circuit will appear in the display window.

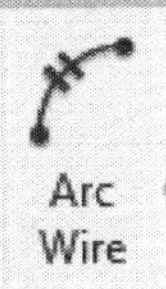

Select **Arc Wire** from the ribbon.

Alternatively, you can select the Arc Wire icon on the preview to convert the preview to place arc wires.

This places wires based on the preview.

7.

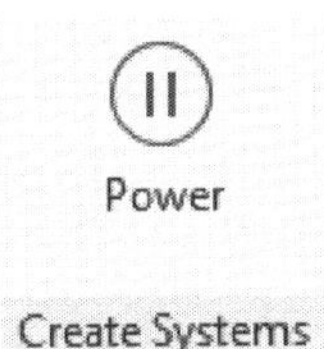

Zoom into **OFFICE 103**.

Hold down the **CTL** key and select the three duplex receptacles in the room. *Do not select the receptacle on the east wall.*

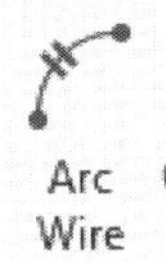

Create Systems Select the **Power** button on the ribbon.

8.

A preview of the circuit will appear in the display window. Select **Arc Wire** from the ribbon or use the convert to wire icon.
This places wires based on the preview.

9.

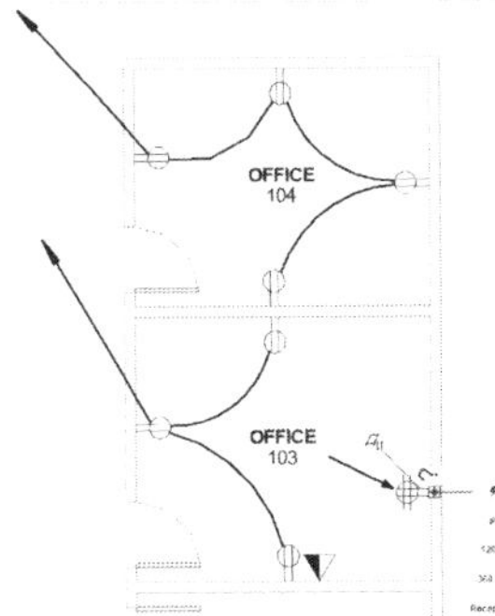

Locate the quadruple receptacle in OFFICE 103.

Click on the bottom connector point.

10.

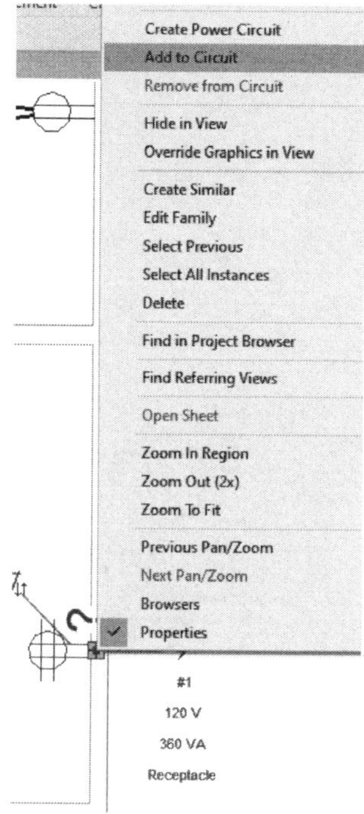

Right click and select **Add to Circuit**.

Select one of the duplex receptacles in the room.

Select the **Arc Wire** tool or use the convert to wire icon to place a wire.

Click ESC to exit the command.

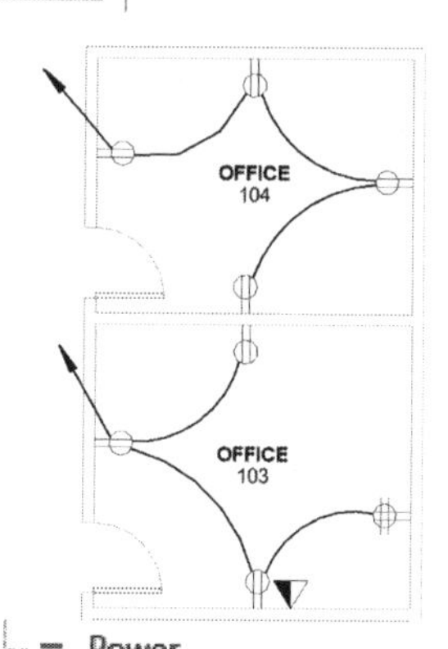

This is what has been done so far.

11.

Open the **EL – Level 1** Ceiling Plan under Power.

12.

Hold down the CTL key.

Select the two lighting fixtures in OFFICE 104.

Power

Select the **Power** button on the ribbon.

13.  Set the Panel to **HA** on the ribbon.

14. 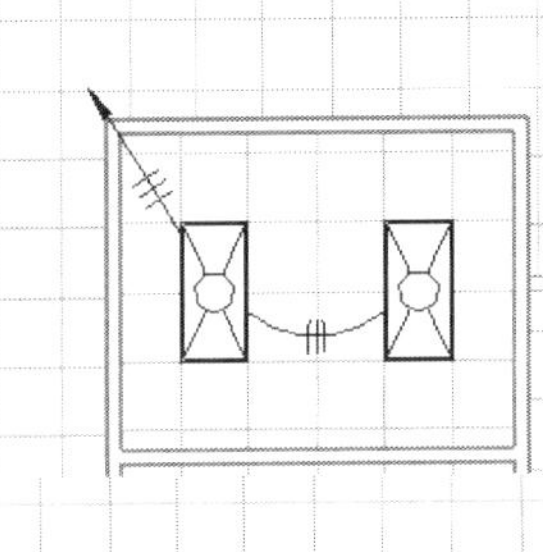 A preview of the circuit will appear in the display window. Select **Arc Wire** from the ribbon.

Arc
Wire

15. The circuit is placed.

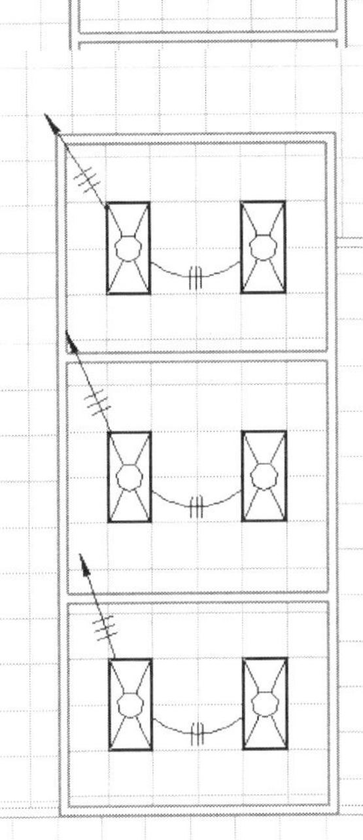

16. Repeat to place circuits in OFFICE 103 and 102.

17. 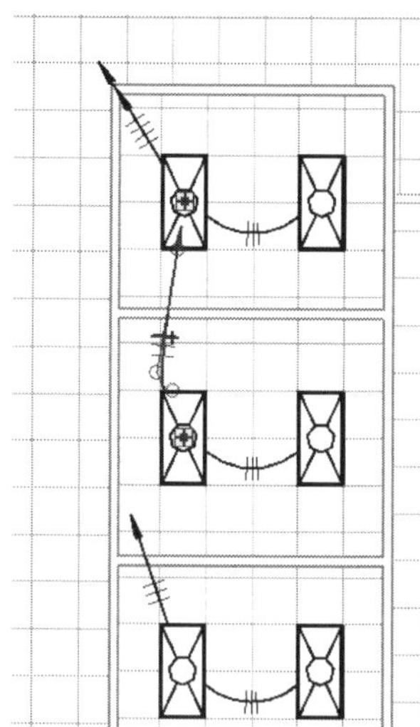 Select the home run wire in OFFICE 103 and drag to connect to the left light fixture in OFFICE 104.

Save as *ex4-6.rvt*.

A **switch leg** is the wire (or set of wires) that runs from a power source (usually a ceiling light box or junction box) down to a wall switch and back to the load (like a light fixture).

Exercise 4-7:

Defining Switch Legs

Drawing Name: *lighting_switch_legs.rvt*
Estimated Time: 25 minutes

This exercise reinforces the following skills:

- ❏ Switch Systems
- ❏ Wires
- ❏ Filters
- ❏ View Overrides

1.  Go to the Insert ribbon.

   Click **Manage Links**.

2.   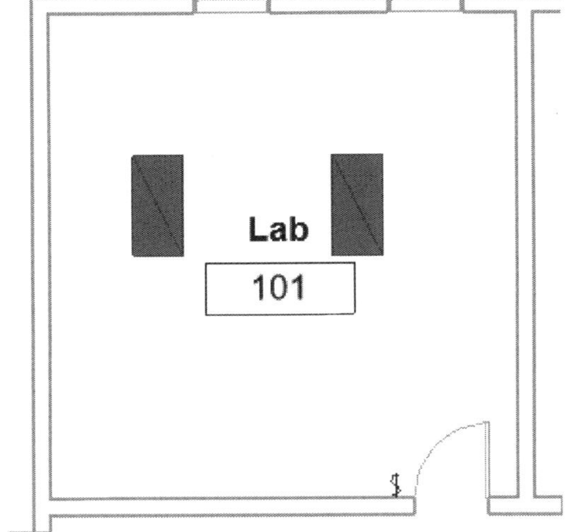

Select **Reload From**.

Locate *Simple-Building-Arch.rvt* and select **Open**.

Close the dialog once the file is loaded.

3.   Hold down the CTL key or use a window to select the lighting fixtures in Lab – Room 101.

4.   Select the **Switch Systems** tab on the ribbon.

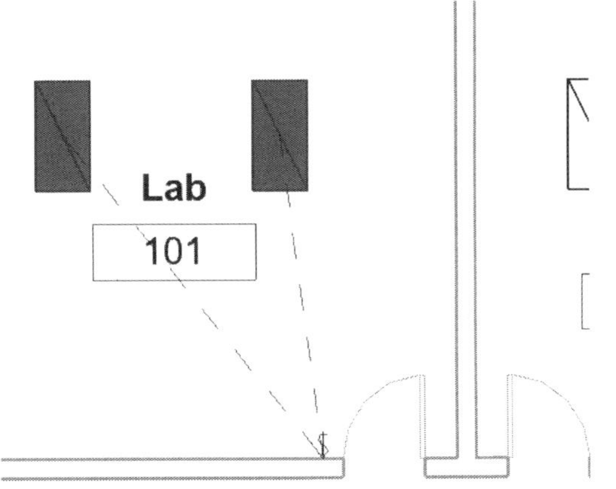

The circuit displays showing that the light fixtures are connected to the switch next to the door.

5.

On the Properties palette, notice that the Switch ID is blank.

Click **ESC** to release the selection.

6.

Select the switch in the Room 101.

Type **SW1** as the Switch ID in the Properties palette.

Click **ESC** to release the selection.

7. Activate the Systems ribbon.

Select the **Arc Wire** tool.

8.

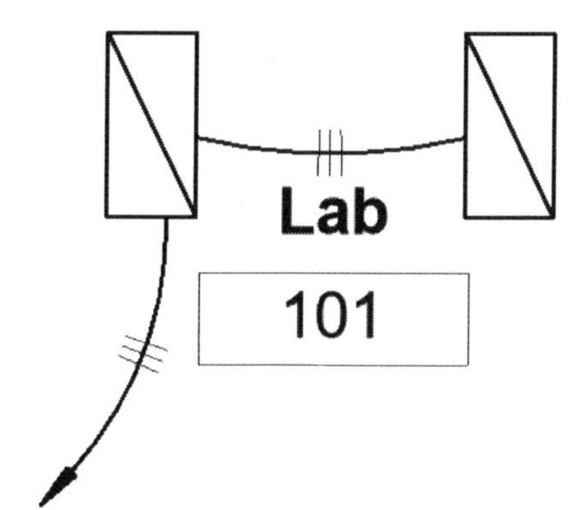

Draw a wire between the two light fixtures.

Draw a home run wire from the left light fixture pointing to the lower left corner of the room.

Cancel out of the command.

Hint: *Click on the connection points on the devices to place the wires.*

9.

Select one of the arc wires you just placed.

On the Properties palette, select **Edit Type**.

10. Select **Duplicate.**

11.

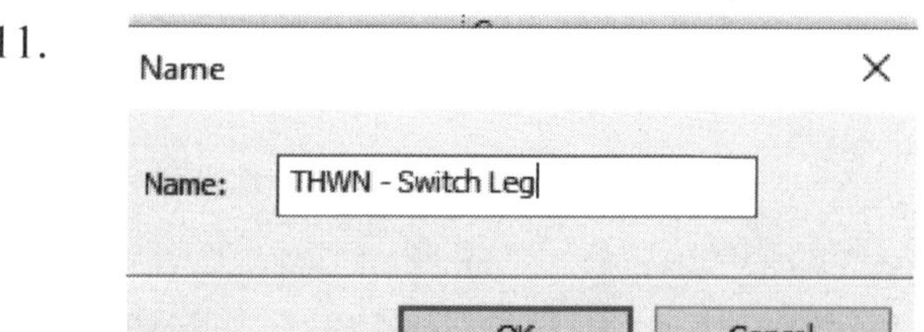

Type **THWN – Switch Leg.**

Click **OK.**

12.

Type Comments
URL
Description   Switch Leg
Assembly Description

Type **Switch Leg** in the Description field.

Click **OK** to close the dialog.

13.

Wire Types
THWN

Assign the wire you selected to use the THWN type using the Type Selector.

14.

Wire   Cable   Conduit
     Tray

Arc Wire

Activate the Systems ribbon.

Select the **Arc Wire** tool.

15.

Wire Types
THWN - Switch Leg

Use the Type Selector to change the wire type to **THWN – Switch Leg.**

16.

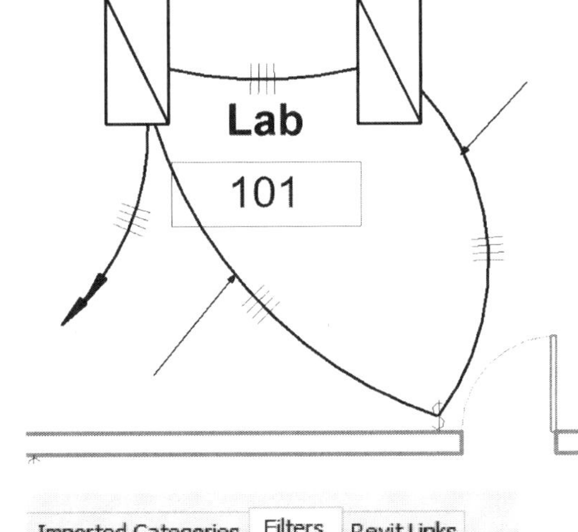

Draw two arc wires from each light fixture to the switch.

Click the connection point on the light fixture. Click a point in the room for the arc. Then click the switch to form the arc.

17.

Imported Categories   Filters   Revit Links

All document filters are defined and modified here   Edit/New...

Type **VV** to open the Visibility/Graphics dialog.

Select the **Filters** tab.

Click **Edit/New** at the bottom of the dialog to access the **Filters** tool.

18.

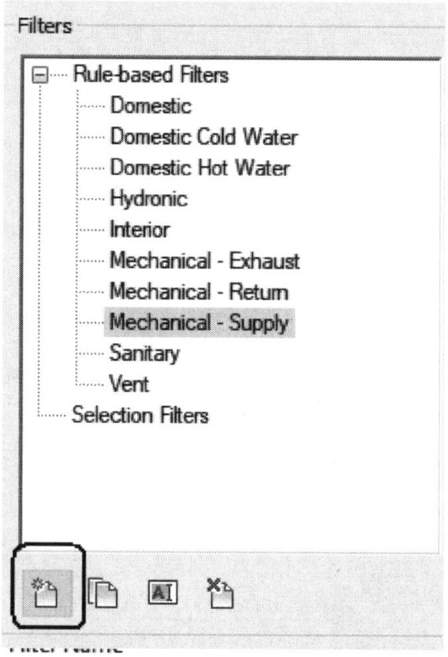

Select **New**.

19.

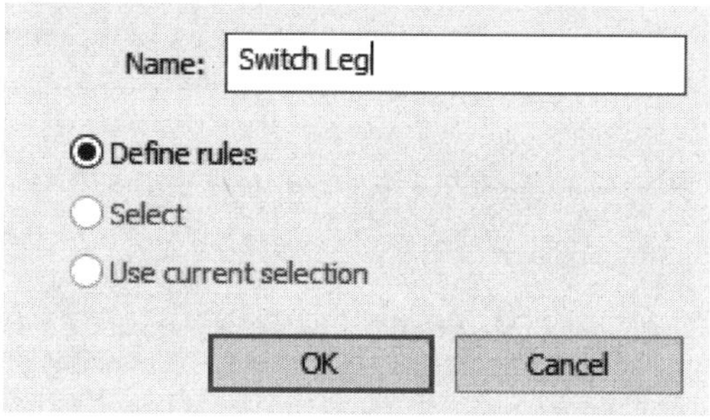

Type **Switch Leg** for the Name.

Click **OK**.

20.

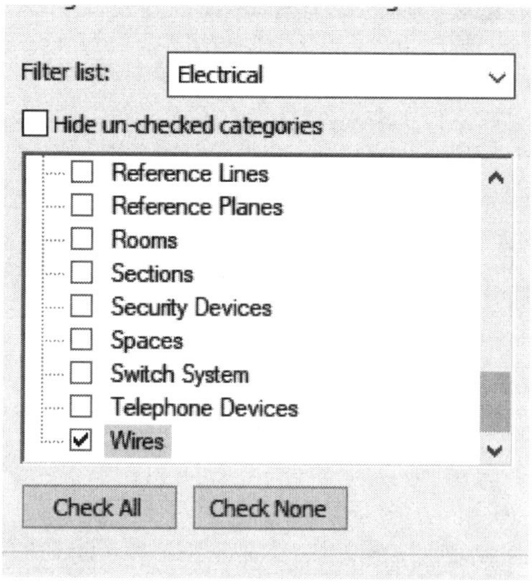

Set the Filter to **Electrical.**

Scroll down.

Enable **Wires** in the category list.

21.

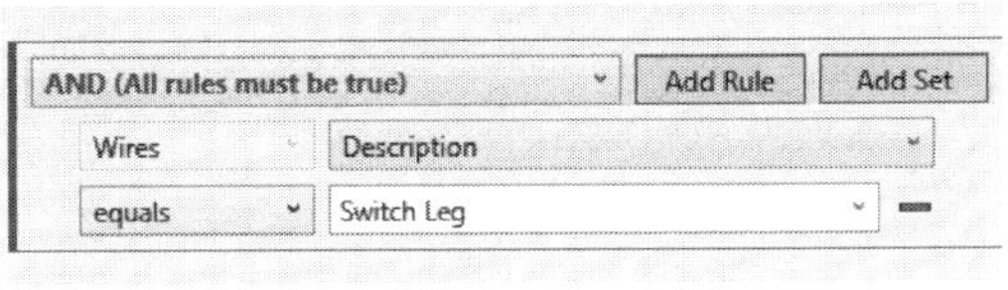

Select **Description**.
Select **equals**.
Select **Switch Leg**.
Click **OK** to create the filter.

22.

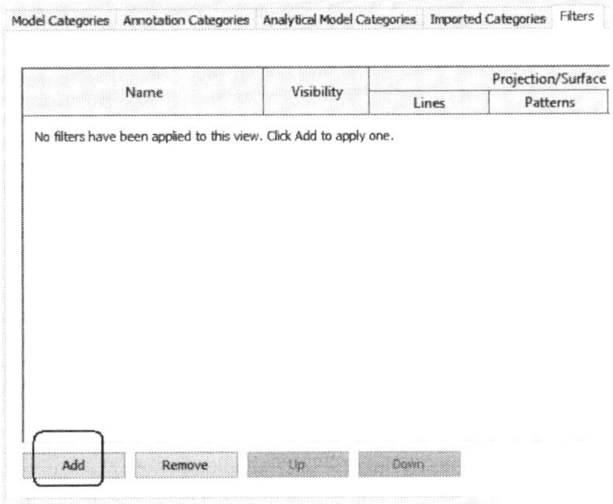

Select **Add** from the bottom of the dialog.

23.

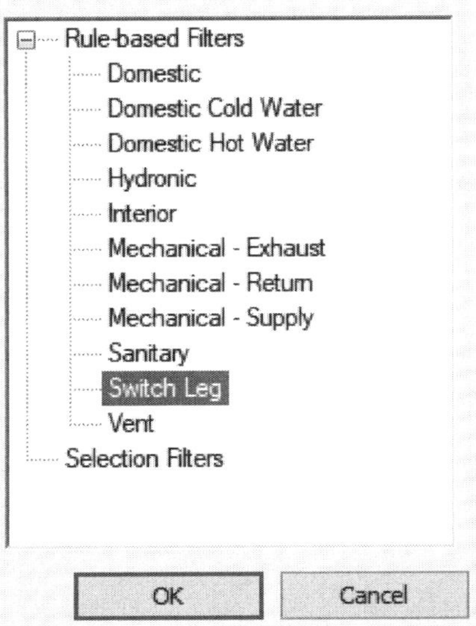

Highlight **Switch Leg**.
Click **OK**.

24.

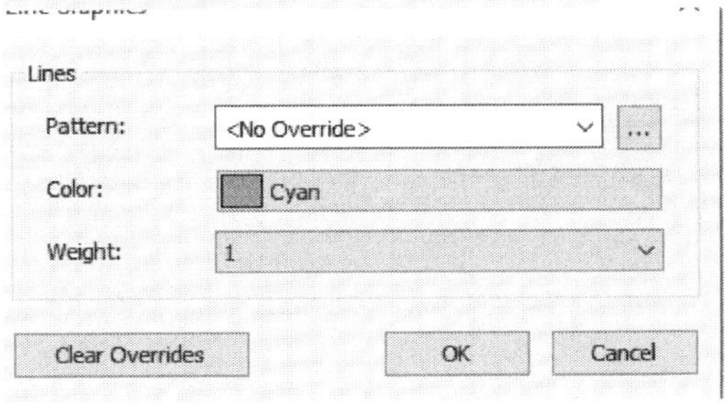

Left click in the Lines column.
Set the Color to **Cyan**.
Set the Weight to **1.**
Click **OK**.

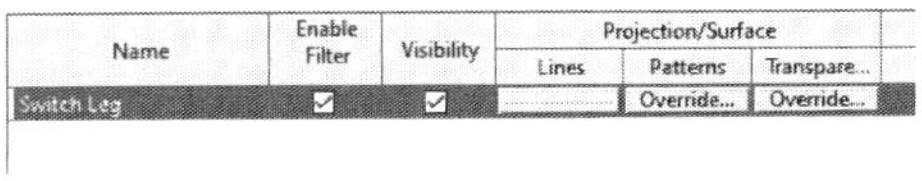

Close the dialog box.

25.

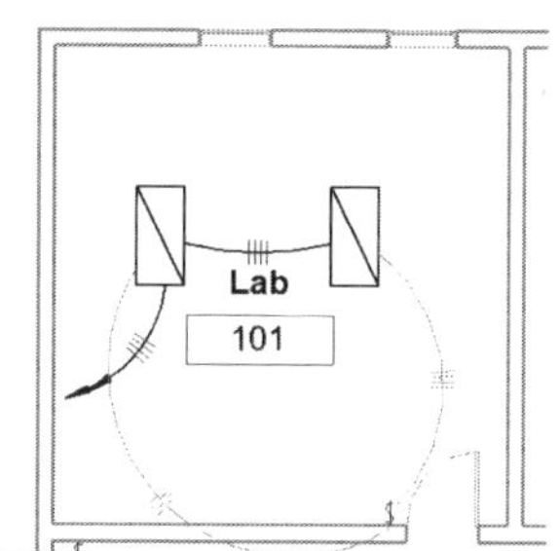

The wire display updates.

26.   Save the file as *ex4-7.rvt*.

A **junction box** is an enclosure (usually metal or plastic) that houses electrical connections. It's where wires are joined (spliced), branched, or transitioned safely.

Exercise 4-8:

Wiring to a Junction Box

Drawing Name: *junction_box_wiring.rvt*
Estimated Time: 30 minutes

This exercise reinforces the following skills:

- ❑ Electrical Fixtures
- ❑ Wires
- ❑ Circuits

1. Open the **East – Elec** elevation view.

2. Set the display to **Wireframe**.

    Notice that there is a floor placed on Level 2 and a ceiling placed on Level 1.

    Notice that ceilings go up and floors go down.

3. Select the **Measure** tool located on the QAT.

4.

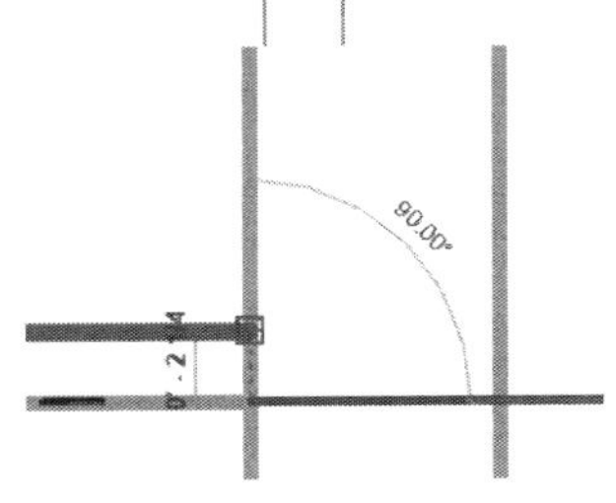

Measure between the floor and the ceiling to determine how much space you have for electrical equipment. There is a 1' 3 ¾" air space between the floor and the ceiling.

5.

Measure the thickness of the ceiling.
To verify, select the ceiling.

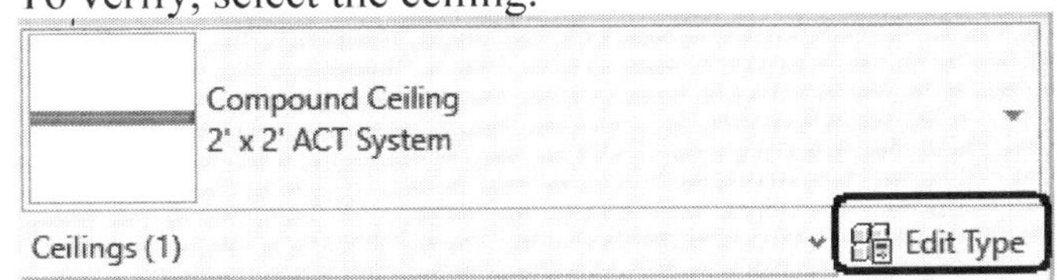

Select **Edit Type** on the Properties palette.

6.

Locate the thickness value of the ceiling.

The thickness is 2 ¼".

This means that any electrical equipment should be placed at 8' 2 ¼" elevation from Level 1.

Type Parameters

Parameter	Value
Construction	
Structure	Edit...
Thickness	0' 2 1/4"

Click **OK** to close the Type Properties dialog.
Press **ESC** to release the selection.

7.

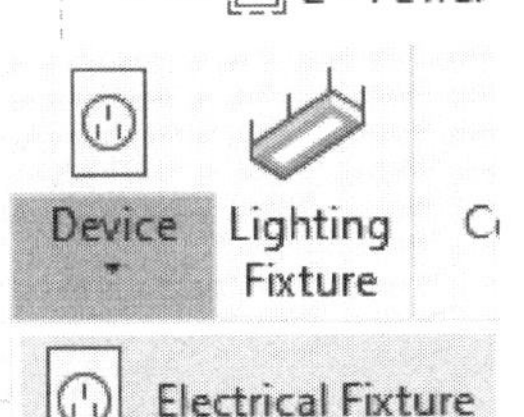

Open the **1 – Power** floor plan.

8.

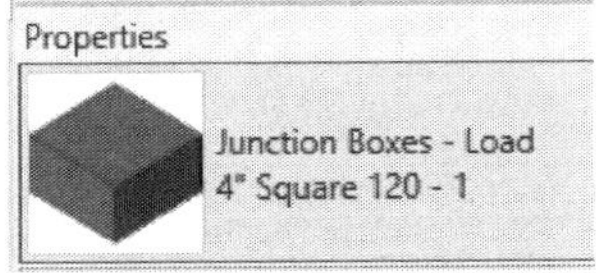

Switch to the **Systems** ribbon.

Select **Electrical Fixture** on the Device fly-out.

9.

Locate the **4" Square 120 -1 Junction box** using the Type Selector.

10. 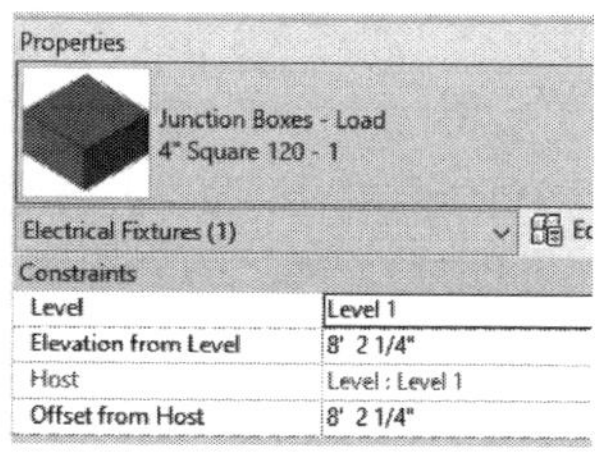

On the Properties palette:

Set the Elevation from level to **8' 2 ¼"**.

11. 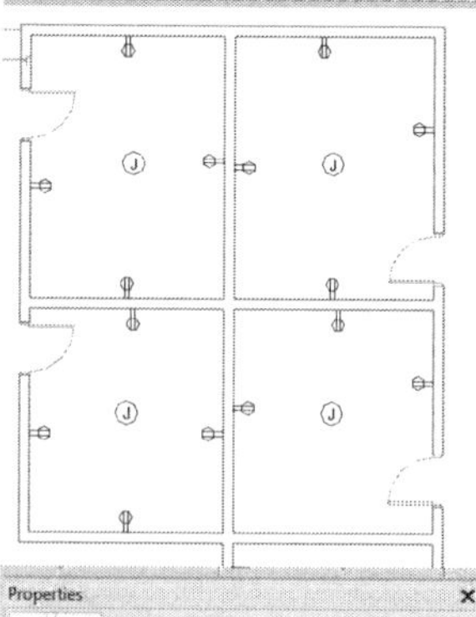

Place a junction box in the center of each of the rooms shown.

12. 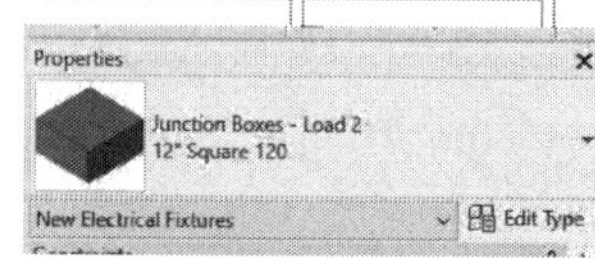

Locate the **12" Square 120 Junction box** using the Type Selector.

13. 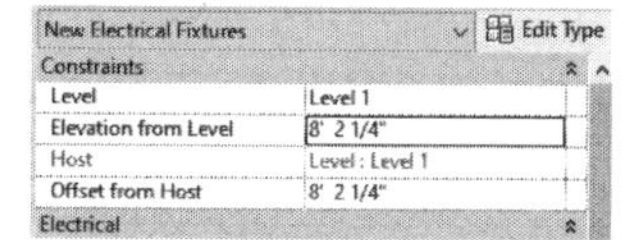

On the Properties palette:
Set the Elevation from level to **8' 2 ¼"**.

14. 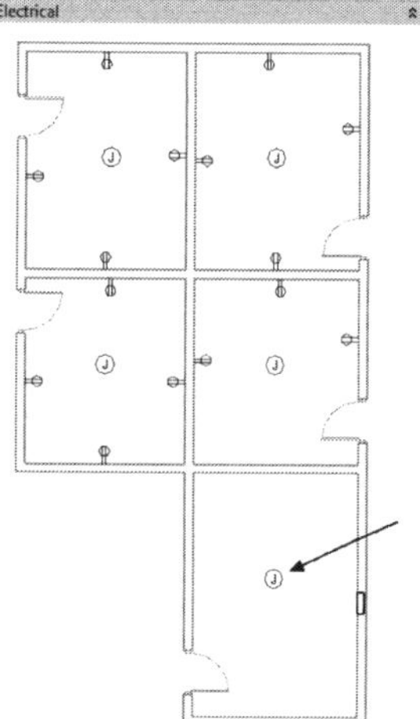

Place the 12" square junction box in the center of the lower room.

Click ESC to exit the command.

15. 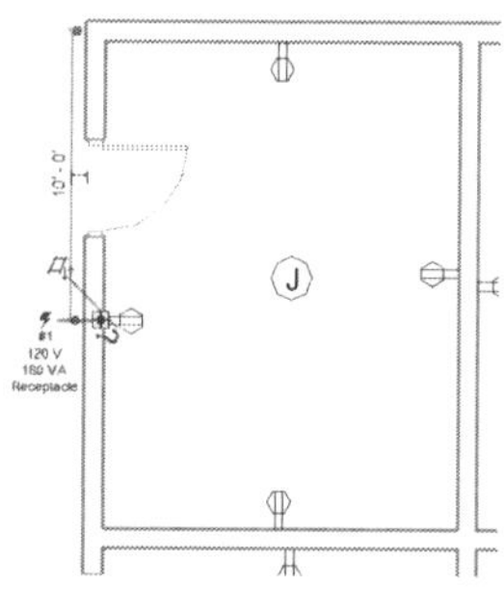

Select the receptacle on the west wall in the upper left room.

16. 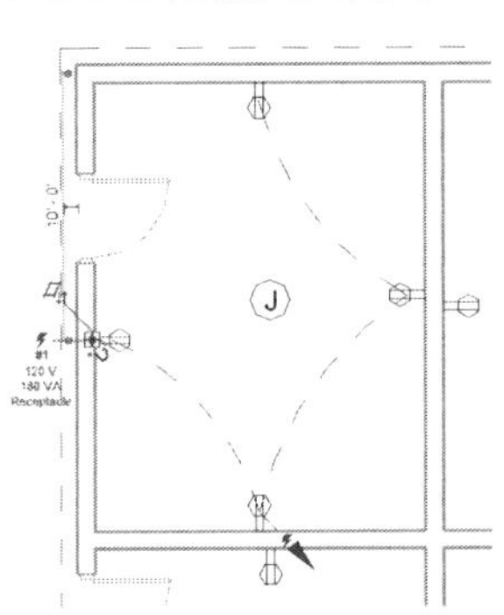 Select the **Electrical Circuits** tab on the ribbon.

17. *A preview will display showing the receptacles are connected.*

Edit Circuit

Select **Edit Circuit** on the ribbon.

18. 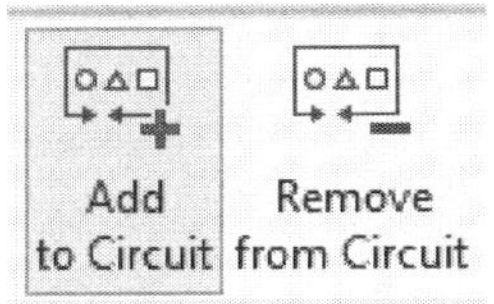 Verify that **Add to Circuit** is enabled on the ribbon.

Notice that the receptacles are in the foreground and all the other devices are grayed out. Anything that is not part of the circuit is faded.

Select the junction box in the center of the room to add it to the circuit.

19. 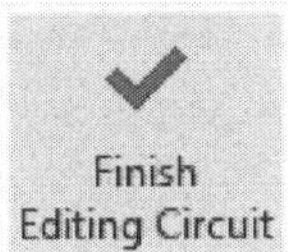 Select **Finish Editing Circuit** on the ribbon.

20. 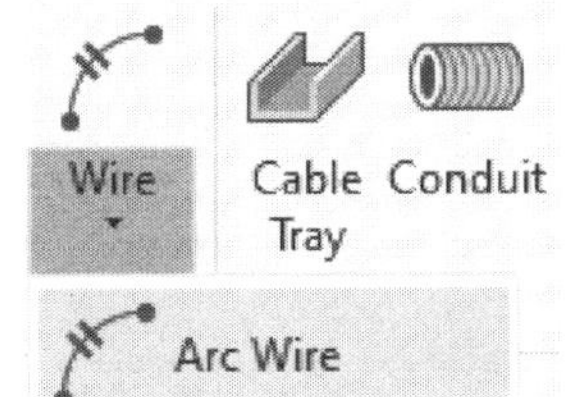 Select **Arc Wire** from the ribbon.

21. 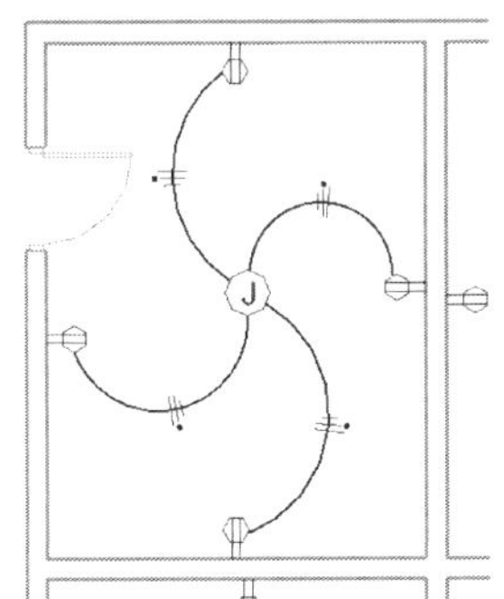 Draw a wire from each receptacle to the junction box in the middle of the room.

Hint: *When placing the wires, be sure to look for the connection snaps before clicking to place.*

22.

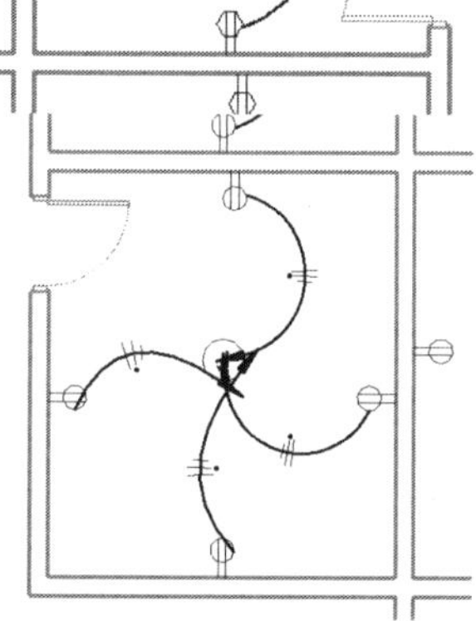

Draw a wire from each receptacle to the junction box in the middle of the upper right room.

23.

Draw a wire from each receptacle to the junction box in the middle of the lower left room.

24. Draw a wire from each receptacle to the junction box in the middle of the lower right room.

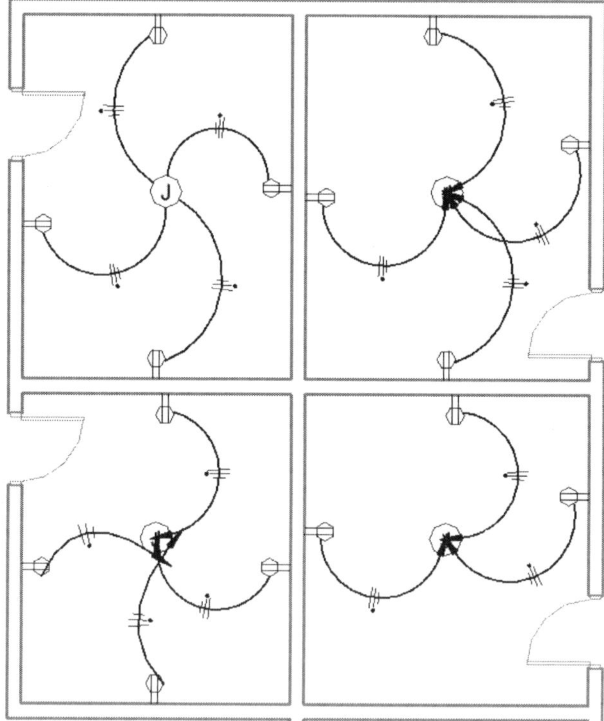

25. Draw a wire between the lower left room junction box and the upper left room junction box.

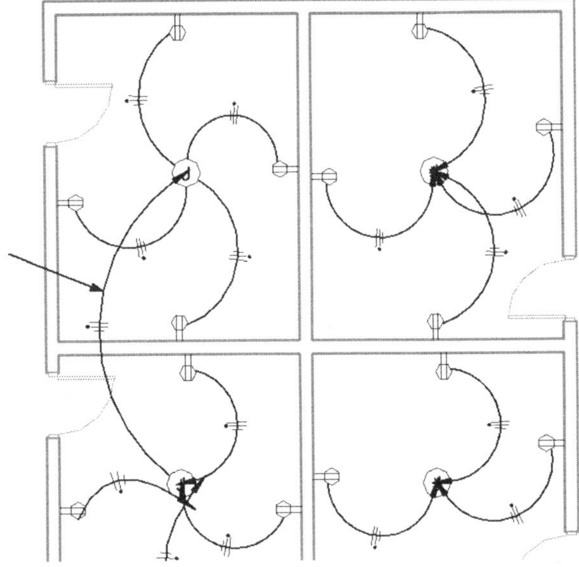

26. Draw a wire between the lower right room junction box and the upper right room junction box.

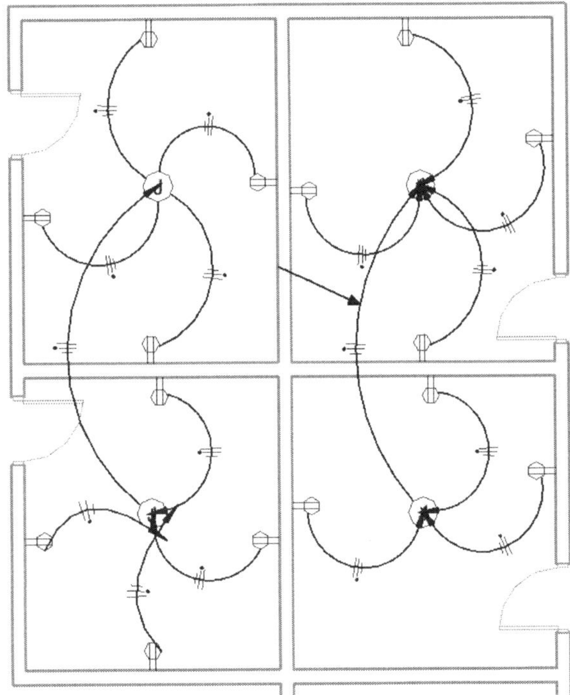

27.

Draw a wire from the lower left room to the 12" junction box.

Draw a wire from the lower right room to the 12" junction box.

ESC out of the command.

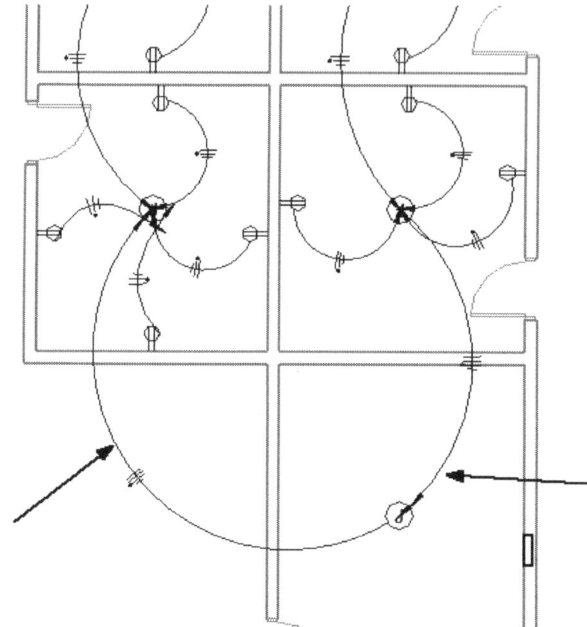

28.

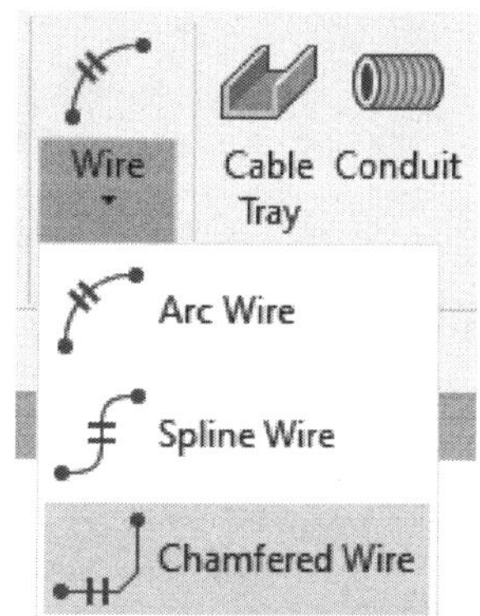

Select the **Chamfered Wire** tool from the ribbon.

29.

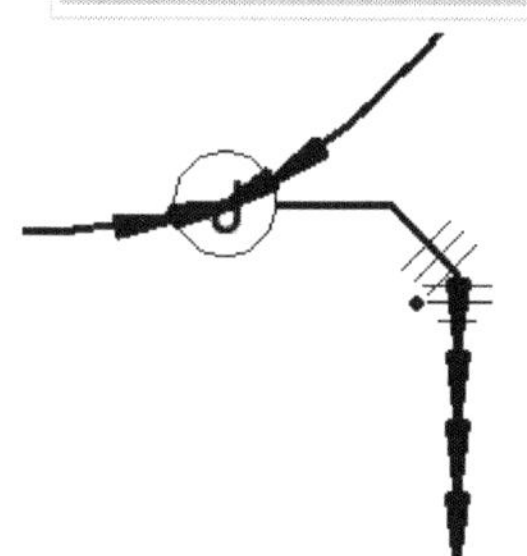

Select the 12" junction box as the starting point for the chamfered wire.

Left click to the right of the junction box.

Move the mouse down and left click again to place the home run wire.

ESC out of the command.

Your view should look similar to this.

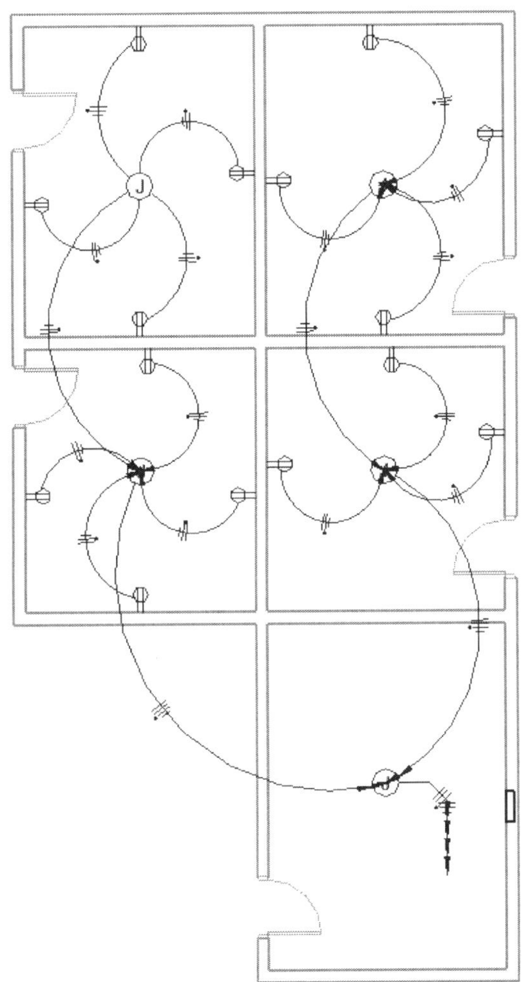

30. 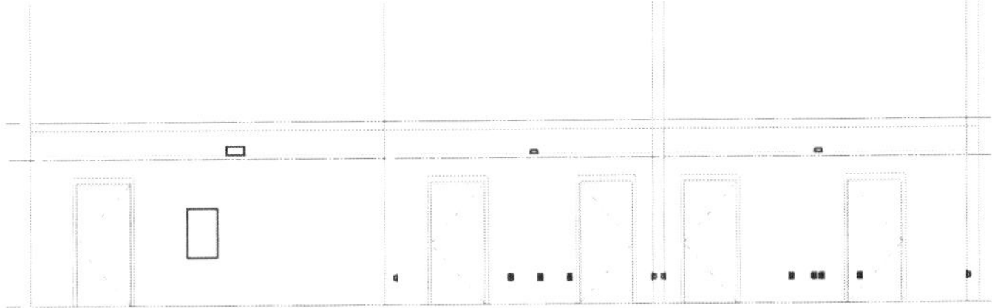

Open the **East – Elec** elevation view.

31. You see the junction boxes placed on the ceilings of each room.

Notice that you don't see the wires. This is because wires are view-specific. They are only visible in the view where they are placed.

Save as *ex4-8.rvt*.

Lab Exercise

Open *wiring_lab.rvt*.

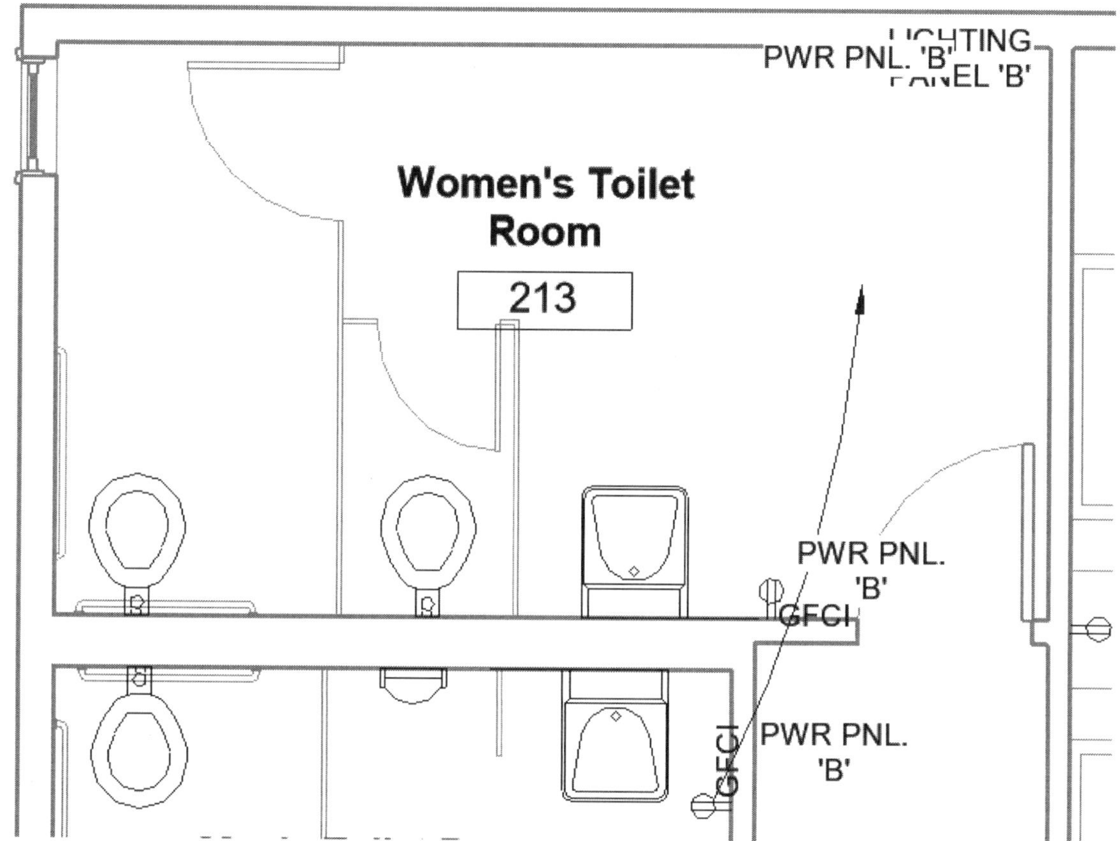

Assign the GFCI receptacle in WOMEN'S ROOM 213 & MEN'S ROOM 212 to PWR PNL B.

Add an arc wire.

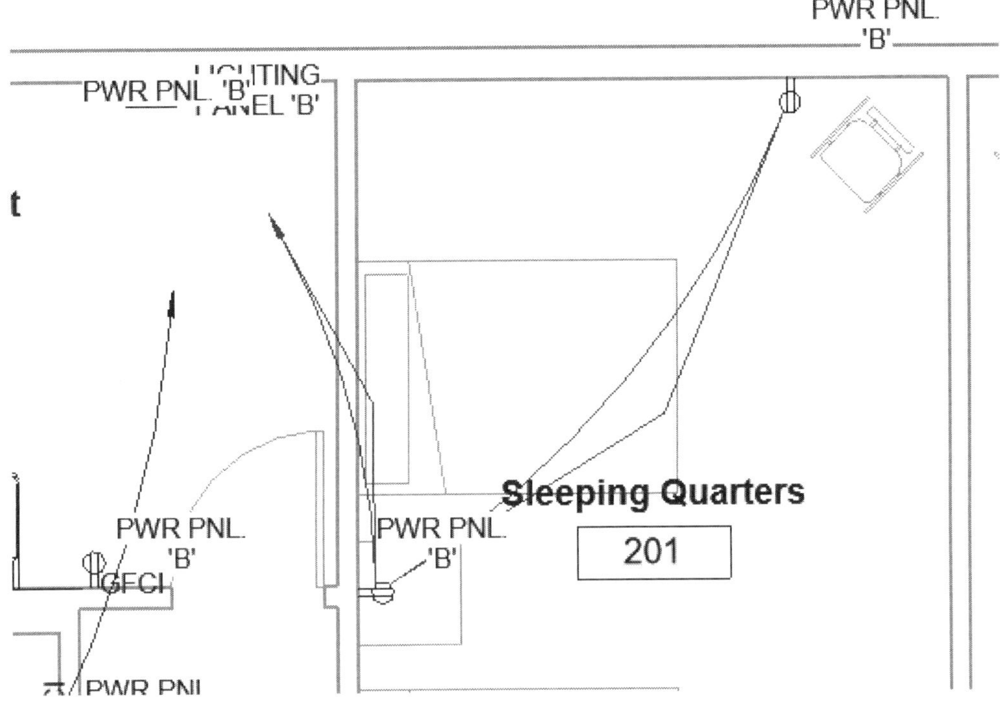

Assign the receptacle in SLEEPING QUARTERS 201 to PWR PNL B.

Add an arc wire.

Continue through the Main Floor floor plan assigning receptacles to panels and adding wires.

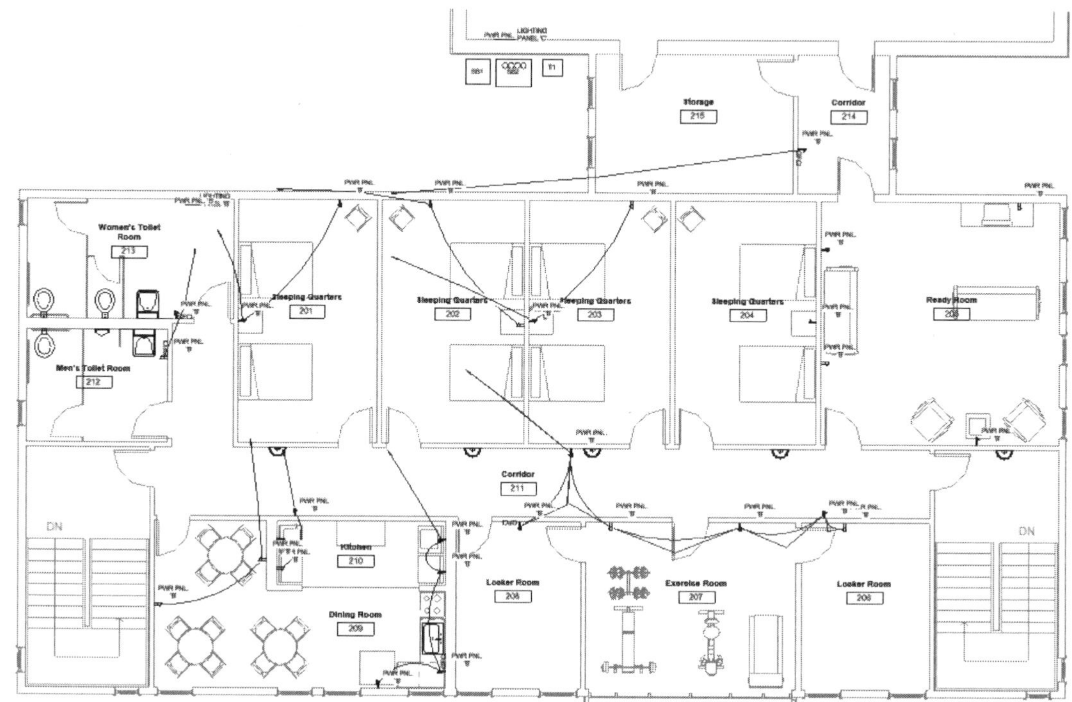

Create a duplicate view of the Main Floor Lighting Ceiling Plan.

Rename the view **Main Floor Lighting**.

Turn off the visibility of elevations, sections, roofs, ceilings, and reference planes.

Add circuits to the lighting fixtures. Connect the lighting fixtures to LIGHTING PANEL B.

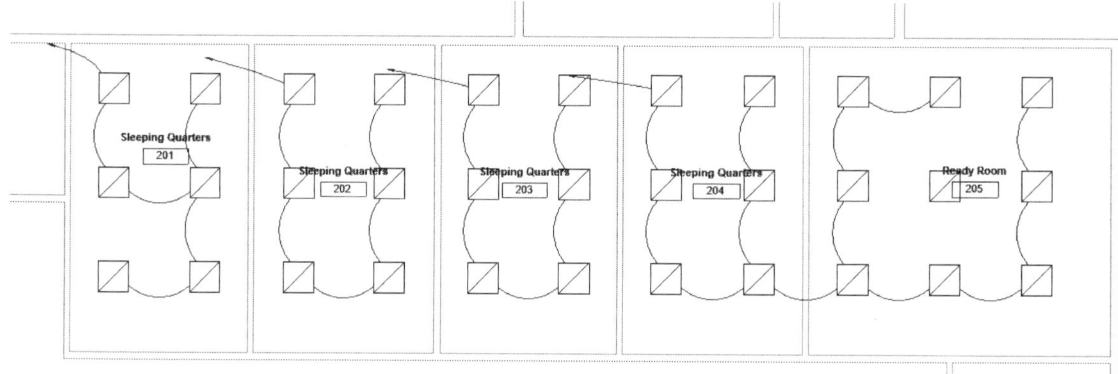

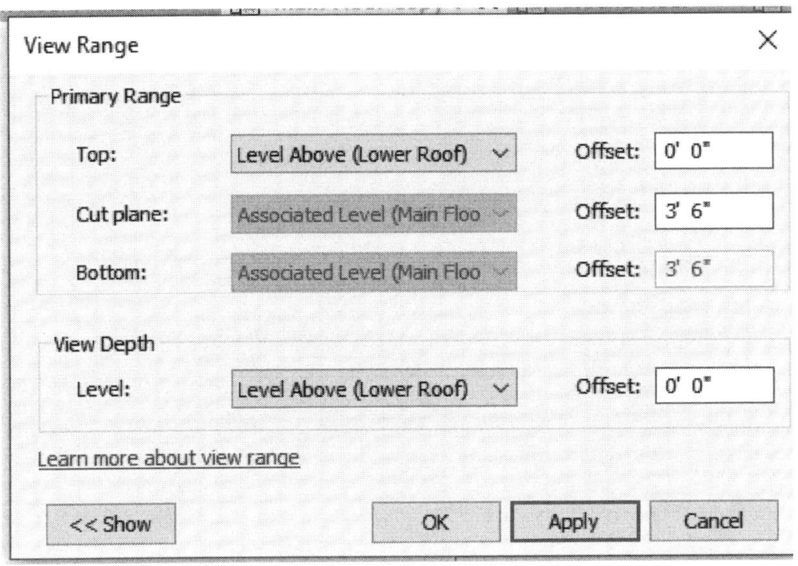

Change the View Range for the Main Floor Lighting Ceiling Plan so that the Cut Plane is set to 3' 6". *This allows you to see any switches which are placed.*

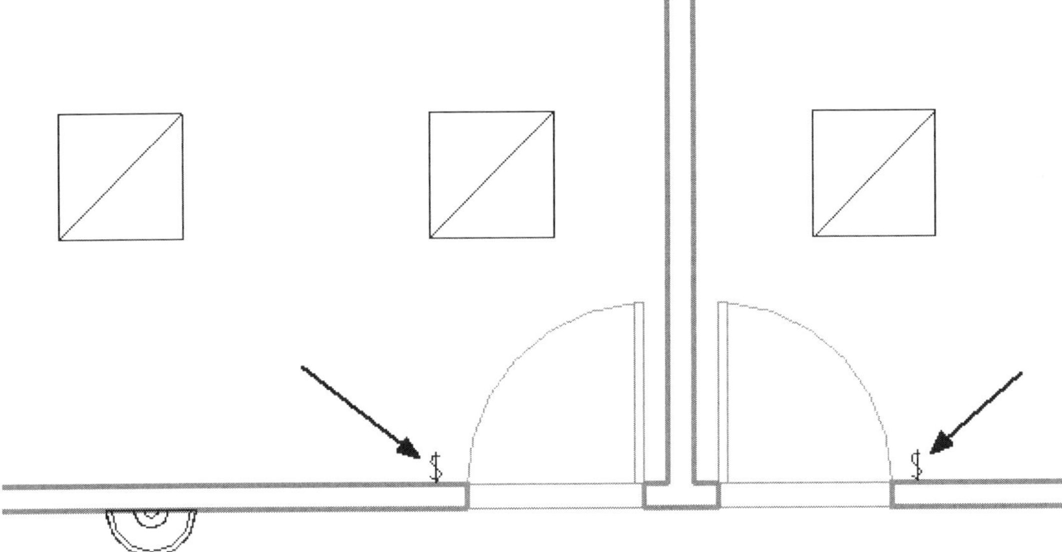

Add single pole light switches to each room.

Connect the light fixtures to the switches.

Create switch leg wires to differentiate between the wires going from the light fixture to the switch and the wiring between the light fixtures.

Notes:

4-42

Conduits

An electrical conduit is a tube used to protect and route electrical wiring in a building or structure. Most conduits use PVC piping, which is rigid. Revit allows you to define different conduit types and sizes.

Revit allows you to apply EMT (electrical metallic tubing), IMC (intermediate metal conduit), RMC (rigid metal conduit), RNC Schedule 40 (rigid nonmetallic conduit) or RNC Schedule 80 (rigid nonmetallic conduit) to your conduit families. RNC Schedule 40 is Heavy Wall PVC piping standard. RNC Schedule 80 is an Extra Heavy Wall standard. RNC Schedule 40 is listed for underground applications encased in concrete and can also be used in exposed or concealed areas above ground. RNC Schedule 80 is used in areas where it may be subjected to physical damage. You have the ability to create and apply your own conduit standards. For example, if you wanted to use GRC (galvanized rigid conduit), you would have to create that standard before you can apply it to a conduit family.

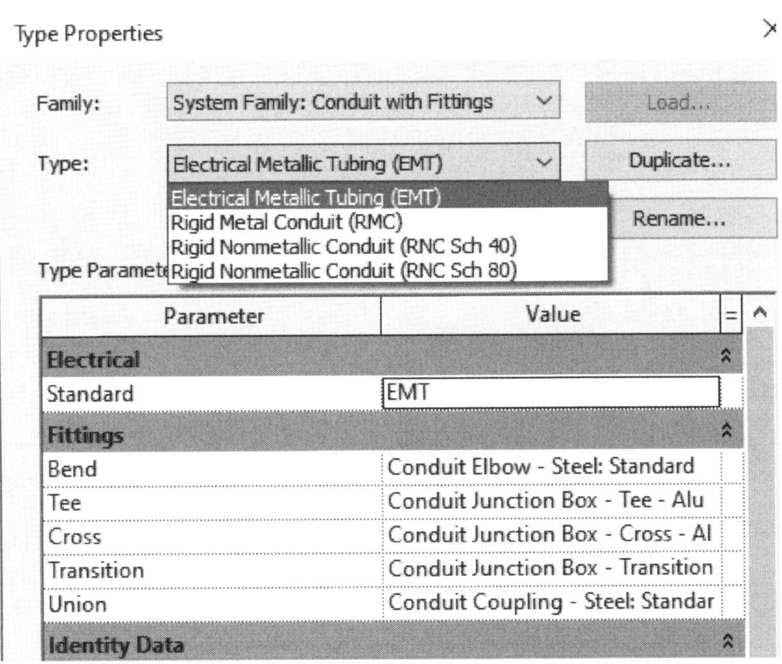

Conduits are system families, so any conduit definitions you create are local to the active project only. I recommend that you define your conduit families for your projects and place them in your templates, so you don't have to redefine them for each project.

You can change the elevation of a conduit as you are placing it by changing the off-set value in the drop-down. Revit will automatically insert the proper fittings and vertical conduits to transition to the new elevation.

To connect a conduit to equipment or to a device, the object must have a conduit connector available. When you select the object, you can right click the conduit connector and choose the option to draw conduit from the connector. You can connect to equipment in plan view, elevation view or 3D view.

In most projects, you will want to assign colors to your conduits to make them easier to identify. You need to create a family type for each conduit color you want to use. In order to see the different colors, you need to define a View Filter and then apply it to your view. You may want to create a view template to make it easier for you to assign the view filter to your views displaying conduits.

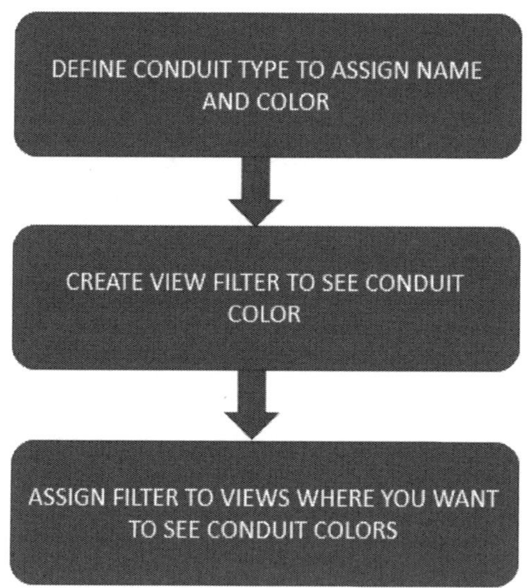

Conduit Settings

Electrical Settings

	Setting	
Hidden Line	Use Annot. Scale for Single Line Fittings	☐
General	Conduit Fitting Annotation Size	0' 0 1/8"
Angles	Conduit Size Prefix	
Wiring	Conduit Size Suffix	ø
Voltage Definitions	Conduit Connector Separator	-
Distribution Systems		
Cable Tray Settings		
Rise Drop		
Single Line Symbology		
Two Line Symbology		
Size		
Conduit Settings		
Rise Drop		
Single Line Symbology		
Two Line Symbology		
Size		
Load Calculations		
Panel Schedules		
Circuit Naming		

Use Annot. Scale for Single Line Fittings	Specifies whether conduit fittings are drawn at the size specified by the Conduit Fitting Annotation Size parameter. Changing this setting does not change the plotted size of components already placed in a project.
Conduit Fitting Annotation Size	Specifies the plotted size of fittings drawn in single-line views. This size is maintained regardless of the drawing scale.
Conduit Size Prefix	Specifies the symbol preceding the conduit size.
Conduit Size Suffix	Specifies the symbol following the conduit size.
Conduit Connector Separator	Specifies the symbol used to separate information between 2 different connectors.

Access conduit settings on the Electrical Settings dialog. To open the dialog, type ES.

Conduit Settings – Rise Drop

Setting		Specifies the plotted size of rise/drop symbols drawn in single-line views. This size is maintained regardless of the drawing scale.
Conduit Rise/Drop Annotation Size	1/8"	

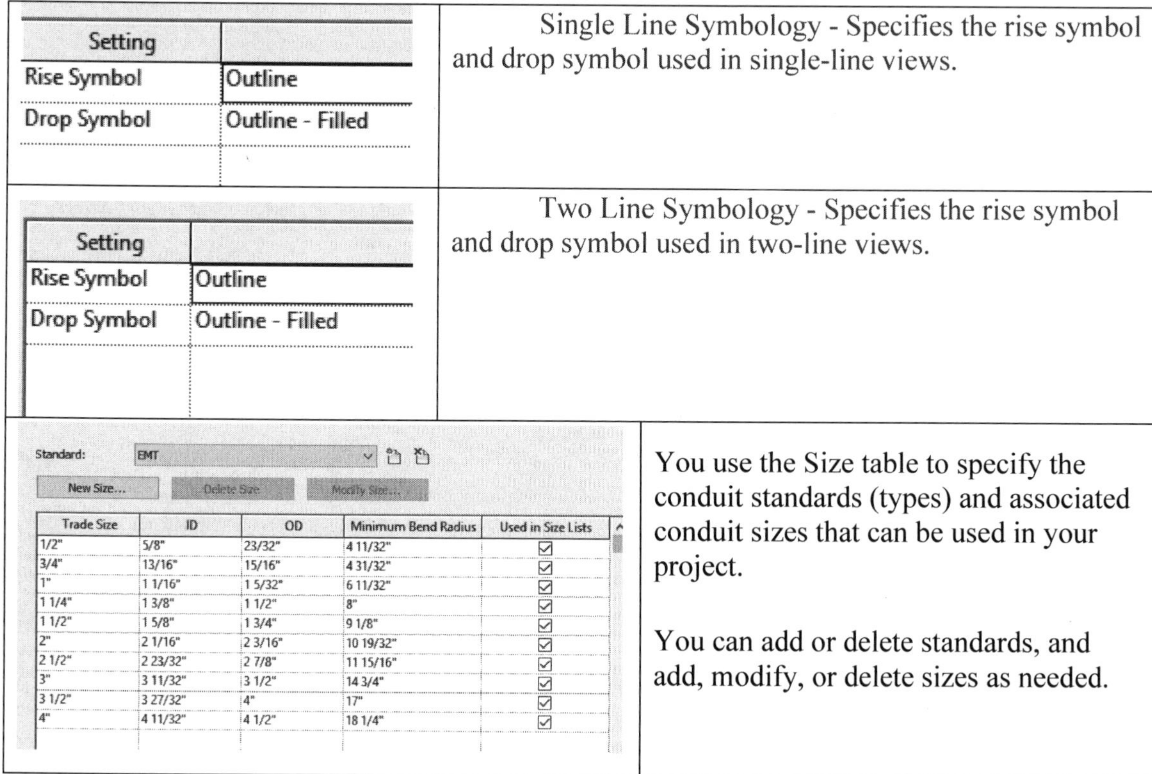

Setting	
Rise Symbol	Outline
Drop Symbol	Outline - Filled

Single Line Symbology - Specifies the rise symbol and drop symbol used in single-line views.

Setting	
Rise Symbol	Outline
Drop Symbol	Outline - Filled

Two Line Symbology - Specifies the rise symbol and drop symbol used in two-line views.

Standard: EMT

New Size...   Delete Size   Modify Size...

Trade Size	ID	OD	Minimum Bend Radius	Used in Size Lists
1/2"	5/8"	23/32"	4 11/32"	☑
3/4"	13/16"	15/16"	4 31/32"	☑
1"	1 1/16"	1 5/32"	6 11/32"	☑
1 1/4"	1 3/8"	1 1/2"	8"	☑
1 1/2"	1 5/8"	1 3/4"	9 1/8"	☑
2"	2 1/16"	2 3/16"	10 19/32"	☑
2 1/2"	2 23/32"	2 7/8"	11 15/16"	☑
3"	3 11/32"	3 1/2"	14 3/4"	☑
3 1/2"	3 27/32"	4"	17"	☑
4"	4 11/32"	4 1/2"	18 1/4"	☑

You use the Size table to specify the conduit standards (types) and associated conduit sizes that can be used in your project.

You can add or delete standards, and add, modify, or delete sizes as needed.

Conduit Settings – Angles

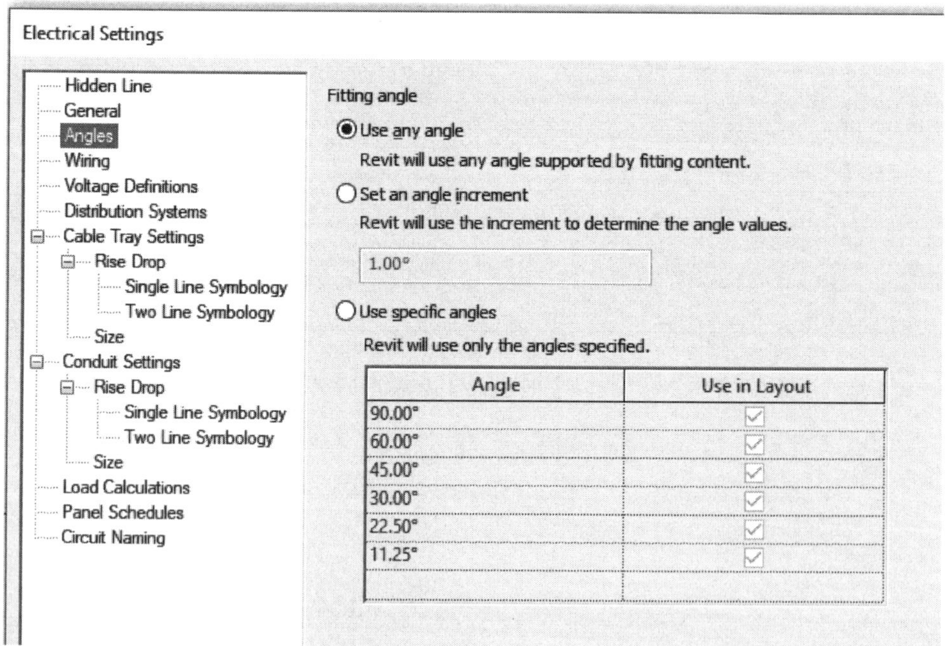

Angle	Use in Layout
90.00°	☑
60.00°	☑
45.00°	☑
30.00°	☑
22.50°	☑
11.25°	☑

Specify the allowable angles to be used for conduits, cable trays, etc. based on the equipment to be installed.

Exercise 5-1:

Creating a Conduit Standard

Drawing Name: *conduit_GRC.rvt*
Estimated Time: 5 minutes

This exercise reinforces the following skills:
- Electrical Settings
- Conduits

1.   Open **Level 1- Rooms** floor plan.

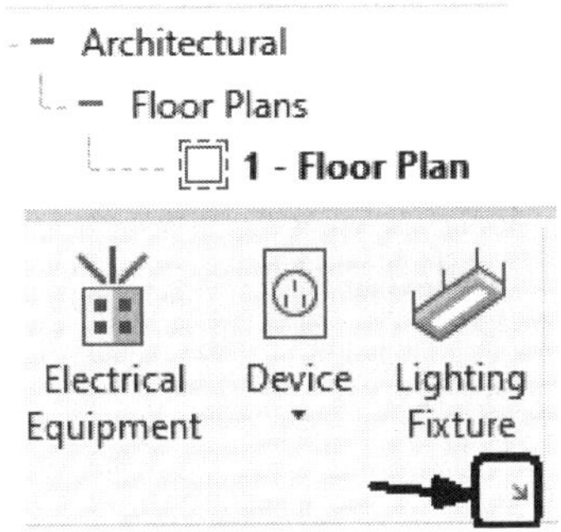

2.   Switch to the Systems ribbon.
Open the Electrical Settings panel.

3.   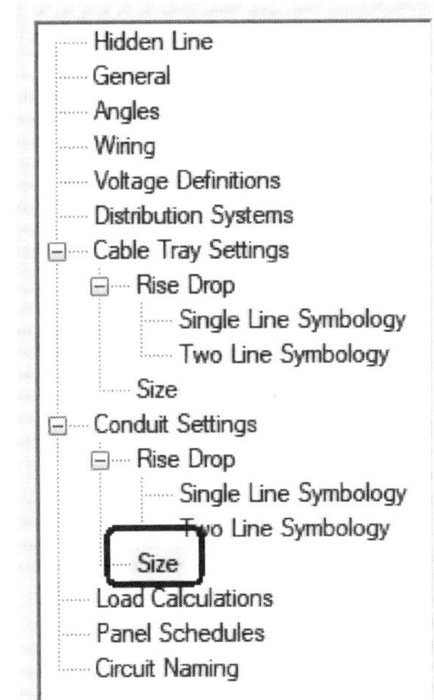

Highlight **Size** in the left panel.

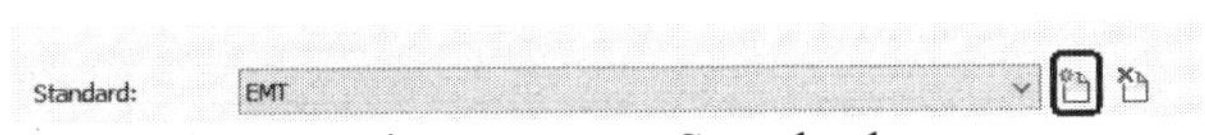

Select the **New** icon next to Standard.

4.

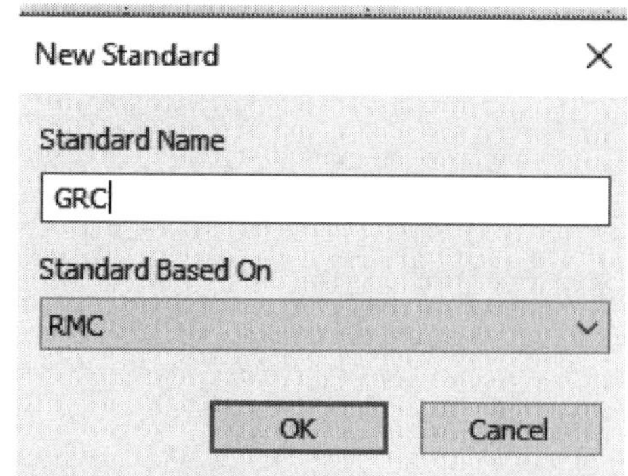

Type **GRC** for the Standard Name.

Select **RMC** (Rigid Metal Conduit) for the Standard Based On value.

Click **OK**.

5.   Close the dialog.

Exercise 5-2:

Creating a Conduit Family

Drawing Name: *Conduit_family.rvt*
Estimated Time: 15 minutes

This exercise reinforces the following skills:
- ❑ Electrical Settings
- ❑ Conduits
- ❑ System Families

1.   Open **1- Power** floor plan.

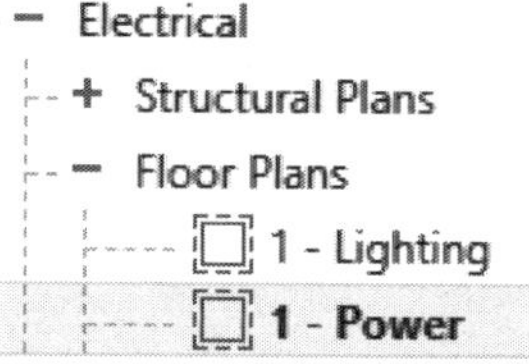

2.

Switch to the **Systems** ribbon.

Select the **Conduit** tool on the Electrical panel.

3.

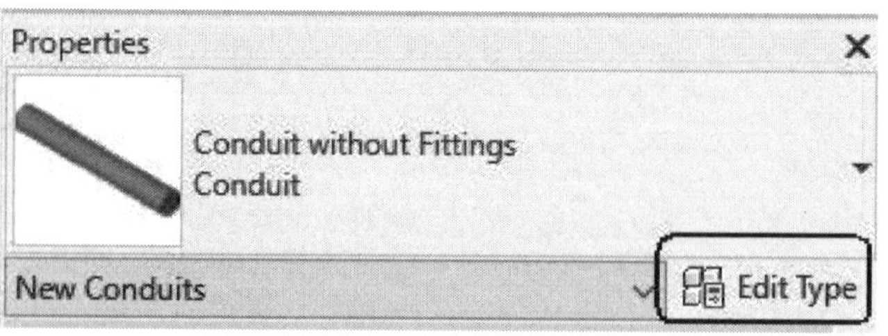

Select the **Conduit without Fittings** using the Type Selector.

Click **Edit Type**.

4.

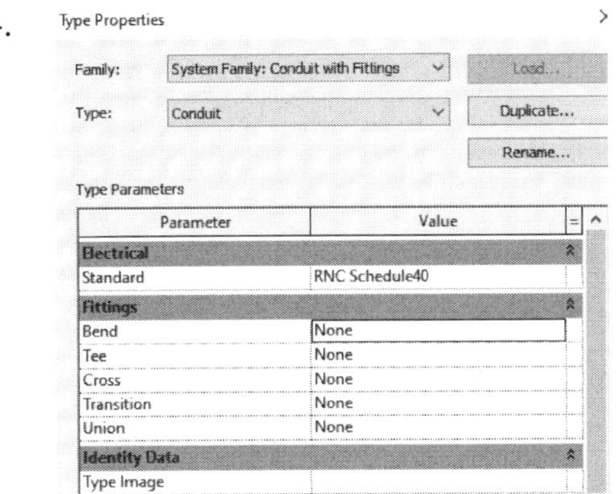

Under Standard:
Select **RNC Schedule40**.

This is a Rigid Non-metal conduit, usually PVC pipe.

Notice that no fittings are loaded for this family.

5.

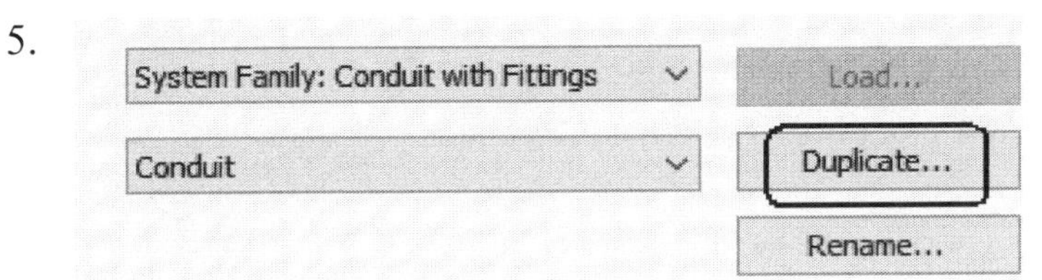

Select **Duplicate.**

6.

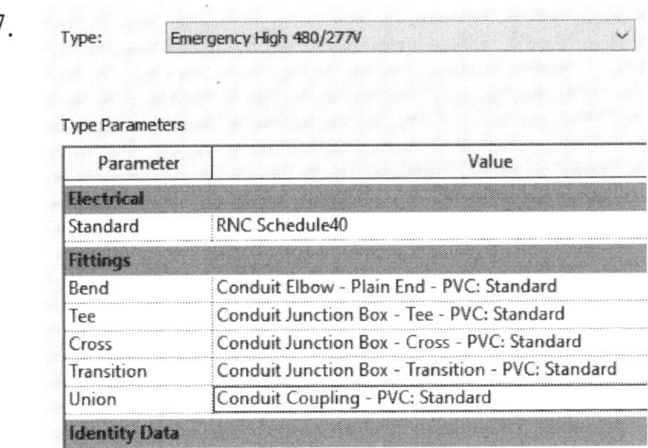

Type **Emergency High 480/277V** in the Name field.

Click **OK**.

7.

Using the drop-down next to each field:

Assign **the Conduit-Elbow – Plain End- PVC: Standard** to the Bend fitting.
Assign the **Conduit Junction Box – Tee -PVC: Standard** to the Tee fitting.
Assign the **Conduit Junction Box – Cross -PVC: Standard** to the Cross fitting.
Assign the **Conduit Junction Box – Transition -PVC: Standard** to the Transition fitting.
Assign the **Conduit Coupling -PVC: Standard** to the Union fitting.

8. In the Description field, type **Red**.

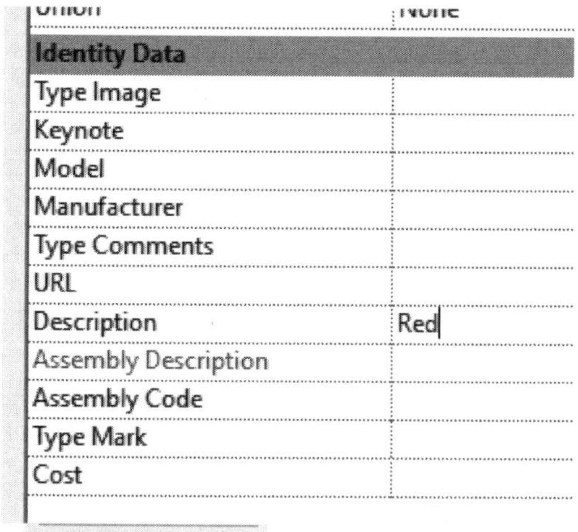

9. Select **Duplicate.**

10. Type **Emergency Low 120/208V** in the Name field.

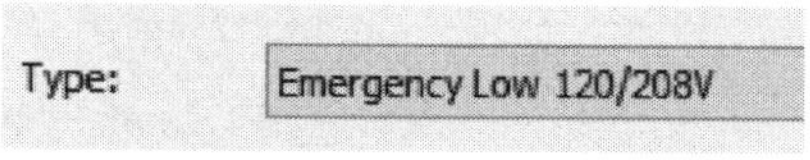

Click **OK**.

11. In the Description field, type **Magenta**.

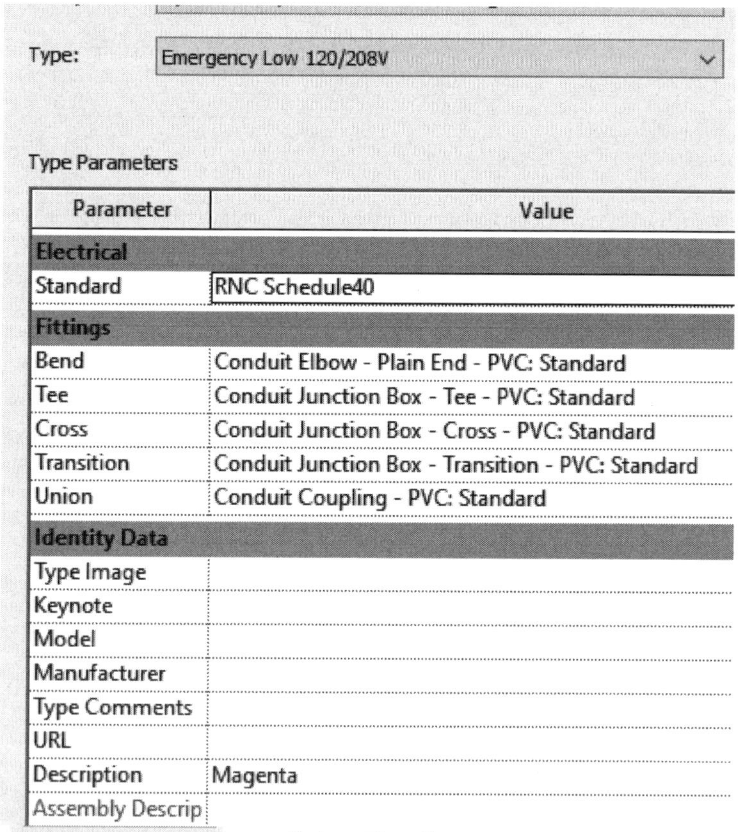

12. Select **Duplicate.**

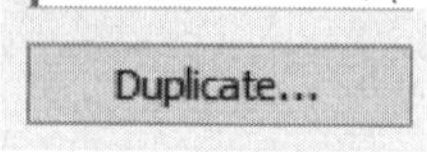

13.   Type **Normal High 480/277V** in the Name field.

Name: Normal High 480/277V

Click **OK**.

14.   In the Description field, type **Cyan**.

Type: Normal High 480/277V

Type Parameters

Parameter	Value
Electrical	
Standard	RNC Schedule40
Fittings	
Bend	Conduit Elbow - Plain End - PVC: Standard
Tee	Conduit Junction Box - Tee - PVC: Standard
Cross	Conduit Junction Box - Cross - PVC: Standard
Transition	Conduit Junction Box - Transition - PVC: Standard
Union	Conduit Coupling - PVC: Standard
Identity Data	
Type Image	
Keynote	
Model	
Manufacturer	
Type Comments	
URL	
Description	Cyan
Assembly Descrip	

15.   Select **Duplicate.**

Duplicate...

16.   Type **Normal Low 120/208V** in the Name field.

Name: Normal Low 120/208V

Click **OK**.

17.

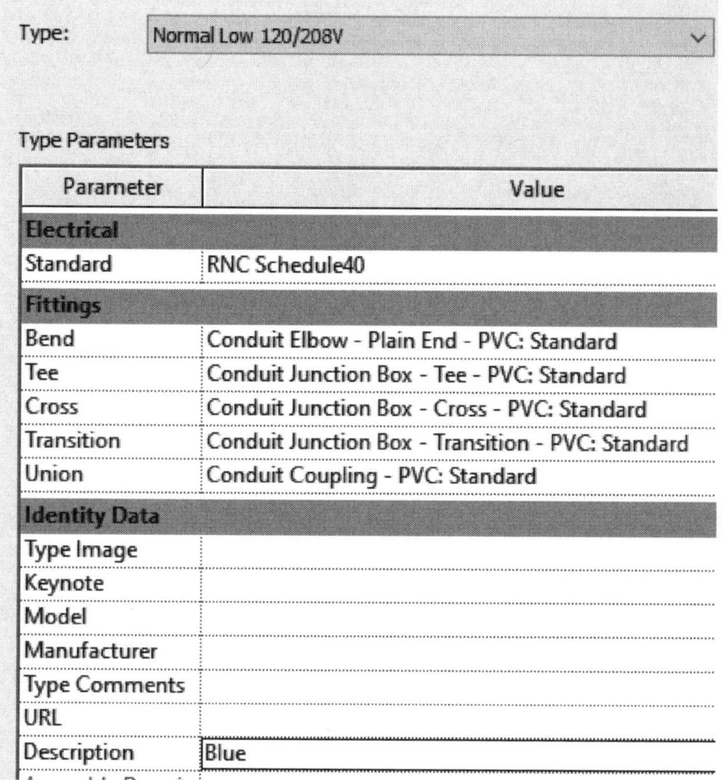

In the Description field, type **Blue**.

Press **OK** to close the dialog.

We have created four conduit types:
- Emergency High (Red)
- Emergency Low (Magenta)
- Normal High (Cyan)
- Normal Low (Blue)

18. Save as *ex5-2.rvt*.

Filters provide a way to override the graphic display and control the visibility of elements that share common properties in a view.

For example, if you need to change the line style and color for different conduit types, you can create a filter that selects all conduits in the view that have the color 'red' in the description parameter. You can then select the filter, define the visibility and graphic display settings (such as line style and color), and apply the filter to the view. When you do this, all conduits that meet the criteria defined in the filter update with the appropriate visibility and graphics settings. You need to set up the view filters and then apply those filters to each view in order to display the conduits with the correct colors and linetypes.

Exercise 5-3:

Defining View Filters

Drawing Name: *Conduit_views.rvt*
Estimated Time: 20 minutes

This exercise reinforces the following skills:
- View Filters
- Conduits

1. Open **Vault Level** floor plan.

   Floor Plans
   - 1 - Lighting
   - 1 - Power
   - 2 - Lighting
   - 2 - Power
   - Grading and Foundation
   - Half-Stairs
   - Parking Lot
   - Trench
   - Vault Level

2. 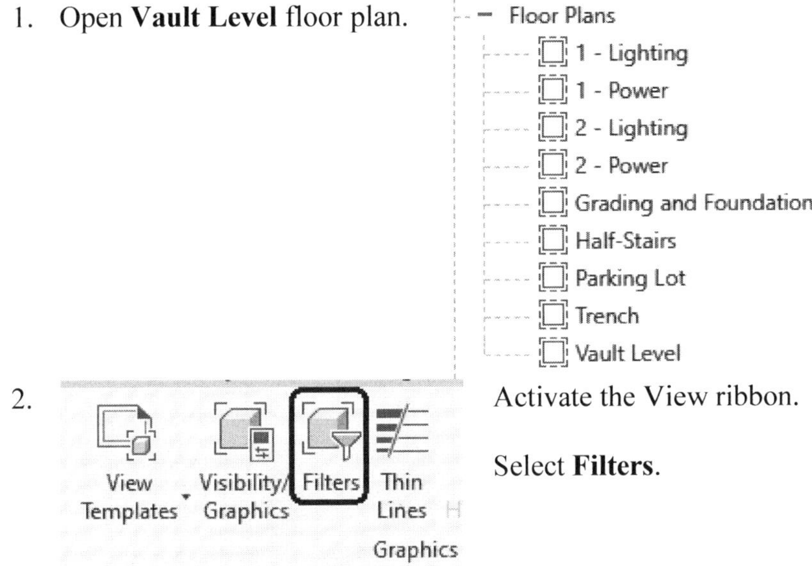 Activate the View ribbon.

   Select **Filters**.

3.

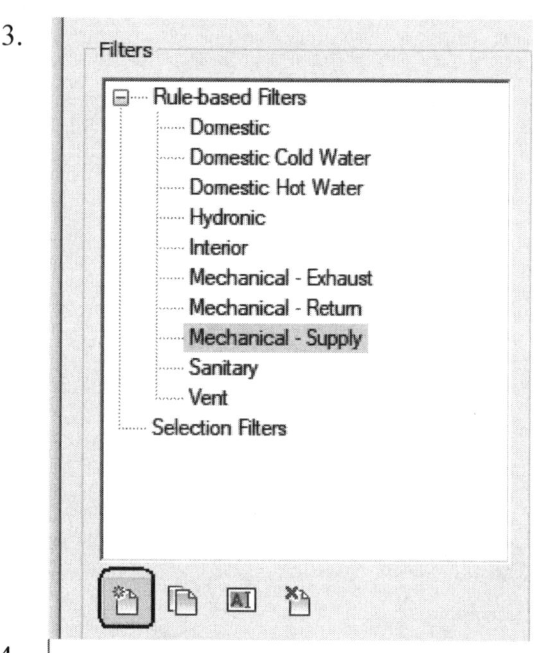

Click the **New** filter icon located at the lower left of the Filters palette.

4.

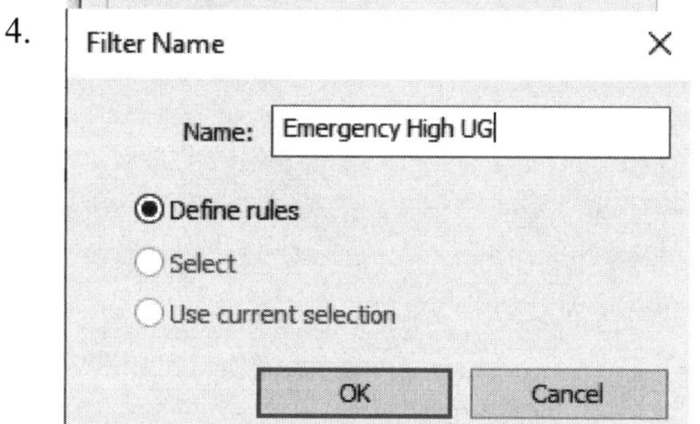

Type **Emergency High UG** in the Name field.

This filter will control the display properties for the underground emergency high conduit.

Click **OK**.

5.

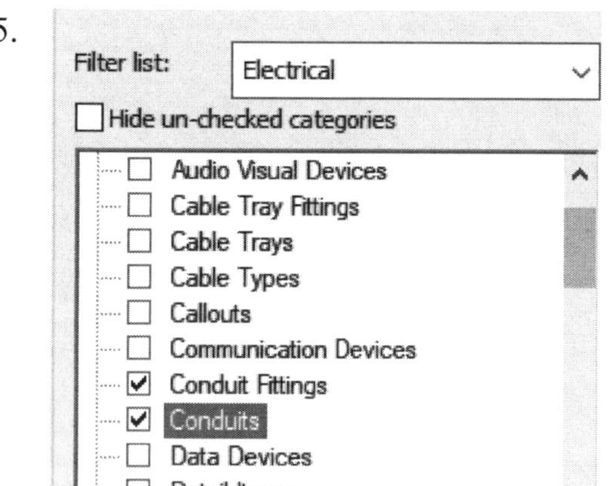

Place a check next to **Conduits** and **Conduit Fittings** in the Category panel.

6.

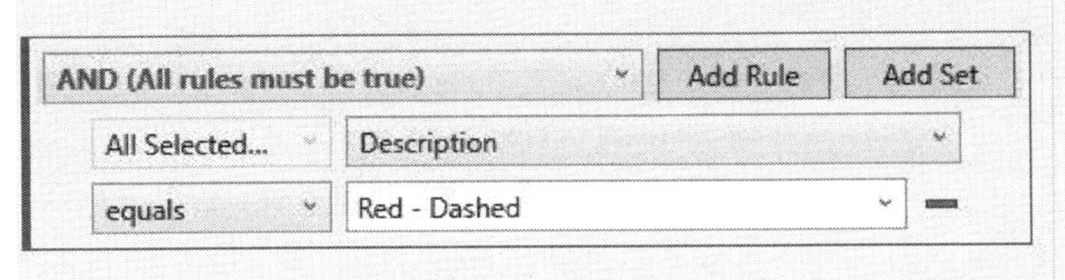

Select **Description** from the parameter list.

Select **equals**.

Select **Red-Dashed**.

Click **Apply**.

You can use the drop-down list to determine which criteria to use.

7.

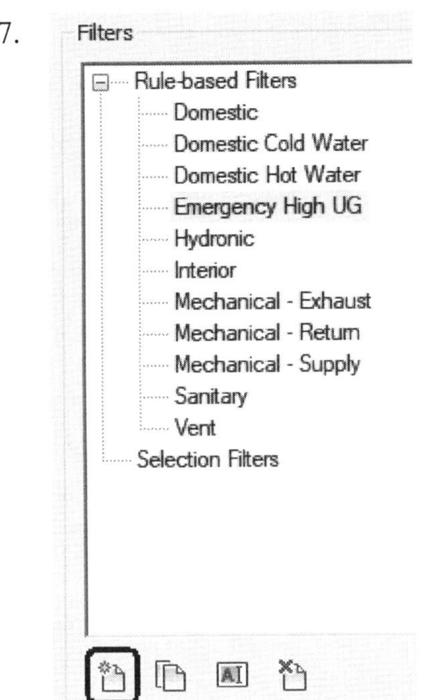

Clicking Apply keeps the dialog open and allows you to continue creating filters.

Click the **New** filter icon located at the lower left of the Filters palette.

8.

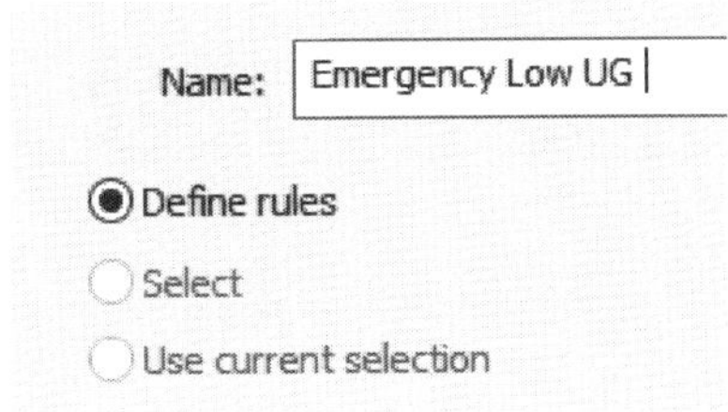

Type **Emergency Low UG** in the Name field.

This filter will control the display properties for the underground emergency low conduit.

Click **OK**.

9.

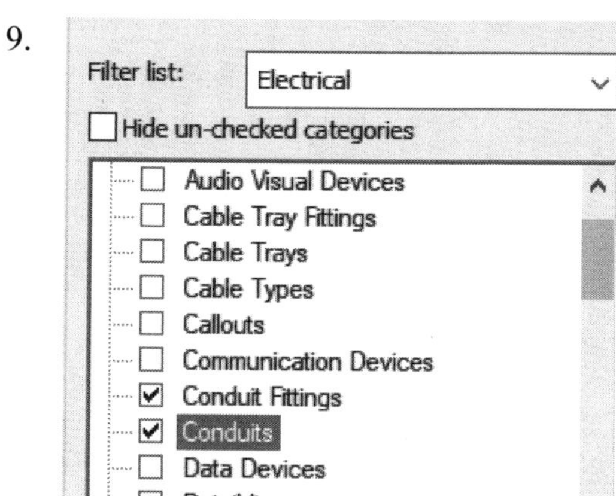

Place a check next to **Conduits** and **Conduit Fittings** in the Category panel.

10.

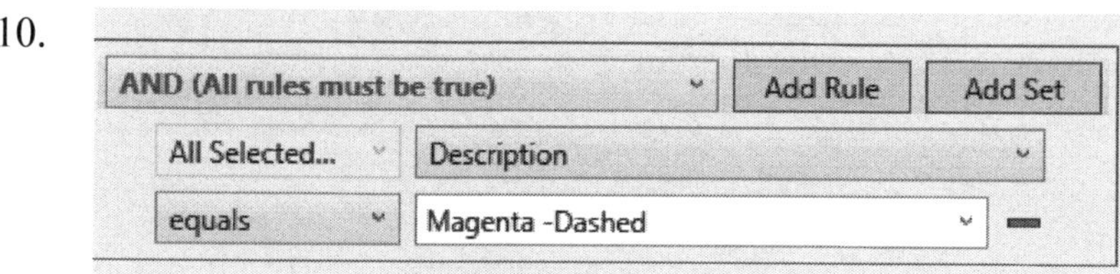

Select **Description** from the parameter list.

Select **equals**.

You can use the drop-down list to determine which criteria to use.

Select **Magenta-Dashed**.

Click **Apply**.

11. 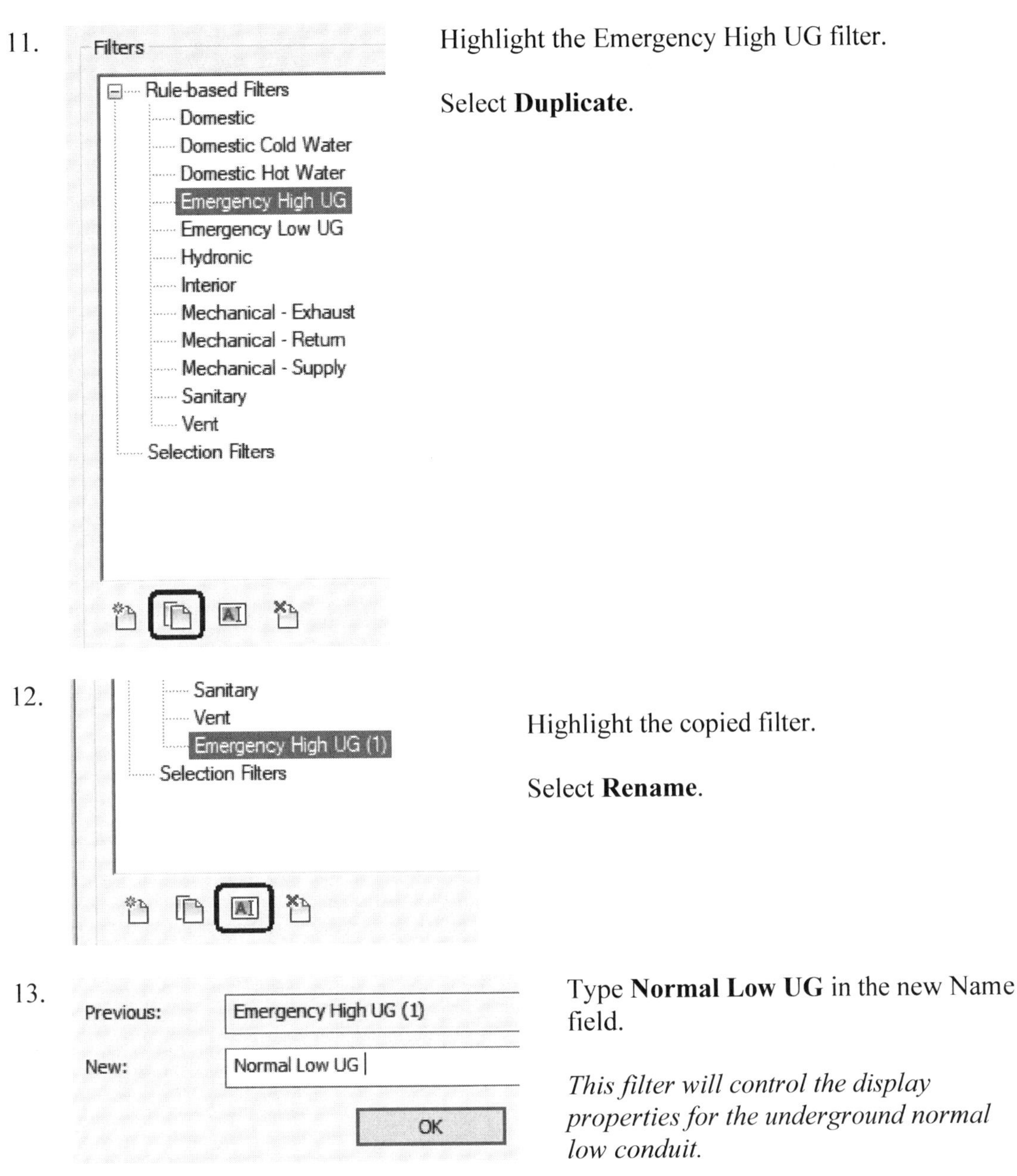

Highlight the Emergency High UG filter.

Select **Duplicate**.

12. Highlight the copied filter.

Select **Rename**.

13. Type **Normal Low UG** in the new Name field.

This filter will control the display properties for the underground normal low conduit.

Click **OK**.

14.

Because you used DUPLICATE, the conduits and conduit fittings categories are already selected.

15.

Because you used DUPLICATE, the filter rules are already set up.

Change the color and linetype to **Blue-Dashed**.

Click **Apply**.

16.

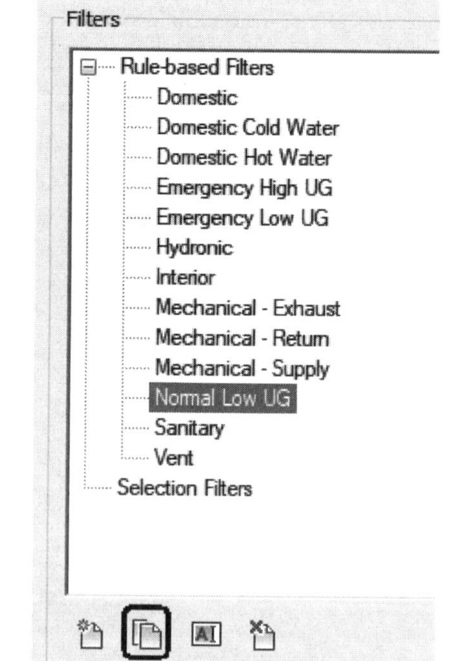

Highlight the **Normal Low UG** filter.

Select **Duplicate**.

17. Highlight the copied filter.

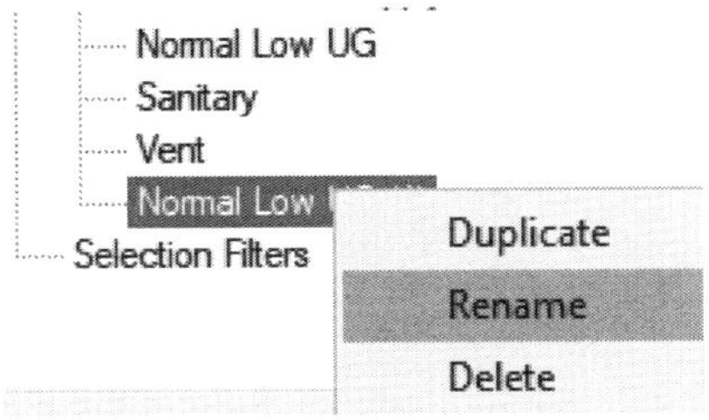

Right click and select **Rename**.

18. Type **Normal High UG** in the new Name field.

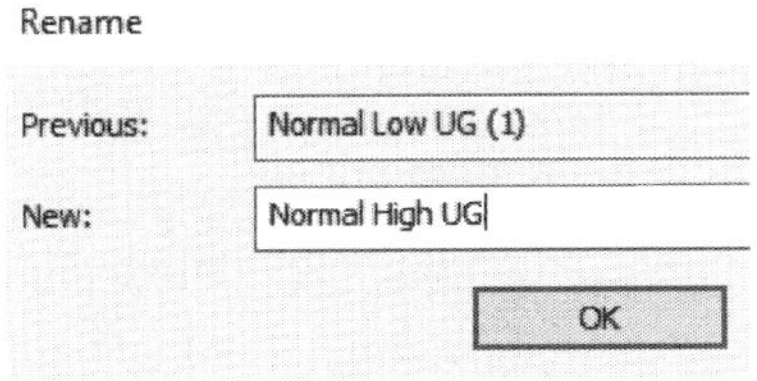

This filter will control the display properties for the underground normal high conduit.

Click **OK**.

19. Verify that Conduit Fittings and Conduits are checked.

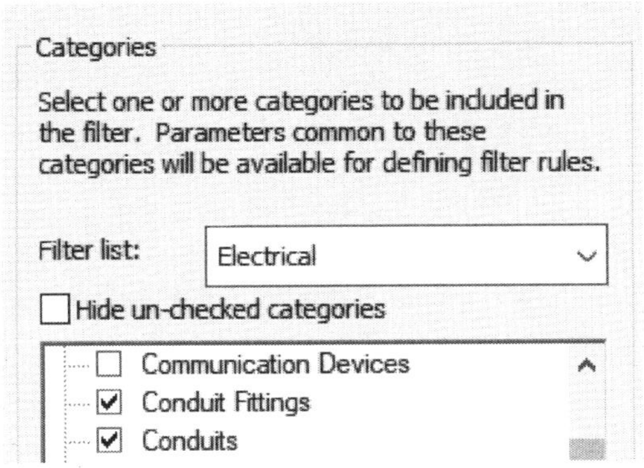

20. Because you used DUPLICATE, the filter rules are already set up.

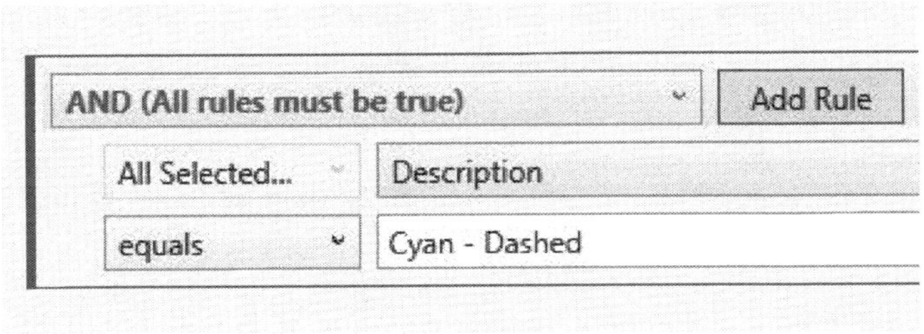

Change the color and linetype to **Cyan-Dashed**.

Click **Apply**.

21.

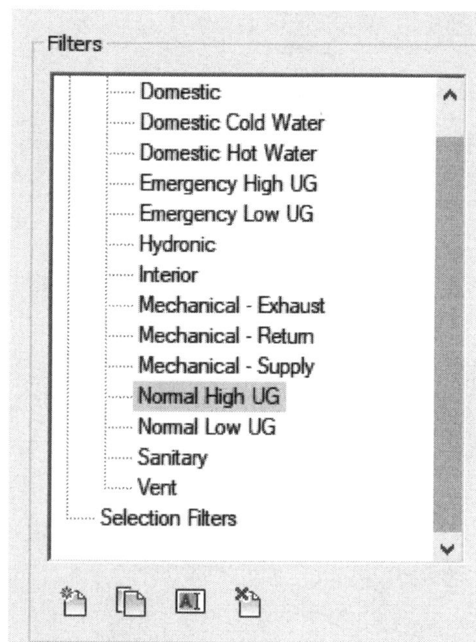

Check the filters list and verify that you have defined four filters:

- Emergency High UG
- Emergency Low UG
- Normal High UG
- Normal Low UG

Click **OK** to close the Filters palette.

22.   Save as *ex5-3.rvt*.

Exercise 5-4:

Applying View Filters to a View

Drawing Name: *conduit_view_setting.rvt*
Estimated Time: 10 minutes

This exercise reinforces the following skills:
- View Filters
- Conduits

1.   Open **Vault Level** floor plan.

Hint: You can type vault to search for the view.

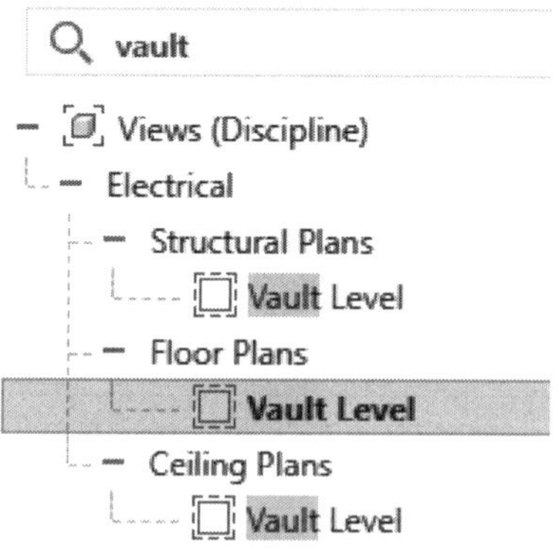

2.  Switch to the View ribbon.

Visibility/ Graphics

Select the **Visibility/Graphics** tool.
You can also access the Visibility/Graphics palette by typing VV.

3.  Select the **Filters** tab.

s   Filters

4.  Click **Add.**

Add

5.

Select one or more filters to insert.

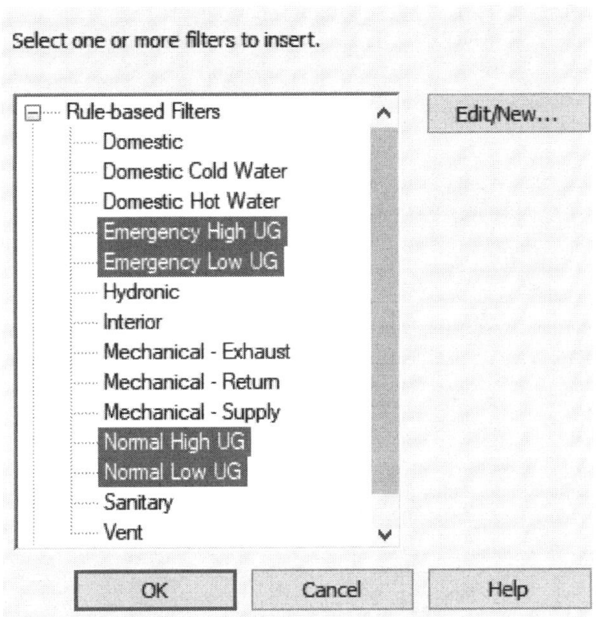

Hold down the CTL key and select the four filters used for conduits:

- Emergency High UG
- Emergency Low UG
- Normal High UG
- Normal Low UG

Click **OK.**

6. 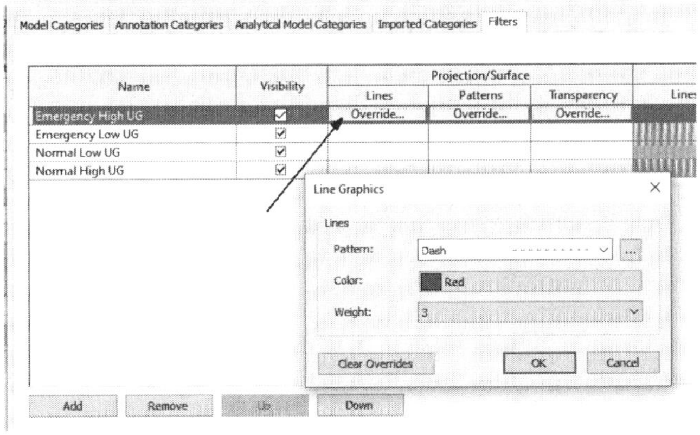 Highlight the **Emergency High UG** conduit filter.

Click in the cell in the Lines column.
Set the Pattern to **Dash**.
Set the Color to **Red**.
Set the Weight to **3**.

Click **OK.**

7.

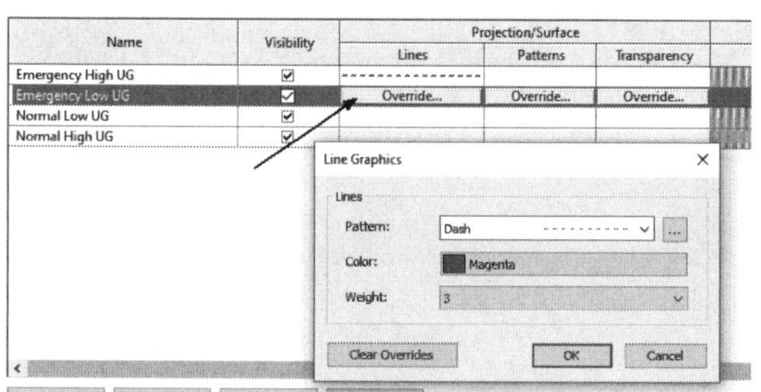

A preview of how the conduit will be displayed is shown.

8.

Highlight the **Emergency Low UG** conduit filter.

Click in the cell in the Lines column.
Set the Pattern to **Dash**.
Set the Color to **Magenta**.
Set the Weight to **3**.

Click **OK**.

9.

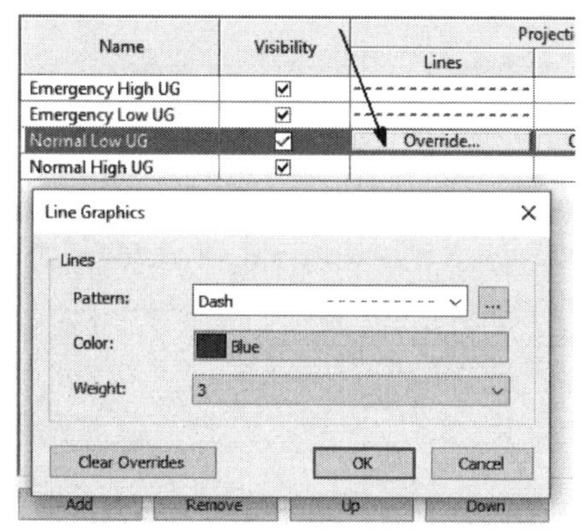

Highlight the **Normal Low UG** conduit filter.

Click in the cell in the Lines column.
Set the Pattern to **Dash**.
Set the Color to **Blue**.
Set the Weight to **3**.

Click **OK**.

10.

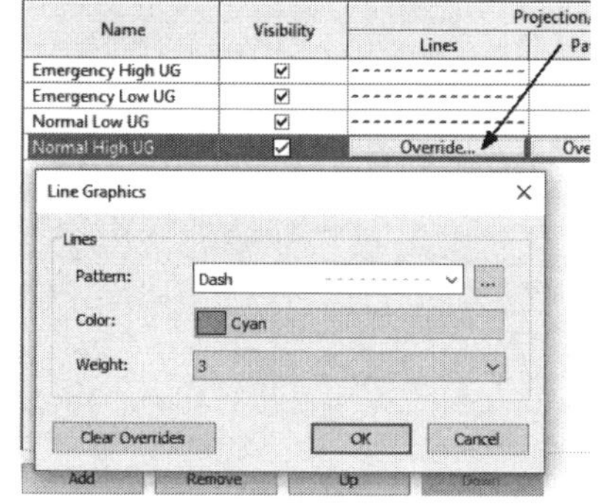

Highlight the **Normal High UG** conduit filter.

Click in the cell in the Lines column.
Set the Pattern to **Dash**.
Set the Color to **Cyan**.
Set the Weight to **3**.

Click **OK**.

11.

Name	Enable Filter	Visibility	Proj
			Lines
Emergency High UG	☑	☑	------------
Emergency Low UG	☑	☑	------------
Normal Low UG	☑	☑	------------
Normal High UG	☑	☑	------------

Verify that all four filters have been defined correctly.

Click **OK**.

12. Save as *ex5-4.rvt*.

Exercise 5-5:

Placing Conduits

Drawing Name: *add_conduit_2.rvt*
Estimated Time: 15 minutes

This exercise reinforces the following skills:
- Conduit Fittings
- Conduits

1. 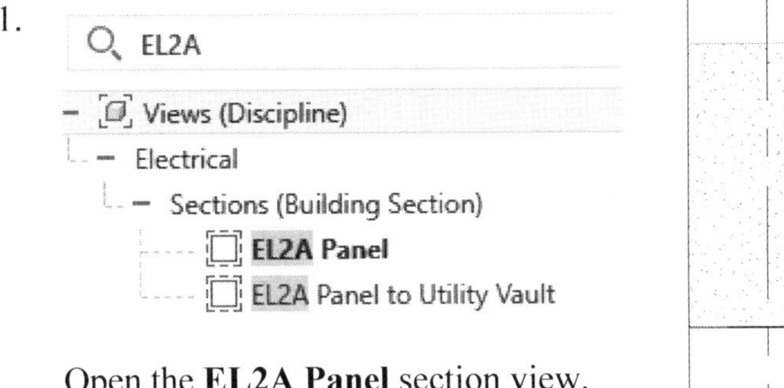 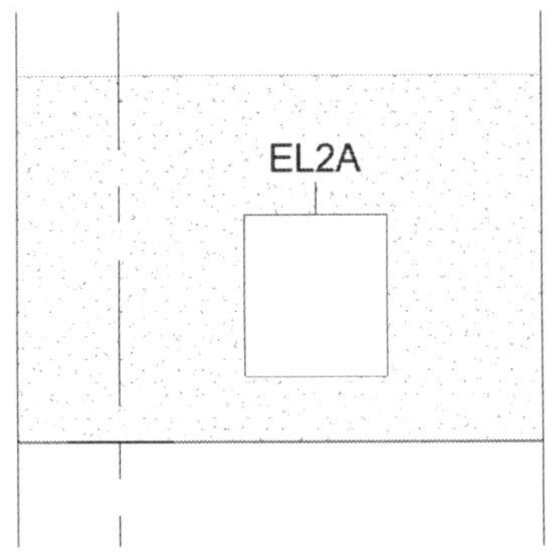

   Open the **EL2A Panel** section view.

2. 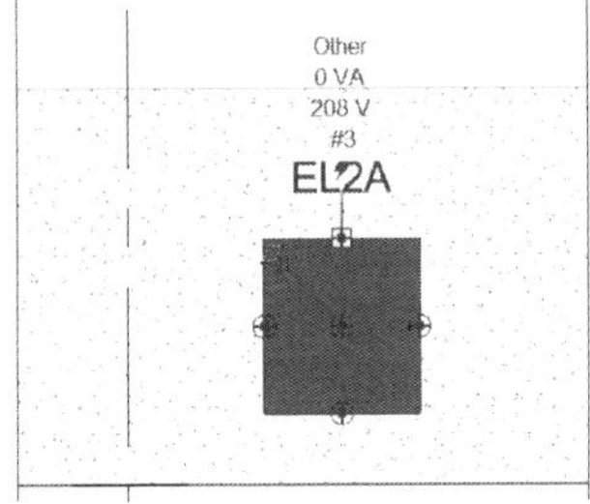 Select the panel so it is highlighted.

3.

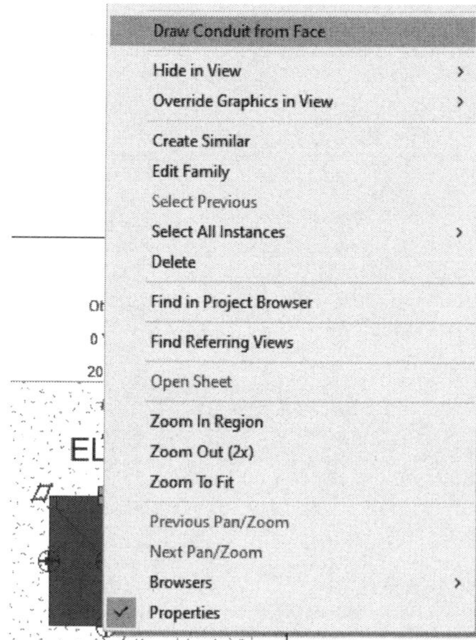

Select the bottom connector.
Right click and select **Draw Conduit from Face**.

4.

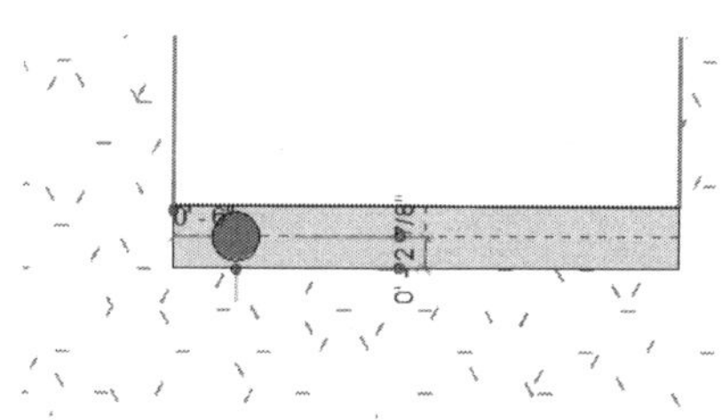

Adjust the position of the connector so it is 6" from the left side.

5.

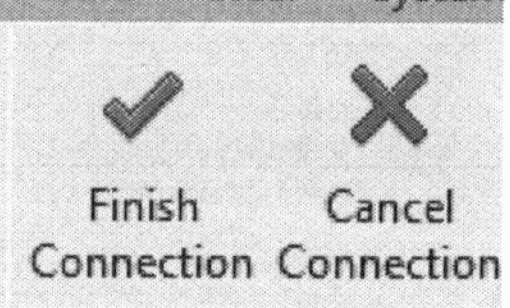

Click on **Finish Connection** on the ribbon.

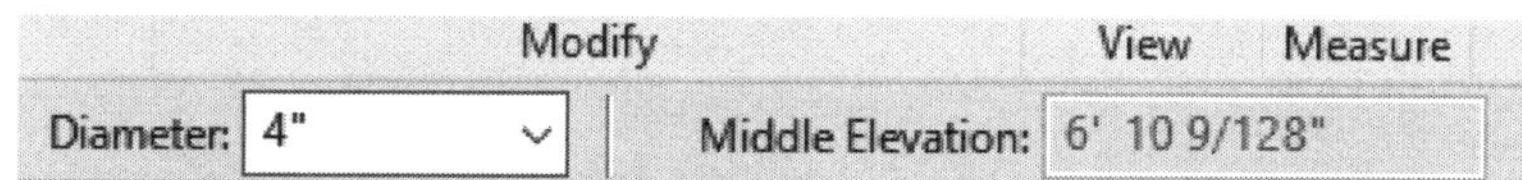

6.   On the Options bar: Set the diameter to **4"**.

7.

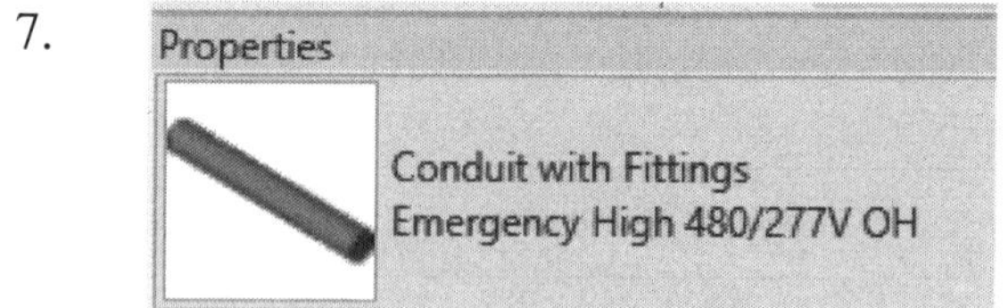

Using the Type Selector on the Properties palette:
Set the Conduit Type to **Emergency High 480/277V OH**.

8.

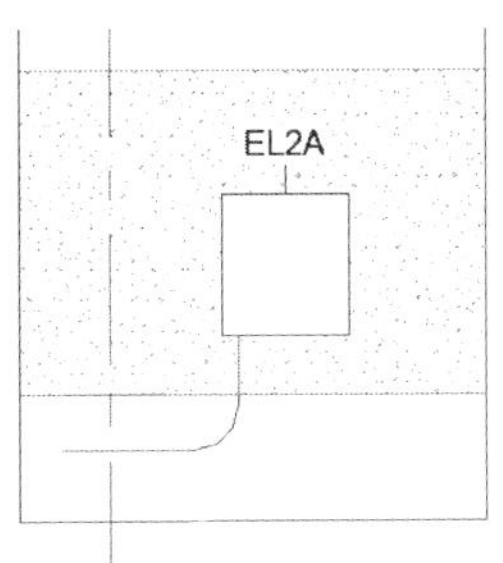

Draw the conduit down 3' 6" and to the left.

Notice the conduit is the correct color, but not the fitting.
Cancel out of the command.
Select the fitting.

9.

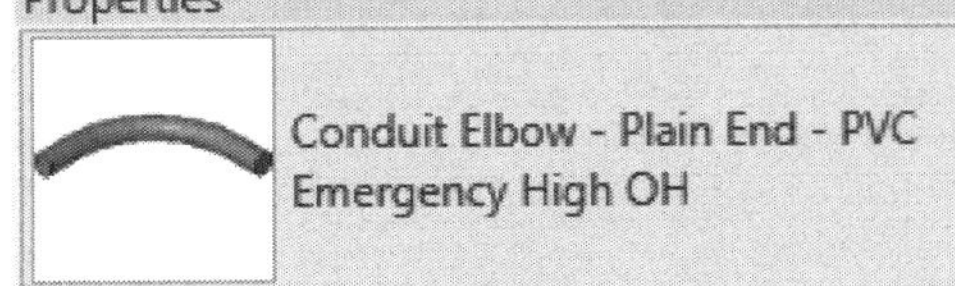

Use the Type Selector to set the fitting to
Conduit Elbow – Plain End – PVC Emergency High UG.

Hint: Look towards the bottom of the list or use search.

10.

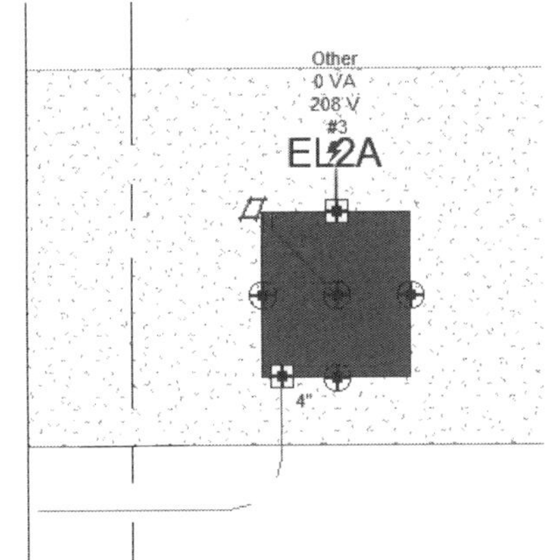

Select the panel so it is highlighted.

11.

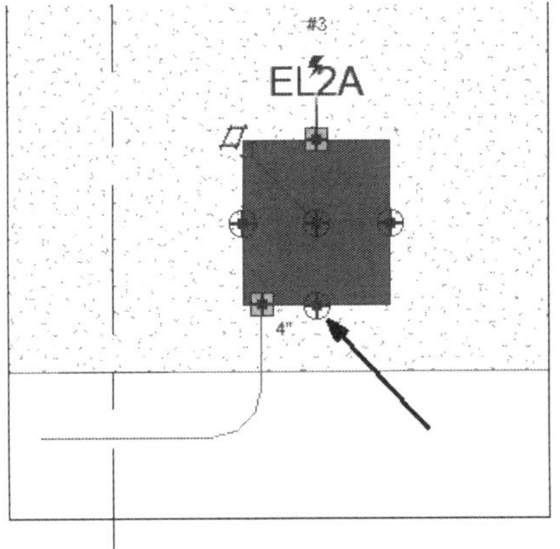

Select the bottom center connector.

Notice there is a new connector available on the bottom face.

Right click and select **Draw Conduit from Face**.

12.

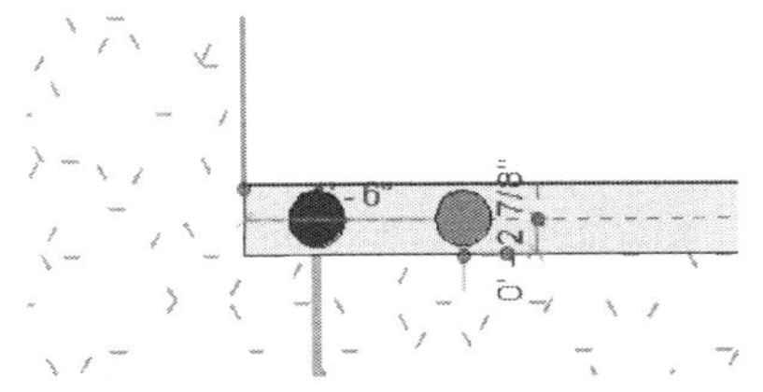

Adjust the position of the connector so it is 1' 6" from the left side.

13. 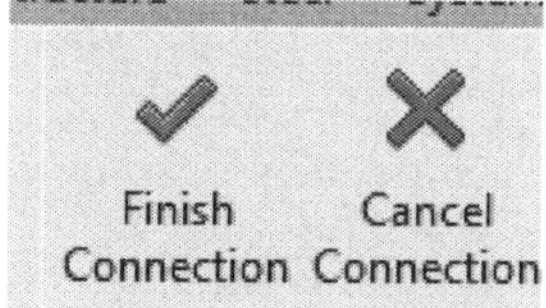

Click on **Finish Connection** on the ribbon.

14. 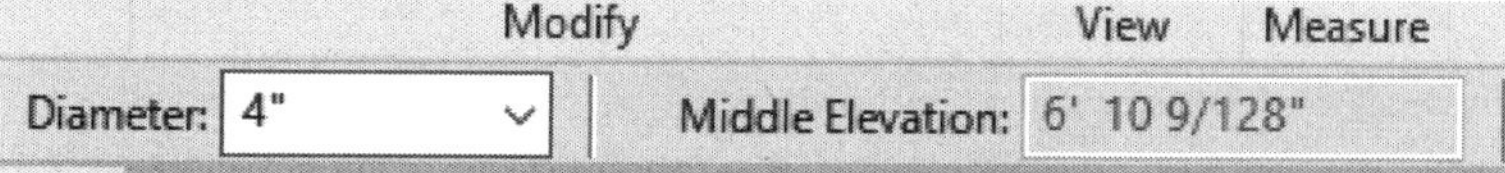

15. On the Options bar: Set the diameter to **4"**.

16. 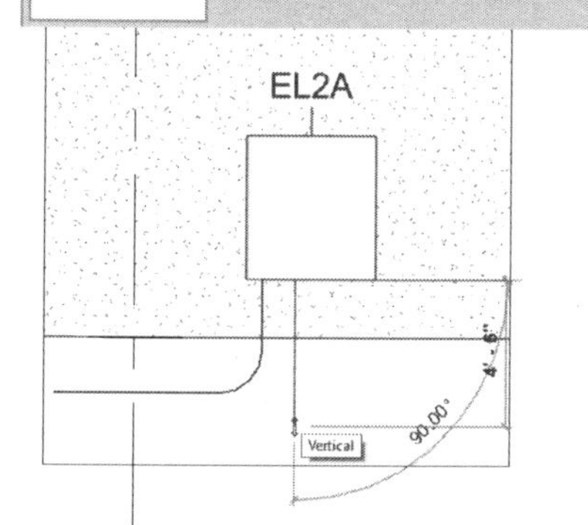

Using the Type Selector on the Properties palette: Set the Conduit Type to **Emergency Low 120/208V OH**.

17.

Draw the conduit down 4' 6" and to the left.

Notice the conduit is the correct color, but not the fitting.

Cancel out of the command.

Select the fitting.

18. 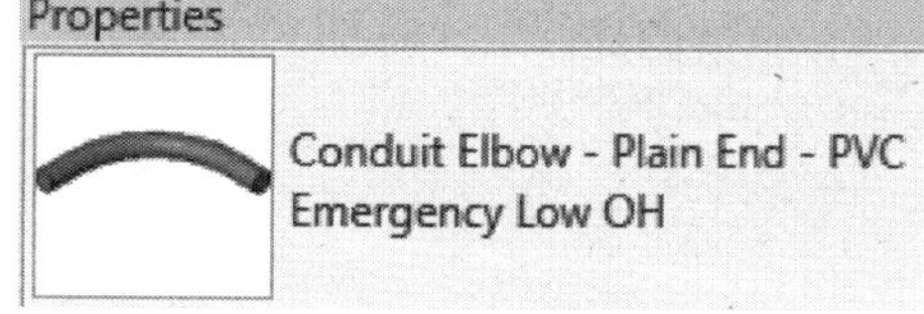

Use the Type Selector to change the fitting to **Emergency Low UG.**

The color should update.
Left click in the window to release the selection.

19. 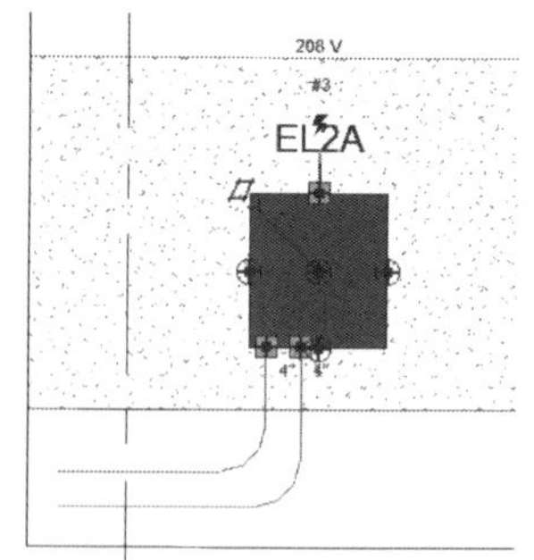

Select the panel so it is highlighted.

20.

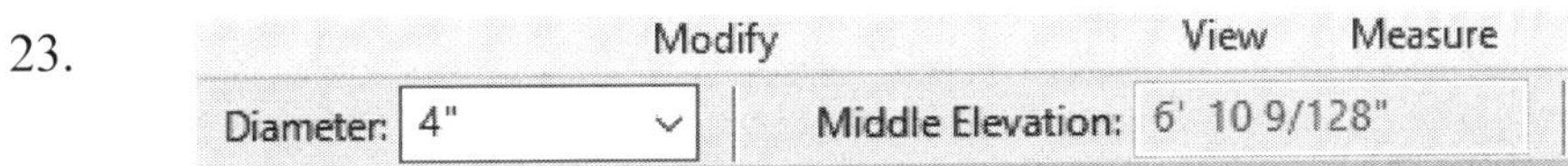

Select the bottom connector that doesn't have a conduit attached.

Notice there is a new connector available on the bottom face.

Right click and select **Draw Conduit from Face**.

21.

Adjust the position of the connector so it is 2' 6" from the left side.

22.

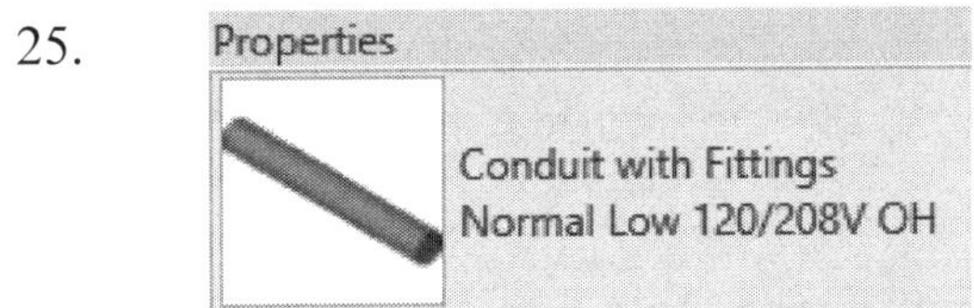

Click on **Finish Connection** on the ribbon.

23.

Modify	View	Measure

| Diameter: | 4" | Middle Elevation: | 6' 10 9/128" |

24.   On the Options bar: Set the diameter to **4"**.

25.

Properties

Conduit with Fittings
Normal Low 120/208V OH

Using the Type Selector on the Properties palette: Set the Conduit Type to **Normal Low 120/208V OH**.

26.

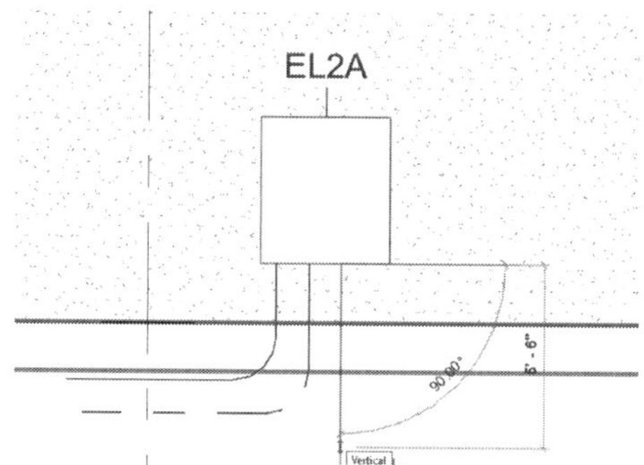

Draw the conduit down 5' 6" and to the left.

Notice the conduit is the correct color, but not the fitting.

Cancel out of the command.

Select the fitting.

27.

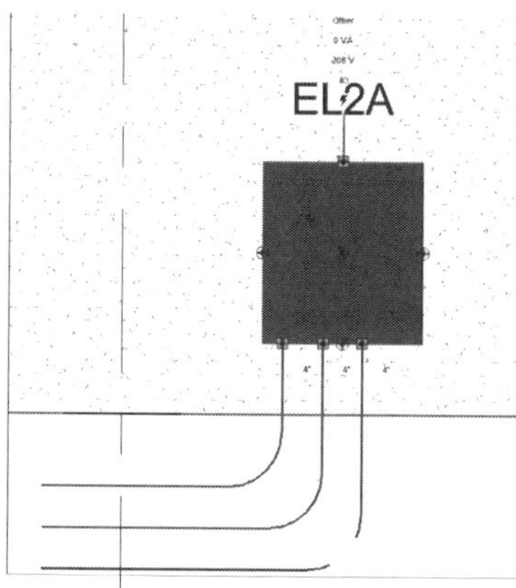

Use the Type Selector on the Properties panel to change the fitting to use the **Normal Low UG** fitting type.
Release the selection.

28.

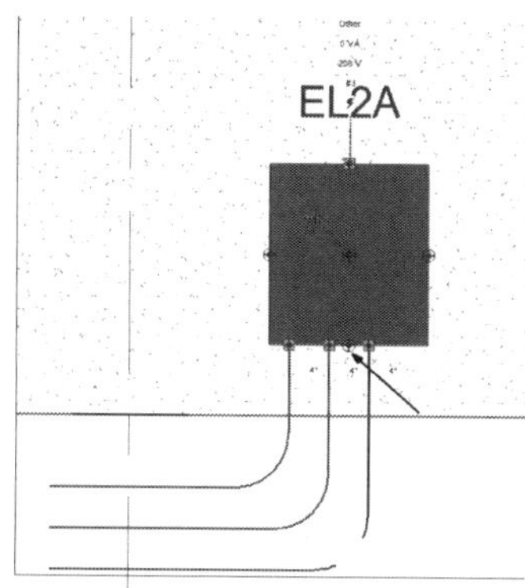

Select the panel so it is highlighted.

29.

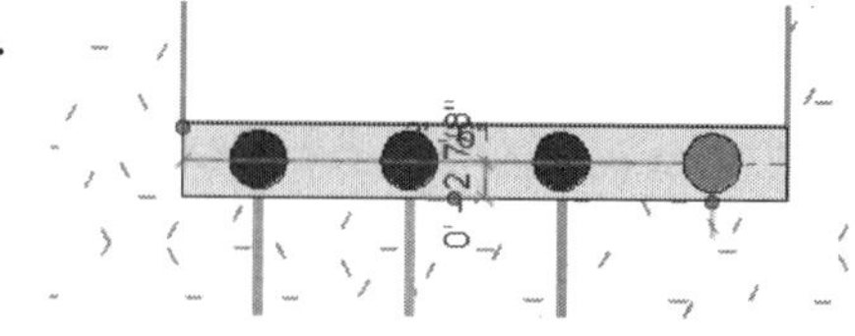

Select the bottom connector that doesn't have a conduit attached.

Notice there is a new connector available on the bottom face.

Right click and select **Draw Conduit from Face**.

30.

Adjust the position of the connector so it is 3' 6" from the left side.

31.  Click on **Finish Connection** on the ribbon.

32. 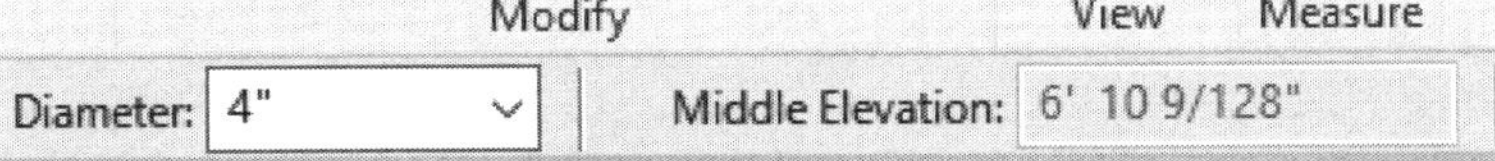

33. On the Options bar: Set the diameter to **4"**.

34. 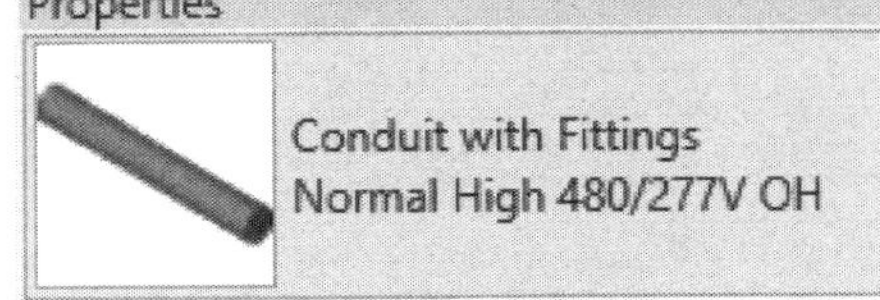 Using the Type Selector on the Properties palette: Set the Conduit Type to **Normal High 480/277V OH.**

35. 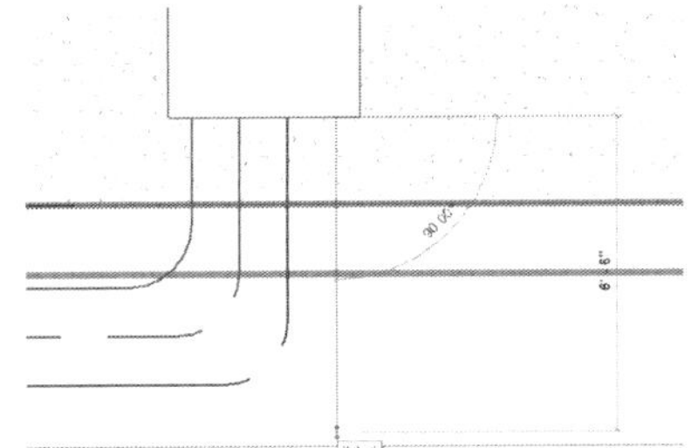 Draw the conduit down 6' 6" and to the left.

Notice the conduit is the correct color, but not the fitting. You may need to drag the cropping for the view down to see the conduit.

Cancel out of the command.

Select the fitting.

36. 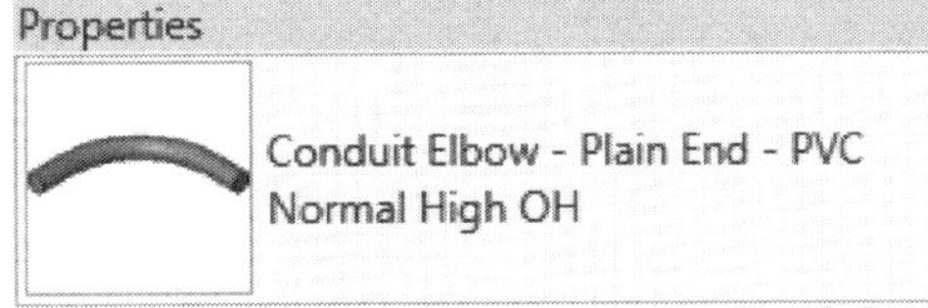 Use the Type Selector on the Properties panel to change the fitting to use the **Normal High OH** fitting type.

37. 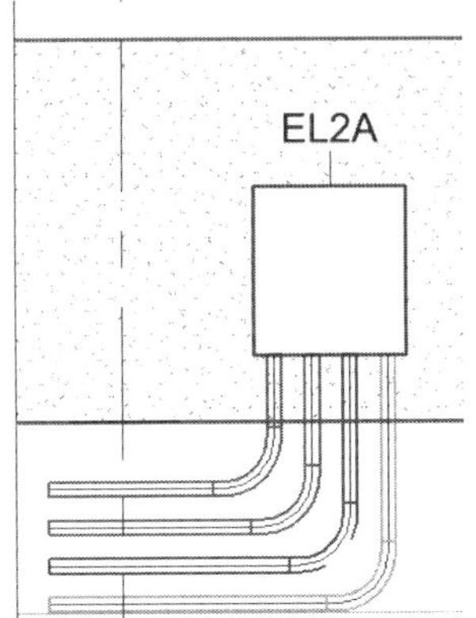 You should have four conduits from the panel.

Each conduit should display a different color.

You can use the Type Selector to change the conduits to display as underground or overhead.

Use the Display Bar to change the Detail Level to Fine to see how the conduit display changes.

Save as *ex5-5.rvt*.

Exercise 5-6:

Assigning Conduit Fittings to Conduit Families

Drawing Name: *conduit_types.rvt*
Estimated Time: 15 minutes

This exercise reinforces the following skills:
- Conduit Fittings
- Conduits

1. Open the **EL2A Panel** section view.

   - Sections (Building Section)
     - EL2A Panel
     - Main Electrical Room 1

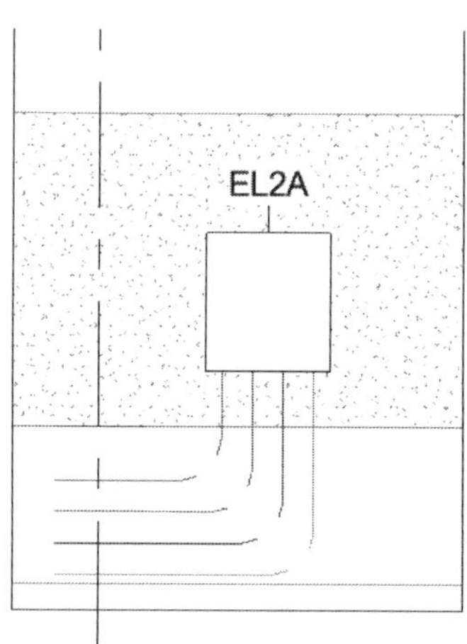

2. In the Project Browser:

   Enable the **Families** filter.

   Locate and expand the *Conduit with Fittings* category.

3.

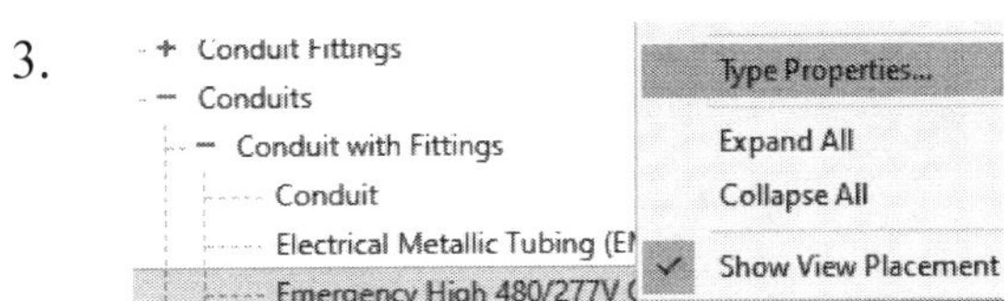

Highlight the **Emergency High 480/277V OH** family.

Right click and select **Type Properties**.

4.

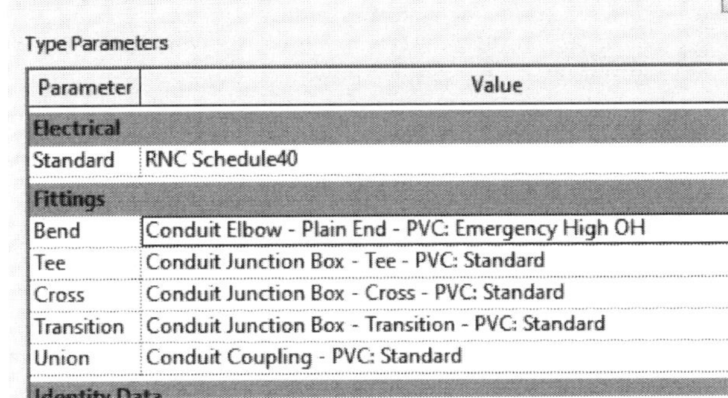

For the Bend parameter, use the drop-down list to select the **Emergency High OH** Conduit Elbow.

Press **Apply**.

5.

Select **Emergency High 480/277V UG** from the Type drop-down list.

6.

Parameter	Value
Electrical	
Standard	RNC Schedule40
Fittings	
Bend	Conduit Elbow - Plain End - PVC: Emergency High UG
Tee	Conduit Junction Box - Tee - PVC: Standard
Cross	Conduit Junction Box - Cross - PVC: Standard
Transition	Conduit Junction Box - Transition - PVC: Standard
Union	Conduit Coupling - PVC: Standard
Identity Data	

For the Bend parameter, use the drop-down list to select the **Emergency High UG** Conduit Elbow.

Press **Apply**.

7.

Select **Emergency Low 120/208V OH** from the Type drop-down list.

8.

Type: Emergency Low 120/208V OH

Type Parameters

Parameter	Value
Electrical	
Standard	RNC Schedule40
Fittings	
Bend	Conduit Elbow - Plain End - PVC: Emergency Low OH
Tee	Conduit Junction Box - Tee - PVC: Standard
Cross	Conduit Junction Box - Cross - PVC: Standard
Transition	Conduit Junction Box - Transition - PVC: Standard
Union	Conduit Coupling - PVC: Standard

For the Bend parameter, use the drop-down list to select the **Emergency Low OH** Conduit Elbow.

Press **Apply**.

9.

Family: System Family: Conduit with Fittings

Type: Emergency Low 120/208V UG

Select **Emergency Low 120/208V UG** from the Type drop-down list.

10.

Type: Emergency Low 120/208V UG

Type Parameters

Parameter	Value
Electrical	
Standard	RNC Schedule40
Fittings	
Bend	Conduit Elbow - Plain End - PVC: Emergency Low UG
Tee	Conduit Junction Box - Tee - PVC: Standard

For the Bend parameter, use the drop-down list to select the **Emergency Low UG** Conduit Elbow.

Press **OK**.

11. Save as ex5-6.rvt.

Exercise 5-7:
Adding a Conduit

Drawing Name: *add_conduit.rvt*
Estimated Time: 30 minutes

This exercise reinforces the following skills:
- ❑ Conduit Fittings
- ❑ Conduits

1. 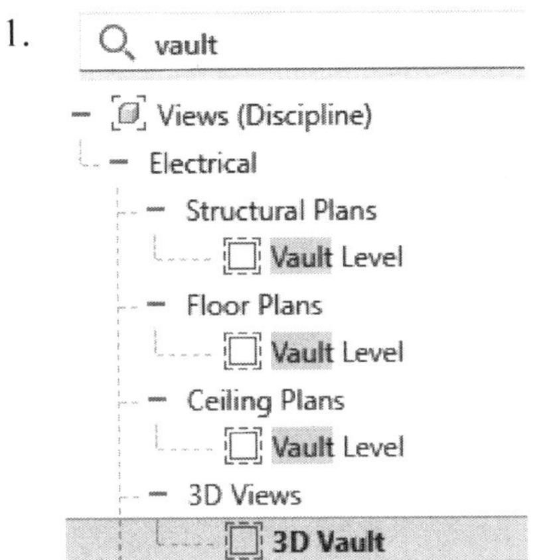
Type **vault** in the search field in the Project Browser.

Open the **3D Vault** view.

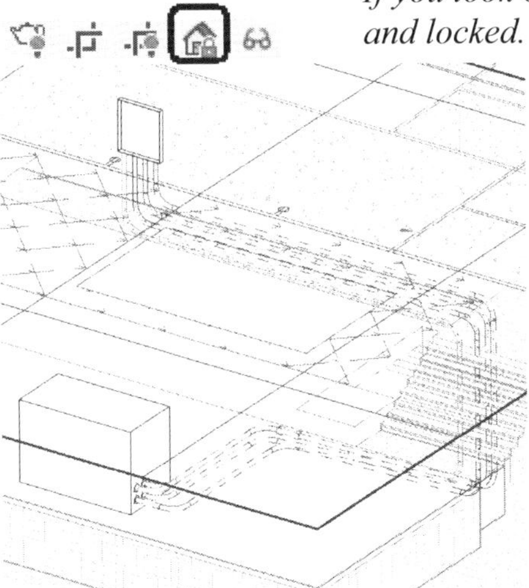

If you look on the display bar, you see that the 3D view is saved and locked. This means you can't modify this view.

We want to place a conduit using the existing conduit to connect to the utility vault located below ground.

This is what it should look like when we are done.

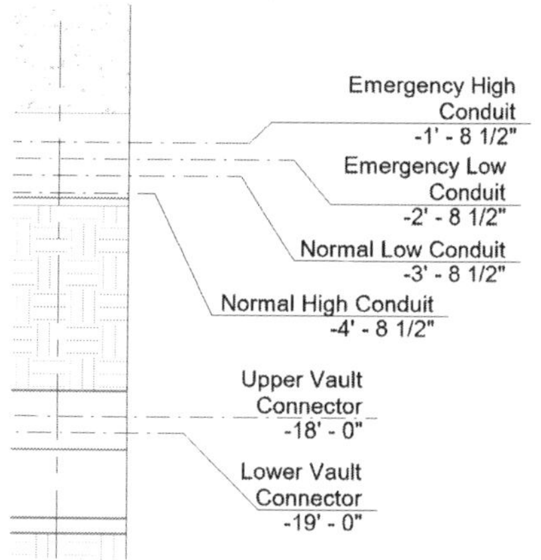

I have added levels on the EL2A Panel to Utility Vault section view to help you see how far down you need to bring the conduits to align them with the connectors located at the utility vault.

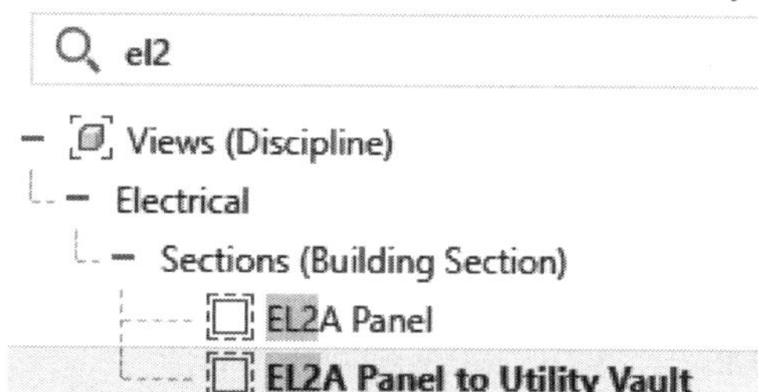

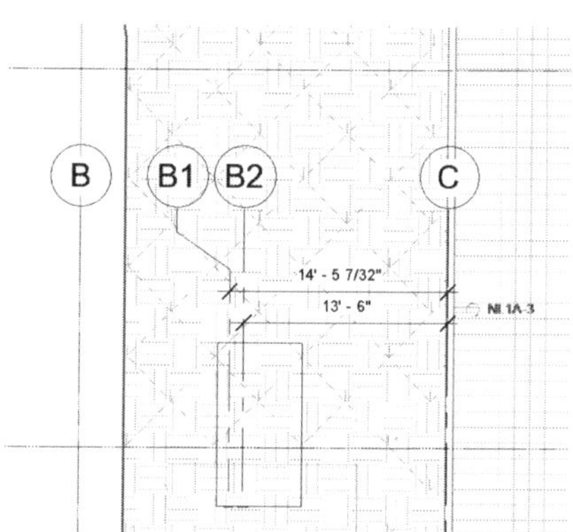

If you activate the Vault Level Floor plan view, you see how far from the wall center each set of connectors is located.

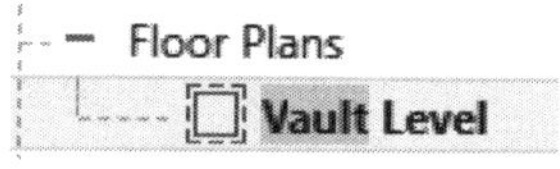

The vault has two rows of connectors with two connectors on each row – a total of four connectors for the four conduits.

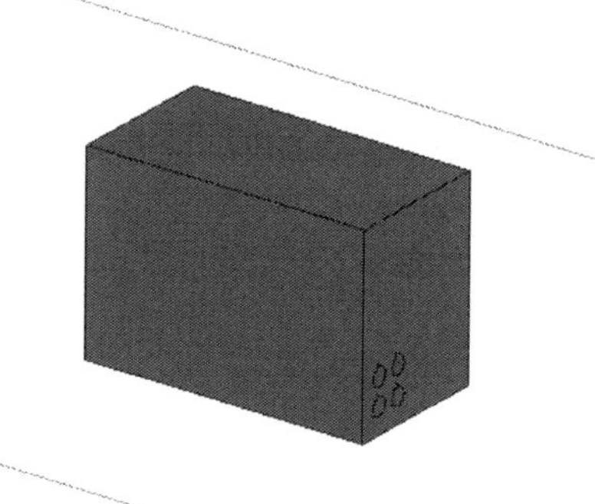

2.   Open the **EL2A Panel to Utility Vault** SectionView.

3.

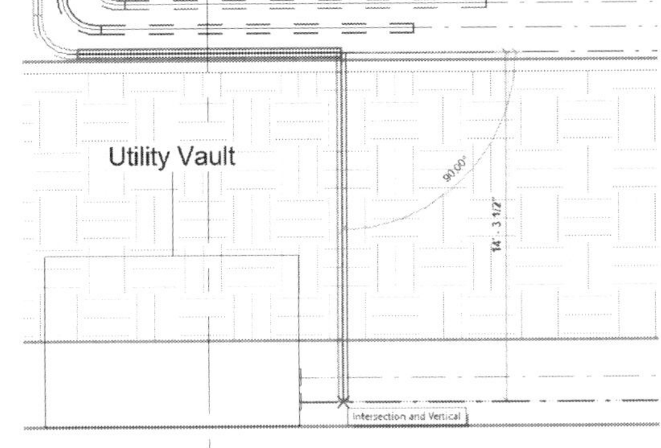

To continue an existing conduit:

Select the end point of the **Normal High** cyan conduit.

When you select the conduit, you will see the conduit type.

Right click and select **Draw Conduit**.

4.

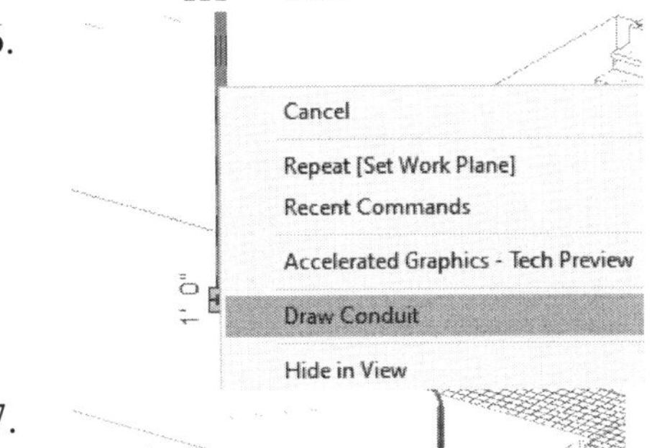

Draw the conduit down towards the vault level.

Draw the conduit down **14' 3 1/2"** to the lower vault connector level.

Cancel out of the command.

5.

Switch to the **3D Vault** view.

6.

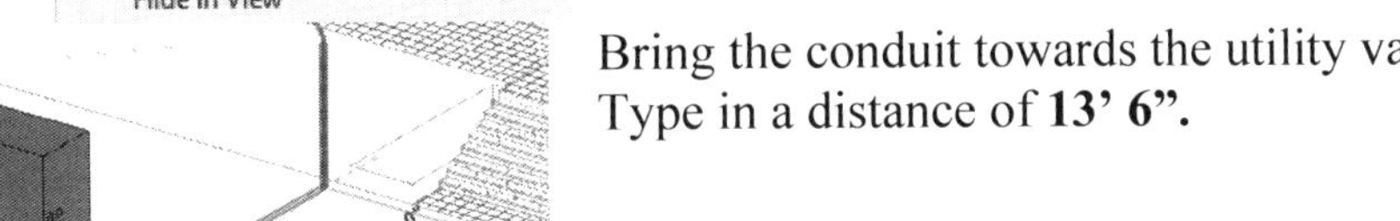

Select the end of the conduit.
Right click and select **Draw Conduit**.

7.

Bring the conduit towards the utility vault.
Type in a distance of **13' 6"**.

8.

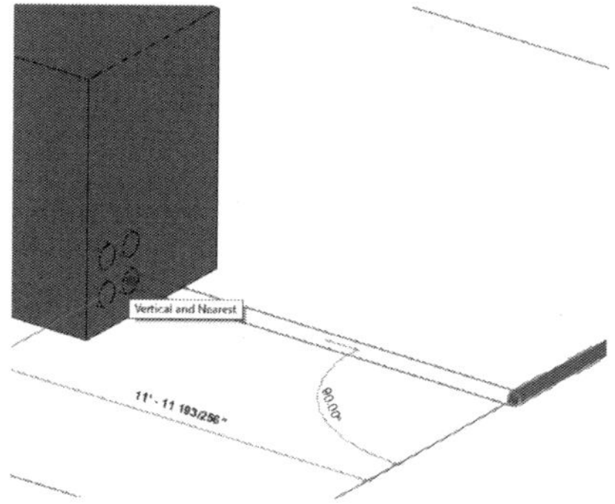

Select the lower right connector on the vault.

9. Select Connector

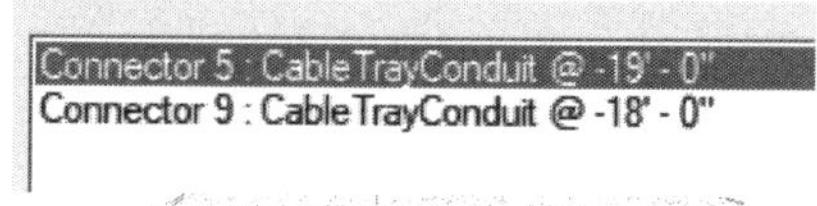

Select **Connector 5**.

Click **OK**.

The conduit should look similar to this image.

10. 3D Views
— 3D Conduit_1
— 3D Vault
— 3D Vault Elevation
— {3D}

Switch to the **3D Conduit_1** view.

You can see how the conduit was routed between the panel and the utility vault.

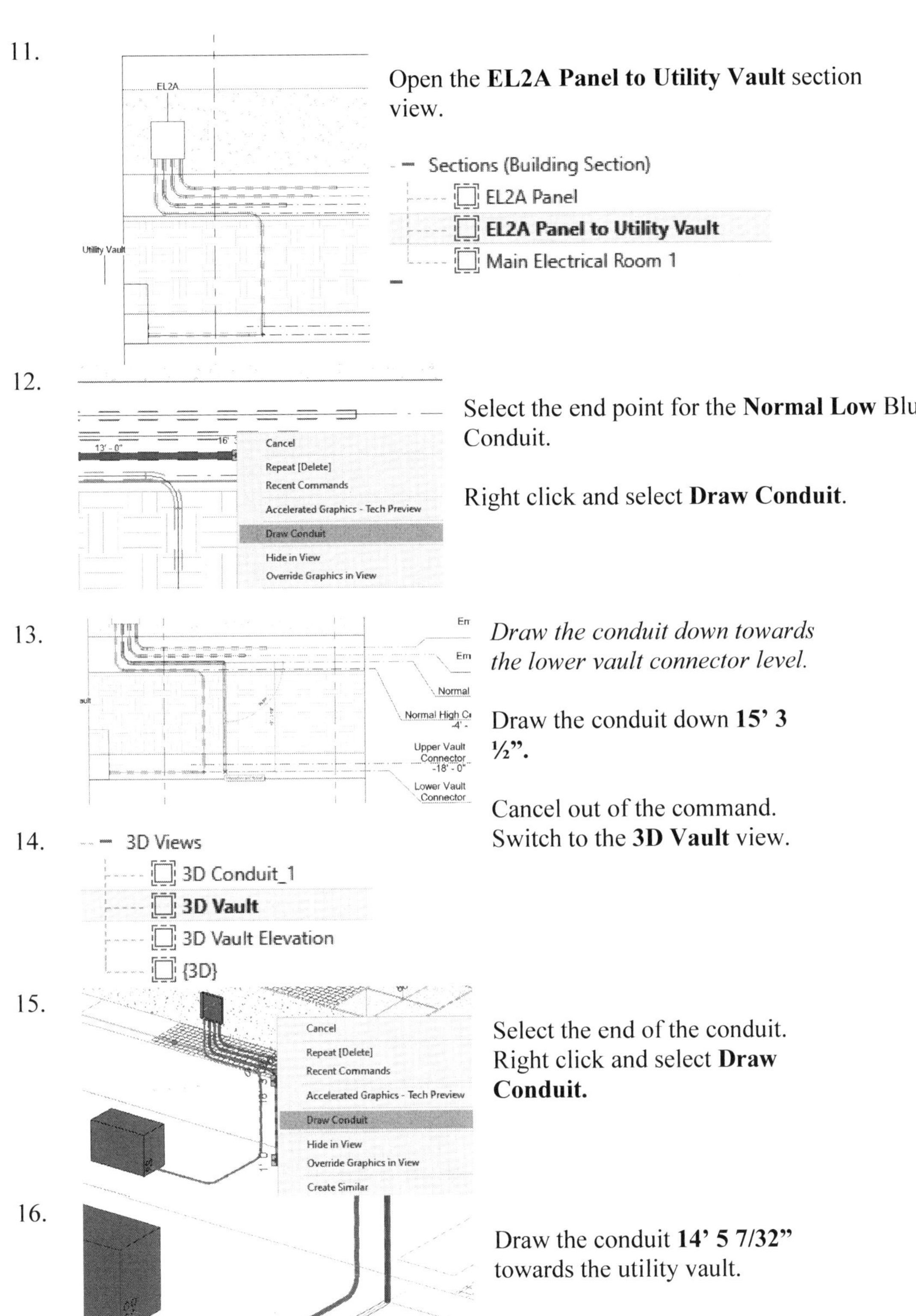

11. Open the **EL2A Panel to Utility Vault** section view.

— Sections (Building Section)
  — EL2A Panel
  — **EL2A Panel to Utility Vault**
  — Main Electrical Room 1

12. Select the end point for the **Normal Low** Blue Conduit.

Right click and select **Draw Conduit**.

13. *Draw the conduit down towards the lower vault connector level.*

Draw the conduit down **15' 3 ½"**.

Cancel out of the command. Switch to the **3D Vault** view.

14. — 3D Views
  — 3D Conduit_1
  — **3D Vault**
  — 3D Vault Elevation
  — {3D}

15. Select the end of the conduit. Right click and select **Draw Conduit.**

16. Draw the conduit **14' 5 7/32"** towards the utility vault.

17.

Select the lower left connector on the vault.

18.

Click **Connector 6.**

Click **OK**.

19.

Switch to the **3D Conduit 1** view.

Your view should look similar to this.

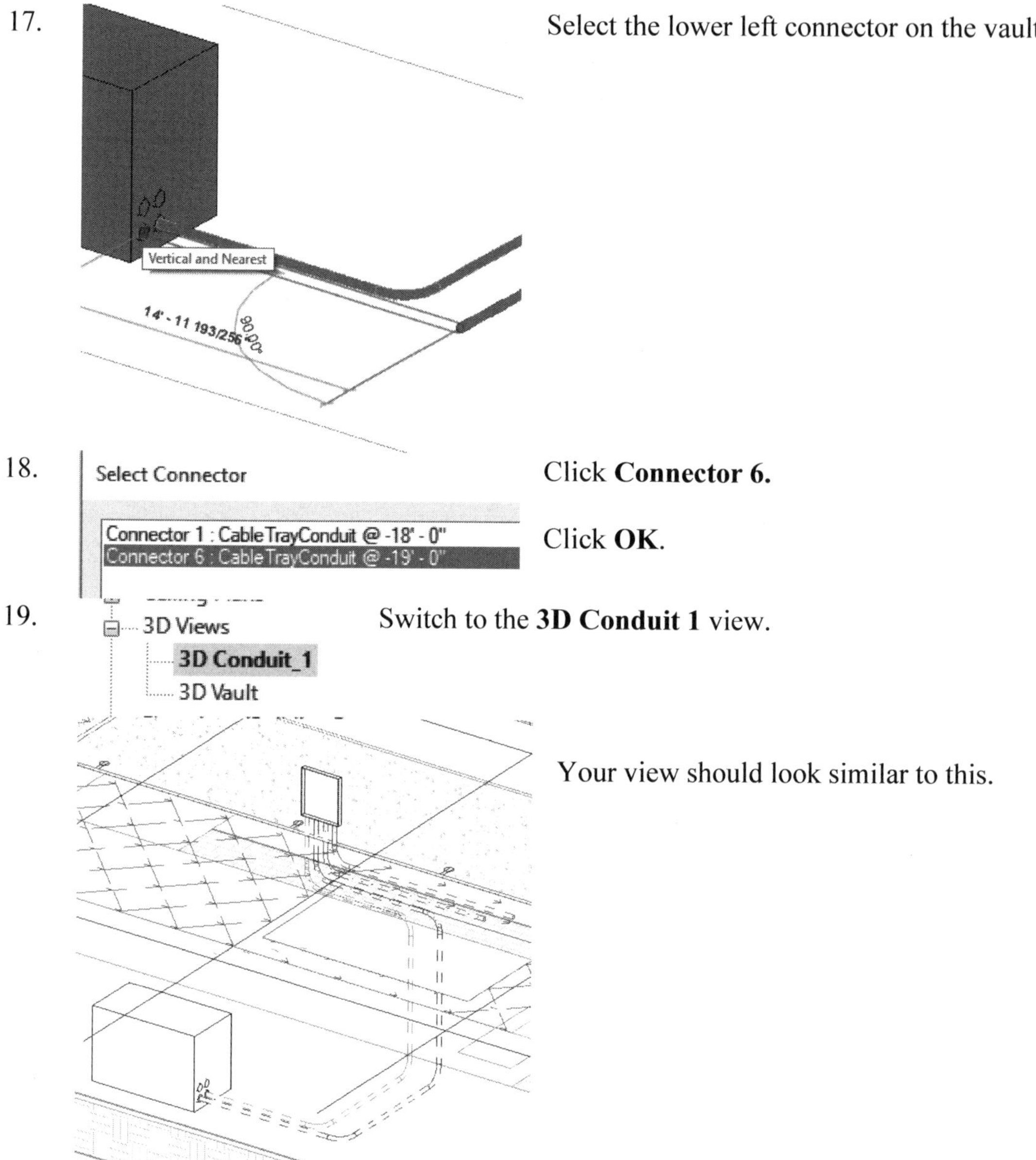

20. 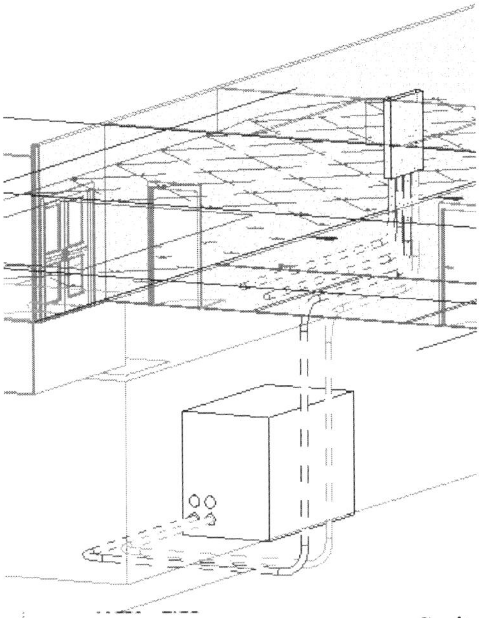 Orbit the view around so you can see how the conduits are routed.

21. 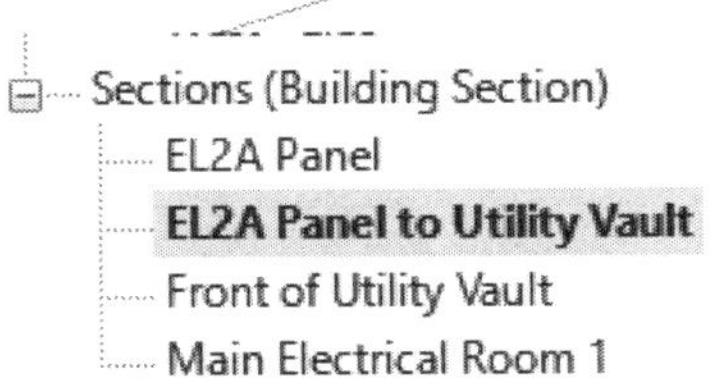 Switch to the **EL2A Panel to Utility Vault** section view.

Sections (Building Section)
- EL2A Panel
- **EL2A Panel to Utility Vault**
- Front of Utility Vault
- Main Electrical Room 1

22. 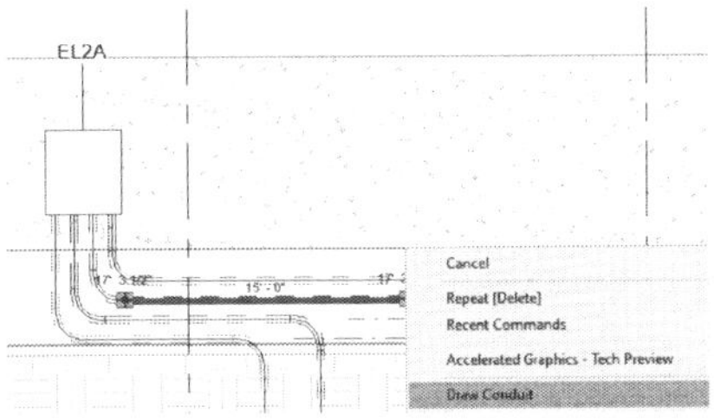 Select the end point for the **Emergency Low Magenta Conduit**.

Right click and select **Draw Conduit**.

23. 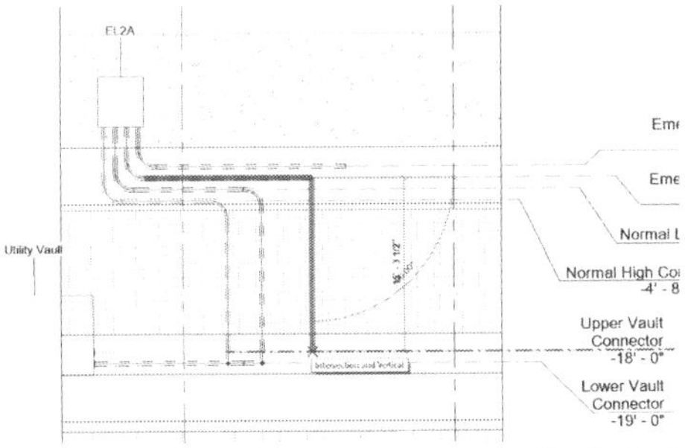 Draw the conduit straight down to the Upper Vault Connector level.

Cancel out of the command.

24. 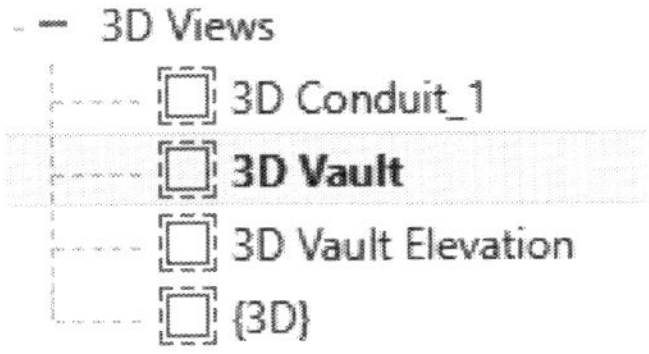 Switch to the **3D Vault** view.

3D Views
- 3D Conduit_1
- **3D Vault**
- 3D Vault Elevation
- {3D}

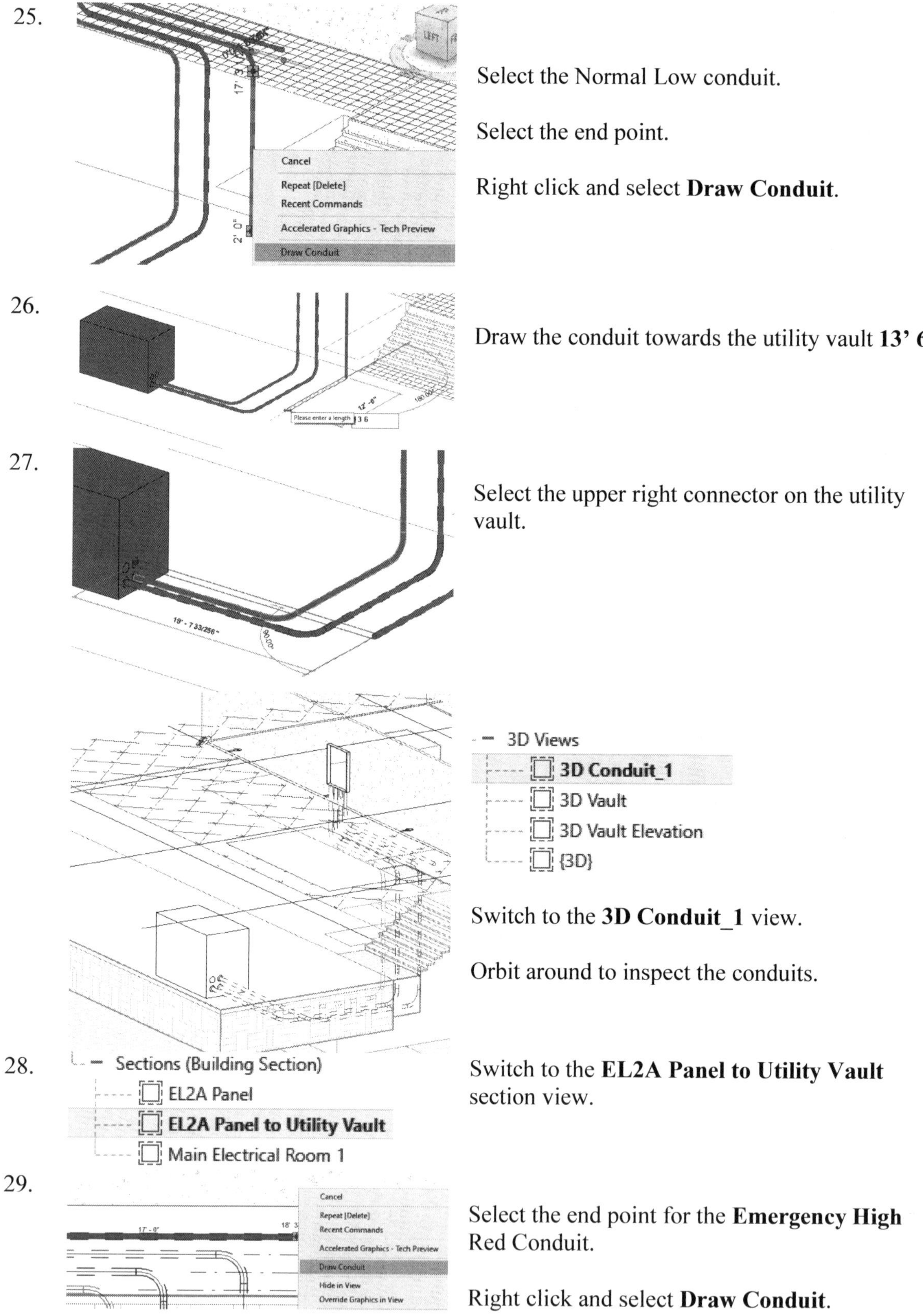

25. Select the Normal Low conduit.

Select the end point.

Right click and select **Draw Conduit**.

26. Draw the conduit towards the utility vault **13' 6"**.

27. Select the upper right connector on the utility vault.

Switch to the **3D Conduit_1** view.

Orbit around to inspect the conduits.

28. Switch to the **EL2A Panel to Utility Vault** section view.

29. Select the end point for the **Emergency High Red Conduit**.

Right click and select **Draw Conduit**.

30. 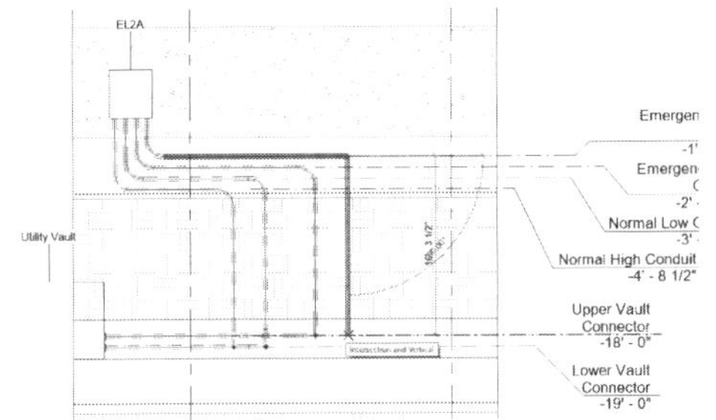

Draw the conduit straight down to the Upper Vault Connector level.

Cancel out of the command.

31. 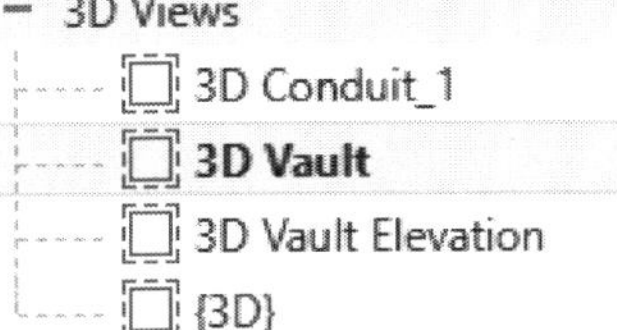

Switch to the **3D Vault** view.

32. 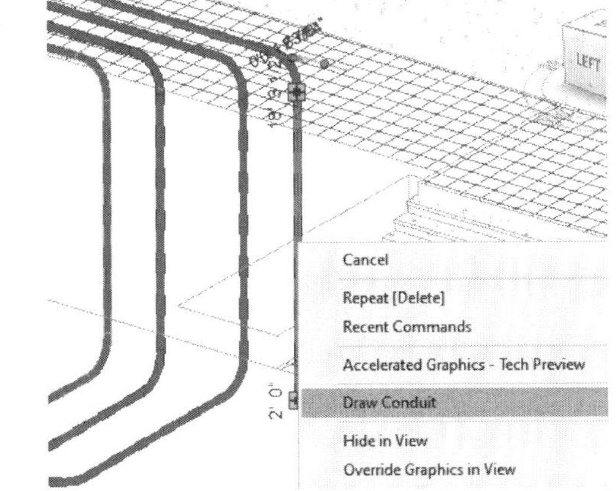

Select the Emergency High conduit.

Select the end point.

Right click and select **Draw Conduit**.

33. 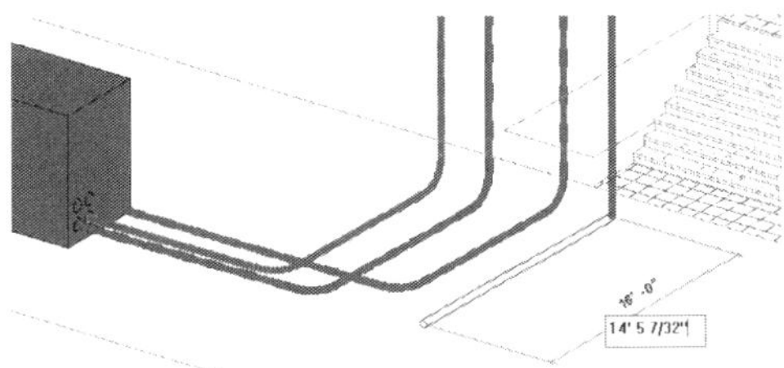

Draw the conduit towards the utility vault **14' 5 7/32"**.

34. 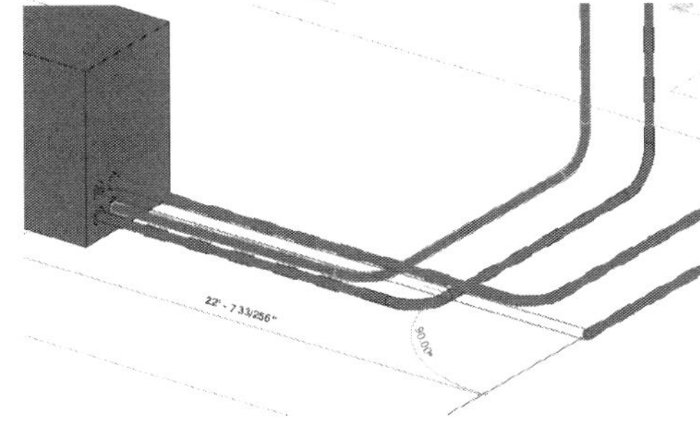

Continue drawing the conduit.
Select the upper left connector on the utility vault.

Cancel out of the command.

35.

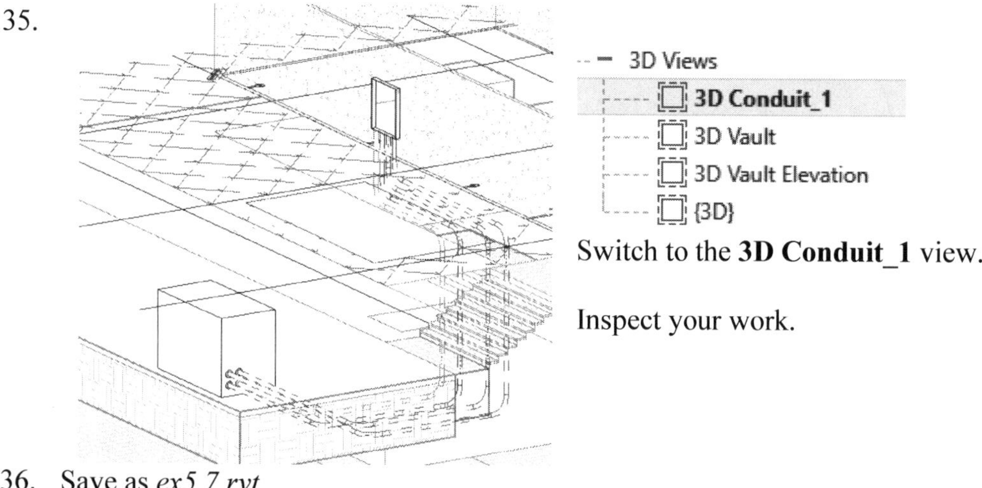

Switch to the **3D Conduit_1** view.

Inspect your work.

36.   Save as *ex5.7.rvt*.

Exercise 5-8:
Adding Parallel Conduits

Drawing Name: *parallel_conduits.rvt*
Estimated Time: 15 minutes

This exercise reinforces the following skills:
- Conduit Fittings
- Conduits

1.

Open the **Main Electrical Room 1** section view.

2.

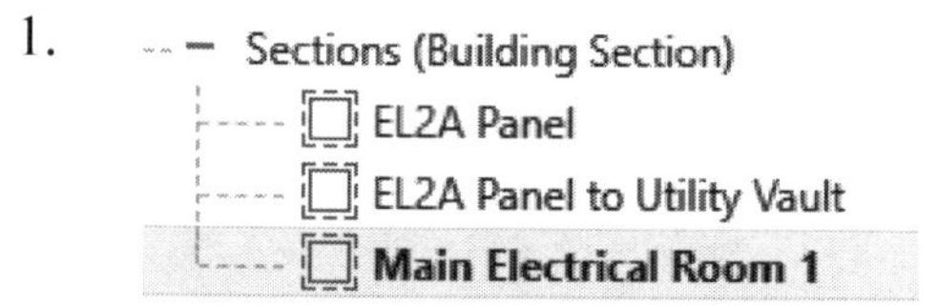

Select the panel labeled **NL1A.**

3.

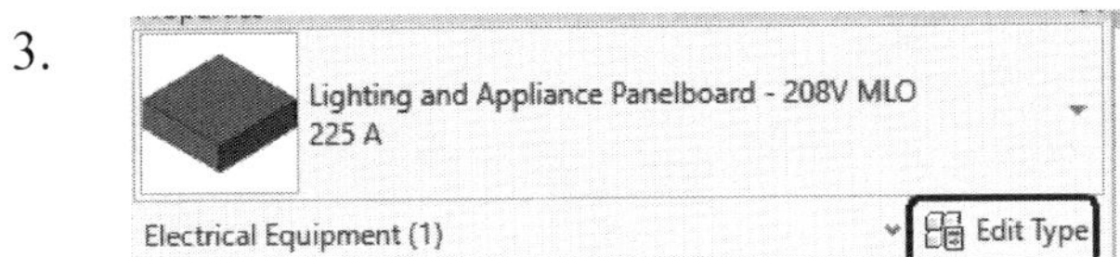

Select **Edit Type** on the Properties panel.

4.

Dimensions	
Width	4' 0"
Depth	0' 5 3/4"
42 Circuit Height	3' 5"
30 Circuit Height	2' 8"
24 Circuit Height	2' 8"
12 Circuit Height	2' 8"

Change the Width to **4' 0"**.

Press **OK**.

The panel size adjusts.

5.

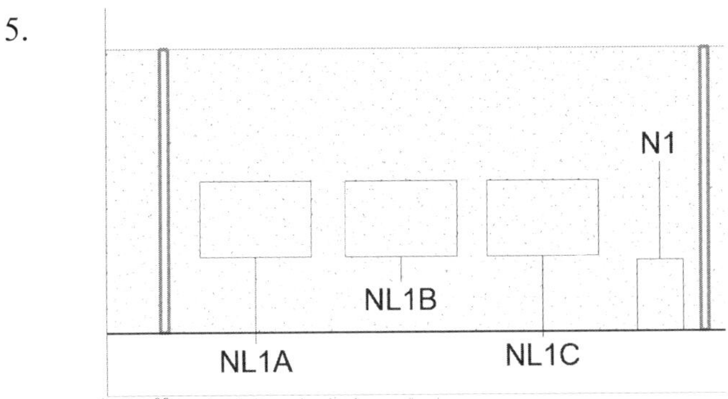

Adjust the position of the panels so they fit inside the room properly.

Select the panel labeled **NL1A.**

6.

Select the top connector on the panel.
Right click and select **Draw Conduit from Face**.

7.

Adjust the position of the connector 6" from the left side.

8.

Select **Finish Connection** on the ribbon.

Finish
Connection

9.

Properties

Conduit with Fittings
Emergency High 480/277V OH

Select the Conduit to **Emergency High 480/277V OH** using the Type Selector on the Properties panel.

10.

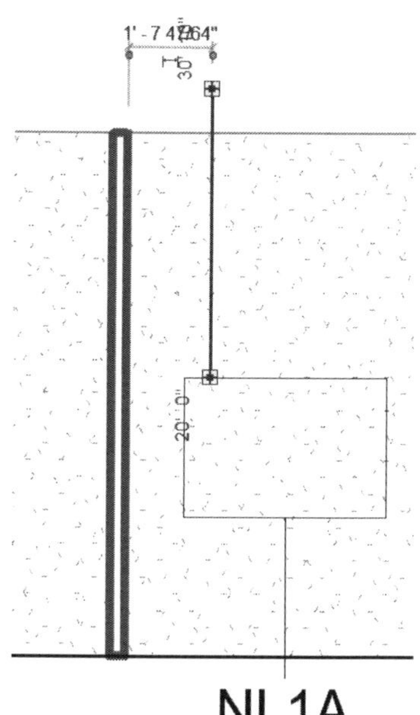

Draw the conduit straight up to the ceiling.

Press Cancel to exit the command.

11.

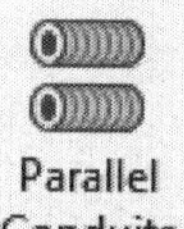

Switch to the Systems ribbon.

Select **Parallel Conduits**.

12.

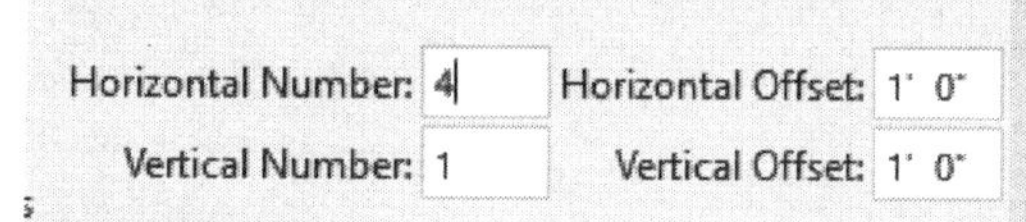

On the ribbon:
Set the Horizontal Number to 4.
Set the Horizontal Offset to 1' 0".
Set the Vertical Number to 1.
Set the vertical Offset to 1' 0".

13.

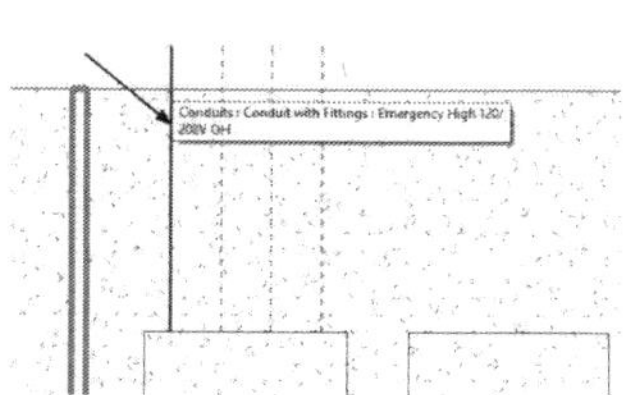

Select the conduit that was placed and check the preview placement of the new conduits.

Left click to place the new conduits.

Cancel out of the command.

14.

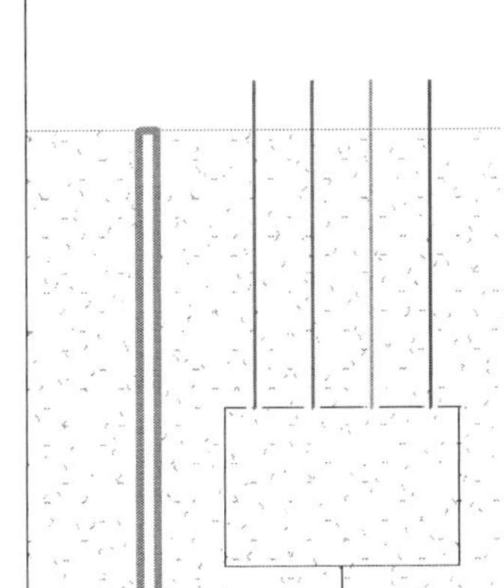

The conduits that were placed are all using the Emergency High conduit type.

Use the Type Selector to change the conduits so that they are from left to right:

- Emergency High OH (Red)
- Emergency Low OH (Magenta)
- Normal High OH (Cyan)
- Normal Low OH (Blue)

15.

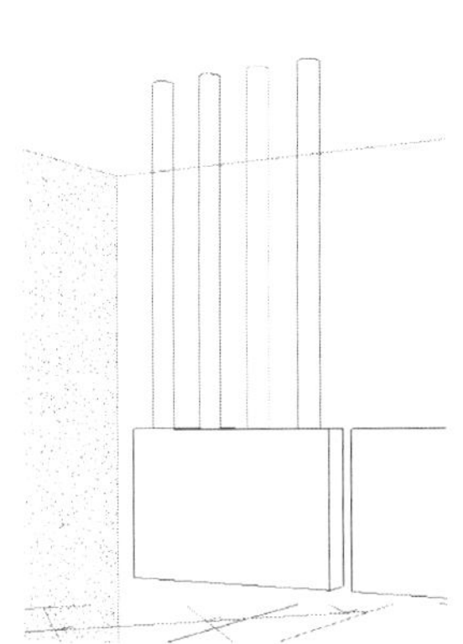

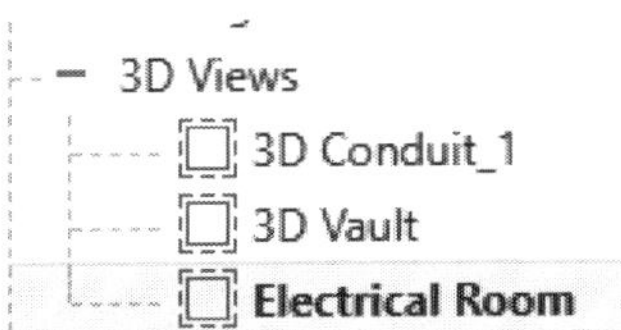

Switch to the **Electrical Room** 3D view to inspect your conduits.

Save as *ex5-8.rvt*.

Exercise 5-9:
Using View Templates

Drawing Name: *conduit_view_templates.rvt*
Estimated Time: 15 minutes

This exercise reinforces the following skills:
- Visibility Graphics Overrides
- Visibility Graphics Filters
- View Templates

1. 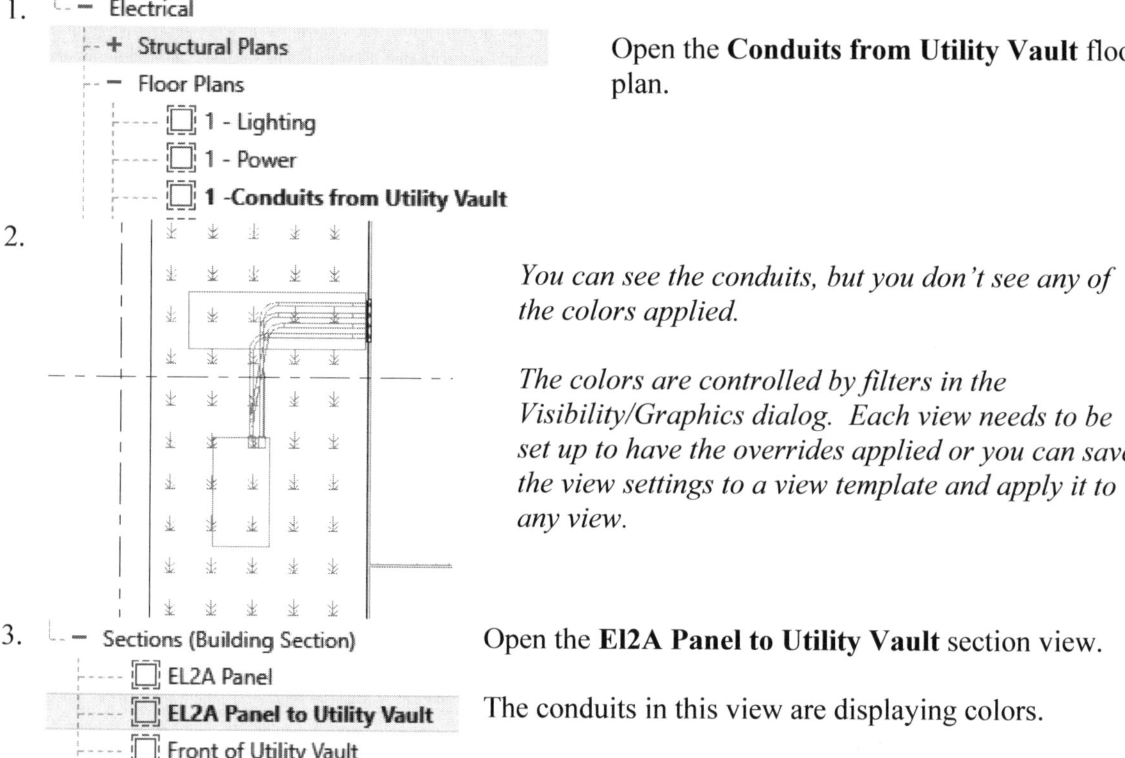

   Open the **Conduits from Utility Vault** floor plan.

2. *You can see the conduits, but you don't see any of the colors applied.*

   The colors are controlled by filters in the Visibility/Graphics dialog. Each view needs to be set up to have the overrides applied or you can save the view settings to a view template and apply it to any view.

3. Open the **El2A Panel to Utility Vault** section view.

   The conduits in this view are displaying colors.

4.
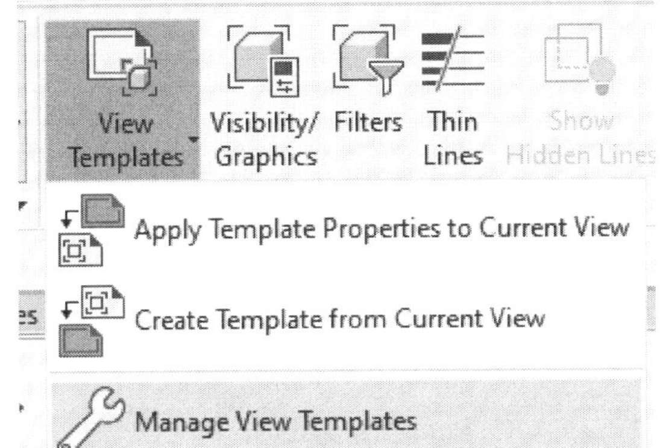

Look under Identity Data in the Properties panel.

A View Template called Conduit Overrides has been applied to this view.

5.

Switch to the **View** ribbon.

Under View Templates, select **Manage View Templates**.

6.
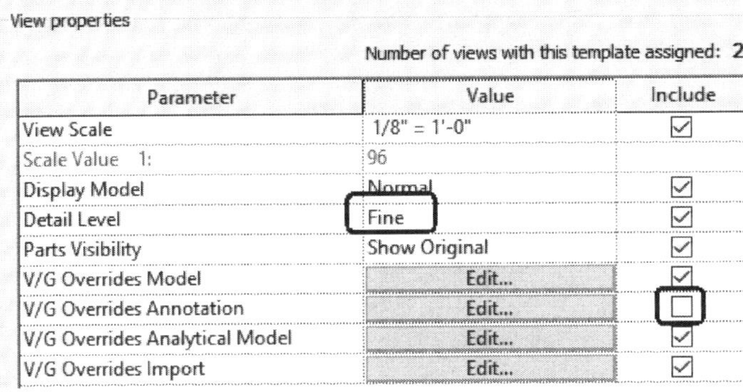

Highlight **Conduit Overrides**.

Notice that there is no check next to the Annotations category.

Notice the Detail Level is set to Fine.

7.

V/G Overrides Model	Edit...	☑
V/G Overrides Annotation	Edit...	☐
V/G Overrides Analytical Model	Edit...	☑
V/G Overrides Import	Edit...	☑
V/G Overrides Filters	Edit...	☑

Click on **Edit** next to **V/G Overrides Filters**.

8.

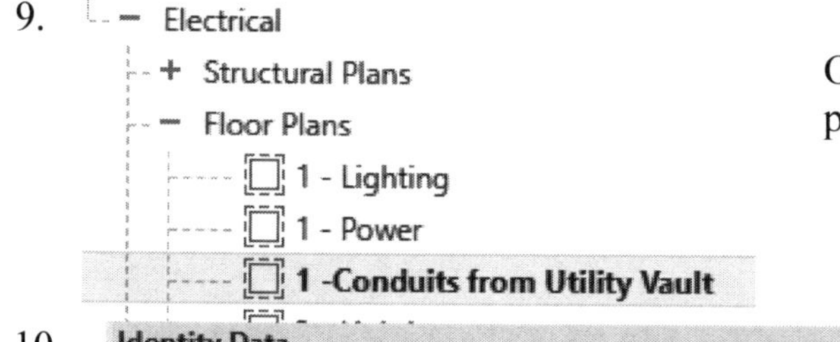

Name	Enable Filter	Visibility	Proje	
			Lines	
Emergency High UG	☑	☑	--------	C
Emergency Low UG	☑	☑	---------	
Normal Low UG	☑	☑	---------	
Normal High UG	☑	☑	-- -- -- -- --	
Emergency High OH	☑	☑	————	
Emergency Low OH	☑	☑	————	
Normal High OH	☑	☑	————	
Normal Low OH	☑	☑	————	

Notice the filters that have been applied in this view template.

Click **OK**.

Click **OK** to close the dialog.

9.

— Electrical

   + Structural Plans

   — Floor Plans

      1 - Lighting

      1 - Power

      1 -Conduits from Utility Vault

Open the **Conduits from Utility Vault** floor plan.

10.

Identity Data

View Template	<None>
View Name	1 -Conduits from Utility Vault
Dependency	Independent

Locate the **View Template** parameter under Identity Data.

Click on the **<None>** button.

11.

View templates

Discipline filter:

<all>

View type filter:

<all>

Names:

<None>
3D Conduit Views
Architectural Elevation
Architectural Plan
Architectural Presentation 3D
Architectural Presentation Elevation
Architectural Reflected Ceiling Plan
Architectural Section
Conduit Overrides
Electrical Ceiling

Set the View type filter to **all**.

Highlight the **Conduit Overrides** template.

12.

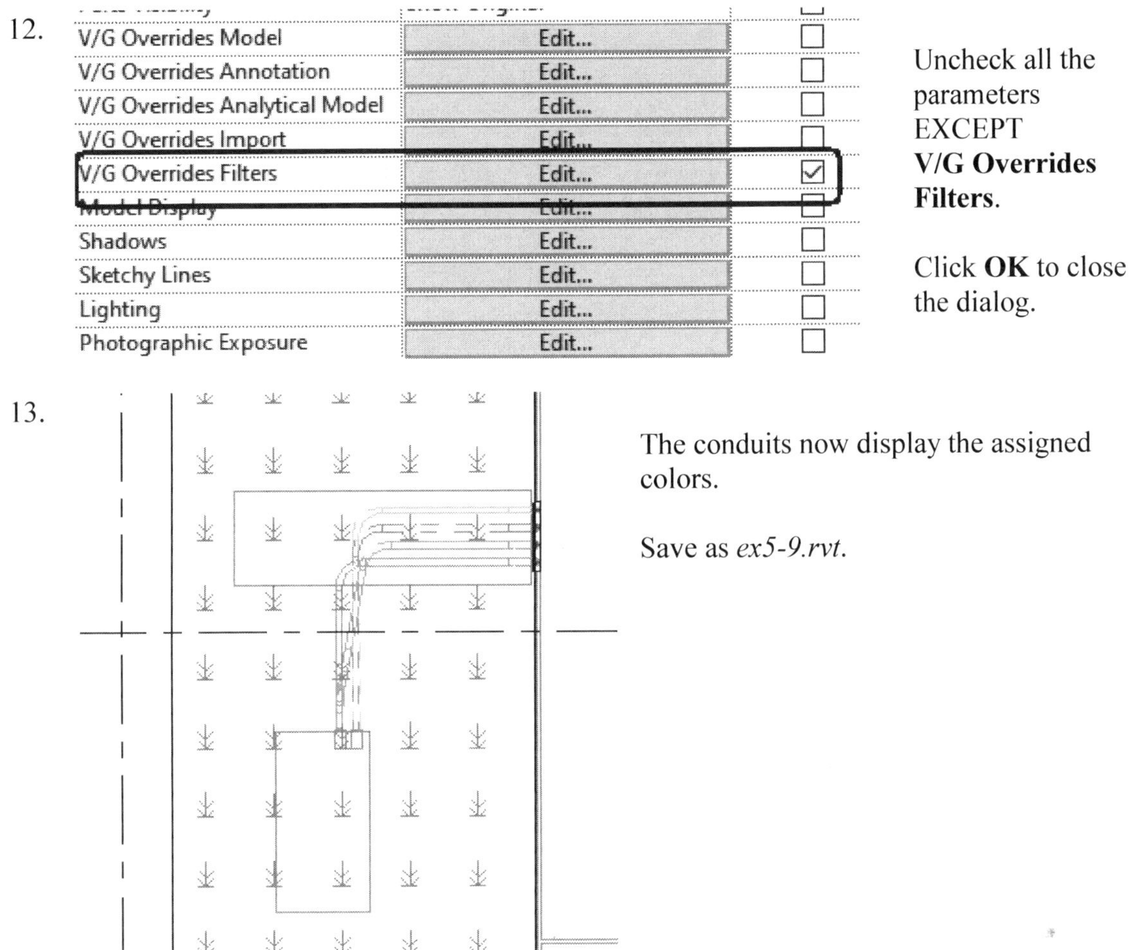

V/G Overrides Model	Edit...	☐
V/G Overrides Annotation	Edit...	☐
V/G Overrides Analytical Model	Edit...	☐
V/G Overrides Import	Edit...	☐
V/G Overrides Filters	Edit...	☑
Model Display	Edit...	☐
Shadows	Edit...	☐
Sketchy Lines	Edit...	☐
Lighting	Edit...	☐
Photographic Exposure	Edit...	☐

Uncheck all the parameters EXCEPT **V/G Overrides Filters**.

Click **OK** to close the dialog.

13.

The conduits now display the assigned colors.

Save as *ex5-9.rvt*.

Revit doesn't have an easy way to create a conduit run schedule when using conduits with fittings. The easiest method is to define shared or project parameters. Shared parameters are saved to an external text file that can be accessed from any project. Project parameters are saved internally to a project file, but can be copied from one project to another using Transfer Project Standards.

Exercise 5-10:

Assign a Conduit Run Name to a Conduit Run

Drawing Name: *conduit run names.rvt*
Estimated Time: 15 minutes

This exercise reinforces the following skills:
- Parameters
- Conduits with fittings

1. Activate the Manage ribbon.

   Select **Project Parameters**.

2. 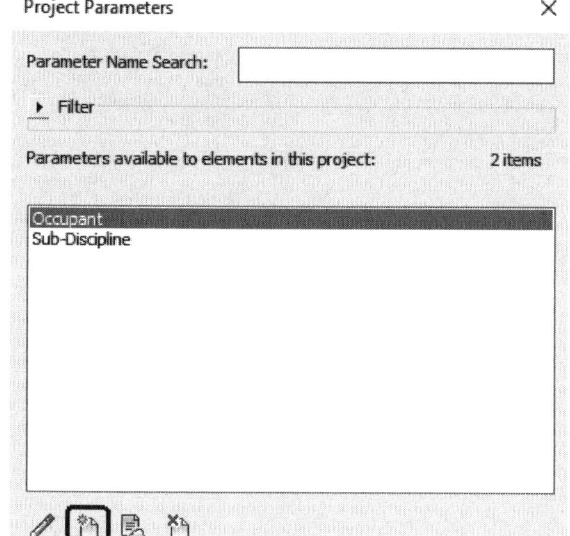

   There are already two project parameters defined in the project.

   Click **New.**

3. Verify that Project parameter is enabled.

   Note that project parameters are only available in this file.

4.

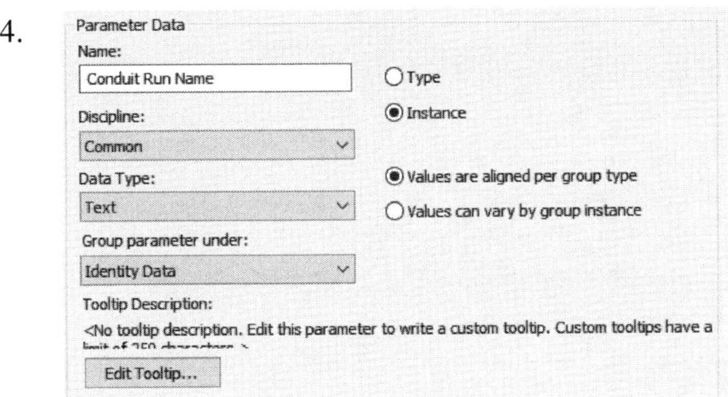

Type **Conduit Run Name** for the Name.
Set the Type of Parameter to **Text**.
Group the parameter under **Identity Data.**
Enable **Instance**.

5.

Enable **Conduit Fittings, Conduit Runs**, and **Conduits** in the Categories list.

Click **OK**.

6.

The parameter is listed and will now be added to the enabled categories.

Click **New.**

7.

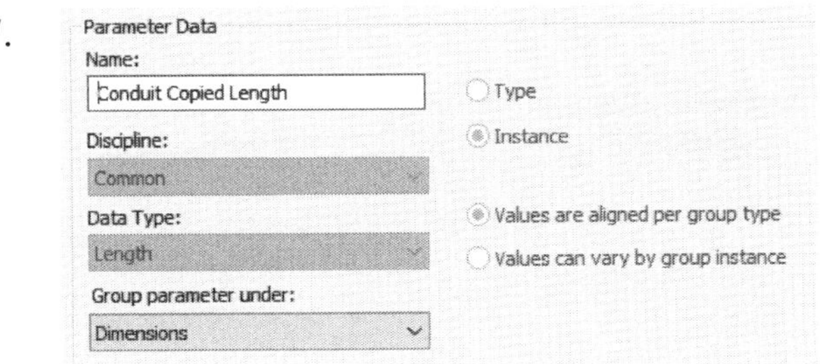

Type **Conduit Copied Length**.
Group under **Dimensions**.

8.

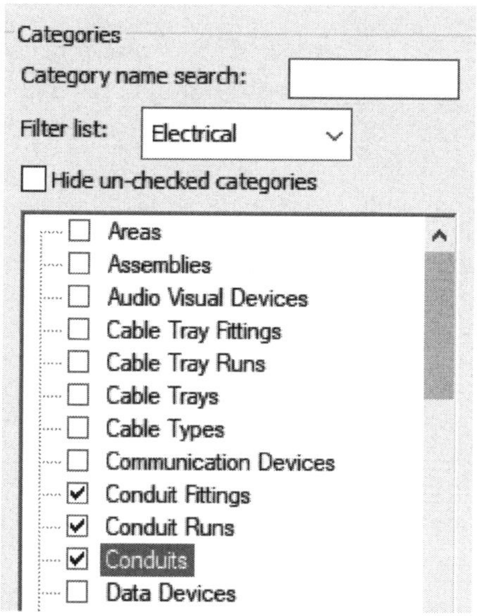

Enable **Conduit Fittings, Conduit Runs**, and **Conduits** in the Categories list.

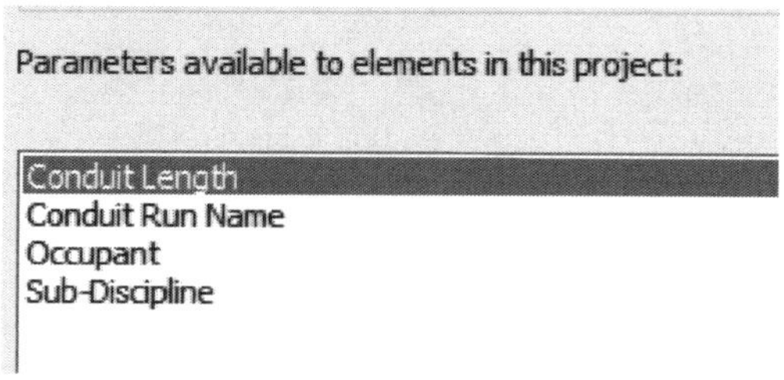

Click **OK**.

9. Open the **3D Vault** view under Electrical.

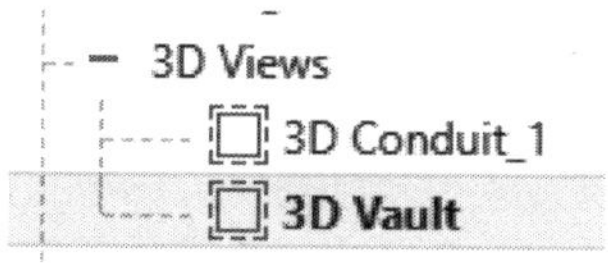

10. Set the Display to **Fine** and **Hidden Line**.

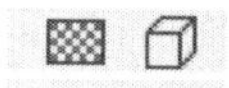

11.

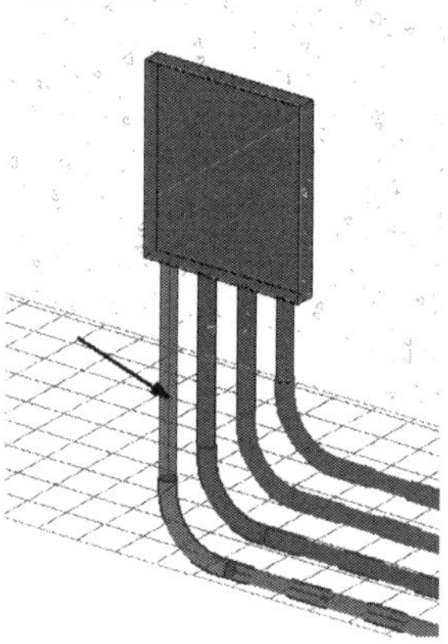

Hover over the start of the Normal High (Cyan) Conduit run.

Press the TAB key.

The entire conduit run is highlighted.

Left click to select.

12.

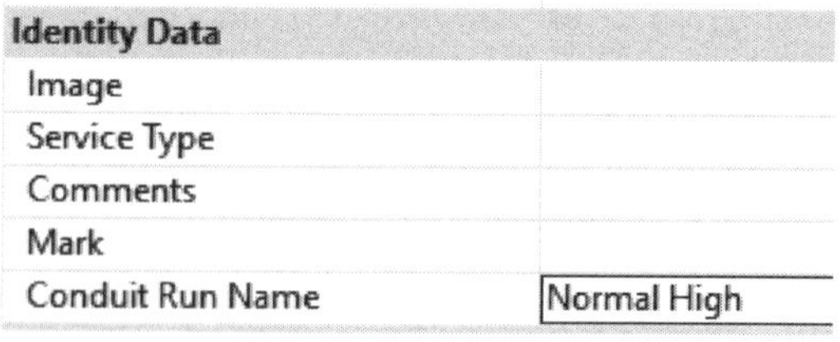

Type **Normal High** for the Conduit Run Name in the Properties palette.

Make sure you press ENTER after you type in the name or the value may not "stick".

Press ESC to release your selection.

13.

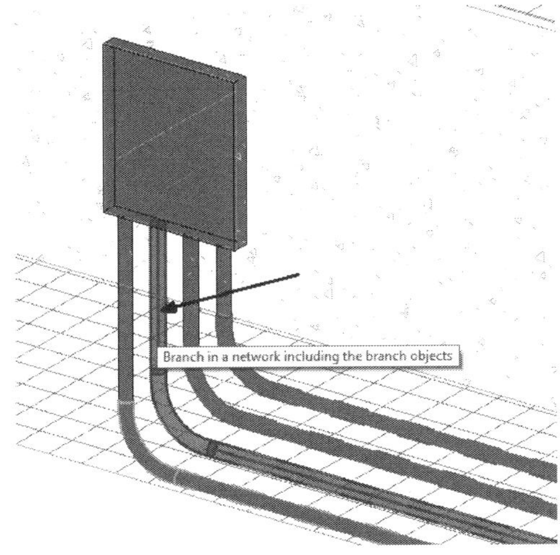

Select the start of the Normal Low (Blue) Conduit run.

Press the TAB key.

The entire conduit run is highlighted.

Left click to select.

You can also hold down the CTL key and select each segment.

14.

Identity Data	
Image	
Service Type	
Comments	
Mark	
Conduit Run Name	Normal Low

Type **Normal Low** for the Conduit Run Name in the Properties palette.

Press ESC to release your selection.

15.

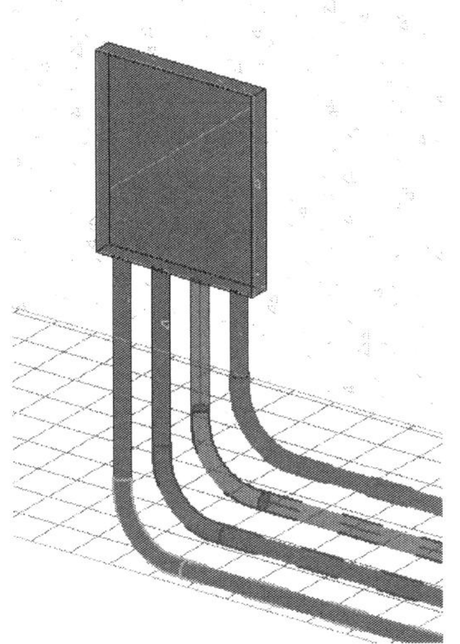

Select the start of the Emergency Low (Magenta) Conduit run.

Press the TAB key.

The entire conduit run is highlighted.

Left click to select.

16.

Identity Data	
Image	
Service Type	
Comments	
Mark	
Conduit Run Name	Emergency Low

Type **Emergency Low** for the Conduit Run Name in the Properties palette.

Press ESC to release your selection.

17.

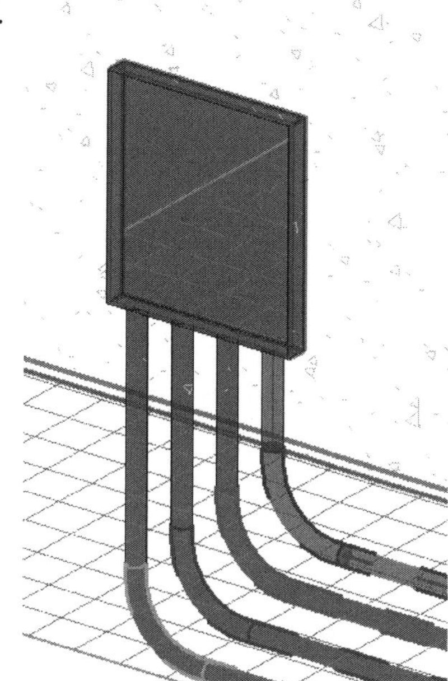

Select the start of the Emergency High (Red) Conduit run.

Press the TAB key.

The entire conduit run is highlighted.

Left click to select.

18.

Identity Data	
Image	
Service Type	
Comments	
Mark	
Conduit Run Name	Emergency High

Type **Emergency High** for the Conduit Run Name in the Properties palette.

Press ESC to release your selection.

19. Save as *ex5-10.rvt*.

Revit won't allow users to add the length of conduits to fittings to get the length of a conduit run. So, we will use the Conduit Copied Length parameter to total the lengths of the conduits and the fittings.

We can use Dynamo to copy the Length value of each conduit to the Conduit Length parameter.

Exercise 5-11:

Using Dynamo

Drawing Name: *parameter dynamo.rvt*
Estimated Time: 15 minutes

This exercise reinforces the following skills:
- Parameters
- Conduits with fittings
- Dynamo

1.  Activate the Manage ribbon.

   Select **Dynamo**.

2. 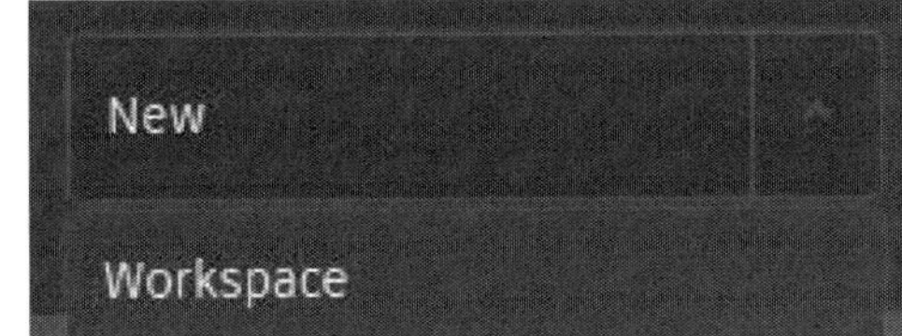 Select **New→Workspace.**

3. 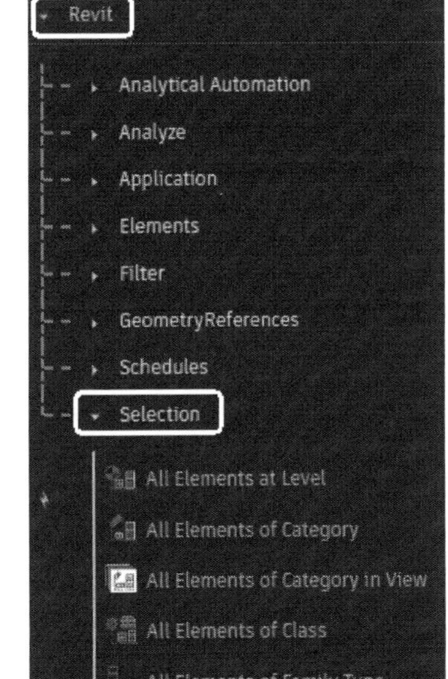 Under **Revit**, locate **Selection** and then **Categories**.

4.

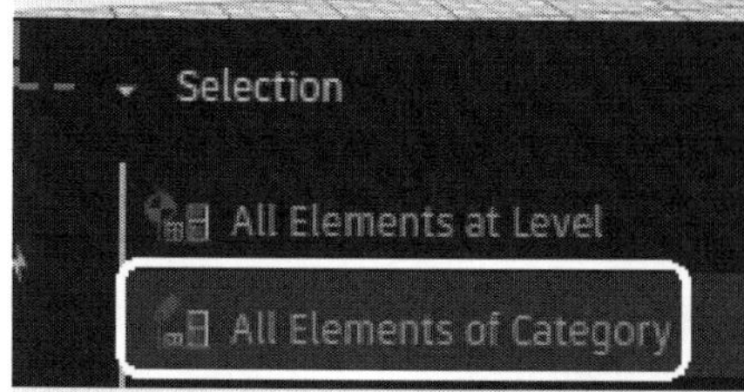

Locate **Conduits**.

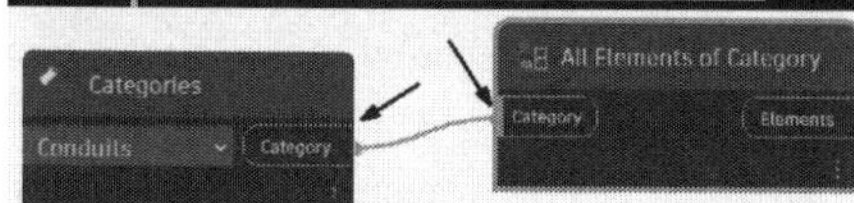

5.

Select **All Elements of Category**.

This selects all conduits in the project.

6.

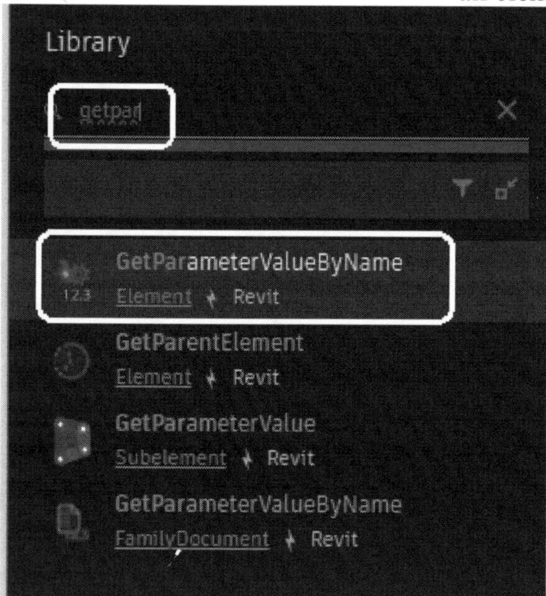

Click the box that says Category on the Categories rectangle.
You will see a blue wire.
Click on the blue bar on the left of the Category box for all elements of category.

7.

Type **getpar** in the search field.

Click **GetParameterValueByName**.

8. 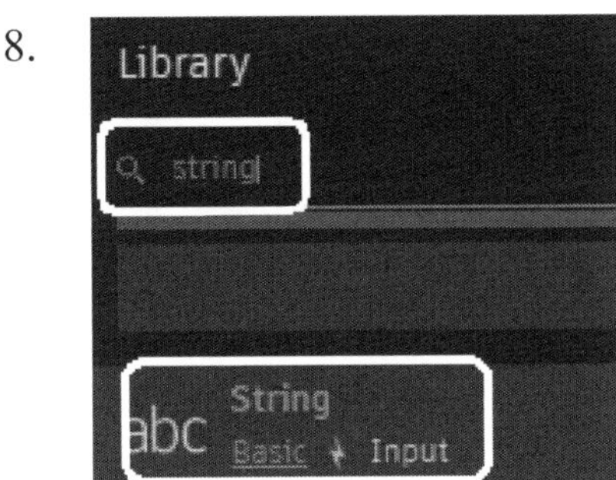

Type **string** in the search field.

Click **String (Basic Input).**

9. 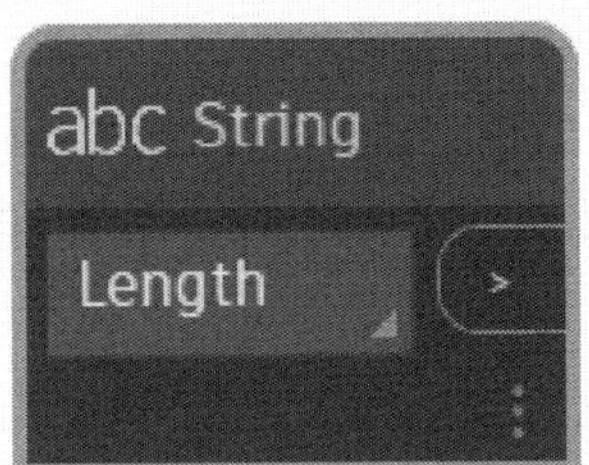

Type **Length** in the String field.

10. 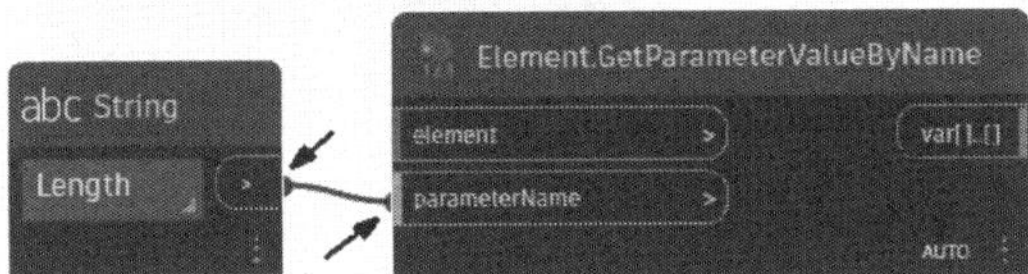

Click the small > box on the Length string box.
You will see a blue wire.
Click the box to the left of the parameterName Element box.

You have now connected the Length value to the parameterName.

11. 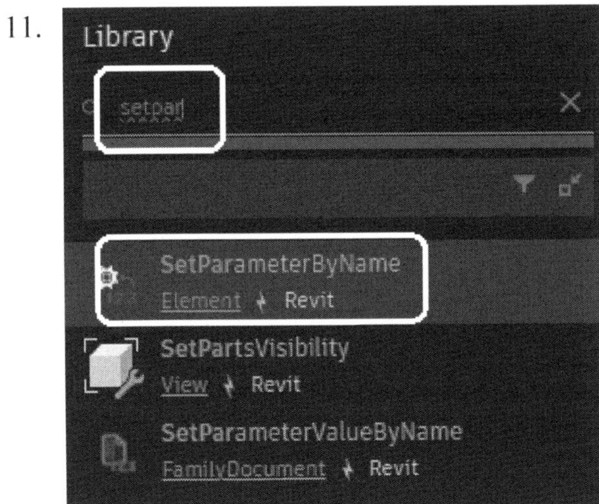

Type **setpar** in the search field.

Click **SetParameterByName (Element Revit).**

12. 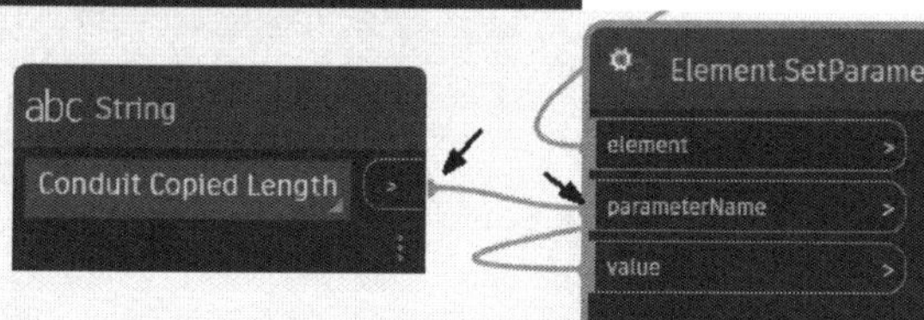
Type **string** in the search field.

Click **String (Basic Input).**

13.
Type **Conduit Copied Length** in the String field.

14.
Click the small > box on the Conduit Length string box.
You will see a blue wire.
Click the box to the left of the Element.SetParameterByName box.

You have now connected the Conduit Copied Length value to the parameter name.

15. 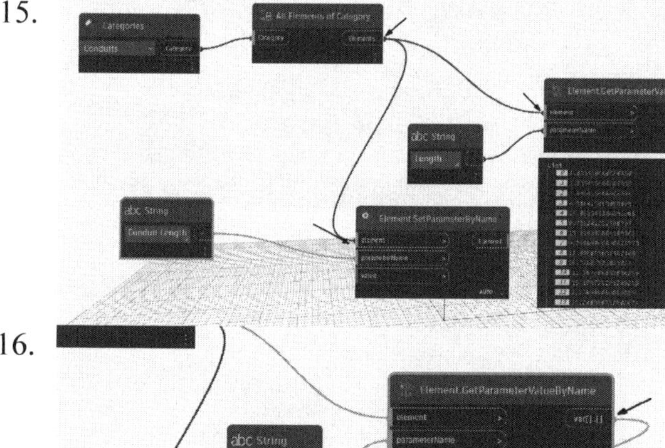
You can move the boxes around to make it easier to create connections.

Connect the element box on the All Elements of Category box to the element box on Element.GetParameterValueByName and the element box on Element.SetParameterValueByName.

16.
Create a connection between the var[] box on Element.GetParameterValueByName and value on Element.SetParameterValueByName.

17. 
Save the file as **conduitlength.dyn**.

18. Return to the Revit project.

19. 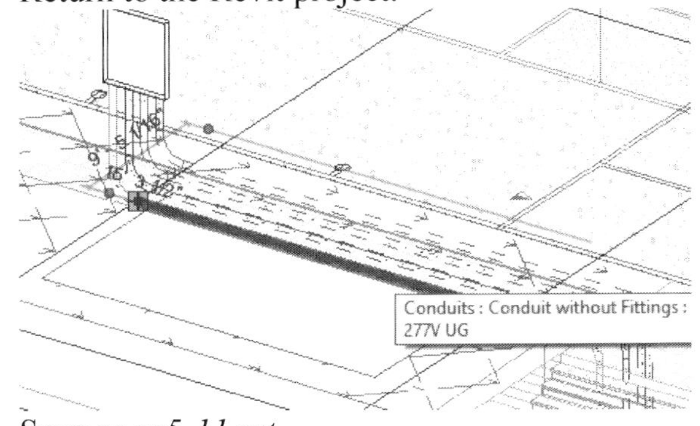

Select a conduit.

| Length | 28' 0 63/64" |
| Conduit Length | 28' 0 63/64" |

Look in the Properties panel.
The Length value has been copied over for all the conduits.

20. Save as *ex5-11.rvt*.

Exercise 5-12:
Modify a Conduit Fitting

Drawing Name: *conduit fitting.rvt*
Estimated Time: 10 minutes

This exercise reinforces the following skills:
- Parameters
- Conduits with fittings

1. 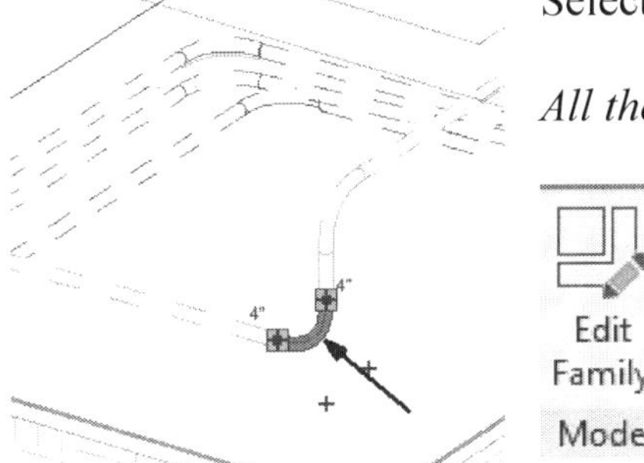

Select one of the elbows in the conduit.

All the elbows are the same size and type.

Edit
Family

Mode

Select **Edit Family** on the ribbon.

2. Click **Family Types** on the ribbon.

3. Click **New Parameter**.

4.

Parameter Data	
Name: Elbow Extension	○ Type
Discipline: Common	● Instance
Data Type: Length	☐ Reporting Parameter
Group parameter under: Dimensions	(Can be used to extract value from a geometric condition and report it in a formula or as a schedulable parameter)

Type **Elbow Extension.**
Enable **Instance.**
Set Data Type to **Length.**

Click **OK.**

The elbows used are comprised of an arc with a short line on either end to create a sweep. The elbow extension is the lengths of the short lines on either side of the arc.

5.

Dimensions		
Elbow Extension	0' 0"	= size_lookup(Conduit Size Lookup, "CLgt", 0.46 * Nominal Diameter + 1 105/256", Nominal Diameter)
Nominal Radius (default)	1/4"	=
Nominal Diameter (default)	1/2"	= Nominal Radius * 2
Fitting Outside Diameter (default)	215/256"	= size_lookup(Conduit Size Lookup, "FOD", 1.06 * Nominal Diameter + 37/128", Nominal Diameter)
Conduit Length (default)	1 1/2"	= size_lookup(Conduit Size Lookup, "CLgt", 0.46 * Nominal Diameter + 1 105/256", Nominal Diameter)
Center to End (default)	5 1/2"	= Bend Radius Label * tan(Angle / 2) + Conduit Length
Bend Radius (default)	4"	= size_lookup(Conduit Size Lookup, "BRad", 4.45 * Nominal Diameter + 207/256", Nominal Diameter)
Angle (default)	90.00°	=

6. Copy and paste the formula in the Conduit Length parameter to the Elbow Extension parameter.

The Conduit Length parameter is only measuring the length of one line used to create the sweep.

7.

Conduit Length (default)	3 101/256"	= (Elbow Extension * 2) + pi() * Nominal Radius * Angle / 180°

This adds the two extension lines plus the elbow curve to get the total elbow length.

Type the following formula into the Conduit Length parameter:
(Elbow Extension * 2) + pi() * Nominal Radius * Angle / 180°

Click **OK.**

8.

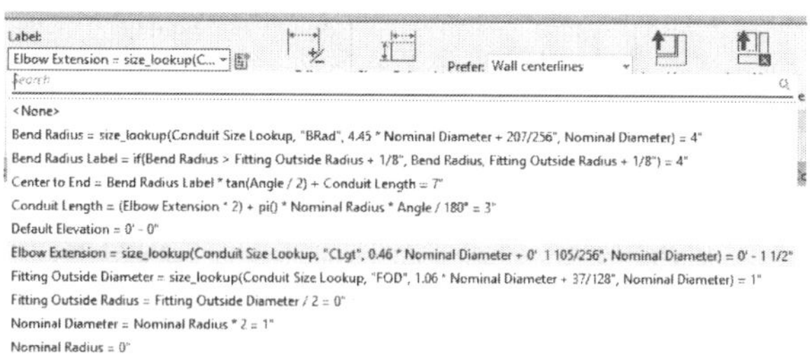

Switch to the Ref Level view.
Select the dimension that is labeled Conduit Length.

Change the label to use the **Elbow Extension** parameter.

9. Save the family to your exercise folder.

Load into Project and Close

Click **Load into Project and Close** to load into the active project.

10. 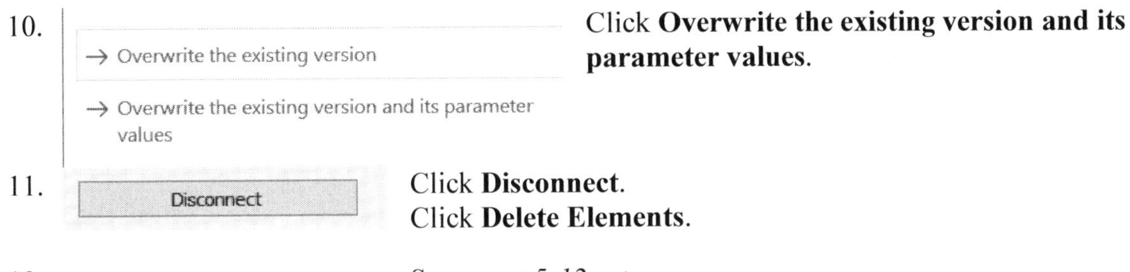
Click **Overwrite the existing version and its parameter values**.

11. Click **Disconnect**.
Click **Delete Elements**.

12. Save as *ex5-12.rvt*.

Exercise 5-13:

Using Dynamo (Reprised)

Drawing Name: *dynamo fitting.rvt*
Estimated Time: 15 minutes

This exercise reinforces the following skills:
- Parameters
- Conduit fittings
- Dynamo

1. Open the **3D Conduit_1** 3D View

2. 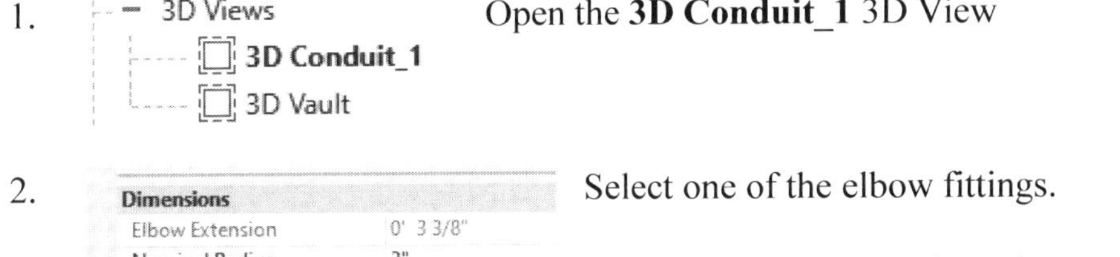
Select one of the elbow fittings.

Note there is a value of Conduit Length that is empty.

We can use Dynamo to copy the value over.

3. Activate the Manage ribbon.

Select **Dynamo**.

4.

Select **New→Workspace.**

5.

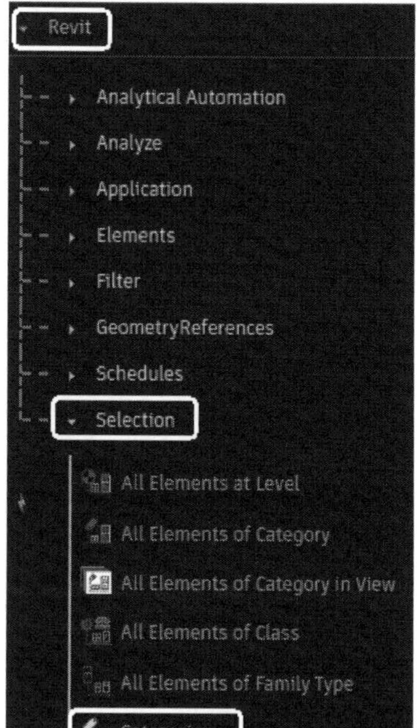

Under **Revit**, locate **Selection** and then **Categories**.

6.

Locate **Conduit Fittings**.

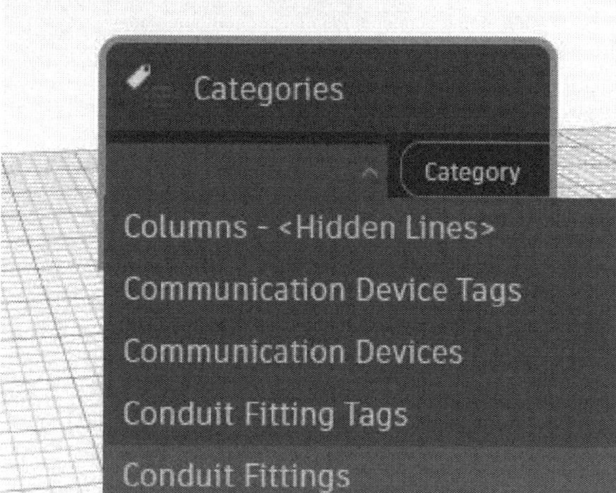

7.

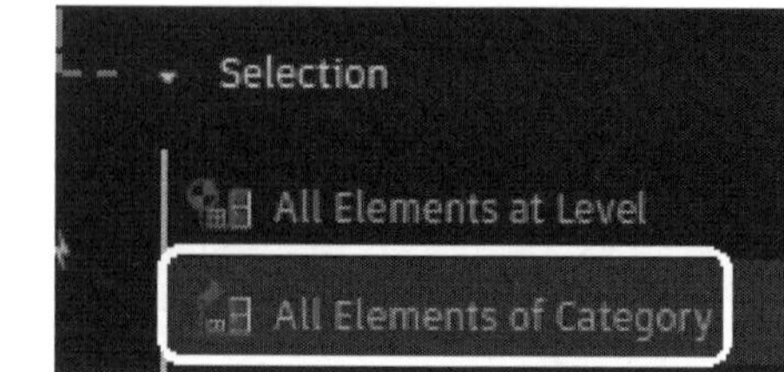

Select **All Elements of Category**.

This selects all conduits in the project.

8.    Click the box that says Category on the Categories rectangle.
You will see a blue wire.
Click on the blue bar on the left of the Category box for all elements of category.

9. 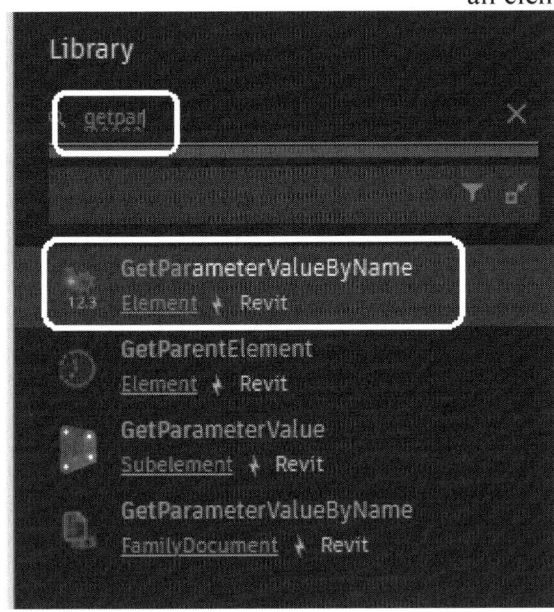   Type **getpar** in the search field.

Click **GetParameterValueByName**.

10. 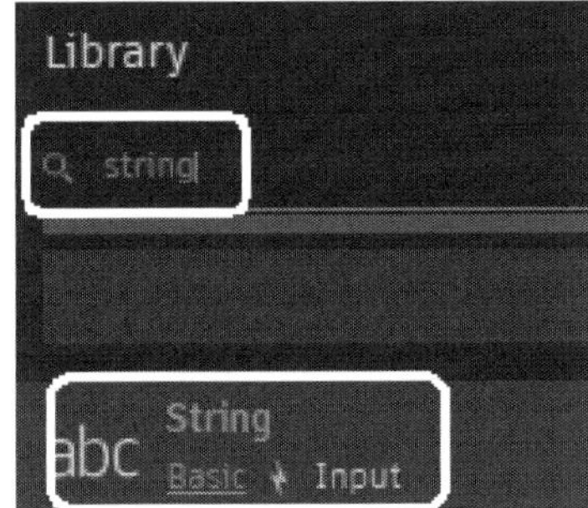   Type **string** in the search field.

Click **String (Basic Input).**

11. 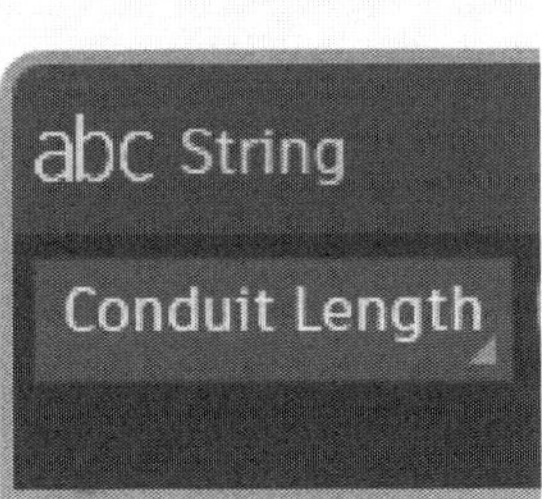   Type **Conduit Length** in the String field.

12.

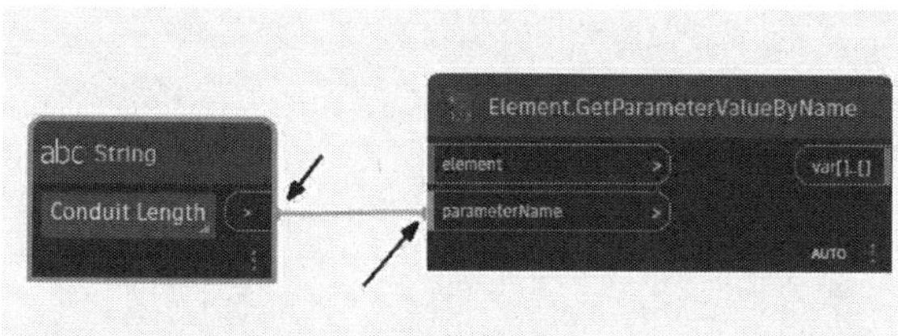

Click the small > box on the Conduit Length string box.
You will see a blue wire.
Click the box to the left of the parameterName Element box.

You have now connected the Conduit Length value to the parameterName.

13.

Type **setpar** in the search field.

Click **SetParameterByName (Element Revit).**

14.

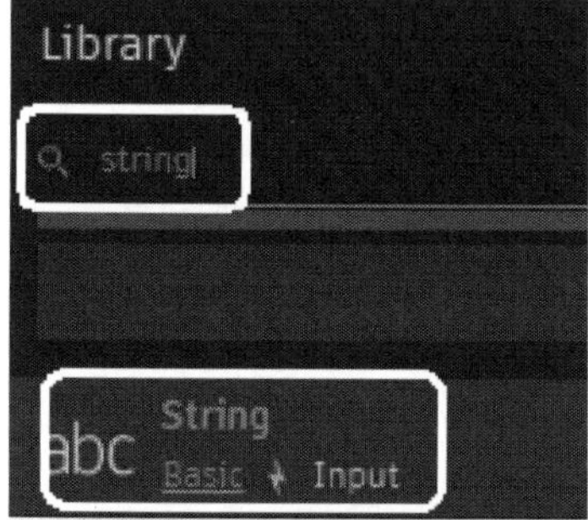

Type **string** in the search field.

Click **String (Basic Input).**

15.

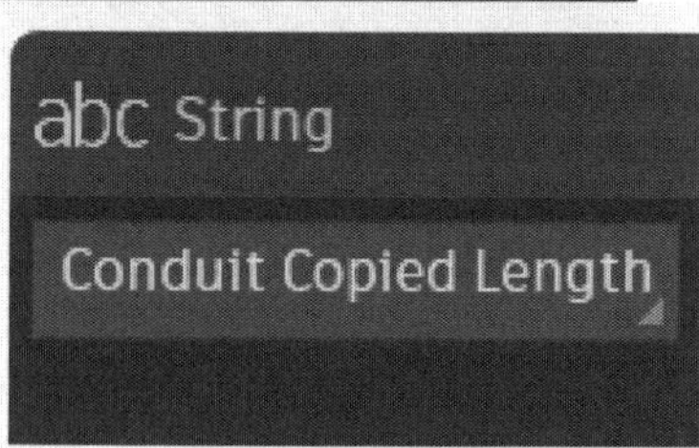

Type **Conduit Copied Length** in the String field.

16.

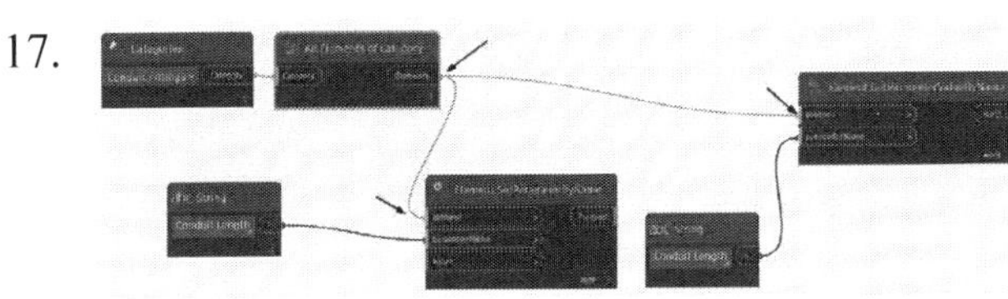

Click the small > box on the Conduit Copied
Length string box.
You will see a blue wire.
Click the box to the left of the
Element.SetParameterByName box.

*You have now connected the Conduit Copied
Length value to the parameter name.*

17.

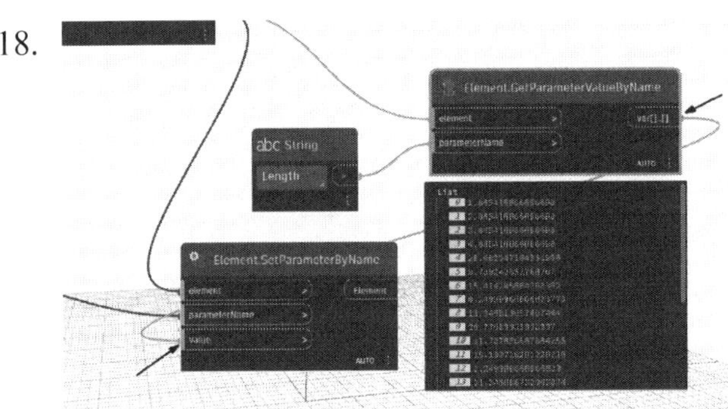

You can move the boxes around to make it
easier to create connections.

Connect the element box on the All Elements
of Category box to the element box on
Element.GetParameterValueByName and the
the element box on
Element.SetParameterValueByName.
Create a connection between the var[] box on
Element.GetParameterValueByName and
value on
Element.SetParameterValueByName.

18.

19.

File name:	conduitlength
Save as type:	Dynamo Workspace (*.dyn)

Save the file as **fittinglength.dyn**.

Close Dynamo.

20. Return to the Revit project.

21.

Fitting Outside Diameter	4 1/2"
Conduit Length	9 57/64"
Center to End	25 57/64"
Bend Radius	16"
Angle	90.00°
Size	4"ø-4"ø
Conduit Copied Length	9' 10 179/256"

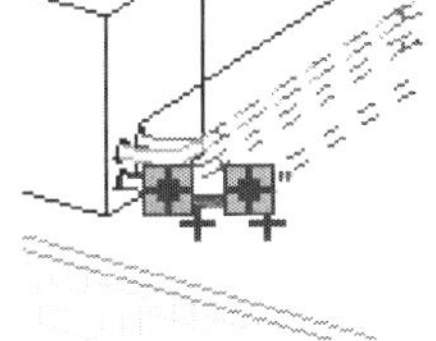

Select an elbow fitting.

Look in the Properties panel.
The Conduit Length value has been copied over for
all the conduit fittings.

22. Save as *ex5-13.rvt*.

Exercise 5-14:

Create a Conduit Run Schedule

Drawing Name: *conduit run schedule.rvt*
Estimated Time: 15 minutes

This exercise reinforces the following skills:
- ❑ Parameters
- ❑ Conduits with fittings
- ❑ Schedules

1. 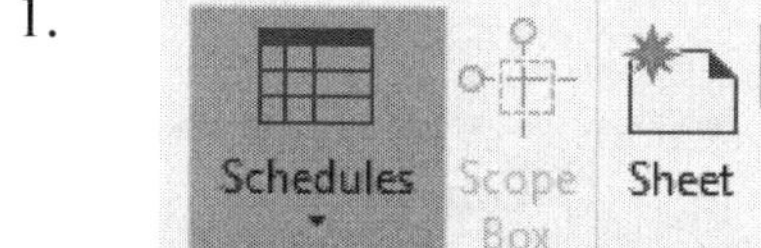

   Switch to the View ribbon.

   Select **Schedules/Quantities**.

2. 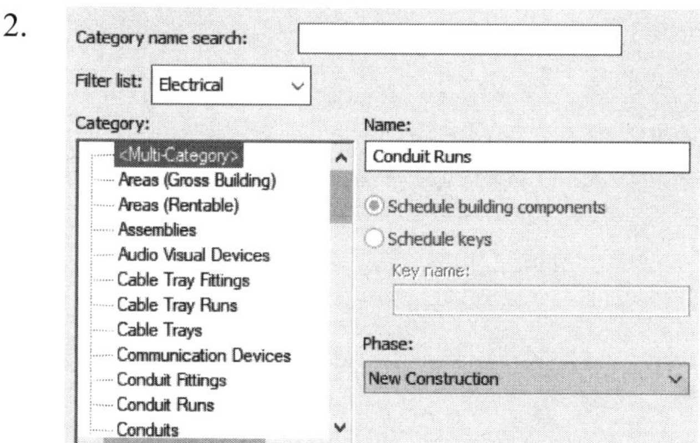

   Highlight **Multi-Category**.in the Category pane.

   Type **Conduit Runs** in the Name field.

   Click **OK.**

3. Scheduled fields (in order):

   Conduit Run Name
   Family and Type
   Conduit Copied Length

   Select the following fields:
   - Conduit Run Name
   - Family and Type
   - Conduit Copied Length

   Reorder the fields as shown.

4. 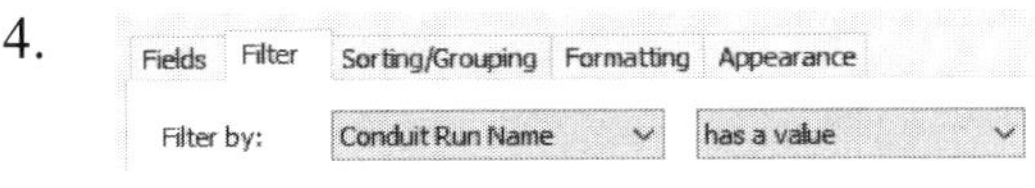

Select the **Filter** tab.

Filter by **Conduit Run Name**
Has a value.

This means any elements with a Conduit Run Name assigned won't be included in the schedule.

5. 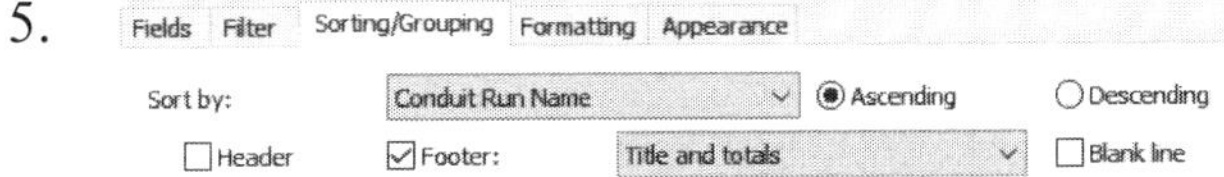

Select the Sorting/Grouping tab.

Set Sort by: **Conduit Run Name**.

Enable **Footer: Title and totals**.

Select the **Conduit Copied Length** field.

Change the Heading to **Conduit Length**.
Enable **Calculate totals**.

Click **OK.**

6. 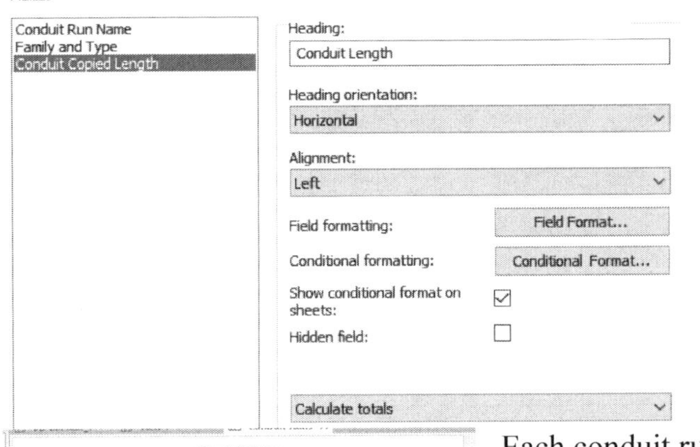

Each conduit run is listed and you see the totals for each conduit run.

Save as *ex5-14.rvt*.

Exercise 5-15:

Create a Conduit Saddle

Drawing Name: *conduit_saddle.rvt*
Estimated Time: 25 minutes

This exercise reinforces the following skills:
- Conduits
- Electrical Fixtures

1. 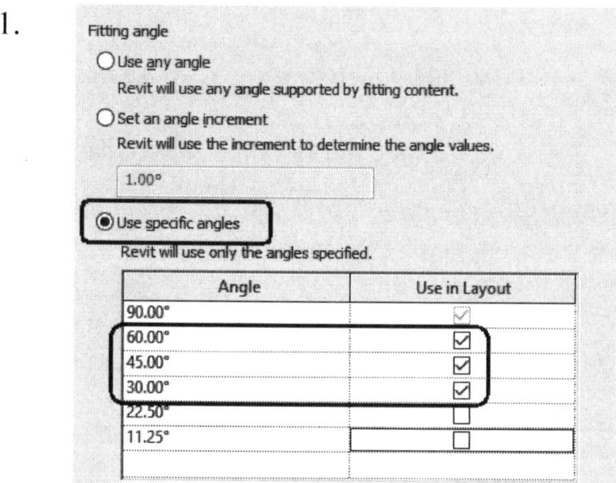

Type **ES** to open the Electrical Settings palette.

Electrical Settings

Highlight **Angles**.

Enable **Use specific angles**.

90° is enabled by default.
Enable 60°, 45°, and 30°.

Click **OK**.

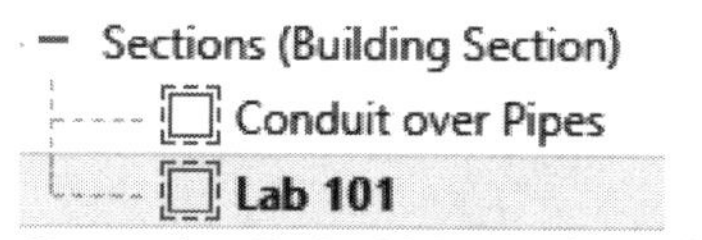

Open the **Lab 101** section view.

Notice that the top of the ceiling is located at 8' 3" above Level 1.

2. 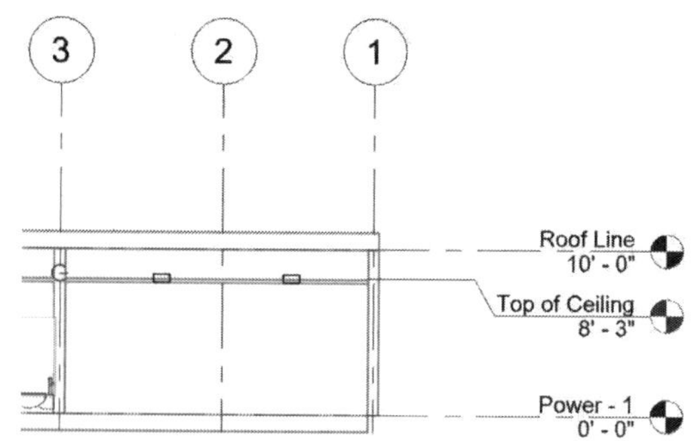

3.

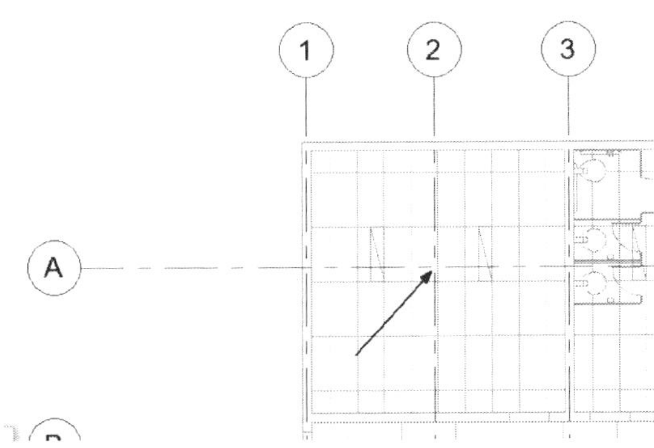

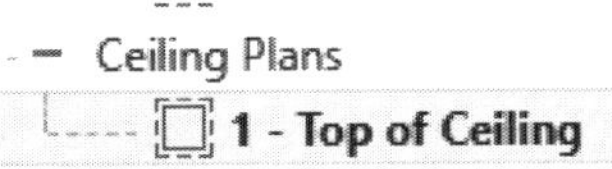

Open the **1 – Top of Ceiling** ceiling plan under Power.

Locate the intersection of Grids A and 2.

We are going to place a junction box at this intersection.

4.

Select the **Place a Component** tool from the Architecture ribbon.

It is useful to use this tool if you don't know how an element is defined.

5.

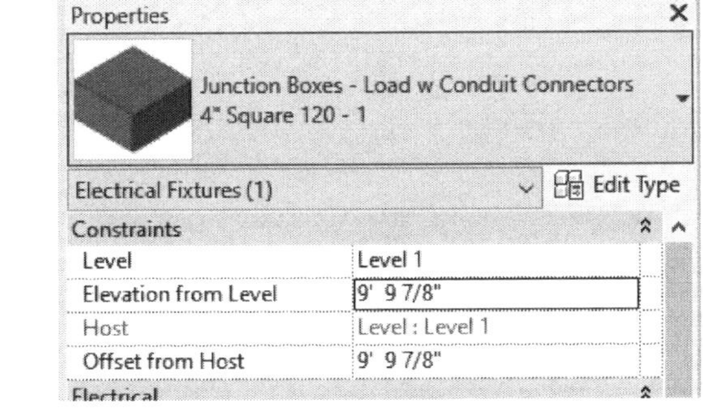

Select the **Load w Conduit Connectors 4"
Square 120 Junction Box**.

Set the Elevation from Level to **9' 9 7/8"**.

This places it above the piping.

Place the component at A2.

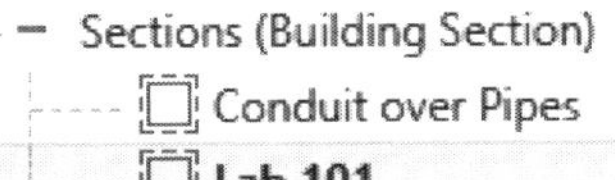

Switch to the Lab 101 Section view and verify the placement of the junction box.

It should be attached to the roof joist.

6.

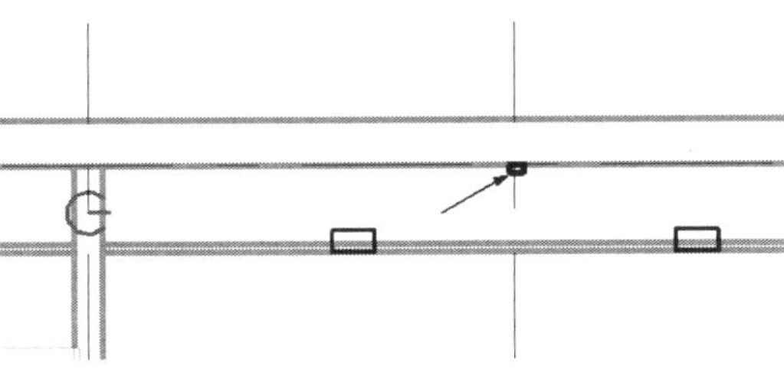

The green circle on the left is the pipe.
Select the pipe.

Our conduit needs to go below this pipe.

7. On the Options bar:

Notice that the pipe has a diameter of 6"
and has a middle elevation of 8' 11".

8.

If you look on the Properties palette, you see the bottom of the pipe is located at 8' 7 15/16".

The top of the ceiling is at 8' 3".

This means we can place the bottom part of the conduit saddle at 8' 5".

9.

Switch back to the **1 – Top of Ceiling** view.

Select the junction box to activate the connectors.

You should see five connectors – one at the top and one on each side.

10.

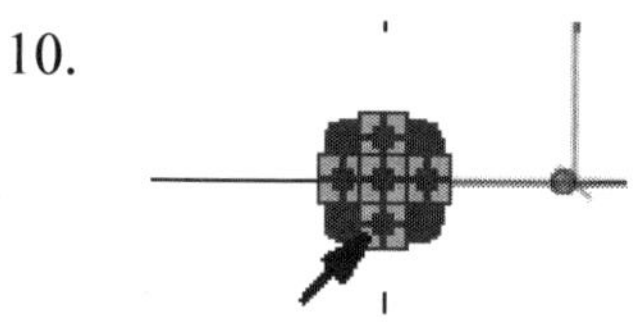

Select the south/bottom connector.

Right click and select **Draw Conduit.**

11.

On the Option bar:
Set the conduit diameter to **1"**.
Set the Middle Elevation to **9' 10 15/16"**.

12.

Use the Type Selector to place a **Conduit without Fittings (RNC Sch 40)**.

13.

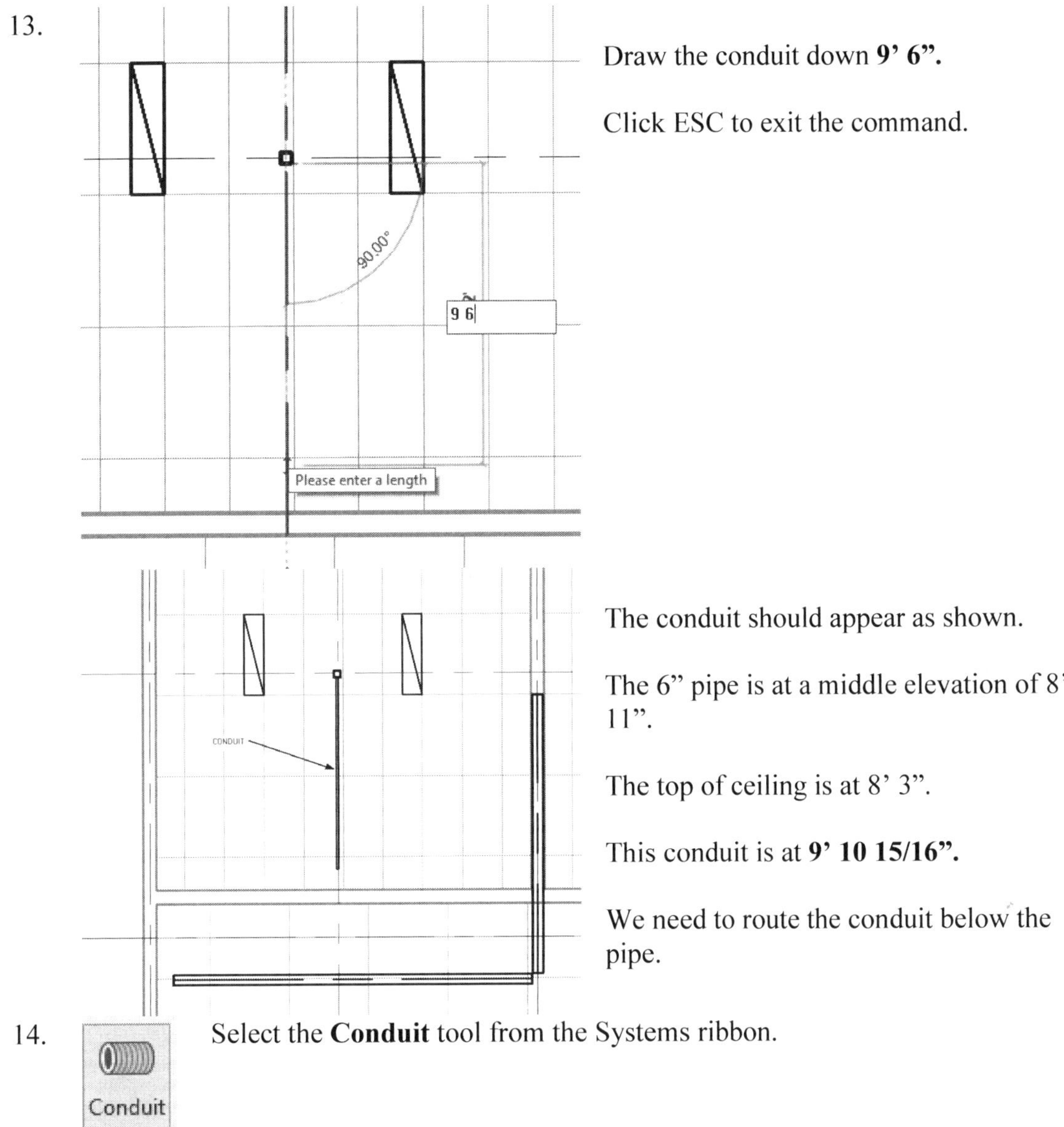

Draw the conduit down **9' 6"**.

Click ESC to exit the command.

The conduit should appear as shown.

The 6" pipe is at a middle elevation of 8' 11".

The top of ceiling is at 8' 3".

This conduit is at **9' 10 15/16"**.

We need to route the conduit below the pipe.

14. Select the **Conduit** tool from the Systems ribbon.

15.

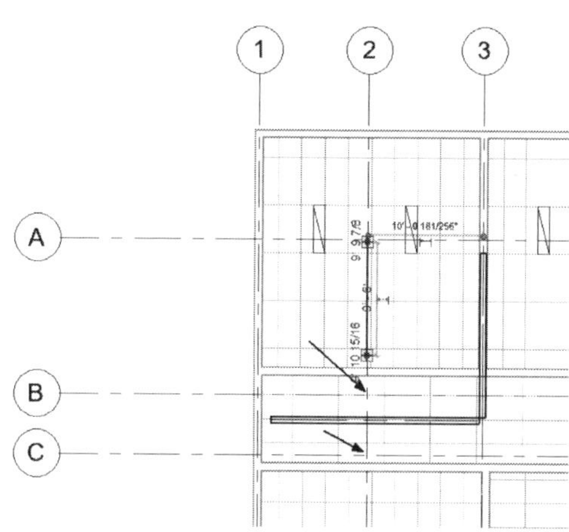

Draw the conduit from B2 to C2.

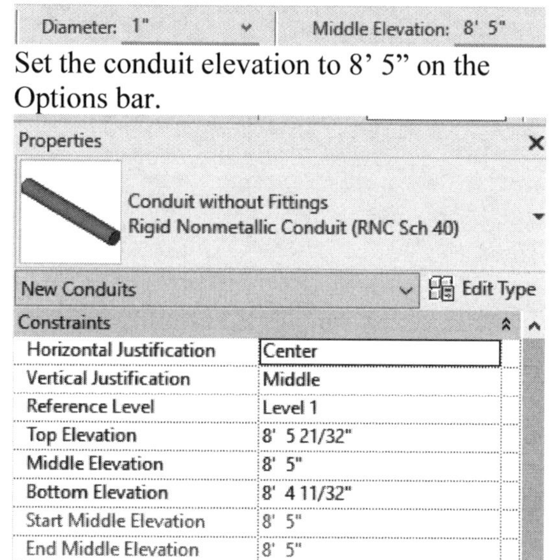

Set the conduit elevation to 8' 5" on the Options bar.

If you look on the Properties palette, you can confirm the elevation.

Cancel out of the command.

16.

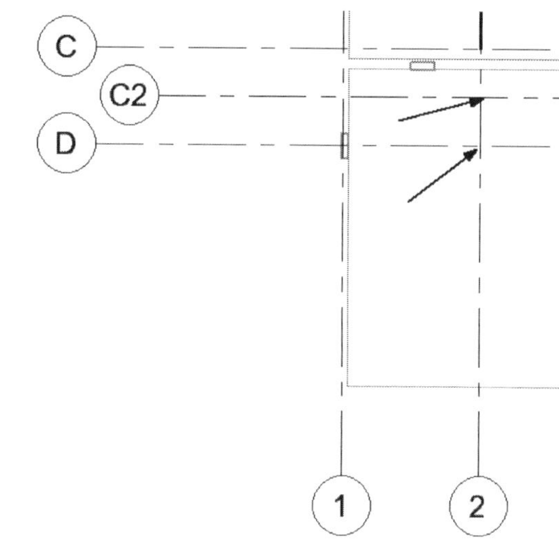

Type **CN** to start the Conduit command.

Draw a conduit from C2-2 to D2 at an elevation of **9' 10 15/16"**.

Cancel out of the command.

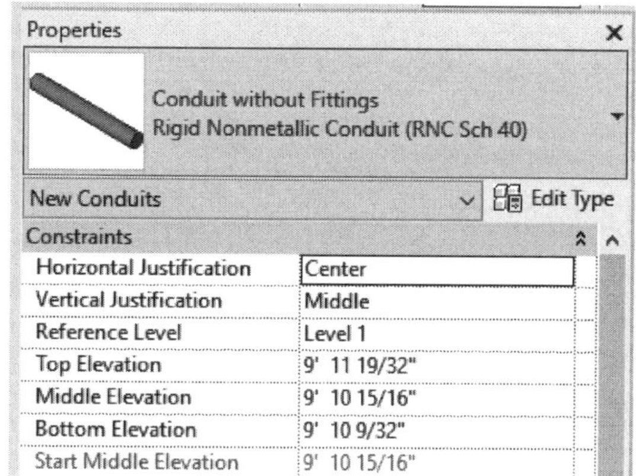

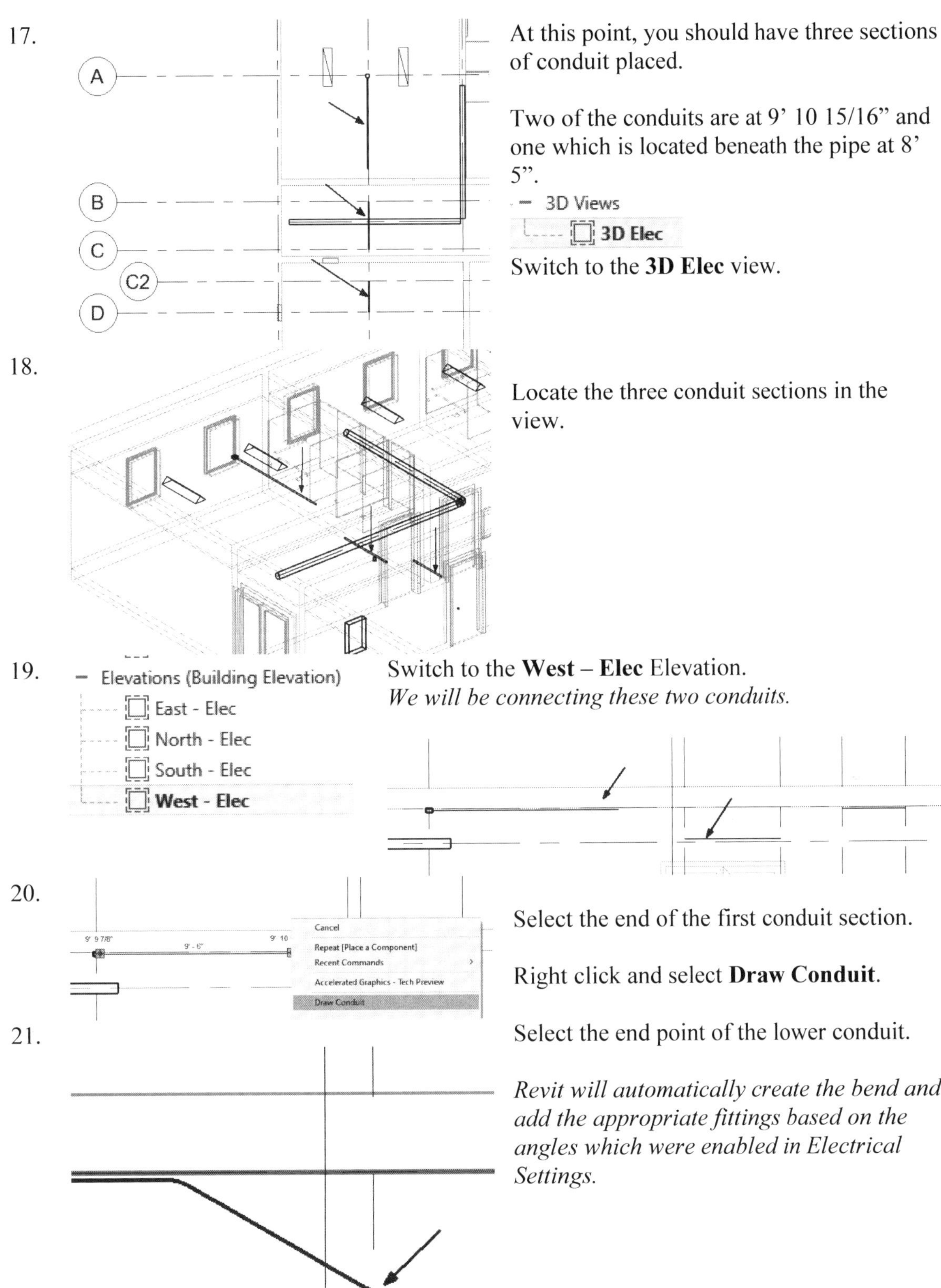

17. At this point, you should have three sections of conduit placed.

Two of the conduits are at 9' 10 15/16" and one which is located beneath the pipe at 8' 5".

Switch to the **3D Elec** view.

18. Locate the three conduit sections in the view.

19. Switch to the **West – Elec** Elevation.
We will be connecting these two conduits.

20. Select the end of the first conduit section.

Right click and select **Draw Conduit**.

21. Select the end point of the lower conduit.

Revit will automatically create the bend and add the appropriate fittings based on the angles which were enabled in Electrical Settings.

22.

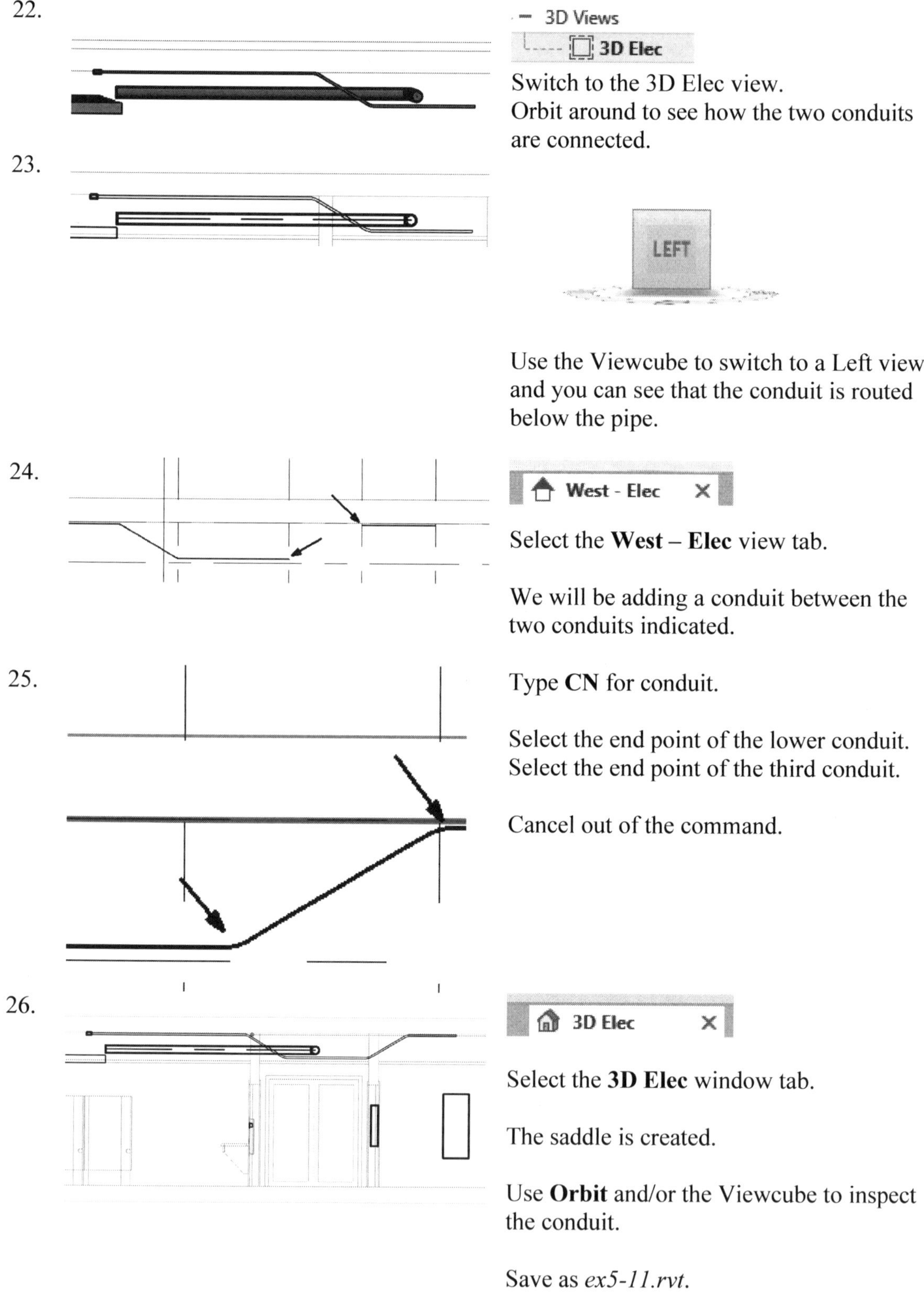

Switch to the 3D Elec view.
Orbit around to see how the two conduits
are connected.

23.

Use the Viewcube to switch to a Left view
and you can see that the conduit is routed
below the pipe.

24.

Select the **West – Elec** view tab.

We will be adding a conduit between the
two conduits indicated.

25.

Type **CN** for conduit.

Select the end point of the lower conduit.
Select the end point of the third conduit.

Cancel out of the command.

26.

Select the **3D Elec** window tab.

The saddle is created.

Use **Orbit** and/or the Viewcube to inspect
the conduit.

Save as *ex5-11.rvt*.

Challenge Exercise:

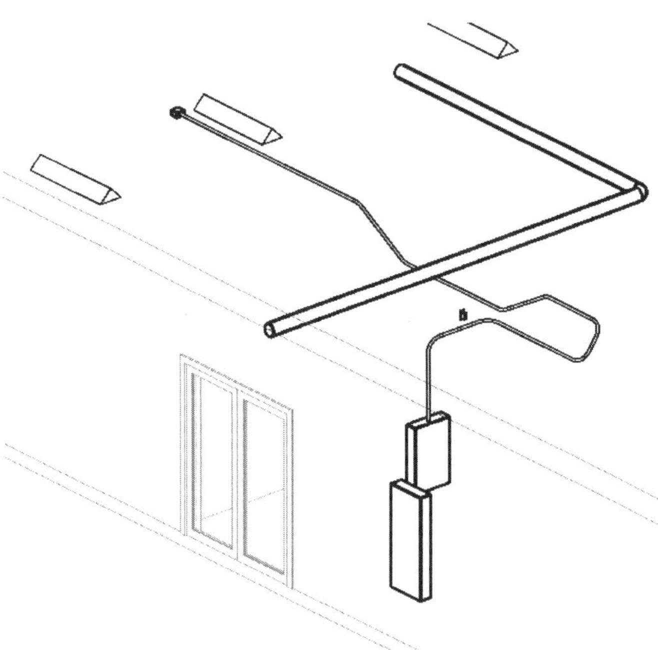

See if you can connect the top connector on the LP1-A panel to the conduit you created.

Hint: *Make sure you provide plenty of space for fittings to be added.*

Switch to the **Conduit over Pipes** section view and draw a section of conduit straight up 3'3".

Then try to connect the two ends of conduit.

Exercise 5-16:

Create a Conduit Roll

Drawing Name: *conduit_roll.rvt*
Estimated Time: 20 minutes

This exercise reinforces the following skills:
- ❑ Conduits
- ❑ Electrical Fixtures

1.

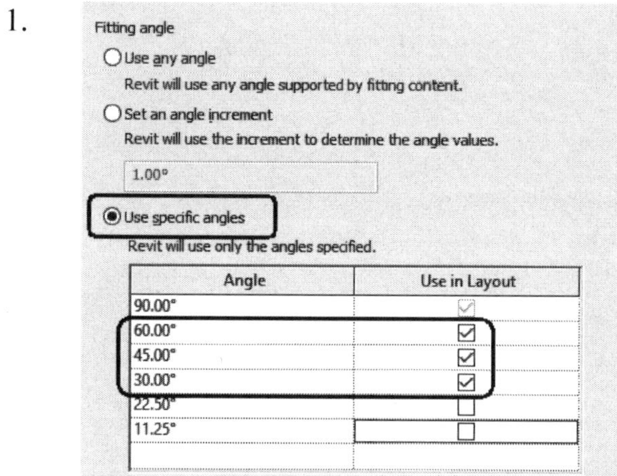

90° is enabled by default.

Type **ES** to open the Electrical Settings palette.

Electrical Settings

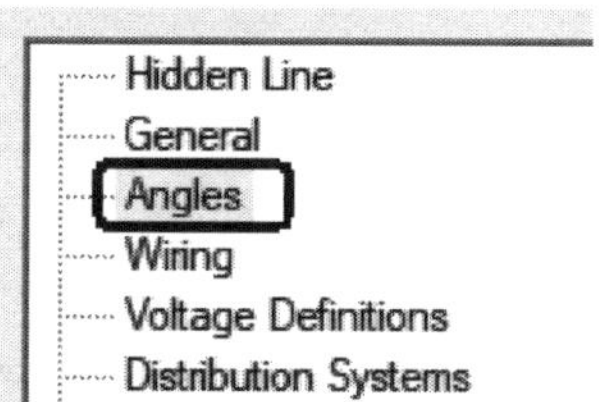

Highlight **Angles**.

Enable **Use specific angles**.
Enable 60°, 45°, and 30°.
Click **OK**.

2.

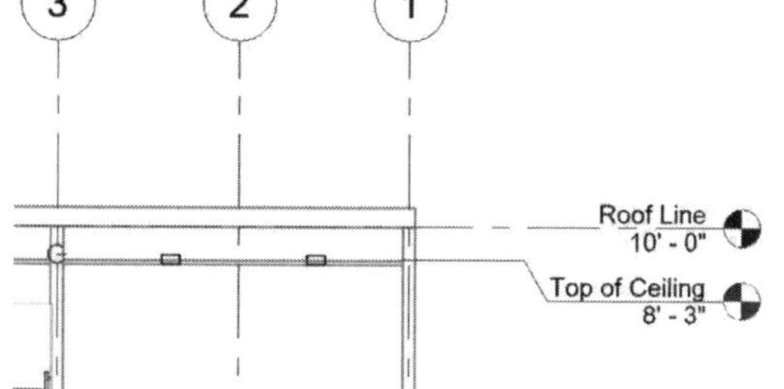

Sections (Building Section)
    Conduit over Pipes
    Front of LP1-A Panel
    Lab 101

Open the **Lab 101** section view.

Notice that the top of the ceiling is located at 8' 3" above Level 1.

3.

Ceiling Plans
1 – Top of Ceiling

Open the **1 – Top of Ceiling** ceiling plan under Power.

Locate the intersection of Grids A and 2.

We are going to place a junction box at this intersection.

4.

Switch to the **Systems** ribbon.

Select the **Electrical Fixture** tool.

5.

Select the **Load w Conduit Connectors 4" Square 120 Junction Box**.

Set the Elevation from Level to **9' 9 7/8"**.

This places it above the piping.

Place the component at A-2.
Cancel out of the command.

6.

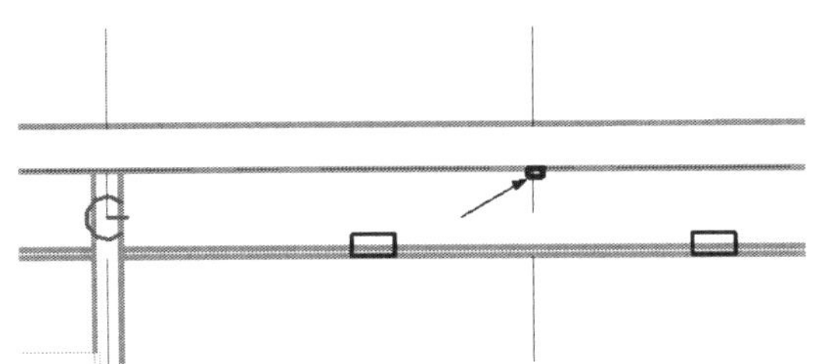

Switch to the Lab 101 Section view and verify the placement of the junction box.

It should be attached to the roof joist.

The green circle on the left is the pipe.

7.

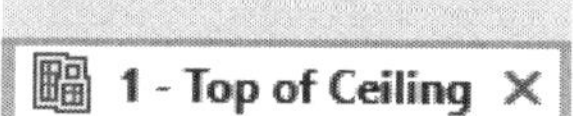

Our conduit needs to go below this pipe.

Select the pipe.
On the Options bar:
See that the pipe has a diameter of 6" and has a middle elevation of 8' 11".

8.

| Pipe Types | |
| Standard | |

Pipes (1)

Constraints
Horizontal Justification	Center
Vertical Justification	Middle
Reference Level	Level 1
Upper End Top Elevation	9' 2 1/16"
Middle Elevation	8' 11"
Lower End Bottom Elevation	8' 7 15/16"
Lower End Invert Elevation	8' 8 33/256"
Slope	0" / 12"

If you look on the Properties palette, you see the bottom of the pipe is located at 8' 7 15/16".

The top of the ceiling is at 8' 3".

This means we can place the bottom part of the conduit saddle at 8' 5".

9.

🔲 1 - Top of Ceiling ✕

Switch back to the **1 – Top of Ceiling** view.

Select the junction box to activate the connectors.

You should see five connectors – one at the top and one on each side.

10.

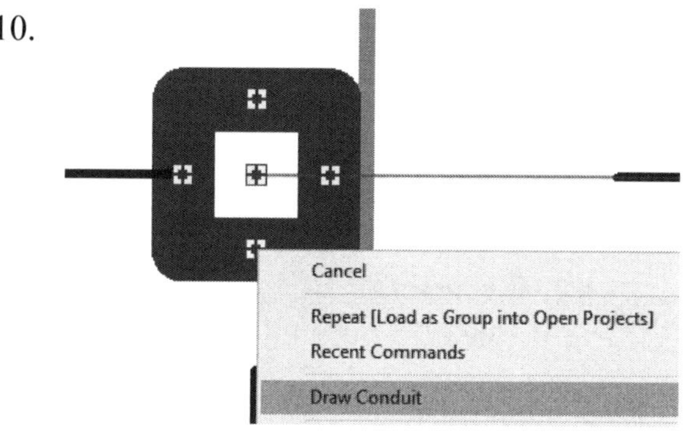

Select the south/bottom connector.

Right click and select **Draw Conduit.**

11.

Diameter: 1"   Middle Elevation: 9' 10 15/16"

On the Option bar:
Set the conduit diameter to **1"**.
Set the Middle Elevation to **9' 10 15/16".**

12.

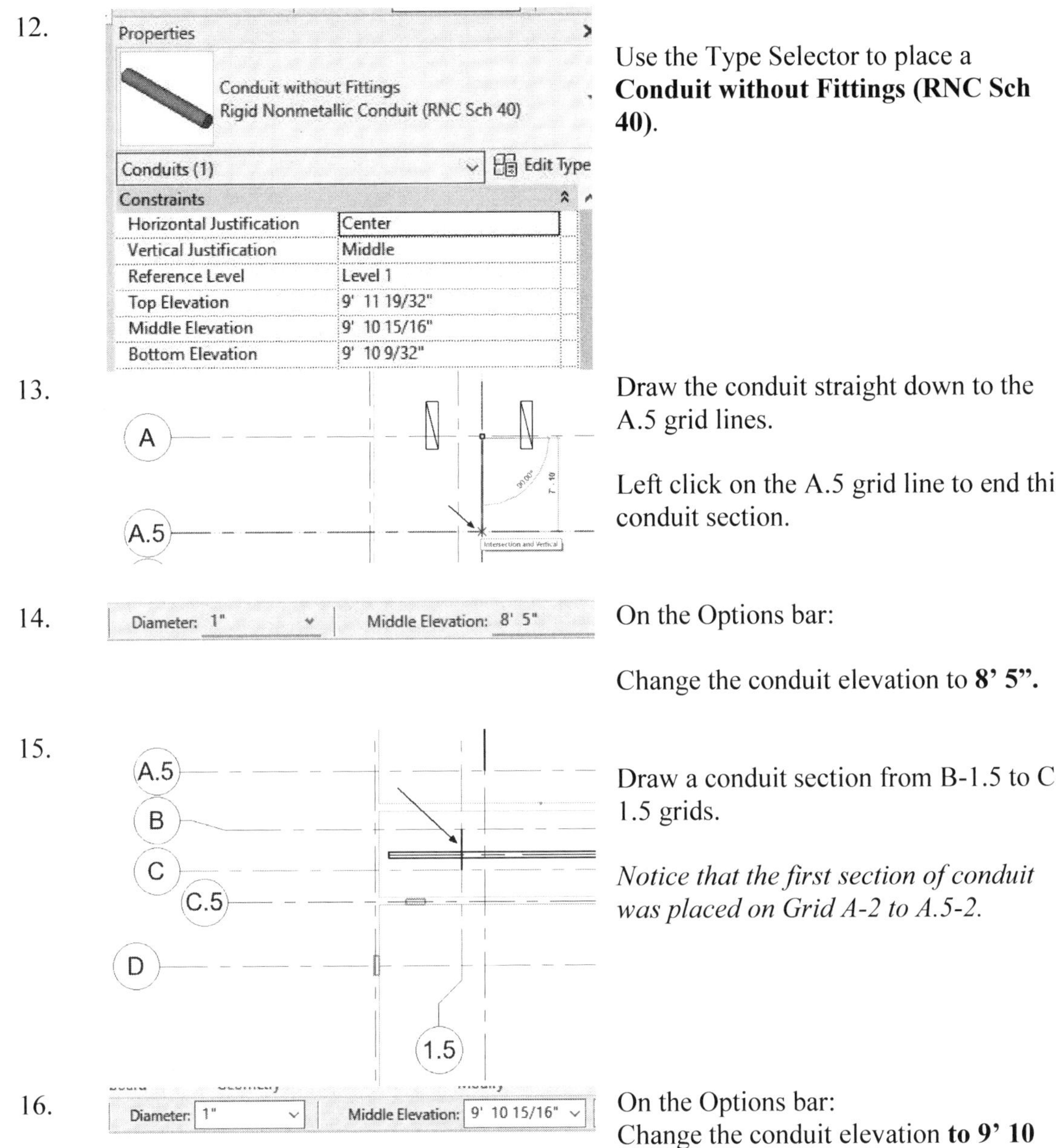

Use the Type Selector to place a
Conduit without Fittings (RNC Sch 40).

13. Draw the conduit straight down to the A.5 grid lines.

Left click on the A.5 grid line to end this conduit section.

14. On the Options bar:

Change the conduit elevation to **8' 5"**.

15. Draw a conduit section from B-1.5 to C-1.5 grids.

Notice that the first section of conduit was placed on Grid A-2 to A.5-2.

16. On the Options bar:
Change the conduit elevation **to 9' 10 15/16"**.

17.

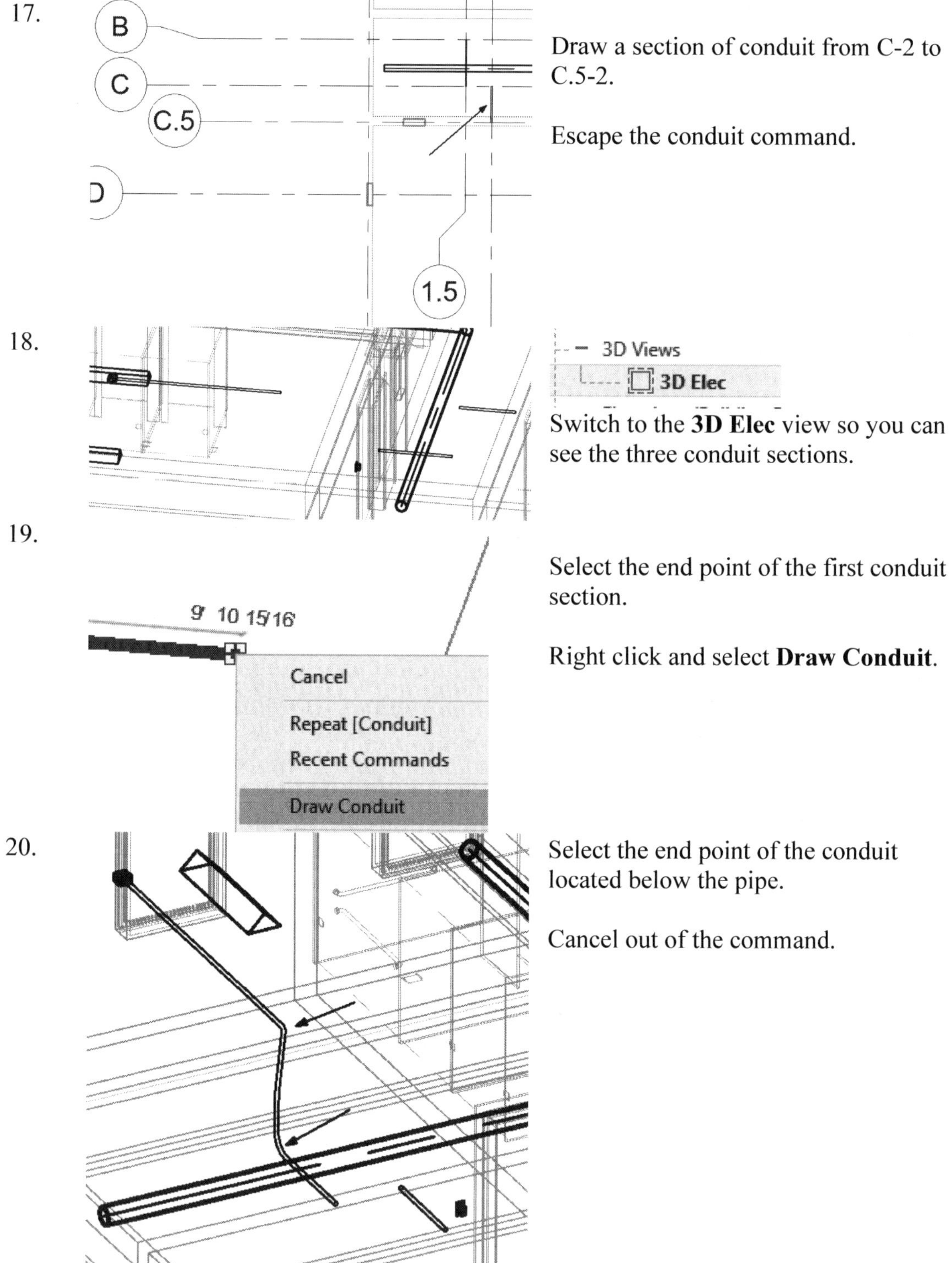

Draw a section of conduit from C-2 to C.5-2.

Escape the conduit command.

18.

Switch to the **3D Elec** view so you can see the three conduit sections.

19.

Select the end point of the first conduit section.

Right click and select **Draw Conduit**.

20.

Select the end point of the conduit located below the pipe.

Cancel out of the command.

21. 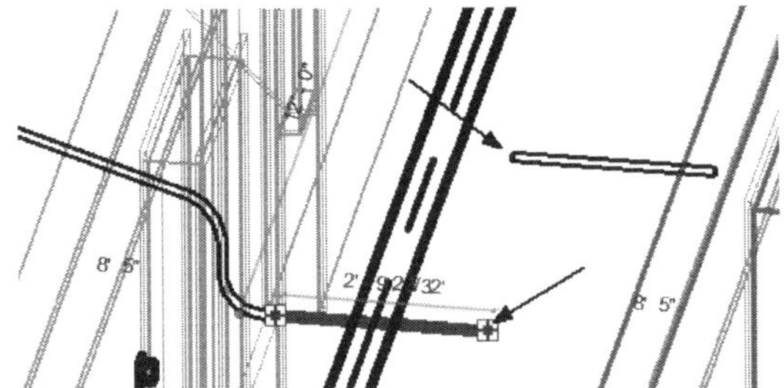

Select the end point of the lower conduit section.

Right click and select **Draw Conduit**.

Select the endpoint of the third conduit section.

Cancel out of the command.

22. 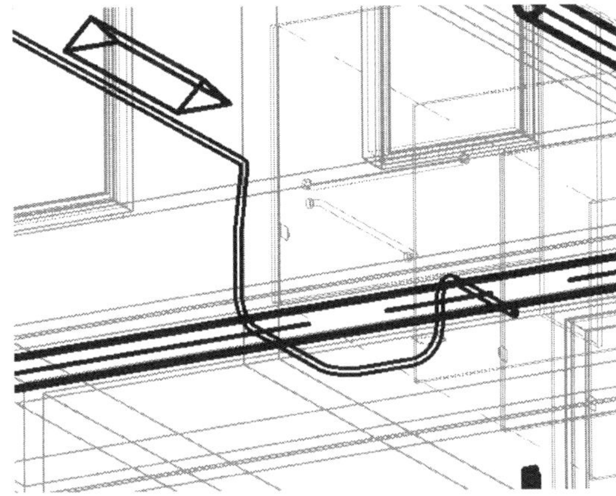

Orbit around to inspect how the conduit was routed.

Save as *ex5-12.rvt*.

Challenge Exercise:

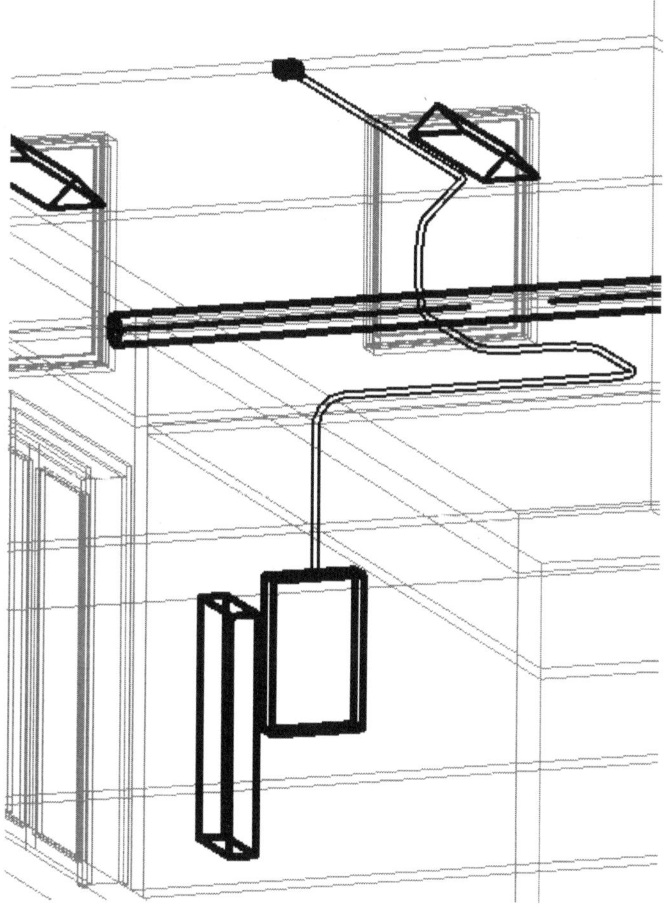

See if you can connect the top connector on the LP1-A panel to the conduit you created.

Hint: *Make sure you provide plenty of space for fittings to be added.*

Switch to the Front of LP1-A Panel section view and draw a section of conduit straight up 1'3".

Then try to connect the two ends of conduit.

Exercise 5-17:

Place a Conduit through a Pipe

Drawing Name: *pipe and conduit.rvt*
Estimated Time: 10 minutes

This exercise reinforces the following skills:
- ❑ Conduits
- ❑ Electrical Fixtures

1. 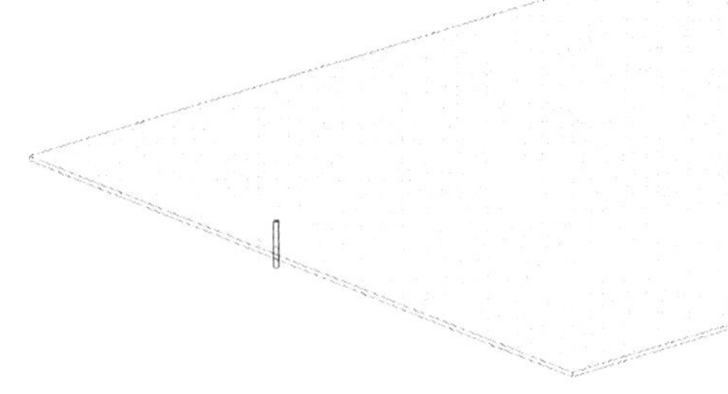

   Open the 3D view.

   There is a 6" pipe and a 6" thick concrete slab.

   We want to run a conduit through the pipe.

2. 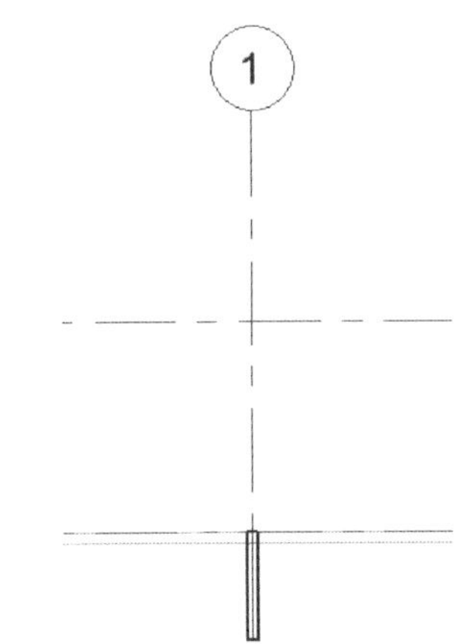

   Switch to an **East – Elec** elevation.

   The pipe is aligned with Grid 1.

   Move the grid bubble up so you can see the pipe clearly.

3.   1/8" = 1'-0" ▦ ⬡   Set the Detail Level to **Fine**.
   Set the Display to **Wireframe**.

4. 
   Conduit

   Select the **Conduit** tool from the Systems ribbon or type CN to start the conduit command.

5.

Set the conduit diameter to 4" on the Options bar.

6.

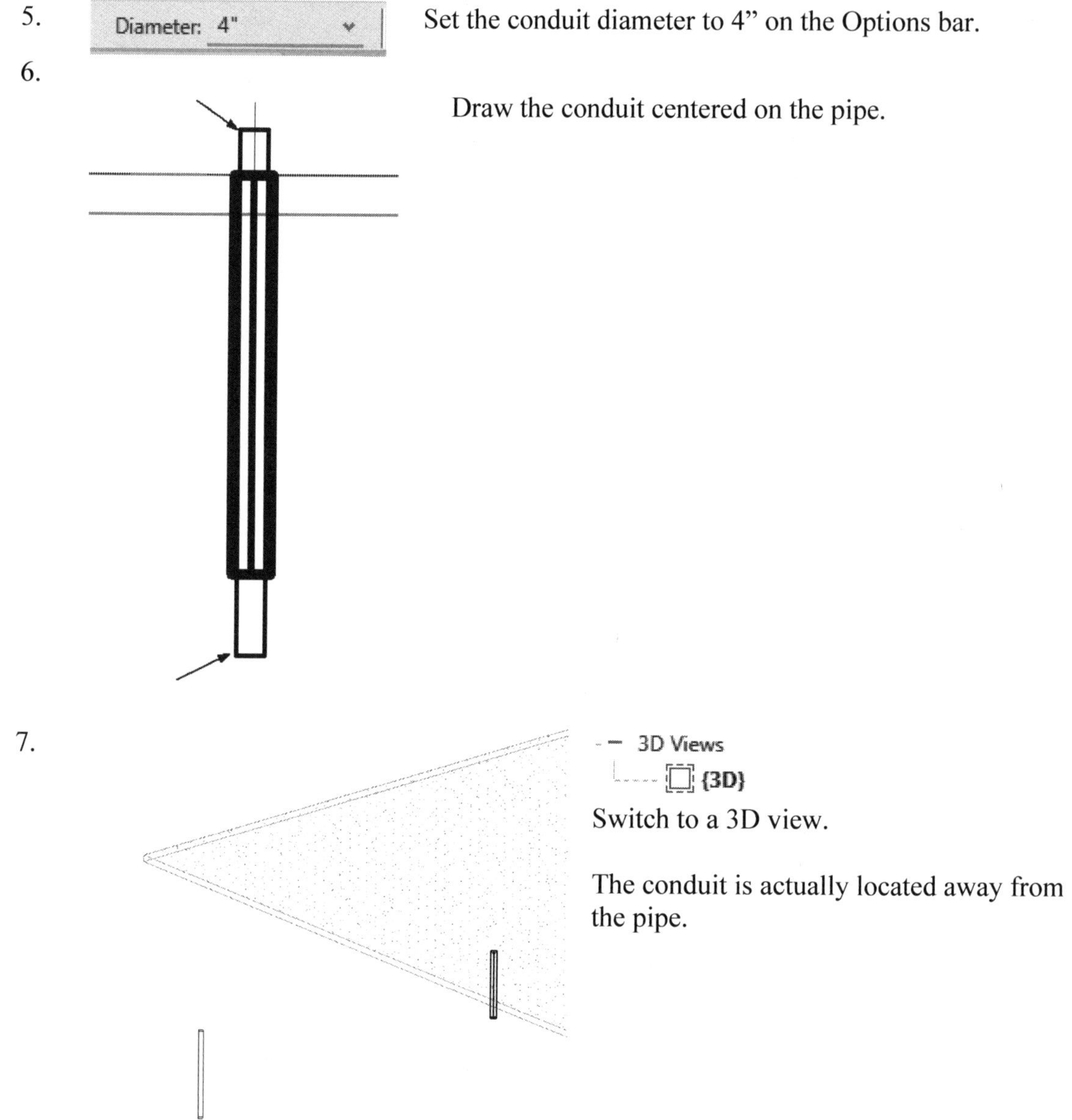

Draw the conduit centered on the pipe.

7.

Switch to a 3D view.

The conduit is actually located away from the pipe.

8.

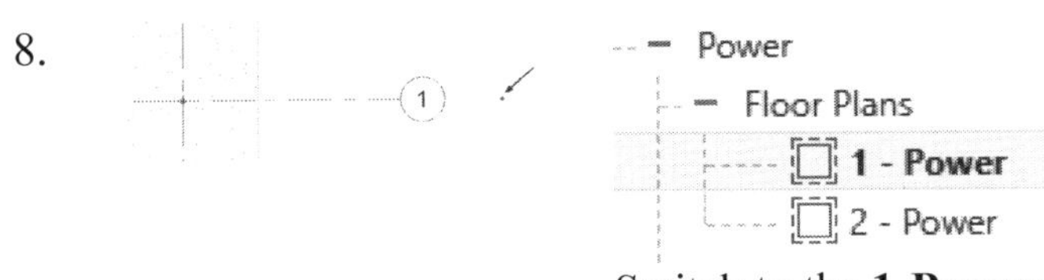

Switch to the **1-Power** floor plan view.

You should see the conduit located to the right of the grid 1 bubble. You may need to zoom in to see it.

9. Activate the **Modify** ribbon.
Select the **ALIGN** tool.

10.

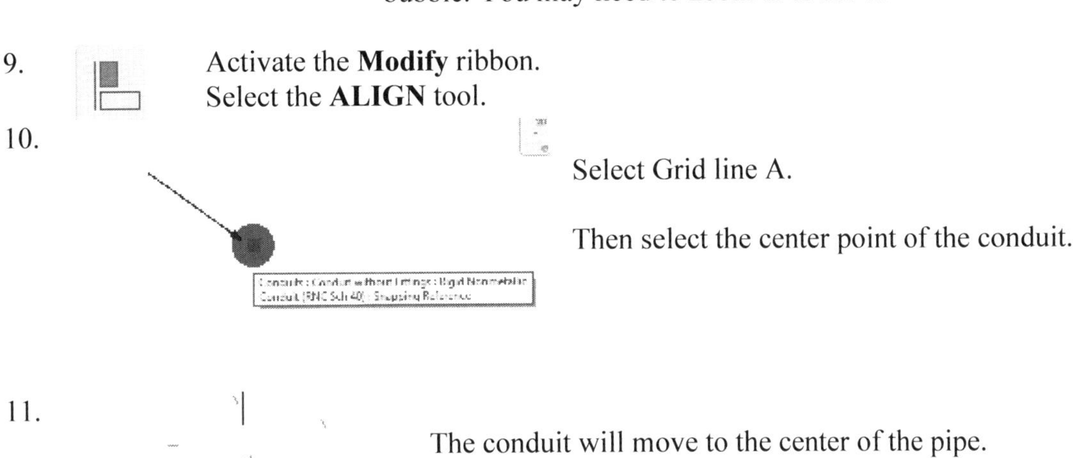

Select Grid line A.

Then select the center point of the conduit.

11. The conduit will move to the center of the pipe.

12.

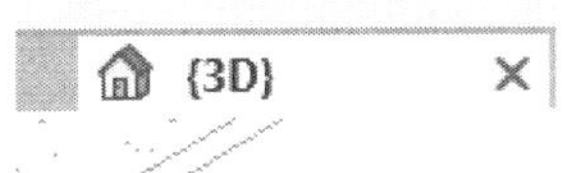

Switch to a 3D view.

Verify that the conduit is inserted into the pipe.

Save as *ex5-13.rvt*.

Lab Exercises

Open Electrical Project_conduit.rvt.

Open the Manage Links dialog.

Reload the linked files: Architectural.rvt and Structural.rvt.

Open the Electrical Power, Floor Plan Level 1.

Zoom in on the ELECTRICAL Room 107.

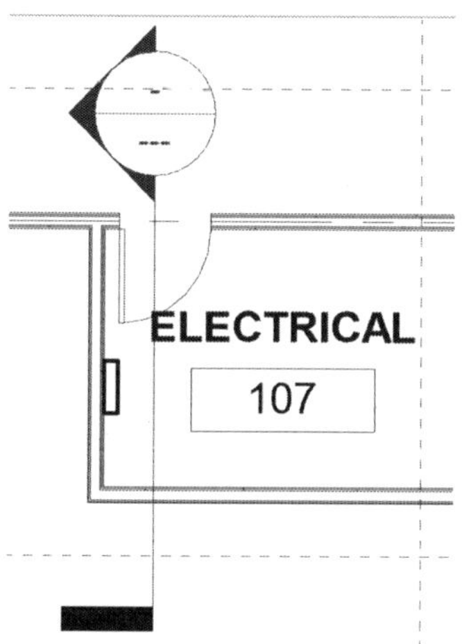

Create a section view to see an elevation of the electrical panel.

Open the new section.

Rename it Electrical Room elevation.

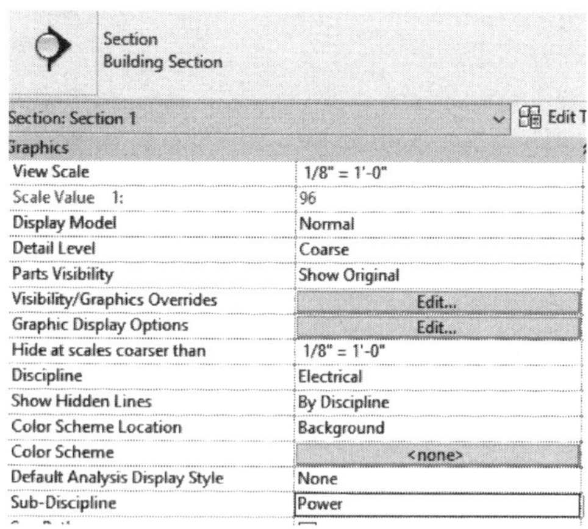

Change the sub-discipline of the view to Power so it sorts correctly in the project browser.

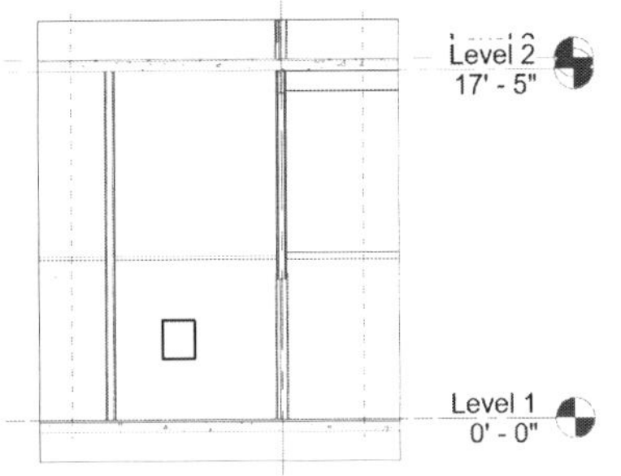

Adjust the crop region for the view.

Set the Detail Level to Fine.

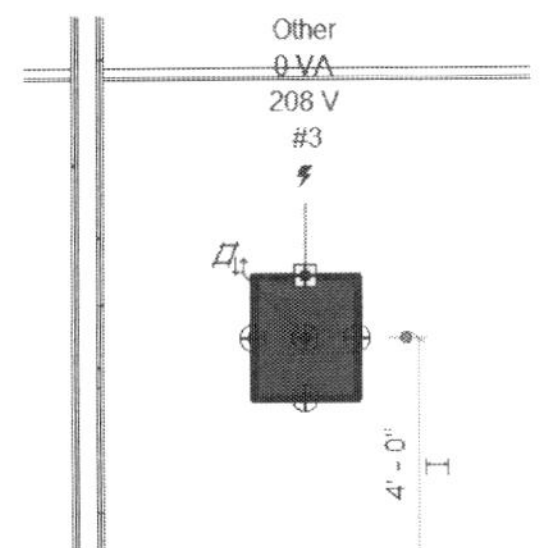

Select the panel so you can see the connectors.

Locate the connector using the right side connector.

Change the conduit diameter to 4".

Draw a conduit as shown.

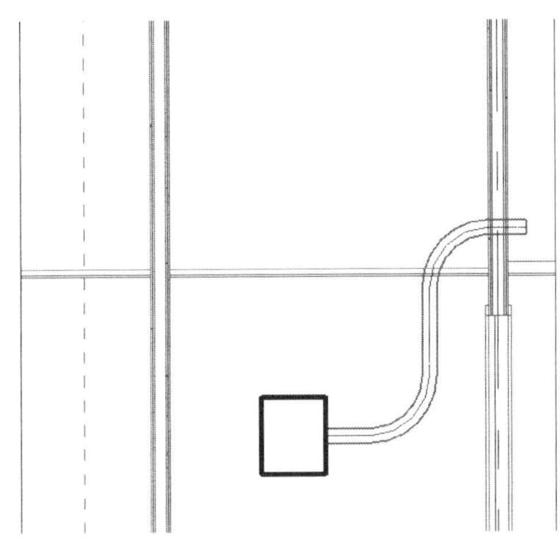

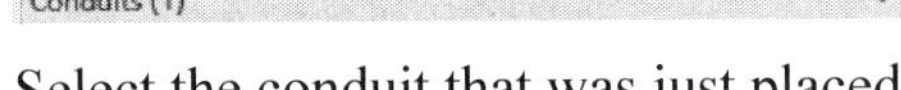

Select the conduit that was just placed.

Define four new conduit types called
- **Emergency High – OH**
- **Emergency High – UG**
- **Emergency Low – OH**
- **Emergency Low- UG**

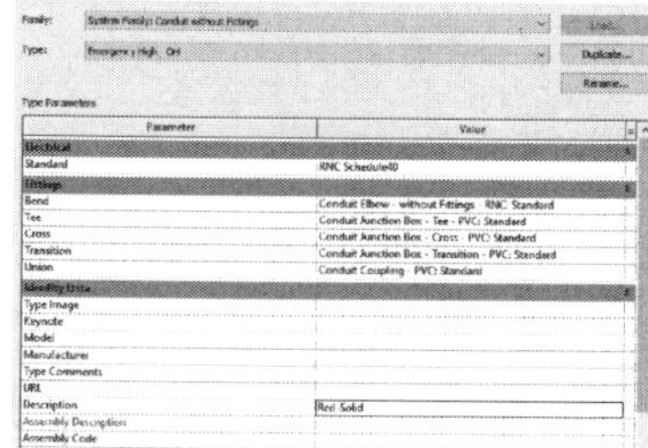

The descriptions for each type should be:

- Emergency High OH – Red Solid
- Emergency High UG – Red Dashed
- Energency Low OH – Magenta Solid
- Emergency Low UG – Magenta Dashed

Hint: *You can use Transfer Project Standards using ex5-10.rvt to import the definitions and then verify the definitions.*

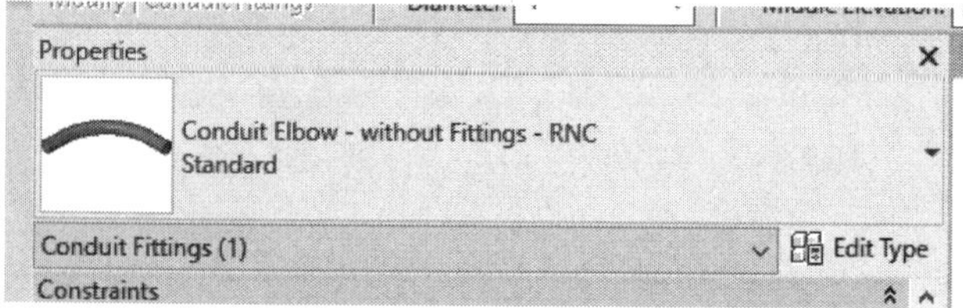

Select the conduit elbow that was just placed.

Define four new conduit fitting types called
- **Emergency High – OH**
- **Emergency High – UG**
- **Emergency Low – OH**
- **Emergency Low- UG**

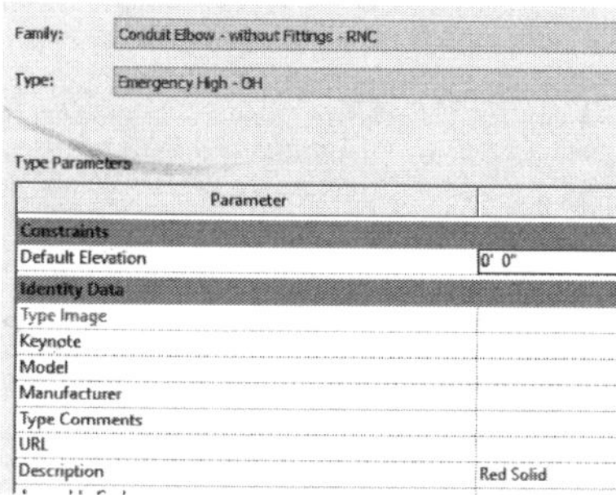

The descriptions for each type should be:

- Emergency High OH – Red Solid
- Emergency High UG – Red Dashed
- Energency Low OH – Magenta Solid
- Emergency Low UG – Magenta Dashed

Change the family definitions for the Emergency High and Emergency Low conduits to use the correct fittings.

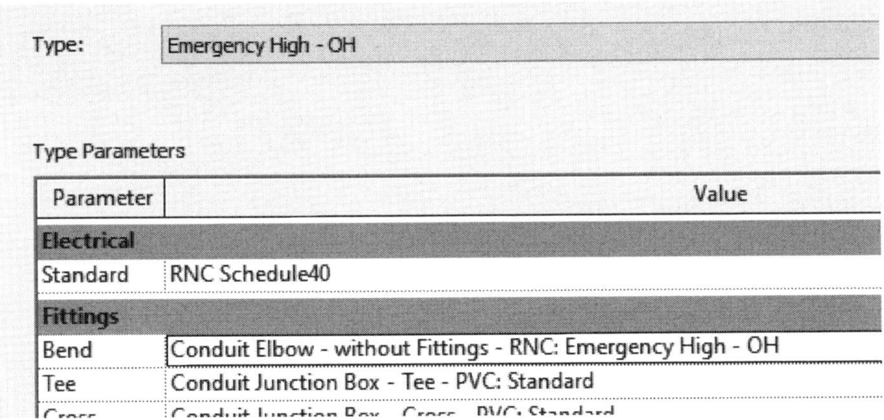

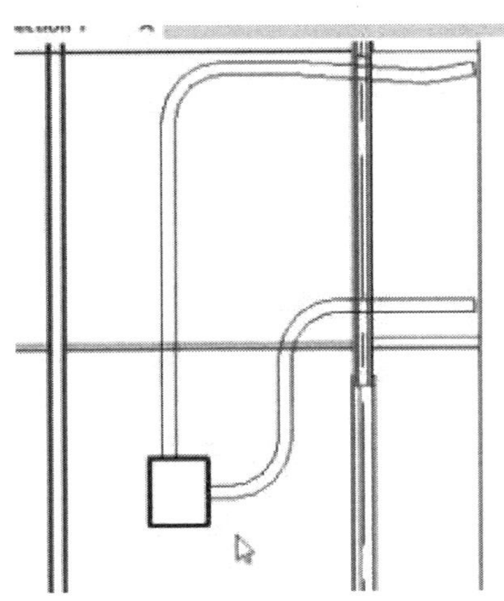

Define filters to display the conduits using the appropriate colors, linetypes, and lineweights.

Hint: *You can use Transfer Project Standards using ex5-10.rvt to import the definitions and then verify the definitions.*

Place an emergency low conduit using the top connector on the panel.

Adjust the location of the connector so it is 1' 2" from the right side.

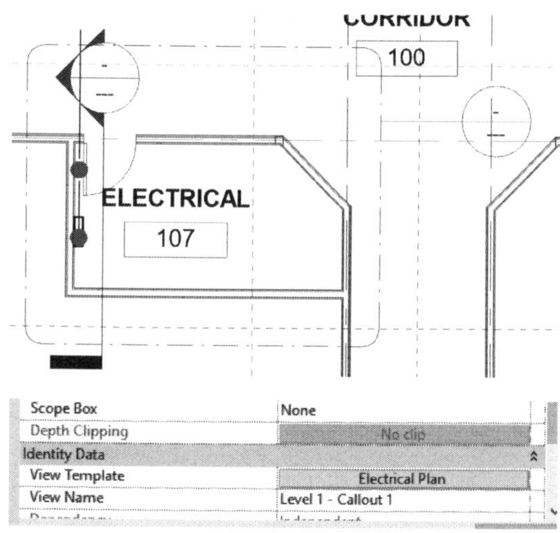

Add a callout view to Level 1 Power floor plan around the electrical room 107.

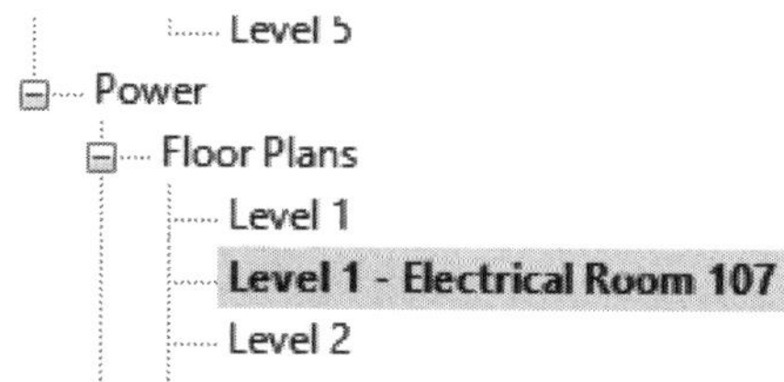

Scope Box	None
Depth Clipping	No clip
Identity Data	
View Template	Electrical Plan
View Name	Level 1 - Callout 1

Open the Callout View.

Rename the CalloutView Electrical Room 107.

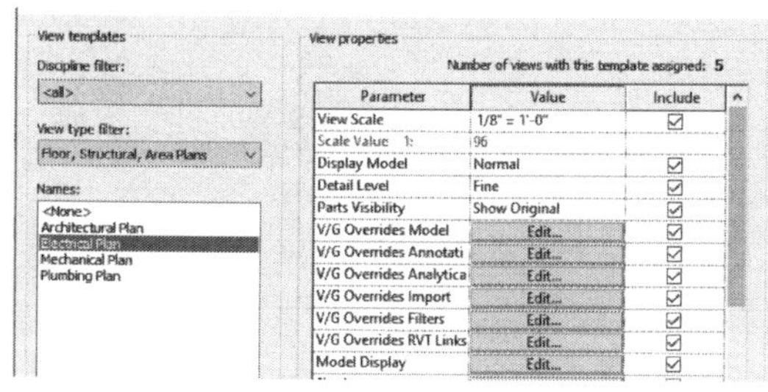

Select the Electrical Plan view template used on the Callout view.

Change the Detail Level to Fine.

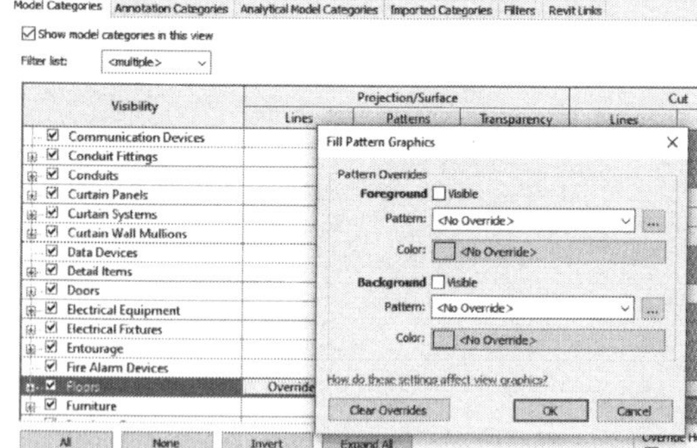

Select the V/G Overrides Model button.

Change the Floors under Model Categories by selecting override under Patterns.

Disable the visibility of the foreground and background patterns.

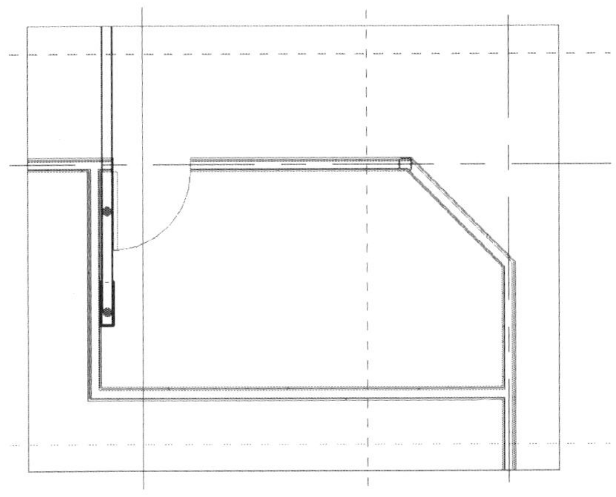

The callout view appearance should no longer display the hatch patterns for the floors.

Go to the Systems ribbon.

Select the **Conduit** tool.

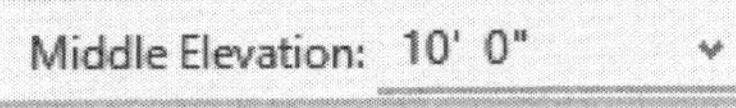

Set the Middle Elevation to **10' 0"** above the level.

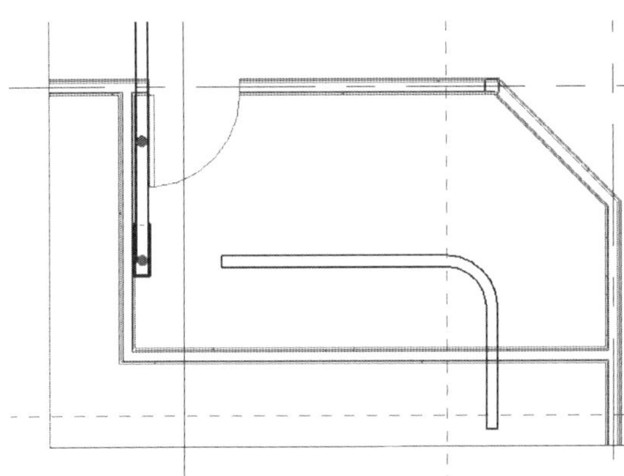

Select the Emergency High OH conduit family.

Align the start of the conduit with the end of the connector.

Start the conduit about 5' to the right of the panel, drawing the conduit horizontally 9' and then draw a vertical conduit down.

Hint: *Draw a model line to help locate the start of the conduit and then erase the line once the conduit is placed.*

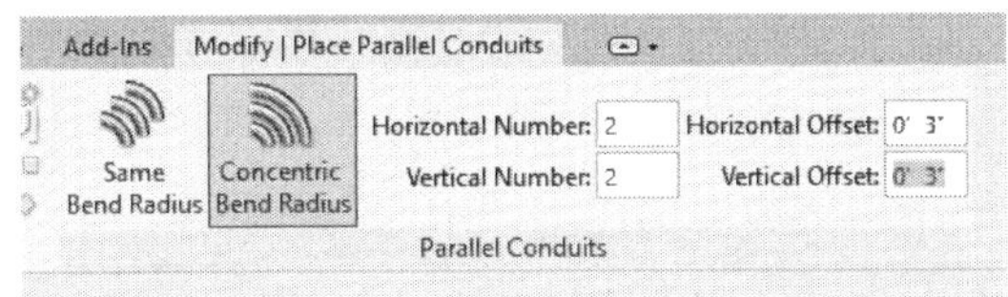

Use the Place parallel conduits tool to place two horizontal and two vertical conduits.

Enable Concentric Bend Radius.

Set the Horizontal Offset to 3".

Set the Vertical Offset to 3".

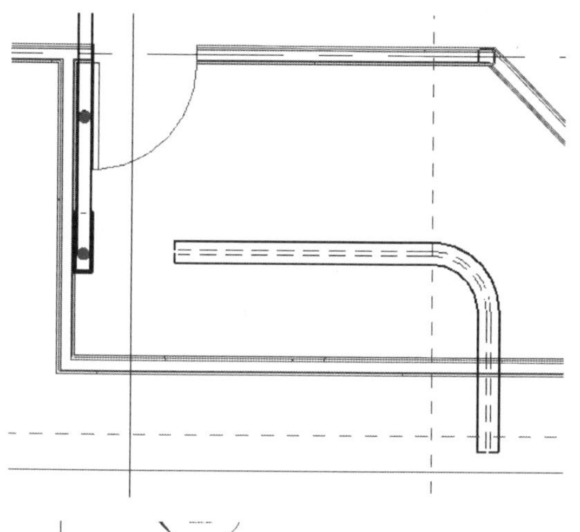

Use the TAB key to select the entire conduit run.

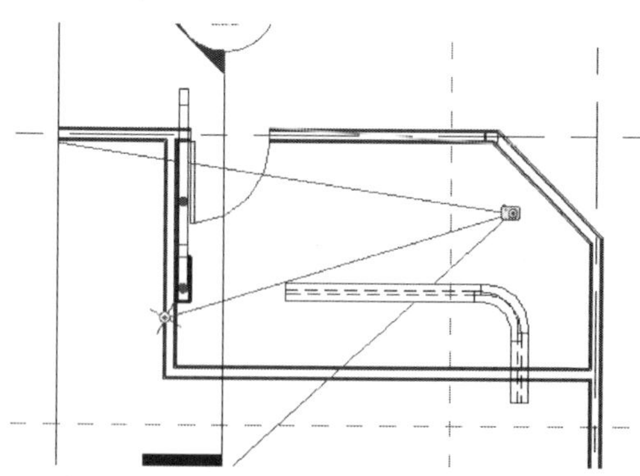

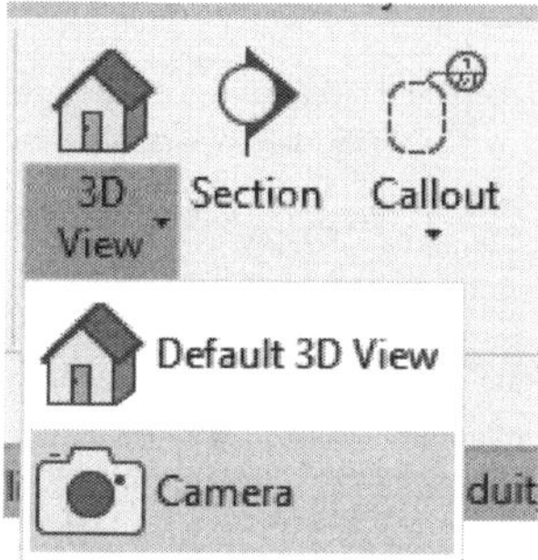

Select Camera under 3D View on the View ribbon.

Place a camera in the Level 1 – Electrical Room floor plan. Point the camera towards the panel.

Rename the 3D view **3D Panel and Conduits**.

Change the Sub-discipline for the view to **Power** so it is organized correctly in the Project Browser.

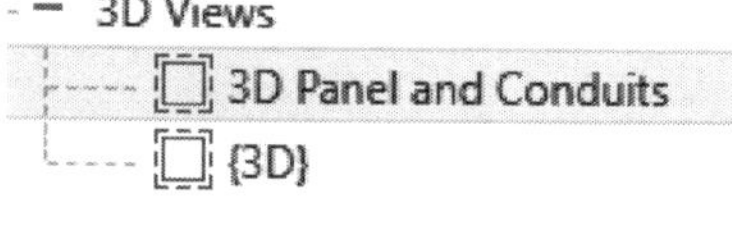

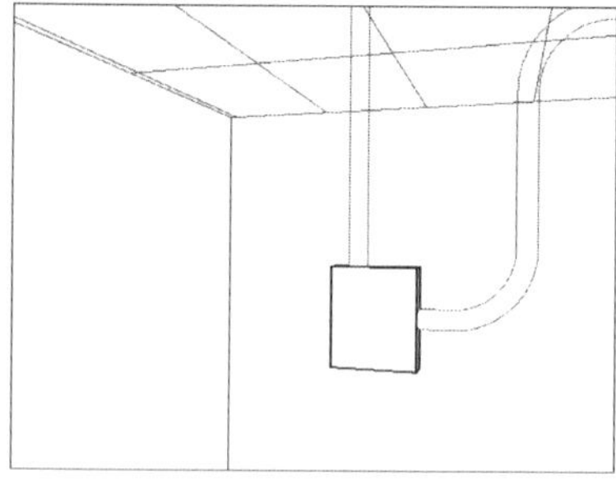

Create a view template to apply filters to your conduits.

Apply the view template to a 3D view.

Lesson

06

Schedules

With equipment, devices, and lights in place, creating schedules helps leverage the database Revit creates to the needs of the designer. MA Lighting fixture schedule can be created the same way the space schedule was created. Panels schedules are a slightly different creature. Select a panel, then pick the Create Panel Schedule tool on the contextual tab. There is a standard template, but custom templates can be created to serve the needs of the individual firms. Once created, Panel schedules become available under their own heading in the Project Browser, similar to other schedules.

Schedules provide information about building elements, such as lighting fixtures, that can be exported to other applications, like Excel, for cost lists, estimates and other quantity tallies. Schedules update automatically when the building model is changed, eliminating the possibility of errors.

A schedule is a formatted view of a building model in tabular format. It is considered a view-element. Each property of an element is represented as a field in the schedule. Schedules can list every instance of an element type in different rows or condense the information to multiple instances of an element in a single row.

Guidelines for working with Schedules

- Create schedules that display only important or critical fields so that the schedules are easy to understand.
- Use the Hidden Field check box on the Formatting tab to hide fields that you want to use but not show in the schedule.
- Use Sorting/Grouping to organize your schedule.
- You can locate elements by using the schedule. Simply highlight the element in the schedule and select Show.

Exercise 6-1:

Creating a Lighting Fixture Schedule

Drawing Name: *schedules.rvt*
Estimated Time: 15 minutes

This exercise reinforces the following skills:
- User Interface
- Ribbon
- System Browser

1. Activate the **View** ribbon.

2. Select **Schedules→Schedule/Quantities**.

3. Highlight **Lighting Fixtures** in the Category pane.

    Enable **Schedule building components**.

    Click **OK**.

    *Hint: You can type **light** in the search field to quickly locate the lighting fixtures category.*

4.

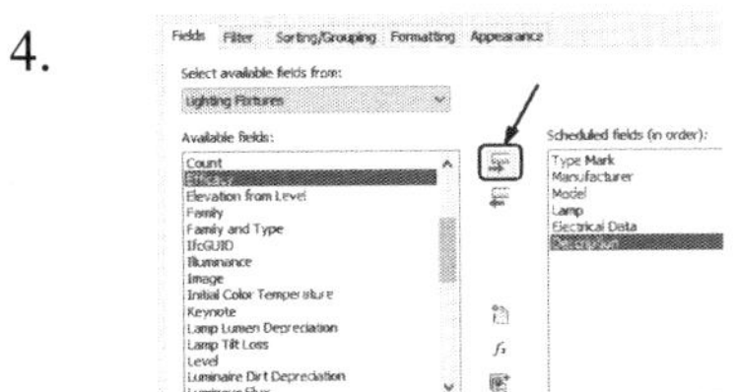

Use the Add tool to add the fields to the schedule. The order of the fields determines their column position in the schedule.

Add the following fields:

- Type Mark
- Manufacturer
- Model
- Lamp
- Electrical Data
- Description

Hint: You can hold down the CTL key to select more than one field at a time. Then use the UP and down controls to re-order the columns.

5.

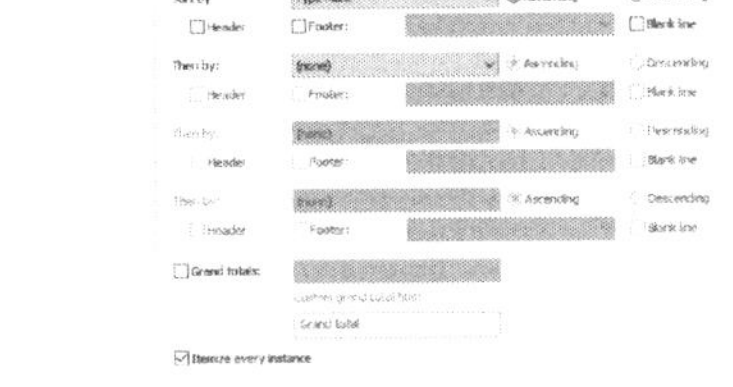

Select the **Sorting/Grouping** tab.

Set Sort by: to **Type Mark**.

Enable **Itemize every instance** at the bottom of the dialog.

Click **OK** to create the schedule.

6.

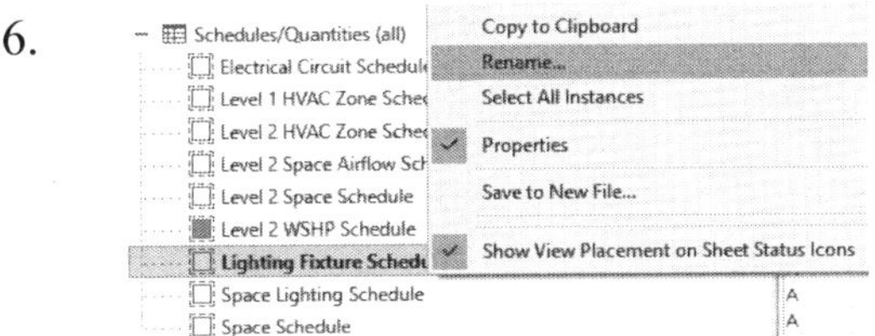

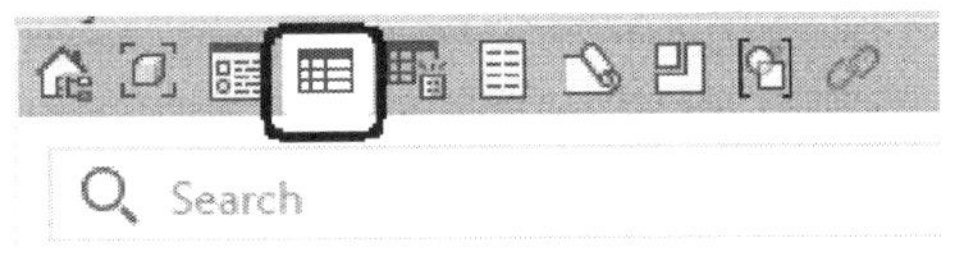

Enable the Schedules filter tab on the Project Browser.

The Lighting Fixture Schedule appears in the browser.

Right click on the Lighting Fixture Schedule and select **Rename**.

7.

Rename **Level 2 – Lighting Fixture Schedule.**

8. 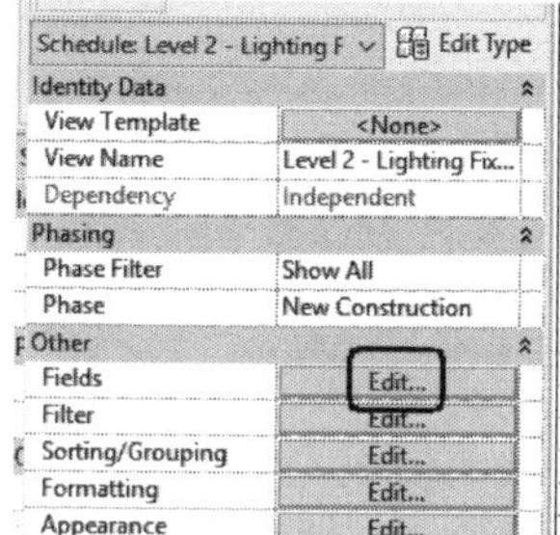 On the Properties palette:

Select **Edit** next to Fields.

9. 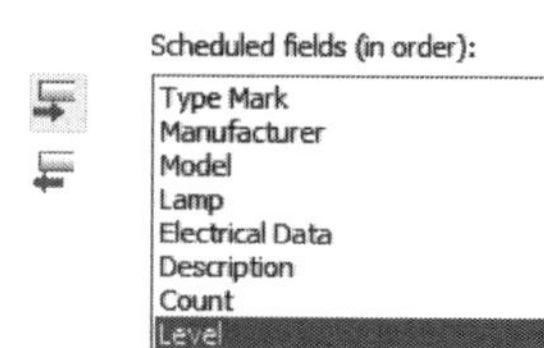 Add **Count** and Level to the selected Fields.

10. Activate the **Filter** tab.

Set Filter by: **Level.**

Select **equals** from the drop-down list.

Set the Level to **Level 2.**

11. Select the **Formatting** tab.

Highlight **Level.**

Enable **Hidden field**.

This means the field will not appear in the schedule, but will be used by the Filter to determine which elements appear in the schedule.

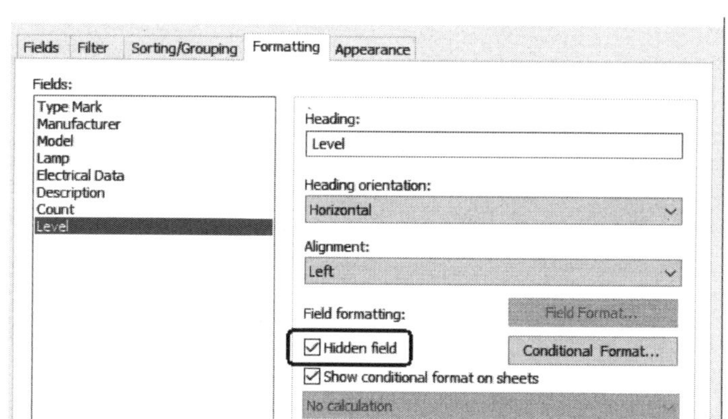

12. Select the **Sorting/Grouping** tab.

Disable **Itemize every instance** at the bottom of the dialog.

Click **OK** to close the dialog.

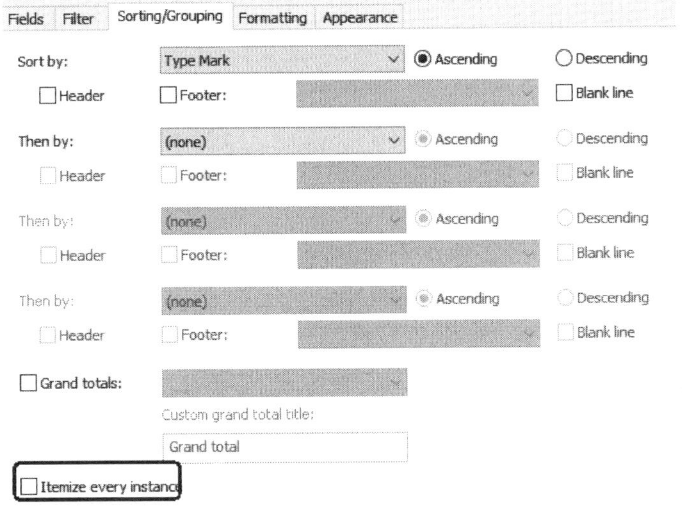

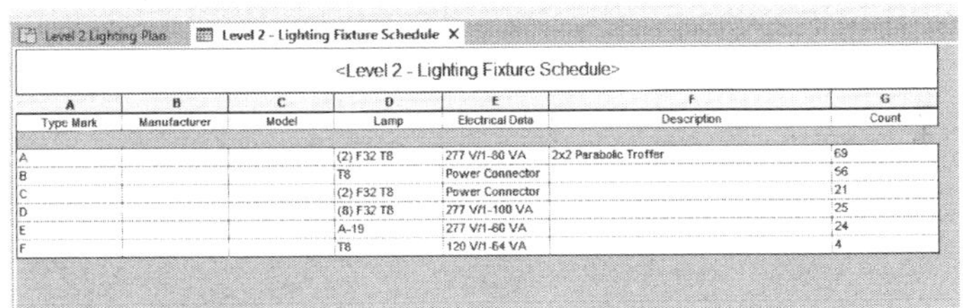

13. The schedule updates.

A	**B**	**C**	**D**	**E**	**F**	**G**
Type Mark	Manufacturer	Model	Lamp	Electrical Data	Description	Count
A			(2) F32 T8	277 V/1-80 VA	2x2 Parabolic Troffer	69
B			T8	Power Connector		56
C			(2) F32 T8	Power Connector		21
D			(8) F32 T8	277 V/1-100 VA		25
E			A-19	277 V/1-60 VA		24
F			T8	120 V/1-64 VA		4

14. Save as *ex6-1.rvt*.

Exercise 6-2:

Creating a Lighting and Power Usage Schedule

Drawing Name: *power_usage.rvt*
Estimated Time: 10 minutes

This exercise reinforces the following skills:
- ❑ Schedules
- ❑ Conditional Format
- ❑ Energy Settings

1. 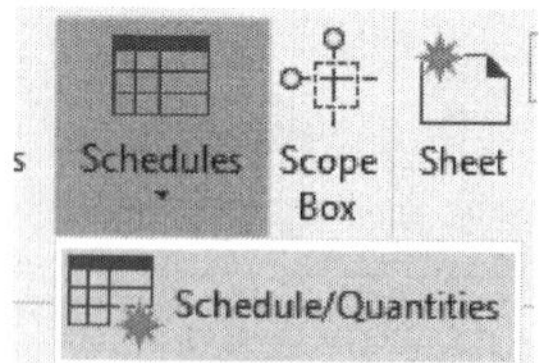 Activate the **View** ribbon.

2. 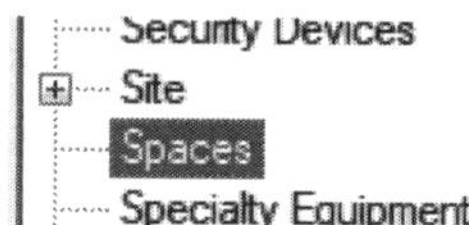 Select **Schedules→Schedule/Quantities**.

3. 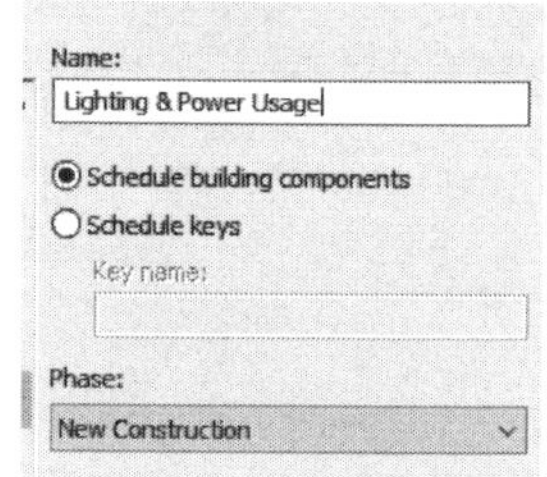 Highlight **Spaces** in the Category pane.

4. Change the Name to **Lighting & Power Usage**.

   Click **OK**.

5. Select the following fields in this order:

   - Name
   - Number
   - Area
   - Actual Lighting Load
   - Actual Lighting Load per Area
   - Actual Power Load
   - Actual Power Load per Area

6. 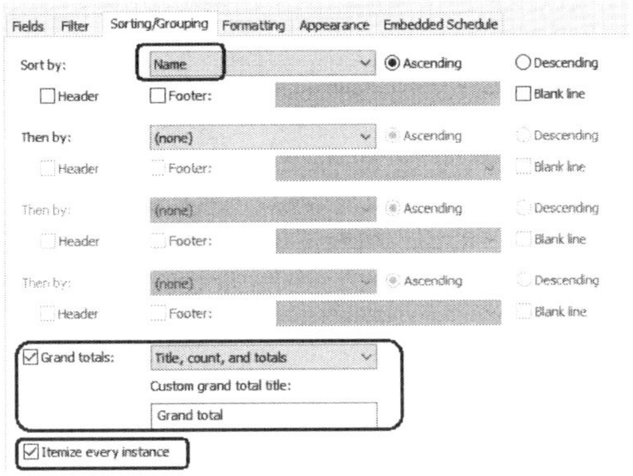 Select the Sorting/Grouping tab.

Sort by: **Name**.

Enable **Grand totals**.

Set to **Title, count, and totals**

Enable **Itemize every instance**.

7. 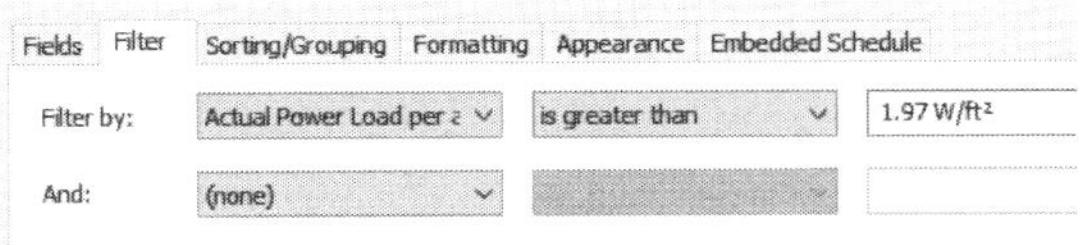 Select the **Filter** tab.

Select **Actual Power Load per Area**

Is Greater Than

Use the drop-down list to select **1.97 W/ft^2**.

Click **OK**.

8. Click **OK** to finish the schedule.

9. 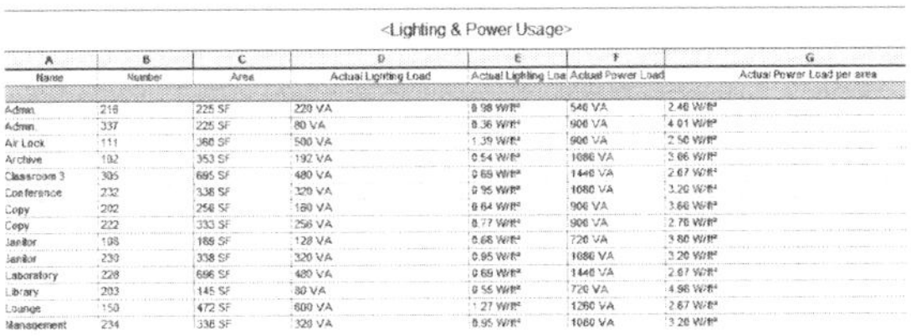 The schedule view opens.

<Lighting & Power Usage>

A	B	C	D	E	F	G
Name	Number	Area	Actual Lighting Load	Actual Lighting Load	Actual Power Load	Actual Power Load per area
Admin	216	225 SF	220 VA	0.98 W/ft²	540 VA	2.40 W/ft²
Admin	337	225 SF	80 VA	0.36 W/ft²	900 VA	4.01 W/ft²
Air Lock	111	360 SF	500 VA	1.39 W/ft²	900 VA	2.50 W/ft²
Archive	102	353 SF	192 VA	0.54 W/ft²	1080 VA	3.06 W/ft²
Classroom 3	305	695 SF	480 VA	0.69 W/ft²	1440 VA	2.07 W/ft²
Conference	232	338 SF	320 VA	0.95 W/ft²	1080 VA	3.20 W/ft²
Copy	202	258 SF	180 VA	0.64 W/ft²	900 VA	3.68 W/ft²
Copy	222	333 SF	256 VA	0.77 W/ft²	900 VA	2.70 W/ft²
Janitor	108	189 SF	128 VA	0.68 W/ft²	720 VA	3.80 W/ft²
Janitor	230	338 SF	320 VA	0.95 W/ft²	1080 VA	3.20 W/ft²
Laboratory	228	696 SF	480 VA	0.69 W/ft²	1440 VA	2.07 W/ft²
Library	203	145 SF	80 VA	0.55 W/ft²	720 VA	4.96 W/ft²
Lounge	150	472 SF	600 VA	1.27 W/ft²	1260 VA	2.67 W/ft²
Management	234	338 SF	320 VA	0.95 W/ft²	1080 VA	3.20 W/ft²

10. Save as *ex6-2.rvt*.

Voltage Drops

Calculating voltage drop is crucial for equipment efficiency and reliability, as excessive drop can cause electrical devices to malfunction, perform poorly, or fail. It is also vital for electrical safety, as excessive voltage drop leads to overheating wires, increasing the risk of fire and electrical accidents. Furthermore, it helps ensure system performance, preventing lights from flickering, motors running hot, and other sensitive components from being damaged. You can use a schedule inside of Revit to help you calculate the voltage drops of a circuit.

Exercise 6-3:

Calculating Voltage Drop of a Circuit

Drawing Name: *voltage drop.rvt*
Estimated Time: 30 minutes

This exercise reinforces the following skills:
- Schedules
- Circuits
- Conductor and Cable Settings
- Wire Types
- Calculated Parameters

1.

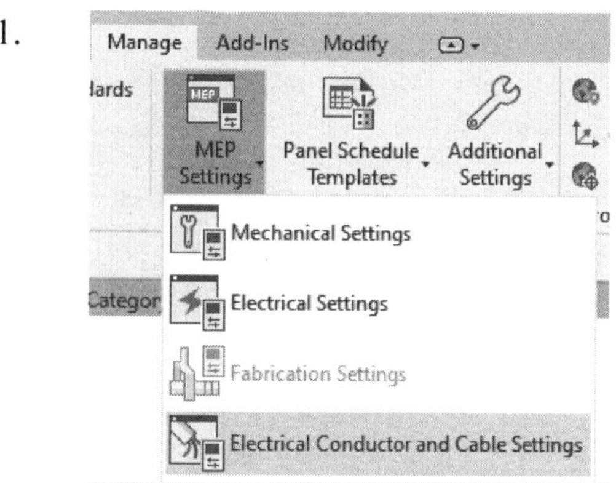

Go to the Manage ribbon.

Go to **MEP Settings→Electrical Conductor and Cable Settings**.

2.

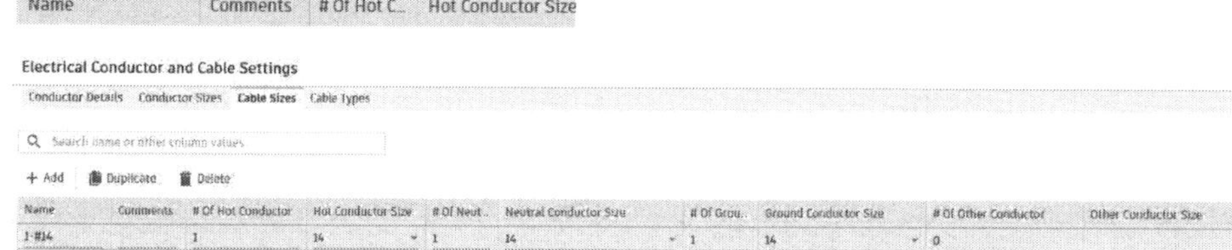

Click the **Cable Sizes** tab.
Select **Add**.

3. Type **1-#14** in the Name column.
Set the # of Hot Conductor to **1**.
Select **14** from the drop-down list to set the hot conductor size.
Repeat for the # of Neutral Conductor and # of Ground Conductor.

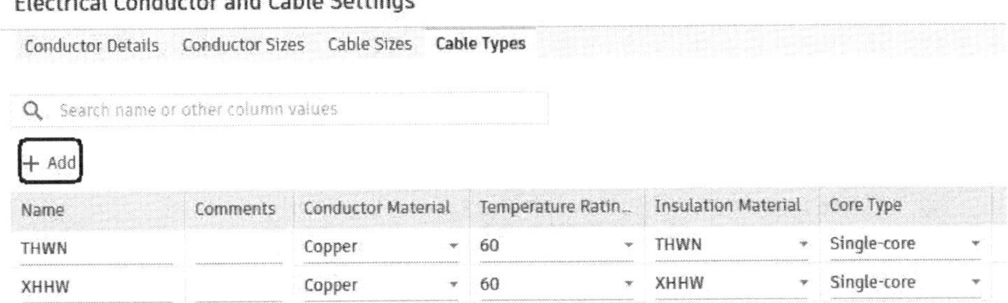

4. Select the **Cable Types** tab.
   Click **Add**.

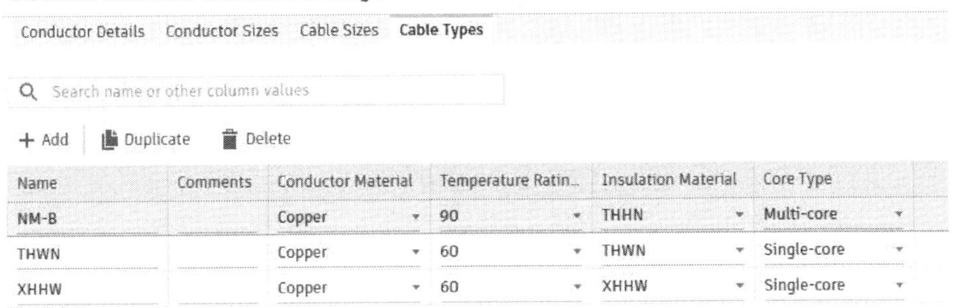

5. Type **NM-B** for the Name.
   Set the Conductor Material to **Copper**.
   Set the Temperature Rating to **90**.
   Set the Insulation Material to **THHN**.
   Set the Core Type to **Multi-Core**.

6. 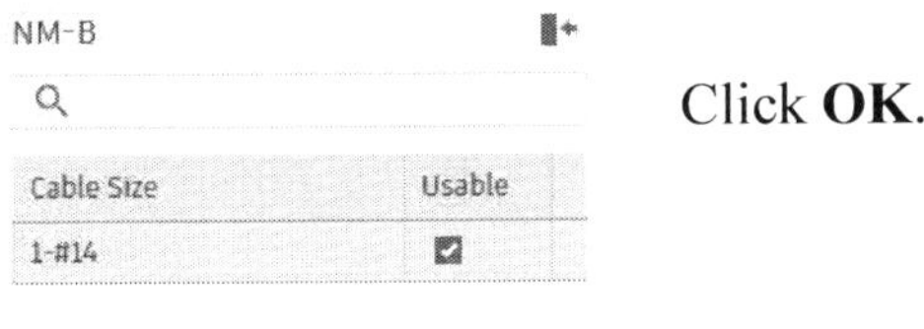   Enable the **1-#14** Cable Size in the right panel.

   Click **OK**.

7.   Open the **1- Lighting** floor plan.

8. 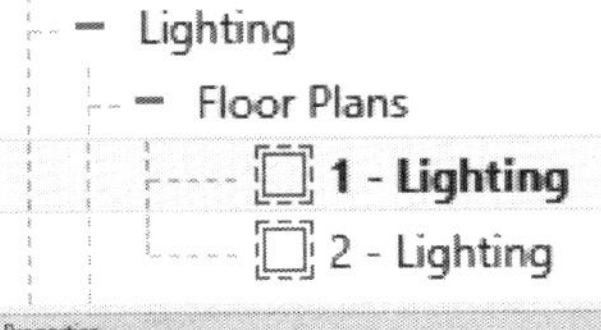   Select one of the wires.
   On the Properties panel:
   Click **Edit Type**.

9.   Select **Duplicate**.

10.   Type **THHN.**

Click **OK.**

11.   Set the Temperature Rating to **90.**
Set the Insulation to **THHN.**

Click **OK.**

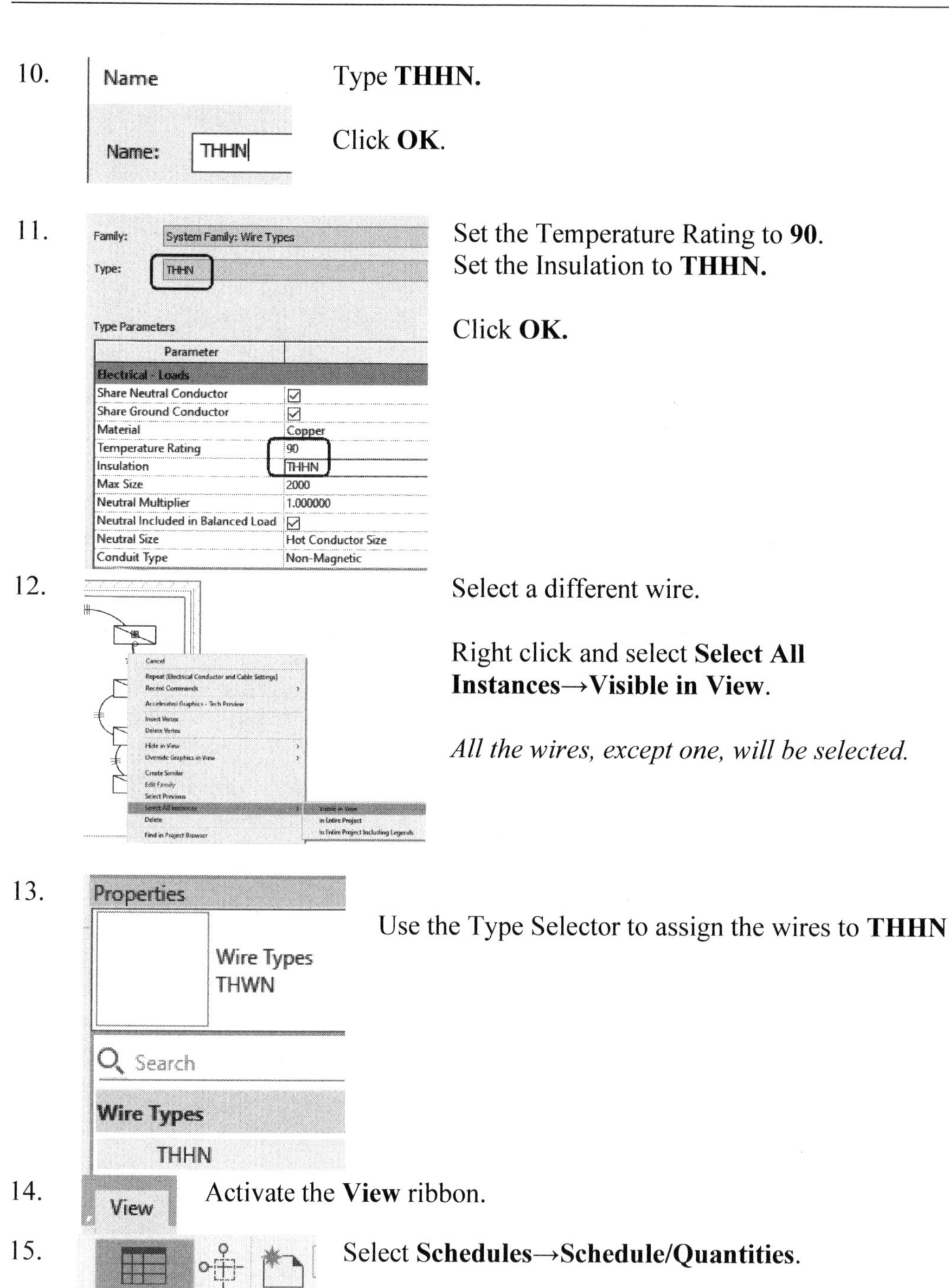

12.   Select a different wire.

Right click and select **Select All Instances→Visible in View**.

All the wires, except one, will be selected.

13.   Use the Type Selector to assign the wires to **THHN.**

14.   Activate the **View** ribbon.

15.   Select **Schedules→Schedule/Quantities**.

16.

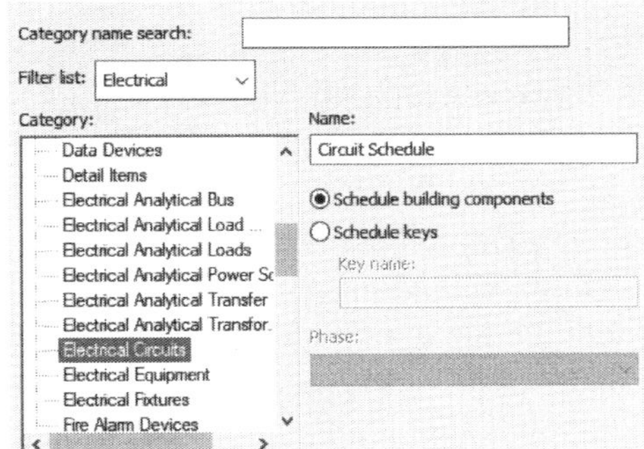

Set the Filter list to **Electrical**.
Highlight **Electrical Circuits**.
Change the Name to **Circuit Schedule**.
Click **OK.**

17.

Scheduled fields (in order):

Panel
Circuit Number
Load Name
Voltage
Number of Elements
Receptacle Connected Apparent Power
Cable Size
Cable Type
Length
Apparent Current Phase B
Rating
Comments

Add the following parameters to the schedule:

- Panel
- Circuit Number
- Load Name
- Voltage
- Number of Elements
- Receptacle Connected Apparent Power
- Cable Size
- Cable Type
- Length
- Apparent Current Phase A
- Apparent Current Phase B
- Rating
- Comments

18.

Select **Calculated Parameter**.

19.

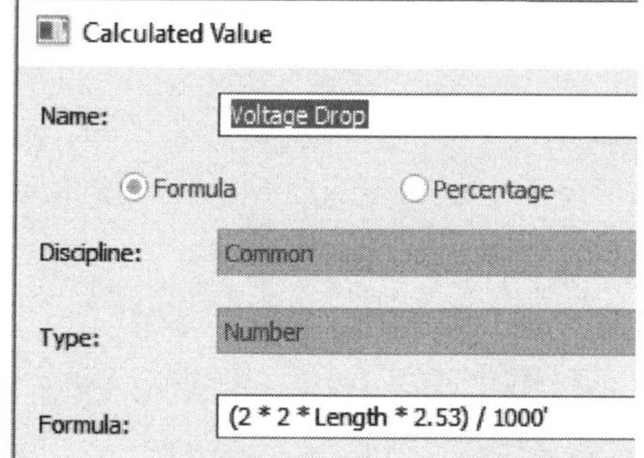

The formula for voltage drop for a single phase circuit using copper wire is:

$$Vd = (2 * I * L * R)/1000$$

Where I is the amperage, L is the length of wire, and R is the resistance.

Type **Voltage Drop** for the Name.
For the formula, type:
(2 * 2 * Length * 2.53)/1000'

I am using 2 as the value for current as that is the value of the apparent phase A current. 2.53 is the resistance for 14AWG wire.

Click **OK.**

20.

Select **Calculated Parameter**.

21.

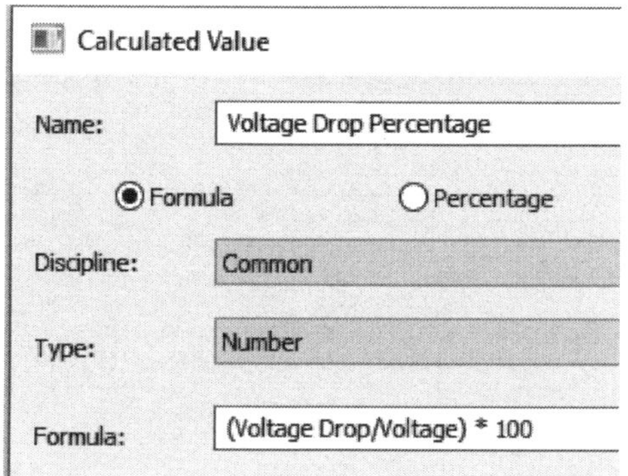

Type **Voltage Drop Percentage** for the Name.
For the formula, type:
(Voltage Drop/Voltage0 * 100.

Click **OK.**

22.

Select **Calculated Parameter**.

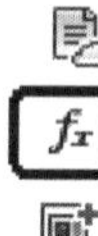

23.

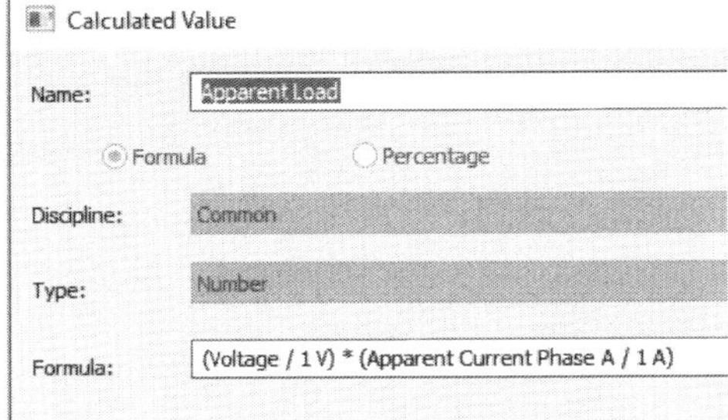

Type **Apparent Load** for the Name.
For the formula, type:
(Voltage/ 1 V) * (Apparent Current Phase A/ 1 A)

You need to divide by 1V and 1A to eliminate an inconsistent units error.

24.

Scheduled fields (in order):

```
Panel
Circuit Number
Load Name
Voltage
Voltage Drop
Voltage Drop Percentage
Number of Elements
Receptacle Connected Apparent Power
Cable Size
Cable Type
Length
Apparent Current Phase A
Apparent Current Phase B
Rating
Comments
Apparent Load
```

Move the Voltage Drop and Voltage Drop Percentage parameters below Voltage.

25.

Scheduled fields (in order):

```
Panel
Circuit Number
Load Name
Voltage
Voltage Drop
Voltage Drop Percentage
Number of Elements
Receptacle Connected Apparent Power
Cable Size
Cable Type
Length
Apparent Current Phase A
Apparent Current Phase B
Rating
Apparent Load
Comments
```

Move **Apparent Load** above Comments.

26. Click the Formatting tab.

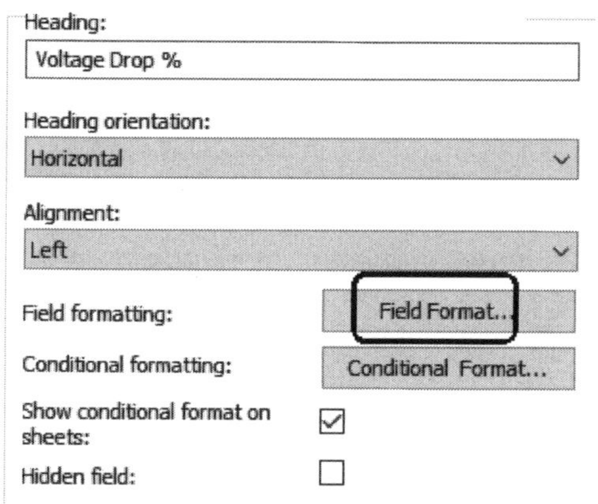

Highlight **Voltage Drop Percentage**. Change the Heading to **Voltage Drop %.**

Click **Field Format.**

27. Uncheck **Use default settings**.

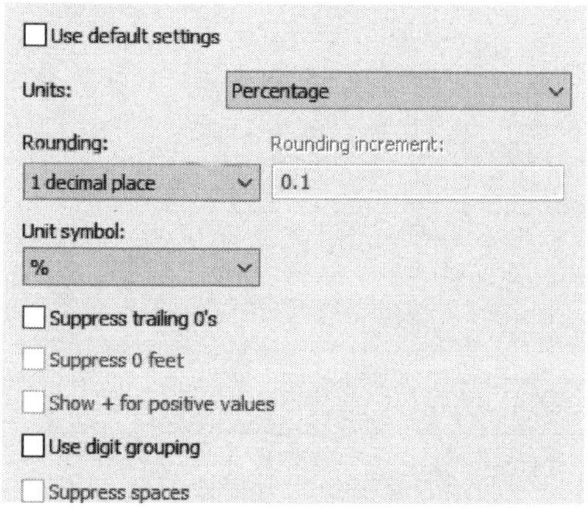

Set Units to **Percentage.**

Set Rounding to **1 decimal place**.

Set the Unit symbol to **%.**

Click **OK**.

28. Highlight **Cable Size**.
Change the Heading to **Wire Size**.

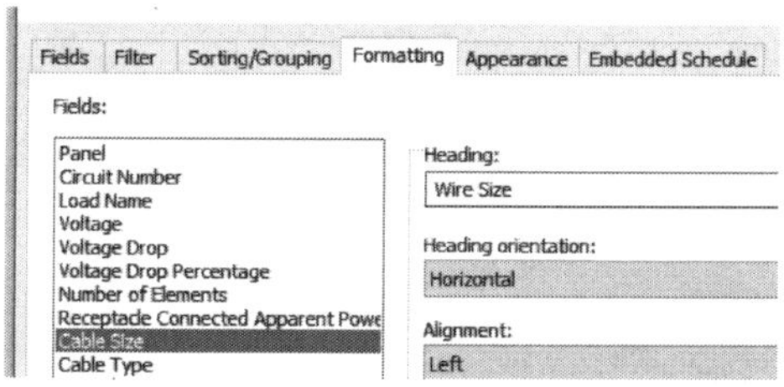

29. Highlight **Cable Type**.
Change the Heading to **Wire Type**.

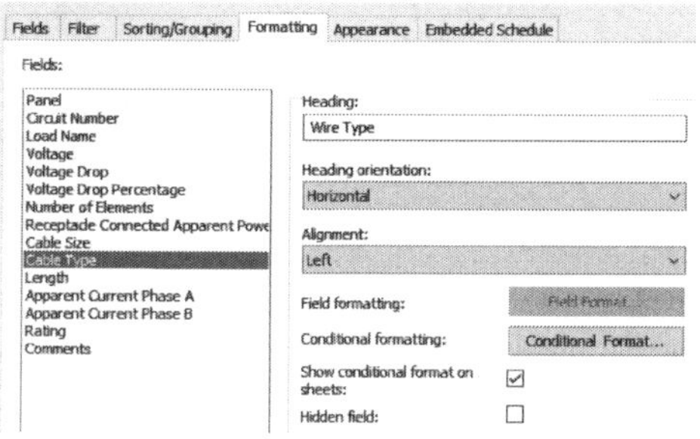

30. 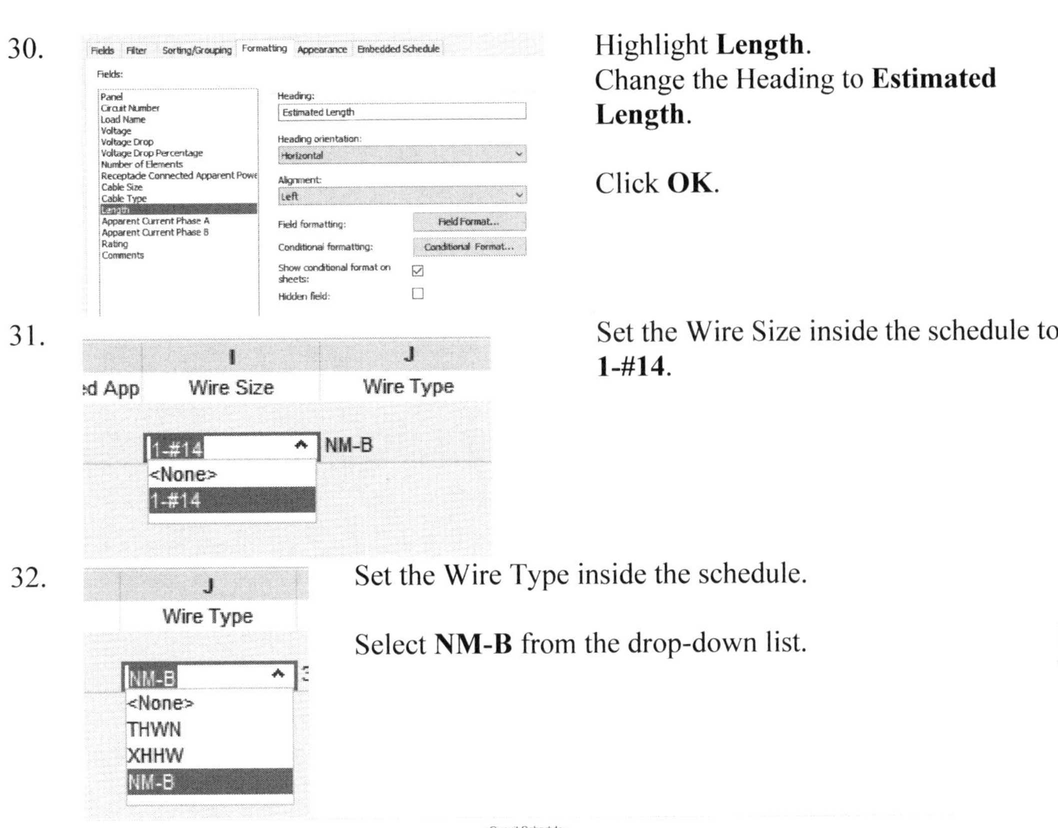 Highlight **Length**.
Change the Heading to **Estimated Length**.

Click **OK**.

31. Set the Wire Size inside the schedule to **1-#14**.

32. Set the Wire Type inside the schedule.

Select **NM-B** from the drop-down list.

33. The schedule is created.
Save as *ex6-3.rvt*.

Sheet Lists

One of the types of schedules available in Revit is sheet lists. A sheet list schedule is built the same way as a component model schedule, but all the relevant parameters are used by sheets. Creating a sheet list is useful for managing your construction documentation and organizing any documentation packages you sent out as it operates as a table of contents.

If you are required to submit a list of all drawings in a submittal package, you can use a Sheet List schedule.

As with most schedules that appear on construction documents, it is good practice to have two different versions of each schedule – one that has all the parameters necessary for tracking the sheets and any revisions and another that is used for the actual documentation package.

Exercise 6-4:

Creating a Sheet List

Drawing Name: *sheet_lists.rvt*
Estimated Time: 5 minutes

This exercise reinforces the following skills:
- Schedules
- Sheets

1. 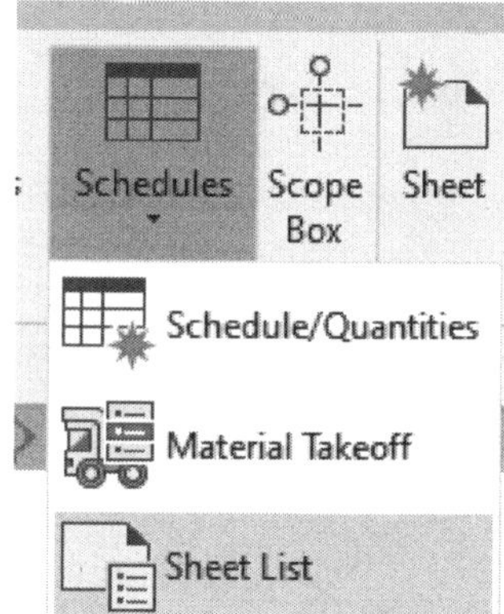   Activate the **View** ribbon.

2.   Go to **Schedules→Sheet List.**

3.   Select the following fields in order:

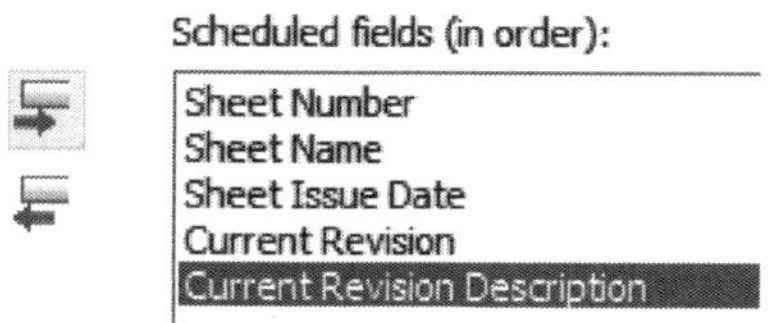

- Sheet Number

- Sheet Name

- Sheet Issue Date

- Current Revision

- Current Revision Description

Click **OK**.

4.   The schedule view opens.

Save as *ex6-4.rvt*.

A	B	C	D	E
Sheet Number	Sheet Name	Sheet Issue Date	Current Revision	Current Revision D
E601	Panel Schedules	02/11/08		
E201	Second Floor Power Plan	02/11/08		
M201	1ST FLOOR NORTH - HVAC	03/05/08		
E301	NORTH LEVEL 1 LIGHTING PLAN	03/05/08		
M601	DUCT SECTIONS	03/05/08		
M701	MECHANICAL SCHEDULES	03/05/08		

Note Blocks

A note block is a schedule of an annotation family that is used in the project. Note Block schedules are useful in managing the plan notes on your construction documents as an alternative to keynotes. As note annotations are placed in a view, they can be given a description. Those descriptions are gathered into the Note Block schedule. A usage parameter can determine on which sheet the note has been placed.

A benefit of creating a Note Block schedule is that if you need to update or delete a note, you can make the desired changes in the schedule and the notes will update across all the sheets.

Exercise 6-5:

Creating a Note Block

Drawing Name: *note_block.rvt*
Estimated Time: 45 minutes

This exercise reinforces the following skills:
- Families
- Symbols
- Schedules
- Sheets

1. 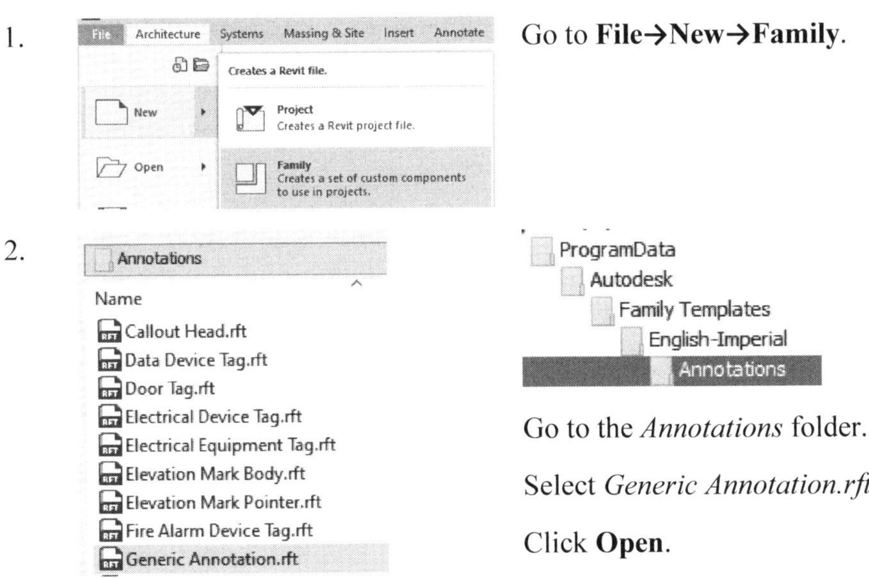

Go to **File→New→Family**.

2. Go to the *Annotations* folder.

Select *Generic Annotation.rft*

Click **Open**.

3.

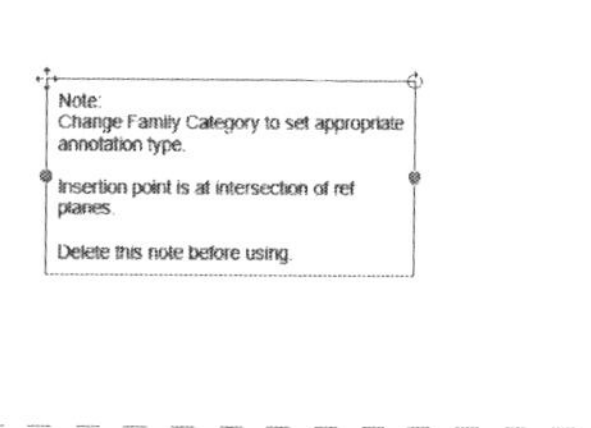

Select the text note and **DELETE**.

4.

Activate the **Create** ribbon.

5.

Select the **Label** tool.

Left click on the intersection of the two reference planes for the insertion point.

6.

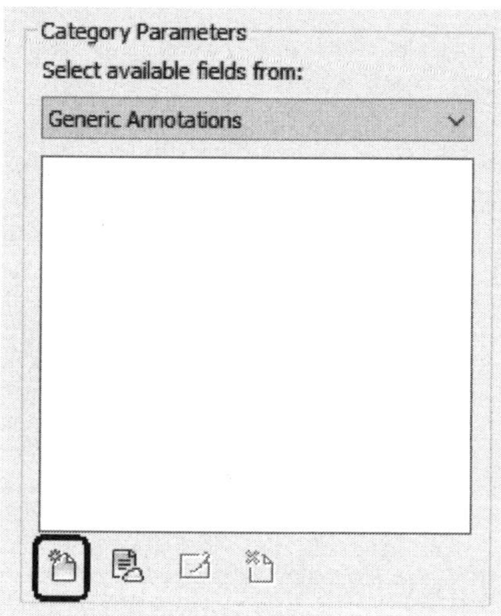

Select **New** located at the bottom left of the dialog.

7.

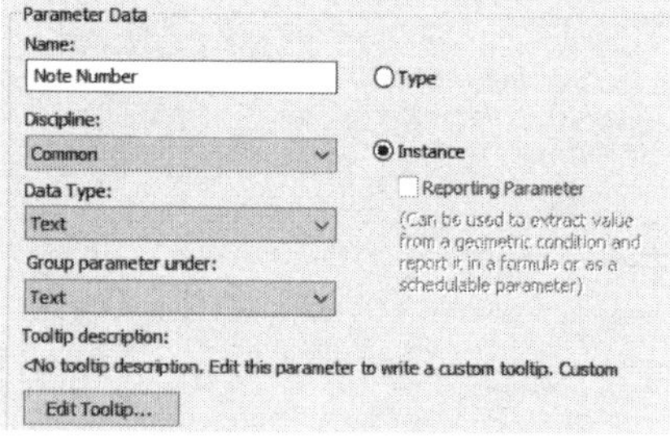

Type **Note Number** for the Name.

Enable **Instance**.

Set the Type of Parameter to **Text**.

Group Parameter under **Text**.

Click **OK**.

8.

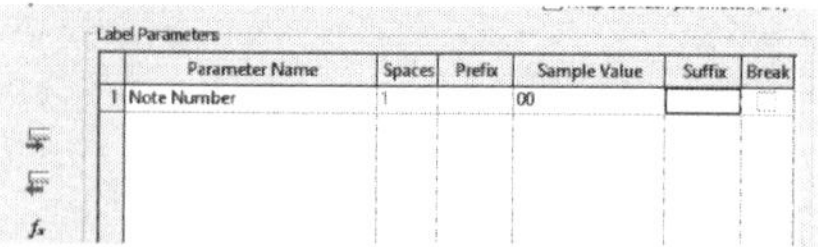

Add to the right panel.

Set the Sample Value to **00**.

9. 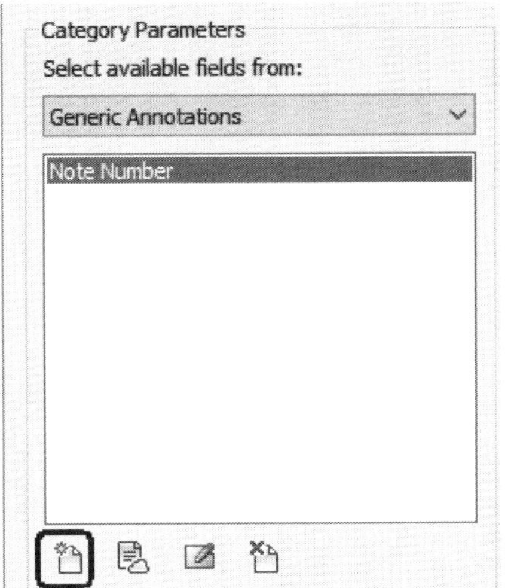

Select **New** located at the bottom left of the dialog.

10. 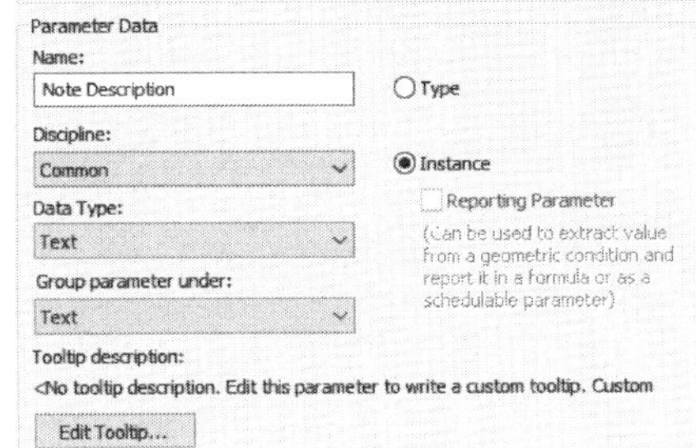

Type **Note Description** for the Name.

Enable **Instance**.

Set the Type of Parameter to **Text**.

Group Parameter under **Text**.

Click **OK**.

We are not placing this label, but it will still be available in the family.

Click **OK**.

Cancel out of the LABEL command.

11. 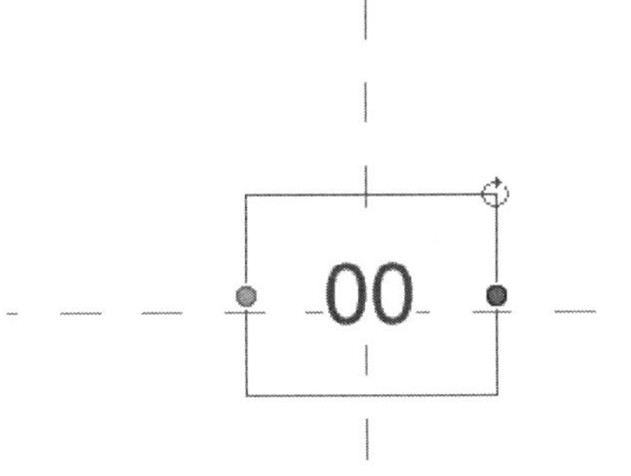

Zoom into the label.

Use the grips to reduce the size of the label.

12. 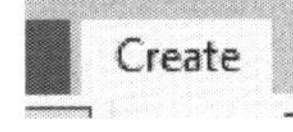 Activate the **Create** ribbon.

13. 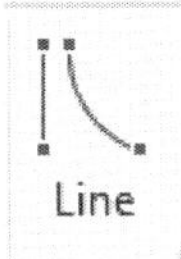 Select the **Line** tool.

14. 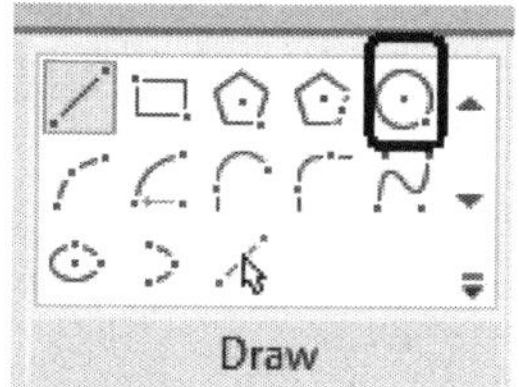
Select the **Circle** tool from the Draw panel.

15. 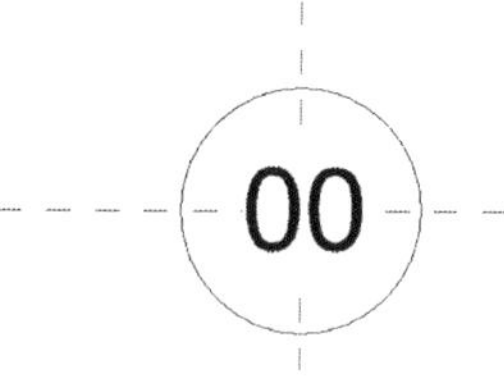
Draw a circle around the label.

Position the label so it is centered in the circle on the intersection.

Save as *Note Block.rfa*.

16. 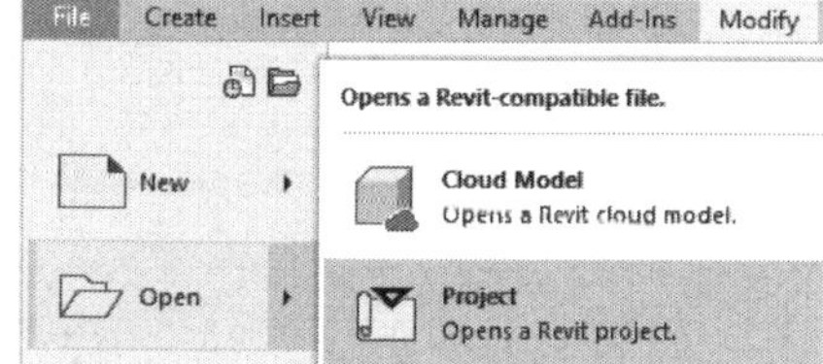
Go to **File**.

Select **Open→Project**.

Open *note_block.rvt*.

17. 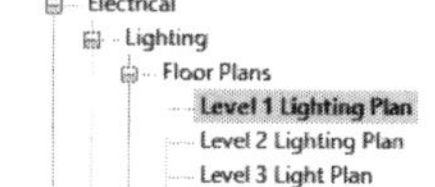
Open **Level 1 Lighting Plan** floor plan.

18.  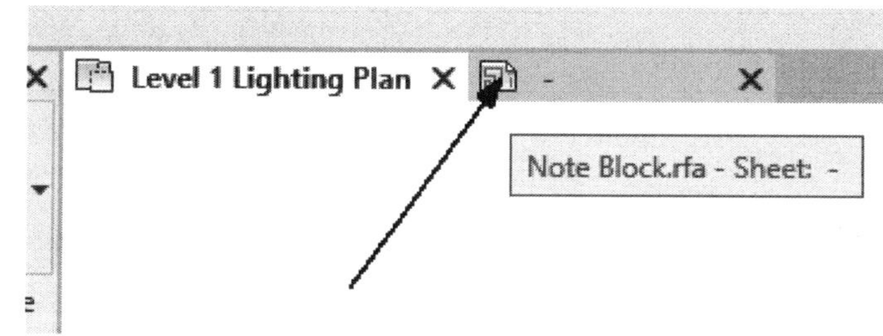

Select the tab for the Note Block.

Select **Load into Project and Close**.

Select the Note_Block project file if a dialog appears.

19. 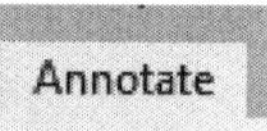
Activate the **Annotate** ribbon.

20. 
Select the **Symbol** tool.

21.

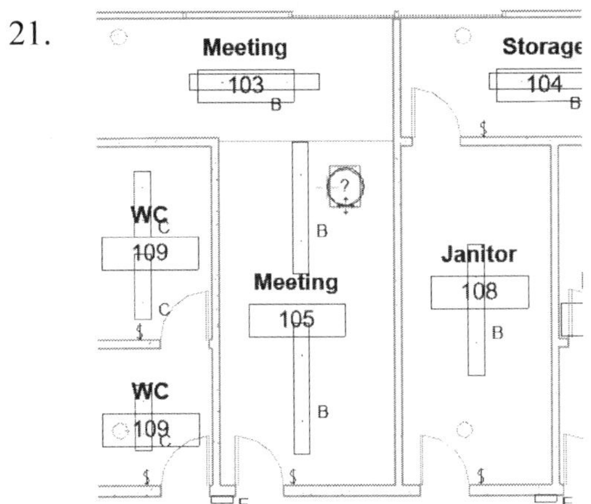

Left click to place in **MEETING 105**.

Cancel out of the command.

22.

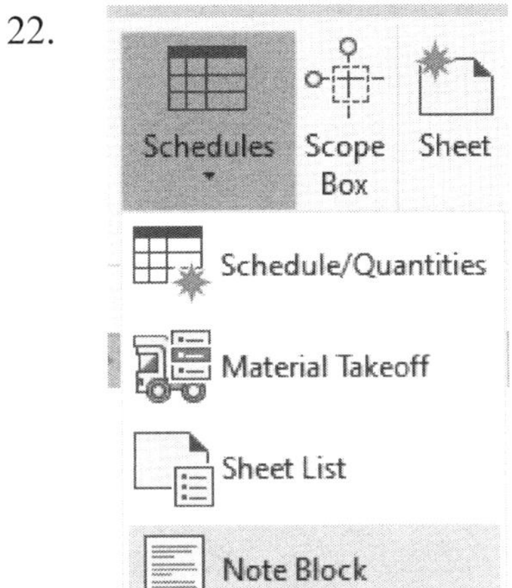

Activate the View ribbon.

Select **Schedules→Note Block**.

23.

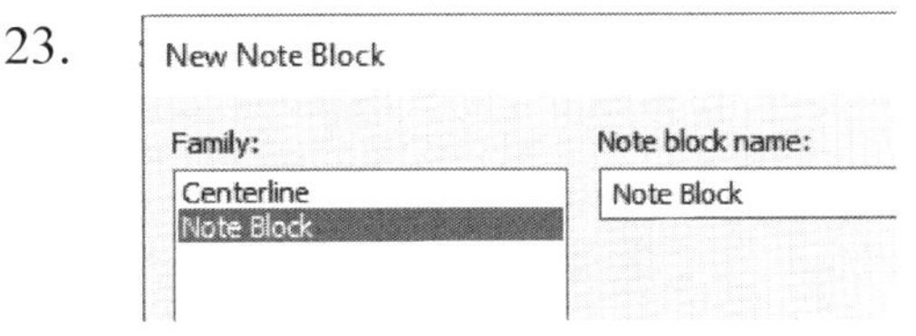

The Note Block that was just placed is listed.

Highlight **Note Block**.

Click **OK**.

24.

Fields   Filter   Sorting/Grouping   Formatting   Appearance

Select available fields from:
Generic Annotations

Available fields: Count, Type
Scheduled fields (in order): Note Number, Note Text

Highlight **Note Number** and **Note Description**.

You can select them together.

Add to the **Scheduled fields**.

Click **OK**.

25. 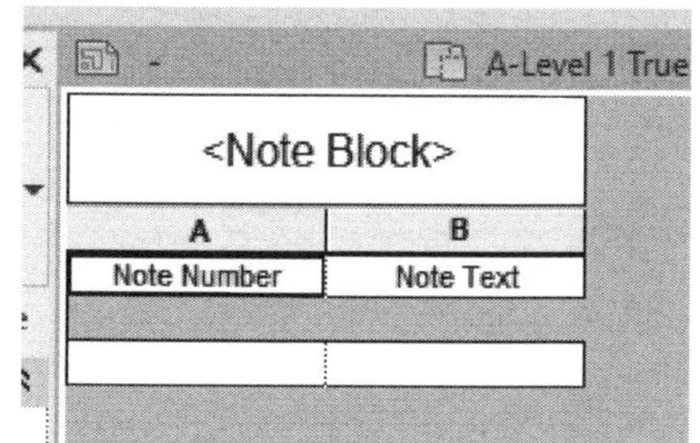

The schedule opens.

The cells are blank because you haven't added anything to the instance properties.

26. 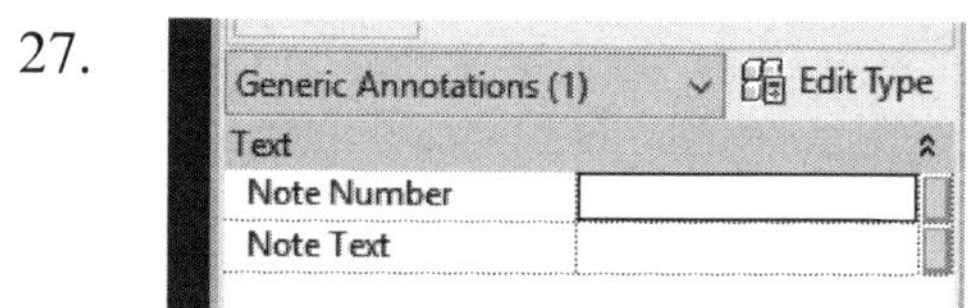 Open **Level 1 Lighting Plan** floor plan.

27. Select the Note Block in MEETING 105.

On the Properties palette:

Note the two instance properties that were created.

28. Type **01** in the Note Number field.

In the Note Description field type:

LIGHTING FIXTURES WITH MORE THAN TWO LAMPS SHALL HAVE THE TWO OUTER LAMPS CONTROLLED BY ONE SWITCH AND INNER LAMP(S) CONTROLLED BY A SECOND SWITCH

29. 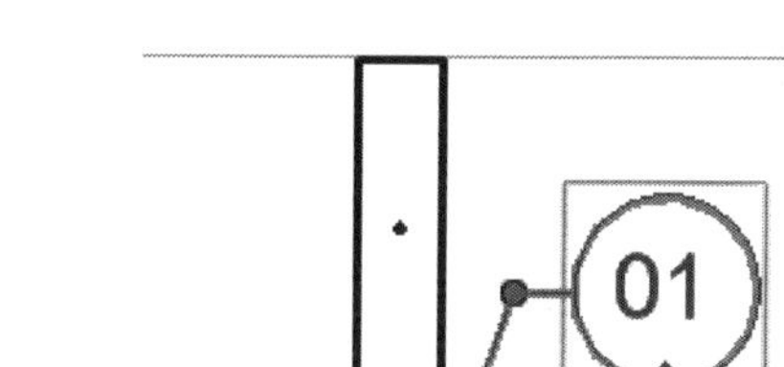

With the note symbol selected, select **Add** leader from the ribbon.

30. 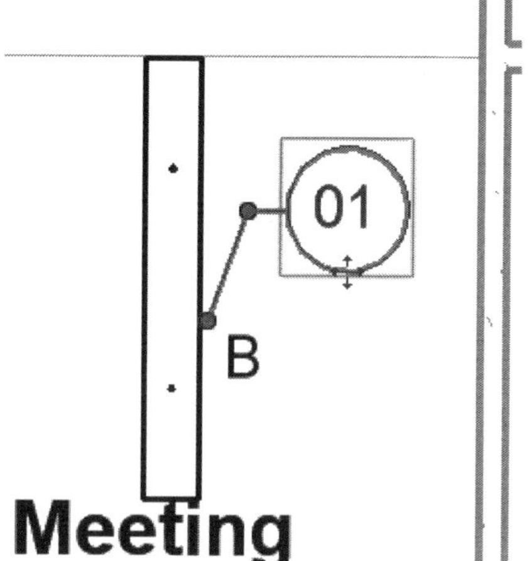

Position the leader so it is attached to the light fixture as shown.

31.  Select **Edit Type** on the Properties palette.

32. 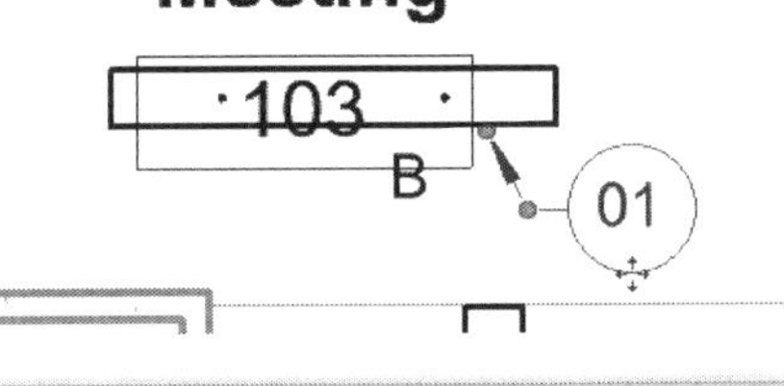 Set the Leader Arrowhead to **Arrow Filled 15 Degree.**

Click **OK.**

33. Verify the note block is still selected.

Select the **Copy** tool from the Modify panel.

34. 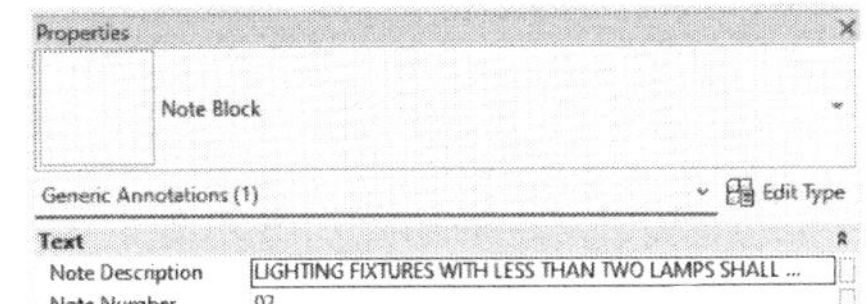 Left click to select a base point.

Left click to place in **MEETING 103.**

Use the grip to adjust the position of the leader to attach to lighting fixture.

35.  In the Properties palette:

Type **02** in the Note Number field.

In the Note Description field type:

LIGHTING FIXTURES WITH LESS THAN TWO LAMPS SHALL BE CONTROLLED BY ONE SWITCH

Release the selection by left clicking in the display window.

36. Select the window tab for the note block schedule.

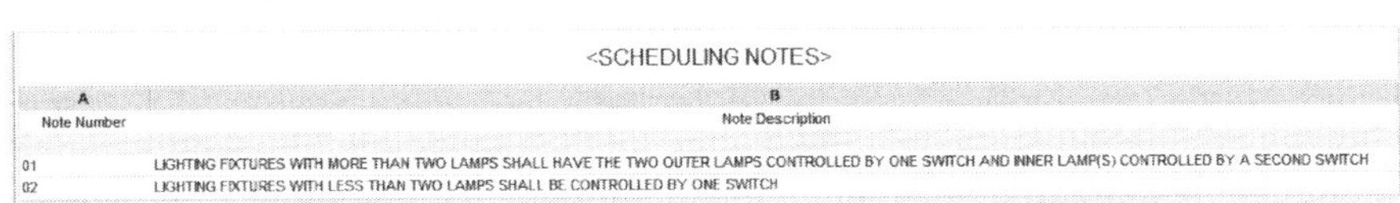

37. Left click on the schedule name and change it to **SCHEDULING NOTES.**

38. 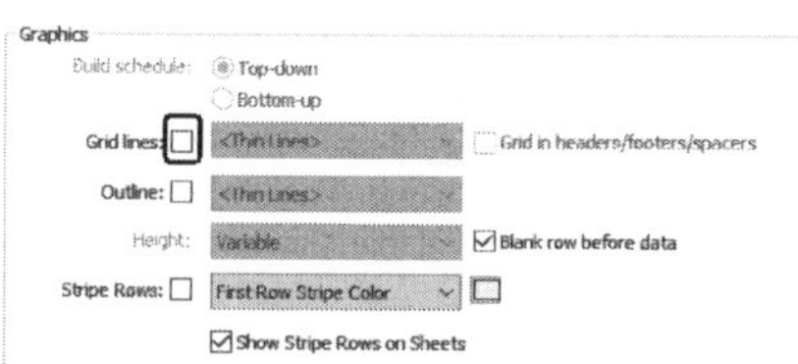

On the Properties palette:

Select **Edit** in the Appearance field.

39. 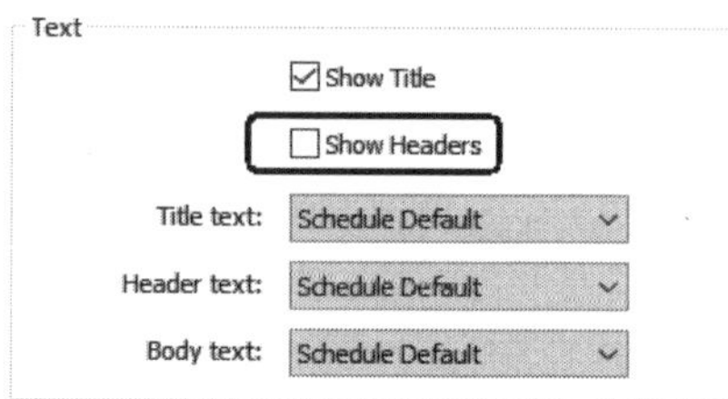

Disable **Grid lines**.

40.

Disable **Show Headers**.

Click **OK**.

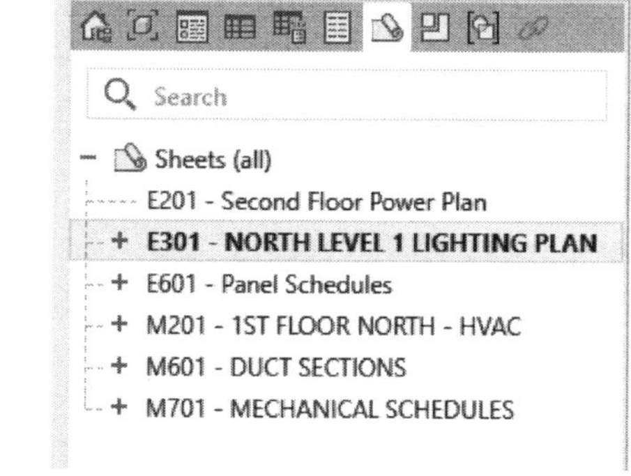

The schedule updates.

41.

Activate the **E301 – NORTH LEVEL 1 LIGHTING PLAN** sheet.

42. 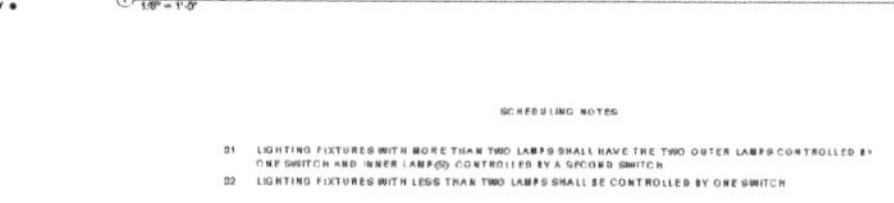

Drag and drop the scheduling notes from the Project Browser on to the sheet.

Save as *ex6-5.rvt*.

Schedule Keys

You can assign a target lighting level for all the spaces to be analyzed. Create a project parameter to be used for your targeted lighting level. This should be an instance parameter as it will be unique to each space element. Set the Discipline of the parameter to Electrical and the type to Illuminance. Group the parameter in the Electrical-Lighting group so that it can be easily located. Name the parameter Required Lighting Level, so the intended use of the parameter is clear. Project parameters can be used in schedules, but they cannot be tagged.

Once you have created the project parameter, you can create another type of schedule to associate lighting levels with types of spaces. This will not be a schedule of building components, but a schedule key.

Creating a schedule key makes it easy to assign target lighting levels to spaces.

Exercise 6-6:

Creating a Schedule Key

Drawing Name: *schedule_key.rvt*
Estimated Time: 20 minutes

This exercise reinforces the following skills:
- Schedules
- Project Parameters
- Spaces

1. 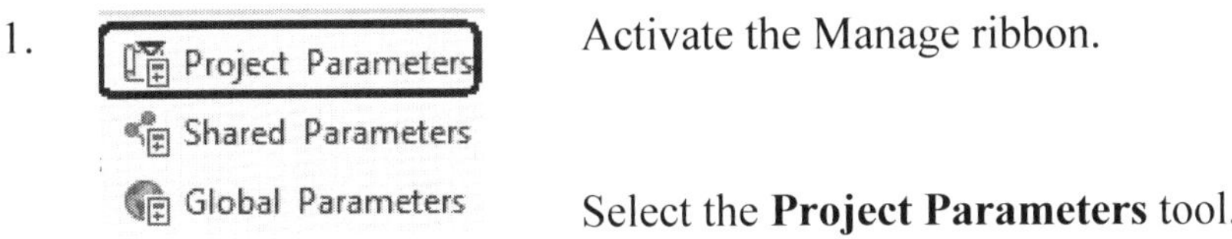

Activate the Manage ribbon.

Select the **Project Parameters** tool.

2. Select **New**.

3.

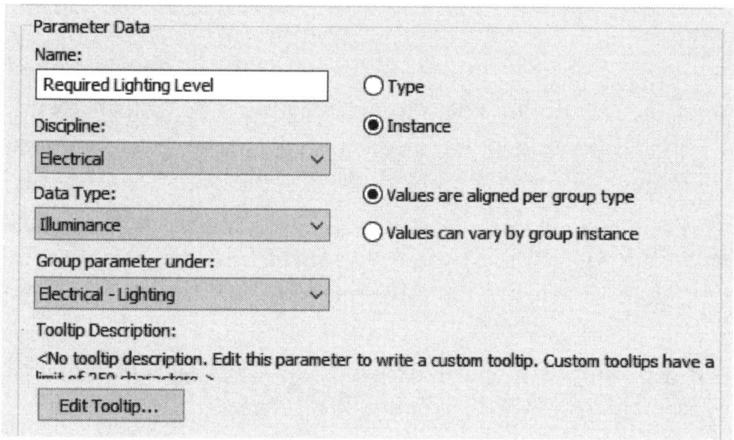

In the Name field:

Type **Required Lighting Level**.

Enable **Instance**.

Under Discipline:

Select **Electrical**.

Under Type of Parameter:

Select **Illuminance**.

Group parameter under **Electrical - Lighting**.

4.

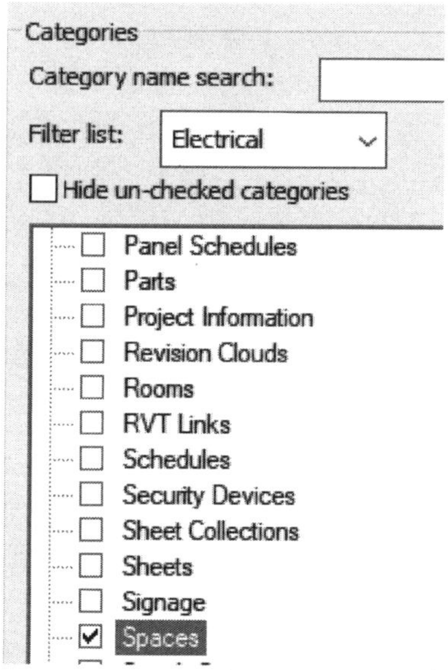

Select **Spaces** in the right Categories pane.

Click **OK**.

5.

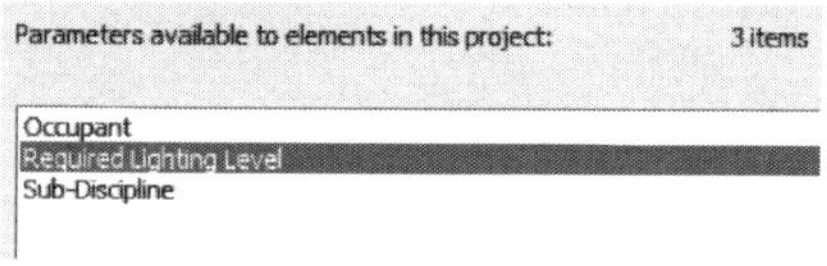

The new parameter is now listed in the dialog.

Click **OK** to close the dialog.

6.  Activate the **View** ribbon.

7. 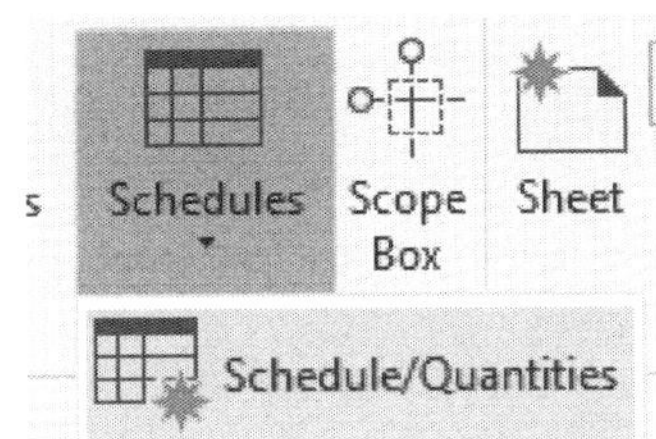 Select **Schedule/Quantities**.

8. 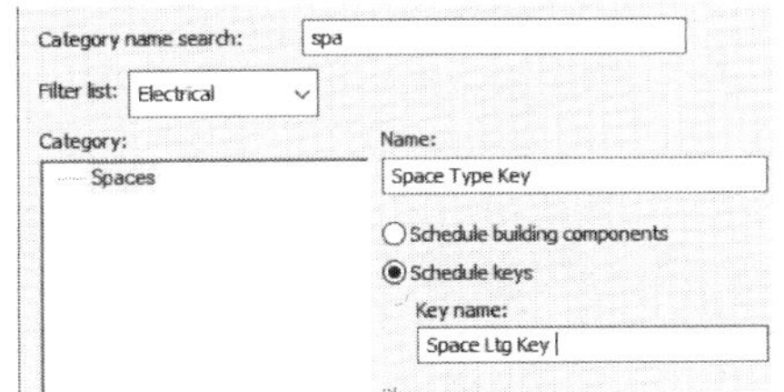 Highlight **Spaces** in the left pane.

In the Name field, type **Space Type Key**.

Enable **Schedule Keys**

Type **Space Ltg Key** in the Key Name field.

Click **OK**.

9. 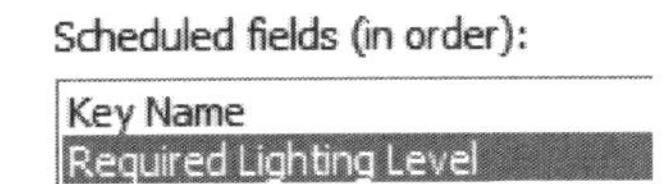 Add **Required Lighting Level** to the scheduled fields.

This is the project parameter you just added.

Click **OK** to create the schedule.

10. 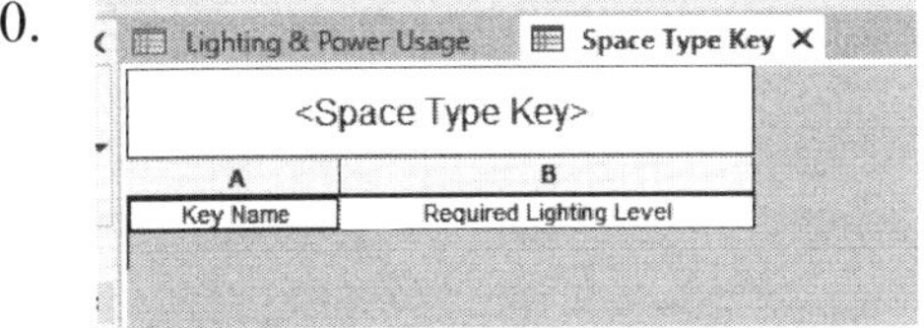 The schedule will not contain any data rows because no values have been assigned to any of the spaces.

11. 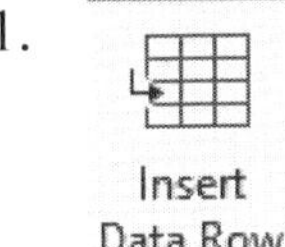 Select **Insert Data Row** from the ribbon.

12. 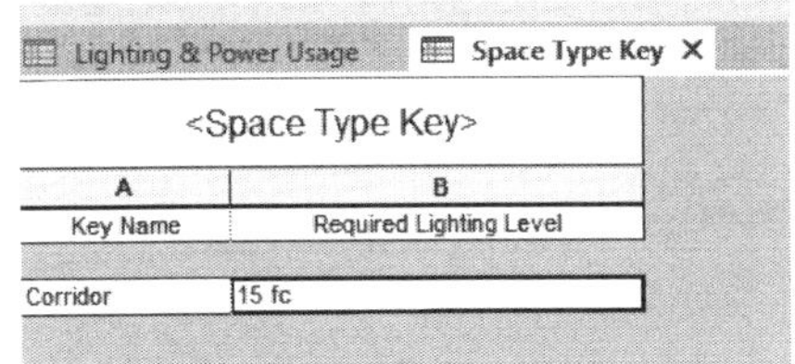 In the new row:

Type **Corridor** for the Key Name.

Type **15 fc** for the Required Lighting Level.

13.

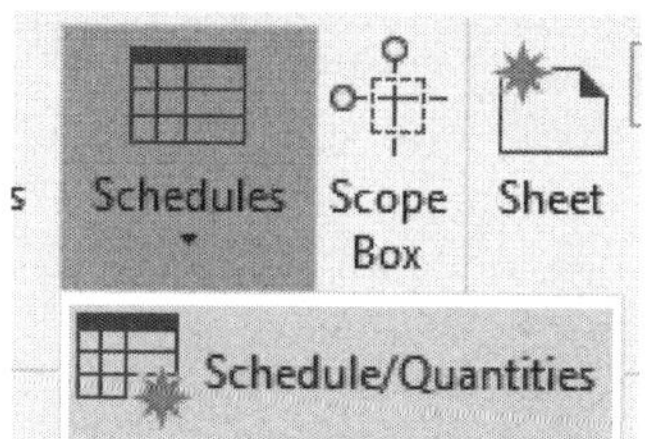

Use the Insert Data Row tool to add more data rows and their values.

This key schedule can now be used with the Lighting Analysis schedule.

14.

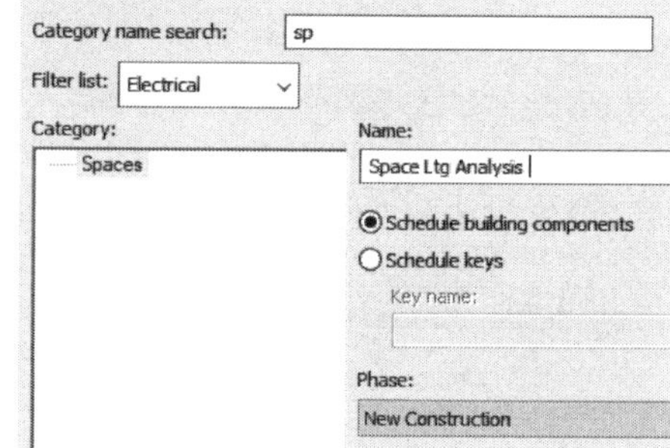

Select **Schedule/Quantities** from the View ribbon.

15.

Highlight **Spaces** in the left Category pane.

Type **Space Ltg Analysis** in the Name field.

Enable **Schedule Building Components**.

Click **OK**.

16.

Select the following fields in order for the schedule:

- Number

- Name

- Space Ltg Key

- Required Lighting Level

- Average Estimated Illumination

- Ceiling Reflectance

- Lighting Calculation Workplane

17. 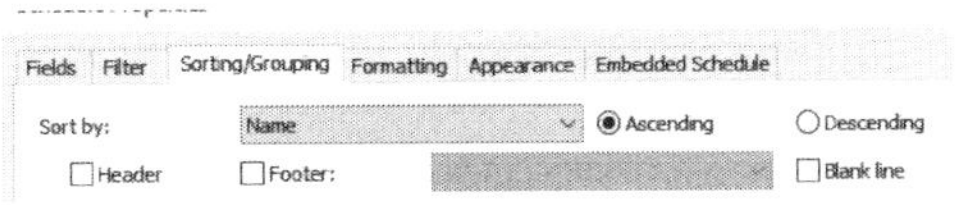

Click Sorting/Grouping.

Sort by **Name.**

Click **OK**.

18. 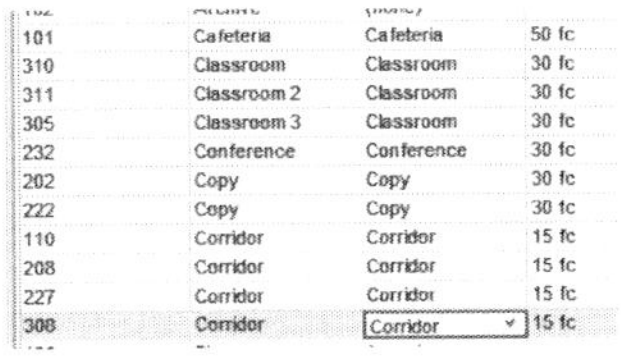

101	Cafeteria	Cafeteria	50 fc
310	Classroom	Classroom	30 fc
311	Classroom 2	Classroom	30 fc
305	Classroom 3	Classroom	30 fc
232	Conference	Conference	30 fc
202	Copy	Copy	30 fc
222	Copy	Copy	30 fc
110	Corridor	Corridor	15 fc
208	Corridor	Corridor	15 fc
227	Corridor	Corridor	15 fc
308	Corridor	Corridor	15 fc

In the Space Ltg Key column, use the drop-down list to assign the correct key to spaces where keys have been provided.

Once the key is assigned, the associated value will appear in the Required Lighting Level column.

19. 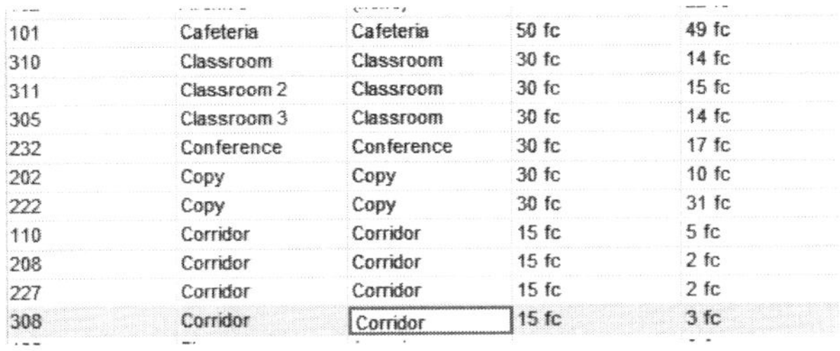

101	Cafeteria	Cafeteria	50 fc	49 fc
310	Classroom	Classroom	30 fc	14 fc
311	Classroom 2	Classroom	30 fc	15 fc
305	Classroom 3	Classroom	30 fc	14 fc
232	Conference	Conference	30 fc	17 fc
202	Copy	Copy	30 fc	10 fc
222	Copy	Copy	30 fc	31 fc
110	Corridor	Corridor	15 fc	5 fc
208	Corridor	Corridor	15 fc	2 fc
227	Corridor	Corridor	15 fc	2 fc
308	Corridor	Corridor	15 fc	3 fc

Reviewing the schedule you can quickly see where you need to make changes in the model.

20. Save as *ex6-6.rvt*.

Exercise 6-7:

Creating a Panel Schedule

Drawing Name: *load_schedule.rvt*
Estimated Time: 10 minutes

This exercise reinforces the following skills:

- ❑ Load Classifications
- ❑ Families
- ❑ Schedules

1. 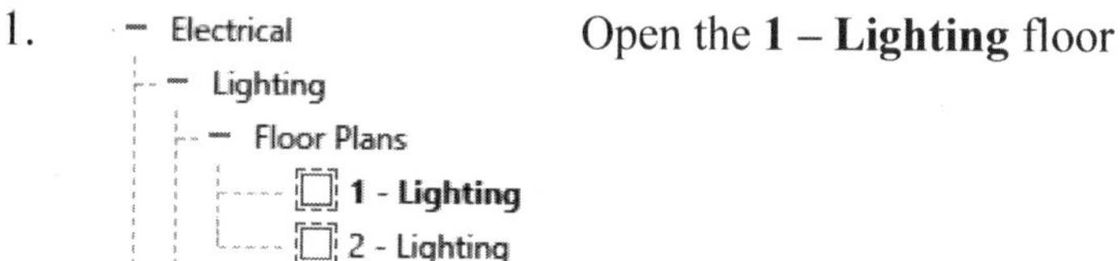 Open the **1 – Lighting** floor plan view.

2. 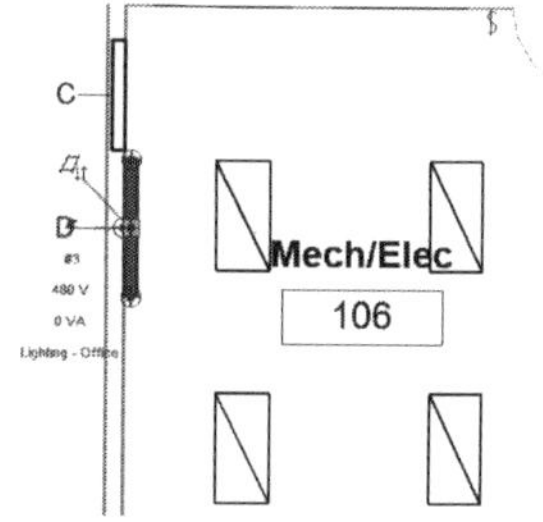 Select **Panel D** in the Mech/Elec Room 106.

3. 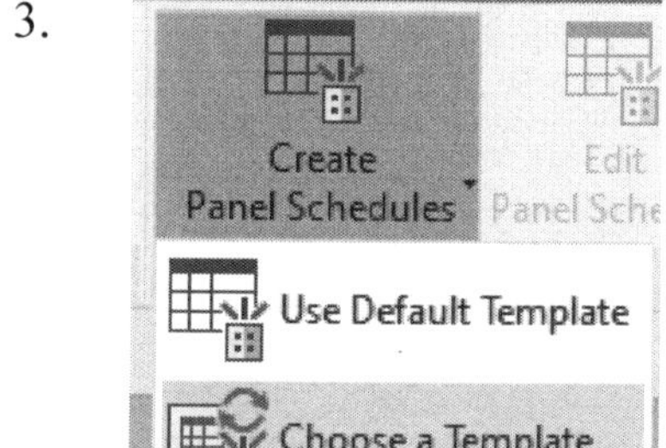 On the ribbon:

    Select **Create Panel Schedules→Choose a Template**.

4. 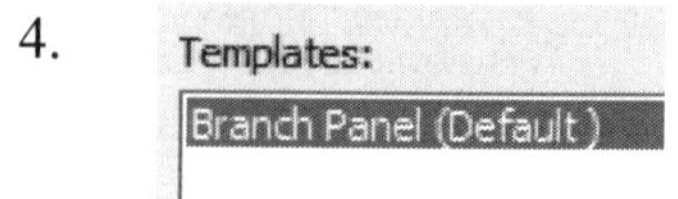 There is only one template available called Branch Panel.

    Highlight this template.

    Click **OK**.

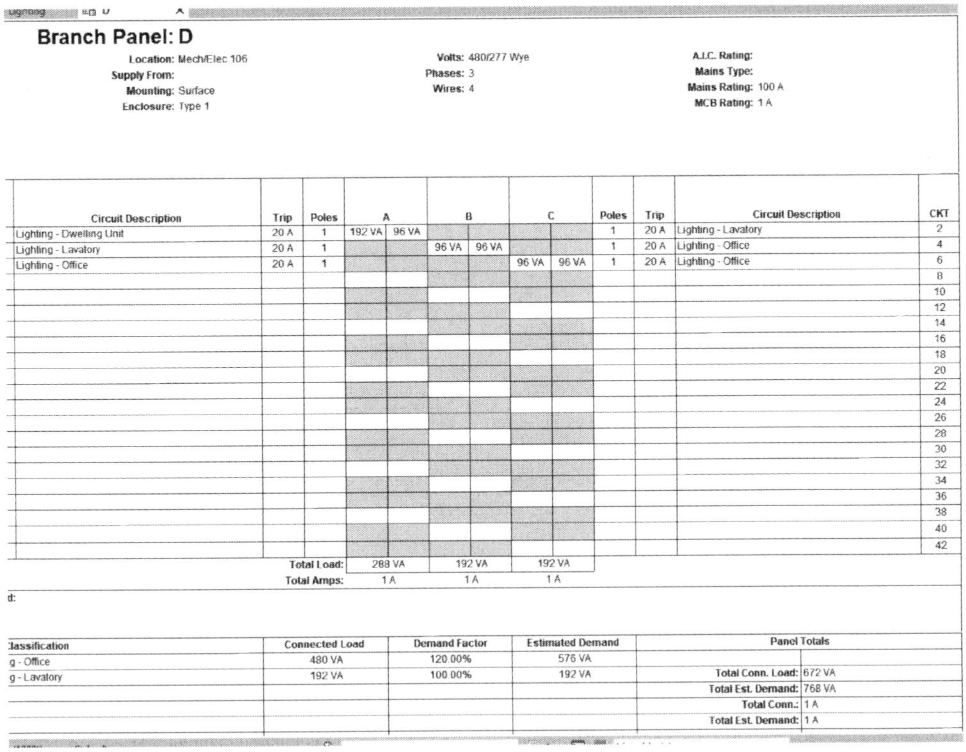

Branch Panel: D

Location: Mech/Elec 106	
Supply From:	
Mounting: Surface	
Enclosure: Type 1	

Volts: 480/277 Wye
Phases: 3
Wires: 4

A.I.C. Rating:
Mains Type:
Mains Rating: 100 A
MCB Rating: 1 A

Circuit Description	Trip	Poles	A		B		C		Poles	Trip	Circuit Description	CKT
Lighting - Dwelling Unit	20 A	1	192 VA	96 VA					1	20 A	Lighting - Lavatory	2
Lighting - Lavatory	20 A	1			96 VA	96 VA			1	20 A	Lighting - Office	4
Lighting - Office	20 A	1					96 VA	96 VA	1	20 A	Lighting - Office	6
												8
												10
												12
												14
												16
												18
												20
												22
												24
												26
												28
												30
												32
												34
												36
												38
												40
												42
	Total Load:		288 VA		192 VA		192 VA					
	Total Amps:		1 A		1 A		1 A					

d:

Classification	Connected Load	Demand Factor	Estimated Demand	Panel Totals	
g - Office	480 VA	120.00%	576 VA		
g - Lavatory	192 VA	100.00%	192 VA	Total Conn. Load:	672 VA
				Total Est. Demand:	768 VA
				Total Conn.:	1 A
				Total Est. Demand:	1 A

5. The schedule opens. You can see which circuits are on each panel and the loads for each panel.

    In Lesson 8, I show you how to create load classifications and assign them to families so they appear properly in schedules.

6. Save as *ex6-7.rvt*.

Exercise 6-8:

Creating a Custom Panel Schedule

Drawing Name: *panel schedule.rvt*
Estimated Time: 30 minutes

This exercise reinforces the following skills:

- Load Classifications
- Panel Schedule Templates
- Schedules
- Sheets

1. 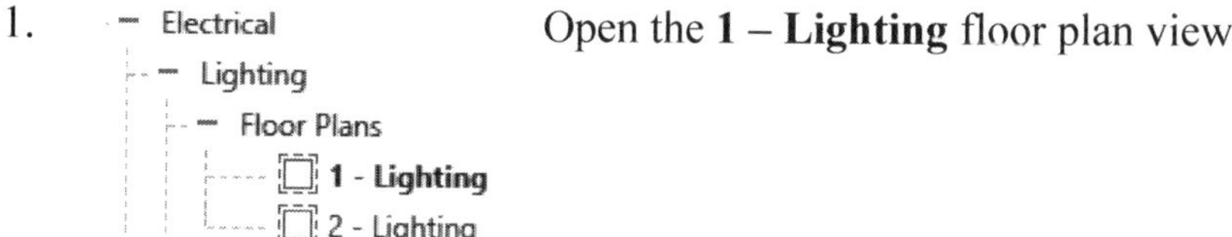

Open the **1 – Lighting** floor plan view.

2. 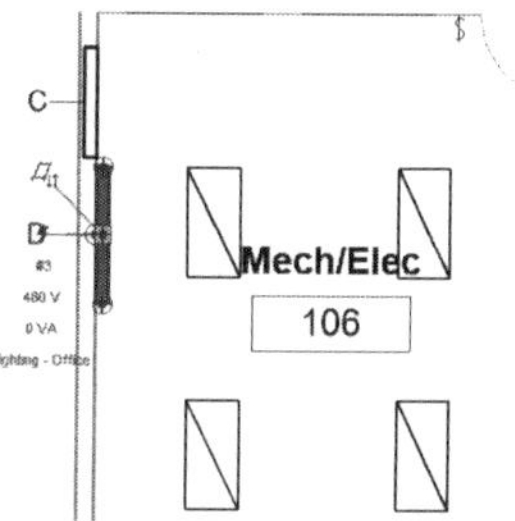

Select **Panel D** in the Mech/Elec Room 106.

3. 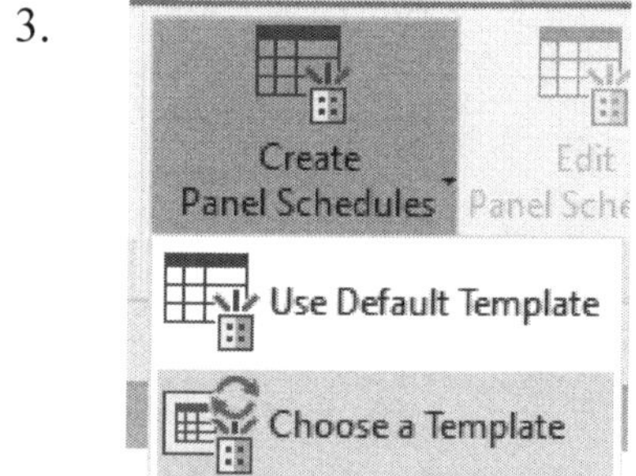

On the ribbon:

Select **Create Panel Schedules→Choose a Template**.

4. 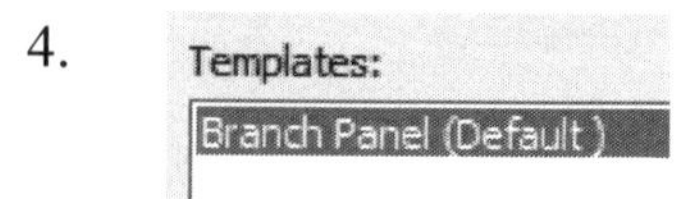

There is only one template available called Branch Panel.

Highlight this template.

Click **OK**.

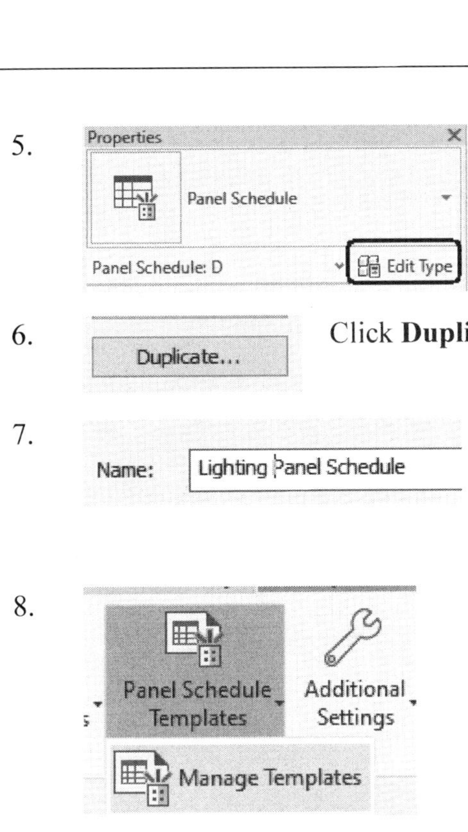

5. The panel schedule view opens.

   Click **Edit Type** in the Properties pane.

6. Click **Duplicate**.

7. Rename **Lighting Panel Schedule**.

   Click **OK**.

   Close the dialog.

8. Switch to the Manage ribbon.

   Select **Panel Schedule Templates→Manage Templates.**

9. Under Template type:

   Select **Branch Panel**.

10. Click **Duplicate** at the bottom of the dialog.

11. 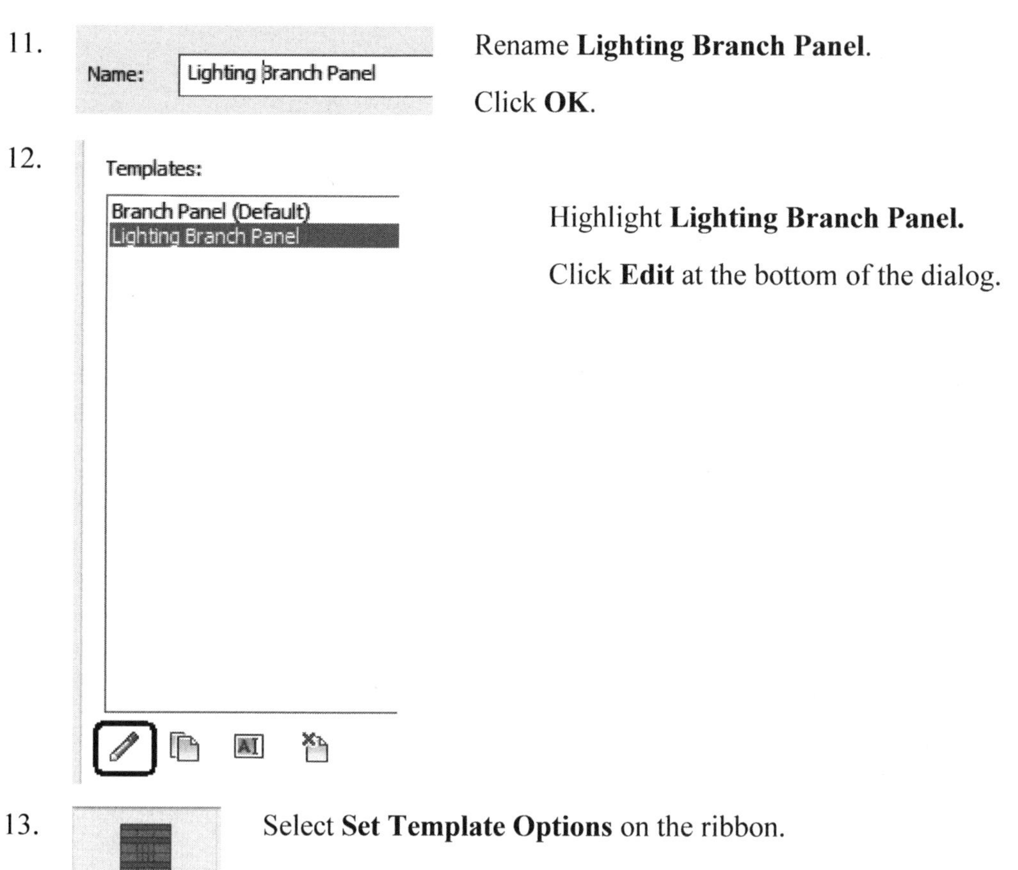

    Rename **Lighting Branch Panel**.

    Click **OK**.

12.   Highlight **Lighting Branch Panel.**

    Click **Edit** at the bottom of the dialog.

13.   Select **Set Template Options** on the ribbon.

14.   Highlight **General Settings**.

    Change the Total width for columns to **6"**.

    Change the Borders to use **Wide Lines**.

15. 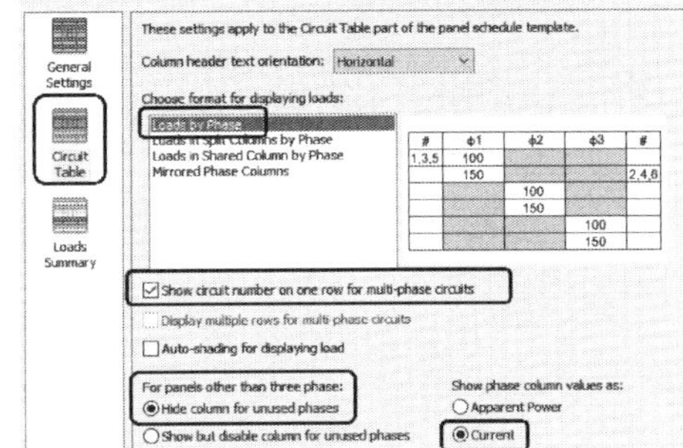 Highlight **Circuit Table**.

Highlight **Loads by Phase**.

Enable **Show circuit number on one row for multi-phase circuits**.

Enable **Hide column for unused phases**.

Enable **Current**.

16. 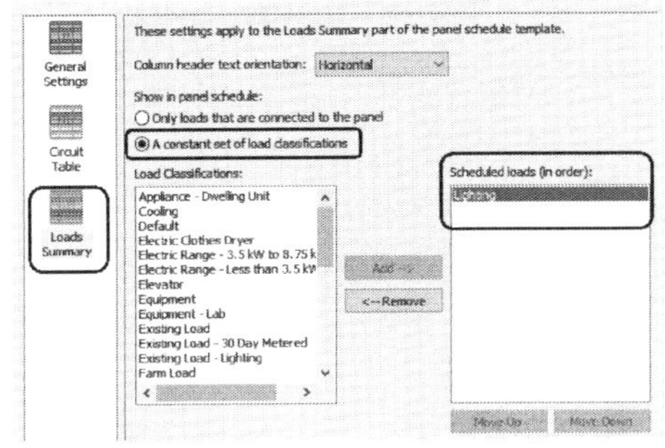 Highlight **Loads Summary**.

Enable **A constant set of load classifications**.

Add **Lighting** to the schedules loads list.

Click **OK**.

17. 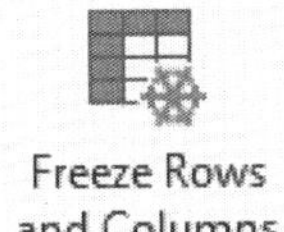 Adjust the column widths.

Click **Freeze Rows and Columns** on the ribbon.

18.  Click **Finish Template**.

19. 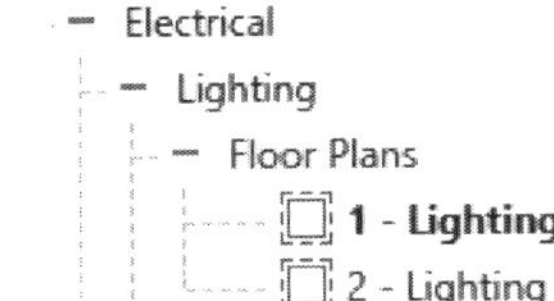 Open the **1 – Lighting** floor plan view.

20. 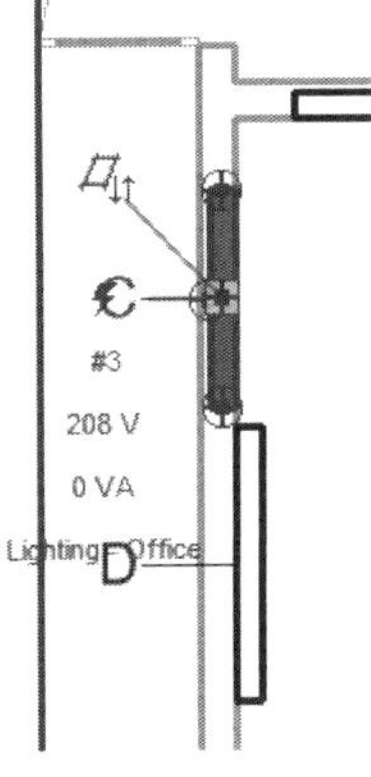 Select **Panel C** in Room 106.

21. 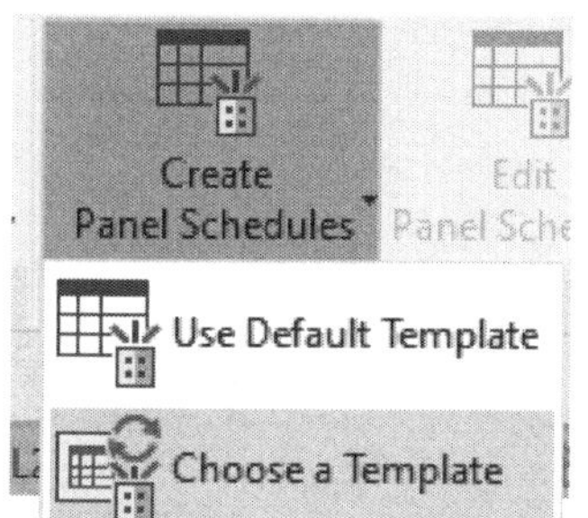 On the ribbon:

Select **Create Panel Schedules→Choose a Template**.

22. 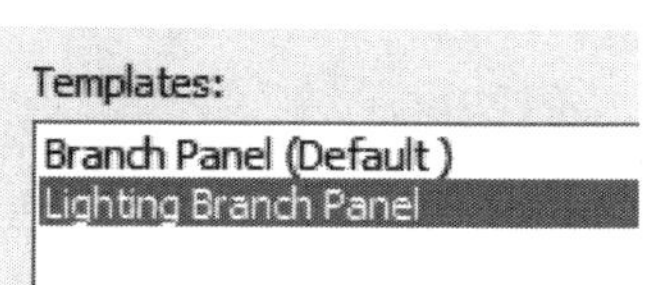 Click **Lighting Branch Panel** template.

Click **OK**.

23. 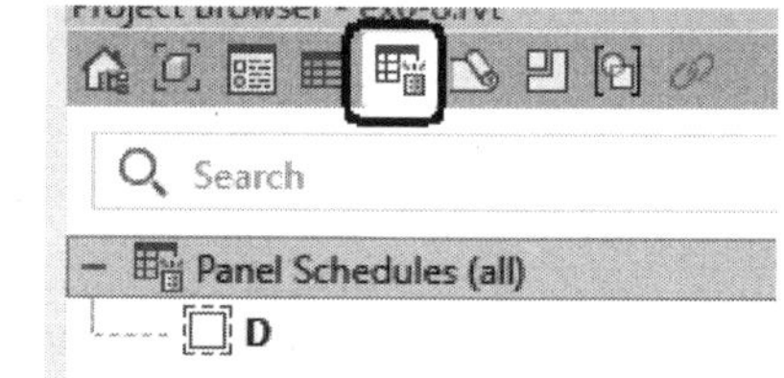 You will see this warning, but it can be ignored.

Close the warning dialog.

24. 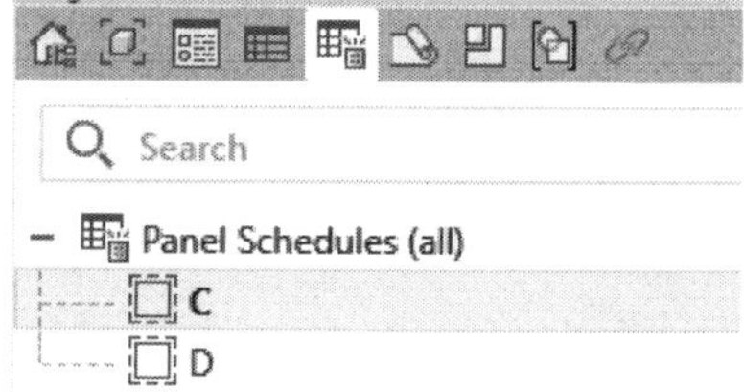 Enable the **Panel Schedules** filter on the Project Browser.

You see the two panel schedules that were created.

25. 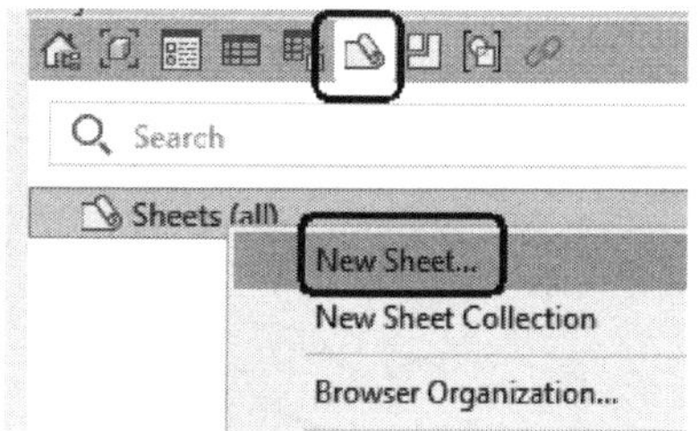 Change the Project Browser filter to **Sheets**.

Highlight **Sheets**.

Right click and select **New Sheet**.

26. 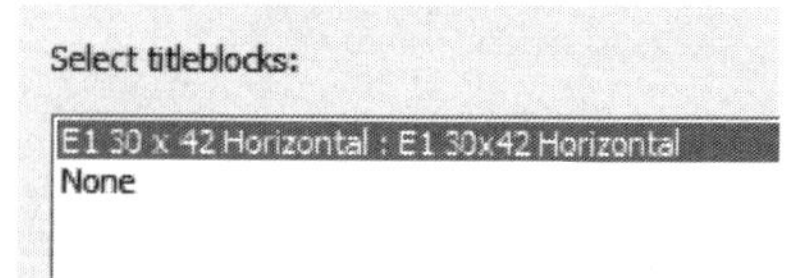 Highlight the **E1** titleblock and click **OK**.

27. 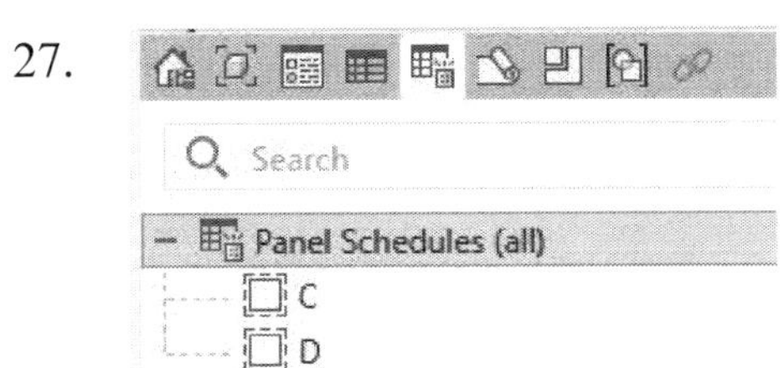 Activate the Panel Schedules filter on the Project Browser.

Drag and drop the two panel schedules onto the sheet.

28. 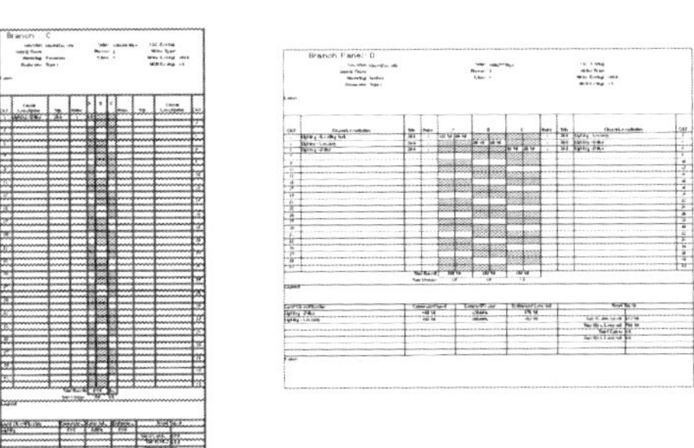 Compare the two panel schedules.

Save as *ex6-8.rvt*.

Lab Exercises

Open *lab_6.rvt*.

Create a lighting fixture schedule as shown.

<table>
<tr><td colspan="4" align="center"><Lighting Fixture Schedule></td></tr>
<tr><td align="center">A</td><td align="center">B</td><td align="center">C</td><td align="center">D</td></tr>
<tr><td align="center">Family and Type</td><td align="center">Panel</td><td align="center">Circuit Number</td><td align="center">Description</td></tr>
<tr><td>Plain Recessed Lighting Fixture: 2x2 - 120</td><td>LIGHTING PANEL "B"</td><td>2</td><td></td></tr>
<tr><td>Plain Recessed Lighting Fixture: 2x2 - 120</td><td>LIGHTING PANEL "B"</td><td>2</td><td></td></tr>
<tr><td>Plain Recessed Lighting Fixture: 2x2 - 120</td><td>LIGHTING PANEL "B"</td><td>2</td><td></td></tr>
<tr><td>Plain Recessed Lighting Fixture: 2x2 - 120</td><td>LIGHTING PANEL "B"</td><td>2</td><td></td></tr>
<tr><td>Plain Recessed Lighting Fixture: 2x2 - 120</td><td>LIGHTING PANEL "B"</td><td>2</td><td></td></tr>
<tr><td>Plain Recessed Lighting Fixture: 2x2 - 120</td><td>LIGHTING PANEL "B"</td><td>2</td><td></td></tr>
<tr><td>Plain Recessed Lighting Fixture: 2x2 - 120</td><td>LIGHTING PANEL "B"</td><td>3</td><td></td></tr>
<tr><td>Plain Recessed Lighting Fixture: 2x2 - 120</td><td>LIGHTING PANEL "B"</td><td>3</td><td></td></tr>
<tr><td>Plain Recessed Lighting Fixture: 2x2 - 120</td><td>LIGHTING PANEL "B"</td><td>3</td><td></td></tr>
<tr><td>Plain Recessed Lighting Fixture: 2x2 - 120</td><td>LIGHTING PANEL "B"</td><td>3</td><td></td></tr>
<tr><td>Plain Recessed Lighting Fixture: 2x2 - 120</td><td>LIGHTING PANEL "B"</td><td>3</td><td></td></tr>
<tr><td>Plain Recessed Lighting Fixture: 2x2 - 120</td><td>LIGHTING PANEL "B"</td><td>3</td><td></td></tr>
<tr><td>Plain Recessed Lighting Fixture: 2x2 - 120</td><td>LIGHTING PANEL "B"</td><td>3</td><td></td></tr>
</table>

If any of the lighting fixtures are not connected to a panel, use the HIGHLIGHT IN MODEL tool to locate the fixture in the model.

Select in the view.
Select POWER from the ribbon.

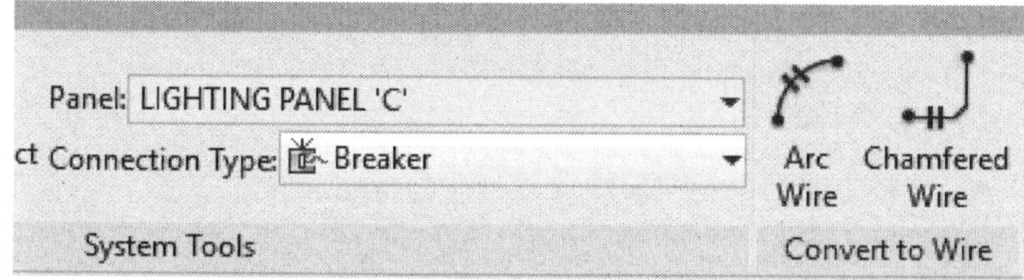

Select the panel to assign.
Add wires.

Return to the schedule and continue assigning light fixtures to panels.

MAIN FLOOR LIGHTING FIXTURES

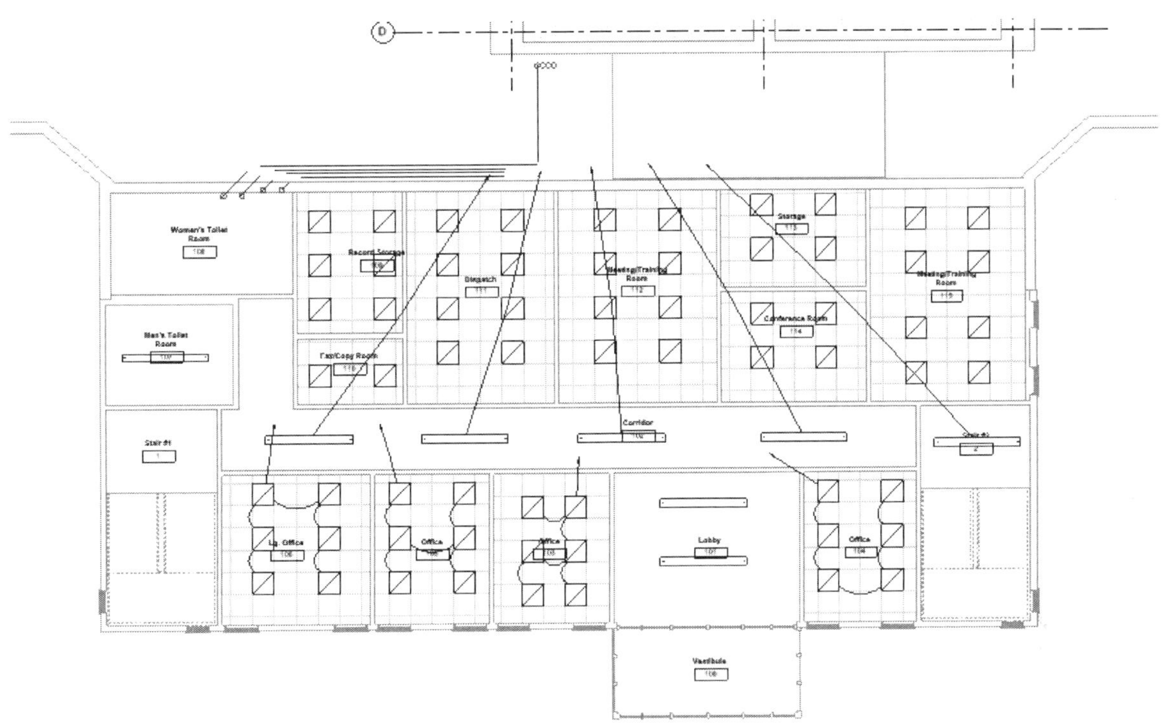

GROUND FLOOR LIGHTING FIXTURES

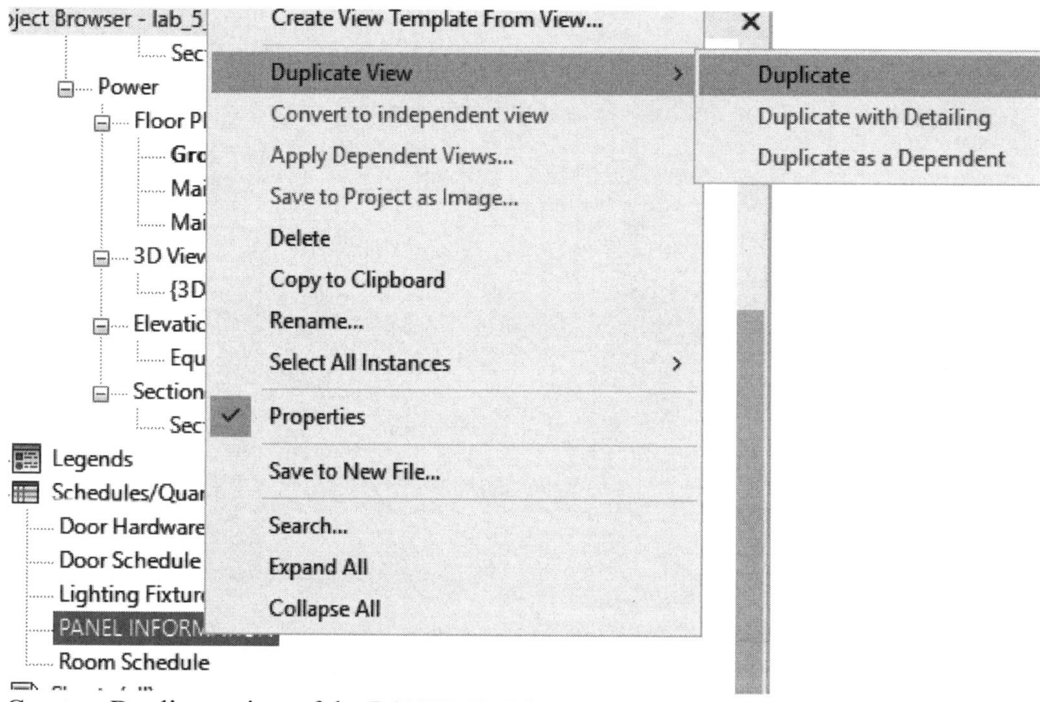

Create a Duplicate view of the PANEL INFORMATION schedule.
Repeat to create a second copy.

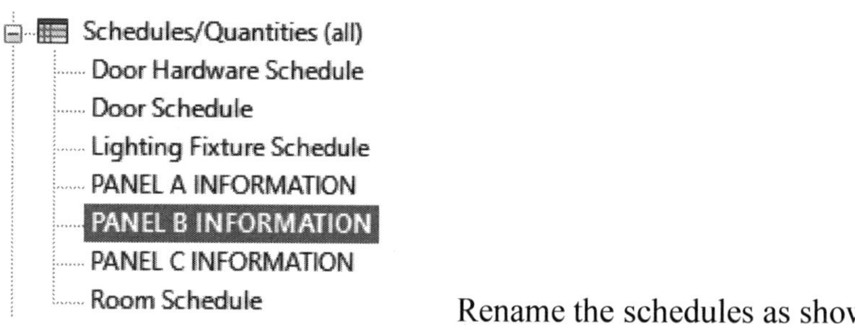

Rename the schedules as shown.

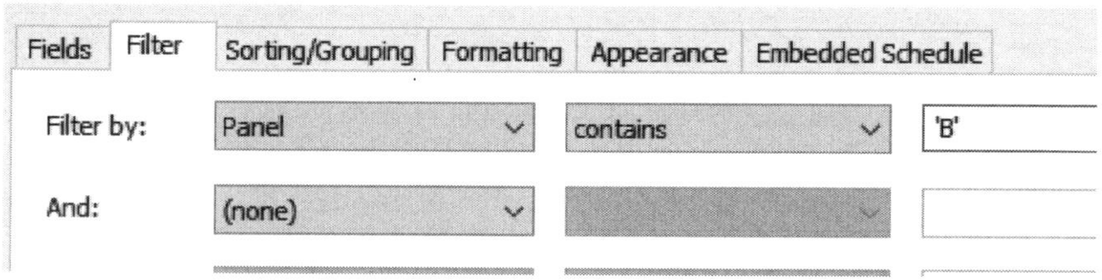

Apply filters so each schedule only lists the required panel.

<PANEL B INFORMATION>

A	B	C	D	E	F
Panel	Load Name	Apparent Load	Rating	Receptacle Connected	Voltage Drop
PWR PNL. 'B'	Receptacle	180 VA	20 A	180 VA	0 V
PWR PNL. 'B'	Receptacle	180 VA	20 A	180 VA	0 V
PWR PNL. 'B'	Receptacle	360 VA	20 A	360 VA	0 V
PWR PNL. 'B'	Receptacle	360 VA	20 A	360 VA	0 V
PWR PNL. 'B'	Receptacle	360 VA	20 A	360 VA	0 V
PWR PNL. 'B'	Receptacle	900 VA	20 A	900 VA	2 V
PWR PNL. 'B'	Receptacle	180 VA	20 A	180 VA	0 V
PWR PNL. 'B'	Receptacle	360 VA	20 A	360 VA	0 V
PWR PNL. 'B'	Receptacle	360 VA	20 A	360 VA	0 V
PWR PNL. 'B'	Receptacle	720 VA	20 A	720 VA	1 V
PWR PNL. 'B'	Receptacle	1080 VA	20 A	1080 VA	2 V
LIGHTING PANEL 'B'	Lighting – Dwelling Unit	372 VA	20 A		0 V
LIGHTING PANEL 'B'	Lighting – Dwelling Unit	372 VA	20 A		0 V
LIGHTING PANEL 'B'	Lighting – Dwelling Unit	372 VA	20 A		0 V
LIGHTING PANEL 'B'	Lighting – Dwelling Unit	372 VA	20 A		0 V
LIGHTING PANEL 'B'	Lighting – Dwelling Unit	372 VA	20 A		1 V

<PANEL C INFORMATION>

A	B	C	D	E	F
Panel	Load Name	Apparent Load	Rating	Receptacle Connected	Voltage Drop
LIGHTING PANEL 'C'	Lighting – Dwelling Unit	372 VA	20 A		0 V
LIGHTING PANEL 'C'	Lighting – Dwelling Unit	930 VA	20 A		1 V
LIGHTING PANEL 'C'	Lighting – Dwelling Unit	2046 VA	20 A		2 V
LIGHTING PANEL 'C'	Lighting – Dwelling Unit	300 VA	20 A		0 V
LIGHTING PANEL 'C'	Lighting – Dwelling Unit	300 VA	20 A		0 V
LIGHTING PANEL 'C'	Lighting – Dwelling Unit	450 VA	20 A		1 V
LIGHTING PANEL 'C'	Lighting – Dwelling Unit	150 VA	20 A		0 V
LIGHTING PANEL 'C'	Lighting – Dwelling Unit	150 VA	20 A		0 V
LIGHTING PANEL 'C'	Lighting – Dwelling Unit	150 VA	20 A		0 V
LIGHTING PANEL 'C'	Lighting – Dwelling Unit	150 VA	20 A		0 V
LIGHTING PANEL 'C'	Lighting – Dwelling Unit	150 VA	20 A		0 V
LIGHTING PANEL 'C'	Lighting – Dwelling Unit	372 VA	20 A		0 V

Notes:

6-42

Lesson

07

Views

You can create different views of the building model, such as plans, sections, elevations, and 3D views.

In the building model, every drawing sheet, 2D view, 3D view, and schedule is a presentation of information from the same underlying building model database.

When you change the building model in one view, Revit propagates those changes throughout the project.

Revit has many different types of views available:

- **Plan Views**
  Two-dimensional views provide a traditional method for viewing a model. These views include floor plans, reflected ceiling plans, and structural plans.

- **Elevation Views**
  View your model from numerous elevation perspectives.

- **Section Views**
  Sections views cut through the model. You can draw them in plan, section, elevation, and detail views. Section views display as section representations in intersecting views.

- **Callout Views**
  A callout shows some portion of another view at a larger scale. In a construction document set, use callouts to provide an orderly progression of labeled views at increasing levels of detail.

- **3D Views**
  Create perspective and orthographic 3D views, and enhance them by adding a background, adjusting the camera position or extents, or changing view properties.

- **Legend Views**
  Create legends to list the building components and annotations used in a project.

- **Drafting Views**
  Drafting Views are details of the building model consisting of 2D elements. The detail views can usually be used across projects to show construction details. They are not associated to the 3D model but can be linked to a callout view. If you have a legacy library of AutoCAD details, they can be imported into Revit drafting views for use in your project.

Exercise 7-1:
Creating a Plan View

Drawing Name: *views.rvt*
Estimated Time: 15 minutes

This exercise reinforces the following skills:
- ❑ Duplicate a View
- ❑ Crop a View
- ❑ Rename a View

1. 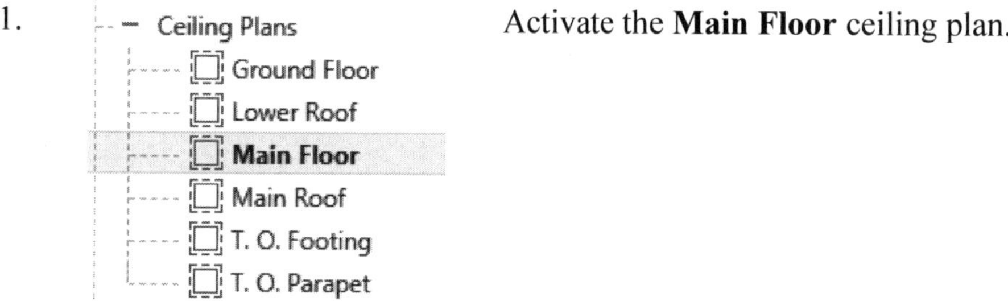

Activate the **Main Floor** ceiling plan.

2. Highlight the Main Floor view name in the Project Browser.

Right click and select **Duplicate View→Duplicate with Detailing**.

When you duplicate a view with detailing, this means you are copying any annotation elements to the new view in addition to the model elements.

3. 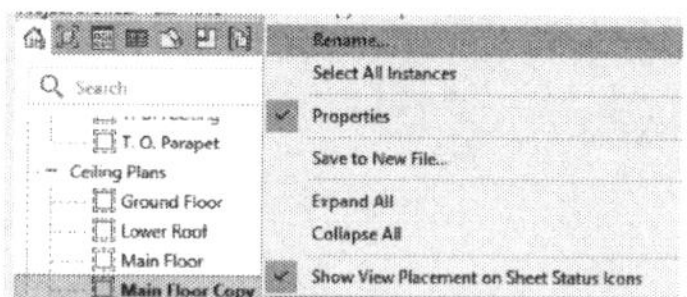

Highlight the copied view.

Right click and select **Rename**.

You can also click F2.

4. 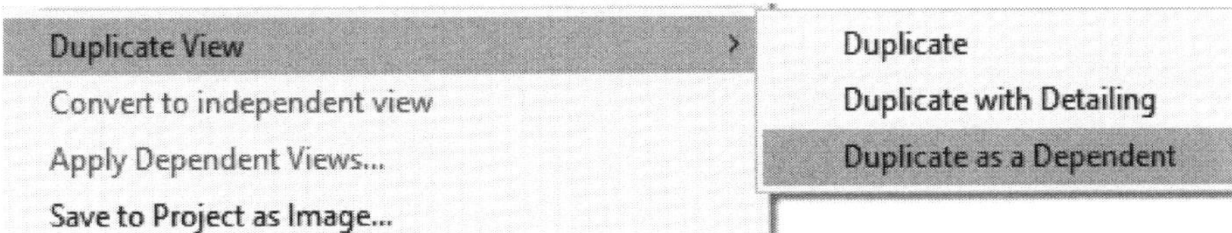   Rename **Main Floor - Annotated**.

5. Highlight the **Main Floor- Annotated** view name in the Project Browser.

Duplicate View	>	Duplicate
Convert to independent view		Duplicate with Detailing
Apply Dependent Views...		Duplicate as a Dependent
Save to Project as Image...		

Right click and select **Duplicate View→Duplicate as a Dependent**.

When you duplicate a view as dependent, it will display the annotations created in the parent view and vice versa.

6. 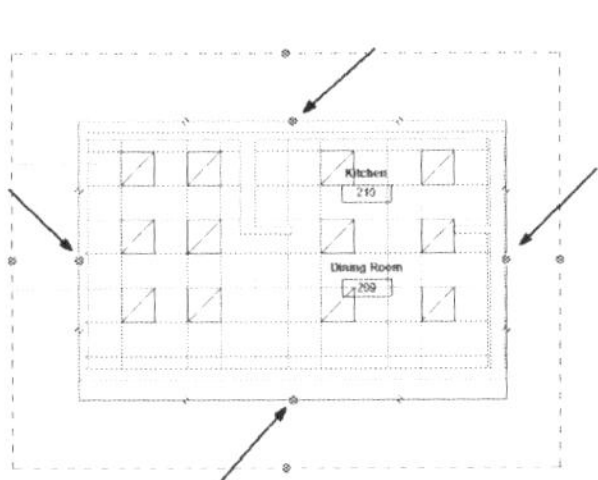   Highlight the dependent view.

Right click and select **Rename**.

7. Rename **Main Floor – Annotated – Dining Room.**

8. Use the grips on the viewport to adjust the viewport size to only include the Dining Room and Kitchen.

9. Select the **Aligned Dimension** tool.

10.

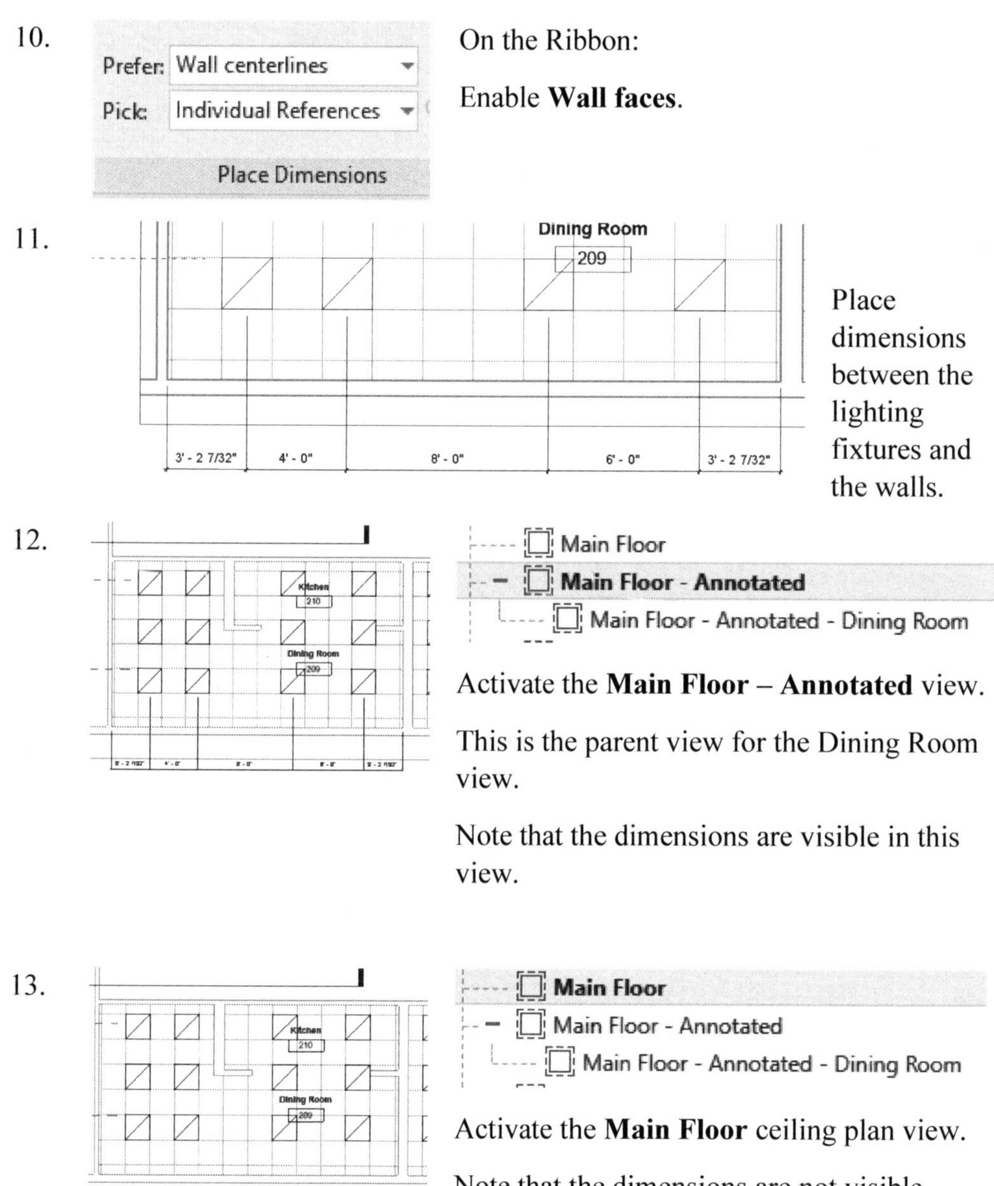

On the Ribbon:

Enable **Wall faces**.

11.

Place dimensions between the lighting fixtures and the walls.

12.

Activate the **Main Floor – Annotated** view.

This is the parent view for the Dining Room view.

Note that the dimensions are visible in this view.

13.

Activate the **Main Floor** ceiling plan view.

Note that the dimensions are not visible.

14.   Save as *ex7-1.rvt*.

Elevation Views

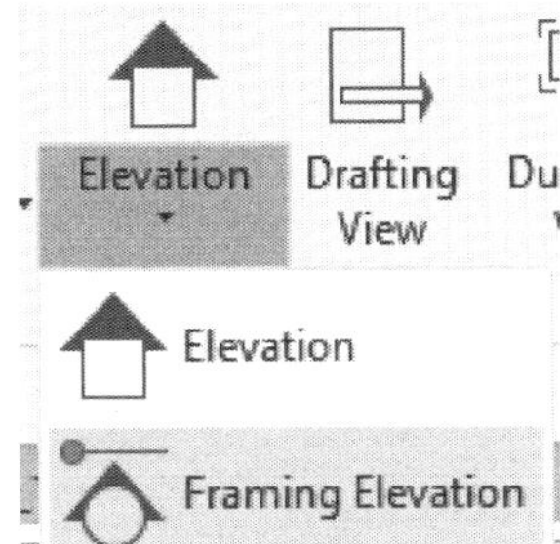

Elevation views are controlled by elevation markers. You can control the visibility of the markers in the Visibility/Graphics dialog on the Annotation tab.

Elevations help clarify relationships between elements as you design and document the building model. In a default template, Revit provides four exterior elevation views. To create additional interior or exterior elevation views, on the View tab, click the Elevation tool. As you place the elevation marker in a plan view, Revit detects model geometry and helps align the elevation marker. To cycle through possible directions for the elevation marker, Click Tab to rotate the elevation marker.

To open the elevation view, double-click the elevation arrow in a drawing or double-click the view name in the Project Browser. As your model changes, Revit automatically updates elevation views.

Electrical designers use elevation views to designate the location of outlets, light fixtures, panels, and other electrical devices.

Exercise 7-2:

Creating an Elevation View

Drawing Name: *elevations.rvt*
Estimated Time: 15 minutes

This exercise reinforces the following skills:
- Views
- Elevation
- Rename View
- Crop View

1. Open the **Main Floor** floor plan.

   Floor Plans
   - Ground Floor
   - Lower Roof
   - **Main Floor**
   - Main Roof

2. 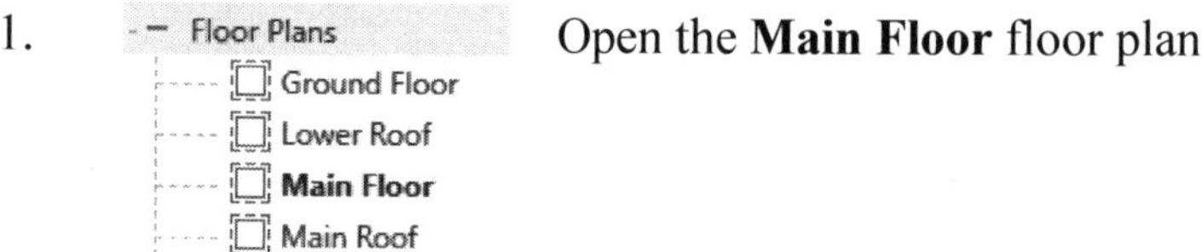 Zoom into the area to the left of **STORAGE 215**.

3. 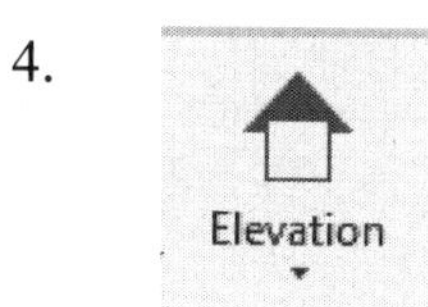 Activate the **View** ribbon.

4. Select **Elevation**.

5. 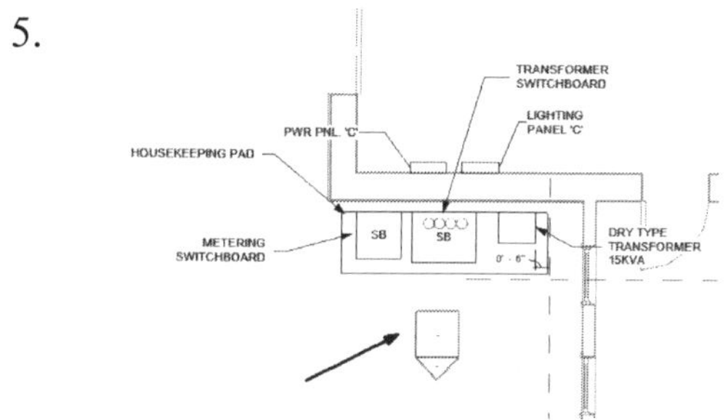 Place the elevation marker below the equipment.

   Cancel out of the command.

6. 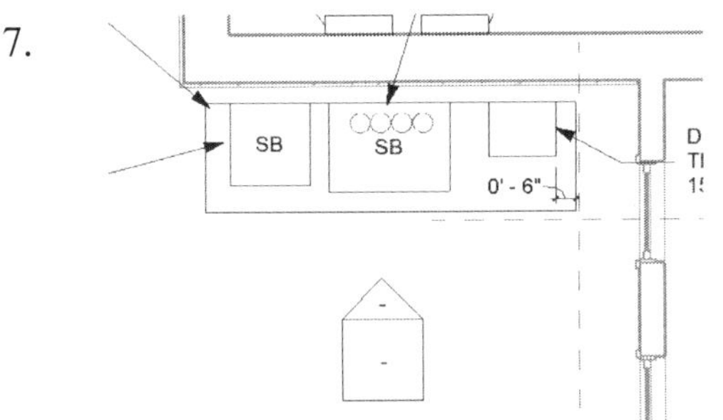

Left click on the square part of the elevation marker.

Place a check mark in the top small square.

This indicates the direction for the view.

Uncheck the small bottom square to delete that view direction.

A dialog will pop up advising the view will be deleted.

Click **OK**.

7. The elevation marker updates with the triangle located at the top of the symbol.

Single left click on the triangle to wake up the crop region.

8. *A crop region displays to show the defined view area.*

Use the grips to adjust the view area.

Double left click on the triangle to open the elevation view.

9. Select the viewport and adjust the outline.

Type **VV** to launch the Visibility/Graphics dialog.

10. 

Activate the Annotation Categories tab.

Disable **Reference Planes** to hide them.

Click **OK**.

11. 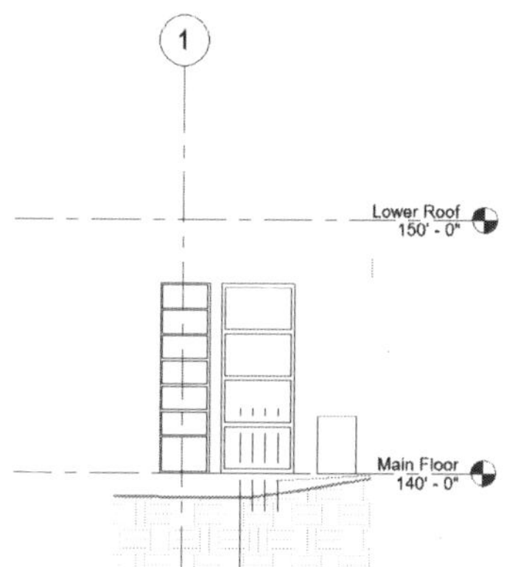

Toggle **Crop Region** off to hide the viewport.

12.

The view should appear similar to this.

13.

Highlight the Elevation view in the Project Browser.

Right click and select **Rename**.

You can also use F2.

14.

Rename **Equipment**.

15. Save as *ex7-2.rvt*.

Section Views

Section Views in Electrical Projects can be used:

- To show conduits, cable trays, and raceways running vertically or horizontally.

- To illustrate panelboards, equipment rooms, and clearances in relation to the building.

- To verify coordination with architectural/structural/MEP systems (avoiding clashes).

- To provide detail for installation, such as mounting heights and routing.

Exercise 7-3:

Creating a Section View

Drawing Name: *section_view.rvt*
Estimated Time: 15 minutes

This exercise reinforces the following skills:
- Creating a Section View
- Controlling the view's crop region window
- Rename a view
- Assign a sub-discipline to a view
- Controlling the visibility of linked file elements
- Adding Tags

1.

Revit could not find or read 1 references. What do you want to do?

Unresolved CAD links or DWF markups will display as they were when the project was last saved.

Click Show Details to view the list of unresolved links.

→ Open Manage Links to correct the problem
  Allows you to specify the location and/or the model you want to reference

→ Ignore and continue opening the project

Click **Open Manage Links to correct the problem**.

2. 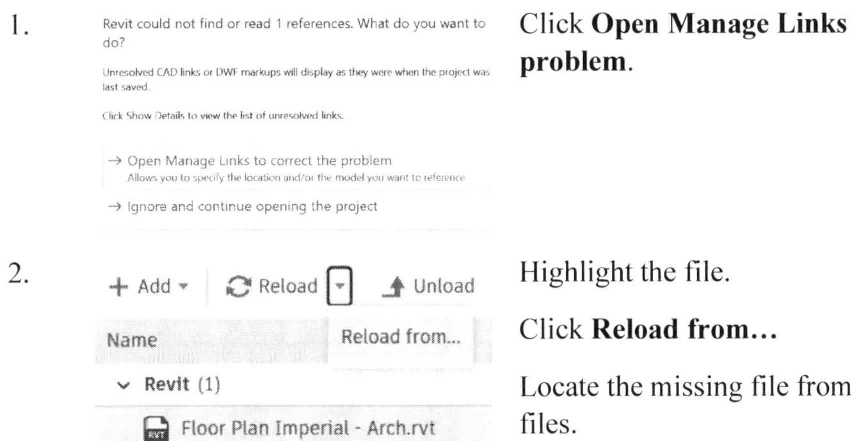

Highlight the file.

Click **Reload from…**

Locate the missing file from the downloaded files.

Click **Open**.

Close the dialog.

3. 

Open the **3rd Floor Lighting Plan** floor plan.

4. Section

Activate the View ribbon.

Select the **Section** tool.

5. 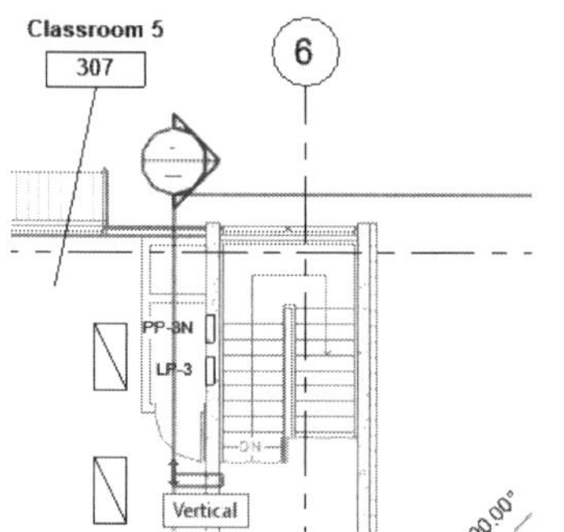

Left click above Classroom 5 to start the section line.

Left click above the door of Classroom 5 to end the section line.

6. 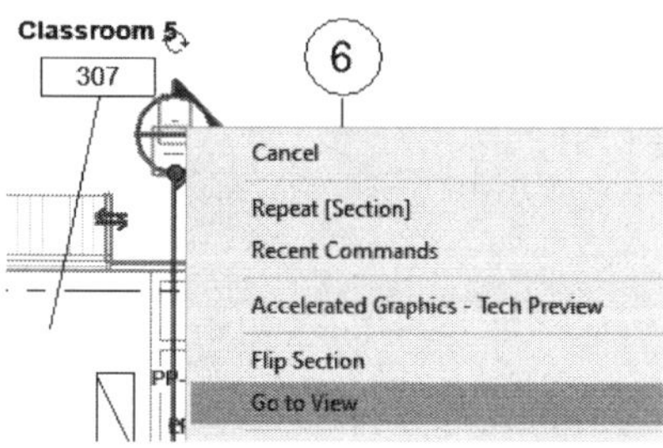

Right click on the section bubble.

Select **Go to View**.

7. 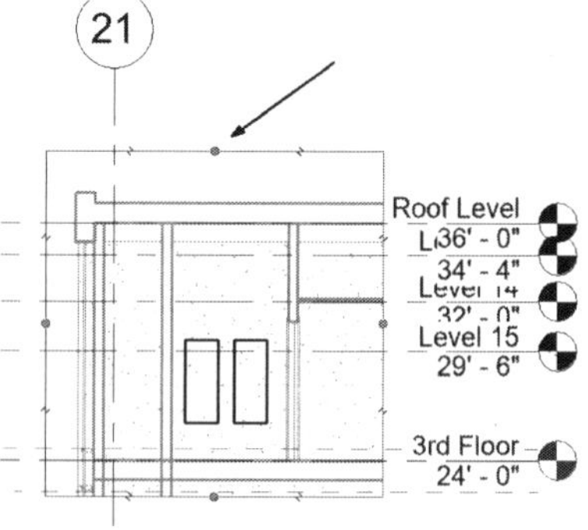

Use the grips on the view crop region to adjust the view so you are only looking at the electrical panels.

8. 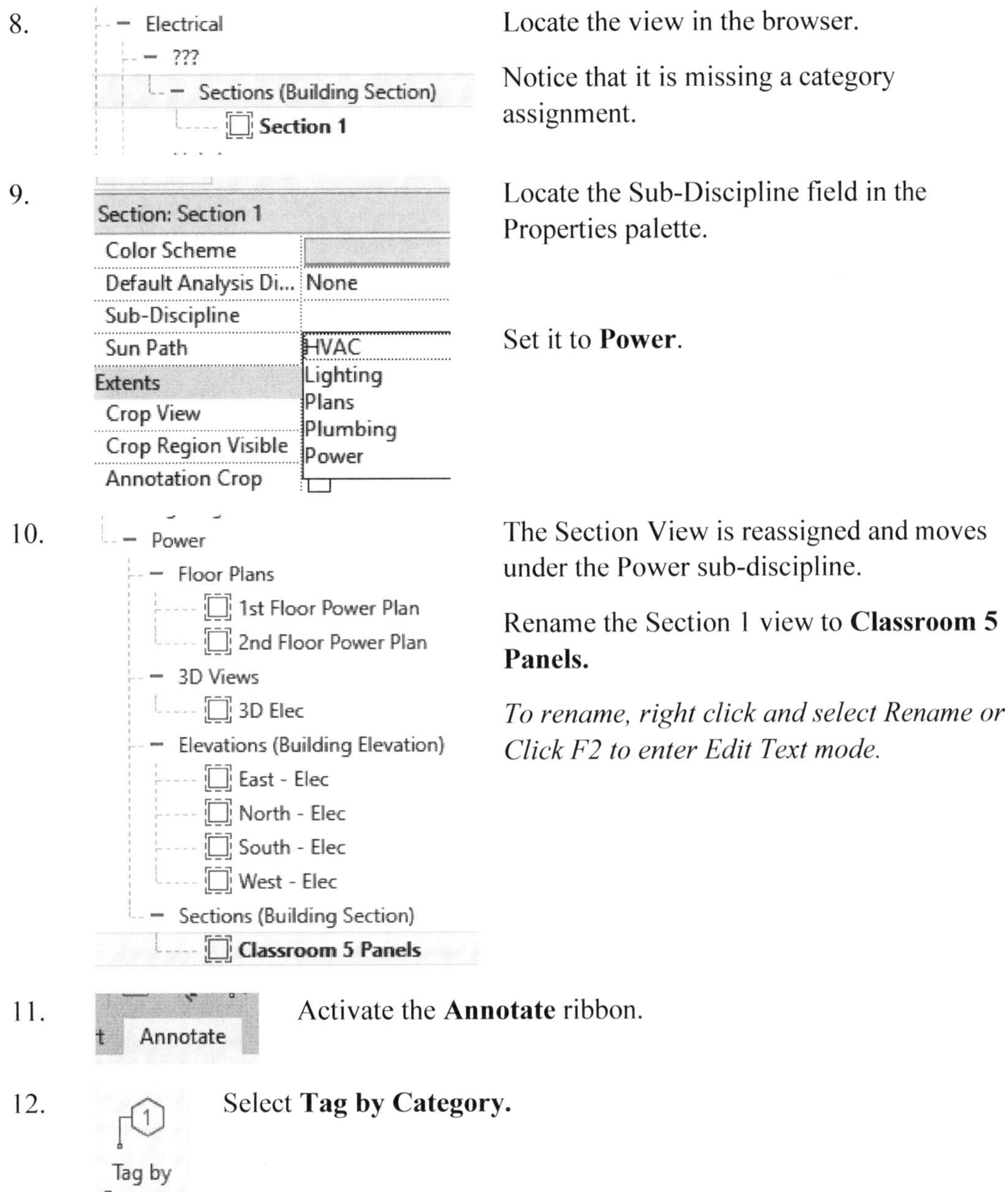 Locate the view in the browser.

   Notice that it is missing a category assignment.

9. Locate the Sub-Discipline field in the Properties palette.

   Set it to **Power**.

10. The Section View is reassigned and moves under the Power sub-discipline.

    Rename the Section 1 view to **Classroom 5 Panels.**

    To rename, right click and select Rename or Click F2 to enter Edit Text mode.

11. Activate the **Annotate** ribbon.

12. Select **Tag by Category.**

13. 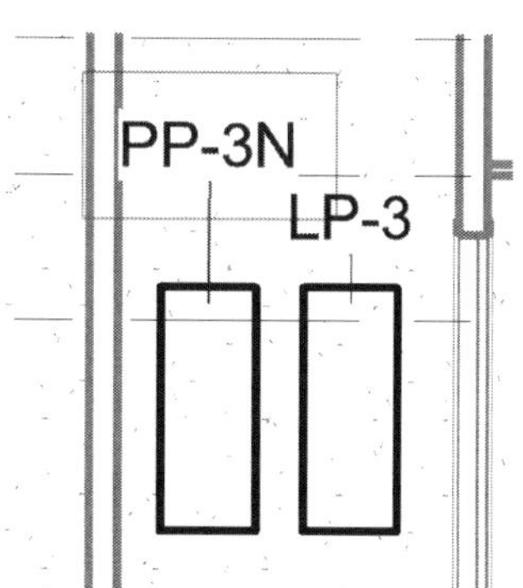

Tag each of the panels with a leader.

14. 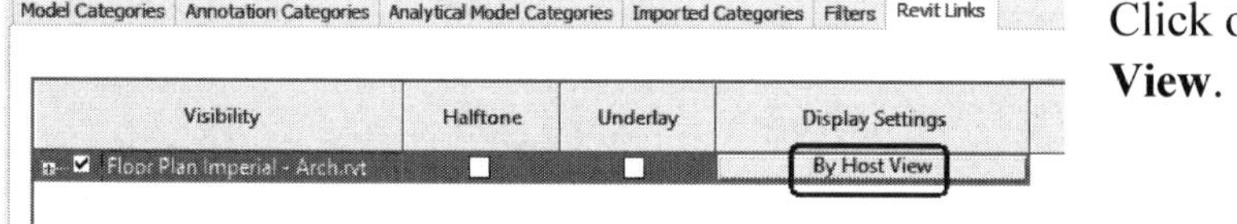

Type **VV** to bring up the Visibility/Graphics palette.

Select the **Revit Links** tab.

15. 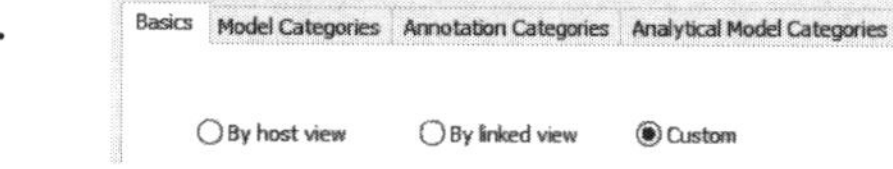

Click on **By Host View**.

16. Click the Basics tab.

Enable **Custom**.

17. 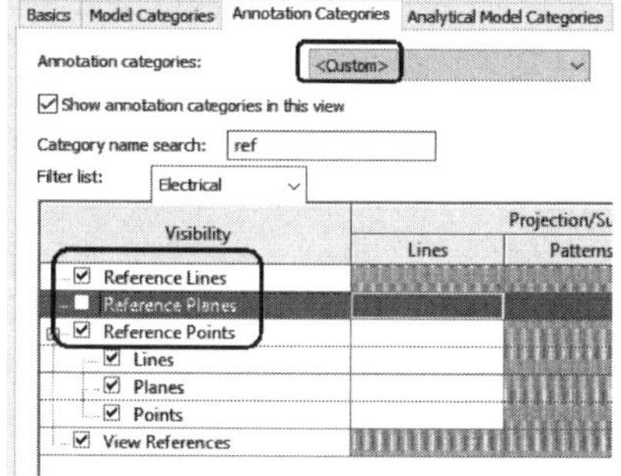

Select the **Annotation Categories** tab.

Set the Annotation categories to **Custom**.

Disable **Levels**.

Disable **Reference Planes**.

Click **Apply**.

18. 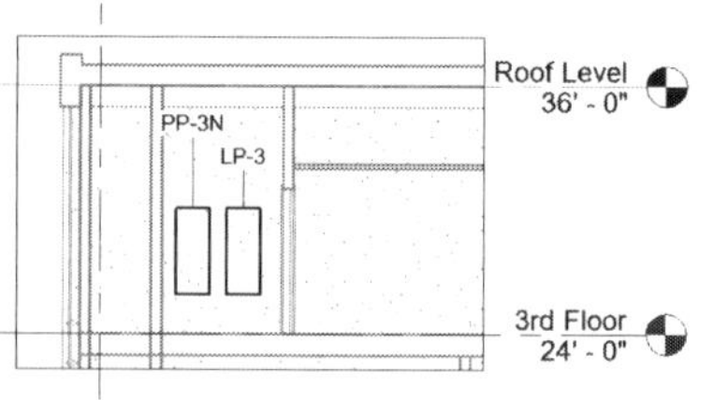

The view updates to display only the levels in the host file.

Click **OK** twice to close the dialog.

19. Save as *ex7-3.rvt*.

Callout Views in Electrical Work

Callout views can be used in the following situations:

1. **Detailing Equipment Connections**
   - Create a callout around a panelboard, switchgear, or piece of equipment to show conduit entries, cable trays, or clearance zones more clearly.
2. **Device Layouts**
   - If a floor plan has many receptacles, data jacks, or switches, a callout can show a room (e.g., a conference room or lab) at a larger scale to clarify mounting locations.
3. **Conduit Routing & Home Runs**
   - Use callouts in congested areas (like electrical rooms or ceilings) where conduit runs overlap.
   - You can detail home runs, junction boxes, or sleeve penetrations without overloading the main plan.
4. **Lighting Details**
   - Callouts are used to show mounting details for special fixtures (pendant lights, emergency fixtures, exit signs) or to enlarge an area with complex switching.
5. **Enlarged Plans for Construction Documents**
   - A callout can generate a **dependent view** (linked to the main floor plan) for enlarged electrical room layouts, ceiling plans, or control zones.

Exercise 7-4:

Creating a Call-out View

Drawing Name: *callout_views.rvt*
Estimated Time: 10 minutes

This exercise reinforces the following skills:
- ❑ View
- ❑ Callouts
- ❑ Crop Region
- ❑ Rename View
- ❑ Dimensions
- ❑ Units

1.

Power
- Floor Plans
  - 1st Floor Power Plan
  - 2nd Floor Power Plan
- 3D Views
  - 3D Elec
- Elevations (Building Elevation)
  - East - Elec
  - North - Elec
  - South - Elec
  - West - Elec
- Sections (Building Section)
  - **Classroom 5 Panels**

Verify that the **Classroom 5 Panels** section view is open.

2.

Open the Insert ribbon.

Click **Manage Links**.

Reload the *Floor Plan Imperial-Arch.rvt* file from the downloaded files.

Close the dialog.

3.

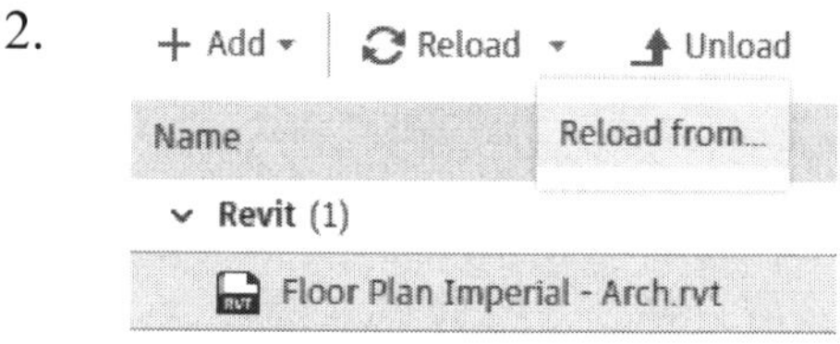

Activate the View ribbon.

Select **Callout →Rectangle**.

4.

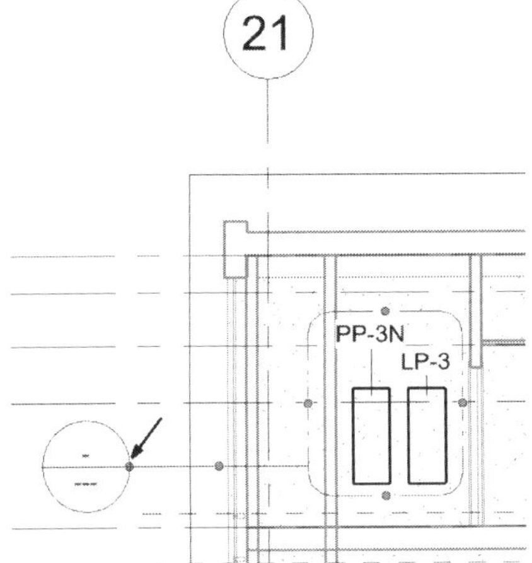

Left click once on the upper left of the panels.

Left click once on the lower right of the panels.

This defines the size of the rectangular callout.

5.

You can use the small grip at the bubble's quadrant to position the bubble on the callout.

6.

Right click on the callout bubble.

Select **Go to View**.

7.

Locate the callout view in the Project Browser.

Rename the callout view – **Classroom 5 Panels Detail.**

8.

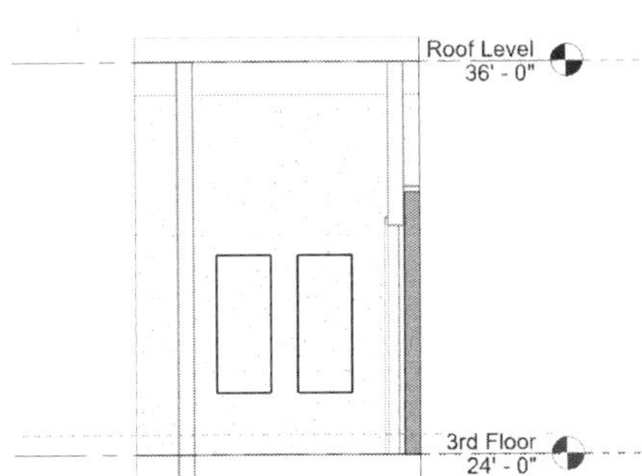

Adjust the crop region so you can see the floor and roof levels.

Notice the panel tags are not visible in the callout view. This is because annotations are view-specific. They are only visible in the view in which they are placed.

9.

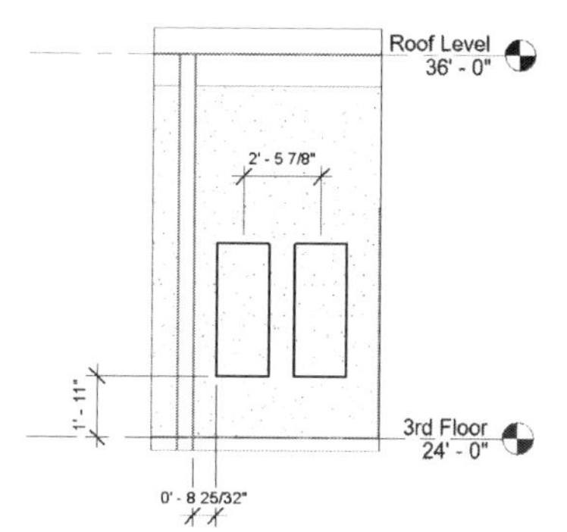

Use **ALIGNED DIMENSION** to add dimensions to indicate the placement of the panels.

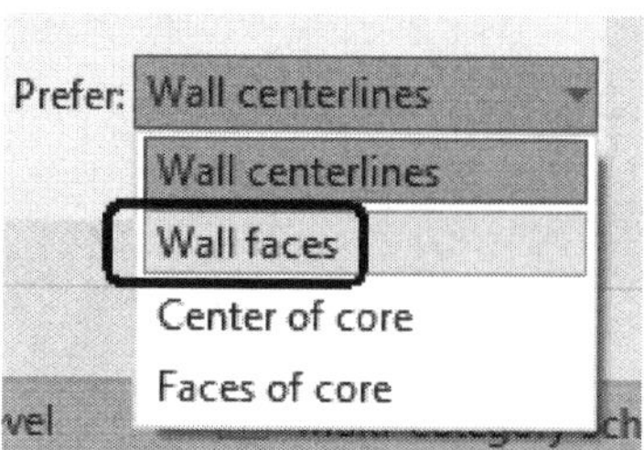

Set **Wall faces** on the ribbon.

10. Select one of the dimensions.

On the Properties palette, select **Edit Type**.

11. Left click on the **Units** format field.

12. Disable **Use project settings**.

Set the Rounding **To the nearest 1/8"**.

Click **OK**.

13.

Text Size	3/32"
Text Offset	1/16"
Read Convention	Horizontal
Text Font	Arial
Text Background	Opaque

Set the Read Convention to **Horizontal**.

Click **OK** to close the Type Properties dialog.

14. Save as *ex7-4.rvt*.

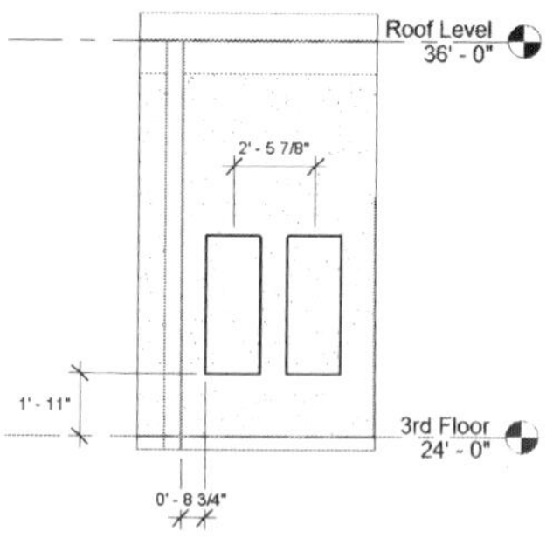

Detail Views in Electrical Design

A detail view is a view of the model that appears as a callout or section in other views. This type of view represents the model at finer scales of detail than in the parent view. Typically, a detail view uses both model and annotation elements.

A detail view can be created as a section or a callout. When created as a callout, the detail can have both section and callout annotations assigned to it. That is, a detail view made as a callout can also show up as a section in views that intersect the callout view extents. For example, you may use a callout to create a detail view of a wall intersection. This same callout can appear as a section view in the overall building section view.

For a detail callout to display in the overall building section view, you must select the Intersecting Views option for the Show In instance parameter. You set this parameter on the Properties palette.

Detail views in electrical work can be useful in the following situations:

1. Equipment Connection Details
- Show how conduits connect to panelboards, switchgear, VFDs, or transformers.
- Add detail lines, annotations, and symbols to clarify connection methods that aren't modeled in 3D.

2. Device & Mounting Details
- Enlarged details of wall-mounted devices: receptacles, switches, data outlets.
- Show mounting height dimensions, back box requirements, and conduit stub-up/down notes.

3. Conduit & Raceway Details
- Show transitions (EMT to flex), expansion fittings, conduit supports, or underground duct banks.
- Useful for construction details that aren't represented well in the model.

4. Lighting Fixture Mounting Details
- Provide ceiling mounting methods, junction box locations, or emergency ballast wiring diagrams.
- Good for coordination with architects and contractors.

5. One-Line or Riser Diagram Enlargements
- Sometimes you'll use detail views as a space to draft portions of a one-line diagram or riser detail that ties back to the modeled systems.

Exercise 7-5:

Creating a Detail View

Drawing Name: *views_detail.rvt*
Estimated Time: 30 minutes

This exercise reinforces the following skills:
- ❑ Section View
- ❑ Add Tags
- ❑ Detail Lines
- ❑ Add Text Notes and callouts

1. Open the **Level 1 Power Plan** view.

2. 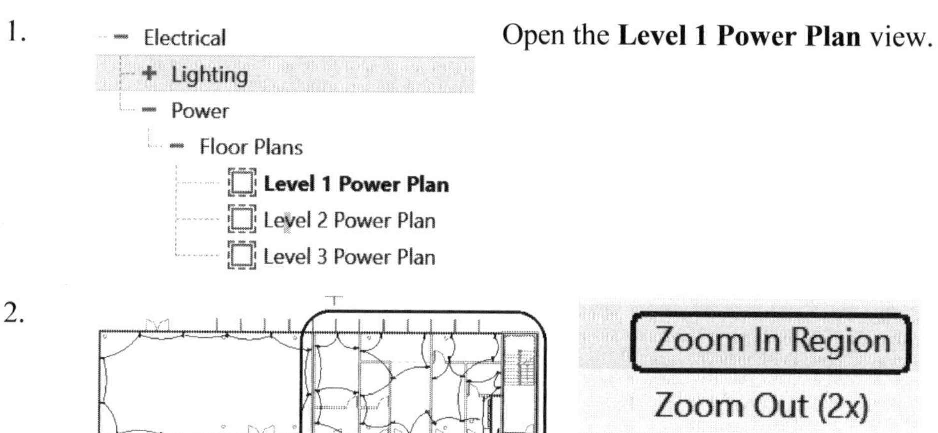

   Use **Zoom In Region** to zoom to the upper right of the model.

3. Activate the View ribbon.

   Select the **Section** tool.

4. On the Properties palette:

   Verify that **Detail View: Detail** is selected.

5. 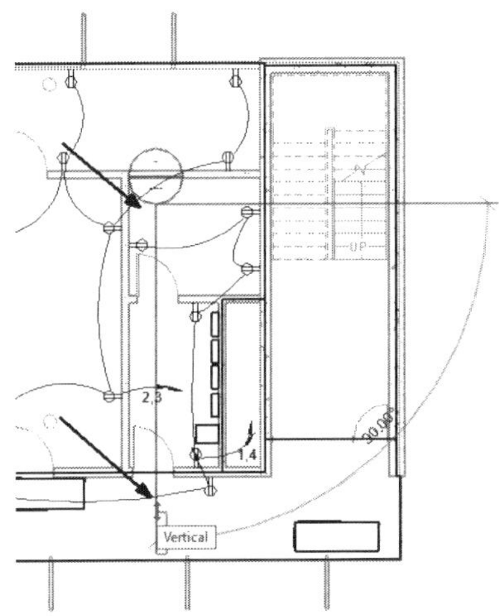

Place a vertical section line looking at the panels.

6. 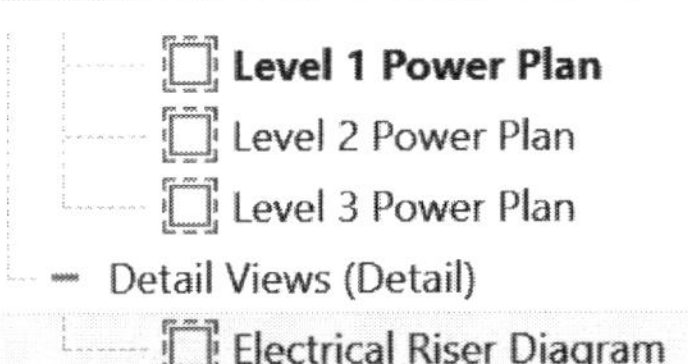

Locate the Detail View in the Project Browser.

Rename to **Electrical Riser Diagram**.

Double left click on the detail view to open.

7. 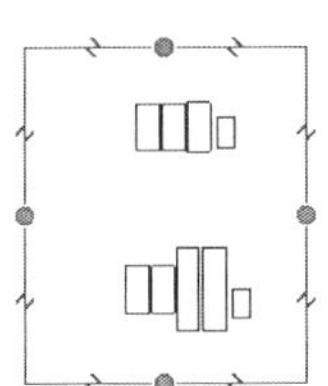

Adjust the crop region to show the electrical panels.

8. 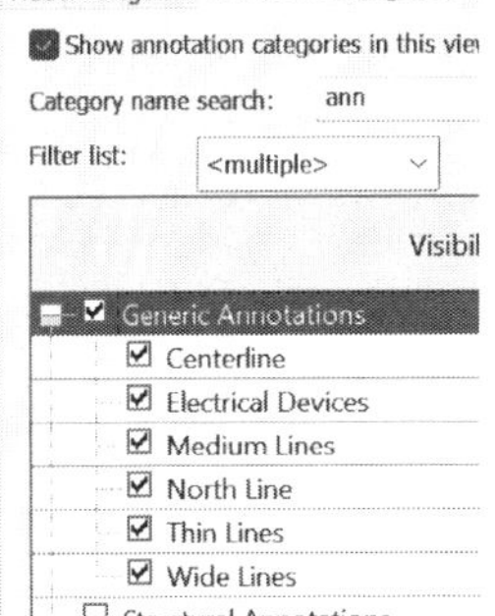

Type **VV** to open the Visibility/Graphics dialog.

Select the Annotation Categories tab.

Enable **Generic Annotations**.

Click **OK**.

9. 

Activate the Annotate ribbon.

Select the **Tag by Category** tool.

10. 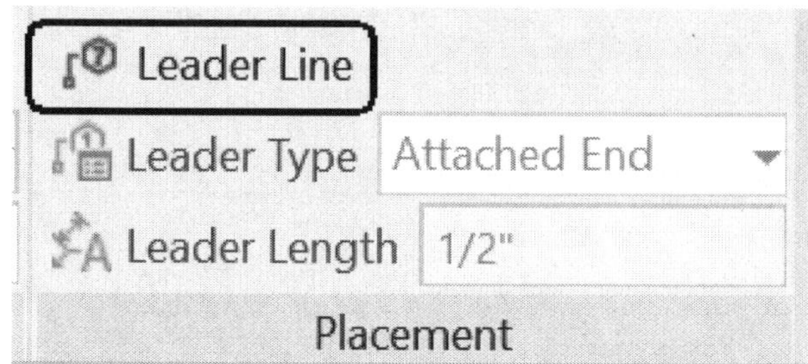 Disable **Leader** on the ribbon.

11. 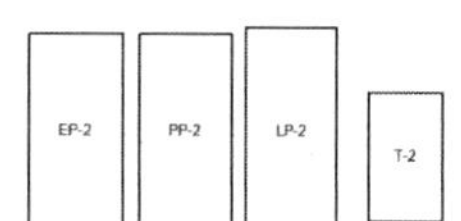 Left click inside of each panel/rectangle to tag.

Click **ESC** to exit the command.

12. 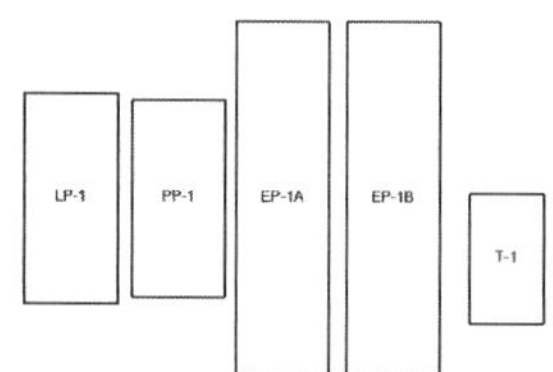 Select the **Detail Line** tool from the Annotate ribbon.

13. 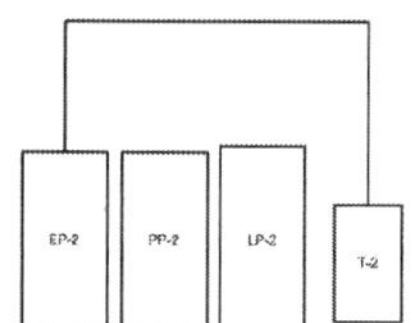 Draw a detail line from EP-2 to T-2 as shown.

You can use the midpoint snap to locate the end points of the line.

14.   Add the detail lines as shown.

Enable **Chain** on the Options bar to automatically stay in the LINE command.

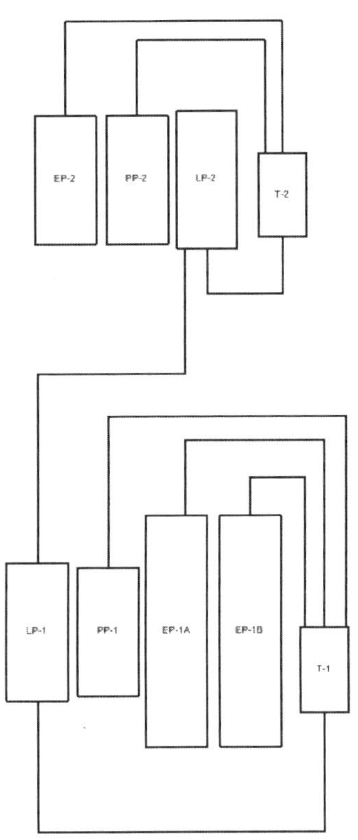

15.   Select the **Detail Line** tool from the Annotate ribbon.

16.   Select the **Rectangle** tool from the Draw panel.

Draw

17.   Draw a 4' 3" wide by 3' 6" high rectangle to the left of the LP-1 panel.

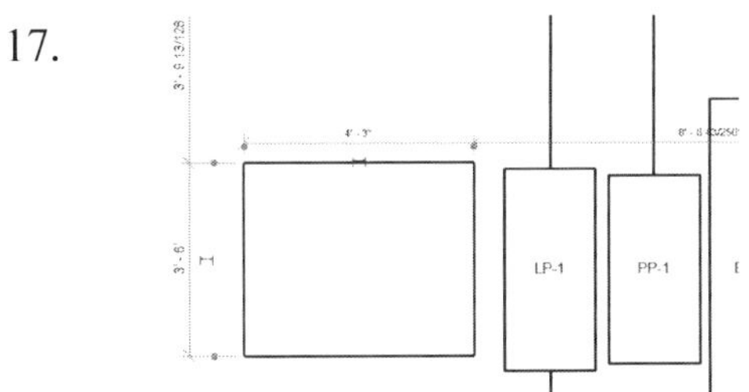

18.

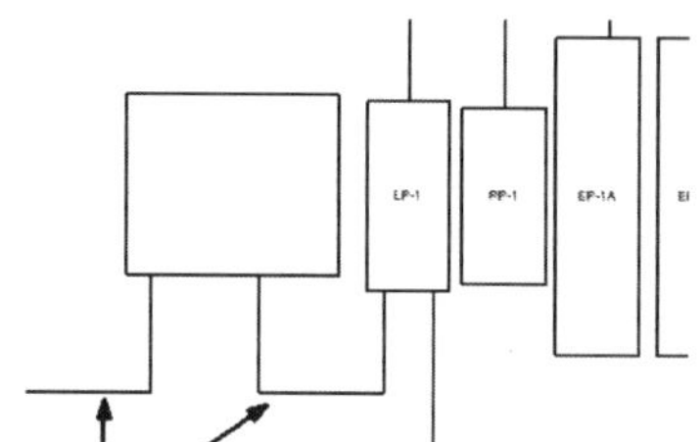

Add detail lines to connect the rectangle to the LP-1 panel and two lines from the rectangle to the left side of the crop region.

19.

Select the **Symbol** tool on the Annotate ribbon.

20.

No Generic Annotations family is loaded in the project. Would you like to load one now?

Click **Yes.**

21.

File name: ground symbol.rfa

Files of type: Family Files (*.rfa)

Locate the *ground symbol* in the downloaded exercise files.

Click **Open.**

22.

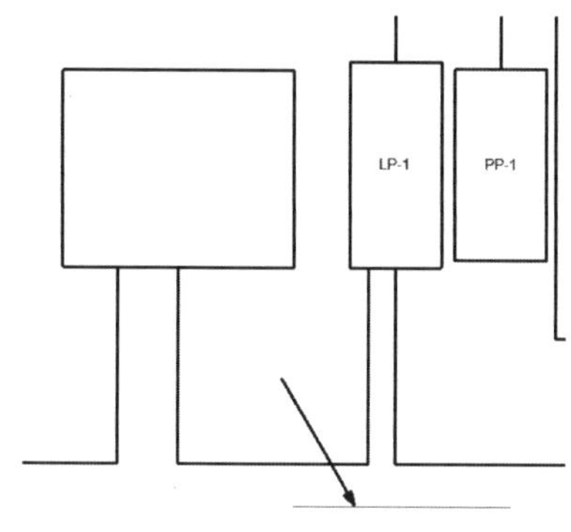

Place the symbol centered below the LP-1 panel.

23.

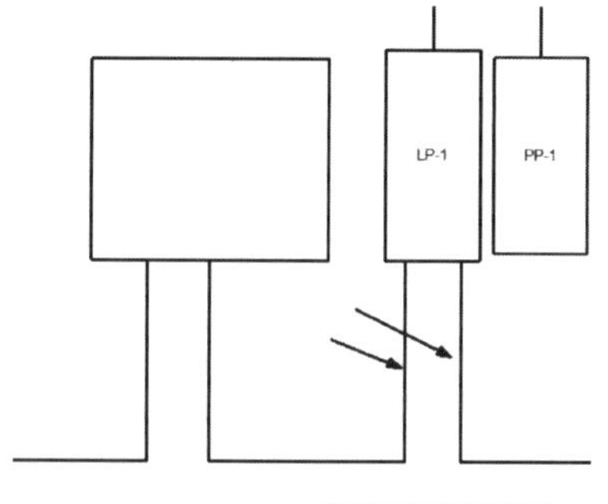

Adjust the lines beneath the LP-1 panel to make room for another connection.

Select the ground symbol.

24. 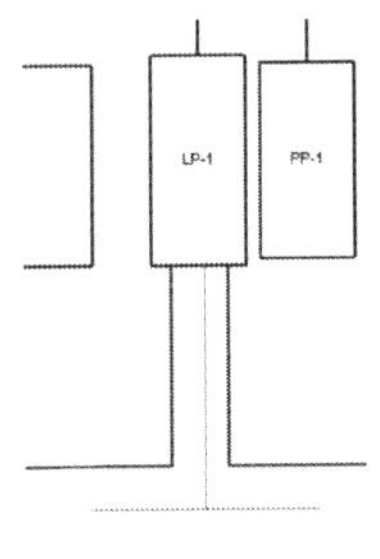 On the ribbon: Enable **Add** Leader.

25. 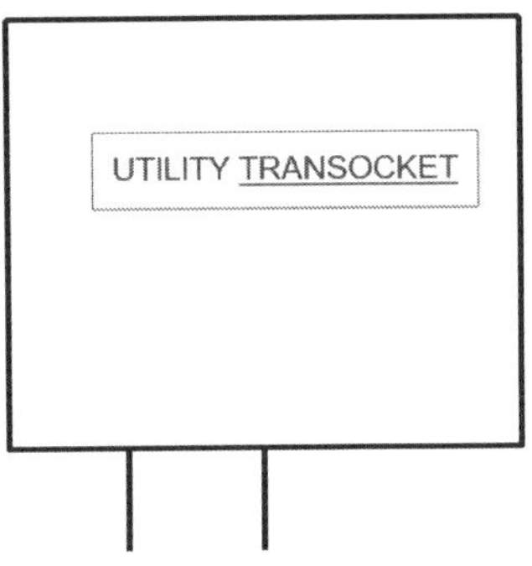 Adjust the leader position to the bottom midpoint of the LP-1 panel.

Position the symbol below LP-1.

26. **A** Text   Select the **Text** tool from the Annotate ribbon.

27. 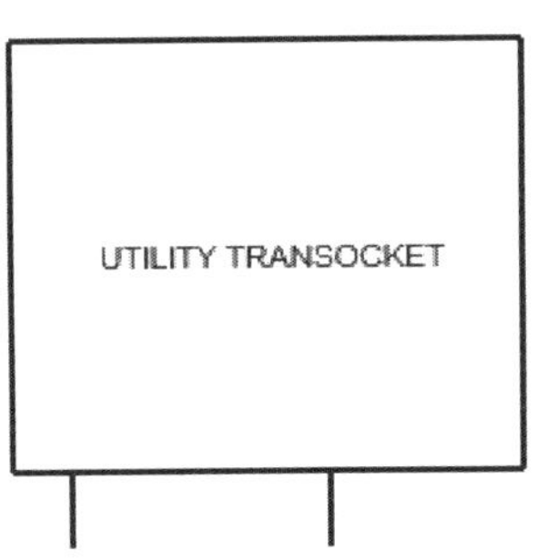

Left click inside the rectangle you placed to locate the test.

Type **UTILITY TRANSOCKET**.

Left click outside of the text box to exit the edit box.

Click ESC or right click and select CANCEL twice to exit the TEXT command.

28.

Click on the text and use the MOVE icon to position the text in the center of the rectangle.

29.

Add text to the wire coming from the left of the Utility Transocket.

The text should read **TO PADMOUNT TRANSFORMER**.

30. **A** Text   Select the **Text** tool from the Annotate ribbon.

31. On the ribbon:

Enable leader.

32.

Left click on the vertical line connecting to the ground to start the leader.

Left click to place the start point of the shoulder.

Left click to start the text.

Type **GROUND ROD**.

Left click outside the text box to exit the text.

Click **ESC** to exit the command.

33.   Save as *ex7-5.rvt*.

Exercise 7-6:

Creating a 3D View

Drawing Name: *3d_view.rvt*
Estimated Time: 20 minutes

This exercise reinforces the following skills:
- View
- Camera
- Properties palette

1. 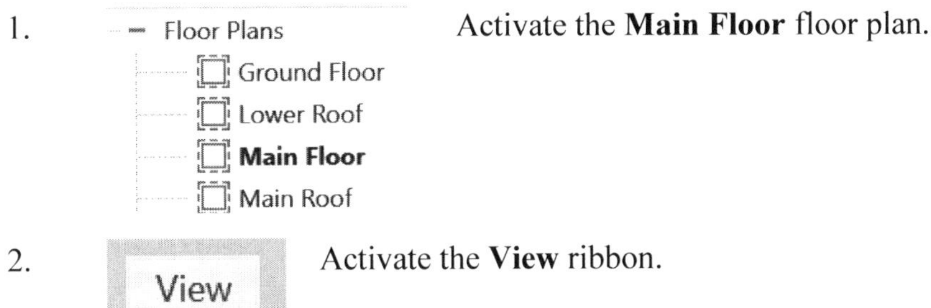

Activate the **Main Floor** floor plan.

2. 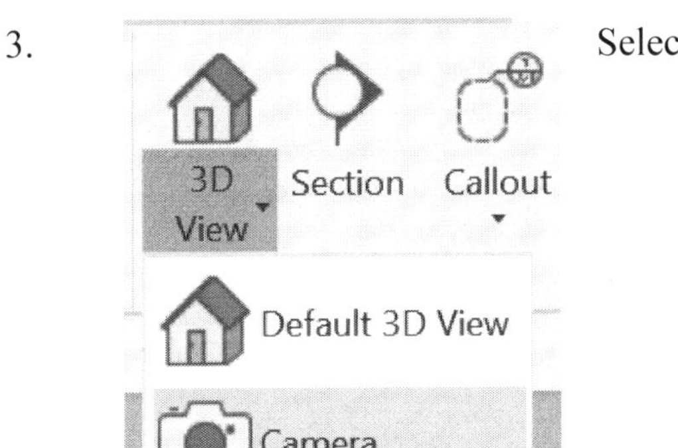

Activate the **View** ribbon.

3. Select **3D View→Camera**.

4.

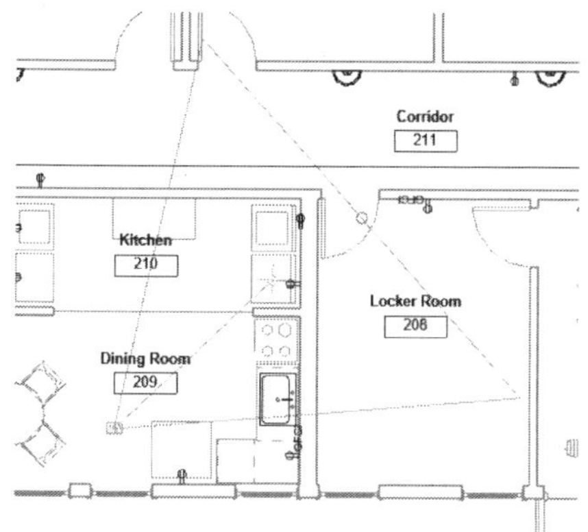

Place a camera in the Dining Room looking towards the kitchen.

5.

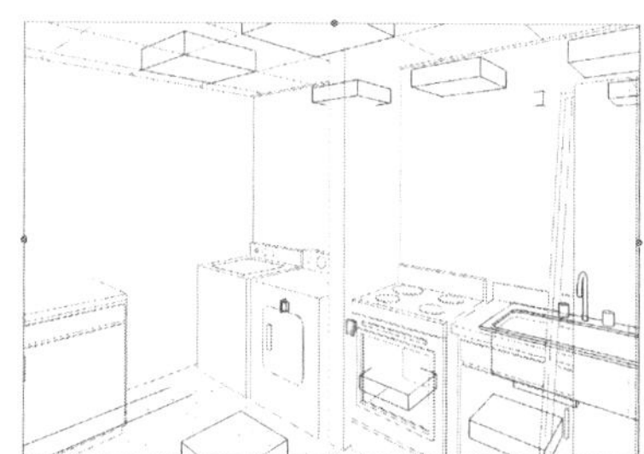

Using grips, adjust the size of the viewport so you can see the kitchen.

6.

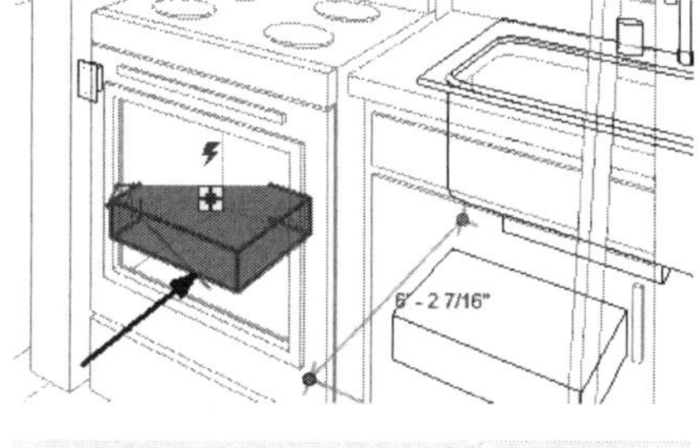

Select the block indicated.

On the Properties panel, it shows that it is a lighting fixture located on the ground floor.

7.

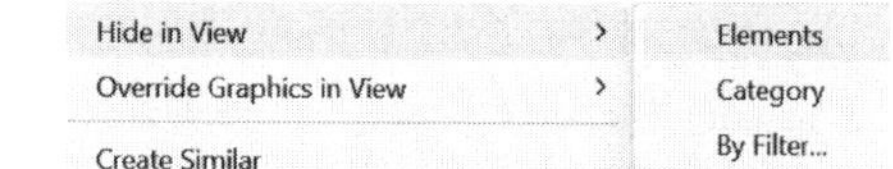

Right click and select **Hide in View→Elements.**

Repeat for the other elements which should not be visible in the view.

8.

You can use the Navigation Wheel located on the right side of the display window to adjust the view further.

Select the Navigation Wheel.

9.

Return to the Main Floor view.

The duplex receptacles need to be adjusted.

10.

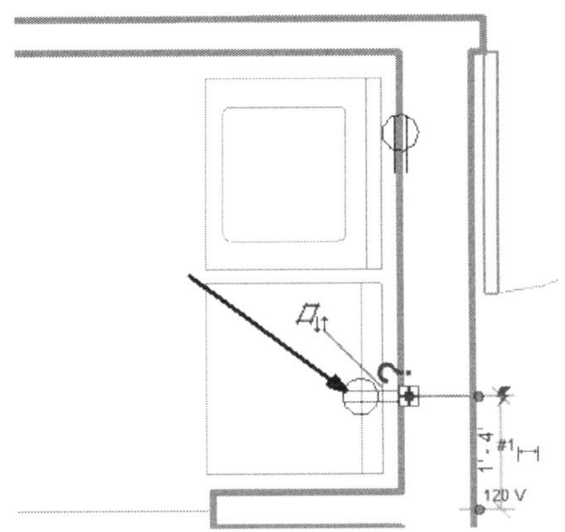

Select the lower receptacle.

On the Properties palette:

11.

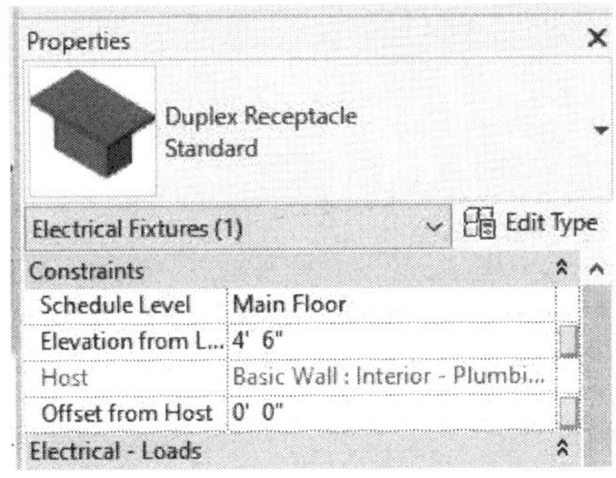

Change the Elevation from Level to **4' 6"**.

Click **ESC** to release the selection.

12.

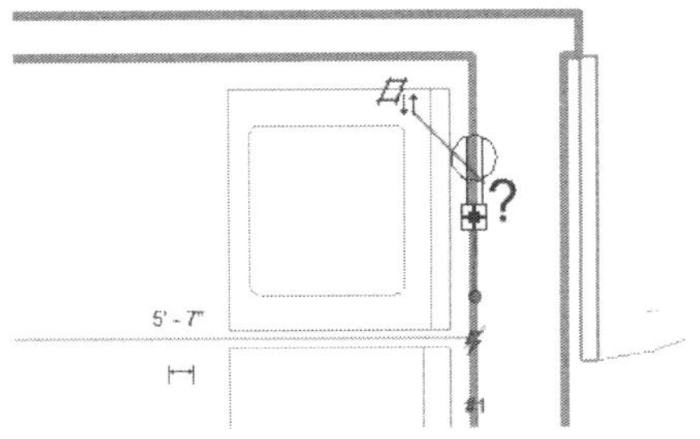

Select the upper receptacle.

13. 

Select **Pick New** from the ribbon.

14. 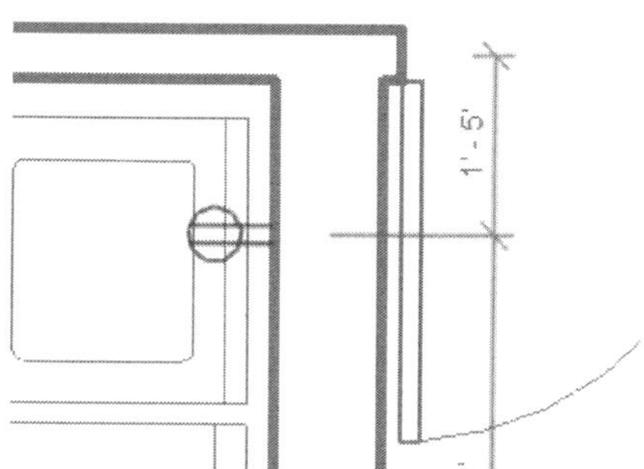

Place it so it is perpendicular to the wall.

15. 

Change the Elevation from Level to **4' 6"**.

Click **ESC** to release the selection.

16. 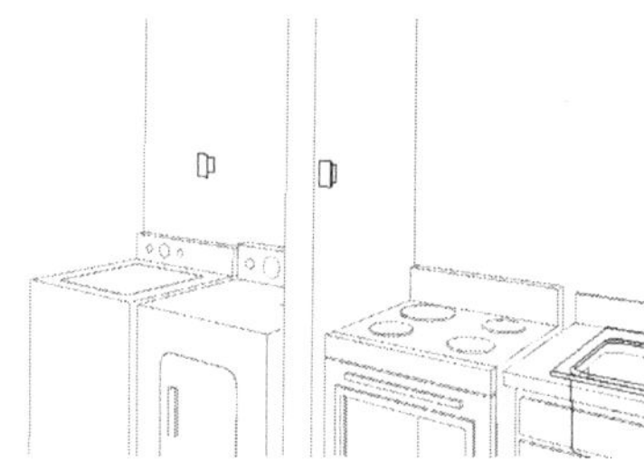

Open the 3D view.

17. The receptacles now look like they are located properly.

Save as *ex7-6.rvt*.

Legends

Legends appear as tables and typically have two columns: one column for graphic symbols and one column with an explanatory description of the symbol. Typical legends include annotations, model elements, line styles, filled regions, and detail lines.

Legends can be placed on multiple sheets in a project. They can also be shared across projects.

Guidelines for Creating Legends

- Set up legends based on the standard documentation of your organization and load them in the project templates. Pre-loaded legends save time and ensure consistency across documentation packages.
- Import CAD files with legends to re-use legacy data.

Because legends use a symbolic 2D graphic of a Revit family, these symbols are view-independent. This means they cannot be rotated. If you need to create a rotated legend symbol of a family, you can edit the existing family or create a drafting view instead of a legend.

Exercise 7-7:

Creating a Legend Symbol

Drawing Name: *legend symbol.rvt*
Estimated Time: 10 minutes

This exercise reinforces the following skills:
- ❑ Legends
- ❑ Views
- ❑ Families
- ❑ Project Browser
- ❑ Reference Planes
- ❑ Labels

1. 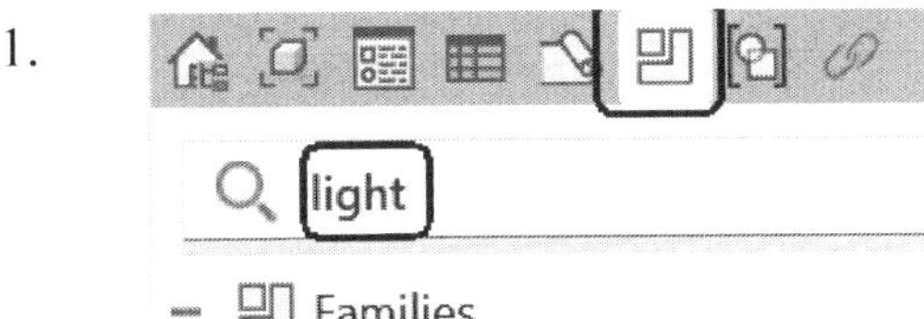

In the Project Browser:
Enable the **Families** filter tab.
Type **light** in the search field.

2.

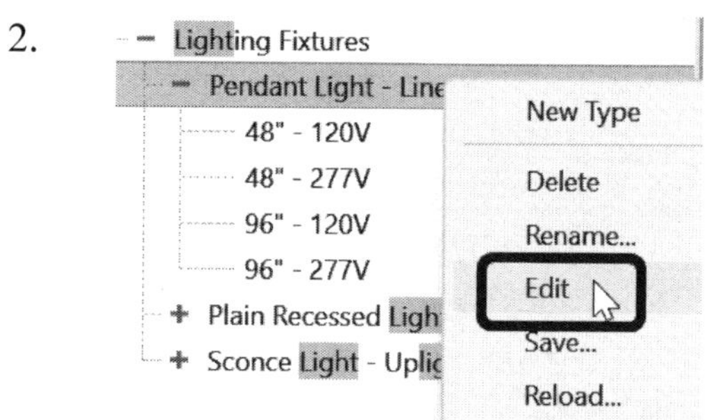

Locate the **Pendant Light – Linear** Lighting Fixture.
Right click and select **Edit**.

3.

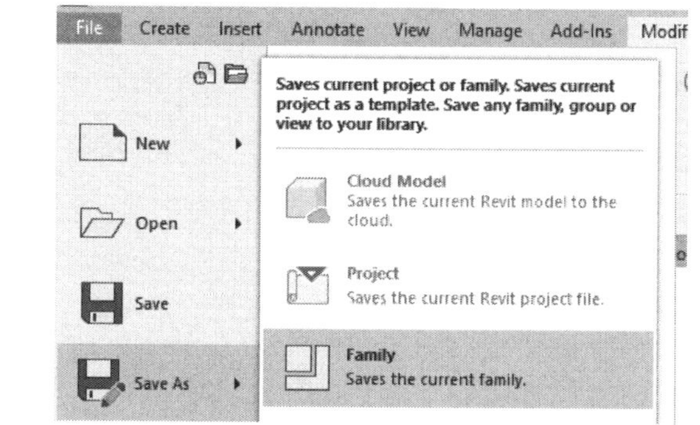

Go to **File→Save As→Family**.

4.

File name:	Pendant Light - Linear - 2 Lamp-legends.rfa
Files of type:	Family Files (*.rfa)

Save as *Pendant Light – Linear -2 Lamp-legends.rfa*.

5.

Open the **Ref. Level** view.

6.

Open the Manage ribbon.

Select **Object Styles**.

7.

Highlight **Reference Planes**.

Click **New** under Modify Subcategories.

8. Type **Legend Ref Plane** for the Name.

Click **OK**.

9. 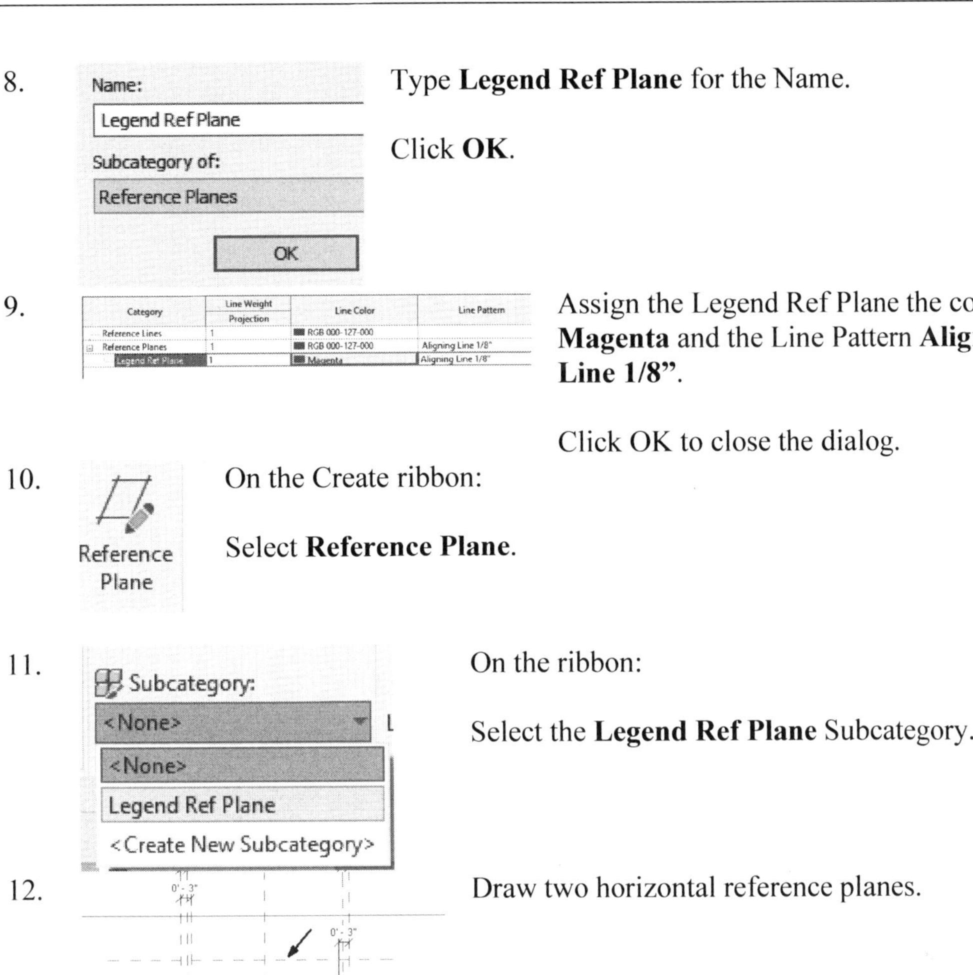

Assign the Legend Ref Plane the color **Magenta** and the Line Pattern **Aligning Line 1/8"**.

Click OK to close the dialog.

10. On the Create ribbon:

Select **Reference Plane**.

11. On the ribbon:

Select the **Legend Ref Plane** Subcategory.

12. Draw two horizontal reference planes.

13.

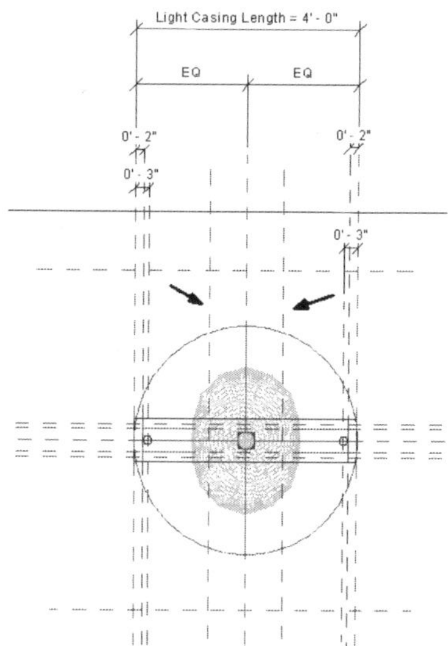

Draw two vertical reference planes.

14.

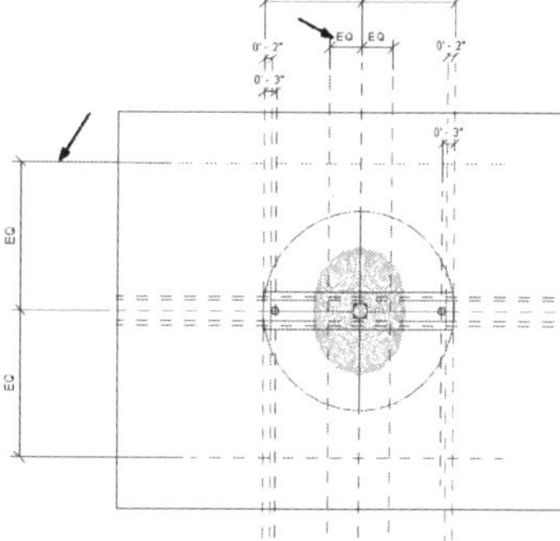

Add continuous dimensions for the width and height.

Set them equal to center the reference planes.

15.

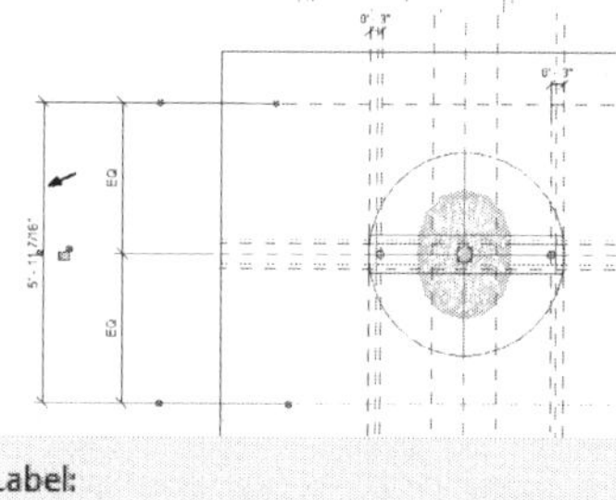

Place an overall height dimension.
Place an overall width dimension.

Cancel out of the command.

16.

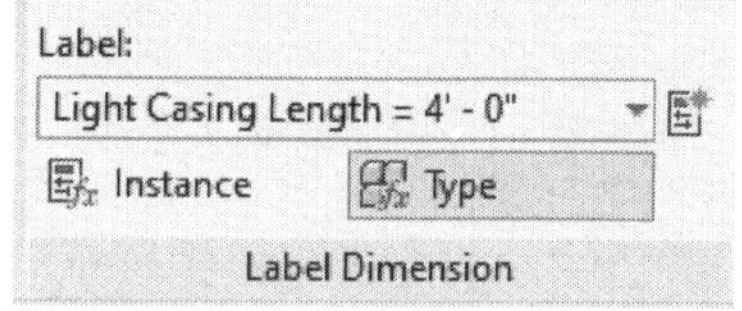

Select the overall height dimension.

Select the extension line, not the text.

On the ribbon, set the dimension equal to the **Light Casing Length**.

17.

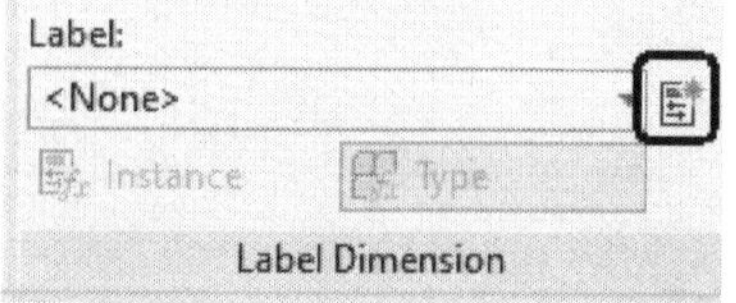

Select the overall width dimension.

Click **New** on the ribbon to create a new parameter label.

18. 

Type **Width** for the Name.
Enable **Type**.

Click **OK**.

19.

On the Create ribbon:

Select **Reference Plane**.

Reference
Plane

20. 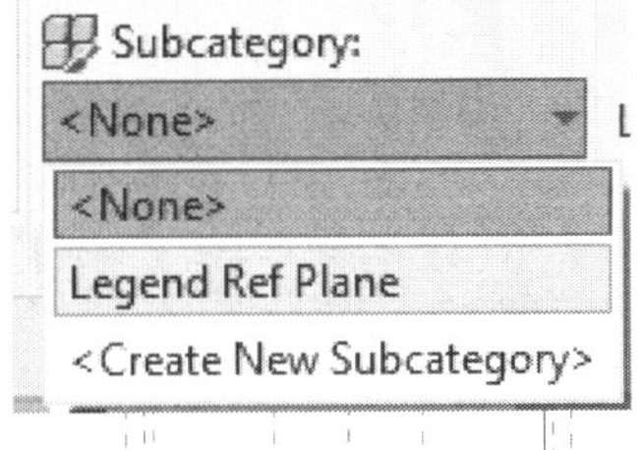

On the ribbon:

Select the **Legend Ref Plane** Subcategory.

21. 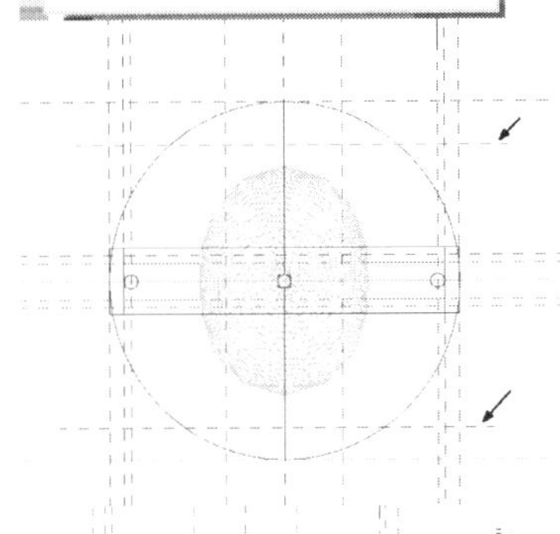

Draw two horizontal reference planes inside the other two horizontal reference planes.

These will be used to locate the circles.

22. 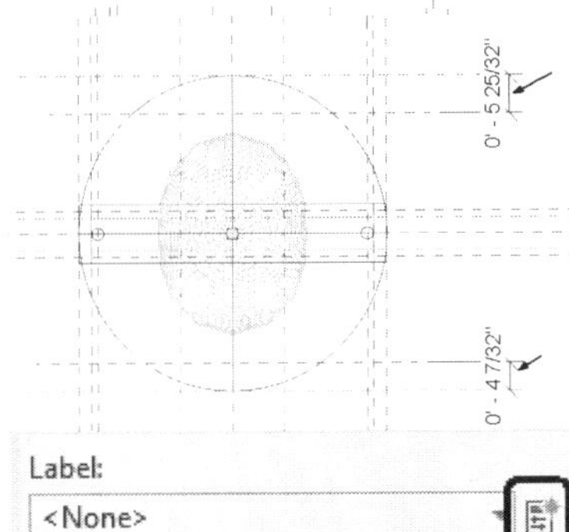

Place two vertical dimensions.

23.

Select the top vertical dimension.

Click **New** on the ribbon to create a new parameter label.

24.

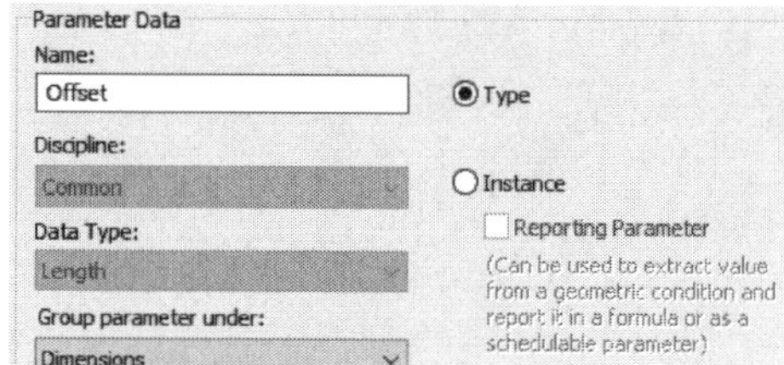

Type **Offset** for the Name.
Enable **Type**.

Click **OK**.

25.

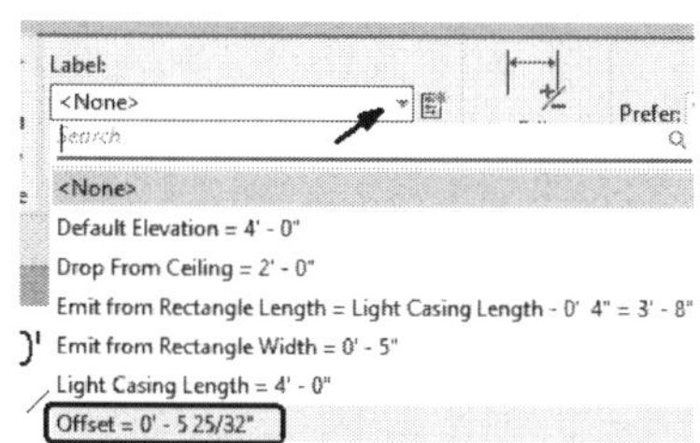

Select the lower vertical dimension.

Assign it the Offset label using the drop-down list on the ribbon.

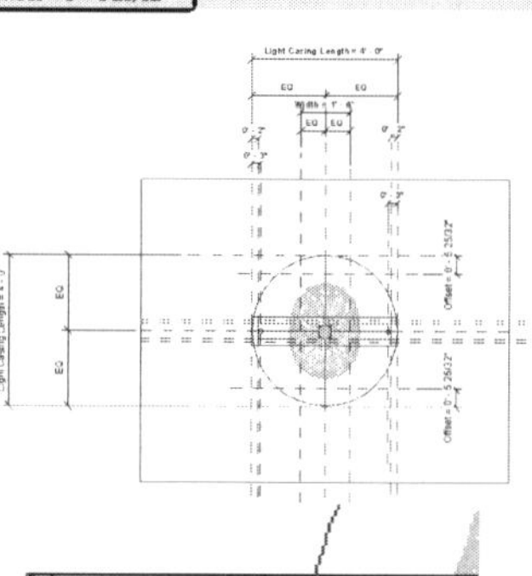

The reference planes should look like this.

26.

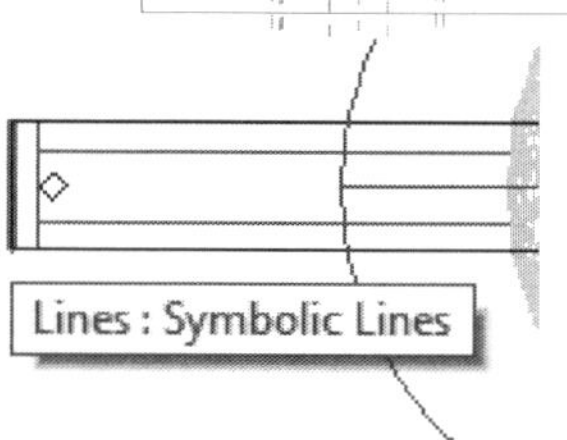

Hover over the outline, you will see the lines are Symbolic Lines. They are not part of the model.

Hover over the circles. They are also Symbolic Lines.

27.

Open the Annotate ribbon.

Select **Symbolic Line**.

28.

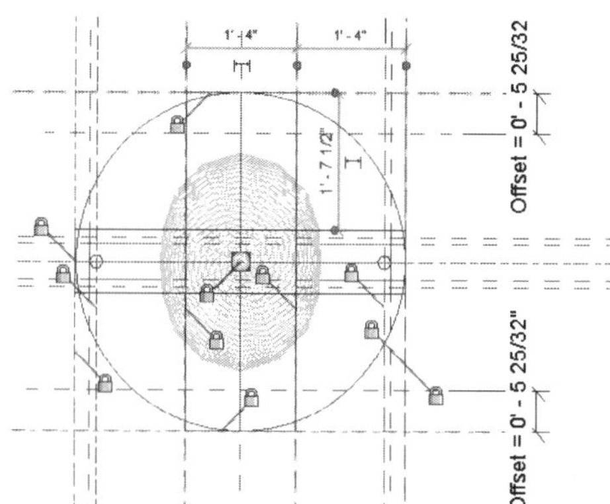

Draw a rectangle centered on the reference planes.

Lock the symbolic lines to the reference planes.

Orient the rectangle 90 degrees from the original symbol.

29.

30. Select circle.

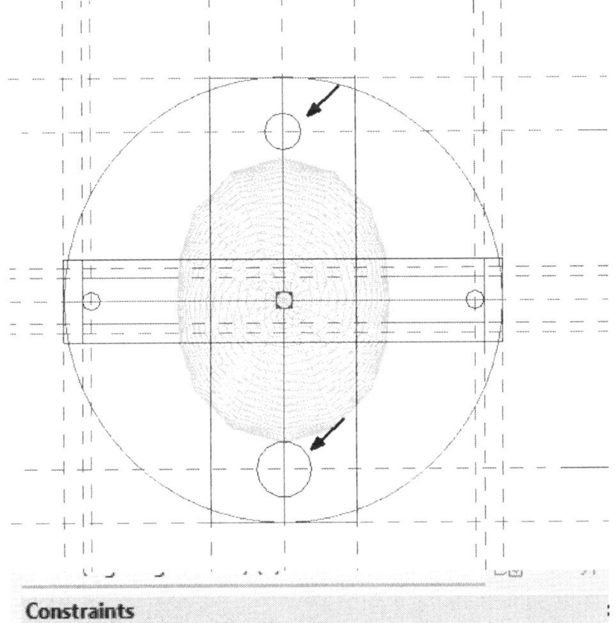

31. Place two circles at the intersection of the offset reference plane and center reference plane.

32. Select the top circle.

In the Properties pane:
Enable **Center Mark Visible**.

Change the radius of the circle to **1"**

Repeat for the bottom circle.

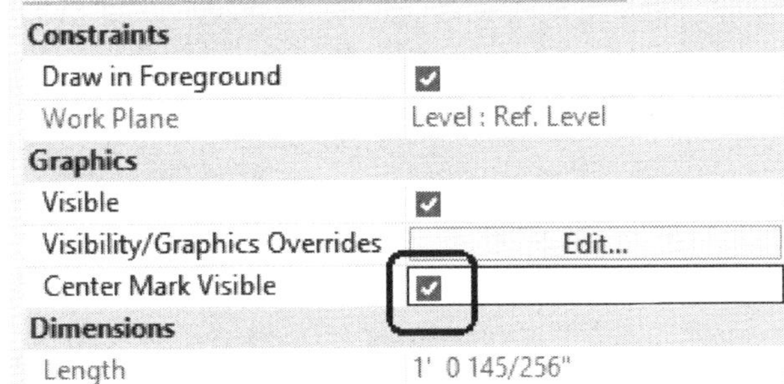

33. Click **Family Types** on the ribbon.

34. Change the Offset to **3"**.
Change the Width to **9"**.
Click **Apply**.

Dimensions	
Light Casing Length	4' 0"
Drop From Ceiling	2' 0"
Offset	0' 3"
Width	0' 9"

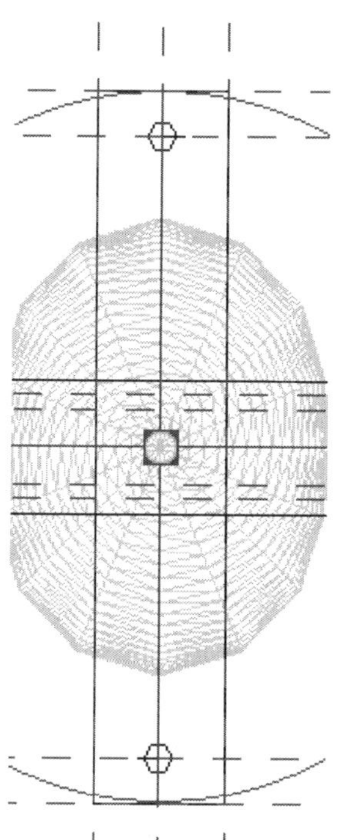

The symbolic lines you drew should adjust.

If they don't, verify that the lines are locked to the reference planes and that the circles are on the intersections.

35. 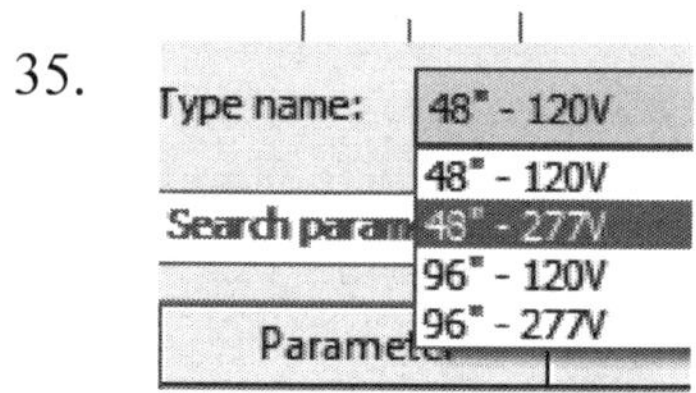

Switch to the next type.
Change the Offset to **3"**.
Change the Width to **9"**.
Click **Apply**.
Repeat for each type.

36. 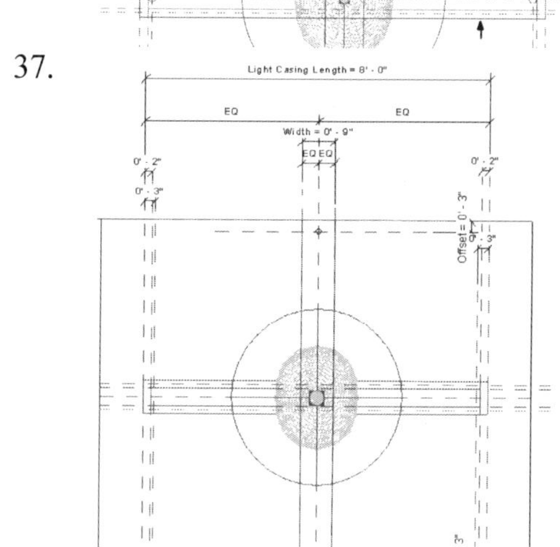

Select the original symbolic lines and delete.

37.

The model elements remain, but the symbolic lines are now oriented 90 degrees.

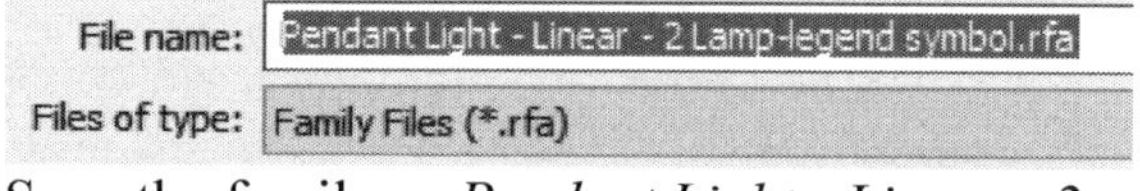

Save the family as *Pendant Light - Linear - 2 Lamp-legend symbol.rfa*.

Close the legend symbol.rvt file.

Exercise 7-8:

Creating a Legend Using Detail Components

Drawing Name: *legends.rvt*
Estimated Time: 15 minutes

This exercise reinforces the following skills:
- Views
- Legend
- Detail Components
- Load Families
- Detail Lines
- Text

1. Go to the Insert ribbon.

   Select **Load Family**.

2. Load the *Pendant Light Linear – 2 Lamp – legend symbol.rfa* file in your exercise folder.

   Click **Open**.
   Go to the Project Browser.
   Enable the **Families** filter.
   Type **lighting** in the search field.

3.

4. Locate the **Pendant Light – Linear – 2 Lamp** family.

   Highlight the **96" -120V** type.

   Right click and **Select all Instances→In Entire Project.**

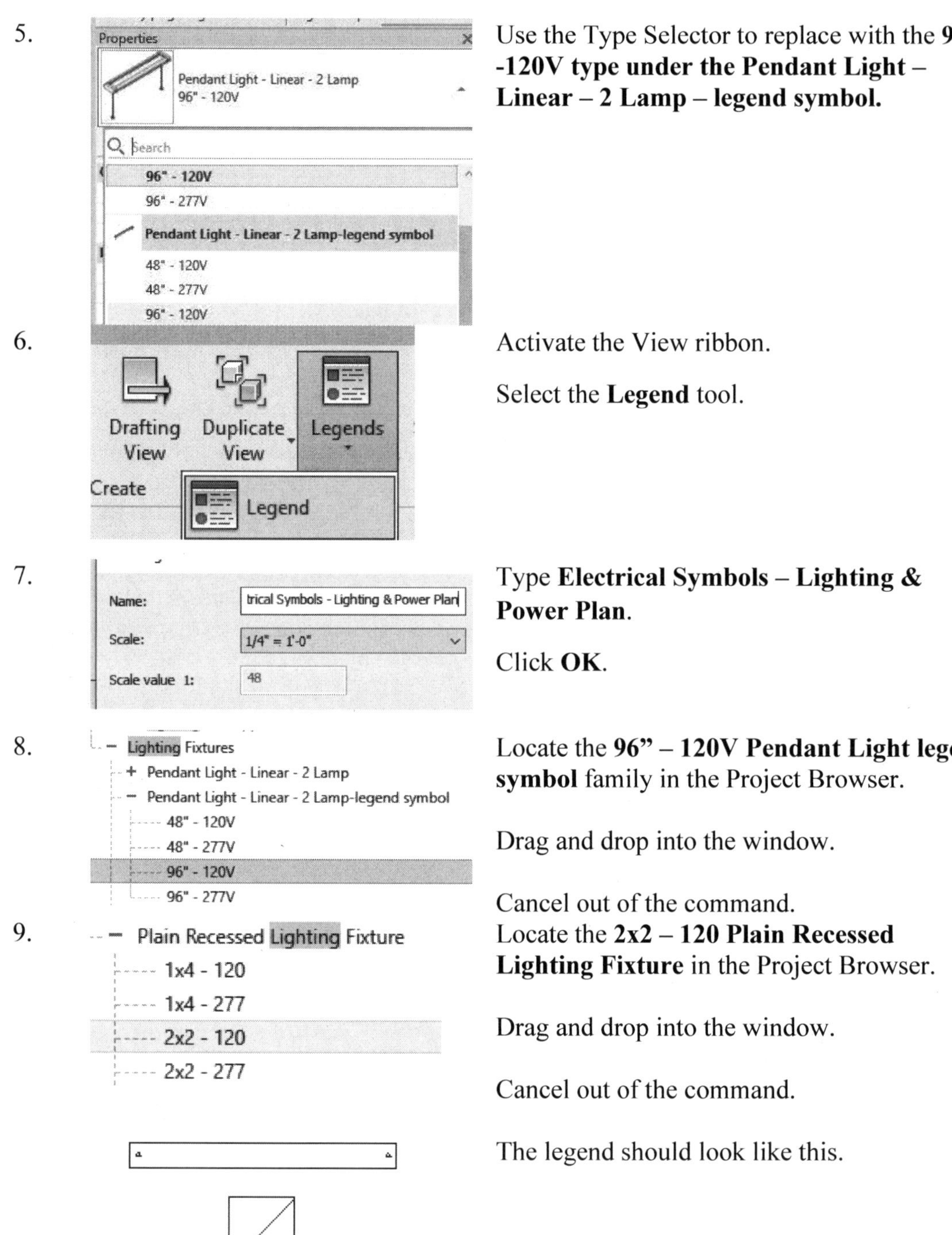

5.   Use the Type Selector to replace with the **96" -120V type under the Pendant Light – Linear – 2 Lamp – legend symbol.**

6.   Activate the View ribbon.

Select the **Legend** tool.

7.   Type **Electrical Symbols – Lighting & Power Plan**.

Click **OK**.

8.   Locate the **96" – 120V Pendant Light legend symbol** family in the Project Browser.

Drag and drop into the window.

Cancel out of the command.

9.   Locate the **2x2 – 120 Plain Recessed Lighting Fixture** in the Project Browser.

Drag and drop into the window.

Cancel out of the command.

The legend should look like this.

10. Go to the Annotate ribbon.

Select **Detail Component**.

11. Select **Load Family**.

12. receptacle symbol.rfa
sconce_light.rfa
Switch.rfa

These are the families that were created in Lesson 2.

Hold down the CTL key and open the receptacle symbol, sconce light, and switch.

13. 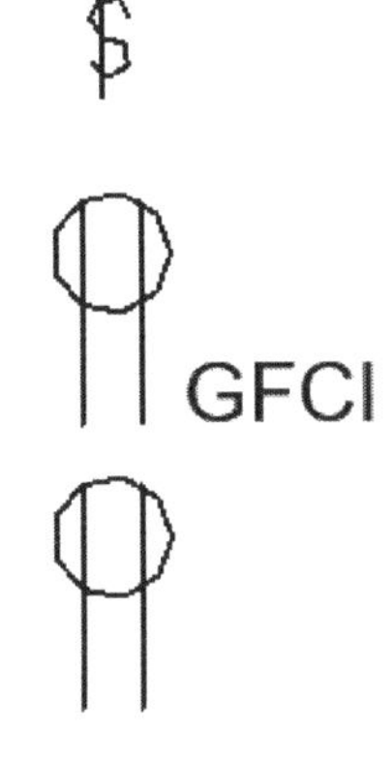

Add the symbols to the legend so it appears as shown.

Use the Type Selector to place the symbols as shown in the view.

receptacle symbol

receptacle symbol

GFCI

Standard

The receptacle symbol has a type that displays the GFCI text and a type that doesn't. Use the Type Selector to show each type.

14. **A** Select the **Text** tool from the Annotate ribbon.

Text

15. 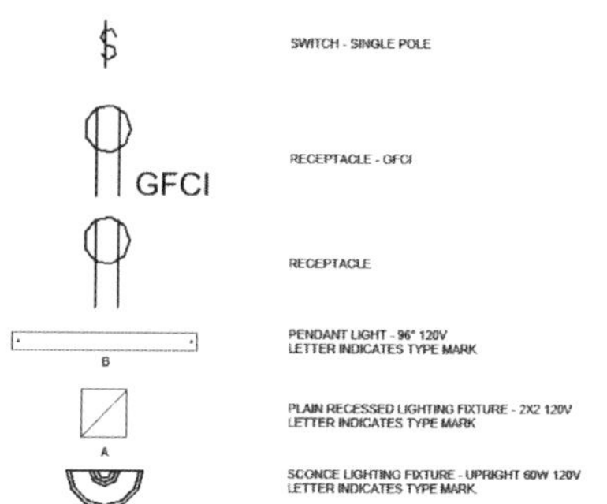

Add the text as shown.

16. 

Detail Line

Select the **Detail Line** tool.

17. 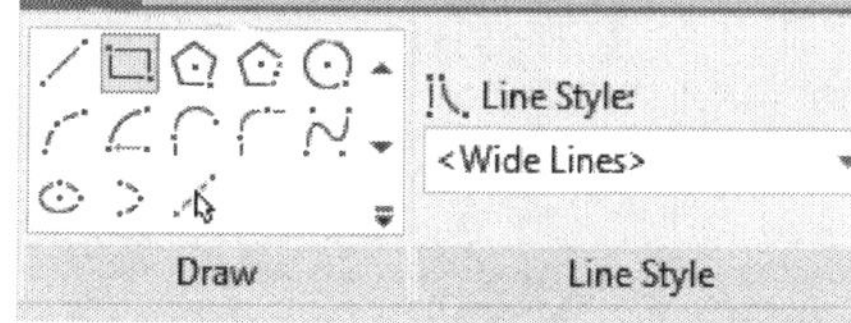

Select the **Rectangle** tool.

Select **Wide Lines**.

18. 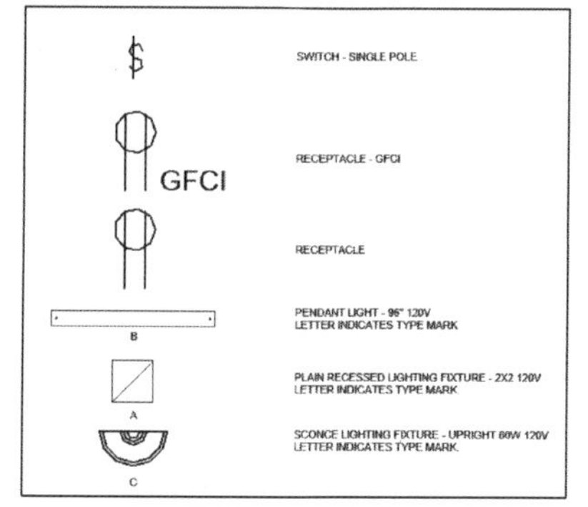

Draw a rectangle around the symbols and text for a border.

19. 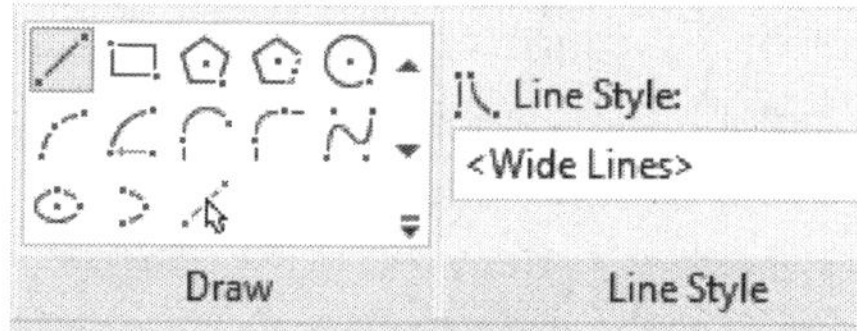

Select the **LINE** tool.

Select **Wide Lines**.

20.

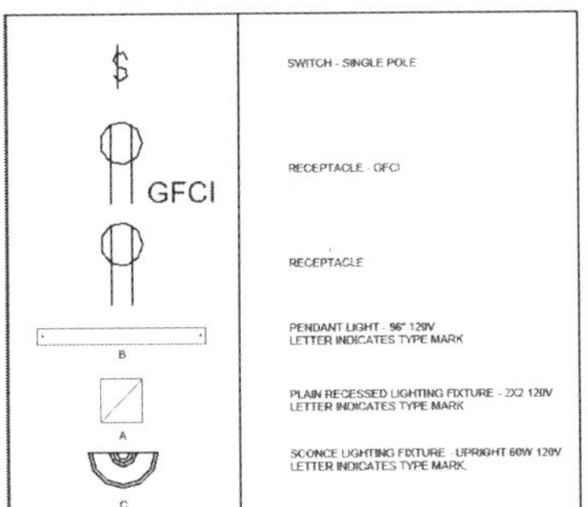

Draw a vertical line to separate the symbols and text.

21.

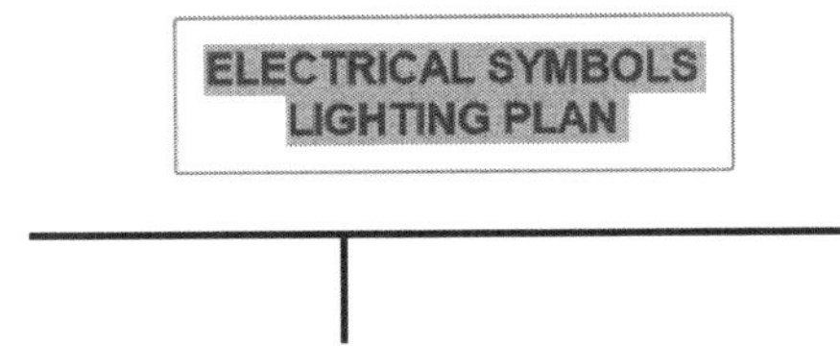

Select the **Text** tool from the ribbon.

Add the legend title to the view.

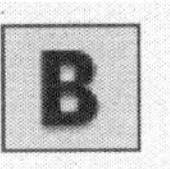

Use the Bold tool.

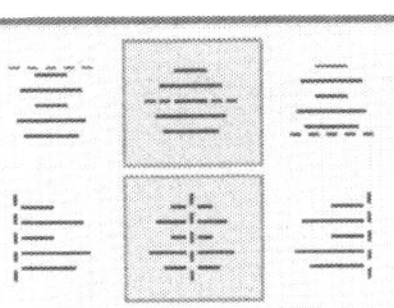

Use the Center Align tool.

22.   Save as *ex7-8.rvt*.

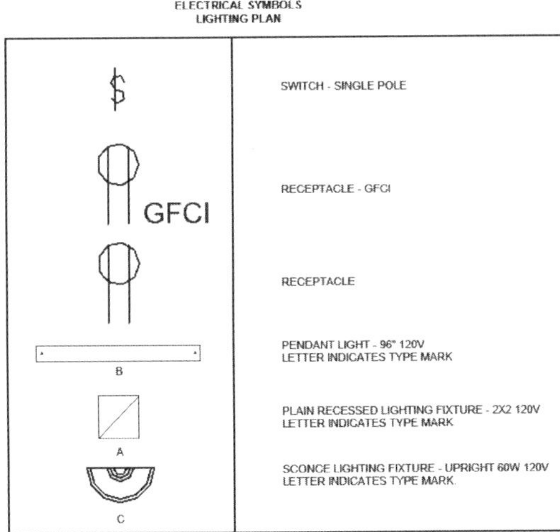

Exercise 7-9:

Creating a Drafting View

Drawing Name: *drafting_view.rvt*
Estimated Time: 60 minutes

This exercise reinforces the following skills:
- Drafting View
- Import AutoCAD Dwg file
- Line Style
- Detail Line
- Filled Region
- Text
- Family Types
- Organizing the Project Browser using Disciplines and Sub-Disciplines

1.   Activate the View ribbon.

   Select the **Drafting View** tool.

2. 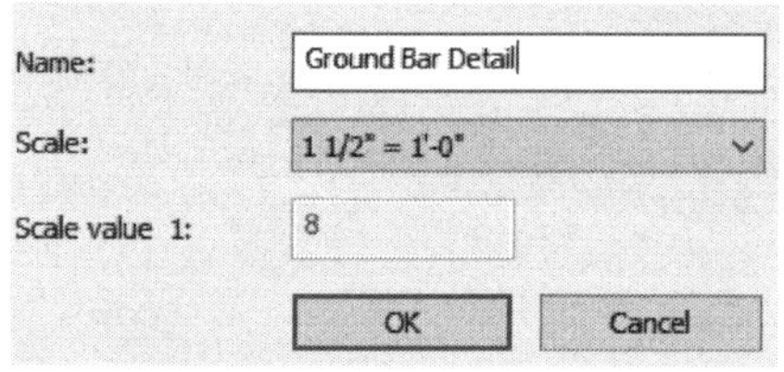 Type **Ground Bar Detail**.

   Click **OK**.

3. 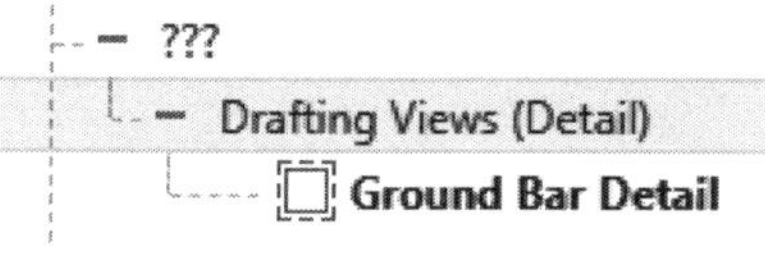 The view is located in the Project Browser under Drafting Views.

4. 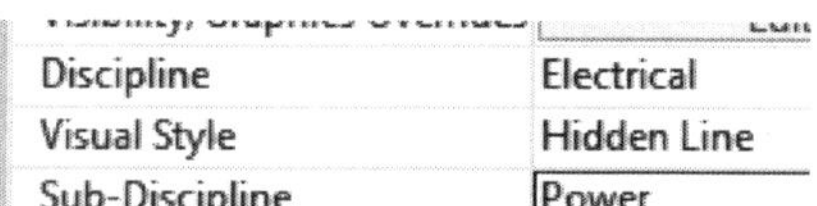 Change the Discipline to **Electrical**.

   Change the Sub-Discipline to **Power**.

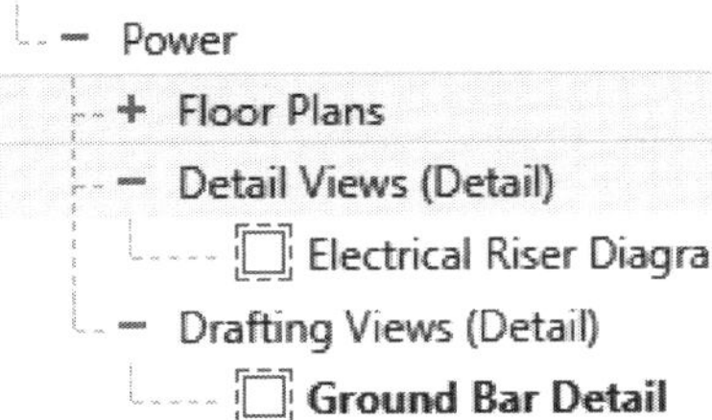

Notice in the Project Browser that the Drafting View has moved position to be under Power.

5. Activate the **Insert** ribbon.

   Select **Import CAD.**

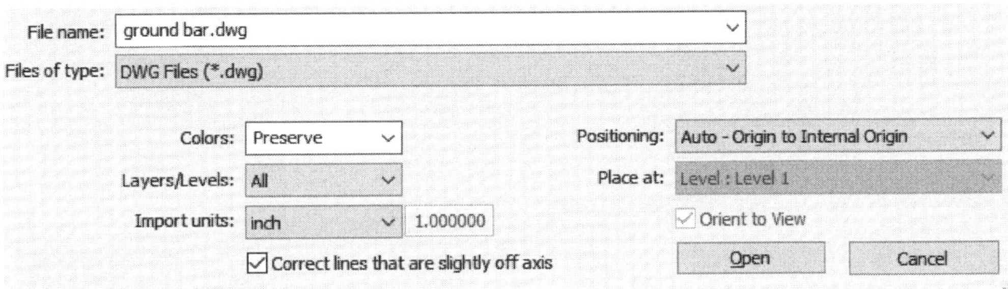

6. Locate the *ground bar.dwg* file.

   Set Colors to **Preserve**.

   Set Layers to **All**.

   Set Import Units to **Inch**.

   Set Positioning to **Auto-Origin to Internal Origin**.

   Click **Open**.

   Note you see a preview of the drawing in the Preview window.

7. Double click the scroll wheel on the mouse to Zoom to Fit.

   Select the imported drawing.

   Select **Partial Explode** from the ribbon.

8.

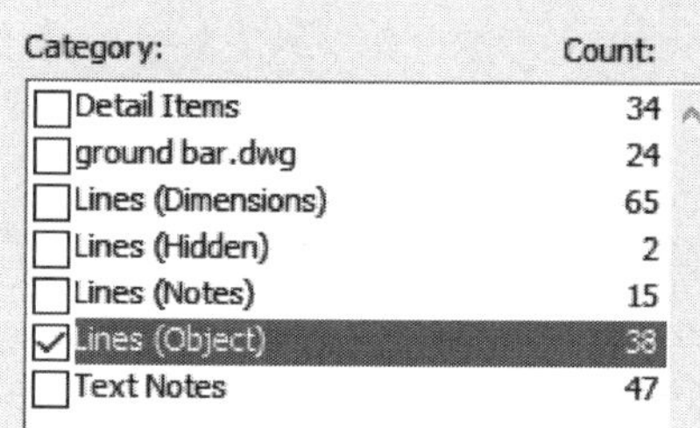

Window around the top view.

Use FILTER to select **Lines (Object).**

Click **OK.**

Note that the AutoCAD objects are designated by their layer name.

9.

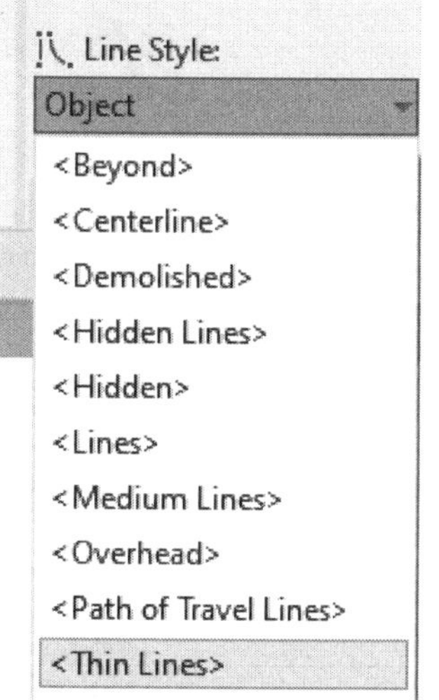

Select **Thin Lines** from the ribbon.

Left click in the window to release the selection.

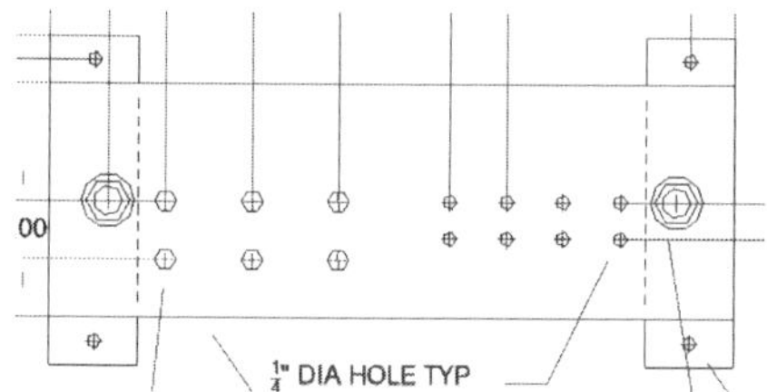

The object looks cleaner since the lines are using Revit line styles.

10.

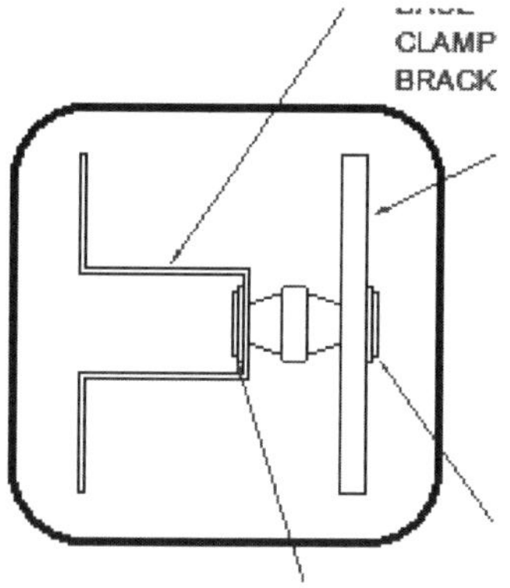

Window around the bottom view.

Use FILTER to select **Lines (Object).**

Click **OK.**

11. 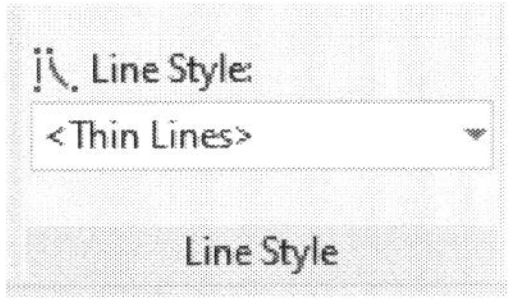 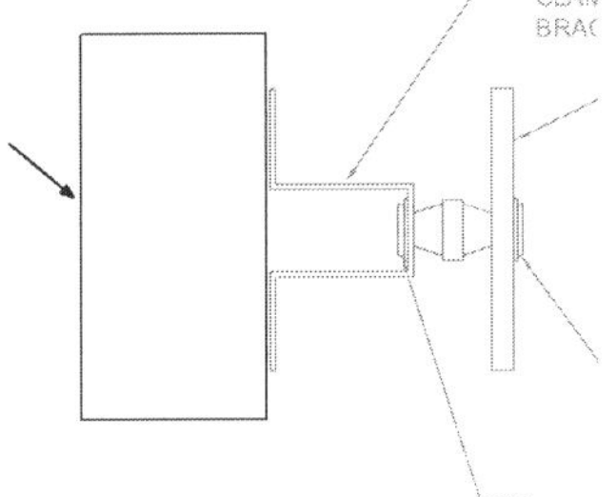 Select **Thin Lines** from the ribbon.

Left click in the window to release the selection.

12. 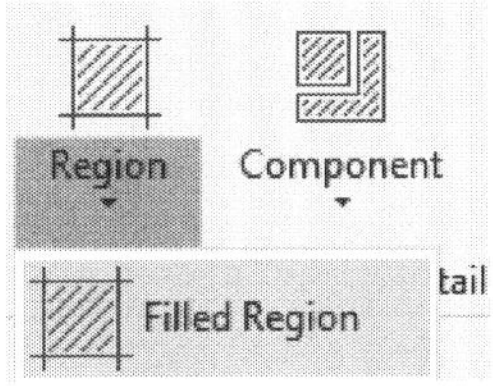 Activate the Annotate ribbon.

Select **Filled Region**.

13.  Select the **Rectangle** tool.

14. Draw a rectangle behind the base clamp/bracket.

15. 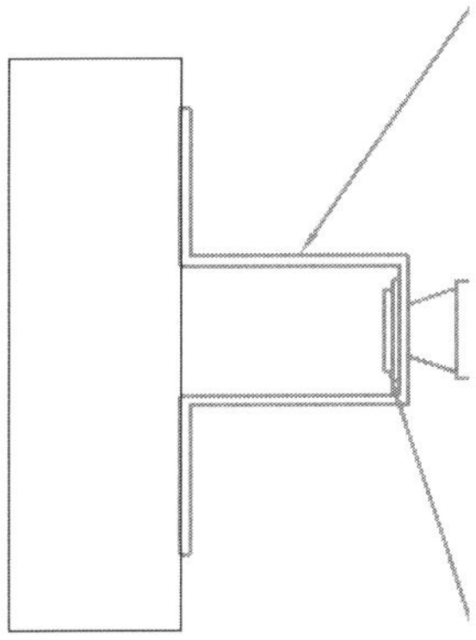 Use ALIGN to position the rectangle so it touches the bracket.

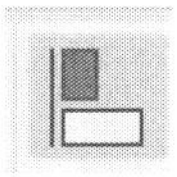

Cancel out of the ALIGN command.

16. 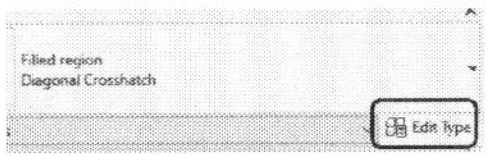  Select **Edit Type** to create a new filled region style.

17. 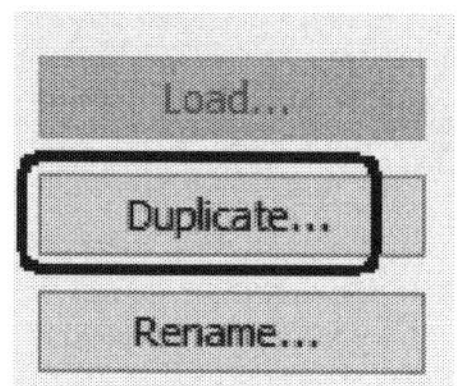 Select **Duplicate**.

18.  Type **Plaster**.

Click **OK**.

19. 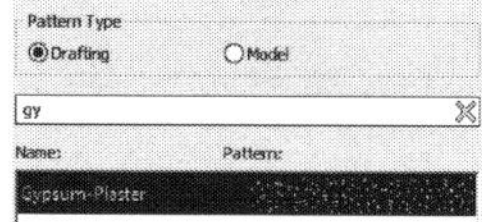 Left click in the **Foreground Fill Pattern** value column.

Select the **Gypsum/Plaster** pattern.

Click **OK**.

20. 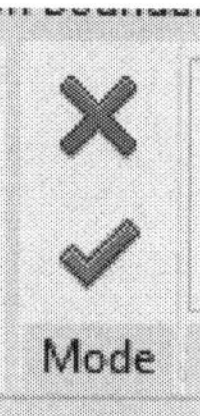 *The fill pattern is displayed in the dialog.*

Click **OK** to close the Type Properties dialog.

21. Click the **Green Check** on the ribbon to close the command.

22. 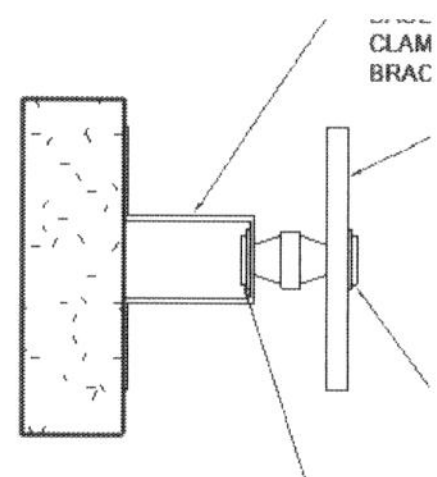 Left click anywhere in the display window to release the selection.

Review the filled region that was placed.

23. 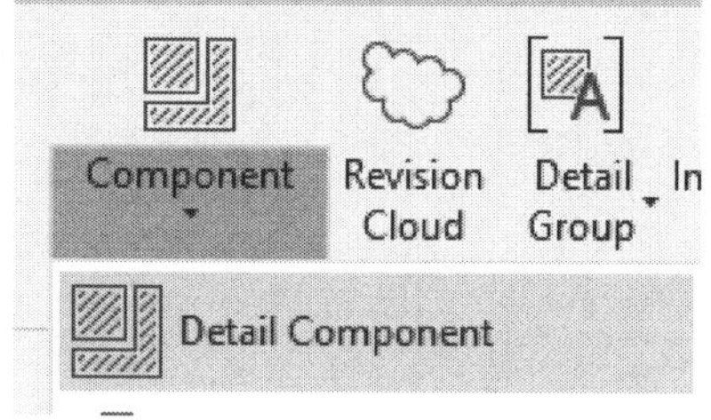 Select **Detail Component** from the Annotate ribbon.

24.  Select **Load Family**.

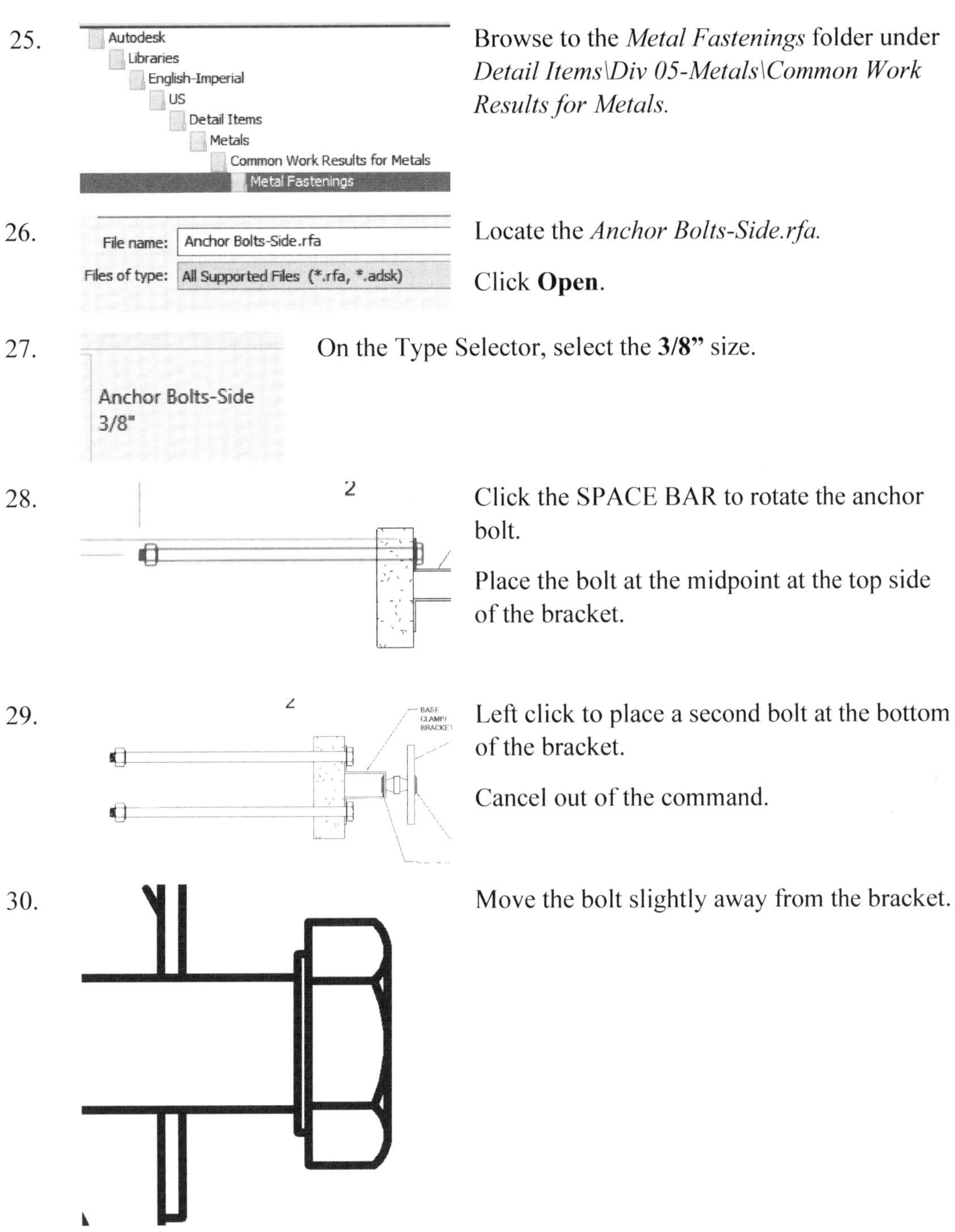

25. Browse to the *Metal Fastenings* folder under *Detail Items\Div 05-Metals\Common Work Results for Metals*.

26. Locate the *Anchor Bolts-Side.rfa*.

    Click **Open**.

27. On the Type Selector, select the **3/8"** size.

28. Click the SPACE BAR to rotate the anchor bolt.

    Place the bolt at the midpoint at the top side of the bracket.

29. Left click to place a second bolt at the bottom of the bracket.

    Cancel out of the command.

30. Move the bolt slightly away from the bracket.

31. Select the **ALIGN** tool on the Modify ribbon.

32.

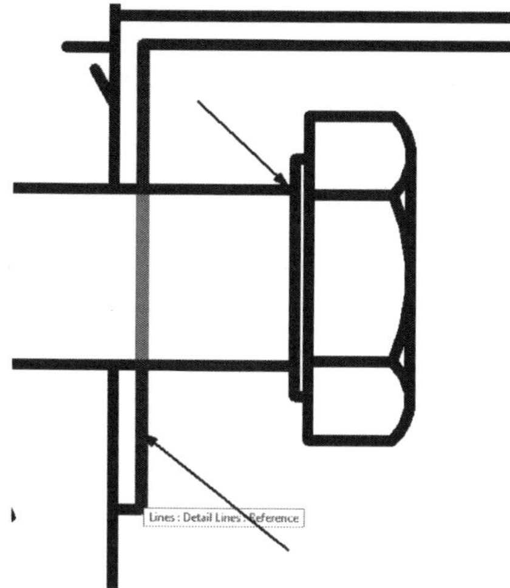

Select the top face of the bracket as the target (the item to be ALIGNED TO).

Select the bottom face of the bolt as the item to shift.

33.

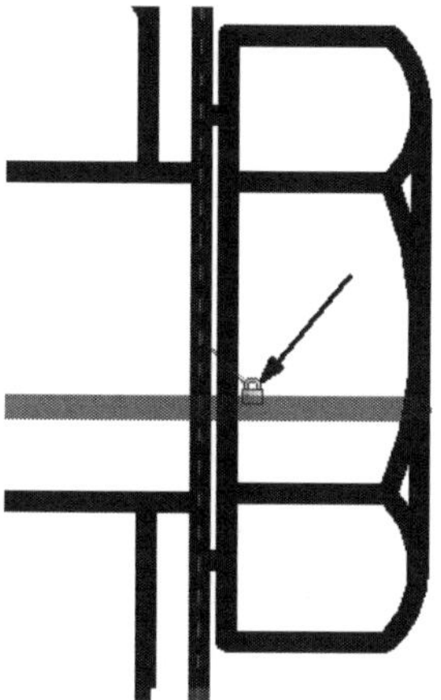

Left click on the LOCK icon to ensure the bolt remains aligned to the bracket.

34.

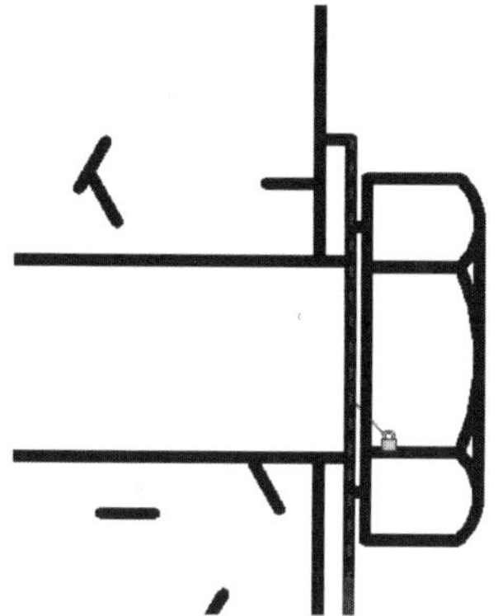

Use the **ALIGN** tool to position the head of the second bolt to the top of the bracket and lock it into position.

By using the LOCK, you ensure the bolt remains in that position.

Click **ESC** to cancel out of the ALIGN command.

35.

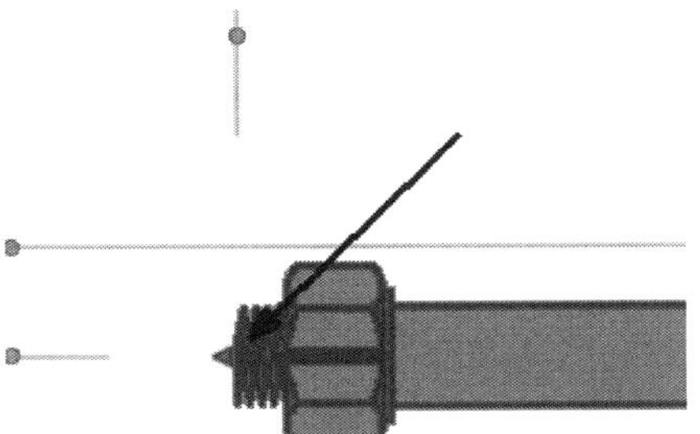

Select the top bolt.

Note there is a grip at the left end that allows you to adjust the length.

36.

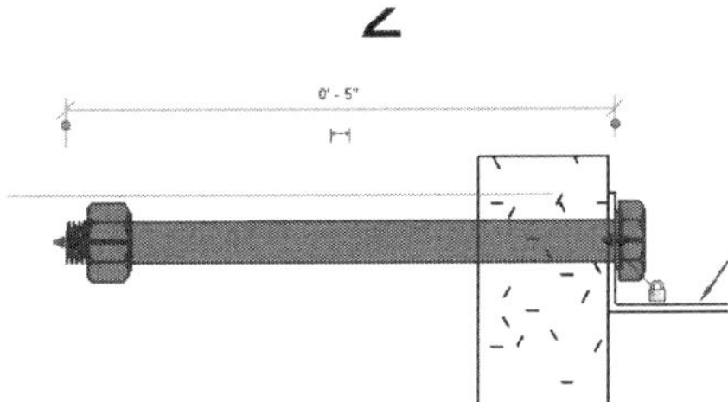

Position the extension lines of the temporary dimension so you can view the length of the bolt.

Then use the left grip to adjust the length to 5".

37.

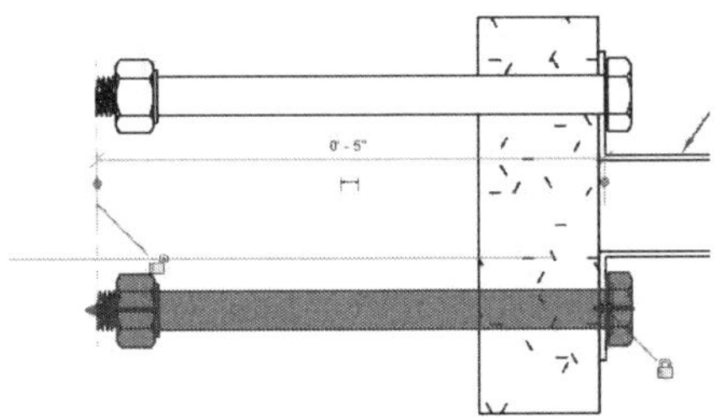

Repeat for the second bolt.

38.

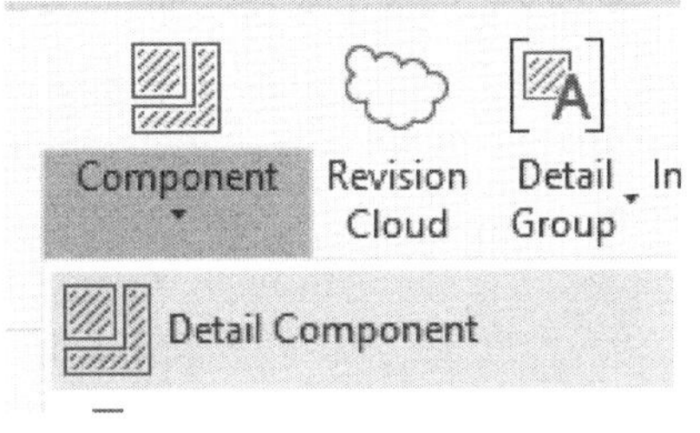

Select **Detail Component** from the Annotate ribbon.

39.

Select **Load Family**.

40. 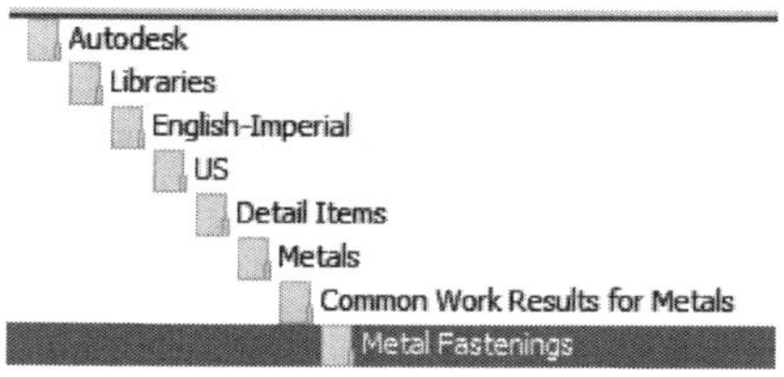 Browse to the *Metal Fastenings* folder under *Detail Items\Div 05-Metals\Common Work Results for Metals.*

41.  Locate the *A325 Bolts-Head.rfa.*

Click **Open**.

42. 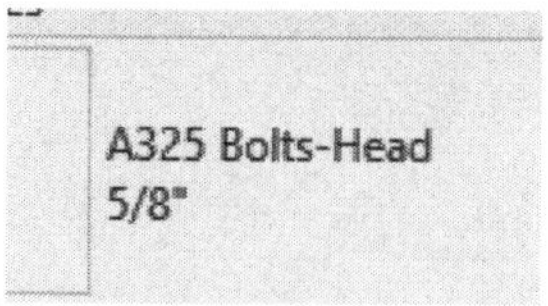 On the Type Selector, select the **5/8"** size.

43. 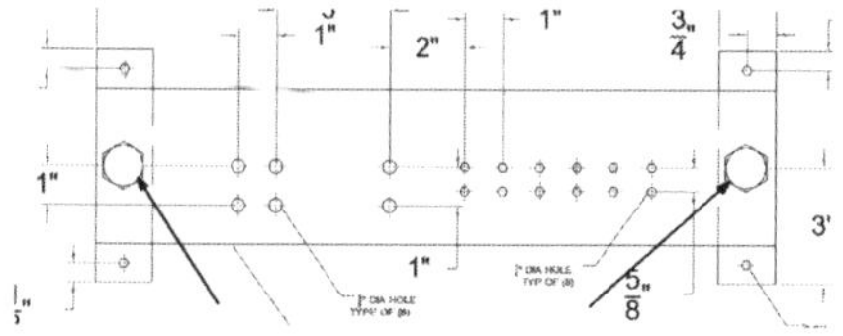 Place a bolt on the middle circle on each side of the ground bar.

Cancel out of the command.

44.  Select the **Text** tool from the Annotate ribbon.

45. 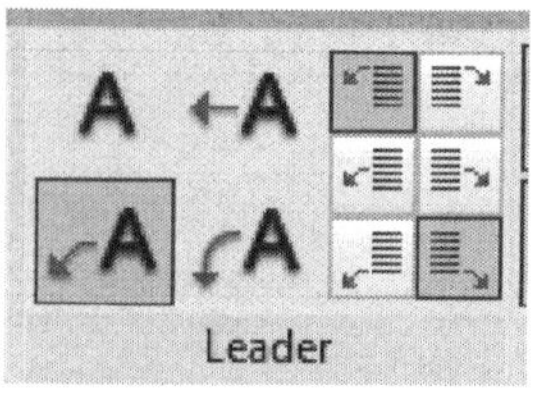 Enable **Leader**.

46.  Select **ground bar–Arial-3** from the Type Selector.

47. 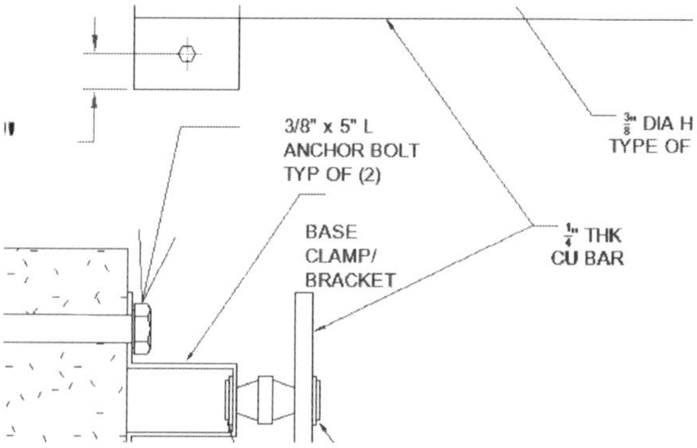 Type **3/8" x 5" L ANCHOR BOLT TYP OF (2)**.

Exit the text command.

48. Save as *ex7-9.rvt.*

Controlling View Display

One method for managing construction documentation is to create a ceiling view that shows only the ceiling objects, not the ceiling grid. This view can be placed on a sheet in the same location as the lighting floor plan view. Revit will automatically snap the view to the same location as the floor plan view so that the views are aligned.

Many architects don't put in the ceilings until later in the design. This can hold up the electrical design. You can place a reference plane at the same height as the future ceiling and mount your lighting fixtures to the reference plane. This will eliminate coordination issues when the architect finally gets around to placing ceilings.

Early in the project, the architect and the electrical designer should agree on who will model the ceilings and place the light fixtures and whether the light fixtures should reside in the architectural model or in the electrical model.

Exercise 7-10:
Controlling the Display in Views

Drawing Name: *view_display.rvt*
Estimated Time: 15 minutes

This exercise reinforces the following skills:
- Duplicate View
- Visibility/Graphics
- Rename View
- Tag All

1. 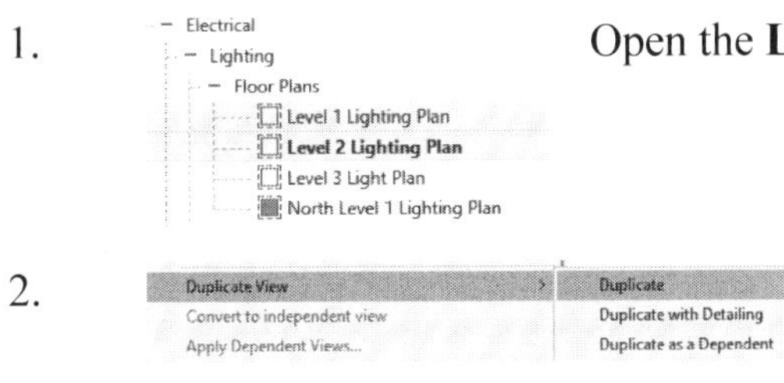
   Open the **Level 2 Lighting Plan** floor plan.

2. Highlight the **Level 2 Lighting Plan** floor plan view in the Project Browser.

   Right click and select **Duplicate View→Duplicate.**

   This will copy the view without annotations.

3. Highlight the copied view.

Right click and select **Rename**.

4. Rename the view **Level 2 Lighting Plan - Annotated**.

5. Select the **Visibility/Graphics** tool from the View ribbon.

6. Disable **Reference Planes** and **Sections** on the Annotation Categories tab.

Click **OK**.

7. 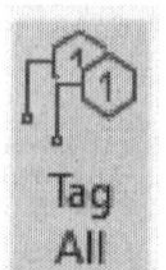

Activate the **Annotate** ribbon.

Select **Tag All**.

8. 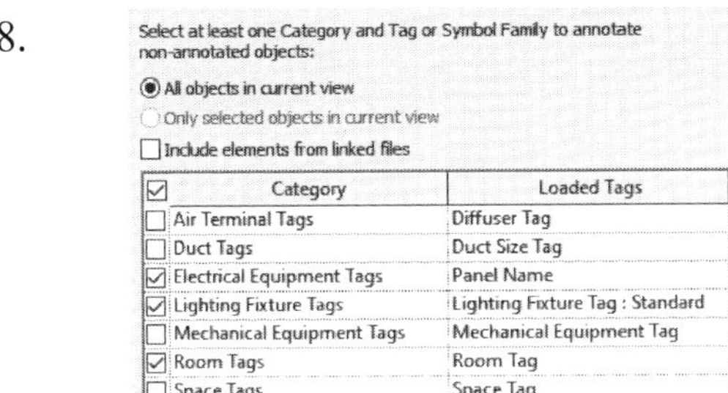

Enable

- Electrical Equipment Tags

- Lighting Fixture Tags

- Room Tags

Click **OK**.

9. 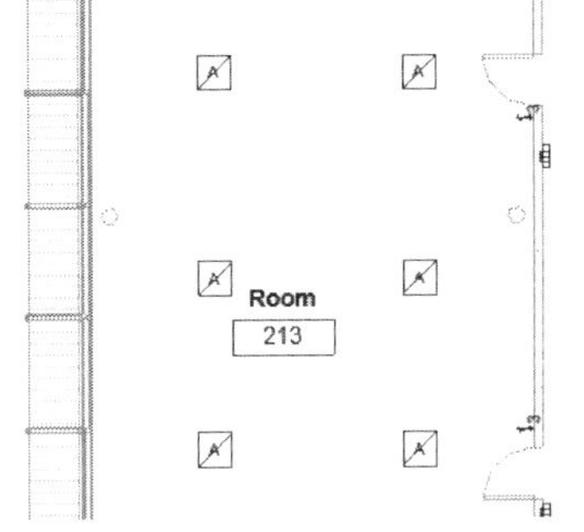

Zoom in to see the lighting fixtures and rooms have been tagged.

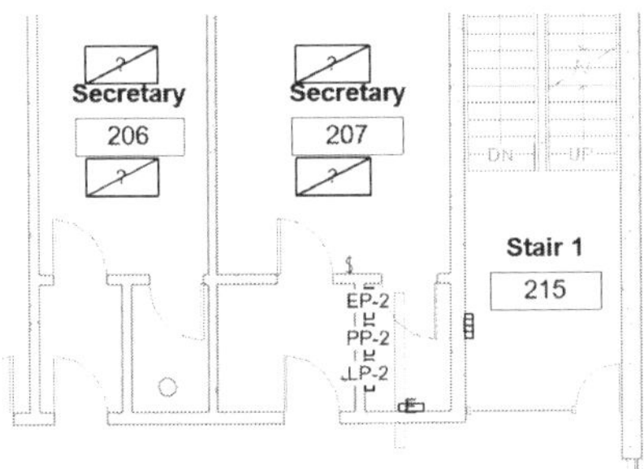

? symbols will appear on tags where the device name has not been designated in the Properties palette.

10. 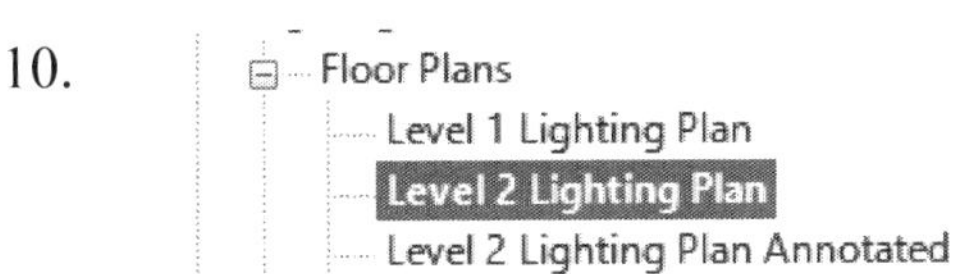

Open the **Level 2 Lighting Plan** floor plan.

Notice how it is different from the Annotated plan.

11. Save as *ex7-10.rvt*.

Exercise 7-11:

Organize Views in the Project Browser

Drawing Name: *project_browser.rvt*
Estimated Time: 20 minutes

This exercise reinforces the following skills:
- Project Parameters
- Project Browser
- Properties

1.  Activate the Manage ribbon.

   Select **Project Parameters**.

2. Select **New**.

3. 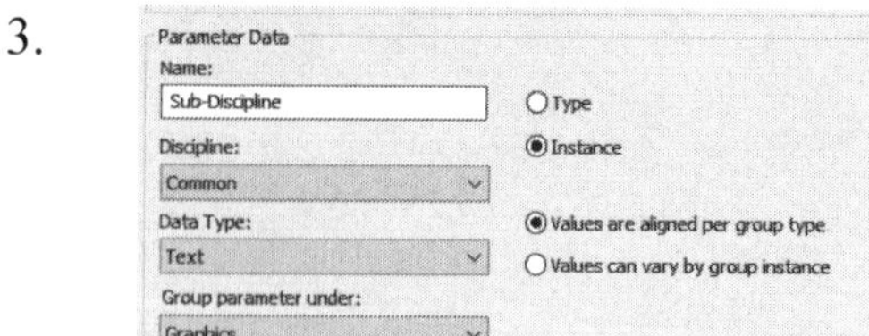 Type **Sub-Discipline** in the Name field.

   Enable **Instance**.

   Select **Text** as Type of Parameter.

   Select **Graphics** for Group parameter under.

4. Enable **Views** in the Categories pane.

   Click **OK**.

15. 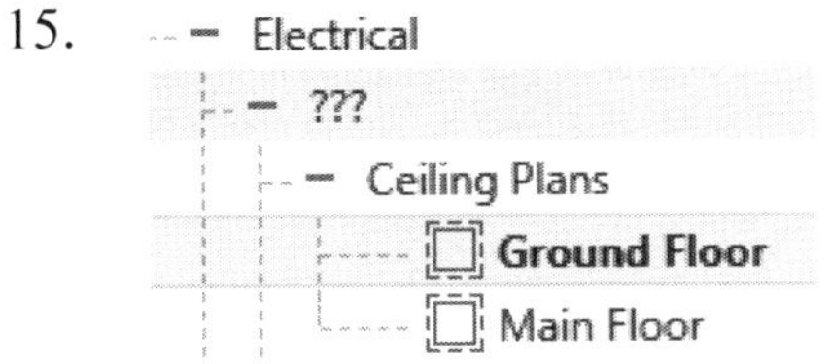

Highlight the **Ground Floor** under Ceiling Plans.

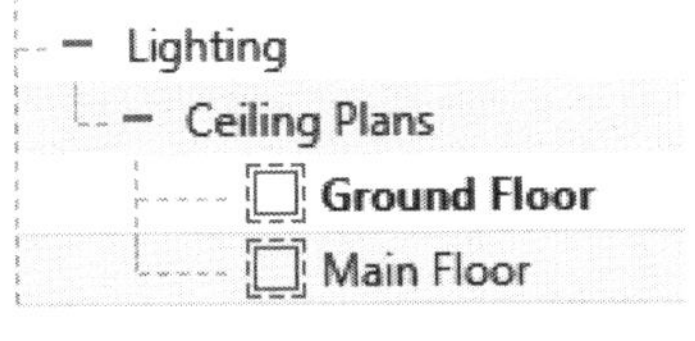

Discipline	Electrical
Show Hidden Lines	By Discipline
Default Analysis Display St...	None
Sun Path	☐
Sub-Discipline	Lighting

In the Sub-Discipline field:

Type **Lighting**.

Click **ENTER** to ensure the value is applied.

16.

The Ground Floor moves under Lighting.

Repeat for the Main Floor ceiling plan.

17. Save as *ex7-11.rvt*.

View Lists

A View List schedule is a type of schedule that helps you keep track of the views within a project.

A View List schedule allows you to quickly view the properties of several views at one time. It allows for quick comparison and editing of multiple views. You can use the View List to verify that the correct views have been placed on each sheet for a submittal package. This means you don't have to inspect each sheet or print out a bunch of paper to check your sheets.

Exercise 7-12:

Create a View List

Drawing Name: *view_list.rvt*
Estimated Time: 10 minutes

This exercise reinforces the following skills:
- ❑ Schedules
- ❑ Views
- ❑ Sheets

1. 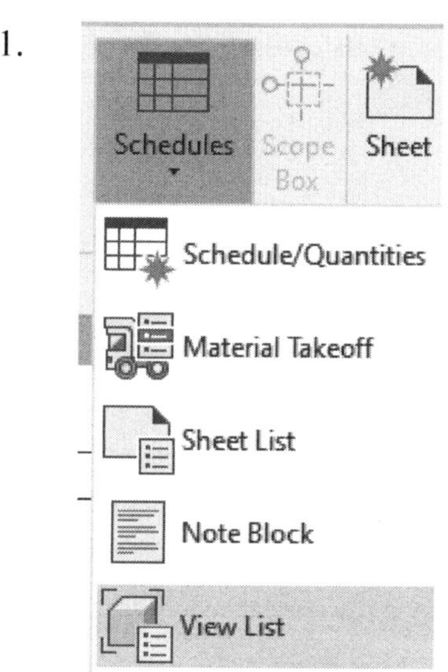

Activate the View ribbon.

Select **View List**.

2.
Scheduled fields (in order):

View Name
View Template
Title on Sheet
Sheet Name
Sheet Number

Select the following fields:

- View Name

- View Template

- Title on Sheet

- Sheet Number

- Sheet Name

3.
Fields | Filter | Sorting/Grouping | Formatting | Appearance

Sort by: Sheet Number ⦿ Ascending
☐ Header ☐ Footer:

On the Sorting/Grouping tab:

Sort by: **Sheet Number.**

Click **OK**.

4.

Main Floor Annotated	None			
Main Floor Lighting Fixtures	None			
Ground Floor Lighting Fixtures	None			
Ground Floor Annotated	None			
Main Floor Lighting Fixtures & Switches	Ceiling Lights &		01	Main Floor Lighting
Ground Floor Lighting Fixtures & Switches	Ceiling Lights &		02	Ground Floor Lighting
Ground Bus Detail	None		05	Details
Panel C	None		06	Panels
Panel A	None	Lighting & Power Panels 'A'	06	Panels
Panel B	None		06	Panels
Recessed Lighting Fixture	None		07	Lighting Fixture Details
Pendant Lighting	None		07	Lighting Fixture Details
Sconce Lighting Fixture - Callout 1	None		07	Lighting Fixture Details

You can see which views have been placed on sheets and which views are still unassigned.

You can assign view templates using the schedule.

5. Save as *ex7-12.rvt*.

View Templates

View templates control the settings of a view. Instead of constantly going into the Visibility/Graphics dialog and turning on and off the visibility of elements, you can save those settings, set up a view template and apply the template to the view.

A view template is a collection of view properties, such as view scale, discipline, detail level, and visibility settings.

Use view templates to apply standard settings to views. View templates can help to ensure adherence to office standards and achieve consistency across construction document sets.

Before creating view templates, first think about how you use views. For each type of view (floor plan, elevation, section, 3D view, and so on), what styles do you use? For example, an electrical designer may use many styles of floor plan views, such as power and signal, lighting fixture, wiring, coordination, and equipment.

You can create a view template for each style to control settings for the visibility/graphics overrides of categories, view scales, detail levels, graphic display options, and more.

Guidelines for View Templates

- Use view templates to ensure project views are consistent.

- Set up view templates in any project templates so new projects have access to those settings.

- Copy view templates from other projects using the Transfer Project Standards tool. This allows you to reuse templates without having to start over from scratch.

- Apply view templates to all views on a sheet by right-clicking on the sheet name in the Project Browser and selecting the Apply View Template to All Views.

- Enable Show Views when applying a view template. This allows you to apply the view settings from another view without saving those settings as a view template.

- Define a default view template for each view type.

Exercise 7-13:

Using a View Template

Drawing Name: *view_template.rvt*
Estimated Time: 30 minutes

This exercise reinforces the following skills:
- Duplicate View
- View Range
- Visibility/Graphics Settings
- View Template
- Edit Circuit

1. Open the **Ground Floor Lighting Fixtures** view.

2. Highlight the view.

   Right click and select **Duplicate→Duplicate with Detailing**.

   This duplicates the view and includes annotations.

3. 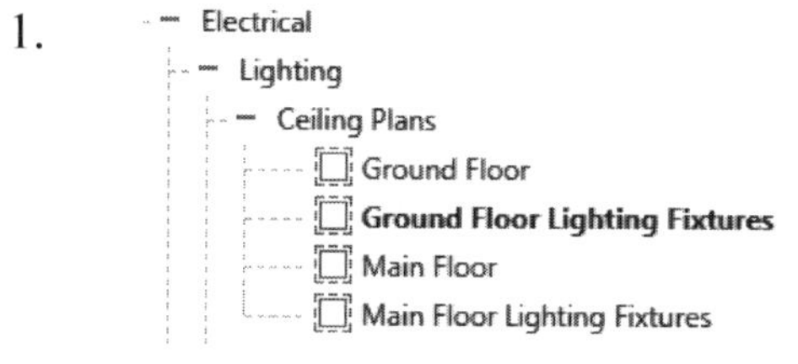

   Right click on the copied view.

   Select **Rename**.

4. Rename **Ground Floor Lighting Fixtures & Switches.**

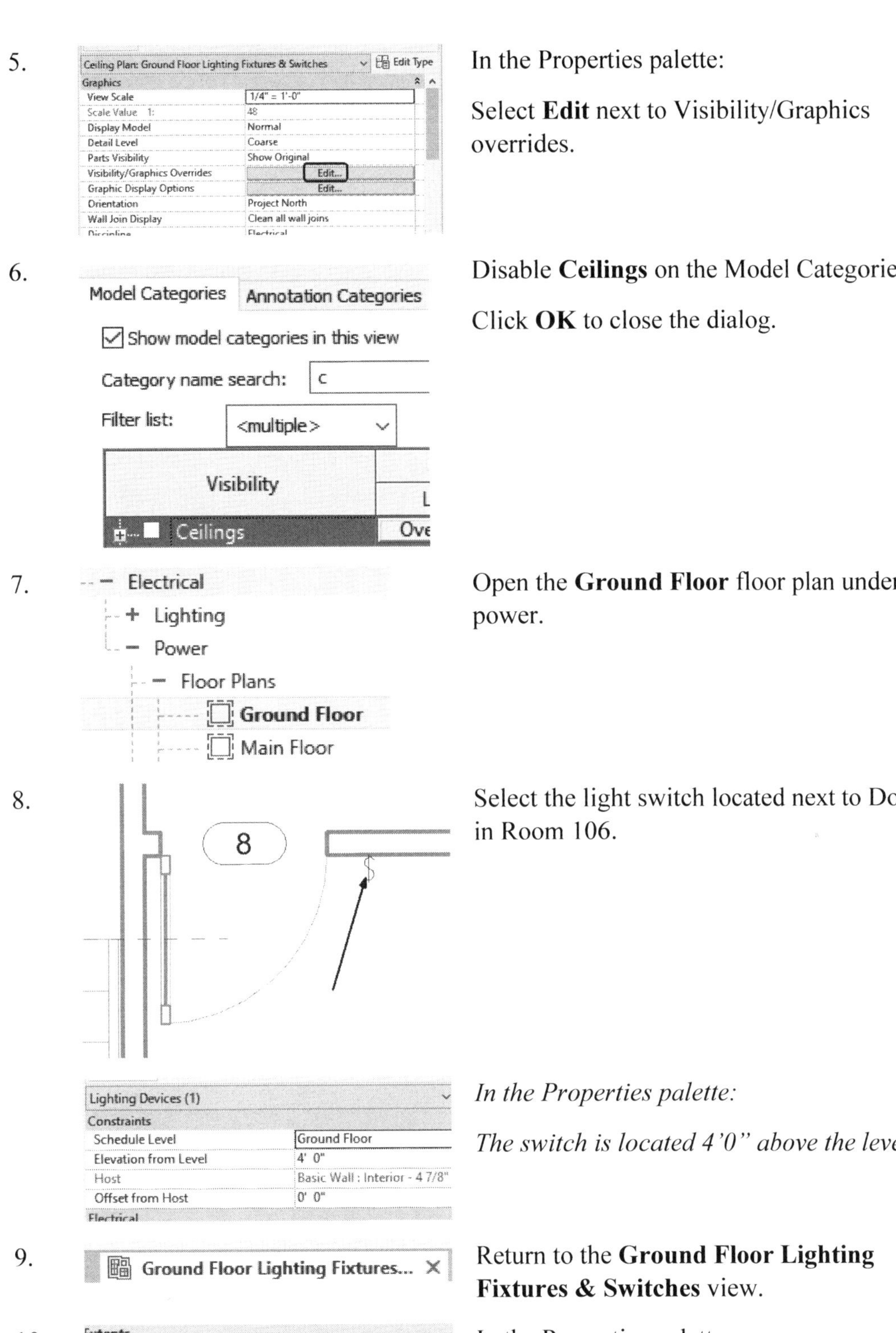

5.   In the Properties palette:

Select **Edit** next to Visibility/Graphics overrides.

6.   Disable **Ceilings** on the Model Categories tab.

Click **OK** to close the dialog.

7.   Open the **Ground Floor** floor plan under power.

8.   Select the light switch located next to Door 8 in Room 106.

In the Properties palette:

The switch is located 4'0" above the level.

9.   Return to the **Ground Floor Lighting Fixtures & Switches** view.

10.   In the Properties palette:

Select **Edit** in the View Range field.

11. 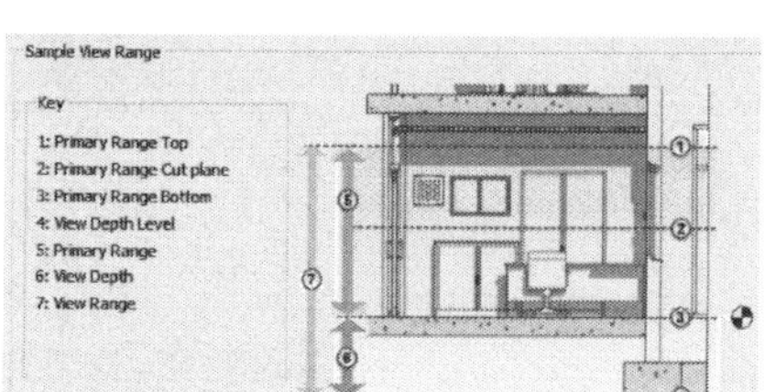

Select the **Show** button on the lower left of the dialog.

The image on the left explains how view range is defined.

12. 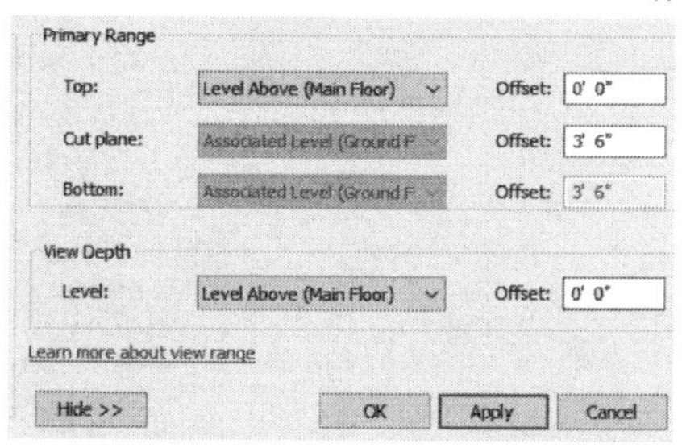

Change the Cut plane to **3' 6"**.

Click **Apply**.

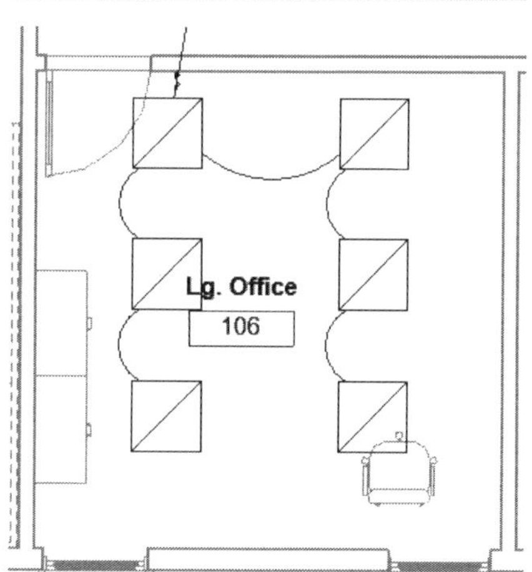

The view updates so that the switches, doors, and furniture are now visible. This is because the cut plane is set lower than the height of the switches.

Click **OK**.

13.

Type **VV** to launch the Visibility/Graphics dialog.

Disable **Furniture and Furniture Systems** on the Model Categories tab.

Click **OK** to close the dialog.

14. 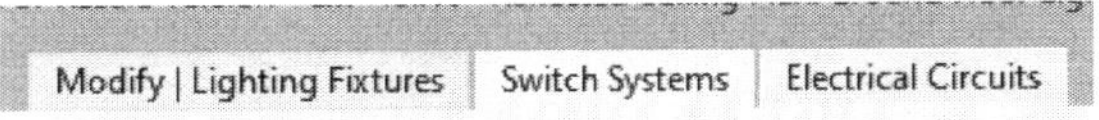

Select the light switch located next to Door 8 in Room 106.

Select the **Power** button on the ribbon.

15. 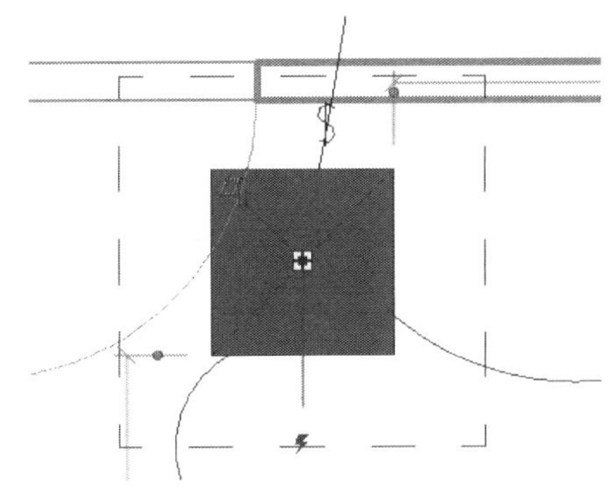

Assign it to the **120V**.

Click **OK**.

Click **ESC** to exit the selection.

16. 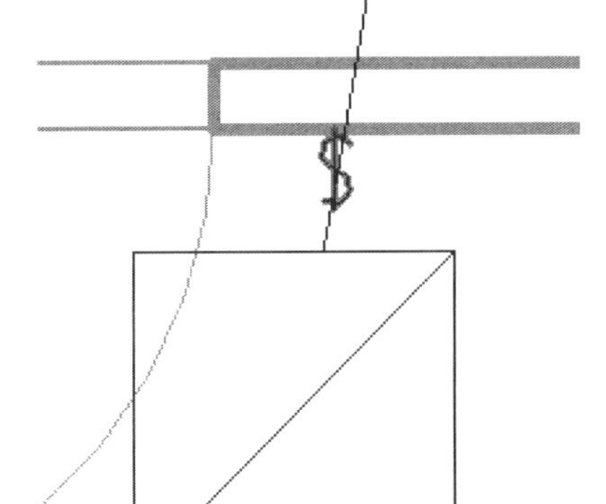

Select one of the light fixtures in Room 106.

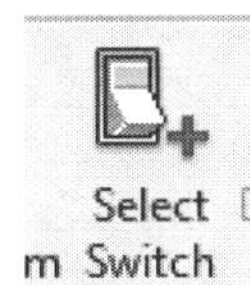

Select the Switch Systems tab on the ribbon.

Select **Select Switch** from the ribbon.

17. 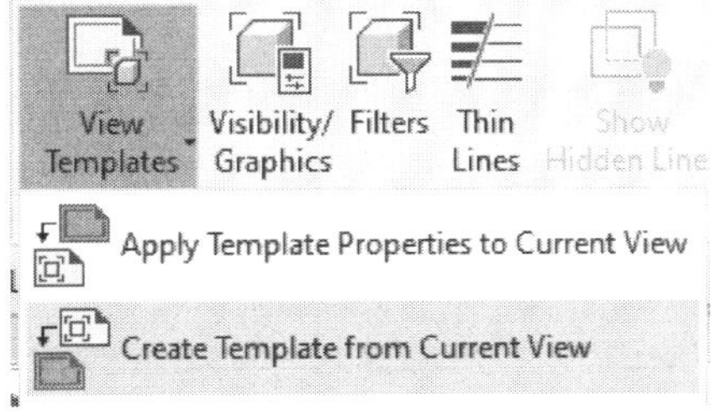

Select the Switch in the room to add it to the circuit.

18.

Activate the View ribbon.

Select **View Templates→Create Template from Current View**.

This saves the view settings of the active view.

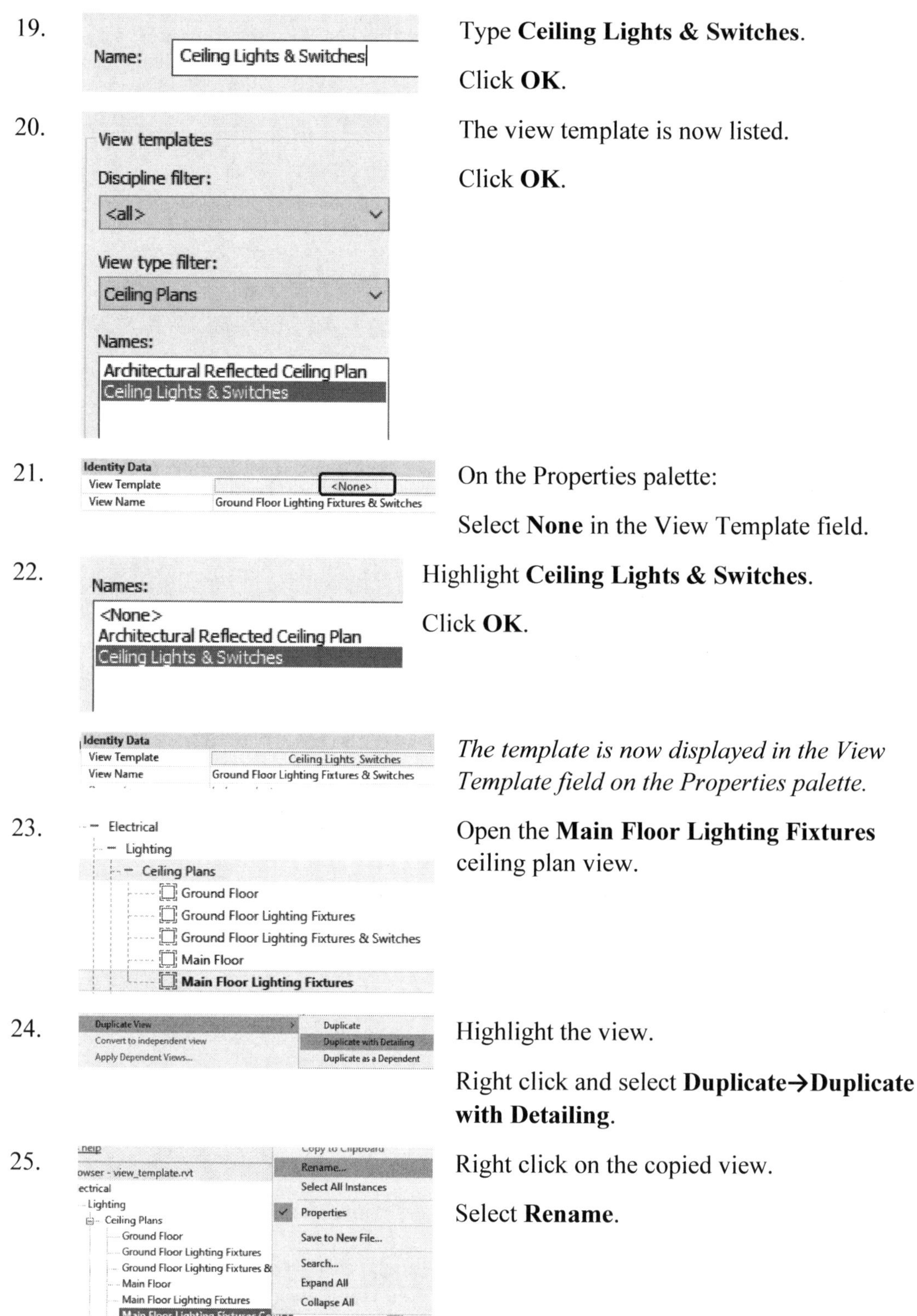

19. Type **Ceiling Lights & Switches**.

Click **OK**.

20. The view template is now listed.

Click **OK**.

21. On the Properties palette:

Select **None** in the View Template field.

22. Highlight **Ceiling Lights & Switches**.

Click **OK**.

The template is now displayed in the View Template field on the Properties palette.

23. Open the **Main Floor Lighting Fixtures** ceiling plan view.

24. Highlight the view.

Right click and select **Duplicate→Duplicate with Detailing**.

25. Right click on the copied view.

Select **Rename**.

26.

Ceiling Plans
  Ground Floor
  Ground Floor Lighting Fixtures
  Ground Floor Lighting Fixtures & Switches
  Main Floor
  Main Floor Lighting Fixtures
  Main Floor Lighting Fixtures & Switches

Rename **Main Floor Lighting Fixtures & Switches.**

27.

Identity Data
View Template   <None>
View Name   Main Floor Lighting Fixtures & Switches

On the Properties palette:

Select **None** in the View Template field.

28.

Names:
<None>
Architectural Reflected Ceiling Plan
Ceiling Lights & Switches

Highlight **Ceiling Lights & Switches**.

Click **OK**.

The template is now displayed in the View Template field on the Properties palette.

You can see the switches and doors, but the furniture is not visible.

29.　Save as *ex7-13.rvt*.

Exercise 7-14:

Modifying View Tag Properties

Drawing Name: *view_tags.rvt*
Estimated Time: 20 minutes

This exercise reinforces the following skills:
- Sheets
- Views
- View Tags

1. 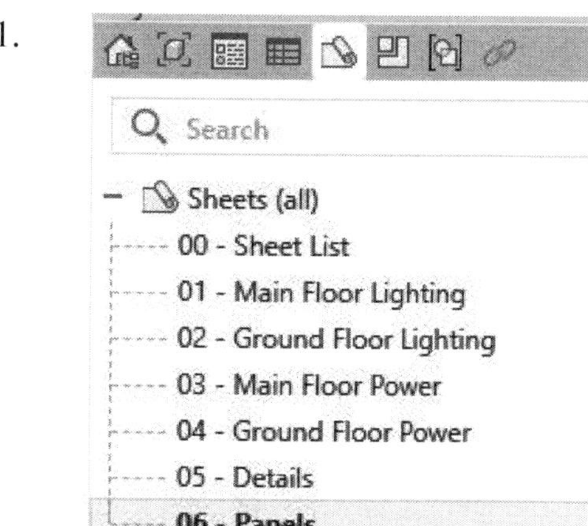
Open the **06 Panels** sheet.

2. Drag **Panel A, Panel B** and **Panel C** views onto the sheet.

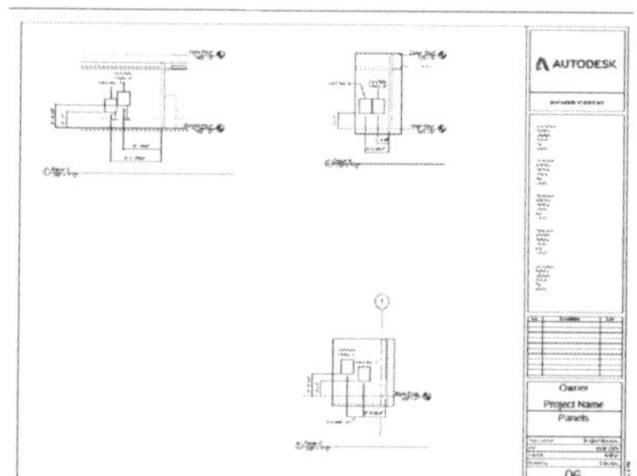

3. 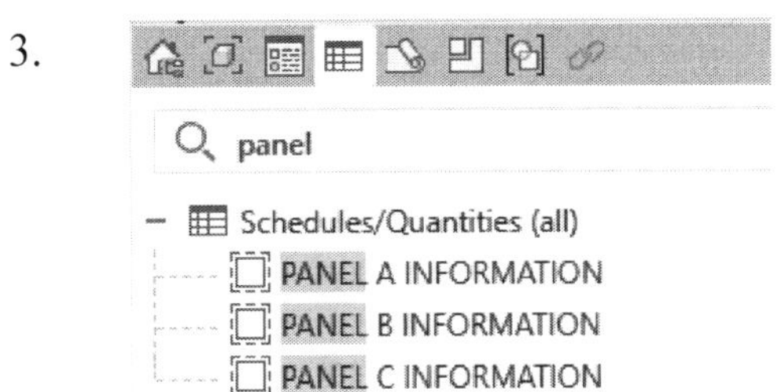

   Drag the three Panel Information schedules (A, B and C) onto the sheet.

4. 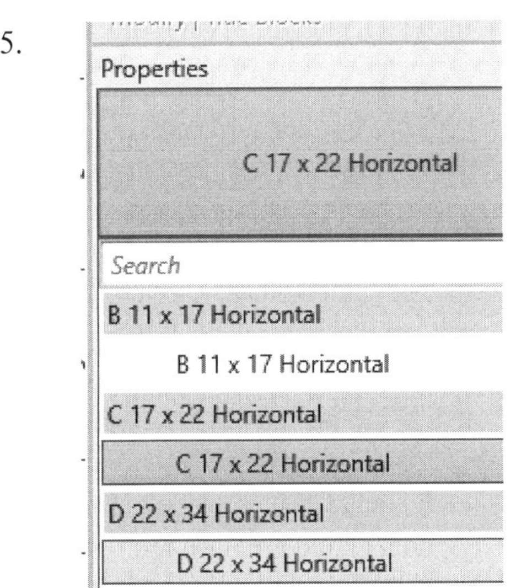

   The views don't all fit on the sheet.

   Select the titleblock.

5. Use the Type Selector on the Properties palette to change to a D size titleblock.

6. 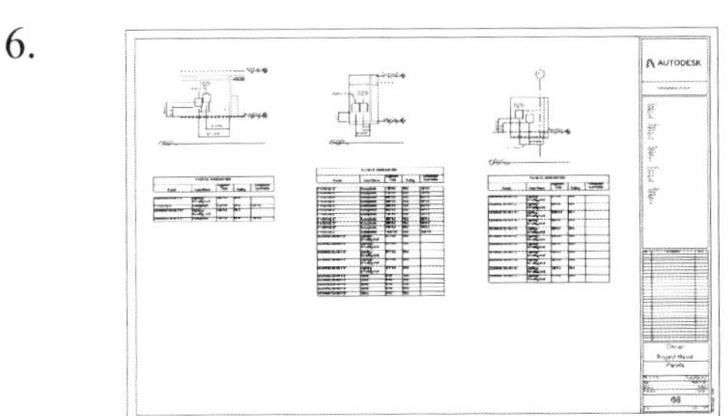

   Reposition the views on the sheet.

7.

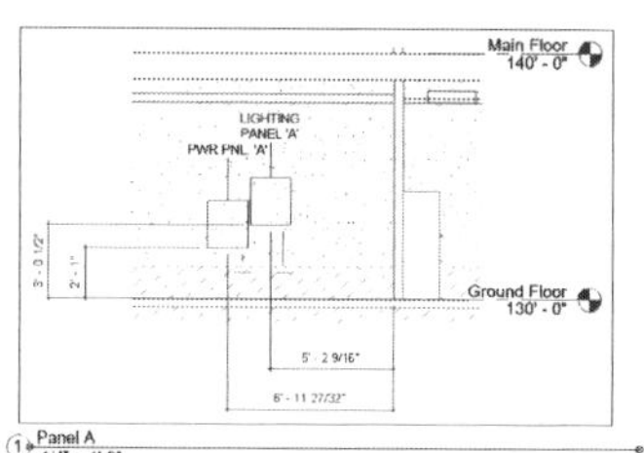

Select the Panel A view.

8.

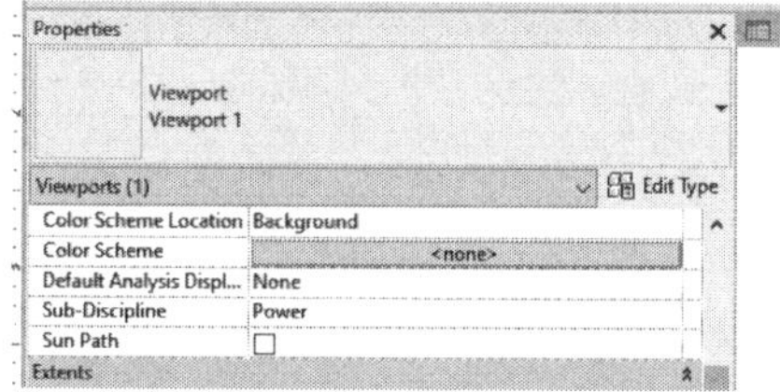

In the Properties palette:

Type **Lighting & Power Panels 'A'** in the Title on Sheet field.

Click **ENTER**.

The View Name remains the same.

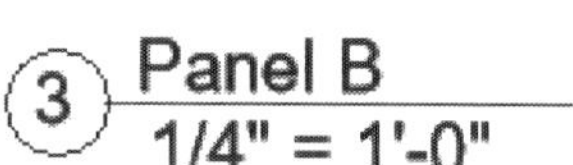

The title bar on the view updates with the new name.

9.

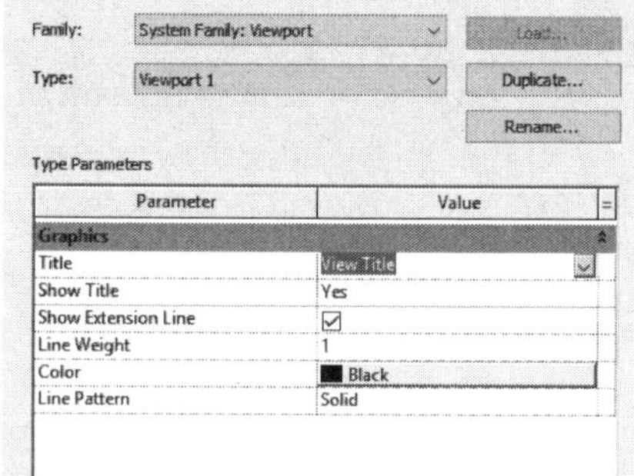

Select the titlebar for Panel B.

On the Properties palette: select **Edit Type**

10.

Note that the Title uses an annotation family called View Title.

Click **OK**.

11.  Activate the Insert ribbon.

Select **Load Family**.

12. 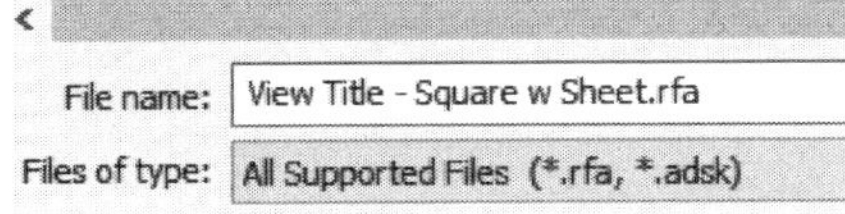 Browse to the Annotations folder.

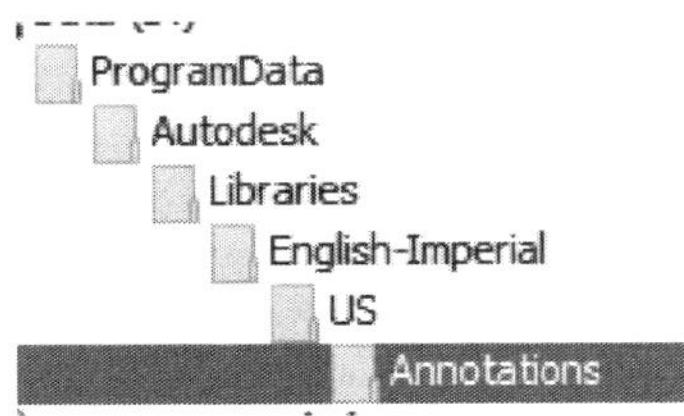

Open the *View Title – Square w Sheet.rfa*.

13. Select the titlebar for Panel B.

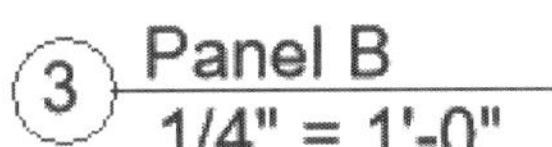

On the Properties palette: select **Edit Type**

14. 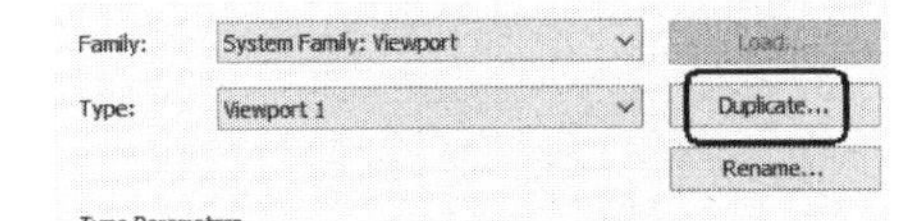 Select **Duplicate**.

15. Type **Viewport w Square**.

Click **OK**.

16. 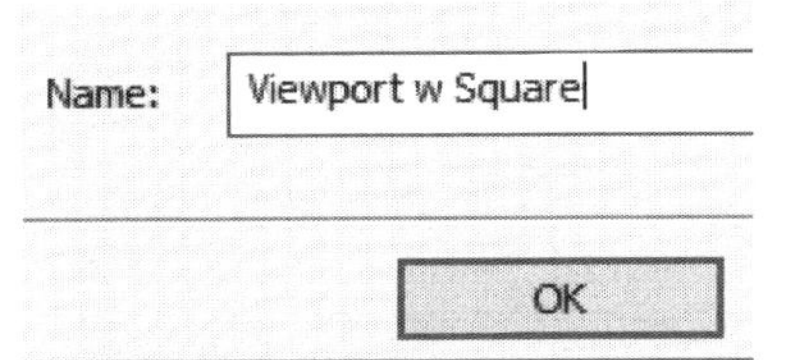 In the Title field:

Select the **View Title – Square w Sheet**.

Click **OK**.

17. The titlebar updates.

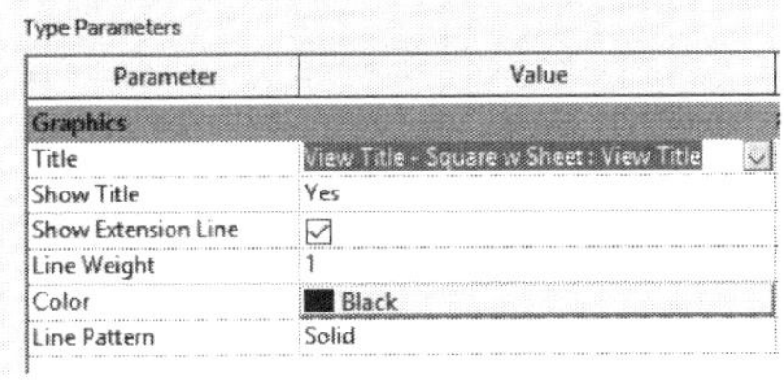

18. Save as *ex7-14.rvt*.

Exercise 7-15:

Create a View Tag Family

Drawing Name: View_Title.rfa
Estimated Time: 15 minutes

This exercise reinforces the following skills:
- Views
- View Tags

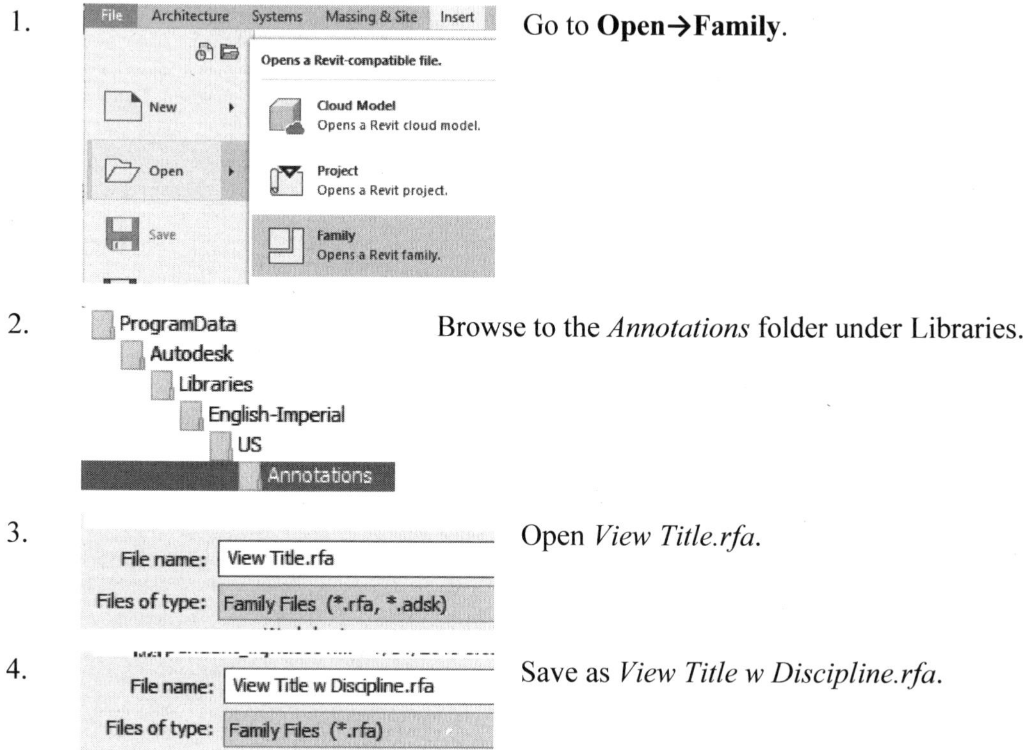

1. Go to **Open→Family**.

2. Browse to the *Annotations* folder under Libraries.

3. Open *View Title.rfa*.

4. Save as *View Title w Discipline.rfa*.

5.

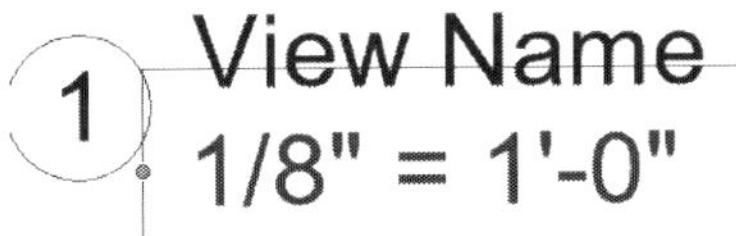

Left click to select the scale label.

View Titles (1)	
Graphics	
Sample Text	1/8" = 1'-0"...
Label	Edit...
Wrap between parame...	☐
Horizontal Align	Left
Vertical Align	Middle
Keep Readable	☑
Visible	☑

On the Properties palette:

Select **Edit** in the Label field.

6.

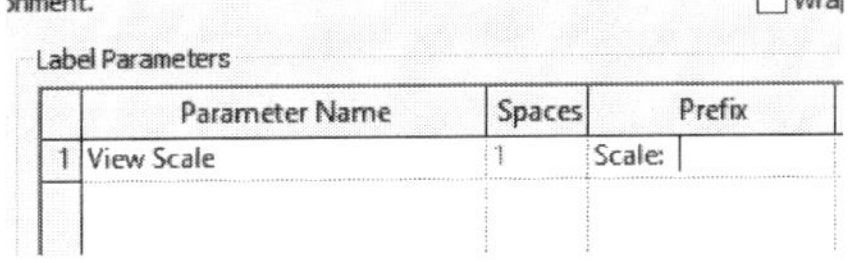

In the Prefix column:

Type **Scale:**

Add two spaces after the colon.

Click **OK**.

7.

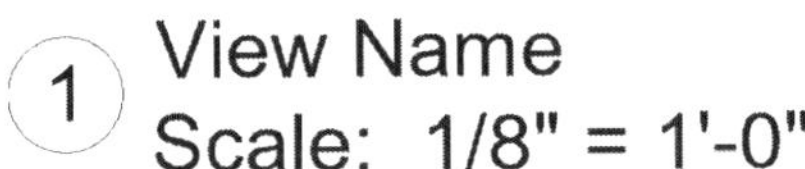

The label updates.

Note the spaces.

Left click anywhere in the display window to release the selection.

8.

Select the **Create** ribbon.

9.

Select the **Label** tool.

Left click above the view name to place the label.

10.

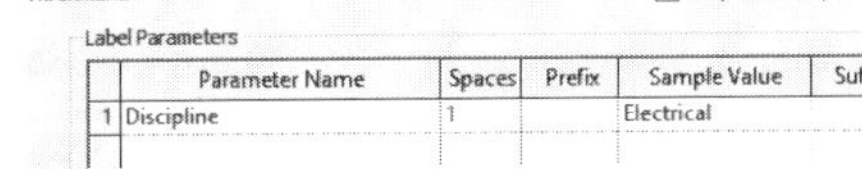

Select **Discipline**.

Type **Electrical** in the Sample Value field.

Click **OK**.

11.

Cancel out of the Label command.

Select the **Discipline** label.

Select **Edit Type** from the Properties palette.

12.   Select **Duplicate**.

13.   Type **Label – Italic** in the Name field.

Click **OK**.

14.   Change the Text Font to **Arial.**

Enable **Italic**.

Click **OK**.

15.   Set the Horizontal Align to Left.

Reposition the Discipline label to align with the other labels.

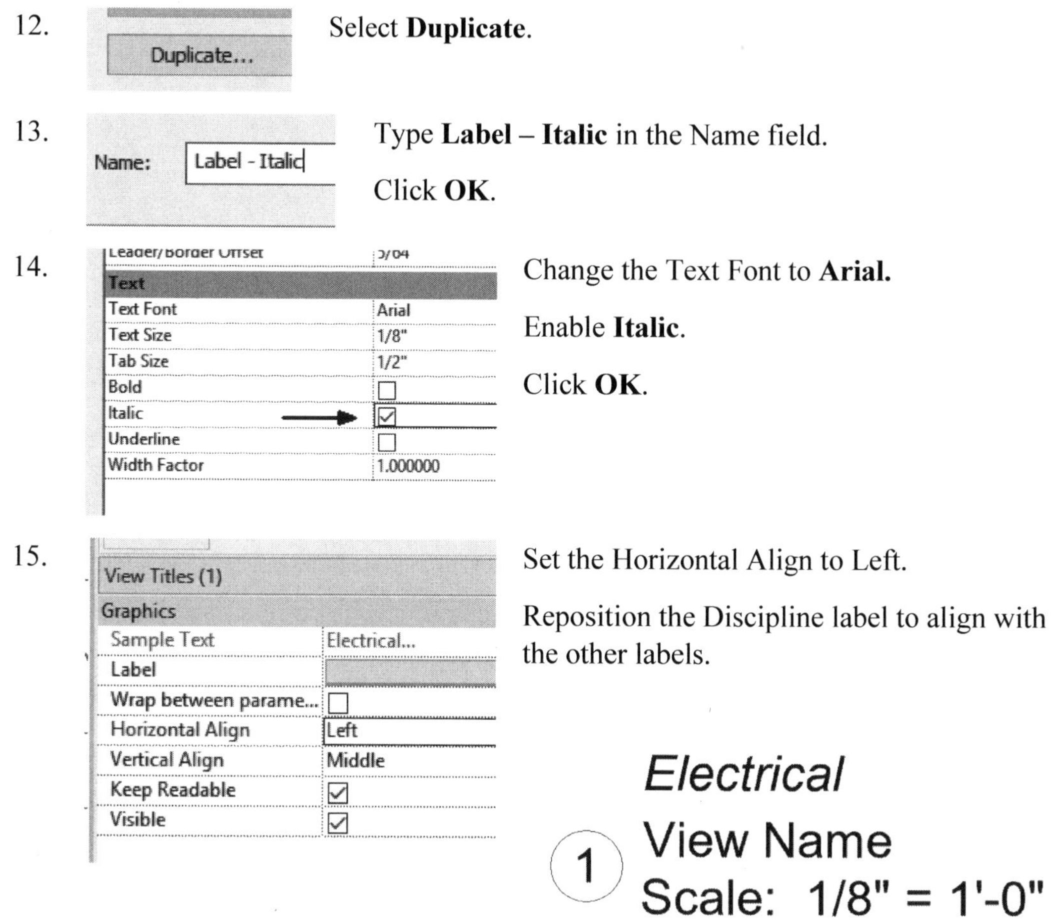

16.   Save the family as **View Title w Discipline**.

Scope Boxes

Scope boxes are used to control the extents of datum elements, like grids, levels and reference planes. Each of these elements can be assigned to a specific scope box, limiting the 3D extents to the dashed green line limit. Scope boxes are not visible when printing.

To create a scope box, you have to use either a Floor Plan View or a Reflected Ceiling Plan View. However, once a scope box is created, it is going to be visible in the other views: sections, callouts, elevations and 3D views. In elevations and sections, the scope box is only going to be visible if it intersects the cut line. You can adjust the extents of the scope box in all views.

The moment a scope box is assigned to a view, the **Crop Region** is locked and can't be modified. Also, you can't use the **Do Not Crop View** tool. To see the whole project in a view, you'll have to create a different plan or remove the scope box temporarily.

A scope box can also be used to control the angle of a view. If you duplicate the view, the extents are assigned to the new scope box. The crop region is automatically adjusted to fit the angle. Removing the scope box from a view will revert the crop angle back to default.

Check the option bar when creating a scope box: you can assign a name to the scope box and enter a height value. If you need to change the height value, switch to an elevation view and use the grips on the scope box to adjust the height.

Exercise 7-16:

Using Scope Boxes

Drawing Name: scope_box.rfa
Estimated Time: 20 minutes

This exercise reinforces the following skills:
- Duplicate Views
- Apply Dependent Views
- Scope Box

1. 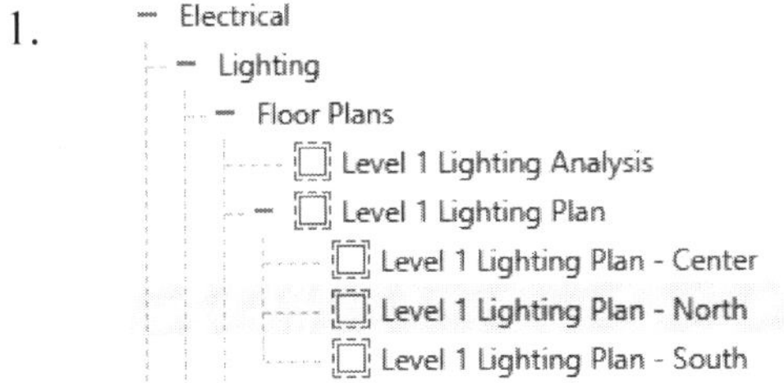

   In the Project Browser:

   Notice that Level 1 Lighting Plan has three dependent views:
   - Center
   - North
   - South

   We want to add three dependent views for Level 2 and Level 3.

2.

> Apply Dependent Views...
> Save to Project as Image...
> Delete
> Copy to Clipboard
> Rename...
> Select All Instances
> ✓ Properties
> Save to New File...
> Expand All
> Collapse Selected
> Collapse All
> ✓ Show View Placement on Sheet Status Icons

Highlight the Level 1 Lighting Plan floor plan.

Right click and select **Apply Dependent Views**.

3.

> The current dependent view layout will be applied to the views selected
>
> Floor Plan: Level 1 Lighting Analysis
> Floor Plan: Level 1 Plumbing Plan
> Floor Plan: Level 1 Power Plan
> Floor Plan: Level 2 Lighting Plan
> Floor Plan: Level 2 Power Plan
> Floor Plan: Level 3 Lighting Plan
> Floor Plan: Level 3 Plumbing Plan

Hold down the **CTL** key.

Select the **Level 2: Lighting Plan** and the **Level 3: Lighting Plan**.

Click **OK**.

4.

> Floor Plans
> ⊟ Level 1 Lighting Analysis
> ⊟ **Level 1 Lighting Plan**
>   Level 1 Lighting Plan - Center
>   Level 1 Lighting Plan - North
>   Level 1 Lighting Plan - South
> ⊟ Level 2 Lighting Plan
>   Level 2 Lighting Plan - Dependent 1
>   Level 2 Lighting Plan - Dependent 2
>   Level 2 Lighting Plan - Dependent 3
> ⊟ Level 3 Lighting Plan
>   Level 3 Lighting Plan - Dependent 1
>   Level 3 Lighting Plan - Dependent 2
>   Level 3 Lighting Plan - Dependent 3

The dependent views are created.
Rename the Dependent views:
- Center
- North
- South

You can use F2 to edit the view name.

5.

> Floor Plans
> + ☐ Level 1 Lighting Analysis
> − ☐ **Level 1 Lighting Plan**
>   ☐ Level 1 Lighting Plan - Center
>   ☐ Level 1 Lighting Plan - North
>   ☐ Level 1 Lighting Plan - South

Open the **Level 1 Lighting Plan**.

6.

Scope Box

Switch to the **View** ribbon.

Select **Scope Box** on the Create panel on the ribbon.

7. 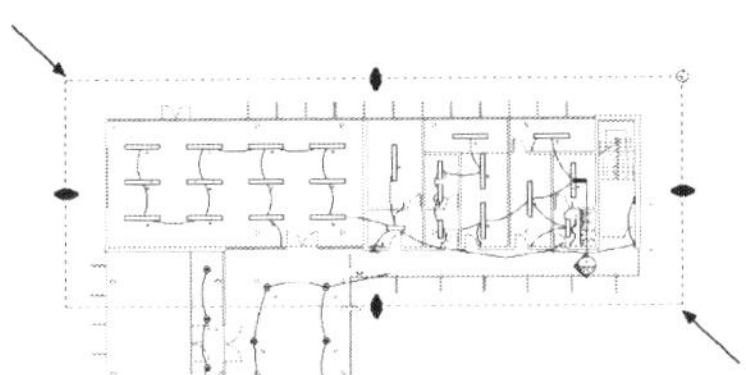 Draw a rectangle around the top section of the floor plan.

8. 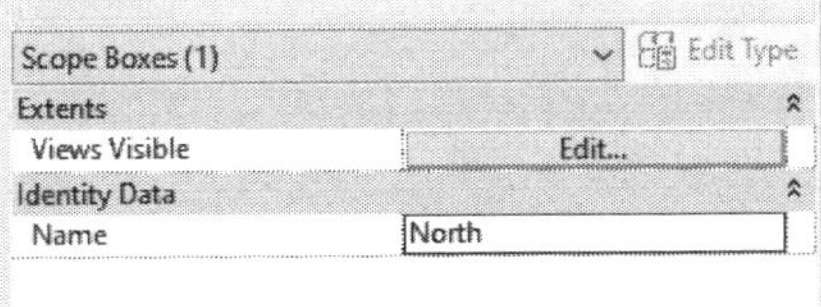 In the Name field, type **North**.

9. 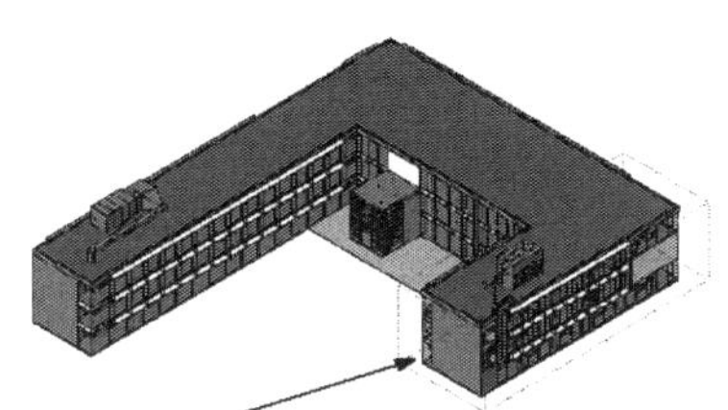

    Switch to a 3D view.

    You can see the scope box around the model.

10. 

    — Floor Plans
       + ☐ Level 1 Lighting Analysis
       — ☐ **Level 1 Lighting Plan**
           ☐ Level 1 Lighting Plan - Center
           ☐ Level 1 Lighting Plan - North
           ☐ Level 1 Lighting Plan - South

    Return to the Level 1 Lighting Plan floor plan.

11. Scope Box

    Switch to the **View** ribbon.

    Select **Scope Box** on the Create panel on the ribbon.

12. 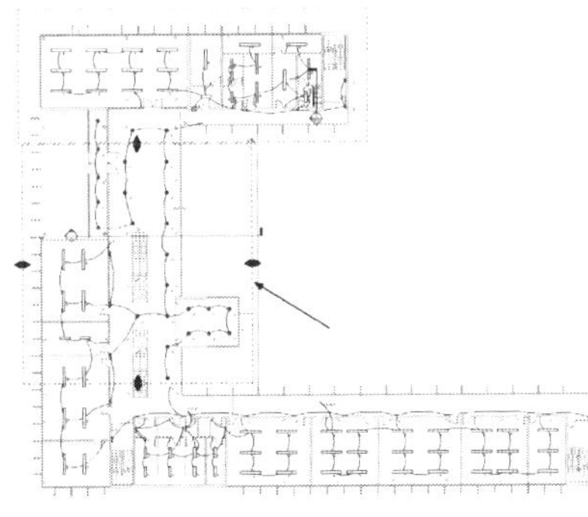 Draw a rectangle around the center section of the floor plan.

13. 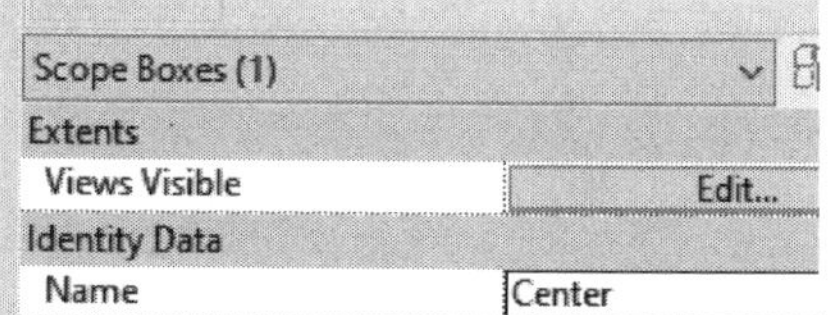
In the Name field, type **Center**.

14. 
Switch to the **View** ribbon.

Select **Scope Box** on the Create panel on the ribbon.

15. 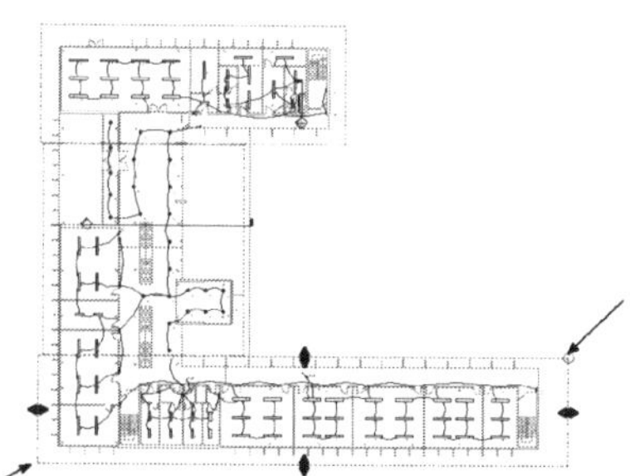
Draw a rectangle around the south section of the floor plan.

16. 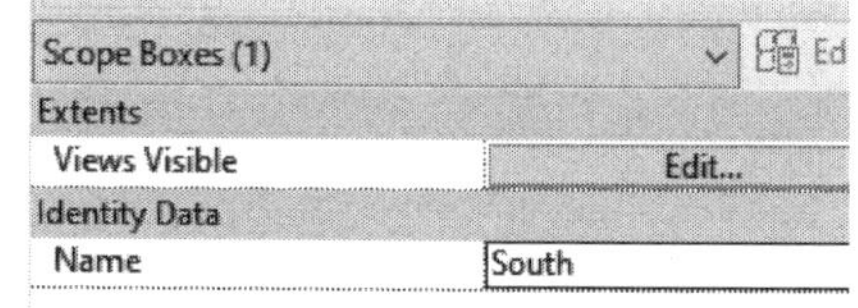
In the Name field, type **South**.

17. 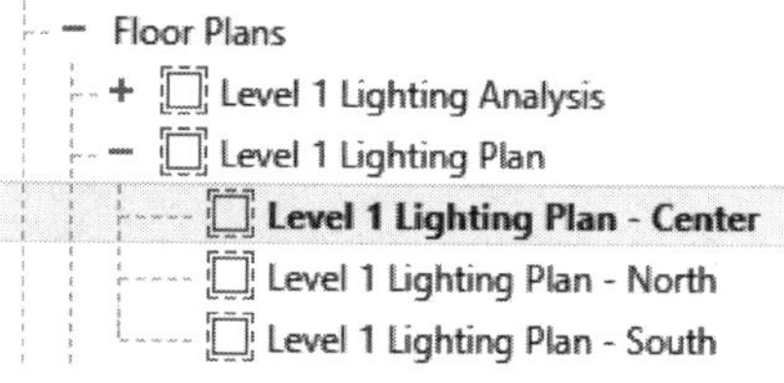
Open the **Level 1 Lighting Plan-Center**.

18.

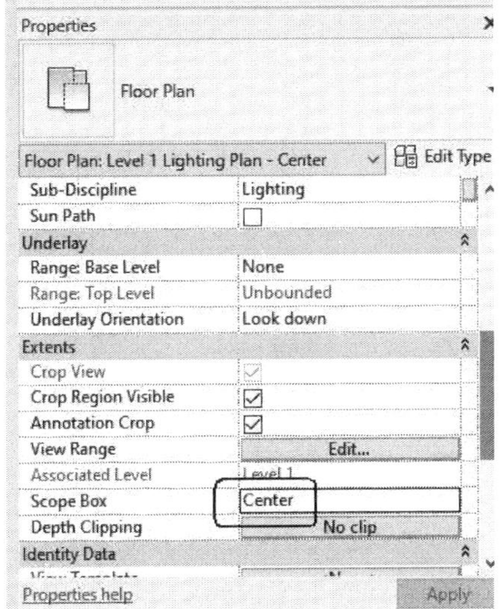

In the Properties palette:

Locate the Scope Box field:

Select **Center** from the drop-down list.

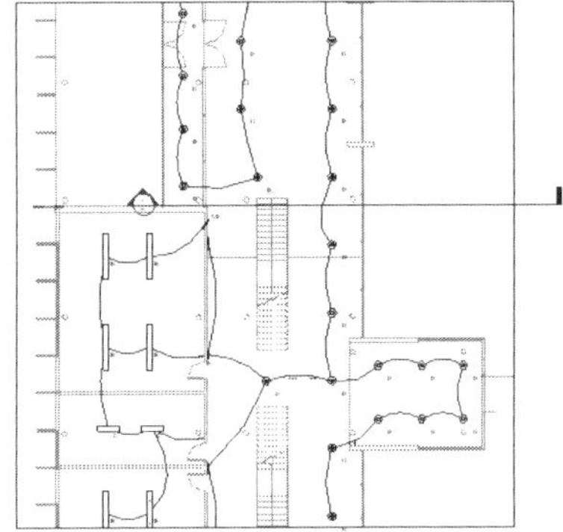

The view displays only the area inside the center scope box.

19. 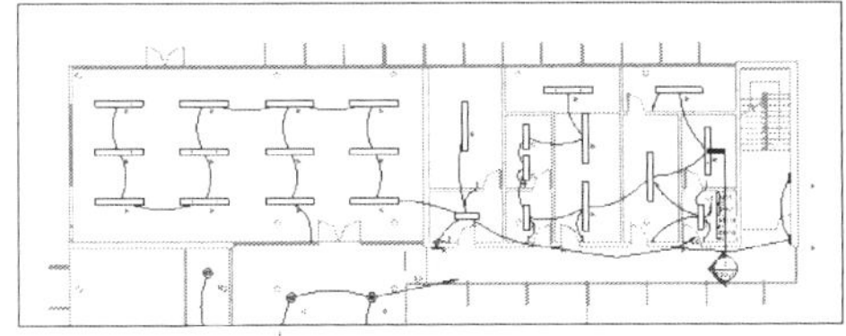

Open the **Level 1 Lighting Plan-North**.

Floor Plans
- + Level 1 Lighting Analysis
- − Level 1 Lighting Plan
  - Level 1 Lighting Plan - Center
  - **Level 1 Lighting Plan - North**
  - Level 1 Lighting Plan - South

20.

In the Properties palette:

Locate the Scope Box field:

Select **North** from the drop-down list.

The view displays only the area inside the North scope box.

21. Open the **Level 1 Lighting Plan-South**.

22. In the Properties palette:

Locate the Scope Box field:

Select **South** from the drop-down list.

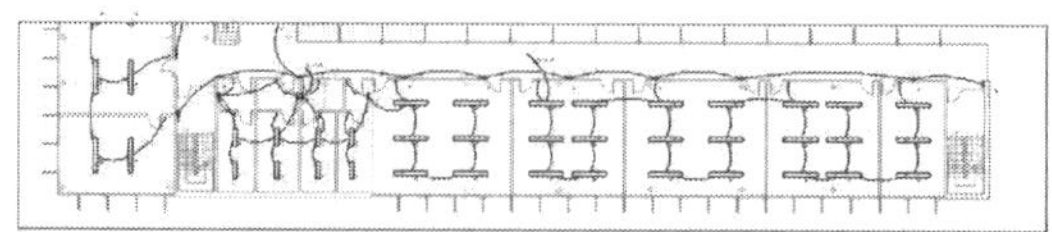

The view displays only the area inside the South scope box.

23. Repeat for the Level 2 Lighting Plan dependent views.

24. Repeat for the Level 3 Lighting Plan dependent views.

25. Save as *ex7-16.rvt*.

Exercise 7-17:

Using Scope Boxes to Control Grid Display

Drawing Name: scope_box_2.rfa
Estimated Time: 20 minutes

This exercise reinforces the following skills:
- Grids
- Scope Box
- Visibility

1. 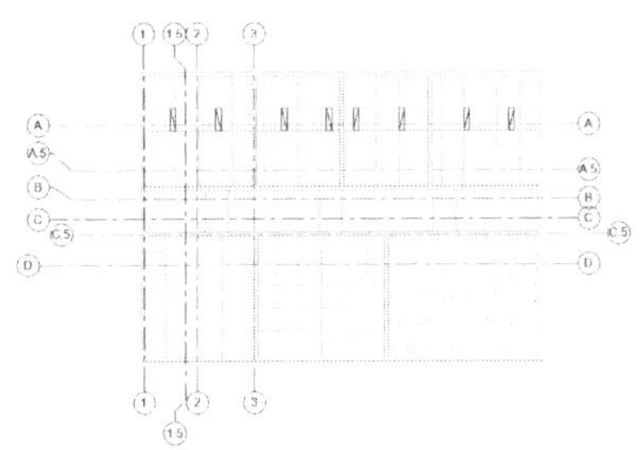

   Locate the ceiling plans under Electrical→Lighting.

2. The plans show several grid lines.

   We can use a scope box to control which grid lines are displayed in a view.

3.

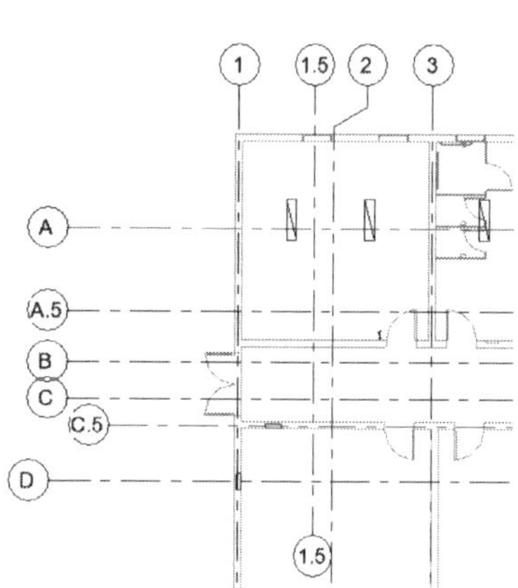

Activate the floor plans under Lighting so you can see how the grids are displayed.

4.

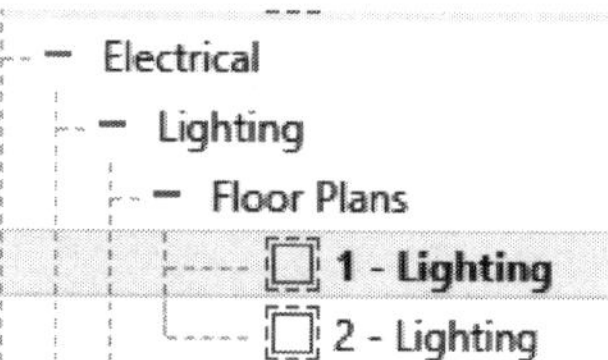

Verify that the **1- Lighting** Floor plan is active.

5.

Select **Scope Box** from the View ribbon.

6.

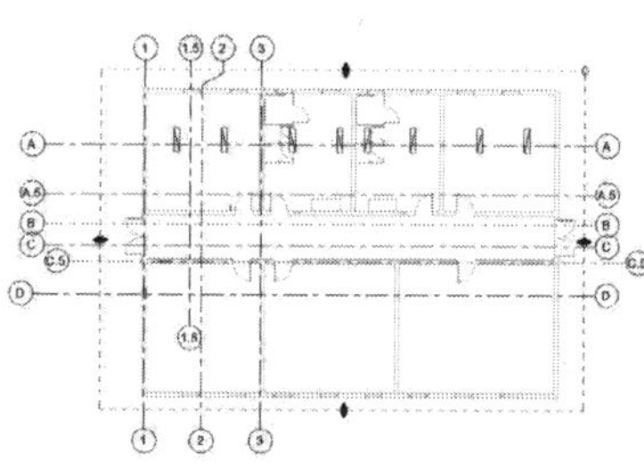

Draw the scope box around the entire building.

7.

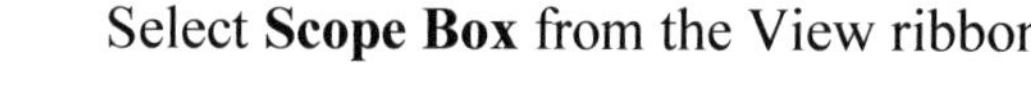

Name the Scope Box **Grids** in the Properties palette.

8.

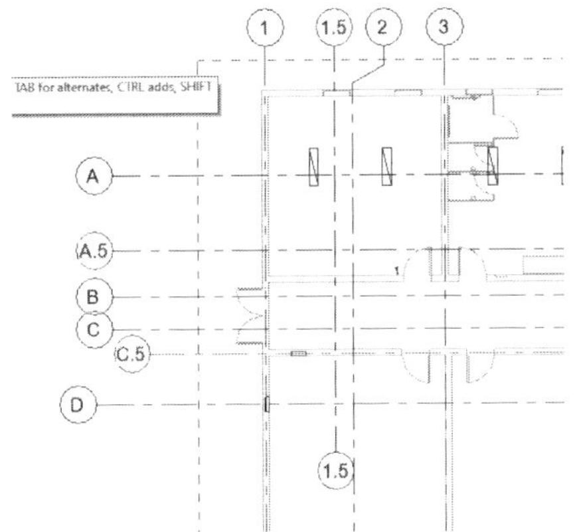

Hold down the CTL key.

Select Grids **1.5**, **A.5** and **C.5**.

Grids (3)	
Extents	
Scope Box	Grids
Identity Data	
Name	<varies>
IFC Parameters	
Export to IFC	By Type
IfcGUID	<varies>

In the Properties palette:

Assign the grids to the Grids **Scope Box**.
Select the Scope Box.

9.

Scope Boxes (1)		
Extents		
Views Visible		Edit...
Height	40' 0"	
Identity Data		
Name	Grids	

In the Properties palette:
Select **Edit** next to Views Visible.

10.

3D View	Section View	Visible	None
Ceiling Plan	1 - Ceiling Mech	Visible	Invisible
Ceiling Plan	2 - Ceiling Mech	Visible	Invisible
Ceiling Plan	1 - Ceiling Elec	Visible	Invisible
Ceiling Plan	2 - Ceiling Elec	Visible	Invisible
Ceiling Plan	1 - Top of Ceiling	Visible	None
Elevation	East - Mech	Invisible	None

Set the grids assigned to the scope box to be invisible in all the ceiling plans except Top of Ceiling.

You can use the CTL key to select more than one view at a time.

11.

Click on the column headers to change the sort order.

View Type	View Name	Automatic visibility	Override
Elevation	West - Plumbing	Invisible	None
Floor Plan	1 - Mech	Visible	Invisible
Floor Plan	2 - Mech	Visible	Invisible
Floor Plan	1 - Lighting	Visible	Invisible
Floor Plan	2 - Lighting	Visible	Invisible
Floor Plan	1 - Plumbing	Visible	Invisible
Floor Plan	2 - Plumbing	Visible	Invisible
Floor Plan	1 - Power	Visible	Invisible
Floor Plan	2 - Power	Visible	Invisible
Floor Plan	1 - Rooms	Visible	Invisible
Section	Conduit over Pipes	Visible	None
Section	Lab 101	Visible	None

Set the selected grids to be invisible in all the floor plans.

Click **OK**.

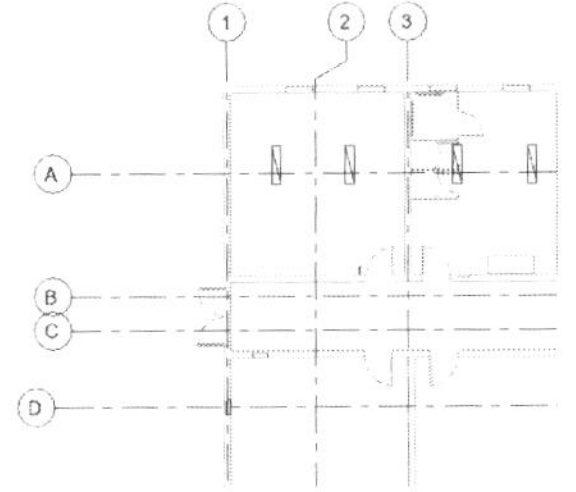

Notice the view updated to not display the selected grids.

12.

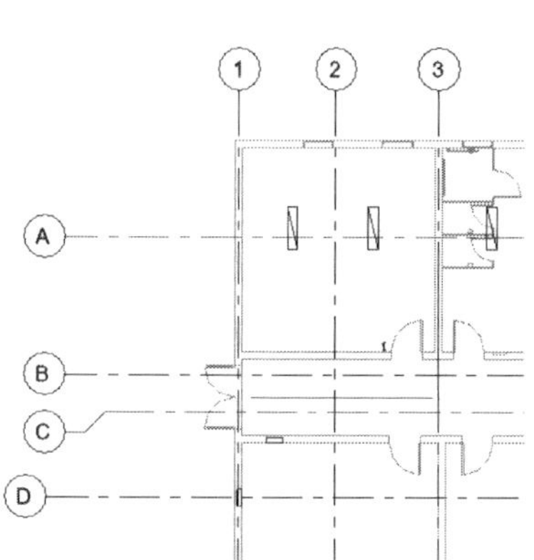

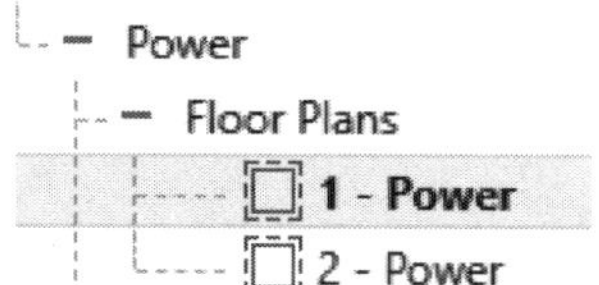

Open the **1-Power** floor plan.

Notice the view updated to not display the selected grids.

13.

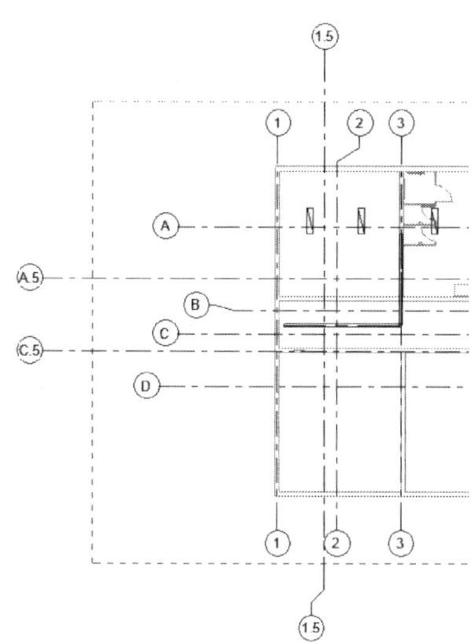

Open the **1-Top of Ceiling** ceiling plan.

Notice the grids and scope box are visible in this view. You may need to zoom out to see the grids.

14. Save as *ex7-17.rvt*.

Lab Exercises

Open Lesson_7_lab.rvt.

Place the Sheet List schedule on the 00 – Sheet List sheet.

Copy the legend from ex7-8.rvt to the active project.

- Start a new legend in the active project.
- Open ex7-8.rvt. Open the legend view.
- Window around the legend to select all the elements.
- Click **CTL-C**.
- Switch back to the lab project.
- Left click in the legend view.
- Click **Ctl-V**.

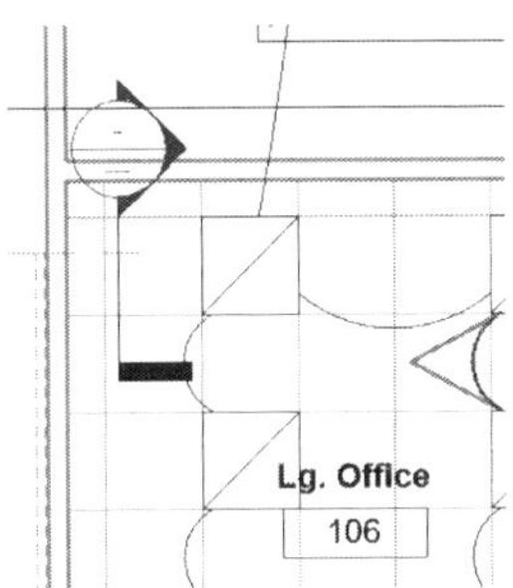

Create a section view of the plain recessed lighting fixture located in ROOM 106.

Assign LIGHTING as the sub-discipline in the view's property palette.

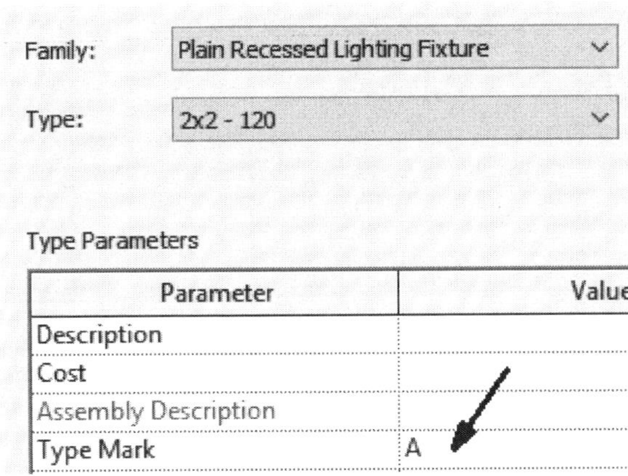

Edit the Plain Recessed Lighting Fixture Type Property to assign a Type Mark.

Repeat for the remaining light fixtures used in the project.

Use type marks that match up with what appears on the legend that was copied over.

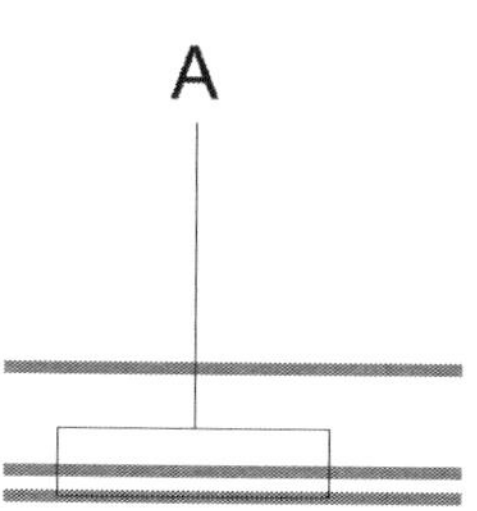

Tag the light fixture in the new section view.

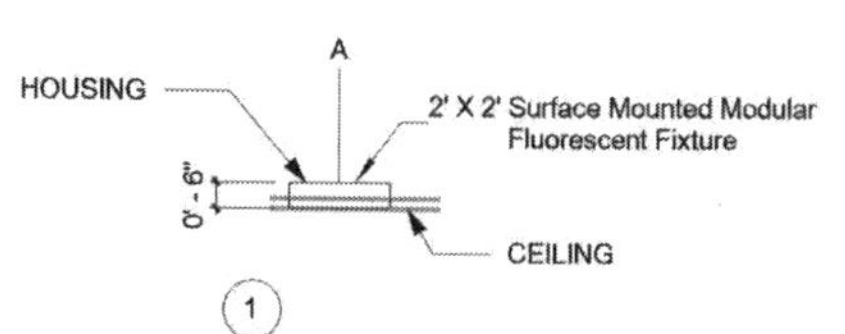

Add annotations including an element keynote, text with leaders note block, and a dimension.

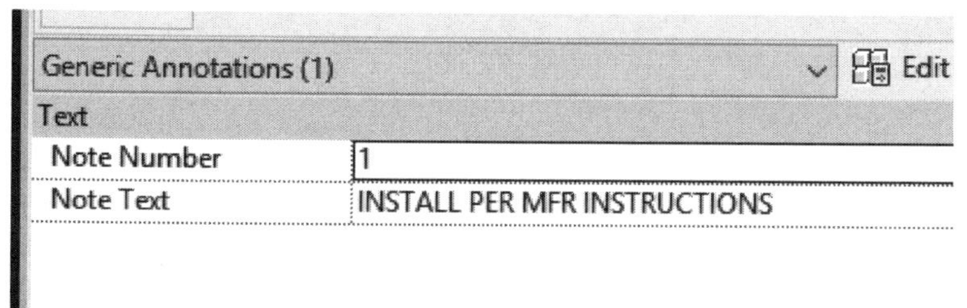

Modify the properties of the note block as shown.

Repeat process to create section views of the other lighting fixtures.

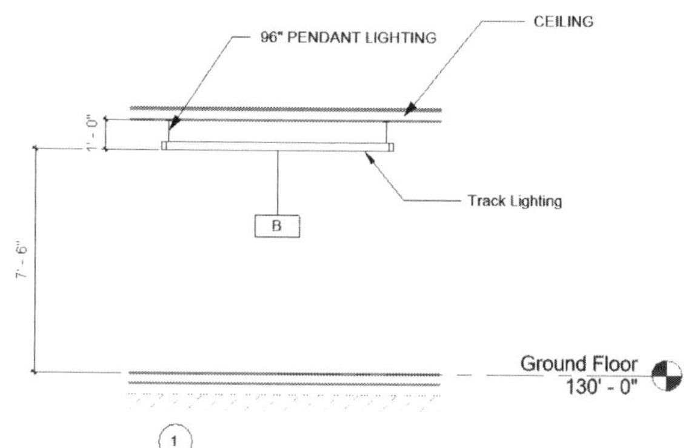

Add annotations including an element keynote, tag, text with leaders note block, and a dimension.

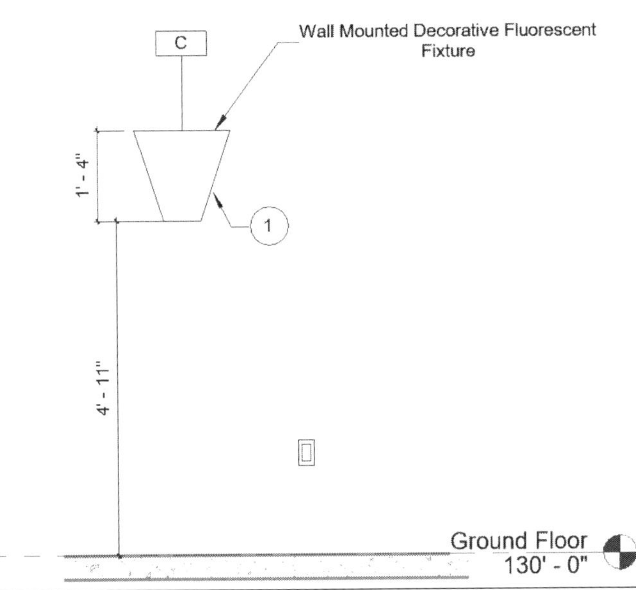

Add annotations including an element keynote, tag, text with leaders note block, and a dimension.

Notes:

Projects

Revit files are called "projects". A project is a building model but also includes metadata such as the size and location of systems, materials used, and annotations. The display settings in a project define the appearance of the model in different views. You have control over how elements are displayed in each view.

Every project starts with a template. The template provides the initial settings, such as display defaults, units, and families which are pre-loaded into the file.

A project is the entire building design as well as the associated documentation (sheets). In most cases, you will be working with an architectural building model provided by an architectural or AEC firm and then linking to that file or modifying the file to add the necessary electrical elements.

You add the parametric building components, such as lighting fixtures and switches, to the project – either working in a separate host file or in the file provided. You then create plan, section, elevation, and 3D views. Any changes made in one view propagate throughout the project and all associated views automatically update reflecting any changes. You then create sheets and place views on the sheets.

Discipline Settings are used to define the appearance and behavior of the system components in electrical systems. After standard settings have been established in your company, they can be configured in a template file, so you don't have to reset them for every project.

Electrical Settings determine the voltage, power distribution systems, wiring, and demand factors for the electrical systems. The Electrical Settings dialog box is used to specify these settings. Electrical settings can be created in template files or copied to other projects using the Transfer Project Settings dialog.

Hidden Line

Electrical Settings

	Setting	
···· Hidden Line	Draw MEP Hidden Lines	☑
···· General	Line Style	<Thin Lines>
···· Angles	Inside Gap	1/16"
···· Wiring	Outside Gap	1/16"
···· Voltage Definitions	Single Line	1/16"
···· Distribution Systems		
⊟··· Cable Tray Settings		

Draw MEP Hidden Lines	A check indicates enabled. No check indicates disabled. If enabled, draws cable trays and conduits using the line style and gaps specified below.
Line Style	Designates the line style to be used for hidden lines
Inside Gap	Specifies the gap for the lines that appear within a crossing segment
Outside Gap	Specifies the gap for the lines that appear outside of crossing segments
Single Line	Specifies the gap for single hidden lines where segments cross

General

Setting	Value
Electrical Connector Separator	-
Electrical Data Style	Connector Description Voltage / Number of Poles – Load
Circuit Description	480V-3P/30A
Circuit Naming by Phase - Phase A Label	A
Circuit Naming by Phase - Phase B Label	B
Circuit Naming by Phase - Phase C Label	C
Capitalization for Load Names:	From Source Parameters
Circuit Sequence:	Numerical (1,2,3,4,5,6,7,8,9,10,11,12)
Circuit Rating	20 A
Circuit Path Offset	9' - 0"

Electrical Connector Separator	Specifies the symbol used to separate rating values
Electrical Data Style	Specifies the style for the electrical data parameter in the Element Properties dialog box
Circuit Description	Specifies the format for circuit descriptions that appear as the Load Name in the panel schedules.
Circuit Naming by Phase – Phase Label (A,B,C)	These values are only used if you specify circuit naming by phase for the panel using the Properties palette.
Capitalization for Load Names	Specifies the format for the Load Name parameter in the instance properties for circuits

Circuit Sequence	Specifies the sequence in which power circuits are created, enabling creation of circuits grouped by phase
Circuit Rating	Specifies the default rating when creating circuits
Circuit Path Offset	Specifies the default offset when placing a circuit path

Voltage Definitions

	Name	Value	Minimum	
1	120	120.00 V	110.00 V	130.00 V
2	208	208.00 V	200.00 V	228.00 V
3	240	240.00 V	220.00 V	250.00 V
4	277	277.00 V	260.00 V	280.00 V
5	480	480.00 V	460.00 V	490.00 V

Name	Identifies a voltage definition
Value	The actual voltage for the voltage definition
Minimum	The lowest voltage rating for electrical devices and equipment that can be used with the voltage definition.
Maximum	The highest voltage rating for electrical devices and equipment that can be used with the voltage definition.

The Voltage Definitions table defines the ranges of voltages that can be assigned to the Distribution Systems available in your project.

Each voltage definition is specified as a range of voltages to allow for differing voltage ratings on devices from various manufacturers. For example, devices used on a 120V distribution system may carry ratings of anywhere from 110V to 130V.

You can create Voltage Definitions and you can delete definitions that are not currently in use with any distribution system.

Revit does not prevent you from specifying unfeasible voltage values. For example, you could configure a distribution system with a L-L Voltage value of 120 and an L-G Voltage value of 480, even though this is physically impossible.

Distribution Systems

	Name	Phase	Configuration	Wires	L-L Voltage	L-G Voltage	High Leg Phase
1	120/208 Wye	Three	Wye	4	208	120	None
2	480/277 Wye	Three	Wye	4	480	277	None

Name	Identifies a distribution system
Phase	Either Three or Single, selected from the drop-down list
Configuration	After you click the value, you can select Wye or Delta, from the drop-down list (three-phase systems only).
Wires	Specifies to the number of conductors (3 or 4 for three-phase, 2 or 3 for single-phase).
L-L Voltage	After you click the value, you can select a Voltage Definition that represents the voltage measured between any two phases. The specification of this parameter depends on the Phase and Wire selections. For example, L-L Voltage is not applicable for a single-phase, 2-wire system.
L-G Voltage	After you click the value, you can select a Voltage Definition that represents the voltage measured between a phase and ground. L-G is always available.
High Leg Phase	The High Leg Phase setting tells Revit which conductor is the "wild leg" in your distribution system. This is important for: • Correct voltage-to-neutral calculations (so you don't accidentally assign 120V loads to the 208V leg). • Panel schedules and circuiting logic (Revit will know which circuits can supply 120V loads). • Code compliance in documentation, since the high leg must be indicated on drawings.

The left-hand navigation tree shows: Hidden Line, General, Angles, Wiring, Voltage Definitions, Distribution Systems, Cable Tray Settings — Rise Drop — Single Line Symbology, Two Line Symbology, Size.

Cable Tray Settings

	Setting	
Hidden Line	Use Annot. Scale for Single Line Fittings	☐
General	Cable Tray Fitting Annotation Size	0' 0 1/8"
Angles	Cable Tray Size Separator	x
Wiring	Cable Tray Size Suffix	ø
Voltage Definitions	Cable Tray Connector Separator	-
Distribution Systems		
Cable Tray Settings		
Rise Drop		
Single Line Symbology		
Two Line Symbology		

Use Annot. Scale for Single Line Fittings	Specifies whether cable tray fittings are drawn at the size specified by the Cable Tray Fitting Annotation Size parameter. Changing this setting does not change the plotted size of components already placed in a project.
Cable Tray Fitting Annotation Size	Specifies the plotted size of fittings drawn in single-line views. This size is maintained regardless of the drawing scale.
Cable Tray Size Separator	Specifies the symbol to be used in showing cable tray sizes. For example, when an x is used, a cable tray that is 12 inches high and 4 inches deep would be shown as 12" x 4".
Cable Tray Size Suffix	Specifies the symbol appended to the cable tray size.
Cable Tray Connector Separator	Specifies the symbol used to separate information between 2 different connectors.

Rise Drop

	Setting		
Hidden Line			Specifies the plotted size of rise/drop symbols drawn in single-line views. This size is maintained regardless of the drawing scale.
General	Cable Tray Rise/Drop Annotation Size	1/8"	
Angles			
Wiring			
Voltage Definitions			
Distribution Systems			
Cable Tray Settings			
Rise Drop			
Single Line Symbology			
Two Line Symbology			

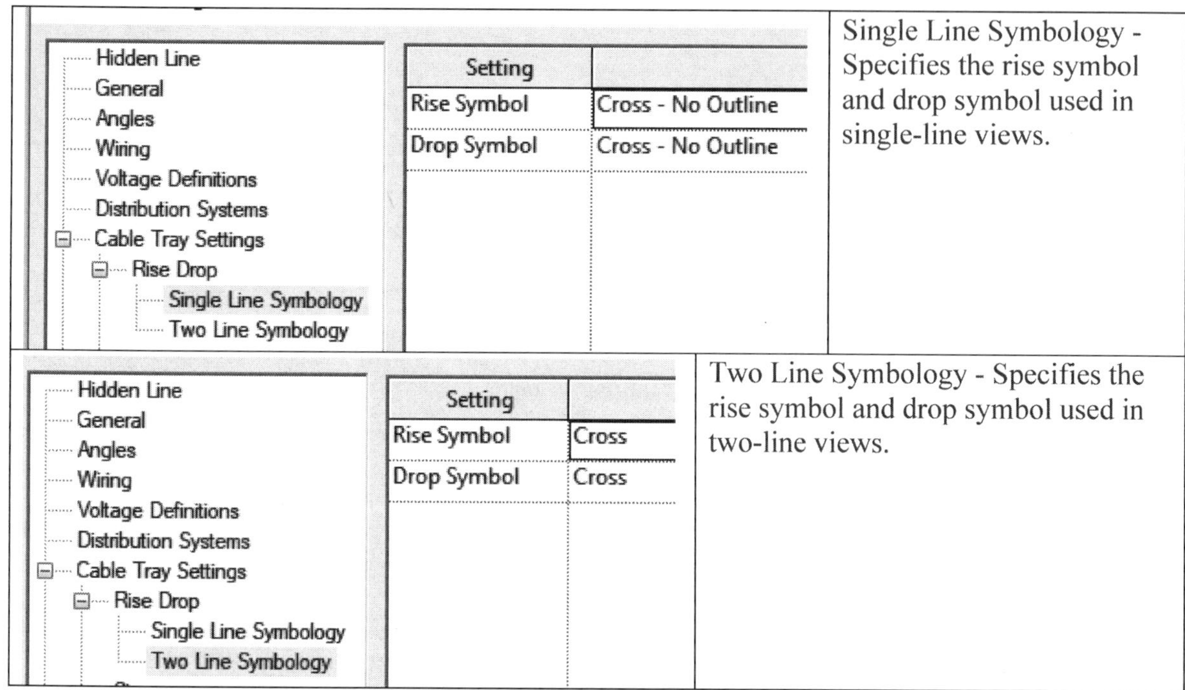

Setting	
Rise Symbol	Cross - No Outline
Drop Symbol	Cross - No Outline

Single Line Symbology - Specifies the rise symbol and drop symbol used in single-line views.

Setting	
Rise Symbol	Cross
Drop Symbol	Cross

Two Line Symbology - Specifies the rise symbol and drop symbol used in two-line views.

Cable Tray Settings – Size

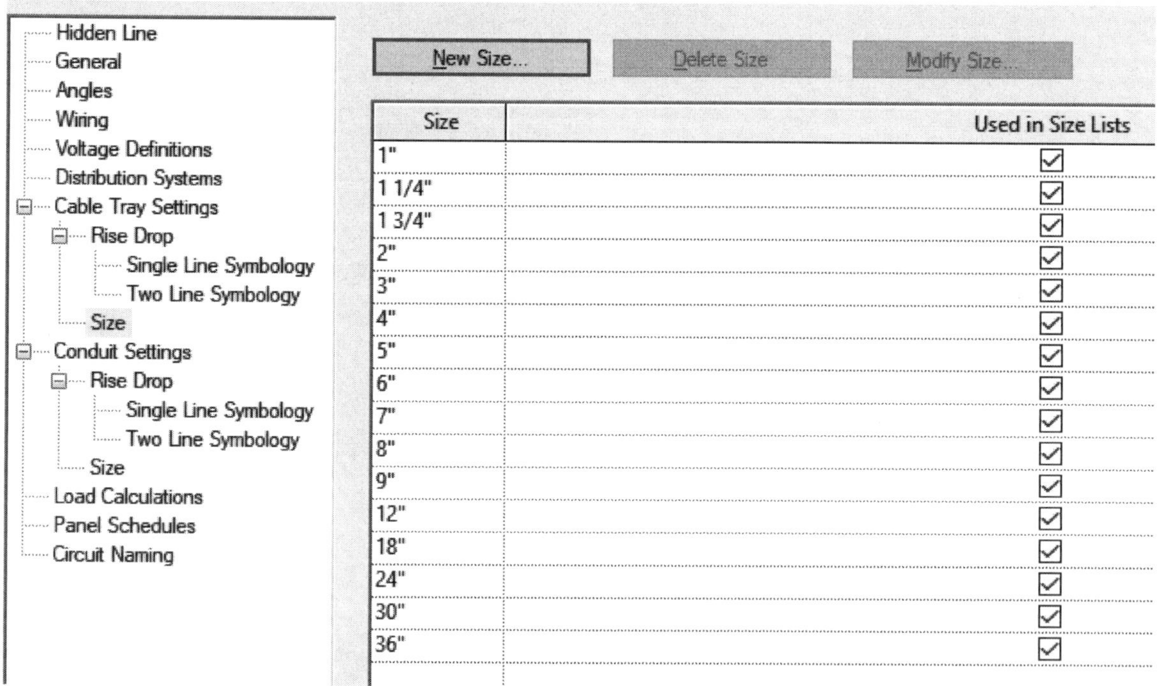

Size		Used in Size Lists
1"		☑
1 1/4"		☑
1 3/4"		☑
2"		☑
3"		☑
4"		☑
5"		☑
6"		☑
7"		☑
8"		☑
9"		☑
12"		☑
18"		☑
24"		☑
30"		☑
36"		☑

You use the Size table to specify the cable tray sizes that can be used in your project.

You can add, modify, or delete sizes as needed. For each cable tray size, the Used in Size Lists parameter specifies that the size is displayed in lists throughout Revit, including the cable tray layout editor and cable tray modify editor.

Load Calculations

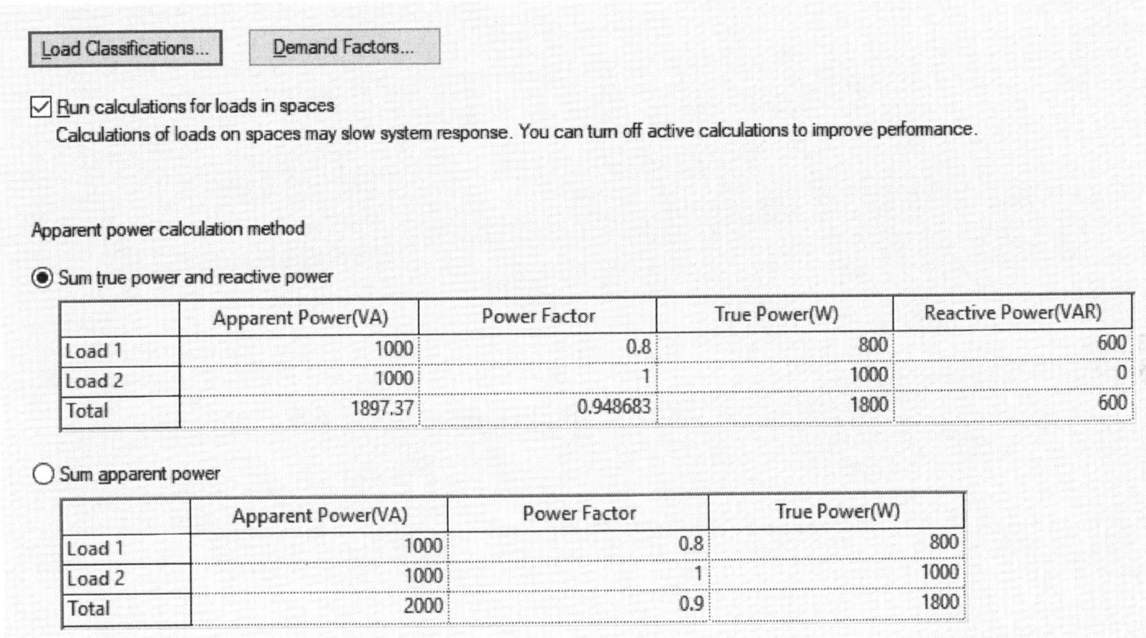

Use the check box to specify whether to enable load calculations for loads in spaces.

Running calculations may slow system response.

- Load Classifications - Click this button to open the Load Classifications dialog.

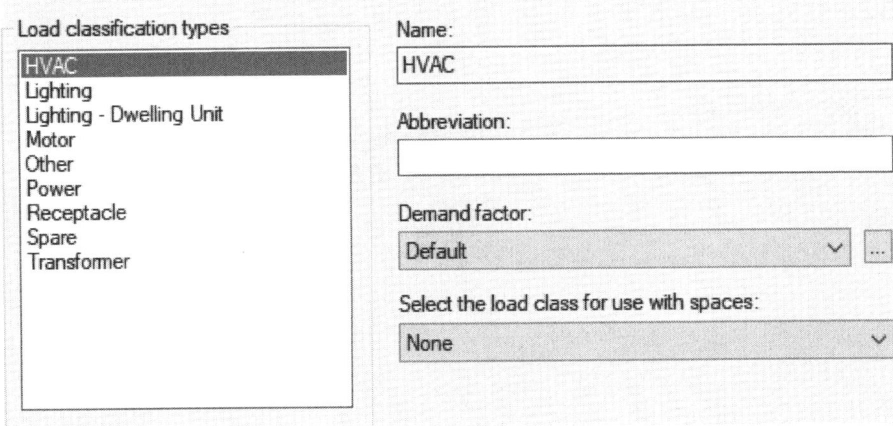

- Demand Factors - Click this button to open the Demand Factors dialog.

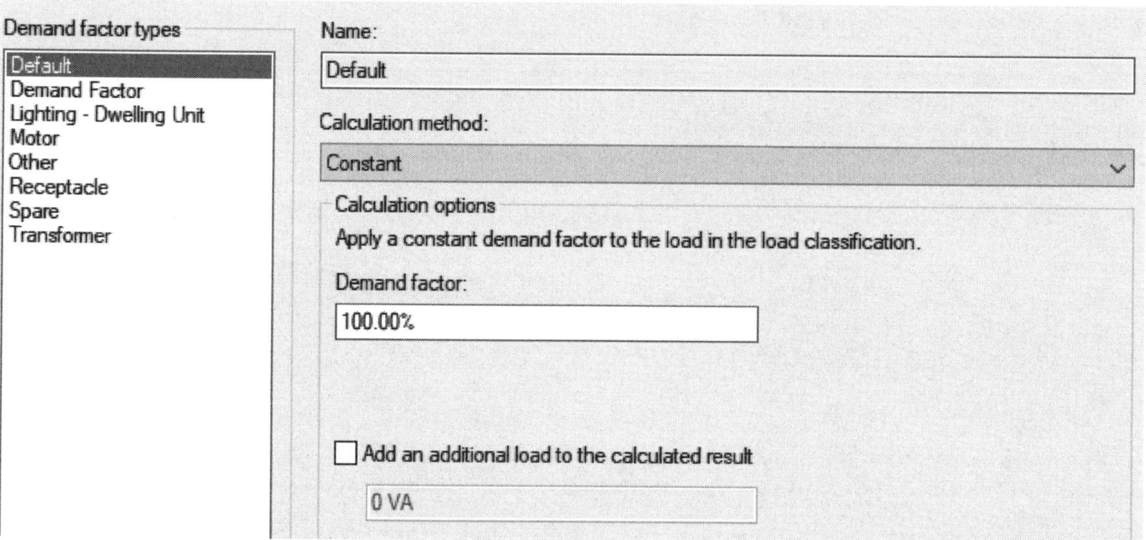

- Run calculations for loads in spaces - Since calculations of loads on space may slow system response, you can disable calculations to improve performance.

- Apparent load calculation method - Specifies how Revit sums electrical loads: Sum true load and reactive load or Sum apparent load. The selected method applies to all loads, circuits, and panels in the model.

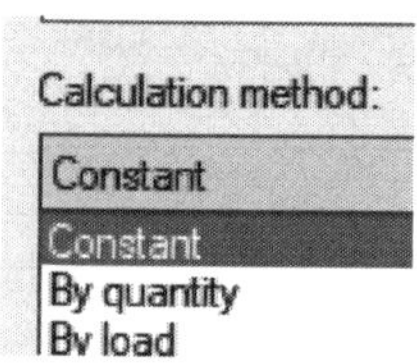

Electrical circuit load capacity is the total amount of power that the building actually will use. In order to decide what size electrical service is needed, one has to do a little math homework. Older buildings often only had a 60-amp electrical service, connected to a fuse panel. Newer buildings have 100- or 200-amp electrical services.

Understanding Electrical Loads

Calculating how much power any electrical appliances use is necessary to calculate this number. As technology continues to advance, more and more electrical loads are added.

Circuits should only be loaded up to 80% of the total circuit capabilities. Having said that, it doesn't mean that you should keep adding additional loads until you get to 80% capacity. Instead, aim for a more reasonable amount, a 60% load if at all possible, allowing for future additional loads. It's better to have too many circuits than too few.

Calculating Capacity

To help you understand the concept, if you have a 15-amp circuit, the safe operating amperage would be no greater than 12 amps. The total wattage would be 1,800 watts, meaning the safe wattage usage would be 1,440 watts. If you had a 1,100-watt hairdryer plugged into this circuit, just one device uses almost the entire desired load capabilities.

If you have a 20-amp circuit, the safe operating amperage would be no greater than 16 amps. The total wattage would be 2,400 watts, meaning the safe wattage usage would be 1,920 watts. In this instance, you could have a hairdryer, radio, and electric razor running on the same circuit, but not much else. That's why there should be additional bathroom circuits to cover lighting, exhaust fans, and heat lamps for drying.

On a 30-amp circuit, the safe operating amperage would be no greater than 24 amps. The total wattage would be 3,600 watts, meaning the safe wattage usage would be 2,880 watts. This information comes in handy with central air conditioners, electric dryers, electric ranges, and electric ovens.

To determine the wattage, you take the voltage times the amperage. Check the tags on all installed appliances for the required amperage rating. Add all of the lighting load by adding the total wattage of the light fixtures.

Most buildings will likely also have 240-volt appliances like water heaters, air conditioners, electric dryers, and electric ranges. These will have an amperage rating label and the wattage can be calculated. The voltage, 240 volts, times the amperage, say 30 amps, will equal the wattage requirements.

Main Circuit Breaker Panel and Sub-Panels

Once you've determined the total load for the building, you'll know what size electrical service you need. Most homes have either a 100-amp or a 200-amp circuit breaker. There may also be additional sub-panels feeding off of the main circuit breaker panel. People often put sub-panels on each floor for easy access to breakers in the event of trouble.

With a large enough main circuit breaker panel, you can add sub-panels to any outbuildings as well. A good rule of thumb is to always have more outlets and service space available for adding circuits and electrical loads.

Panel Schedules

Setting	
Spare Label:	Spare
Space Label:	Space
Include Spares in Panel Totals	☑
Merge multi-poled circuits into a single cell	☐

Spare Label - Specifies default label text to apply to the Load Name parameter for any spare in a panel schedule.

Space Label - Specifies default label text to apply to the Load Name parameter for any space in a panel schedule.

Include Spares in Panel Totals - Specifies whether to include spares in the panel totals when you add load values to spares in a panel schedule.

Merge multi-poled circuits into a single cell - Specifies whether to merge 2 or 3 pole circuits into a single cell in a panel schedule.

Linking Revit Architectural Projects

In most cases, you will work in your own project overlaid over the floor and building plans provided by an architect or an outside party. Close coordination between the two files is essential because if the supplied file changes it may directly affect the placement of electrical components.

When linking files, it is important to consider the hierarchy. Normally, you have a main project file which acts as the host file and then other files are loaded into the host file. Positioning the files is important to ensure that the components line up and are placed correctly. Most users use shared positioning to ensure that the linked files are aligned properly. Another method is to select a specific point or grid intersection and use that to ensure proper alignment.

When you link a Revit project file into a host Revit project file, Revit opens the linked model and retains it in memory. The more linked files, the more resource memory will be used. When you link a file into your host project, the path is saved in the host file. After linking, if the path is changed, you can reload it in the host project file to view the updated linked project file. You can update the path using the Manage Links dialog box.

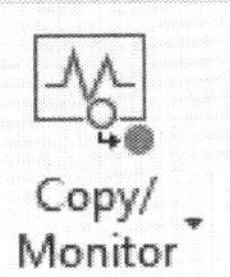

The Copy/Monitor tool is used to copy elements from the linked file to your project. Because many electrical components require a host (for example, an electrical panel needs a wall to mount on), you need to copy any necessary elements into your project. Any copied elements will be monitored by Revit to ensure that if they move or are modified, you are alerted.

Exercise 8-1:

Linking Files

Drawing Name: *linking_revit_models.rvt*
Estimated Time: 25 minutes

This exercise reinforces the following skills:

- ❑ Linking Revit files
- ❑ Changing the display of linked files
- ❑ Monitoring linked files

1. Activate the **Insert** ribbon.

   Select **Manage Links**.

2. **Manage Links**

   Type   All

   ＋ Add ▾

   Revit

   Click **Add→Revit**.

   File name: link_revit_building.rvt
   Files of type: RVT Files (*.rvt)
   Positioning: Auto - Internal Origin to Internal Origin

   Select the *link_revit_building.rvt* file.
   Set the Positioning to **Auto – Internal Origin to Internal Origin**.
   Click **Open**.

3. File name: link_revit_building.rvt
   Files of type: RVT Files (*.rvt)
   Positioning: Auto - Internal Origin to Internal Origin

4. 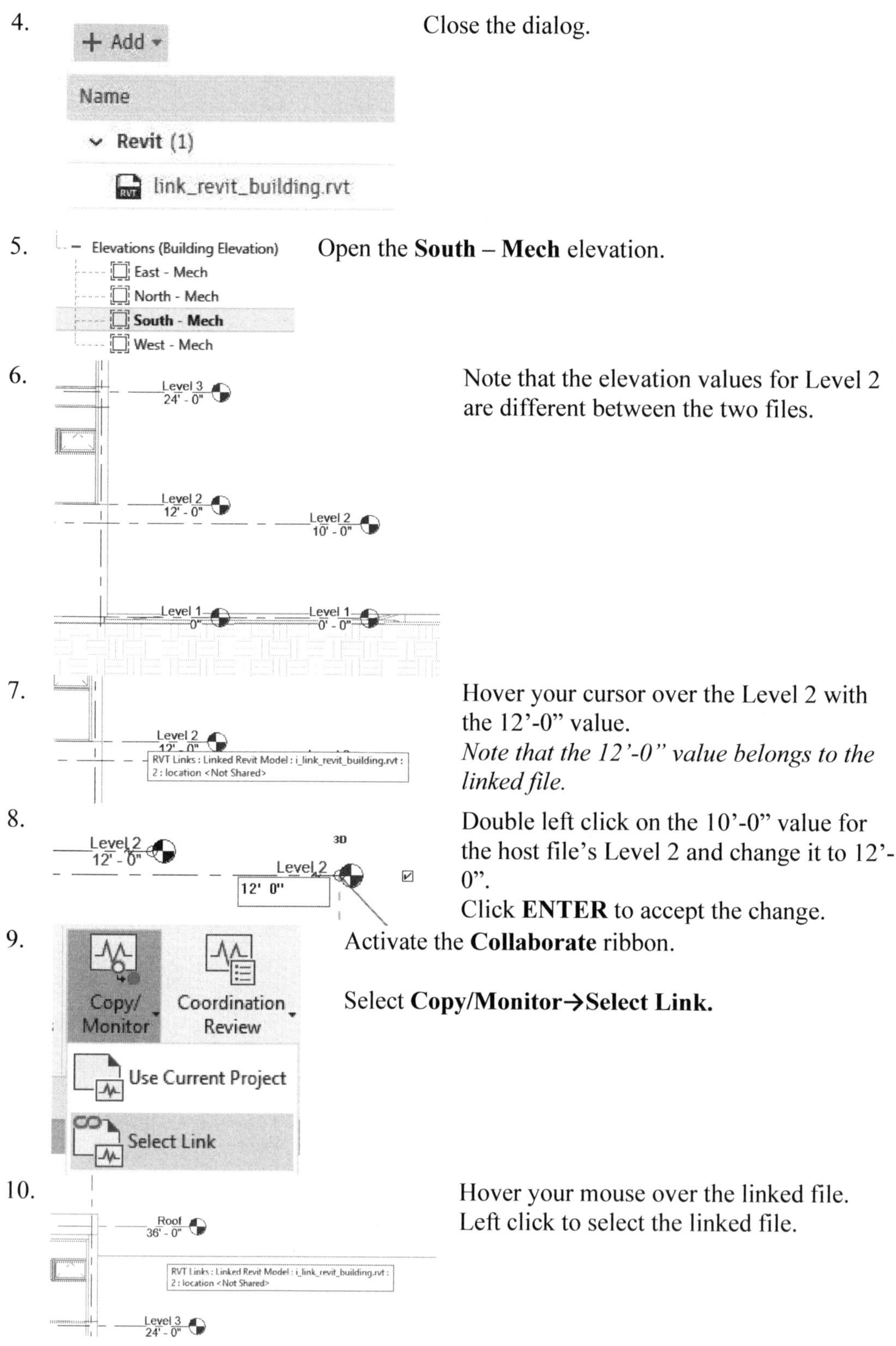 Close the dialog.

5. Open the **South – Mech** elevation.

6. Note that the elevation values for Level 2 are different between the two files.

7. Hover your cursor over the Level 2 with the 12'-0" value.
Note that the 12'-0" value belongs to the linked file.

8. Double left click on the 10'-0" value for the host file's Level 2 and change it to 12'-0".
Click **ENTER** to accept the change.

9. Activate the **Collaborate** ribbon.

Select **Copy/Monitor→Select Link.**

10. Hover your mouse over the linked file.
Left click to select the linked file.

11. 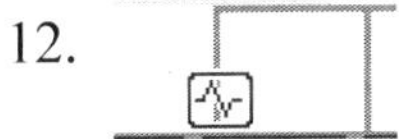 To monitor Level 1 in the linked file and compare it to Level 1 in the host file:
Select the level 1 on the right.
Select the level 1 on the left.

12. *A heartbeat symbol should appear around the middle of the level 1 lines. This indicates the element is being monitored.*

13. Repeat to monitor the Level 2 lines.

14. 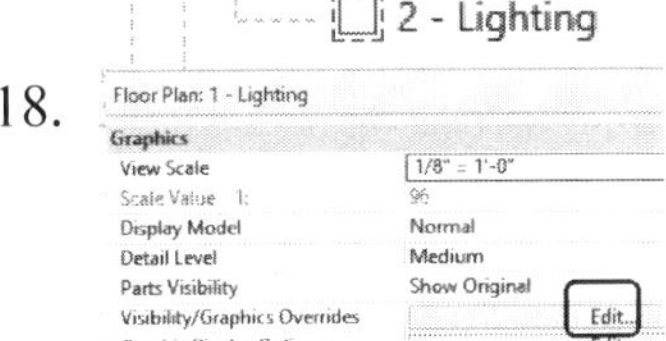 Select **Copy** to copy elements in the linked files into the host file.

15. Select **Level 3** and **Roof** levels to copy into the host file.

16. Select **Finish**.

17. Open the **1 – Lighting floor** plan.

18. Select **Edit** for the Visibility/Graphics Overrides or type **VV** to open the dialog.

19. Select the Revit Links tab.
Note that the Display Settings are set to **By Host View**.

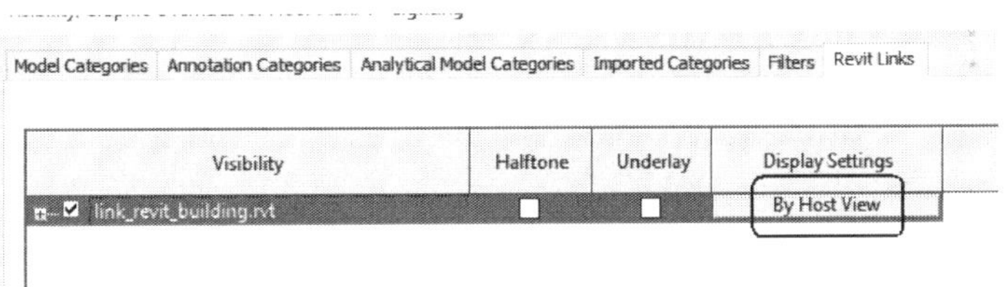

Click the **By Host View** button.

20. On the Basics tab:

Enable **Custom**.

21. Select the **Annotation Categories** tab.

Select Custom for **Annotation Categories.**

22. 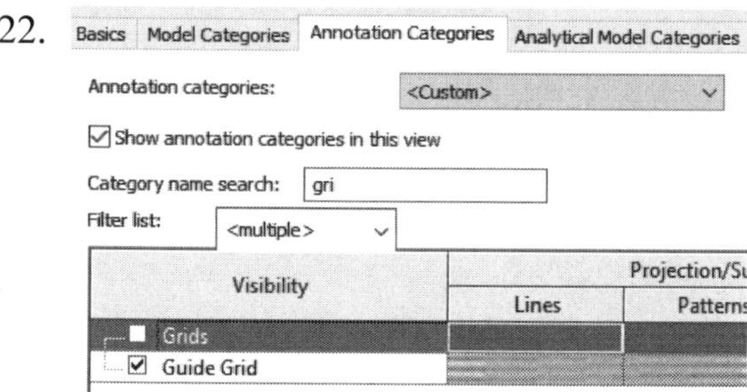 Disable **Grids**.
Click **OK**.
Note that the grids are turned off on the linked file.

23. Close without saving.

Coordination Review Tool

The Coordination Review tool is used when monitored/copied elements in a linked file have been modified. When you re-load a linked file that has been modified, warnings will appear to notify you of any violations. Warnings can also appear when the original element in the linked file is deleted or the copied element in the host file is deleted or modified.

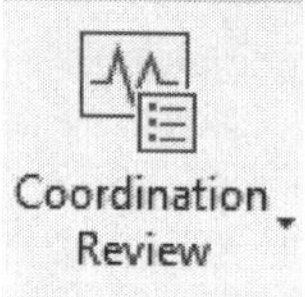

Coordination Review

The Coordination Review tool is available on the Collaborate ribbon.

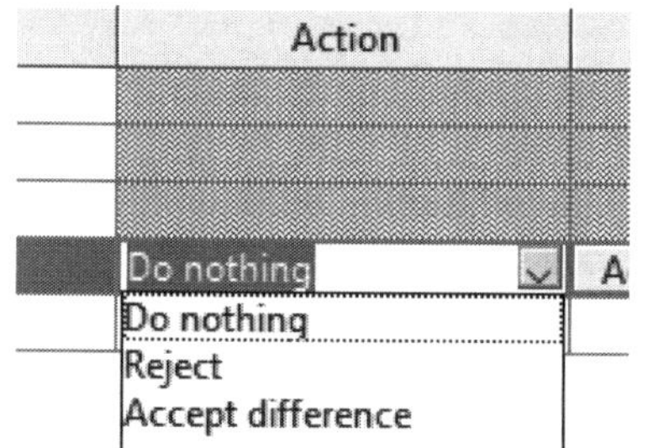

In the Coordination Review dialog box, you can select any of the changes made and select an action to address the change.

Action	Description
Do nothing	Takes no action on the element. This allows you time to message another team member to determine the best course of action regarding the change.
Reject	This command is used when the change made to the host file is correct and the linked file needs to be updated. This option is only available in the Host file.
Accept Difference	This option accepts the changes made in the linked file and updates the affected element in the host file. This option is only available in the Host file.

Exercise 8-2:
Working In a Host File

Drawing Name: *wiring.rvt*
Estimated Time: 30 minutes

This exercise reinforces the following skills:

- Manage Links
- Coordination Review
- Place Components
- Create Circuit
- Add Wires

1.  Activate the **Insert** ribbon.

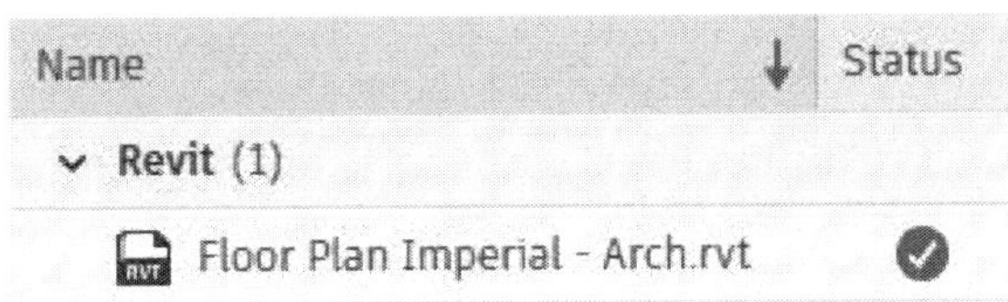

   Select the **Manage Links** tool.
   Note that there is a floor plan file linked to the project.
   You may need to reload the file to point it to the correct link.

2. Click **OK**.
   Close the Manage Links dialog.

3. Open the Collaborate ribbon.

   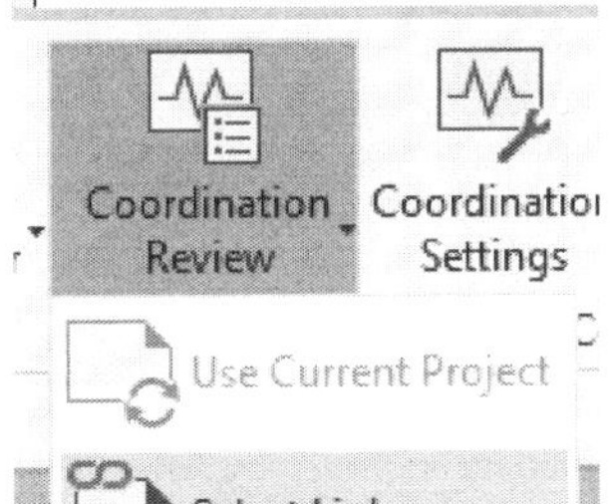

   Click **Coordination Review**→**Select Link**.

   Select the linked file.

4. A list of deleted
   elements is displayed.

   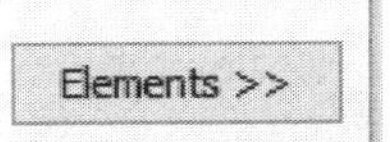

   Click the **Elements**
   button at the bottom of
   the dialog.

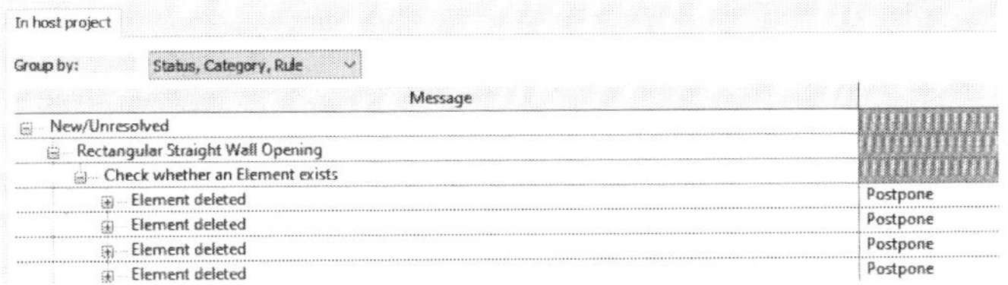

In host project		
Group by:	Status, Category, Rule ∨	
	Message	
New/Unresolved		
Rectangular Straight Wall Opening		
Check whether an Element exists		
Element deleted		Postpone
Element deleted		Postpone
Element deleted		Postpone
Element deleted		Postpone

5. A list of doors that were deleted is displayed.

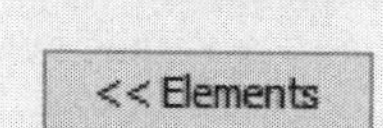

Click the **Elements** button at the bottom of the dialog.

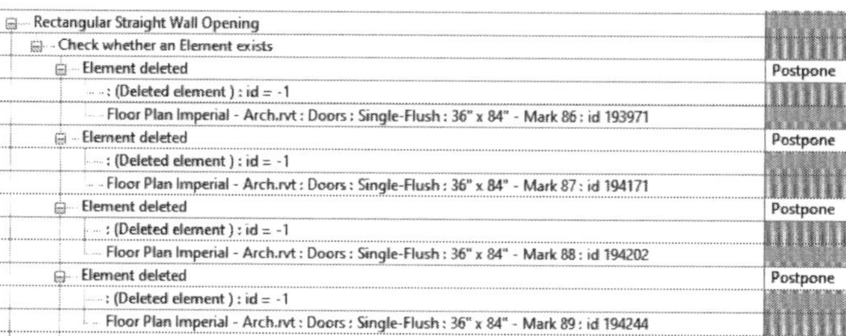

Rectangular Straight Wall Opening	
Check whether an Element exists	
Element deleted	Postpone
: (Deleted element) : id = -1	
Floor Plan Imperial - Arch.rvt : Doors : Single-Flush : 36" x 84" - Mark 86 : id 193971	
Element deleted	Postpone
: (Deleted element) : id = -1	
Floor Plan Imperial - Arch.rvt : Doors : Single-Flush : 36" x 84" - Mark 87 : id 194171	
Element deleted	Postpone
: (Deleted element) : id = -1	
Floor Plan Imperial - Arch.rvt : Doors : Single-Flush : 36" x 84" - Mark 88 : id 194202	
Element deleted	Postpone
: (Deleted element) : id = -1	
Floor Plan Imperial - Arch.rvt : Doors : Single-Flush : 36" x 84" - Mark 89 : id 194244	

6. Highlight the list.

Click in the Action column.
Select **Accept difference**.
Click **Apply**.

7. Expand the first deleted element.
Several walls have been deleted.

New/Unresolved	
Walls	
Check whether an Element exists	
Element deleted	Postpone
: (Deleted element) : id = -1	
Floor Plan Imperial - Arch.rvt : Walls : Basic Wall : CONCRETE AND OUTSULATION : id 140103	
Element deleted	Postpone
Element deleted	Postpone
Element deleted	Postpone
Element deleted	Postpone
Element deleted	Postpone
Element deleted	Postpone

8. Highlight the list.

Click in the Action column.
Select **Accept difference**.
Click **Apply**.

Nothing is left to be reviewed.
Click **OK.**

9. Verify that the **Level 1 Power Plan** floor plan is the active view.

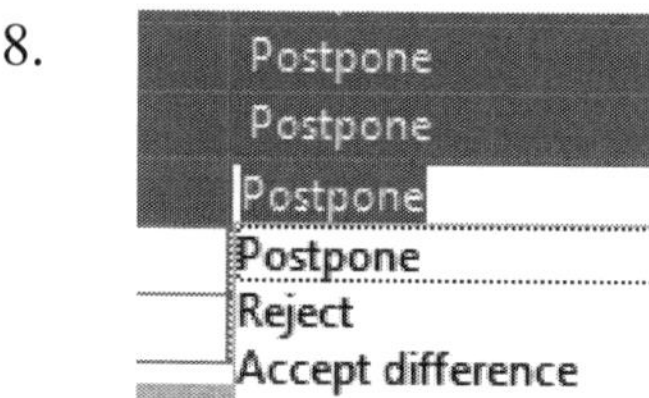

Zoom into the area between Grids 4-6 and 19-21.
There should be several rooms labeled in this area.

10. Activate the **Systems** ribbon.

Select the **Device→Electrical Fixture** tool.

11.

Using the Type Selector, verify that the **Duplex Receptacle – Standard** is active.

12.

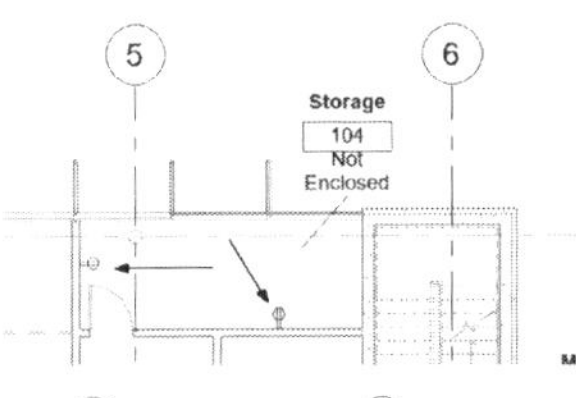

Place two receptacles in Rooms 104.

Use the SPACE BAR to rotate the receptacles as needed prior to placement.

13.

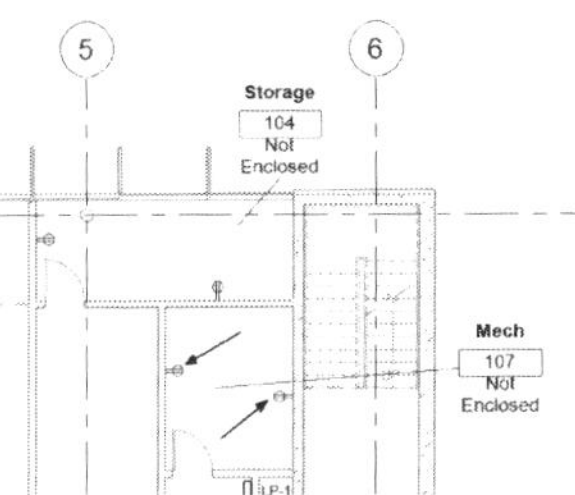

Place two receptacles in Rooms 107.

14.

Place two receptacles in Rooms 108.

Click **ESC** to exit the command.

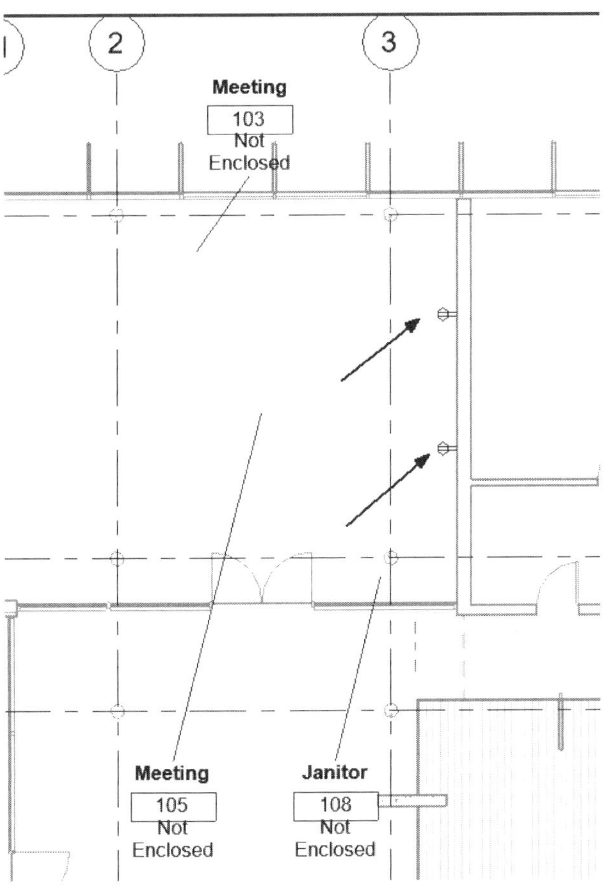

15.   Select one of the receptacles placed in Room 104.

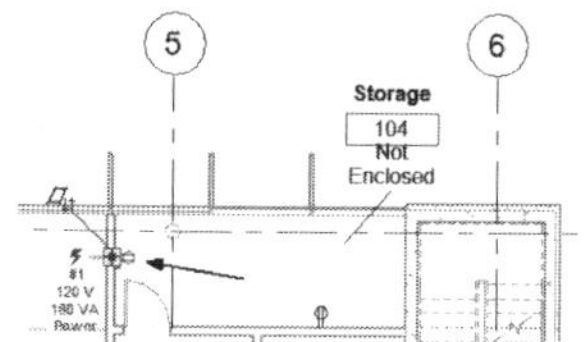

16.  Select the **Power** tool on the Create Systems panel on the ribbon.
This creates an electrical circuit.

17. 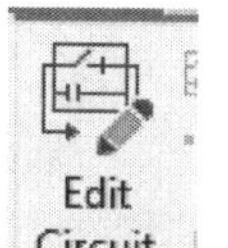 Select the **Edit Circuit** tool on the ribbon.

18.  Verify that **Add to Circuit** is enabled on the ribbon.

19. 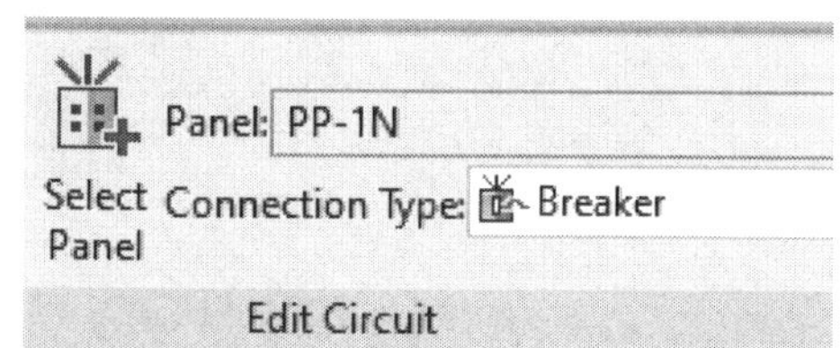   Assign the circuit to Panel: **PP-1N**.

20.  Select the remaining receptacles to be added.
On the Options bar verify that 6 elements have been selected.

21. 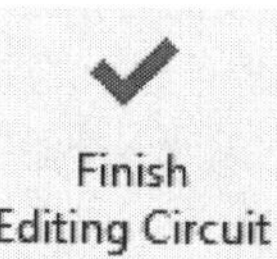 Select **Finish Editing Circuit** from the ribbon.

22. 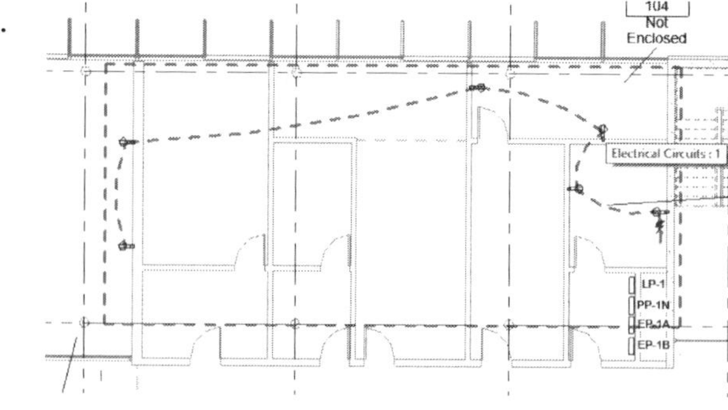 Hover the cursor over one of the power receptacles in Room 104.
Click the **TAB** key.
Dashed lines will appear to indicate the intended wiring for the new circuit.

23. 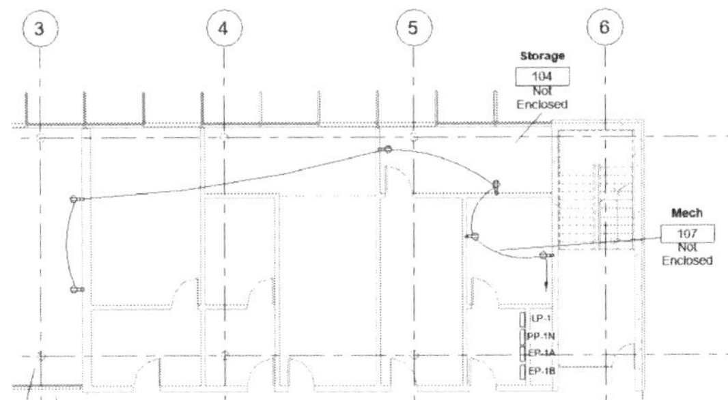 Select **Arc Wire** on the ribbon to add wiring to the circuit.

24. 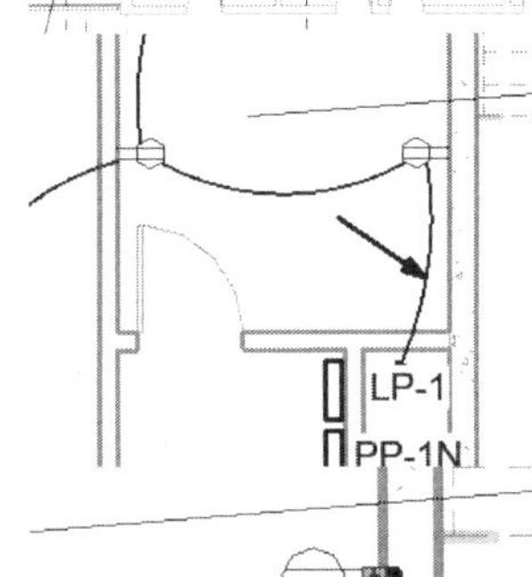 *Wiring is displayed between the receptacles and the panel.*
Note the home run symbol between the panel and one of the receptacles.

25. Select the wire which has the home run symbol.

26. 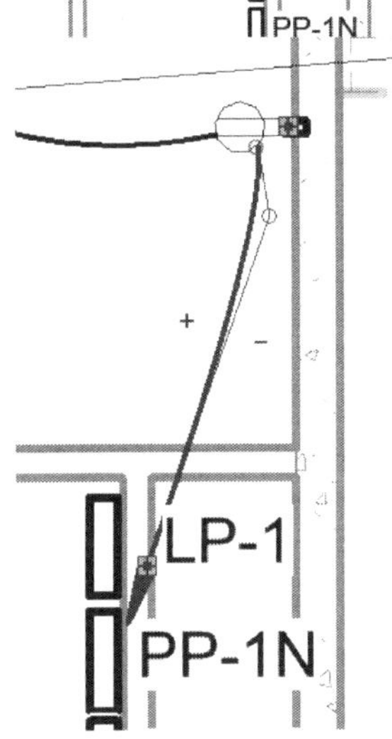 Use the grip to reposition the end of the wire above the assigned panel.

Left click in the window to release the selection.

27. 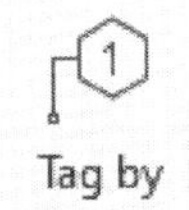 Activate the Annotate ribbon.
Select **Tag by Category**.

28. 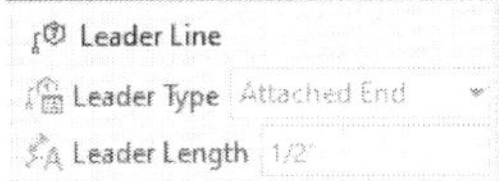 Verify that Leader is disabled on the ribbon.

29.   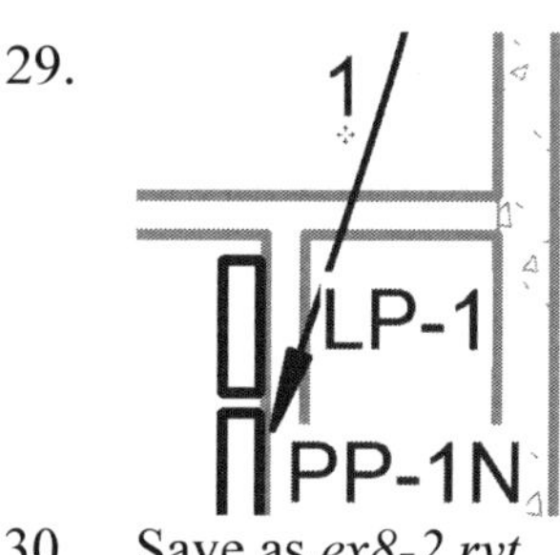 Left click on the home run wire in Room 107 to add a circuit number tag.

Adjust the circuit number tag location so it is easy to read.

30.   Save as *ex8-2.rvt*.

Guidelines for Monitoring Changes in Linked Files

- Use Copy and Monitor to monitor level lines, walls, doors, ceilings, and windows. This ensures that floor to floor heights remain coordinated as well as elements which are used to position electrical components.
- Use the Coordination Review tool to perform coordination reviews and generate reports of any changes made to the host or linked file(s). The reports ensure a paper trail of any changes made by team members and the decisions made regarding those changes.
- Use the Add Comment option in the Review dialog to add comments regarding any changes. These comments are visible to other team members and enhance communication.
- Reload the linked file periodically to check for any changes. Verify that you are using the latest version of the model prior to doing any major work on your host file.

Interference Checks

Interference checks detect overlapping geometry between elements of selected categories. Based on the selection made, the check scans the building to identify pairs of elements that conflict or interfere with each other. You can perform a check within a project or between linked projects.

Interference checks only apply to model elements, so they apply to any view where the model elements are located.

The check generates an interference report that alerts the user to the number of interferences in the model, which may result in construction errors. You can then review the conflicts and determine the best resolution for each conflict.

Interferences are not always visible in existing views. You may need to create new sections or levels to reveal the interference issue.

Guidelines for Checking and Fixing Interference Conditions

- Check for interference early in the design stage. Correcting conflicts is easier when there are fewer elements to evaluate.

- Select a limited number of elements or categories to check to reduce the processing time.

- Refresh an interference report after correcting any interference conditions and run the report a second time to ensure that all conflicts have been resolved.

- Generate an interference report to gather additional input from other team members when you need guidance resolving conflicts.

Exercise 8-3:
Interference Checking

Drawing Name: *interference_checking.rvt*
Estimated Time: 30 minutes

This exercise reinforces the following skills:

- Interference Check
- Resolving Conflicts

1. 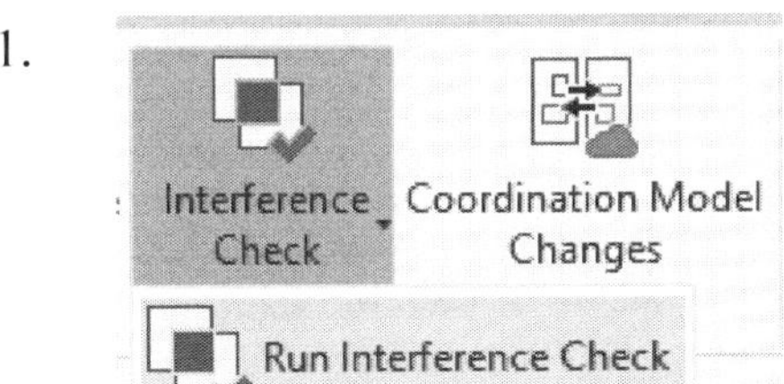 Select the **Collaborate** ribbon.
Select **Run Interference Check** from the ribbon.

2.

Select **Air Terminals, Ceilings, Floors**, and **Walls** from the left pane.

Categories from
Current Project

- ☑ Air Terminals
- ☑ Ceilings
- ☐ Curtain Panels
- ☐ Curtain Wall Mullions
- ☐ Doors
- ☐ Duct Fittings
- ☐ Ducts
- ☐ Electrical Equipment
- ☐ Electrical Fixtures
- ☐ Flex Ducts
- ☑ Floors

3.

Select **Electrical Equipment, Lighting Devices** and **Lighting Fixtures** from the right pane.
We are looking to see if any of the electrical systems have any conflicts.

Click **OK**.

- ☑ Electrical Equipment
- ☐ Electrical Fixtures
- ☐ Flex Ducts
- ☐ Floors
- ☐ Generic Models
- ☑ Lighting Devices
- ☑ Lighting Fixtures
- ☐ Mechanical Equipment

There are several conflicts being reported.

Group by: Category 1, Category ⌄

Message
⊟ Air Terminals
⊞ Lighting Fixtures
⊞ Lighting Fixtures
⊟ Ceilings
⊞ Lighting Fixtures

4.

⊟ Air Terminals
⊟ Lighting Fixtures
Air Terminals : Supply Diffuser - Rectangular Face Round Neck : 24x24 8 Neck - Mark 359 : id 728098
Lighting Fixtures : Recessed Parabolic Light : 2'x4'(2 Lamp) - 120V - Mark 636 : id 808190

Expand the first conflict under Air Terminals.

Highlight the Lighting Fixture.

Show

Select **Show** at the bottom of the dialog.
A view is displayed.
The lighting fixture is right on top of the air terminal.
Zoom out the view a little to get a better idea of the room.
Close the Interference Report dialog.

5.

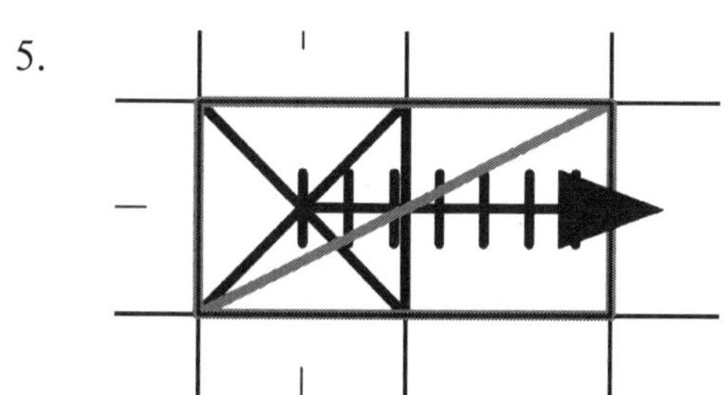

6. 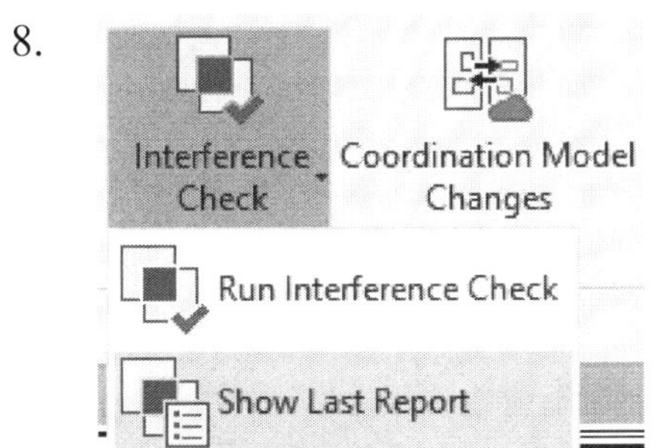 Move the air terminal above the lighting fixture.

7. You can see another conflict in the room to the right.

Move that air terminal as well.

8. Select the Collaborate ribbon.

Select **Interference Check →Show Last Report**.

Interference Check | Coordination Model Changes

Run Interference Check

Show Last Report

9. Refresh

The report still shows there is a conflict between the air terminals and the lighting fixtures.

Click **Refresh**.

The report clears the conflicts with the air terminals, but several conflicts remain.

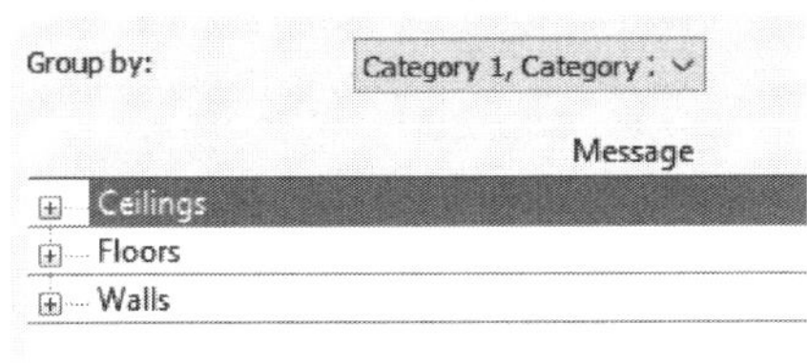

Group by: Category 1, Category : ∨

Message

⊞ Ceilings
⊞ Floors
⊞ Walls

10. 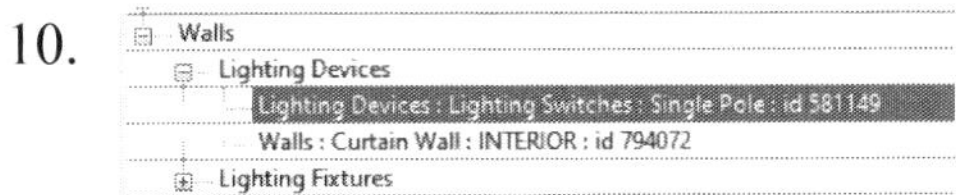 Highlight the first Lighting Device conflict under Walls.

⊟ Walls
⊟ Lighting Devices
Lighting Devices : Lighting Switches : Single Pole : id 581149
Walls : Curtain Wall : INTERIOR : id 794072
⊞ Lighting Fixtures

Show

Select **Show**.

11.

There is no open view that shows any of the highlighted elements. Searching through the closed views to find a good view could take a long time. Continue?

Click **OK** until you find a good view where you can see the conflict.

12.

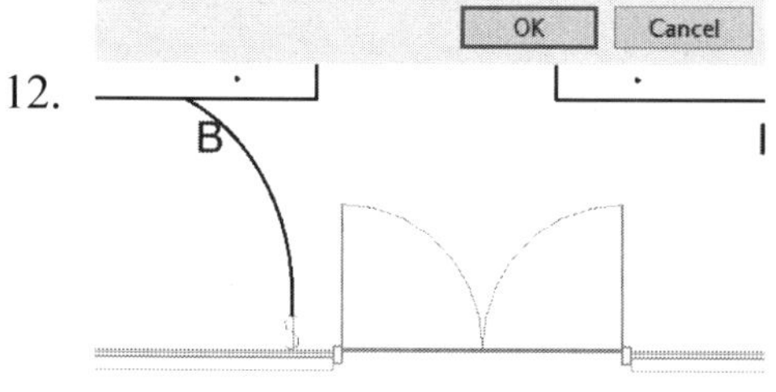

The Level 1 Lighting Plan floor plan opens to show the light switch mounted on the curtain wall is not a good location.
Close the Interference Check dialog.

13.

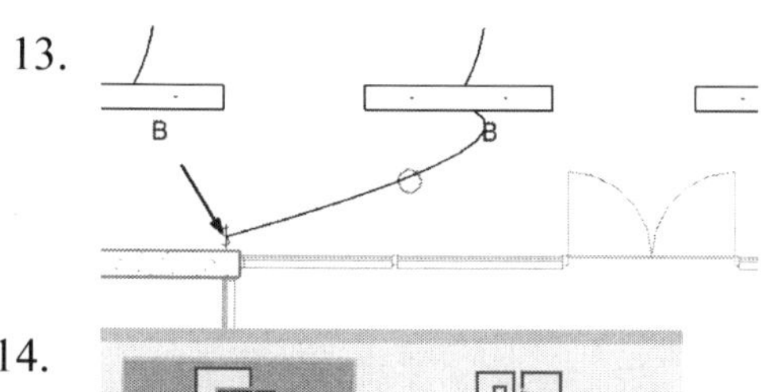

Move the switch to the wall adjacent to the curtain wall.

Use Pick New on the ribbon to select a new host for the switch.

14.

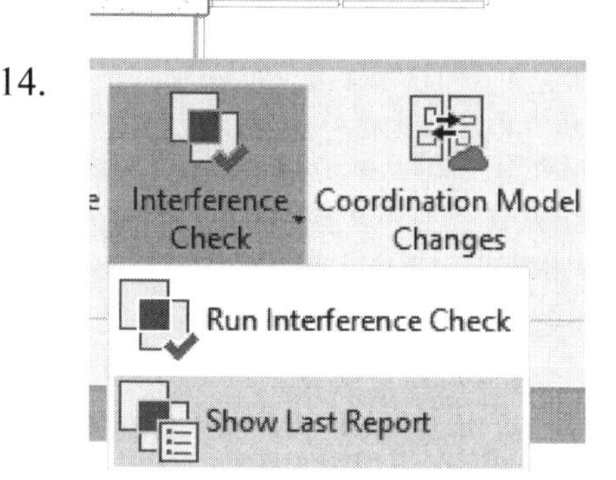

Select **Show Last Report**.

15.

The report still shows there is a conflict between the air terminals and the lighting fixtures.

Click **Refresh**.

16.

The report clears the first conflict with a wall.
Highlight the remaining Lighting Fixture.

Click **Show**.

17.

The Level 2 Ceiling plan opens.

18. 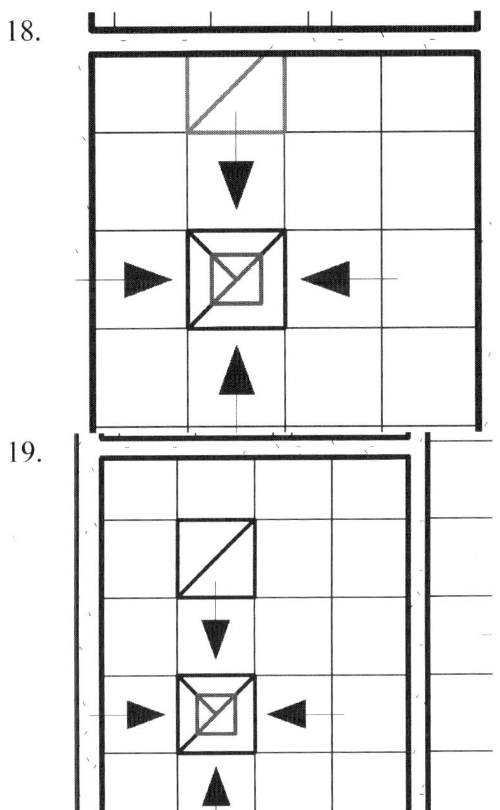

It looks like the lighting fixture doesn't fit properly on the ceiling.
Close the Interference Check dialog.

19. Use the MOVE tool to shift the air terminal down to the center of the ceiling.
Use the MOVE tool to shift the lighting fixture down.

20. On the Collaborate ribbon:
Select **Show Last Report**.

21. *The report still shows there is a conflict between the walls and the lighting fixtures.*

Click **Refresh**.

22. 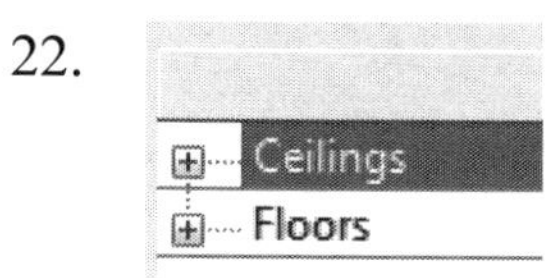   The report clears the wall interference.
Remaining are all the conflicts with the ceilings and floors. These can be fixed during a lab period.

23.   Save as *ex8-3.rvt*.

Load Classifications

Load classification in Revit segments your loads into different classifications. These classifications will be put on your panel schedules and are useful when filling out utility letters at the end of a project. The utility company uses this information to size the transformer at the service entrance. Typically, this information takes a long time to collect; you need to add up all the receptacle loads, lighting loads, largest motor, as well as heating and cooling loads. When done throughout the course of the project, this information is simple to provide.

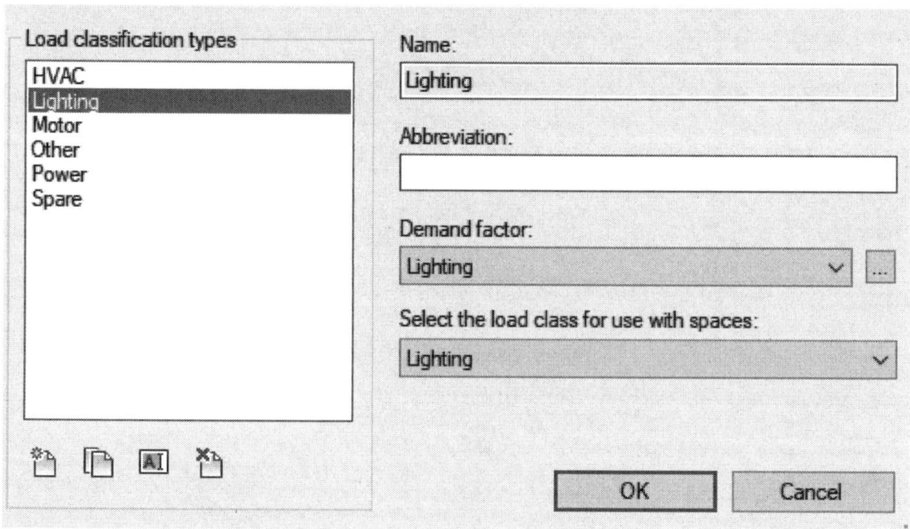

When placing equipment, it is important to make sure that each load is connected to the right classification. Not doing this important step could result in over-sized panels, transformers, and switchboards, which could add tens if not hundreds of thousands of dollars to the electrical costs of the project.

Load classifications also have specific demand factors. Receptacles have a demand factor of 100% for the first 10 kVA then 50% for every VA after. Hospital Lighting has a demand factor of 40% for the first 50 kVA and 20% for every VA after. Make sure you enter the correct demand factor!

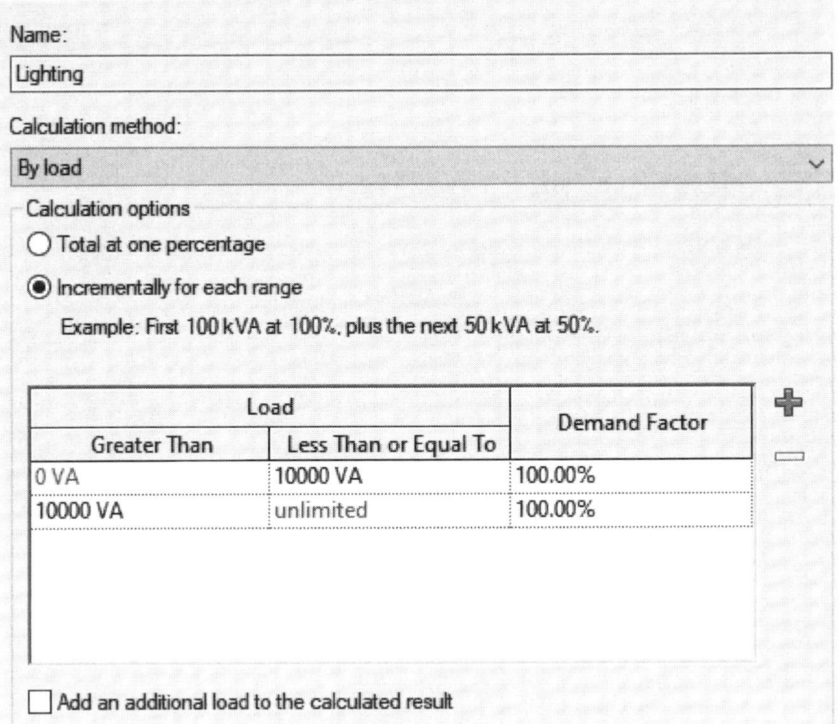

To set your load classifications, you need to:

1. Click on the family.
2. Go to edit type.
3. Click on load classification.
4. There will be a list on the right of the different load classifications in the model.
5. These classifications will be what appears on your panel schedules.
6. Make sure that you have the right demand factor for each classification type; this sets connected vs. demand.
7. Repeat for each family type – lights, receptacles, motor connections, heating and cooling connections.

Exercise 8-4:

Creating Load Classifications

Drawing Name: *load_classifications.rvt*
Estimated Time: 30 minutes

This exercise reinforces the following skills:

- Load Classifications
- Demand Factors
- Families

1. Open the **1 – Lighting** floor plan view.

2. Type **ES** to open **Electrical Settings**.
   Highlight **Load Calculations** in the left panel.
   Click on **Load Classifications**.

3. 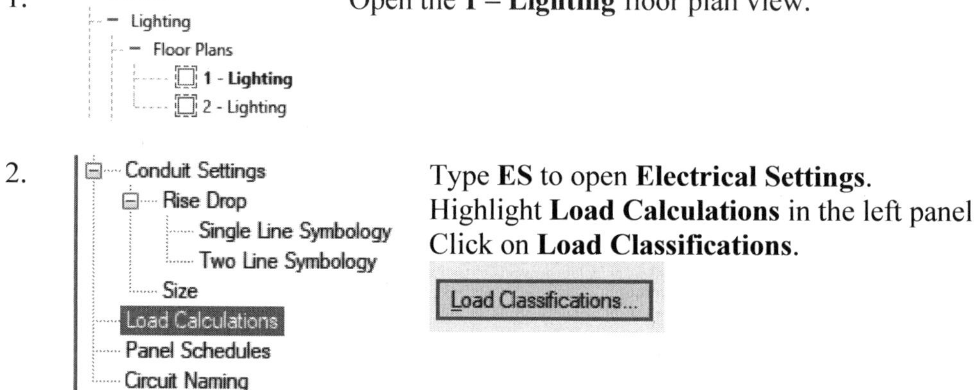
Select the **New** tool.

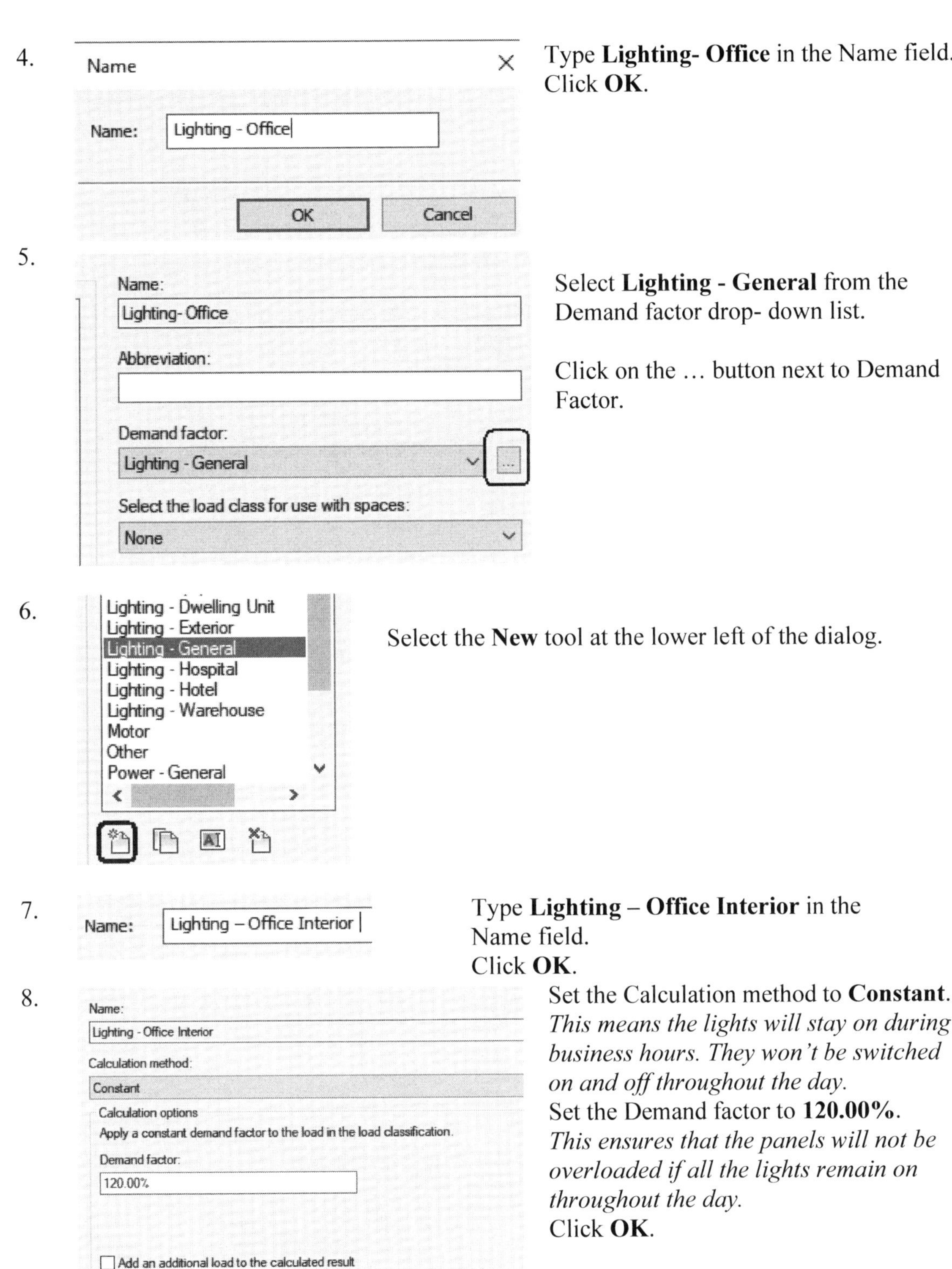

4. Type **Lighting- Office** in the Name field.
Click **OK**.

5. Select **Lighting - General** from the Demand factor drop- down list.

Click on the ... button next to Demand Factor.

6. Select the **New** tool at the lower left of the dialog.

7. Type **Lighting – Office Interior** in the Name field.
Click **OK**.

8. Set the Calculation method to **Constant**. *This means the lights will stay on during business hours. They won't be switched on and off throughout the day.*
Set the Demand factor to **120.00%**. *This ensures that the panels will not be overloaded if all the lights remain on throughout the day.*
Click **OK**.

9. 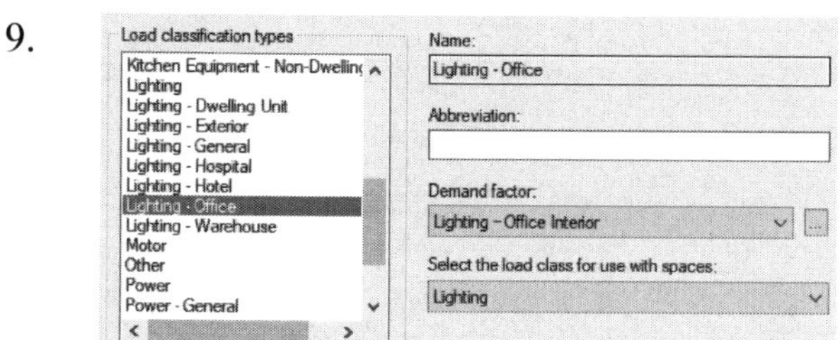

Assign the **Lighting – Office** load classification to use the **Lighting – Office Interior** Demand factor.
Set the load class for use with spaces to **Lighting**.

10. 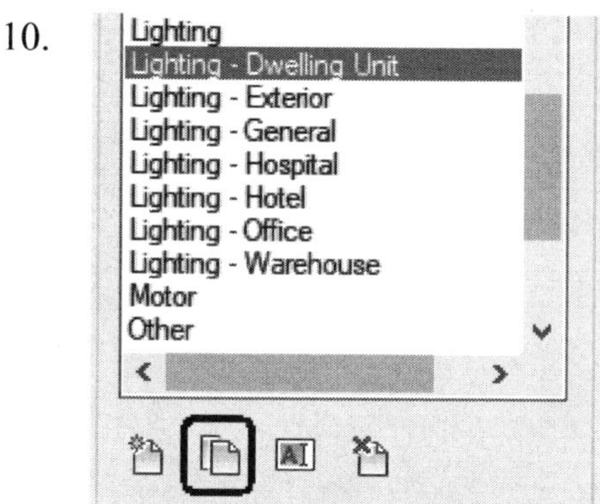

Highlight the **Lighting – Dwelling Unit**.
Select the **Duplicate** tool.

11. 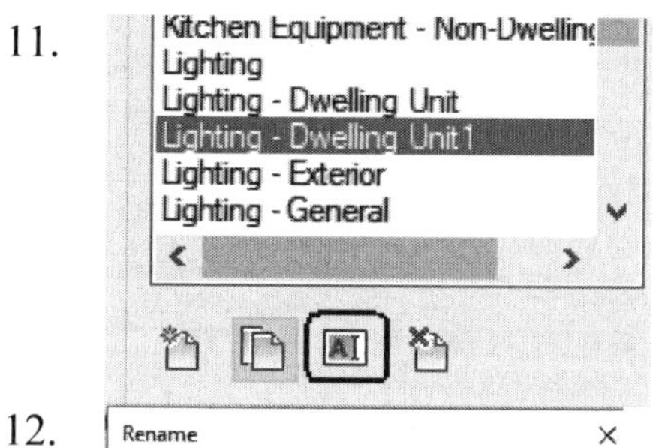

Highlight the copied type.
Select **Rename** or click **F2**.

12. 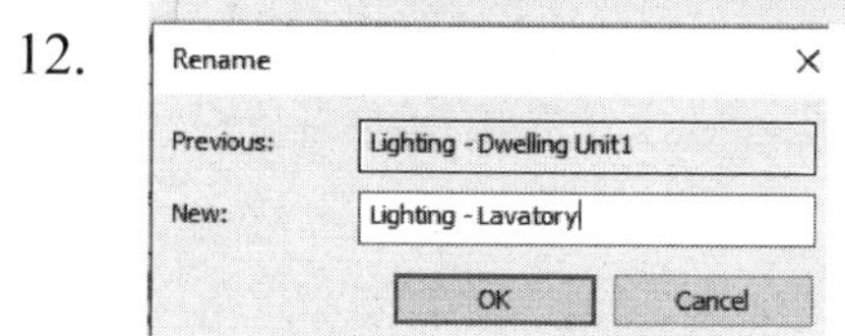

Type **Lighting - Lavatory** in the New Name field.
Click **OK**.

13. 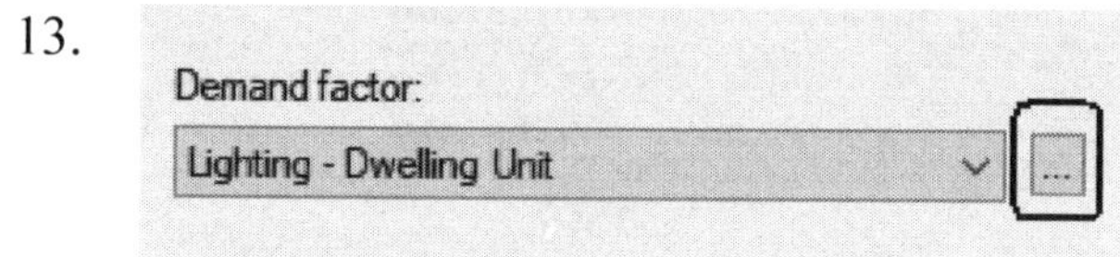

Click on the … button next to Demand Factor.

14.

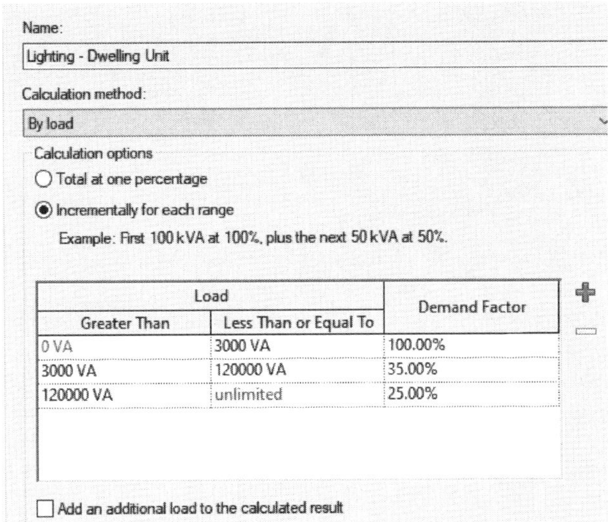

Because lights in homes are turned on and off, the calculation method used is different.
Click **OK**.

15.

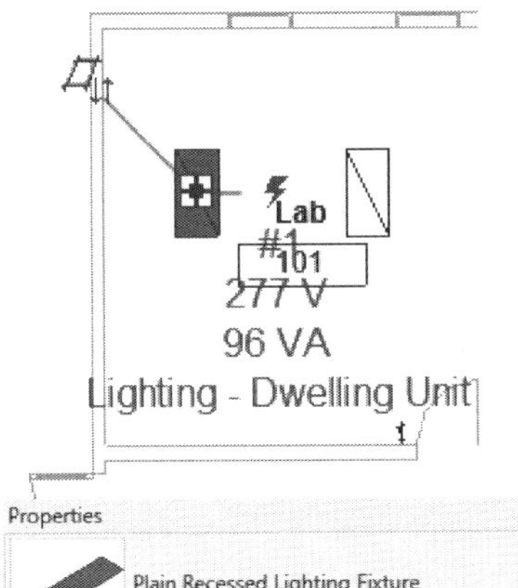

Select the load class for use with spaces.
Set this to **Lighting**.
Click **OK**.

16. Click **OK** to close the dialog.

17.

Select one of the lighting fixtures in **Lab-101**.

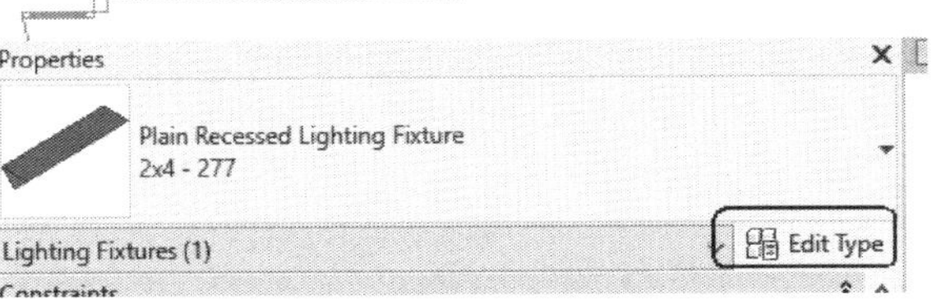

18.

Select **Edit Type** on the Properties palette.

19.

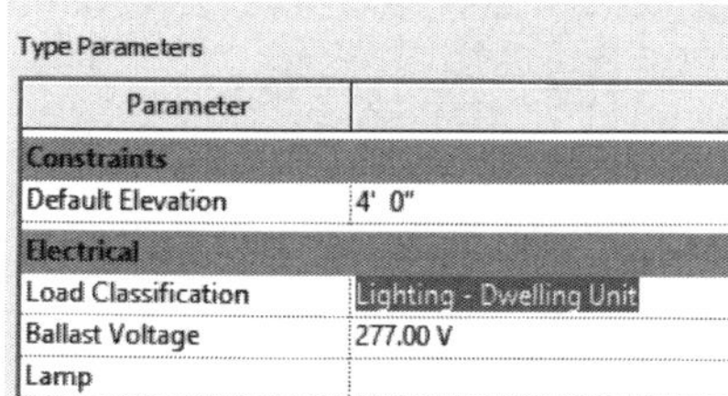

Notice that the current load classification is set to Lighting – Dwelling Unit. This would not be correct, because most people turn the lights in their homes on or off, depending on if they are using the room.

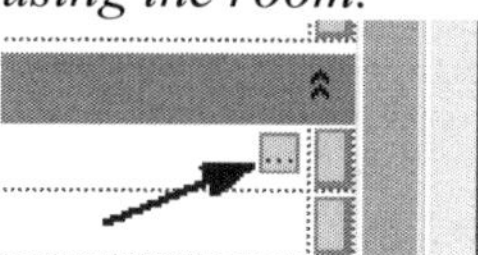

Click on the … button that appears when you left click in that field.

20.

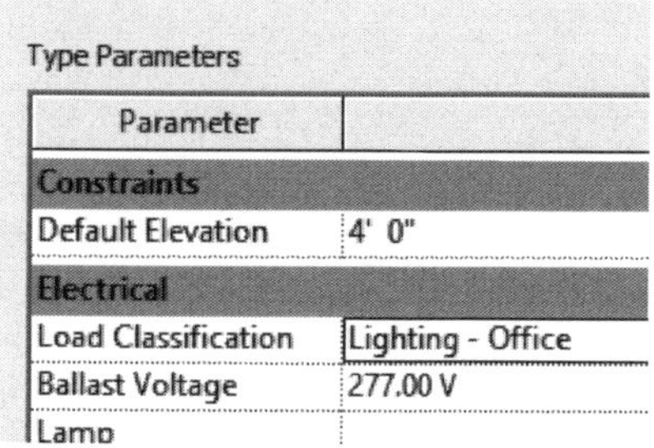

Select the **Lighting – Office** load classification you just created.

Click **OK**.

21.

It updates in the Properties palette.
Click **OK**.

Type Parameters	
Parameter	
Constraints	
Default Elevation	4' 0"
Electrical	
Load Classification	Lighting - Office
Ballast Voltage	277.00 V
Lamp	

22.

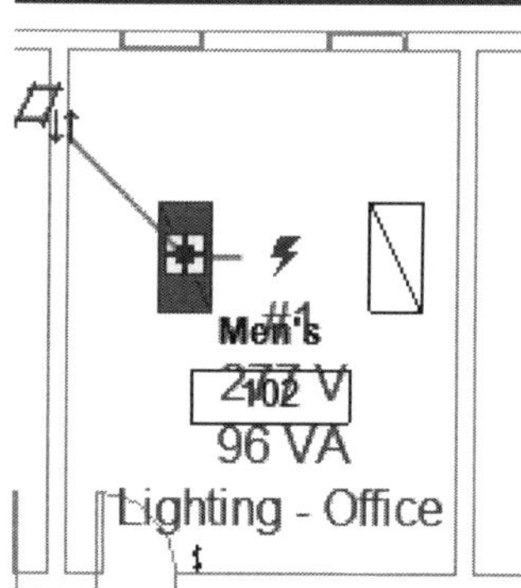

Because this was a type parameter that was changed, it affects all lights that are the same type.
Select a light fixture in the Men's lavatory.

23.

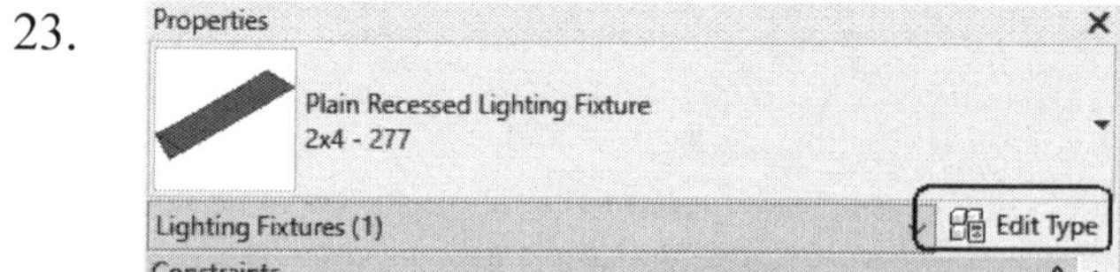

Select **Edit Type** on the Properties palette.

24. 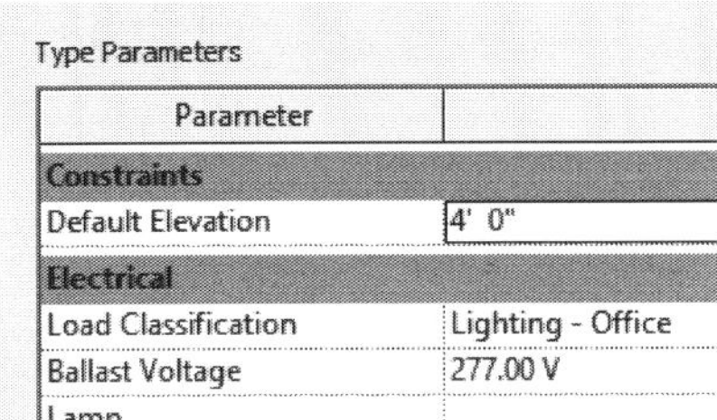

Notice it is using the correct load classification because it is the same type of fixture as it used in Lab - 101.

Some offices have the lights in the bathrooms turn off when not in use. This means you would have to create a different light fixture family using a different load classification.

Click **OK** to close the Type Properties dialog.

25. Click **Duplicate**.

26. Change the name to 2x4 – 277V – Lavatory Use. Click **OK**.

27. Click on the **...** button that appears when you left click in the Load Classification field.

28. Change the Load Classification to **Lighting – Lavatory**.

Click **OK**.
Click **OK** to close the Type Properties dialog.

29. Hold down the CTL key and select the lighting fixtures in the Men's and Women's Lavatories.

30. Use the Type Selector to assign the light fixtures to the Lavatory Use type.

Hint: You can select one of the lavatory light fixtures, right click and select all instances visible in the view to verify that all the light fixtures as using the correct family type.

31. 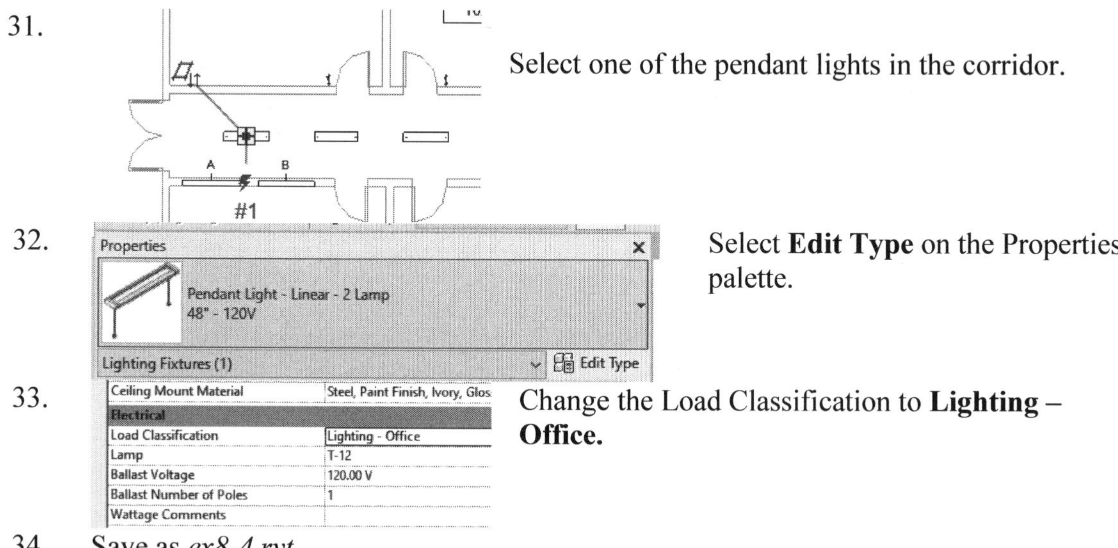   Select one of the pendant lights in the corridor.

32.   Select **Edit Type** on the Properties palette.

33.   Change the Load Classification to **Lighting – Office.**

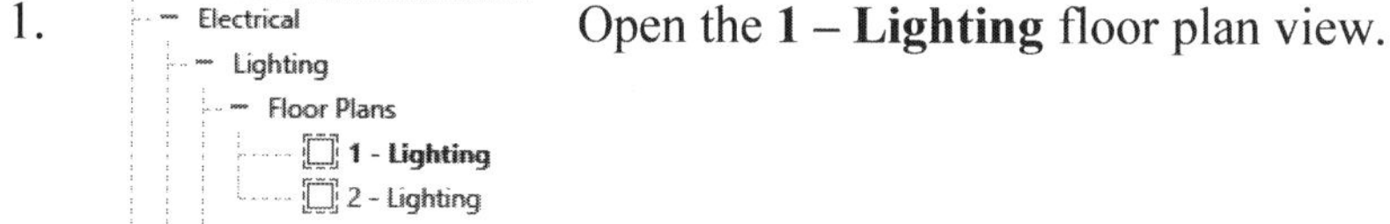

34.   Save as *ex8-4.rvt*.

Exercise 8-5:

Assigning Load Names to a Circuit

Drawing Name: *load_names.rvt*
Estimated Time: 10 minutes

This exercise reinforces the following skills:

- ❑   Load Classifications
- ❑   Load names
- ❑   Circuits

1.   Open the **1 – Lighting** floor plan view.

2.

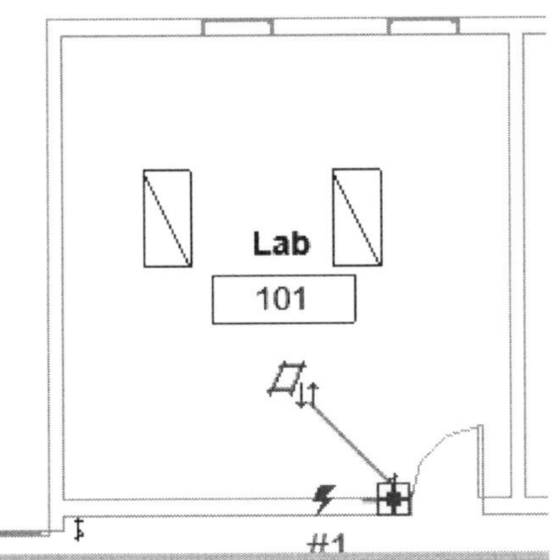

Select the switch in Lab 101.

3. | Modify | Lighting Devices | Switch Systems | Electrical Circuits |

Select the **Electrical Circuits** tab on the ribbon.

4.

Circuit: 2	
Electrical Engineering	
Schedule Circuit Notes	
Electrical - Loads	
Circuit Number	2
Connection Type	Breaker
Load Name	Lighting - Office
Panel	A
System Type	Power

Look in the Properties panel.

*Note the Load Name is set to **Other**.*
Type the Load Name **Lighting – Office**.
Click **ENTER** and Apply to ensure the new name is applied.

Note that the circuit is on Panel A.

Click ESC to release the selection.

5.

Select the switch in Men's 102.

6. | Modify | Lighting Devices | Switch Systems | Electrical Circuits |

Select the **Electrical Circuits** tab on the ribbon.

7.

Circuit: 4	
Electrical Engineering	
Schedule Circuit Notes	
Electrical - Loads	
Circuit Number	4
Connection Type	Breaker
Load Name	Lighting - Lavatory
Panel	A
System Type	Power

*Note the Load Name is set to **Other**.*
Select **Lighting – Lavatory** from the drop-down list to change the Load Name.

Note that the circuit is on Panel A.

Click ESC to release the selection.

8.

Circuit: 2

Electrical Engineering

| Schedule Circuit Notes | |

Electrical - Loads

Circuit Number	2
Connection Type	Breaker
Load Name	Lighting - Office
Panel	A
System Type	Power

Select each switch in the building and assign it to the correct load name.
All the circuits should be assigned to Lighting – Office except for the switches in the lavatories.

Assign Rooms 101 through Rooms 104 to Panel A.

Assign Rooms 106 through Rooms 108 to Panel B. Assign the corridor to Panel B.

Each circuit should be assigned to a panel and a load name.

9.   Save as *ex8-5.rvt*.

Shared Parameters

Shared parameters are parameter definitions that can be used in multiple families or projects.

Shared parameters are definitions of parameters that you can add to families or projects. Shared parameter definitions are stored in a text file independent of any family file or Revit project; this allows you to access the file from different families or projects. The shared parameter is a *definition* of a container for information that can be used in multiple families or projects. The *information* defined in one family or project using the shared parameter is not automatically applied to another family or project using the same shared parameter.

In order for information in a parameter to be used in a tag, it must be a shared parameter. Shared parameters are also useful when you want to create a schedule that displays various family categories; without a shared parameter, you cannot do this. If you create a shared parameter and add it to the desired family categories, you can then create a schedule with these categories. This is called creating a multi-category schedule in Revit.

Most companies will create a single text file which contains all the shared parameters used in projects. This file is then placed on the server and distributed to the different team members so they can use this file and not have to create their own individual shared parameters file. The "shared" in shared parameters means the parameters are shared across families and projects, not that the parameters are shared between team members.

The shared parameters file cannot be easily edited, and it is not recommended for editing. Revit automatically adds formatting and spacing to the txt file when it is created. If you open the file in Word, or even in Notepad, you can corrupt the file. Once you define a parameter, it is not easily modified. If you need to modify a parameter, you will most likely have to delete it and create a new one.

I recommend that companies review the column headers they use in schedules and any columns which are not covered by an existing parameter is a candidate to be used as a shared parameter.

Exercise 8-6:

Creating a Shared Parameter

Drawing Name: *shared_parameters.rvt*
Estimated Time: 15 minutes

This exercise reinforces the following skills:

❑ Shared Parameters

1. Open the **1 – Lighting** floor plan view.

2. Go to the **Manage** ribbon.

   Select **Shared Parameters**.

3. Select **Create.**
   Browse to the folder where you want to save your file.

4. 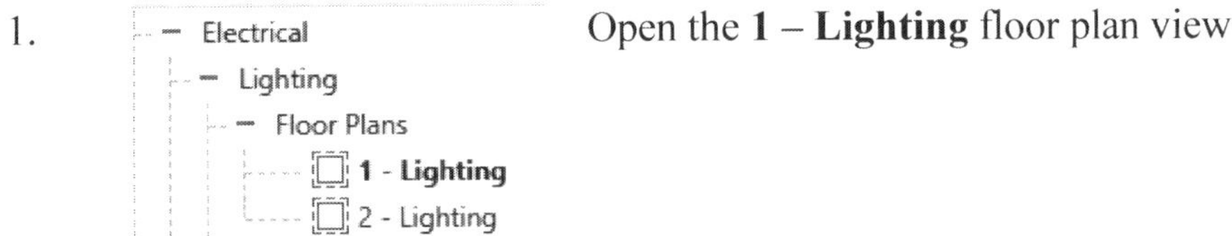

   Type *jatc_parameters.txt* for the file name.

   Click **Save**.

5. 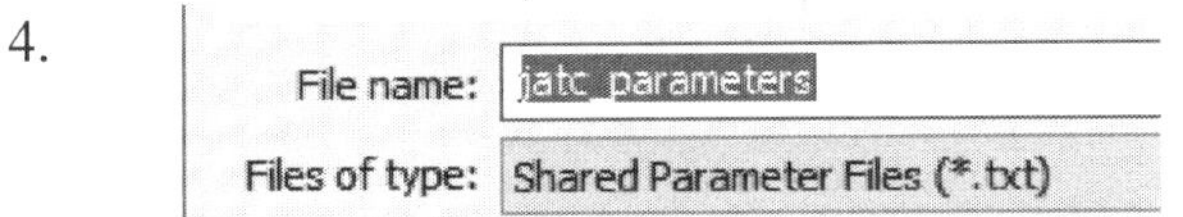

   Select **New** under Groups.

   Shared parameters are organized under Groups to make it easier for users to locate the desired parameters.

6.

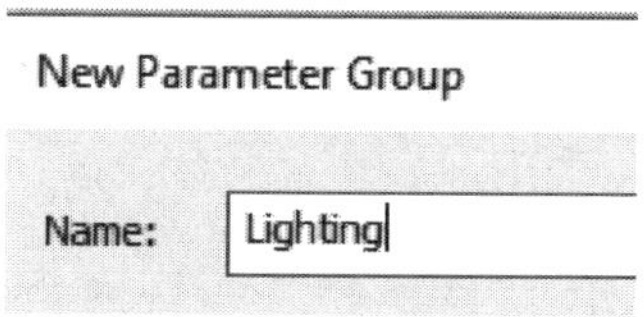

New Parameter Group

Name: Lighting

Type **Lighting** in the Name field.

Click **OK**.

7.

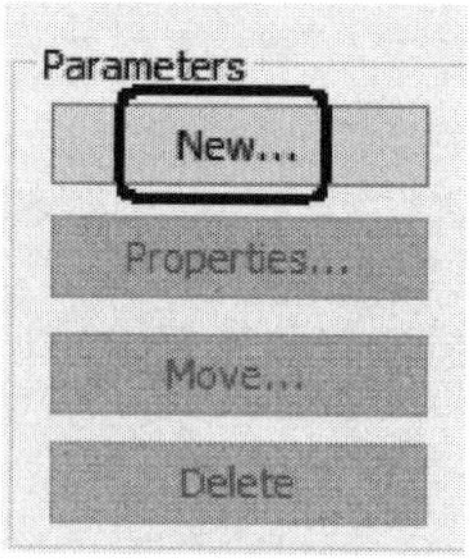

Parameters

New...

Properties...

Move...

Delete

Click **New** under Parameters.

The new parameter will be placed in the Lighting parameter group.

8.

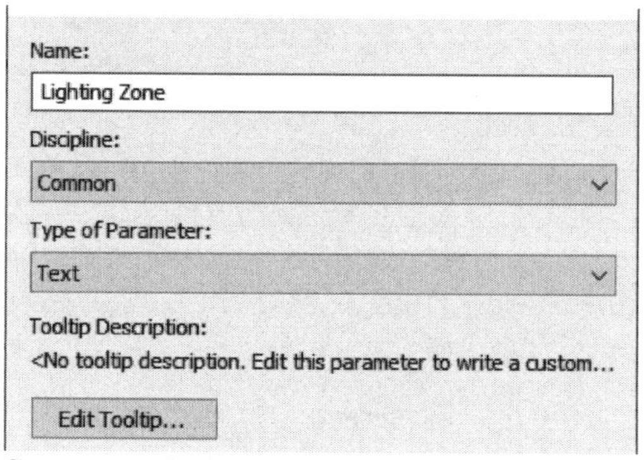

Name:

Lighting Zone

Discipline:

Common

Type of Parameter:

Text

Tooltip Description:

<No tooltip description. Edit this parameter to write a custom...

Edit Tooltip...

Type **Lighting Zone** in the Name field.

Set the Discipline to **Common**.

Set the Type of Parameter to **Text**.

Click **OK**.

Click **OK** to close the dialog.

Save as *ex8-6.rvt*.

Exercise 8-7:

Add a Shared Parameter to a Family

Drawing Name: *shared_parameters.rvt*
Estimated Time: 15 minutes

This exercise reinforces the following skills:

- Shared Parameters
- Families

1. 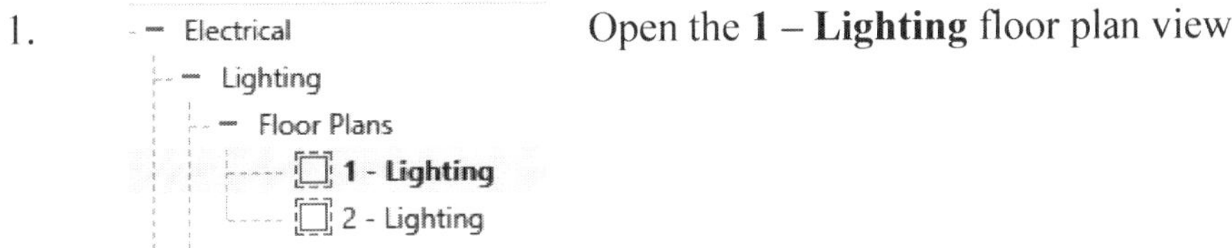

Open the **1 – Lighting** floor plan view.

2. 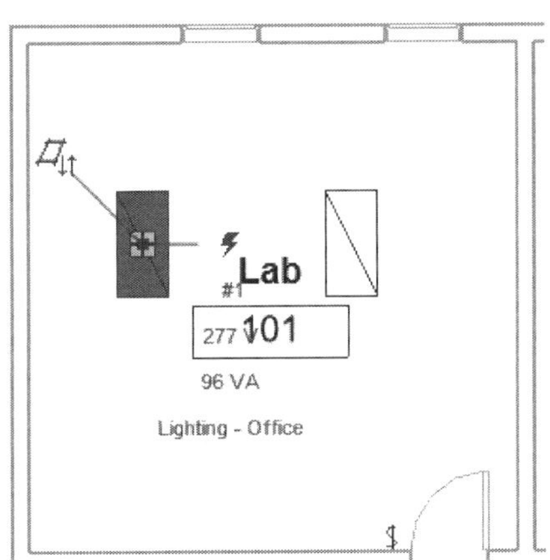

Select the light fixture in Lab 101.

Select **Edit Family** from the ribbon.

3. 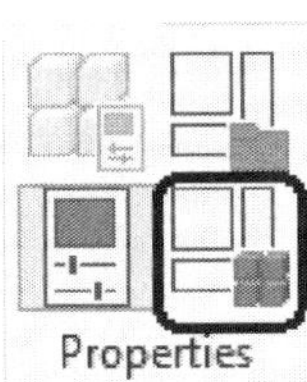

Select **Family Types** on the ribbon.

4.   

This lighting fixture has several types already defined.

We want to add the shared parameter to the 2x4 -277 and the 2x4-277 Lavatory types.

Select the **2x4 – 277** type name from the drop-down list.

5.   Select **New** parameter.

6.   Enable **Shared parameter**.
Click on **Select**.

7.   Switch to the **Lighting Parameter** group.

Highlight **Lighting Zone**.

Click **OK**.

8.   Enable **Instance**.

Group the parameter under **Electrical-Lighting**.

The Discipline and Type of parameter are filled in based on how the shared parameter was defined.

Click **OK**.

9. 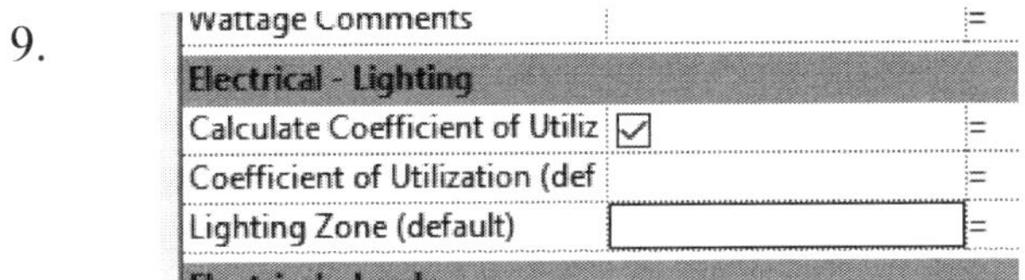 The Lighting Zone parameter appears under the Electrical category.

Because it is an instance parameter, users may wish to fill in a default value.

The parameter is now available to be assigned and used in schedules.

Click **OK**.

10. 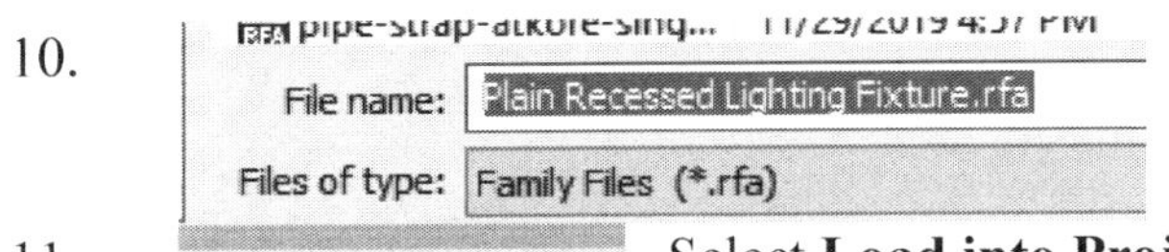 Save the family to your exercise folder.

11. Select **Load into Project and Close**.

12. Select **Overwrite the existing version and its parameter values**.

13. Save as *ex8-7.rvt*.

Switch Legs & Lighting Zones

Adding a switch leg to light fixtures allows you to easily create and change lighting zones within a project. Once a lighting control zone has been established and light fixtures are tied to a specific switch, changing the name of the control zone or adding and removing fixtures becomes as simple as editing a circuit. This allows for easy manipulation of zones, labeling and adding of zones. Here's how you add switch legs:

1. Select the fixtures that you want to be switched together.
2. Add the switch to the switch system.
3. You can now edit the switch system, either adding or removing lights from the system.
4. Select the switch you want to control those lights.
5. In that switch under the instance property of 'Switch ID' enter the lowercase letter that you want to call that switch group.
6. Tag the switch and fixtures with their switch ID.

To change the display of switch legs, use the same workflow that was used to create conduit types.

1. Create a wire type for switch legs.
2. Assign a description for the switch leg wires.
3. Create a filter for the switch leg description.
4. Assign the filter to a view.
5. Use overrides to change the display of the switch leg wires.

Exercise 8-8:

Assigning Lighting Zones to Light Fixtures

Drawing Name: *lighting zones.rvt*
Estimated Time: 10 minutes

This exercise reinforces the following skills:

- ❑ Shared Parameters
- ❑ Families

1. 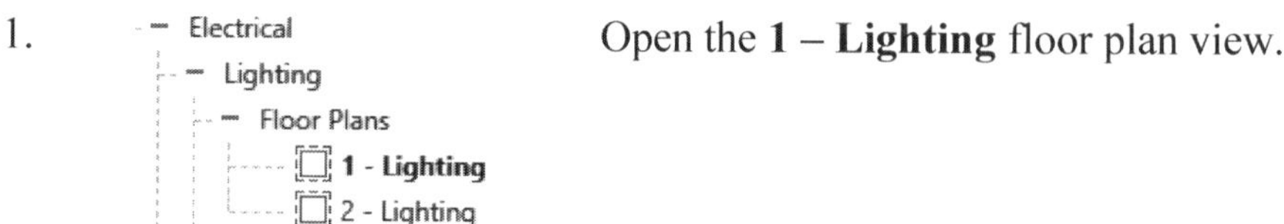

Open the **1 – Lighting** floor plan view.

2.

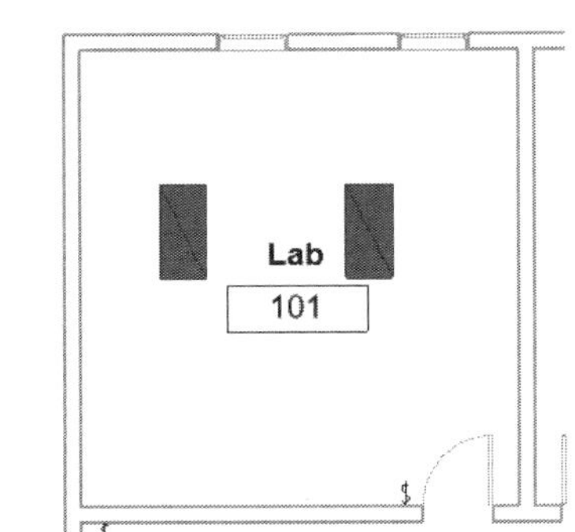

Hold down the CTL key.
Select the Lighting fixtures in Lab -101.

3.

Lighting Fixtures (2)

Constraints	
Schedule Level	Level 1
Elevation from Level	8' 0"
Host	Linked Revit Model : S
Offset from Host	0' 0"
Electrical	
Lighting Zone	Zone 1

In the Properties palette:
Type **Zone 1** for the lighting zone.

4.

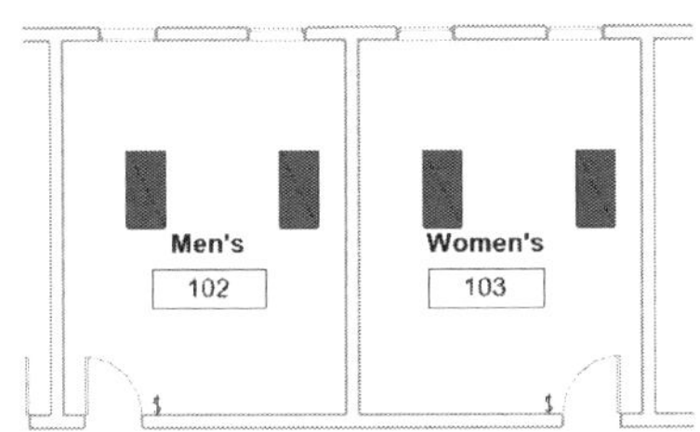

Hold down the CTL key.

Select the lighting fixtures in the two lavatories.

5.

Offset from Host	0' 0"
Electrical	
Lighting Zone	Zone 2
Electrical - Lighting	

In the Properties palette:
Type **Zone 2** for the lighting zone.

6.

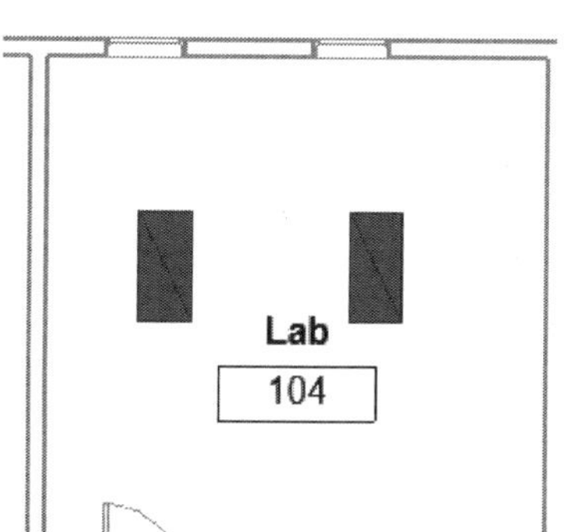

Hold down the CTL key.

Select the Lighting fixtures in Lab -104.

7.

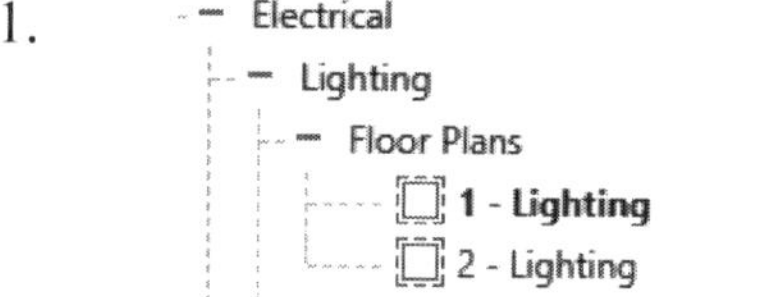

In the Properties palette:
Type **Zone 3** for the lighting zone.

8. Save as *ex8-7.rvt*.

Exercise 8-9:

Creating a Custom Lighting Fixture Tag

Drawing Name: *lighting_fixture tag.rvt*
Estimated Time: 25 minutes

This exercise reinforces the following skills:

- ❑ Lighting Fixture Tags
- ❑ Shared parameters
- ❑ Schedules

1.

```
- Electrical
  - Lighting
    - Floor Plans
        1 - Lighting
        2 - Lighting
```

Open the **1 – Lighting** floor plan view.

2.

Name	Status
+ Add ▾ ⟳ Reload ▾ ⬆ Unload 🗑 Remove	
∨ Revit (1)	
Simple-Building-Arch.rvt	✓

Go to the Insert ribbon.

Use **Manage Links** to Reload From your exercise folder to reload *Simple-Building-Arch.rvt*.

3. Open the View ribbon.

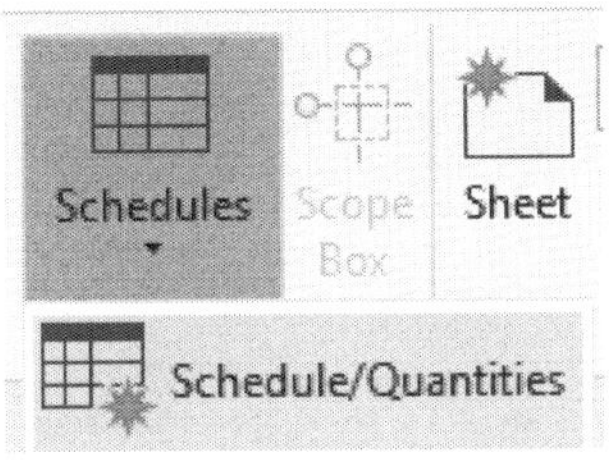

Select **Schedule/Quantities**.

4. Highlight **Lighting Fixtures**.

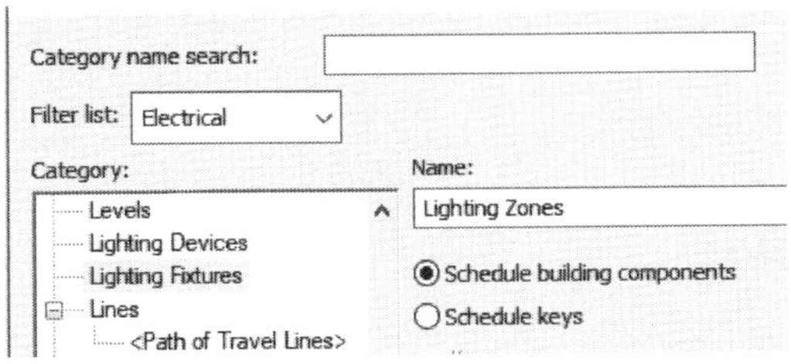

Change the Name to **Lighting Zones**.

Click **OK**.

5. Add the following fields:
- Lighting Zone
- Family and Type
- Count

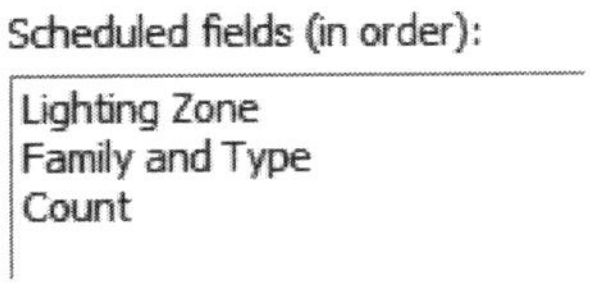

6. Select the **Sorting/Grouping** tab.
Sort by: **Lighting Zone**.
Enable **Footer:**
Select **Title and totals**.
Enable **Itemize every instance**.

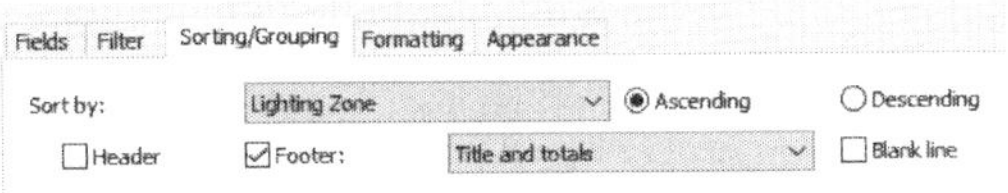

7. Select the **Formatting** tab.
Highlight **Count**.
Change the Heading to **Qty**.
Select **Calculate totals**.

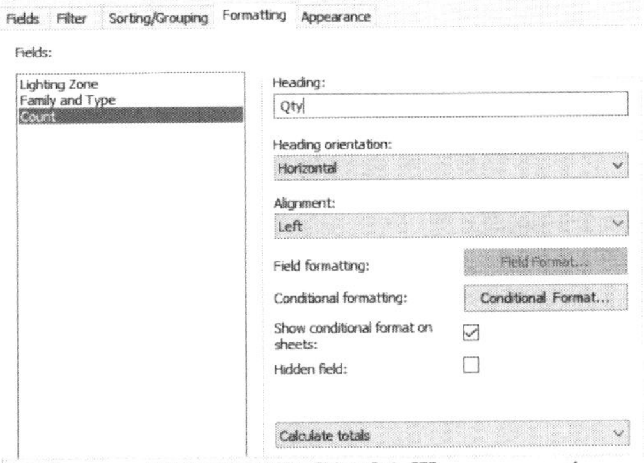

Click **OK**.

8. Some of the fixtures don't have a Lighting Zone assigned.

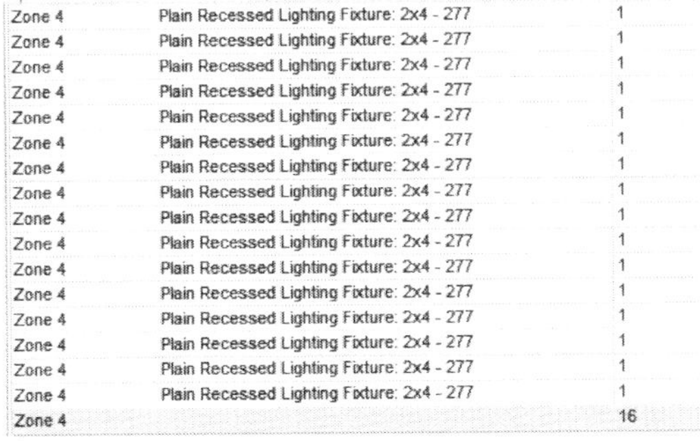

Assign the unassigned Plain Recessed Lighting Fixtures to **Zone 4**.

9.

Zone 5	Pendant Light - Linear - 2 Lamp: 48" - 120V	1
Zone 5	Pendant Light - Linear - 2 Lamp: 48" - 120V	1
Zone 5	Pendant Light - Linear - 2 Lamp: 48" - 120V	1
Zone 5	Pendant Light - Linear - 2 Lamp: 48" - 120V	1
Zone 5	Pendant Light - Linear - 2 Lamp: 48" - 120V	1
Zone 5	Pendant Light - Linear - 2 Lamp: 48" - 120V	1
Zone 5	Pendant Light - Linear - 2 Lamp: 48" - 120V	1
Zone 5	Pendant Light - Linear - 2 Lamp: 48" - 120V	1
Zone 5		8

Assign the Pendant Lights to **Zone 5**.

10.

Switch to the **Annotate** ribbon.

Select **Tag All**.

11.

Enable **Lighting Fixture Tags**.

Select **Lighting Fixture Tag – Boxed**.

12.

Disable **Leader**.

Click **OK**.

13.

Select one of the tags.

Right click and select **Edit Family** or select **Edit Family** from the ribbon.

14.

Select the text.

Select **Edit** next to Label in the Properties palette.

15.

Highlight the **Type Mark** parameter name.

Select the **Remove** button to remove the parameter.

16.

Select **New parameter**.

17.

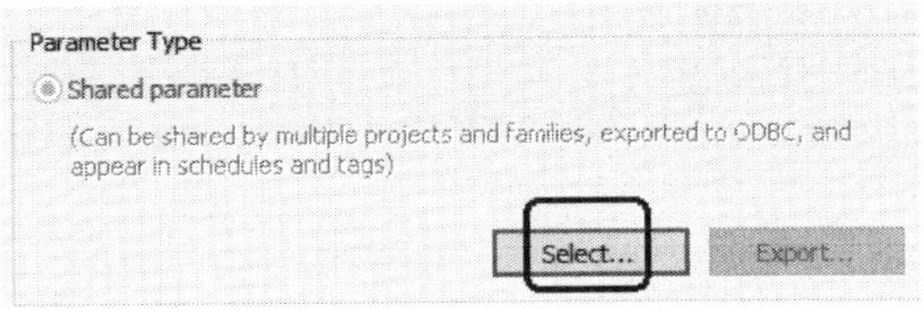

Click **Select.**

18.

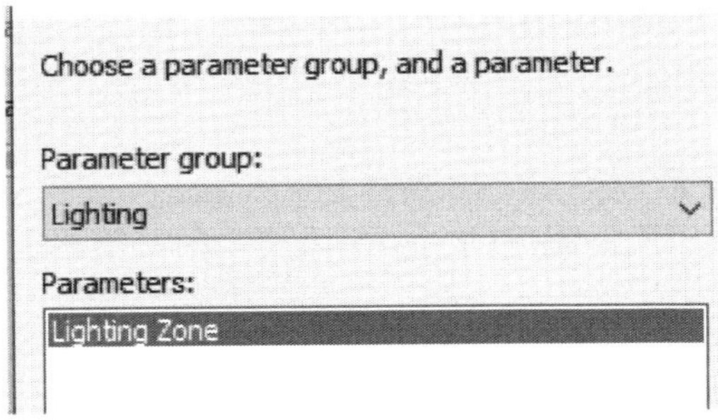

Choose a parameter group, and a parameter.

Parameter group:

Lighting

Parameters:

Lighting Zone

Highlight the **Lighting Zone** parameter.

Click **OK.**

19.

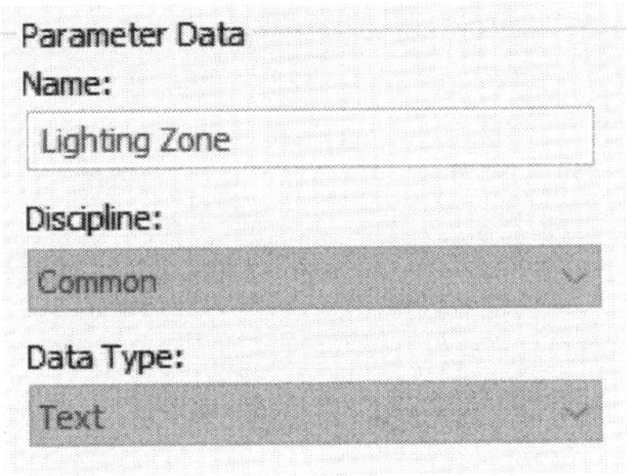

Parameter Data

Name:

Lighting Zone

Discipline:

Common

Data Type:

Text

Click **OK.**

20.

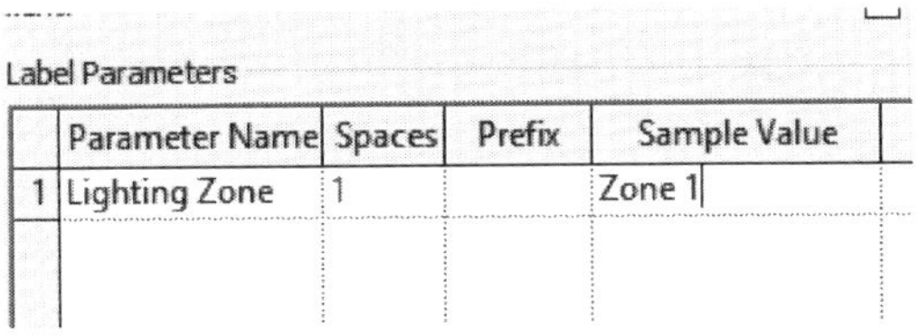

Label Parameters

	Parameter Name	Spaces	Prefix	Sample Value
1	Lighting Zone	1		Zone 1

Highlight **Lighting Zone** and add it to the Label Parameters.

Type **Zone 1** in the Sample Value column.

Click **OK.**

21.

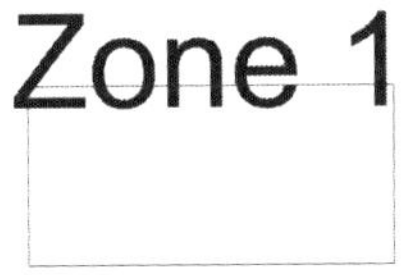

Zone 1

Expand the text box, so it is all one line.

22.

Label

Open the Create ribbon.

Select the **Label** tool.

Left click below the Zone 1 label to place the new label.

23.

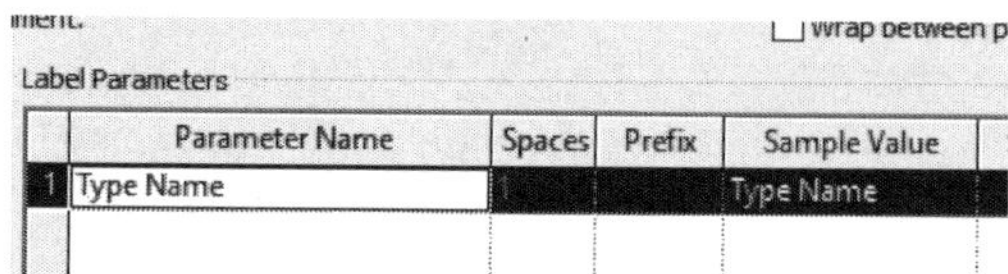

Add **Type Name** to the Label Parameters.
Click **OK**.

24.

Position the Type Name so it is centered under the Zone Name.

25.

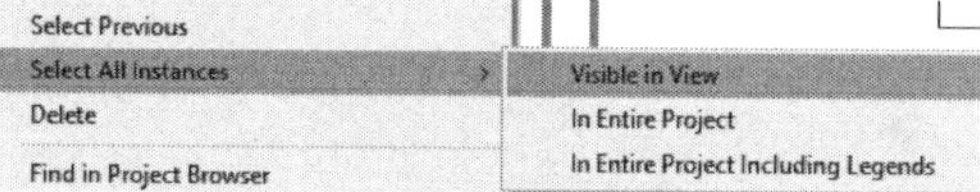

Adjust the box size.
Select a line and then drag it to the desired position.
Save the family as *Lighting Fixture Tag – Zone.rfa.*

26.

Select **Load into Project and Close** from the ribbon.

27.

Select one of the lighting fixture tags.
Right click and select **Select All instances→Visible in View**.
This will select all the lighting fixture tags of that type in this view.

28.

Using the Type Selector, change the tags to **Lighting Fixture Tag – Zone Standard.**

29.

The tags should update with the Lighting Zone information.

Save the file as *ex8-8.rvt*.

Transfer Project Standards

Transfer Project Standards is used to copy system families from one project to another. System families are elements that are defined inside a project and are not loaded from an external file. System families include view templates, walls, conduits, and wires.

You need to have the project open that you want to import into as well as the project you want to transfer from. If the project you are transferring from has a linked file, you can also import families from the linked file without opening that file.

Items which can be copied from one project to another include:

- Family types (including system families, but not loaded families)
- Line weights, materials, view templates, and object styles
- Mechanical settings, piping, and electrical settings
- Annotation styles, color fill schemes, and fill patterns
- Print settings

You may get a prompt during the transfer process alerting that an item being transferred already exists in the new project. You may opt to overwrite, ignore or cancel for the existing elements. You do not get to pick and choose which elements you overwrite if more than one item has been selected to be transferred.

Exercise 8-10:

Transfer Project Standards

Drawing Name: *export standards.rvt*
Estimated Time: 10 minutes

This exercise reinforces the following skills:

- ❑ Project Standards
- ❑ Conduits
- ❑ View Templates

1. 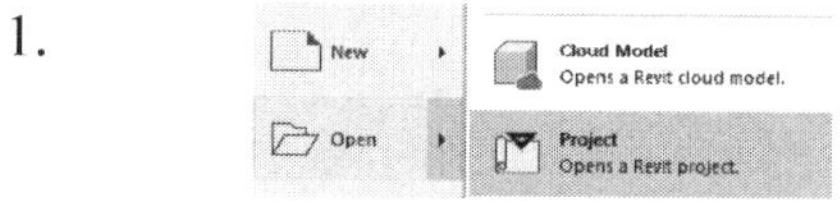 Open the *export standards.rvt file.*
    This is the file we will import standards from.

2.  Start a New Project using the Electrical-Default template.

3. Select the Manage ribbon.

    Select **Transfer Project Standards** from the Settings panel on the ribbon.

4. Select *export standards.rvt* to copy from.

    This file must be open to be selected.

    Click **Check None**.

    Place a check next to:
    - • Conduit Settings
    - • Conduit Sizes
    - • Conduit Standard Types
    - • Conduit Types

5.

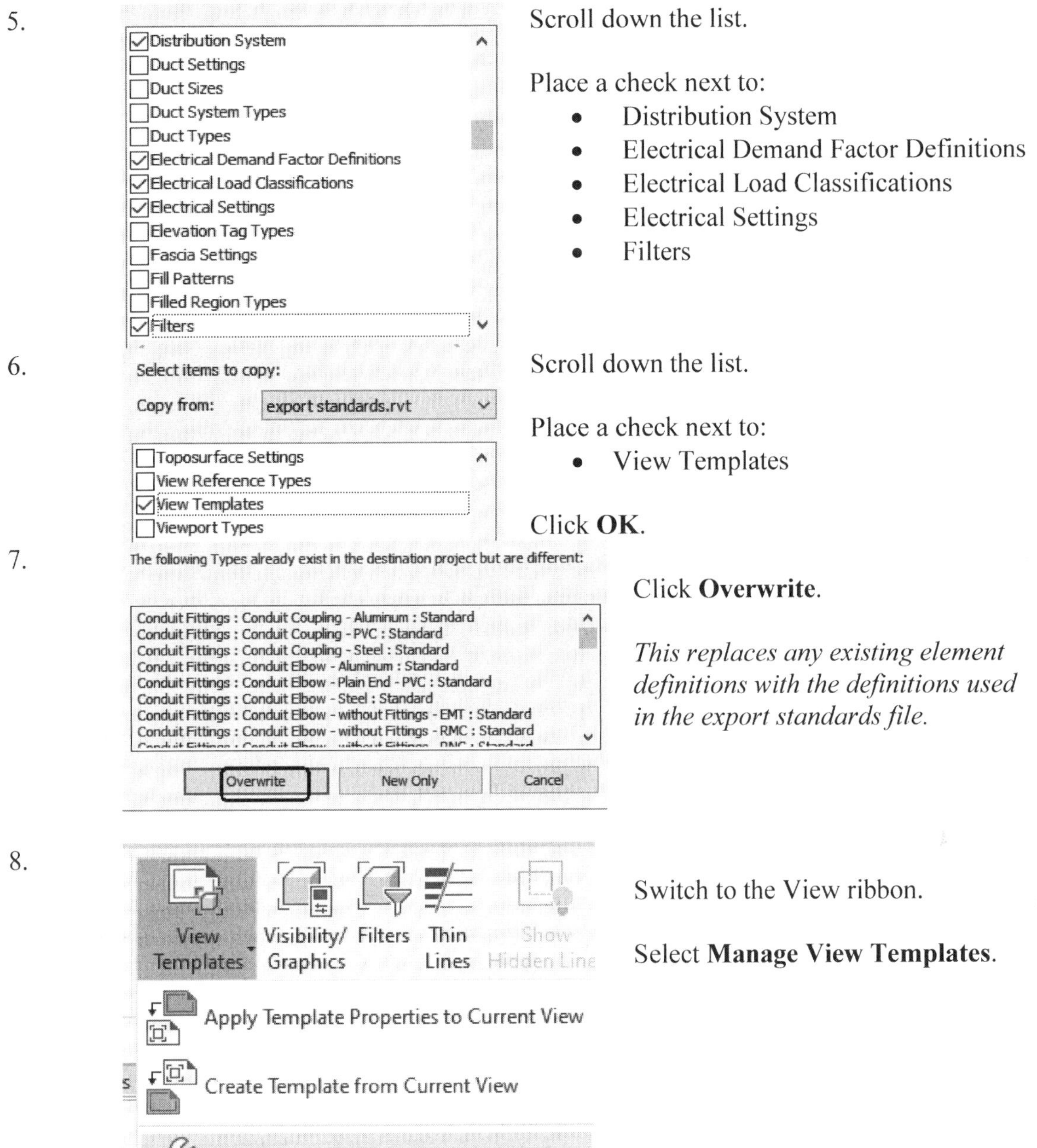

Scroll down the list.

Place a check next to:
- Distribution System
- Electrical Demand Factor Definitions
- Electrical Load Classifications
- Electrical Settings
- Filters

6.

Scroll down the list.

Place a check next to:
- View Templates

Click **OK**.

7.

Click **Overwrite**.

This replaces any existing element definitions with the definitions used in the export standards file.

8.

Switch to the View ribbon.

Select **Manage View Templates**.

9.

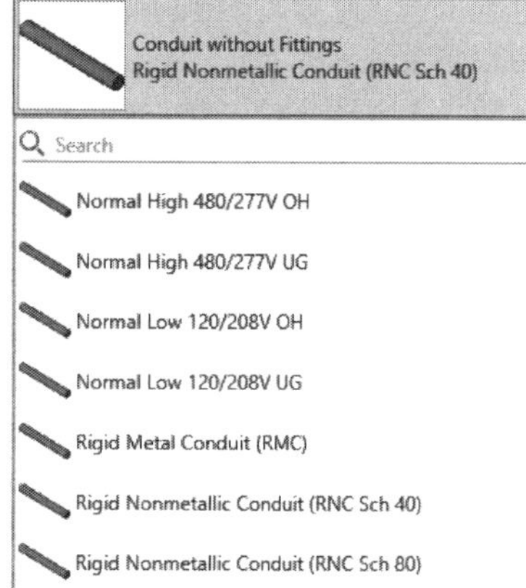

You imported a view template called Conduit Overrides.

Click **OK** to close the dialog box.

10.

Switch to the Systems ribbon.
Select **Conduit**.

11.

Use the Type Selector to see all the conduit types which were imported.

12.

Save as *ex8-9.rvt*.

Shared Coordinates

Coordinates in a file will only be shared, or the files will have shared coordinates after a process of transferring the coordinate system used in a file into another. It does not matter if in two files the location is exactly the same. They will be not sharing coordinates unless the sharing coordinates process has been carried out.

Normally there is one file, and only one, that is the source for sharing coordinates. From this file the location of different models is transferred to them, and after that all files will be sharing coordinates, and be able to be linked with the "Shared Coordinates option".

Revit uses three coordinate systems. When a new project is opened, the three systems overlap. They are:

- The Survey Point
- The Project Base Point
- The Internal Origin

The Survey Point is represented by a blue triangle with a small plus symbol in the center. This is the point that stores the universal coordinate system, or a defined global system of the project to which all the project structures will be referred. The Survey Point is a real-world relation to the Revit model. It represents a specific point on the Earth, such as a geodetic survey marker or a point of reference based on project property lines. The survey point is used to correctly orient the project with other coordinate systems, such as civil engineering software.

- It is the origin that Revit will use in case of share coordinates between models.
- The origin point used when inserting linked files with the Shared Coordinates option.
- The origin point used when exporting with Shared Coordinates option.
- The origin point to which spot coordinates and spot elevations are referenced, if the Survey Point is the coordinate origin in the type properties.
- The origin point to which level elevation is referred, if the SP is the Elevation Base in the level type properties.
- When the view shows the True North, it is oriented according to the Survey Point settings.

The Project Base Point is represented by a blue circle with an x. The position of this point is unique for each model, and this information is not shared between different models. The Project Base point could be placed in the same location as the Survey Point, but it is not usual to work in that way. This point is used to create a reference for positioning elements in relation to the model itself. By default, the Project Base Point is the origin (0,0,0) of the project. The Project Base Point should be used as a reference point for measurements and references across the site. The location of this point does not affect the shared site coordinates, so it should be located in the model where it makes sense to the model; usually at the intersection of two gridlines or at the corner of a building.

- The origin point to which spot coordinates and spot elevations are referenced, if the Project Base Point is the coordinate origin in the type properties.
- The origin point to which level elevation is referred, if the Project Base Point is the Elevation Base in the level type properties.
- When the view shows the Project North, it is oriented according to the Project Base Point.
- If it is not necessary, it is better not to move this point, so that it always is coincident with the third point: the Internal Origin.
- If we have moved the Project Base Point to a different location, it can be placed back to the initial position by right clicking on it when selected, and use **Move to Startup Location.**

The Internal Origin is now visible starting with the 2021 release of Revit. The Internal Origin is coincident with the Survey Point and the Project Base Point when a new project is started. It is displayed with an XY icon. Prior to this release, users sometimes resorted to placing symbols at the internal origin location to keep track of the origin.

- The project should be modeled in a restricted area around the internal origin point. The model should be inside a 20 miles radius circle around the internal origin, so that Revit can compute accurately.

- This is the origin point that is used when inserting external files using the "Internal Origin to Internal Origin" option.

- This is the origin point that is used when copy/pasting model objects from one file into another using the "aligned" option.

- The origin point to which spot coordinates and spot elevations are referenced, if Relative is the coordinate origin in the type properties.

- The origin point used when exporting with Internal Coordinates option.

- Revit API and Dynamo use this point as the coordinates origin point for internal computational calculations.

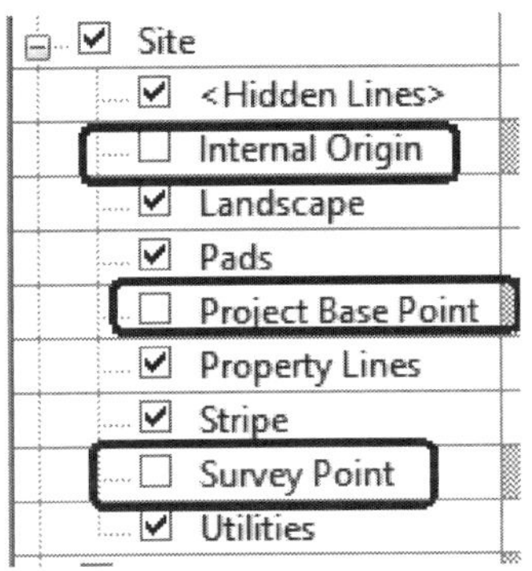

The visibility of these three systems is controlled under the Site category on the Model tab of the Visibility Graphics dialog.

Moving the project base point is like changing the global coordinates of the entire project. Another way of looking at it is if you modify the location of the project base point, you are moving the model around the earth. If you modify the location of the survey point, you are moving the earth around the model.

The benefits of correctly adjusting shared coordinates are not limited to aligning models for coordination but can also position the project in the real world if using proper geodetic data from a surveyor landmark or a provided file with the real-world information present.

To fully describe where an object (a building) sits in 3D space (its location on the planet), we need four dimensions:

- East/West position (the X coordinate)
- North/South position (the Y coordinate)
- Elevation (the Z coordinate)
- Rotation angle (East/West/True North)

These four dimensions uniquely position the building on the site and orient the building relative to a known benchmark as well as other landmarks. Revit allows you to assign a unique name to these four coordinates. Revit designates this collection as a **Shared Site**. You can designate as many Shared Sites as you like for a project. This is useful if you are planning a collection of buildings on a campus. By default, every project starts out with a single Shared Site which is named Internal. The name indicates that the Shared Site is using the Internal Coordinate System. Most projects will only require a single Shared Site, but if you are managing a project with more than one building or construction on the same site, it is useful to define a Shared Site for each instance of a linked file.

For example, in a resort, there may be different instances of the same cabin located across the site. You can use the same Revit file with the cabin model and copy the link multiple times. Each cabin location will be assigned a unique Shared Site, allowing each instance of the linked file to have its own unique location in the larger Shared Coordinate system.

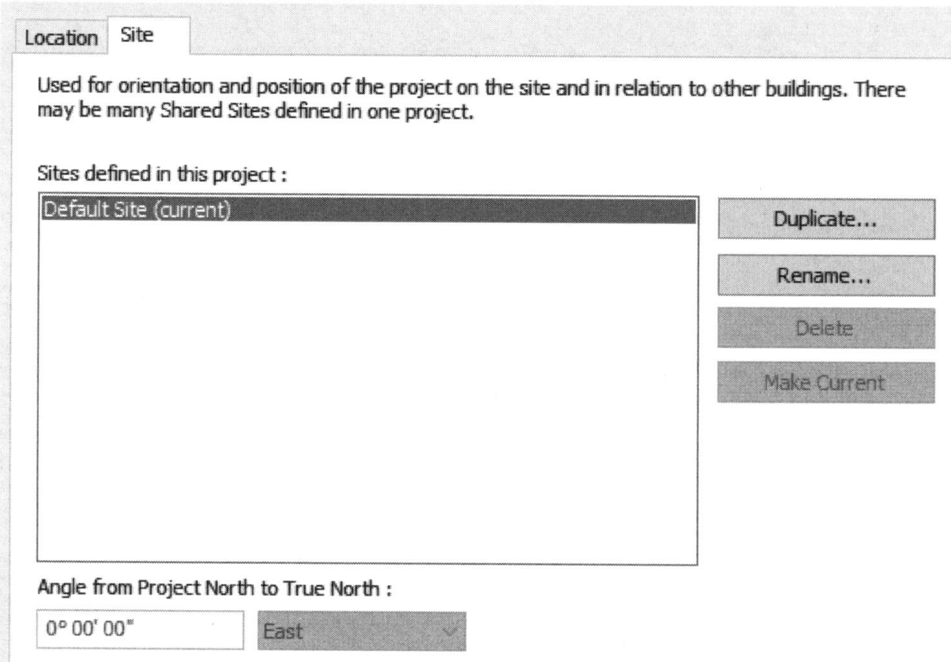

Shared Sites are named using the Location Weather and Site dialog.

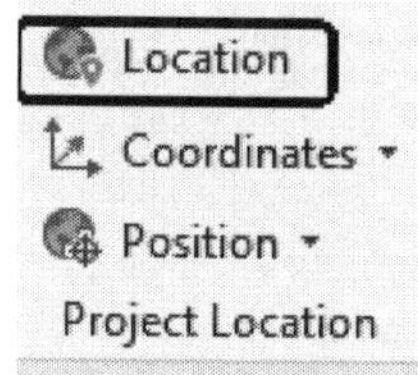

The dialog is opened using the Location tool on the Manage ribbon.

Why setting up shared coordinates is important:

- To properly coordinate the project models to work across platforms, including BIM Track.
- To display the project in its real-world location (including BIM and GIS data overlay).
- To link files together that have different base points (arbitrary coordinate systems).

Shared Coordinates allow you to adjust the reference point from project origin to a shared site point, to make it appear in a different position or with a different angle based on the internal base point. It is important to note that nothing in the Revit model moves when using this system, even if it looks like it moves and/or rotates on the screen. It is just applying an adjustment to the point of origin, so in fact, all elements keep their relation to the internal base point when using this option.

Revit has two different North directions: Project North and True North. True North doesn't change. Project North is used to position the project for sheets and views. This allows the project to be parallel and perpendicular for presentation and modeling purposes. The Project North rotation is referenced to the True North. The model's True North settings are saved and set when shared coordinates are used.

If multiple models are being linked together and need to be positioned appropriately in relation to one another, shared coordinates are required. Most electrical projects use a linked model which contains the architectural model (the floor plan) and sometimes linked models for the plumbing and the structural designs as well.

There are two ways to establish shared coordinates: the push method and the pull method. The push method has the host file determine which shared coordinates should be used and requires all linked files to align with the host file. The pull method takes the shared coordinates from a linked file and adjusts the position of the model elements in the host file. Most BIM projects either have the architect who has designed the floor plan control which coordinates are used when linking to files or the civil engineer who has designed the site survey designate the shared coordinates. Most electrical workers need to "pull" the shared coordinates from the project file provided by either the architect or the civil engineer.

The steps to pull shared coordinates are as follows:

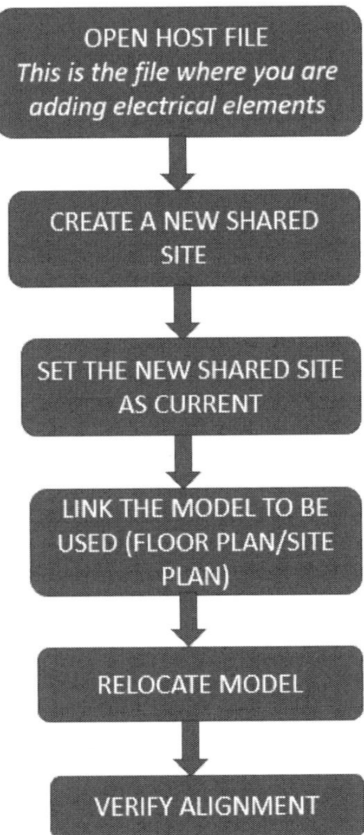

Exercise 8-11:

Understanding Shared Coordinates

Drawing Name: new
Estimated Time: 20 minutes

This exercise reinforces the following skills:

- Shared Coordinate System
- Site Point
- Base Point
- Internal Origin
- Views
- Visibility/Graphics
- Spot Coordinate
- Specify Coordinates at a Point
- Report Shared Coordinates

1. 

   Start a new project using the *Electrical-default* template.

2. 

   Highlight the **1- Lighting** floor plan.

   Right click and select **Duplicate View→Duplicate**.

3. 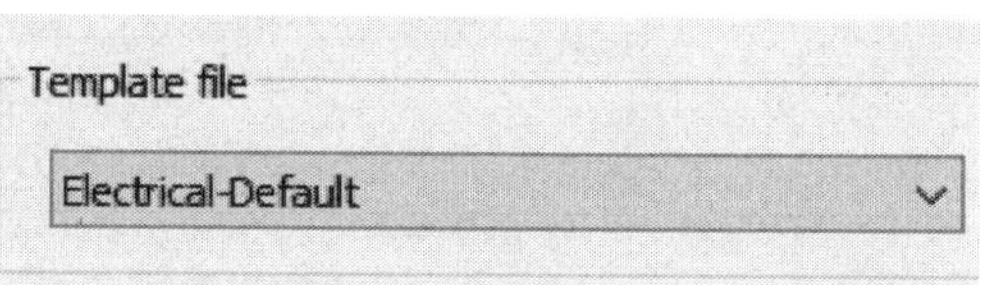

   Set the Discipline to **Coordination**.
   Set the Sub-Discipline to **Site**.

   *You will have to type **Site** in the Sub-Discipline field.*

4. The view will be placed under Coordination/Site.

   Rename the view **Site**.

5.

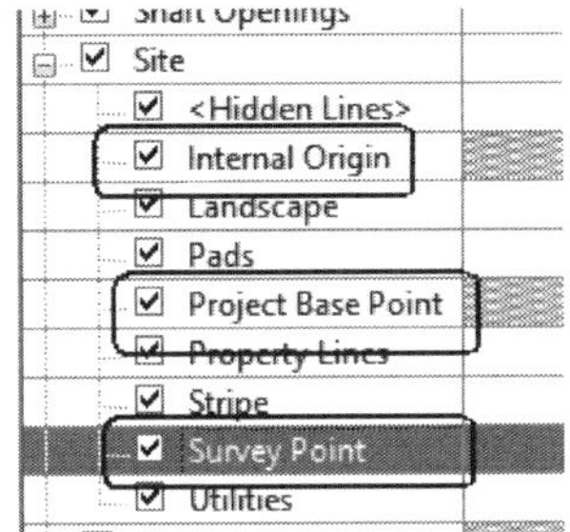

Type **VV** to open the Visibility/Graphics dialog.

On the Model Categories tab:

Enable:
- Internal Origin
- Project Base Point
- Survey Point

These are located under the Site category.

Click **OK**.

The Internal Origin, Project Base Point and Survey Point are all visible.

They are overlaid on top of each other.

6.

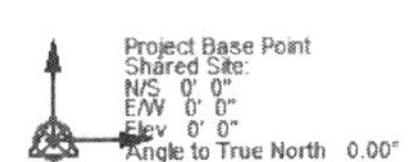

Select the **Project Base Point**.
That's the circle symbol.

The coordinates for the base point are displayed. Note that by default the base point is located at 0,0.

It is also centered on the screen relative to the elevation markers.

We can add a spot coordinate symbol to the project base point to keep track of its location.

Spot coordinates report the North/South and East/West coordinates of points in a project. In drawings, you can add spot coordinates on floors, walls, toposurfaces, and boundary lines. Coordinates are reported with respect to the survey point or the project base point, depending on the value used for the Coordinate Origin type parameter of the spot coordinate family.

7.

Switch to the Annotate ribbon.

Spot
Coordinate

Select the **Spot Coordinate** tool on the Dimension panel.

8.

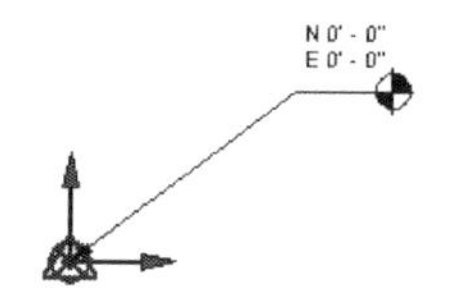

Select the Project Base Point.

Left click to place the spot coordinate.

9.

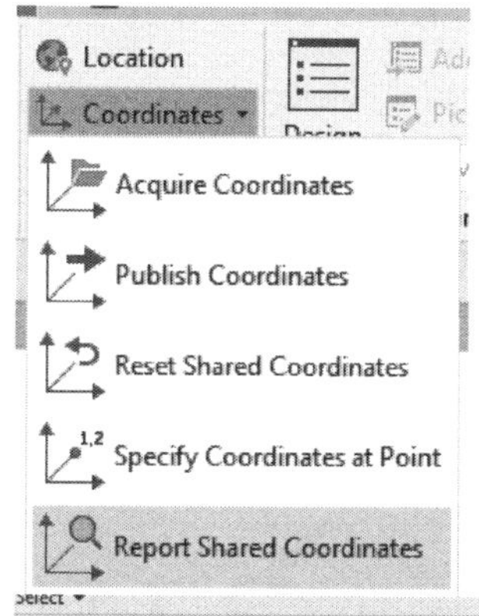

Switch to the Manage ribbon.

Select **Report Shared Coordinates** on the Project Location panel.

Select the Project Base Point.

10.

The coordinates are displayed on the Options bar.

Cancel out of the command.

11.

Select the Project Base Point.

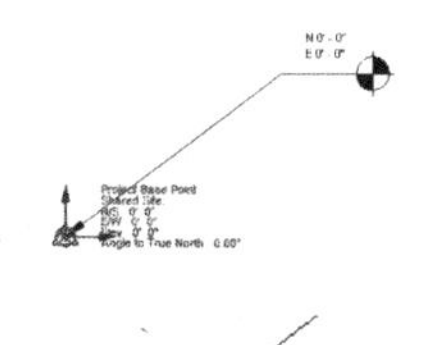

Notice that the coordinates that are displayed are blue. This means they are temporary dimensions which can be edited.

12.

Click on the **E/W** dimension.
Change it to **20' 6"**.
Press **ENTER**.

13.

The location of the project base point shifted to be 20' 6" east of the internal origin/survey point.

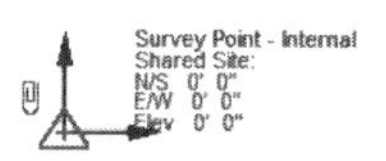

Notice that the spot coordinate value updated.

14.

Left click on the Survey Point.
That's the triangle symbol.
Notice that dimensions are black, which means they cannot be edited.

15.

Drag the survey point away from the internal origin (the XY icon).

Notice that the Project Base Point value updates.

Remember the Survey Point represents a real and known benchmark location in the project (usually provided by the project survey). The Project Base Point is simply a known point on the building (usually chosen by the project team).

Think of the Survey Point as the coordinates in the *World* and the Project Base Point as the local building coordinates.

The Survey Point is always located at 0,0, while the Project Base Point is relative to the Survey Point.

It is called a shared coordinate system because it represents the coordinate system of the world around us and is shared by all the buildings on the site.

16.

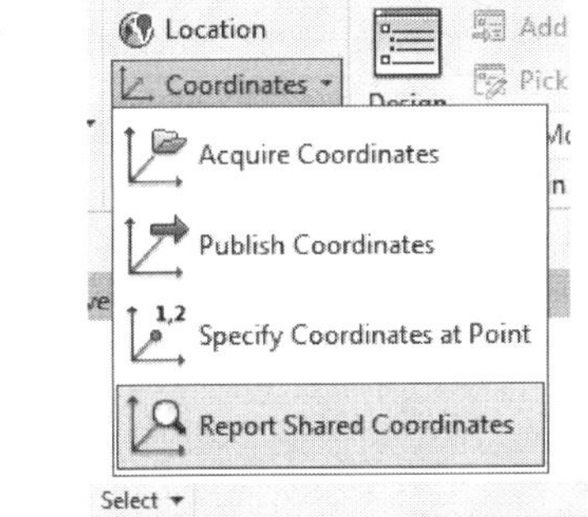

Select **Report Shared Coordinates** on the Project Location panel.

Select the Internal Origin (the XY icon).

17.

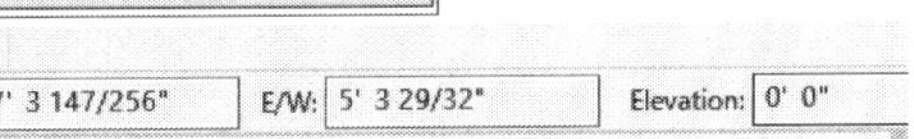

The coordinates are displayed on the Options bar.

Notice that the Internal Origin is located relative to the Survey Point. The Internal Coordinate System represents the building's "local" coordinates.

Cancel out of the command.

18.

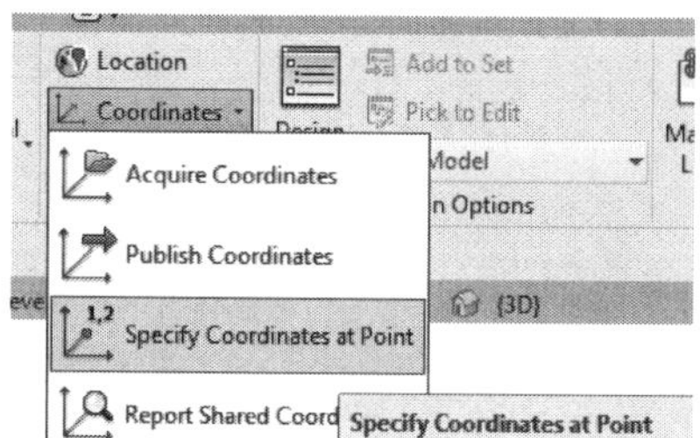

Usually, you will be provided the coordinate information for a project from the civil engineer.

Select **Specify Coordinates at Point**.

Select the Survey Point (the triangle symbol.).

19.

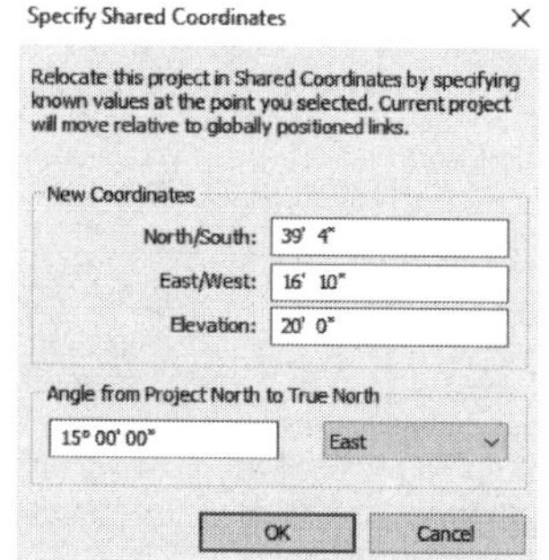

Fill in the Shared Coordinates:

For North/South: **39' 4"**.
For East/West: **16' 0"**.
For Elevation: **20' 0"**.
For Angle from Project North to True North: **15° East**.

Click **OK**.

20.

Zoom out and you will see that the Survey Point's position has shifted.

Note the coordinates for the Project Base Point updated.

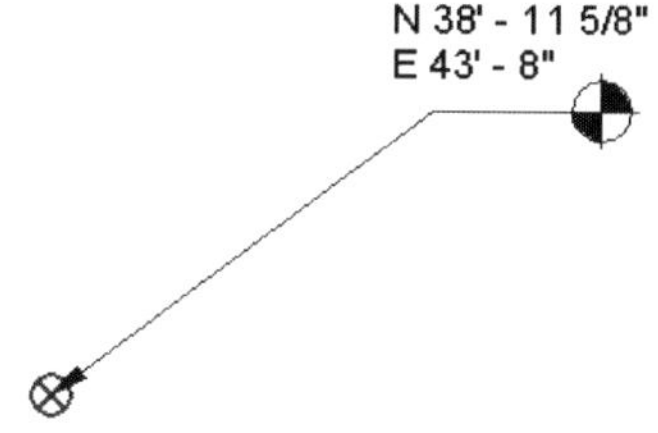

21. Save as *ex8-10.rvt*.

Exercise 8-12:

Understanding Location

Drawing Name: Simple Building-Arch.rvt, electrical plan.rvt
Estimated Time: 20 minutes

This exercise reinforces the following skills:

- Linking Files
- Shared Coordinate System
- Survey Point
- Base Point
- Internal Origin
- Visibility/Graphics

1. Open the *electrical plan.rvt* file.

   This is the host file.

   Open the **Site** floor plan.

2. 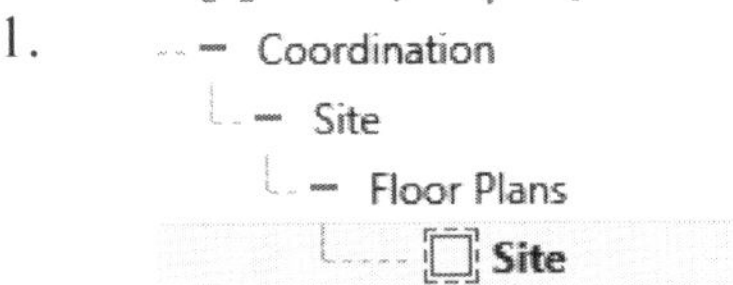

   Open the Visibility/Graphics dialog by typing **VV**.

   On the Model Categories tab:

   Enable:
   - Internal Origin
   - Project Base Point
   - Survey Point

   This is located under the Site category.

   Click **OK** and close the dialog.

3. Activate the **Insert** ribbon.

   Select **Link Revit**.

4.

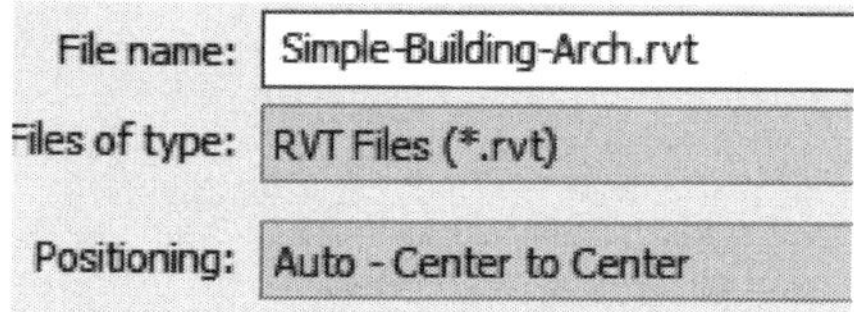

Locate the *Simple-Building-Arch.rvt* file.

Set the Positioning to **Auto – Center to Center**.

Click **Open**.

Many users will be tempted to align the files using Internal Origin to Internal Origin. This is not the best option when we plan to reposition the building on the site plan. Origin to Origin works well when linking MEP files to the Architectural file.

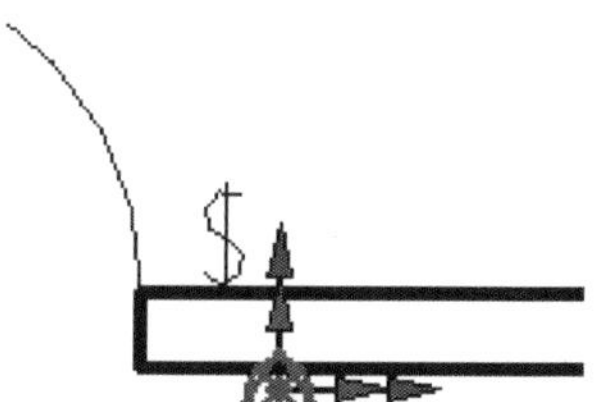

Notice that the linked file's coordinate system is aligned with the host file's coordinate system.

5.

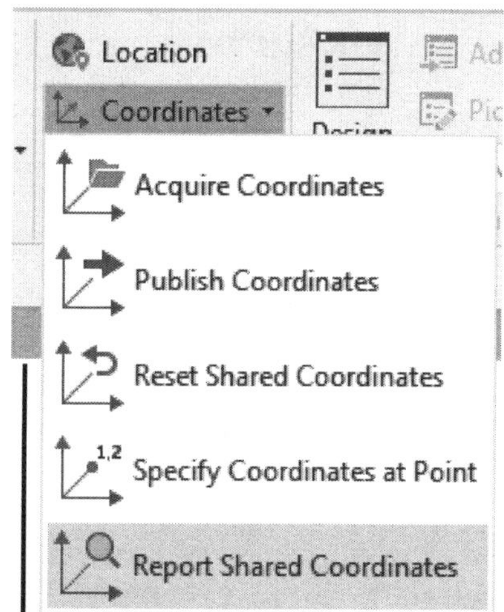

Open the Manage Ribbon.

Select **Coordinates→Report Shared Coordinates.**

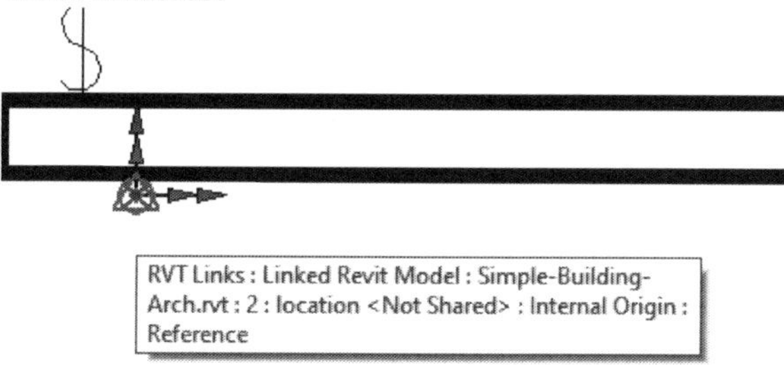

RVT Links : Linked Revit Model : Simple-Building-Arch.rvt : 2 : location <Not Shared> : Internal Origin : Reference

Select the internal origin of the linked file. Click the TAB key until the correct element is displayed. Then click the left mouse button to get the coordinate information.

6.

N/S: 0' 0"   E/W: 0' 0"   Elevation: 0' 7 1/2"

The coordinates of the linked file are listed on the Options bar.

7.

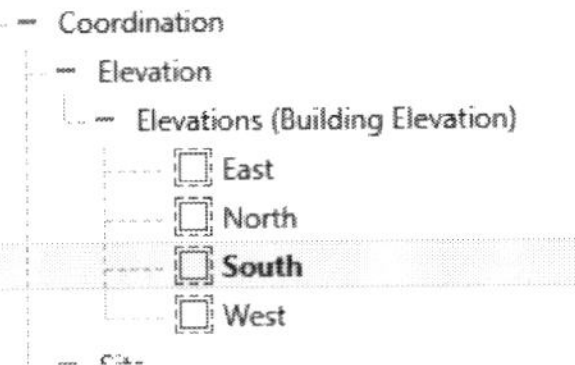

Open the **South** elevation.

Notice that the levels are not aligned between the files.

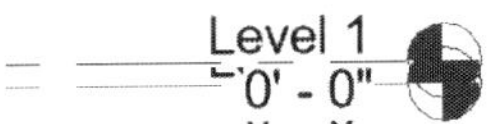

8.

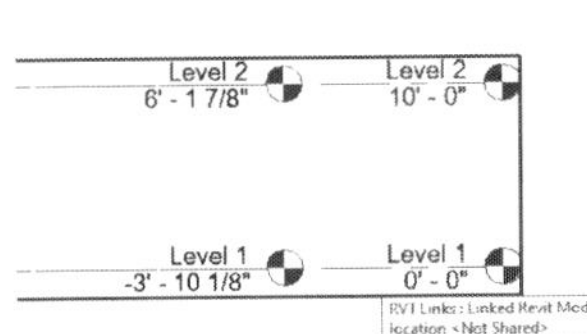

*Use the **ALIGN** tool to move the Level 1 in the linked file to align with Level 1 in the electrical plan file.*

Select the **ALIGN** tool.

Select the Level 1 that is on the electrical plan file as the target.
Select the Level 1 on the host file to be moved.

9. Return to the Site Plan.

Use the TAB key to select the linked file's Project Base Point. Notice that the elevation has updated.

10. Switch to the Manage ribbon.

Select **Acquire Coordinates** and then select the linked file.

11. Coordinates acquired from Simple-Building-Arch.rvt.

GIS Coordinate System: <Unknown>

Click **Close**.

12. Select the Project Base Point for the electrical plan.

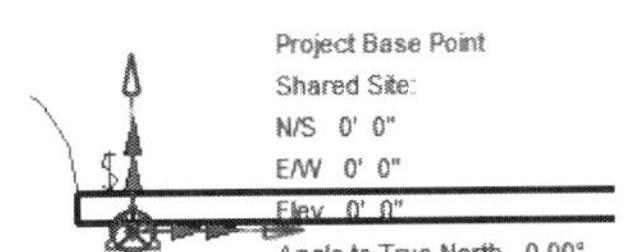

Notice the change to the coordinates.

13.

Use the TAB key until you can select the Project Base Point for the linked file.

Notice it now shows that it is sharing the coordinate system with the host file.

14.   Save the file as *ex8-11.rvt*.

eTransmit

eTransmit allows you to copy a Revit project along with any linked/dependent files to a single folder. This is also useful if you want to create snapshots of your project at different stages of construction.

You can elect to:
- Include related dependent files such as linked models and DWF markups.
- Include supporting files such as documents or spreadsheets.
- Upgrade the Revit (.rvt) model and linked models to the current release.
- Disable worksets.
- Remove unused families, materials, and other objects from the Revit models to reduce file size.
- Delete sheets and specific view types so that the models do not contain unnecessary data.
- Include only the views that are placed on sheets.

Shared parameter files, external font files, and lookup tables are not included in the eTransmit package.

Exercise 8-13:

Transmit a Model

Drawing Name: etransmit.rvt
Estimated Time: 25 minutes

This exercise reinforces the following skills:

❏   eTransmit

1.   Click the Home button until the ribbon appears.

2.   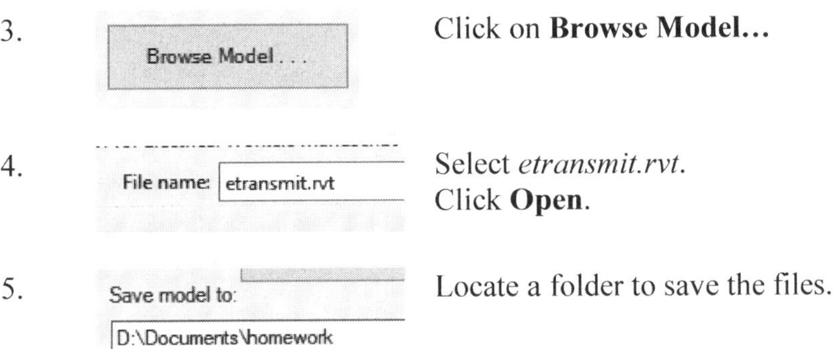
Verify all files are closed.
Select the **Add-Ins** tab on the ribbon.
Select **Transmit a model**.

3.   Click on **Browse Model...**

4.   Select *etransmit.rvt*.
Click **Open**.

5.   Locate a folder to save the files.

6.

Enable:
- Linked Revit models
- CAD links
- DWF markups

Note that you can also add spreadsheets, reports, etc. to the transmittal package using the Add files... button.

7.

Enable **Cleanup**.

Enable **Purge unused**.
This deletes any unused families from the files to reduce file size.

You can also opt to only include the views on sheets.

8.

Click **Transmit model**.

9.

When it is completed, you will see a message with the day's date.

Click **Open folder** to see the etransmit file.

10.

Using File Explorer, locate the eTransmit folder that was created.

11.

That folder includes a folder with the files and a txt file.

Open the txt file.

12.

Note the report lists which files were included as well as which files were excluded.

Annotations, Dimensions, and Symbols

The term 'Annotations' is used in Revit to include several different types of elements:

- Dimensions
- Text Notes
- Keynotes
- Tags
- Symbols

Dimensions

There are three types of dimensions in Revit:

Temporary dimensions are only displayed when elements are selected. They show the position of elements relative to other dimensions. They control the placement of elements. They are not plotted. A dimension symbol appears near the temporary dimension of a selected element. If you left click on the dimension symbol, a permanent dimension is placed.

Permanent dimensions are annotations users place in a view. They are view-specific, and they will be visible when the sheet or view is printed. The value of the permanent dimension is fed from the temporary dimension. In order to change the permanent dimension, the user needs to edit the temporary dimension. If you lock a permanent dimension, the value cannot be changed.

Listening dimensions are the dimensions which appear when placing or modifying an element. Listening dimensions appear in bold and update as elements are created or modified.

Settings can be specified such as snapping points for temporary dimensions.

Guidelines for Working with Dimensions

- Change temporary dimensions to permanent dimensions when you need to refer to the distance frequently while working. You can delete or turn off the visibility of dimensions when they are no longer necessary.
- Add parallel reference planes or model lines at the corners of a room when you want to place dimensions across the corners. You can then turn off the visibility of the planes/model lines.
- Add dimension styles to project templates once you have established a standard.
- Use the Duplicate View tool to create a copy of the view. Have one view with dimensions and annotations and one without. You can also hide individual dimensions by right clicking on a dimension and selecting Hide element.
- Adjust the view scale prior to placing text and dimensions. Text and Dimensions will scale with the view. If you change the view scale, you may need to reposition text and dimensions to maintain clarity.

Exercise 9-1:

Adding Dimensions

Drawing Name: *dimensions_2vt*
Estimated Time: 5 minutes

This exercise reinforces the following skills:

- ❑ Add dimensions to a view

1. 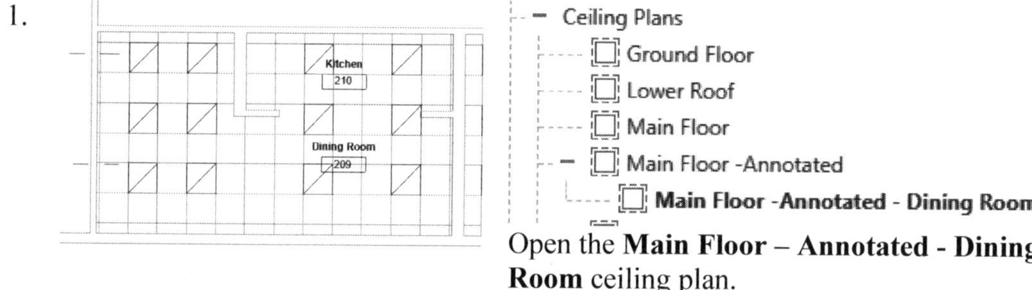

Open the **Main Floor – Annotated - Dining Room** ceiling plan.

2. Activate the **Annotate** ribbon.

Aligned   Select the **ALIGNED** dimension tool on the ribbon.

3. 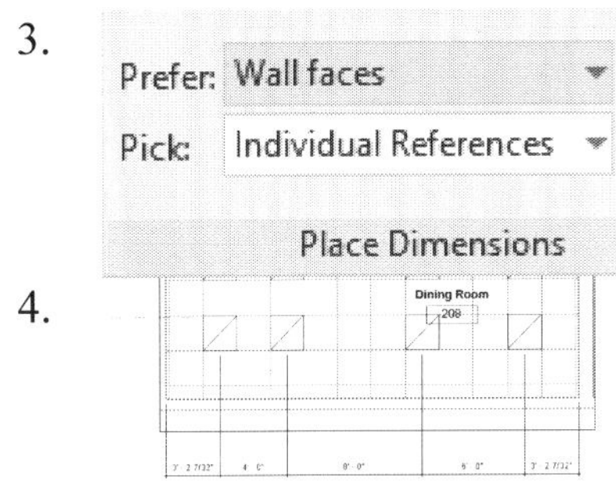

On the ribbon:
Select **Wall faces.**

4. 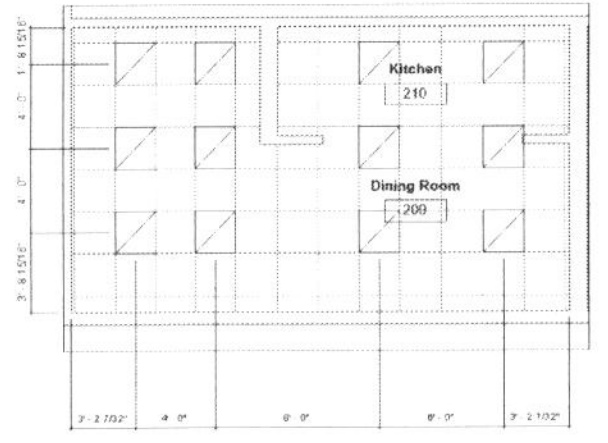

Working from left to right, select the inside wall face on the west wall, select the center of the lighting fixture, select the center of the next light fixture, then the center of the next light fixture, then the center of the next light fixture, then the inside face on the east wall.

Left click below the view to place the dimension.

5. 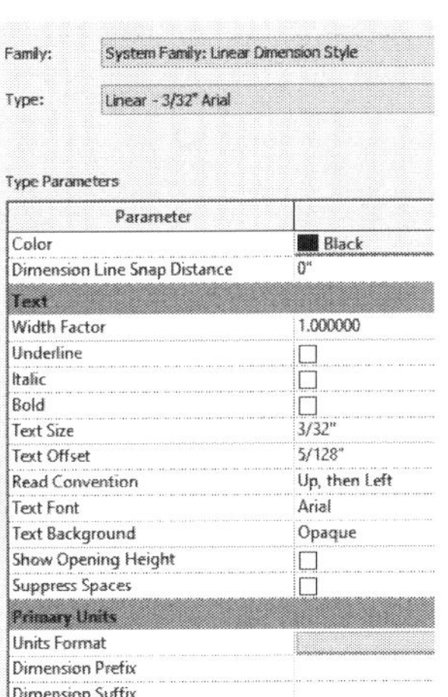

Starting at the inside face of the south wall, place vertical dimensions from the inside wall faces to the lighting fixture centers.

6. Save as *ex9-1.rvt*.

Dimension Types

Revit dimension types are system families. Dimension Types control the dimension units, font, text color, text size, whether the text is bold or italic, arrowhead type, and so on.

Because they are system families, the definitions reside within the project file. They can be copied from one project to another using Transfer Project Standards.

| Family: | System Family: Linear Dimension Style |
| Type: | Linear - 3/32" Arial |

Type Parameters

Parameter	
Color	Black
Dimension Line Snap Distance	0"
Text	
Width Factor	1.000000
Underline	☐
Italic	☐
Bold	☐
Text Size	3/32"
Text Offset	5/128"
Read Convention	Up, then Left
Text Font	Arial
Text Background	Opaque
Show Opening Height	☐
Suppress Spaces	☐
Primary Units	
Units Format	
Dimension Prefix	
Dimension Suffix	

Exercise 9-2:

Create a Dimension Type

Drawing Name: *dimension type.rvt*
Estimated Time: 20 minutes

This exercise reinforces the following skills:

- ❑ Define a new Dimension family type
- ❑ Activate View
- ❑ Deactivate View
- ❑ Type Properties
- ❑ Type Selector

1. 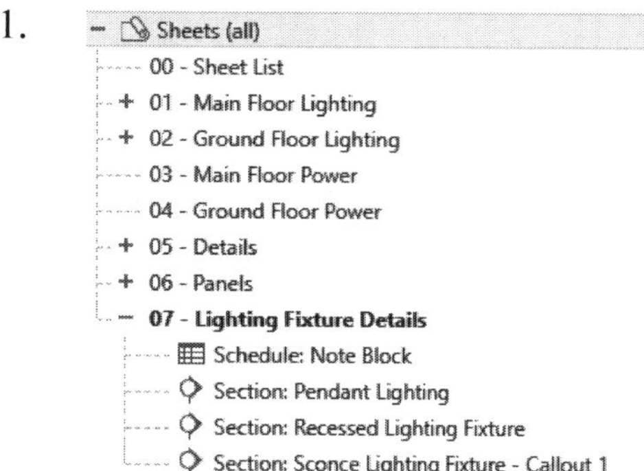

   Open the **07 Lighting Fixture Details** sheet in the Project Browser.

2. 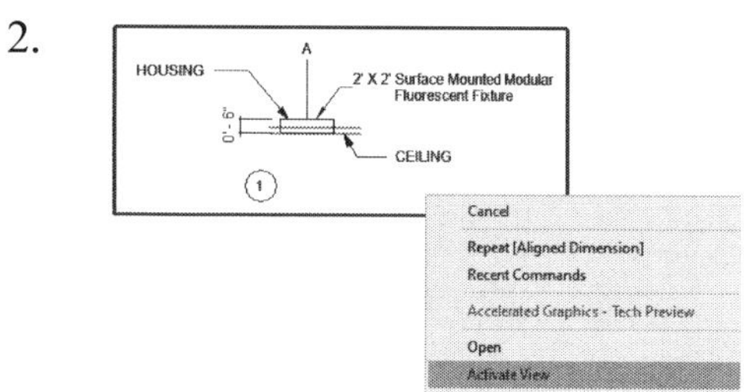

   Highlight the middle view with the recessed lighting fixture.

   Right click and select **Activate View**.

3.

   Select the vertical dimension that displays the height of the lighting fixture.

4.   Select **Edit Type**.

5. Select **Duplicate**.

6. Rename **Linear – 3/32" Tahoma ANSI**.

   Name: Linear - 3/32" Tahoma ANSI

   Click **OK**.

7. Change the Tick Mark to **Arrow Filled 15 Degree.**

Type Parameters	
Parameter	Value
Graphics	
Dimension String Type	Continuous
Leader Type	Arc
Leader Tick Mark	None
Show Leader When Text Moves	Beyond Witness Lines
Tick Mark	Arrow Filled 15 Degree

8. Scroll down the Type Parameters.

Text Size	3/32"
Text Offset	5/128"
Read Convention	Horizontal
Text Font	Tahoma
Text Background	Opaque

   Set the Read Convention to **Horizontal**.

   Set the Text Font to **Tahoma**.

   Click **OK**.

   Review the change to the dimension.

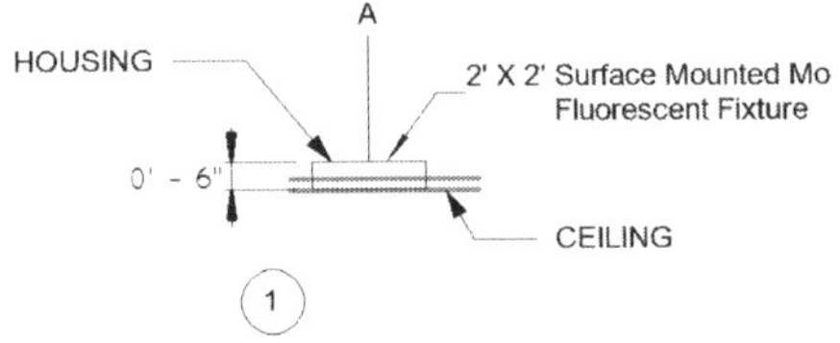

9. Select the vertical dimension that displays the height of the lighting fixture.

10. Select **Edit Type**.

    Edit Type

11. Select **Duplicate**.

12. Rename **Linear – 3/32" Arial ANSI**.

    Name: Linear - 3/32" Arial ANSI

    Click **OK**.

13. Set the Text Font to **Arial**.

Text Offset	5/128"
Read Convention	Horizontal
Text Font	Arial
Text Background	Opaque
Units Format	1' - 5 11/32" (Default)
Alternate Units	None
Alternate Units Format	1235 [mm]
Alternate Units Prefix	

    Left click on the **Units Format** button.

14.

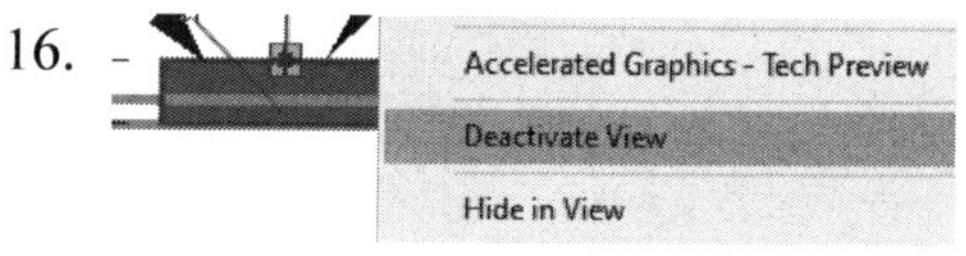

Disable **Use project settings.**

Set the Units to **Inches.**

Set the Rounding to **2 decimal places.**

Click **OK.**

Click **OK** to close the dialog.

15.

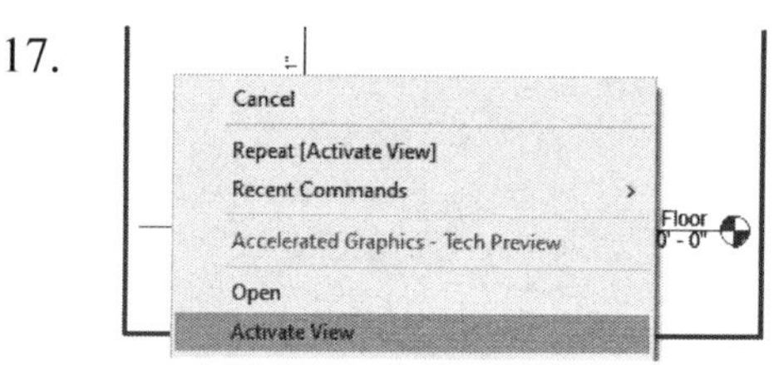

The dimension has updated to the new dimension type.

Use the Type Selector to assign the **Linear – 3/32" Tahoma ANSI** dimension type to the dimension.

16.

Right click on the view and select **Deactivate View.**

17.

Highlight the right view with the sconce lighting fixture.

Right click and select **Activate View**.

18.

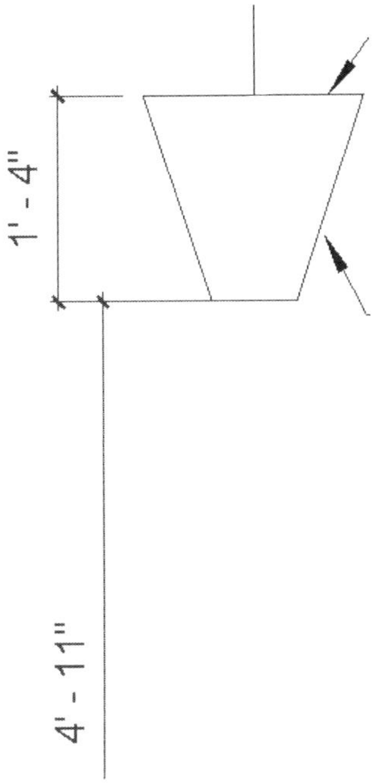

Select the two vertical dimensions.

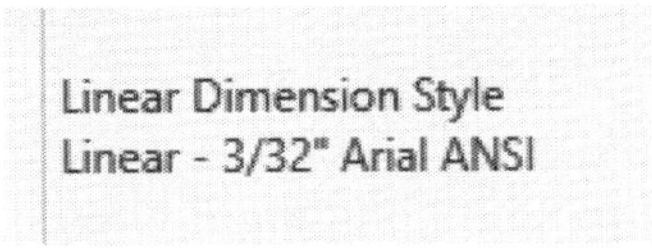

Linear Dimension Style
Linear - 3/32" Arial ANSI

Use the Type Selector to change the dimensions to use the **Linear – 3/32" Arial ANSI** type.

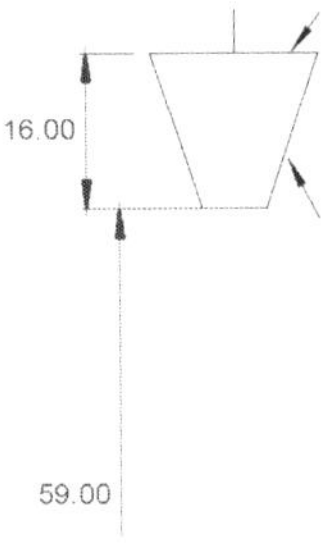

The dimensions update.

19.

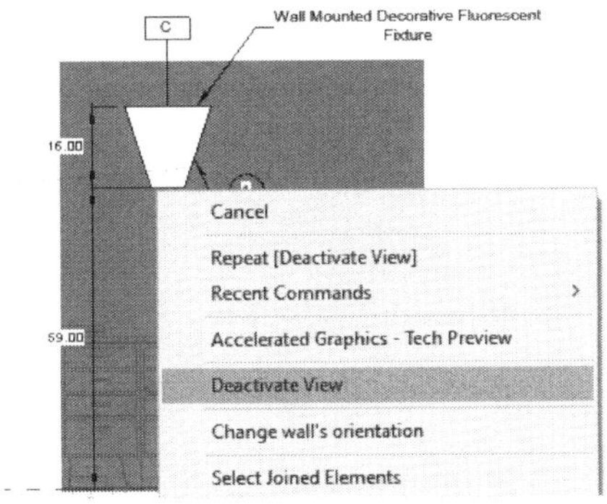

Right click on the view and select **Deactivate View**.

20. Save as *ex9-2.rvt*.

Exercise 9-3:

Modifying Dimensions

Drawing Name: *modify_dimensions.rvt*
Estimated Time: 10 minutes

This exercise reinforces the following skills:

- Place an ALIGNED dimension
- Modifying Dimensions
- Temporary Dimensions

1. 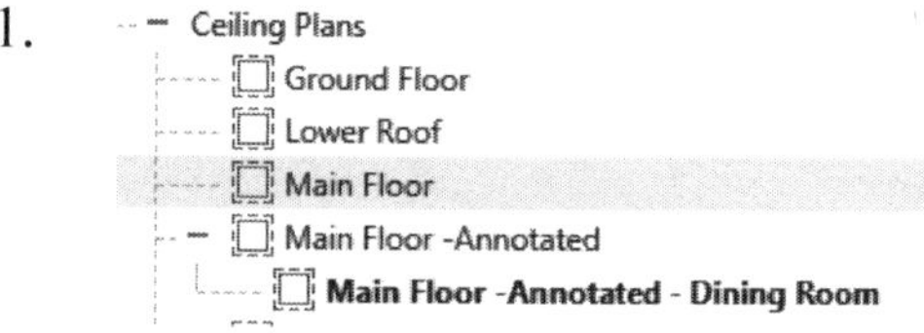

Open the **Main Floor – Annotated - Dining Room** ceiling plan.

2. 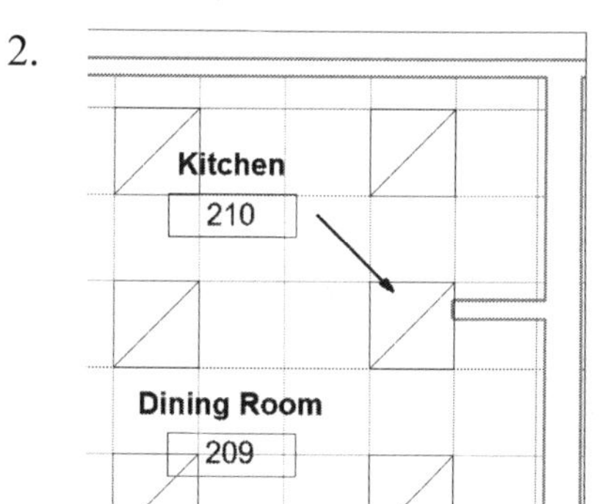

Locate the lighting fixture on the middle right of the Room 210.

It is interfering with the wall and should be moved.

3. 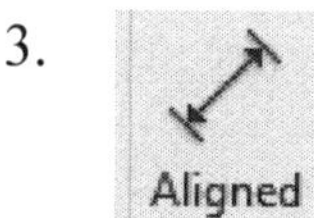

Select the **ALIGNED** dimension tool on the Annotate ribbon.

4. 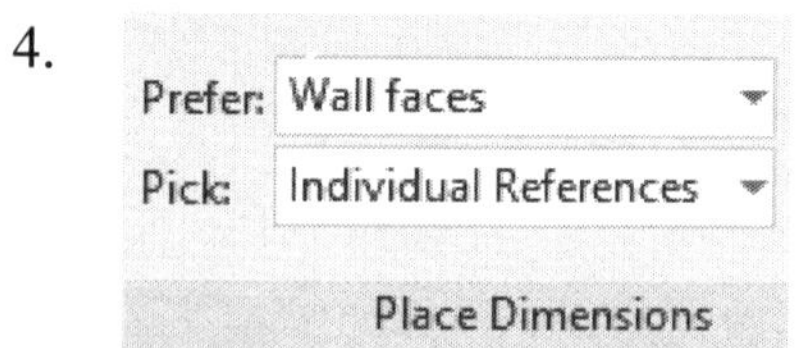

On the ribbon: Select **Wall faces.**

5.

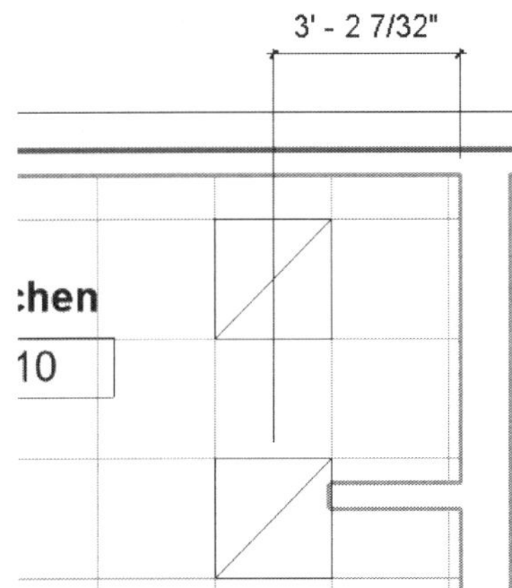

Place a horizontal dimension between the center of the lighting fixture and the inside face of the east wall.

6.

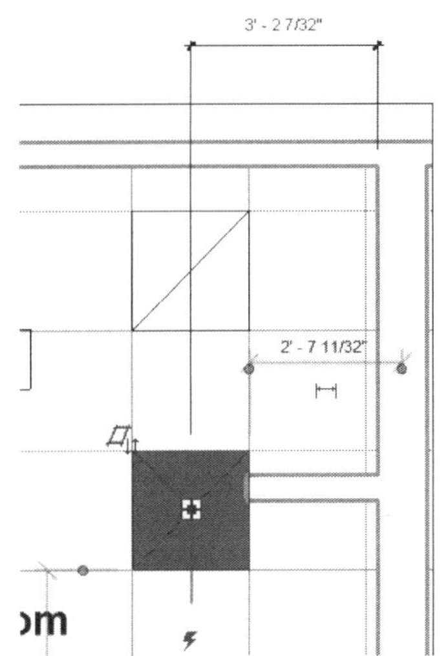

Select the lighting fixture.

Notice that the temporary dimension appears.

7.

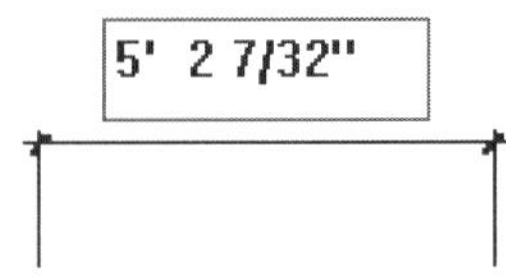

Change the value of the temporary dimension to **5' 2 7/32"**.

Click **ENTER** to update the dimension.

Left click in the window to release the selection.

8.

Notice that the permanent dimension updates.

Save as *ex9-3.rvt*.

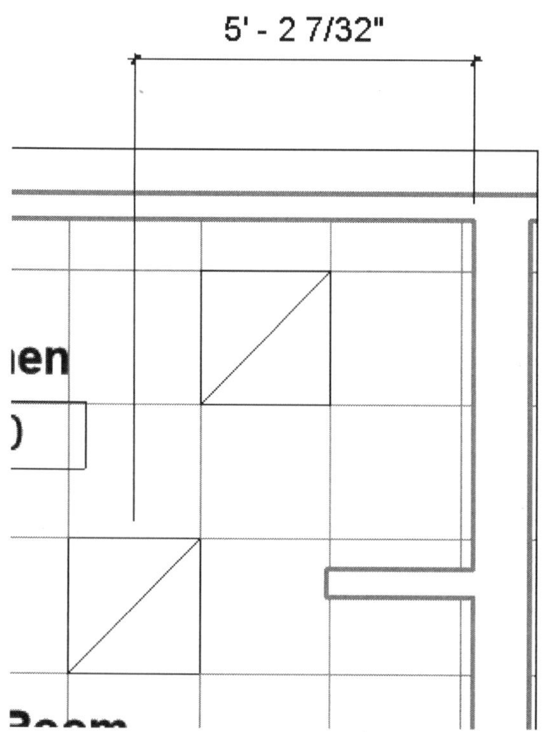

Exercise 9-4:

Create Ordinate Dimensions

Drawing Name: detail_view.rvt
Estimated Time: 30 minutes

This exercise reinforces the following skills:
- ❑ Detail Components
- ❑ Detail Views

1. 

Select **Drafting View** from the View ribbon.

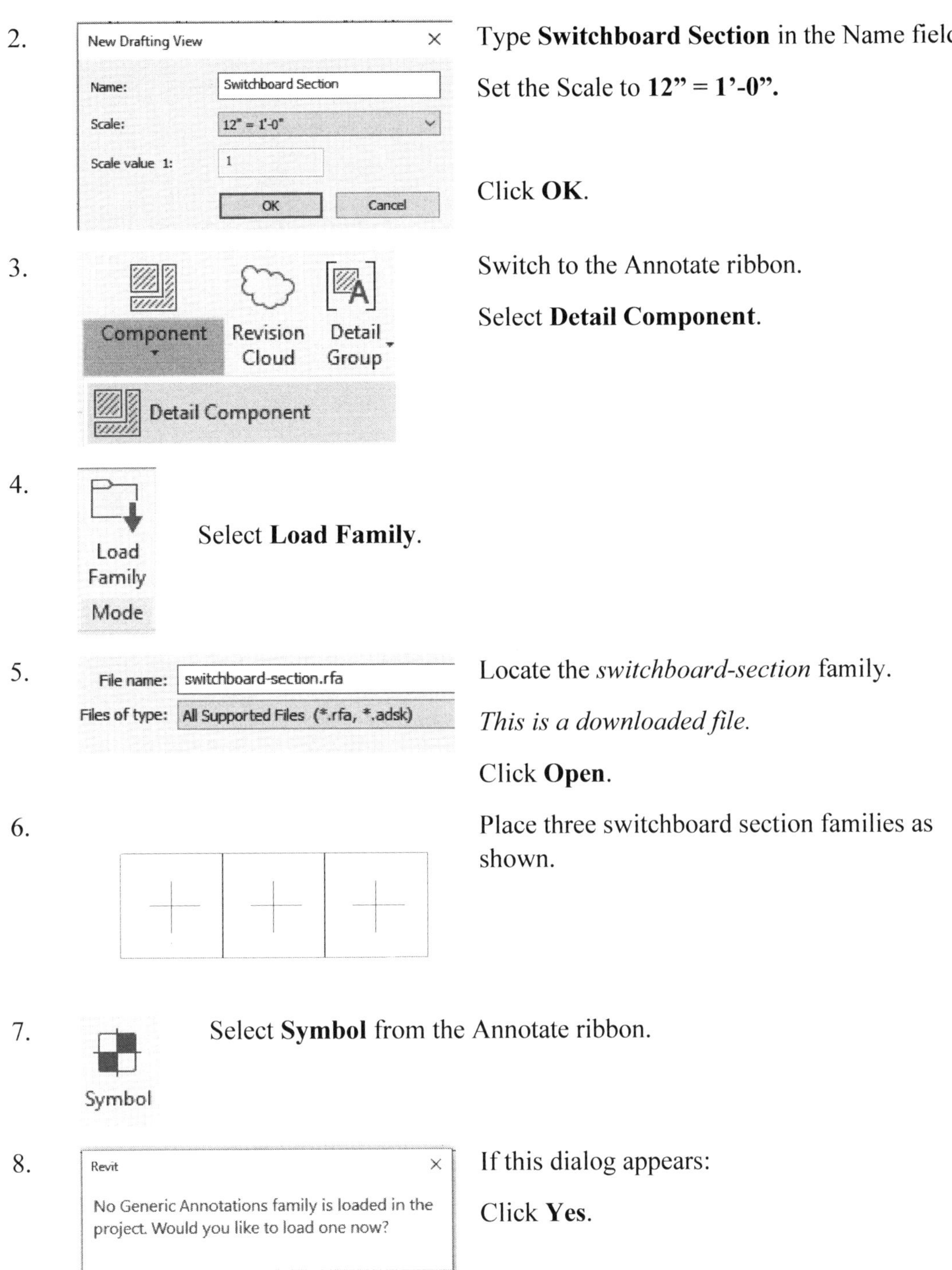

2.   Type **Switchboard Section** in the Name field.

Set the Scale to **12" = 1'-0"**.

Click **OK**.

3.   Switch to the Annotate ribbon.

Select **Detail Component**.

4.   Select **Load Family**.

5.   Locate the *switchboard-section* family.

This is a downloaded file.

Click **Open**.

6.   Place three switchboard section families as shown.

7.   Select **Symbol** from the Annotate ribbon.

8.   If this dialog appears:

Click **Yes**.

9.

Select **Load Family**.

10.

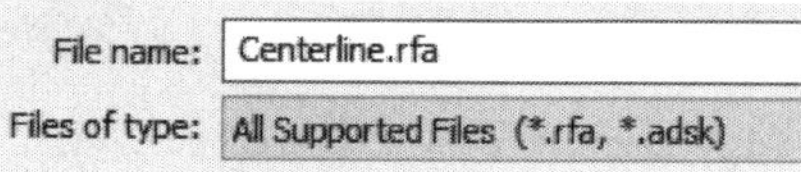

Select *Centerline.rfa* from the downloaded files.

The centerline family provided with Revit uses metric units and is too small for this view.

Click **Open**.

11.

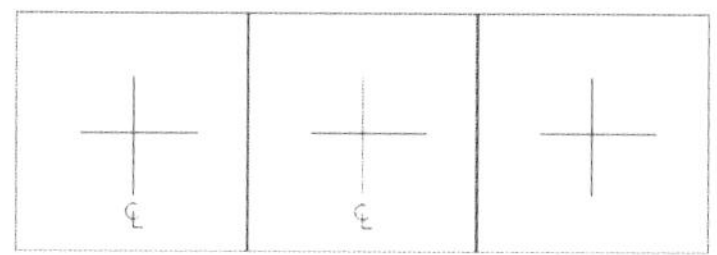

Place the symbol below the center mark you created in the first two squares.

12.

Select **Text** from the Annotation ribbon.

13.

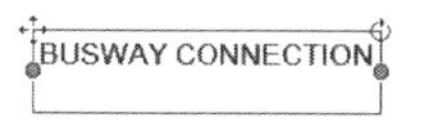

Type BUSWAY CONNECTION for the text value.

Use the grips to set the text to be one line and centered over the square.

14.

Select the text.

On the Properties palette:

Select **Edit Type**.

15.

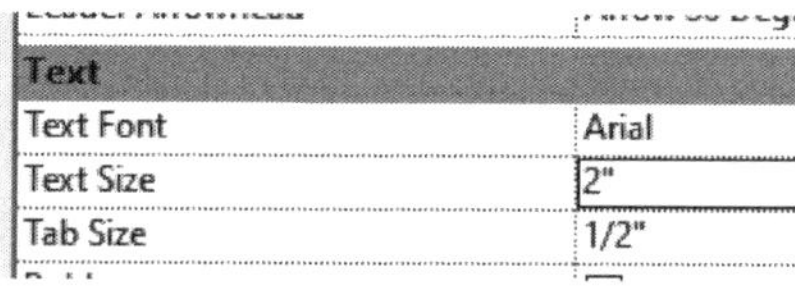

Change the Text Size to **2"**.

Click **OK**.

16.

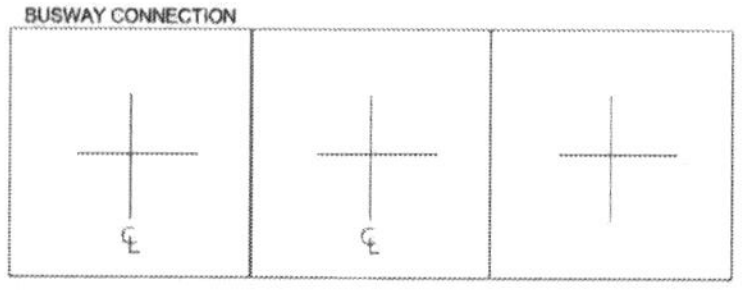

Adjust the position of the text so it is positioned above the first switch section.

17. Copy the text so it is over the second square.

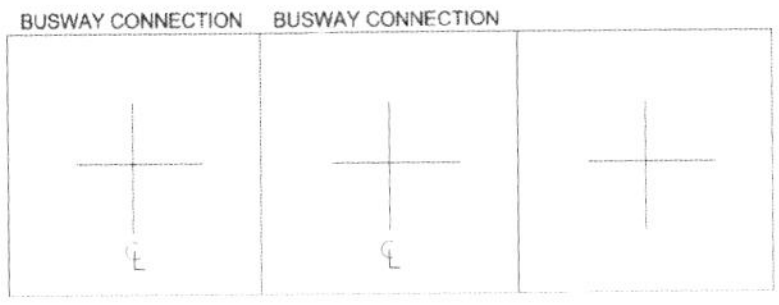

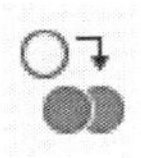

18. **Measure**

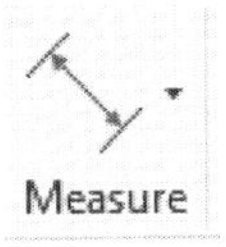

Select **Aligned** dimension.

19. Place a dimension to the left of the first square.

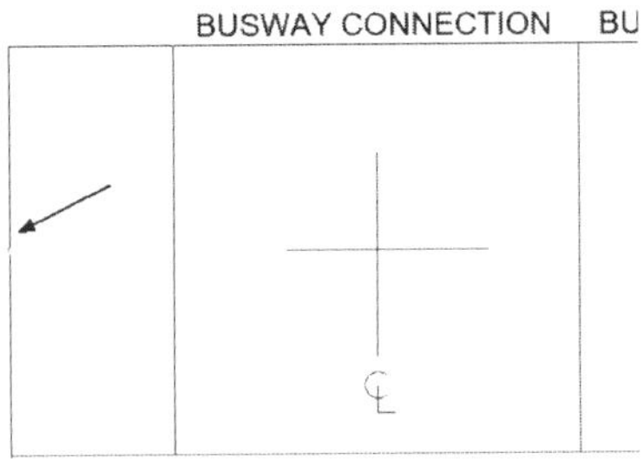

20. **Edit Type**

Select the dimension that was just placed.

Select **Edit Type** on the Properties palette.

21. **Duplicate...**

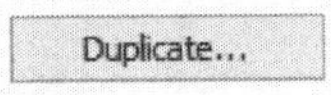

Select **Duplicate**.

22. Name: Ordinate - Arial 2"

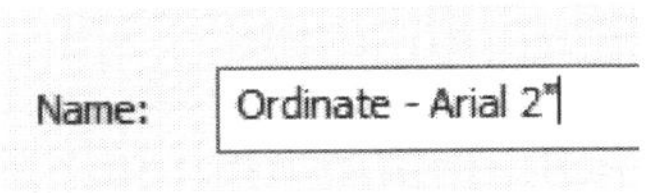

Type **Ordinate – Arial 2"** in the Name field.

Click **OK**.

23. Set the Dimension String Type to **Ordinate**.

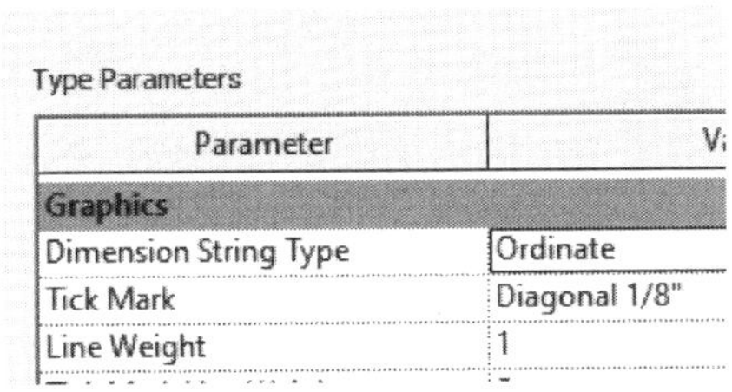

Type Parameters

Parameter	V:
Graphics	
Dimension String Type	Ordinate
Tick Mark	Diagonal 1/8"
Line Weight	1

24. Set the Witness Line Gap to Element to **1"**.

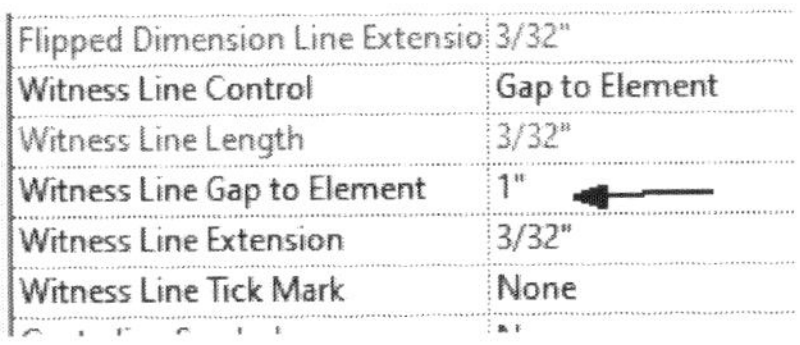 Flipped Dimension Line Extensio	3/32"
Witness Line Control	Gap to Element
Witness Line Length	3/32"
Witness Line Gap to Element	1"
Witness Line Extension	3/32"
Witness Line Tick Mark	None

25. 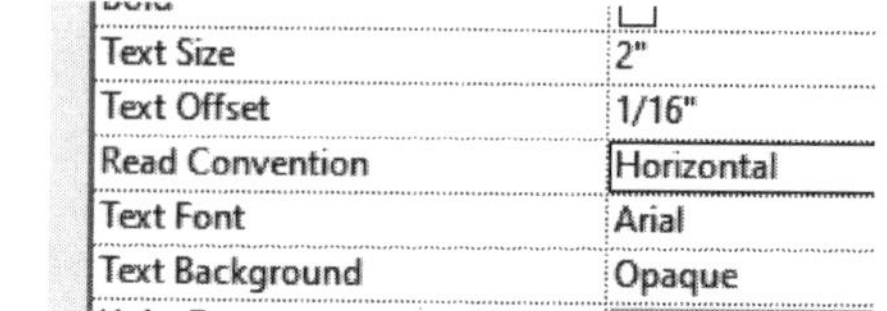

Set the Text Size to **2"**.

26. 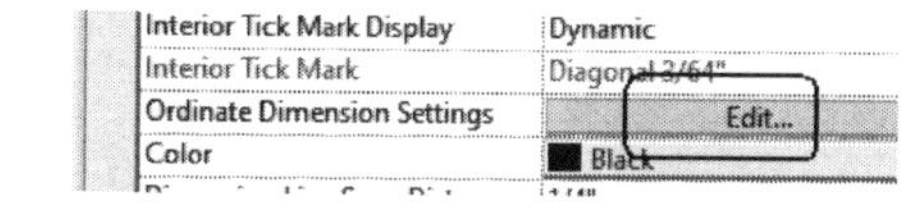

Set the Alternate Units to **Below**.

Set the alternate units to **mm**.

In the Alternate Units Prefix, type **[**.

In the Alternate Units Suffix, type **]**.

This adds brackets around the alternate units.

27. 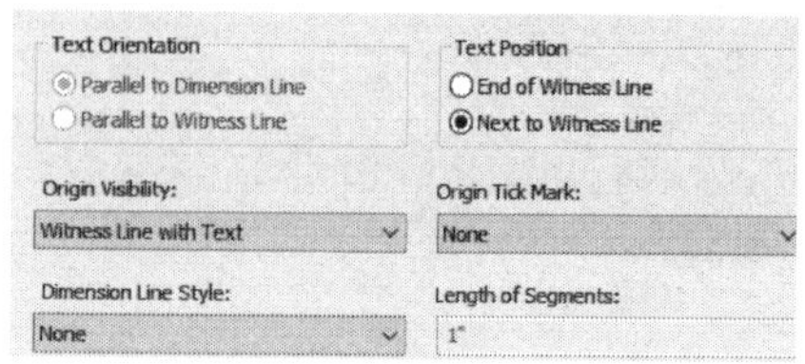

Set the Read Convention to **Horizontal**.

28.

Select **Edit** next to Ordinate Dimension Settings.

29.

Set Text Position to **Next to Witness Line**.

Set Dimension Line Style to **None**.

Set Origin Tick Mark to **None**.

Click **OK**.

30.

Click **OK** to close the dialog box.

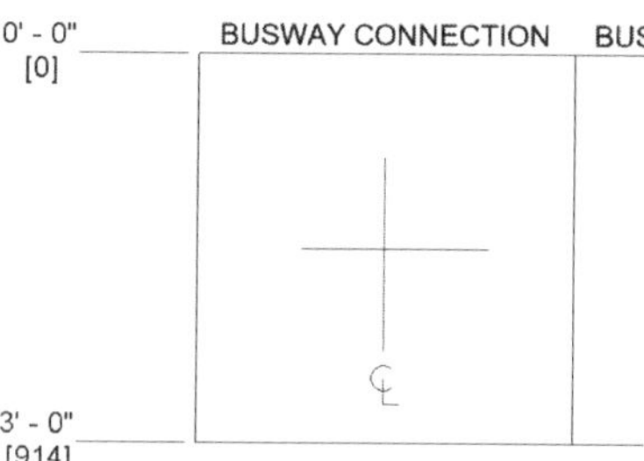

The first line selected when you placed your dimension will be the 0' 0" dimension. If the top line is not designated as the origin, delete the dimension and place again using the Ordinate dimension type.

Delete the aligned dimension that was placed.

Select the top line of the section. Then the bottom line to place the ordinate dimensions.

31.

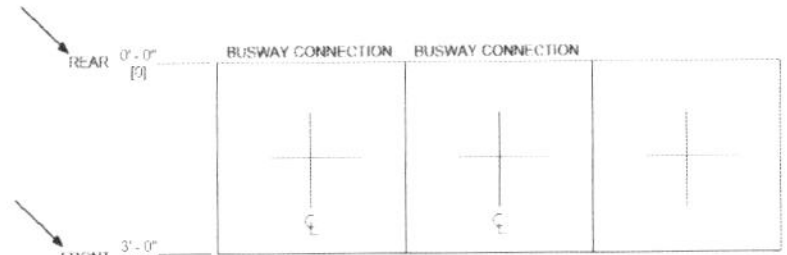

Add text to designate the front and rear of the switchboards.

32.

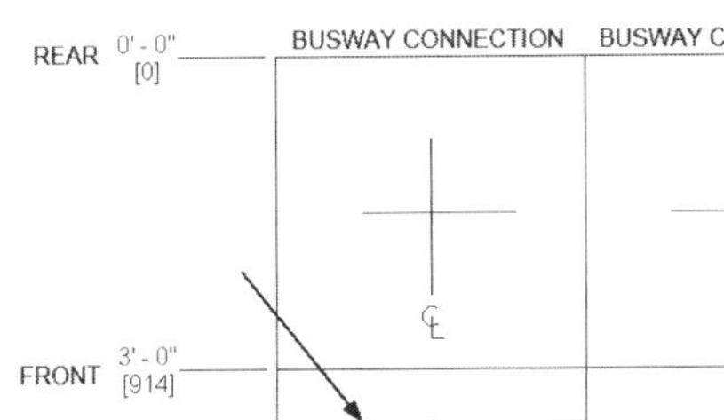

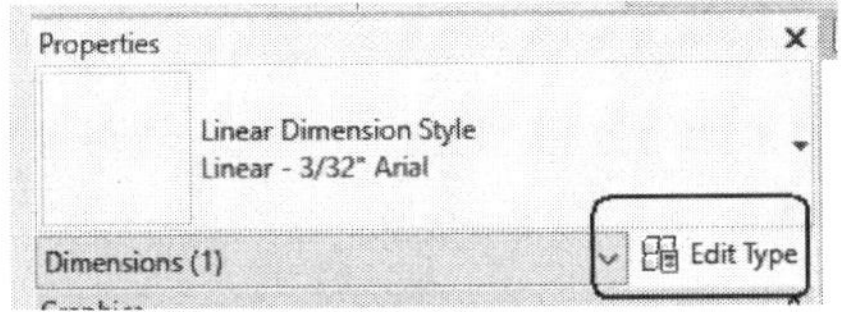

Place an aligned dimension below the first square using the Linear – 3/32" Arial dimension type.

33.

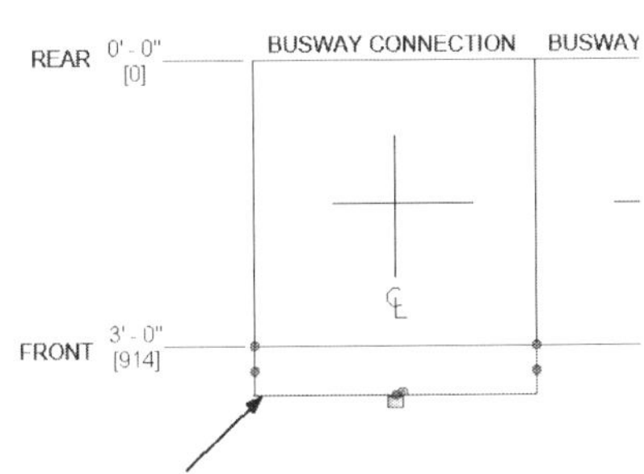

Select the dimension.

Select **Edit Type** on the Properties palette.

34. Select **Duplicate**.

35. Name: Linear - Dual Arial 2"

Type Linear – **Dual Arial 2"** in the Name field.

Click **OK**.

36.

Type Parameters	
Parameter	Value
Graphics	
Dimension String Type	Continuous
Leader Type	Arc
Leader Tick Mark	Arrow Filled 30 Degree
Show Leader When Text Moves	Away From Origin
Tick Mark	Arrow Filled 30 Degree
Line Weight	1
Tick Mark Line Weight	5

Set the Leader Tick Mark to **Arrow Filled 30 Degree**.

Set the Tick Mark to **Arrow Filled 30 Degree**.

37.

Parameter	Value
Flipped Dimension Line Extension	3/32"
Witness Line Control	Gap to Element
Witness Line Length	3/32"
Witness Line Gap to Element	1"
Witness Line Extension	3/32"
Witness Line Tick Mark	None

Set the Witness Line Gap to Element to **1"**.

38. 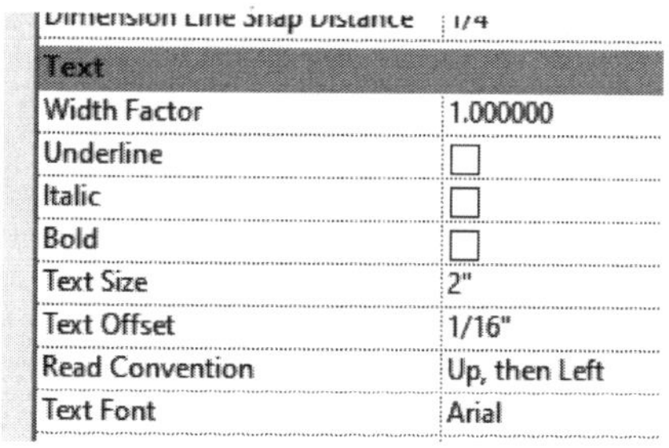 Set the Text Size to **2"**.

Click **OK**.

39. 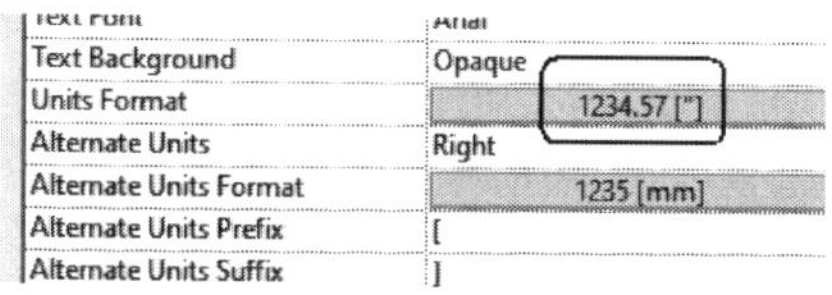 Click on the **Units Format**.

40. 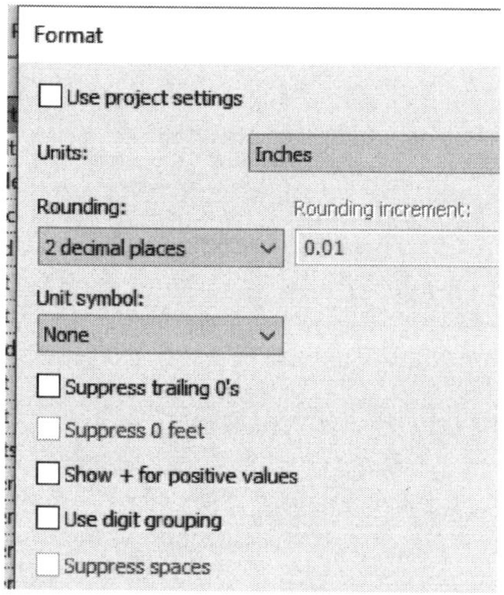 Disable **Use project settings**.

Set the Units to **Inches**.

Set the Rounding to **2 decimal places.**

Click **OK**.

41. 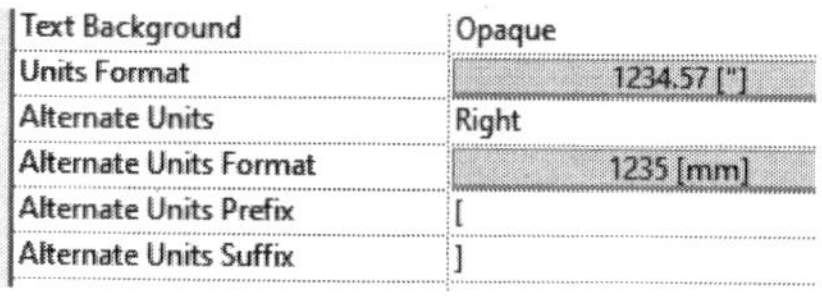 Set the Alternate Units to **Right**.

Set the alternate units to **mm**.

In the Alternate Units Prefix, type **[**.

In the Alternate Units Suffix, type **]**.

This adds brackets around the alternate units.

42. 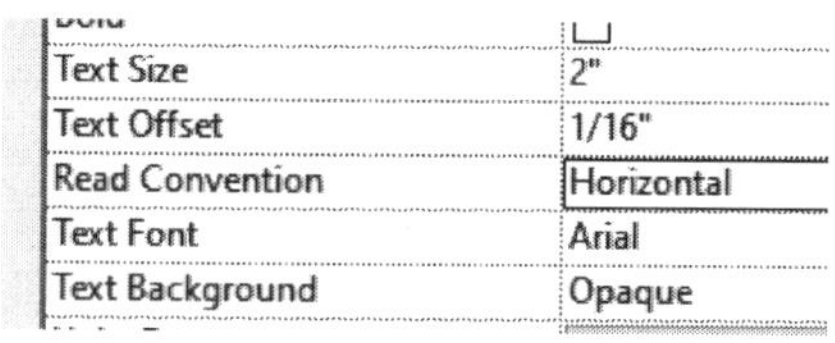 Set the Read Convention to **Horizontal**.

Click **OK**.

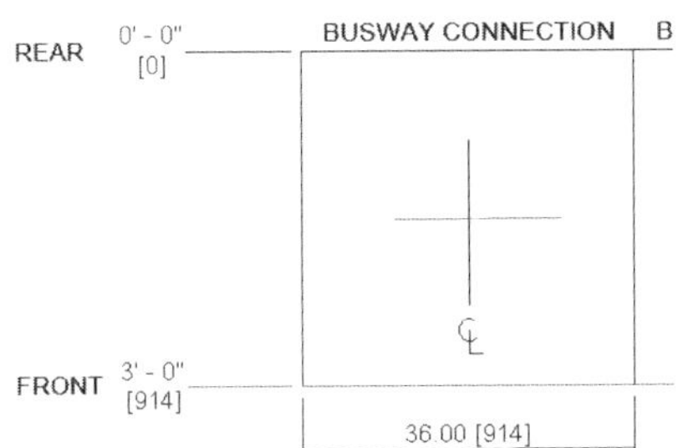

The arrowheads are too small in this dimension.

43. 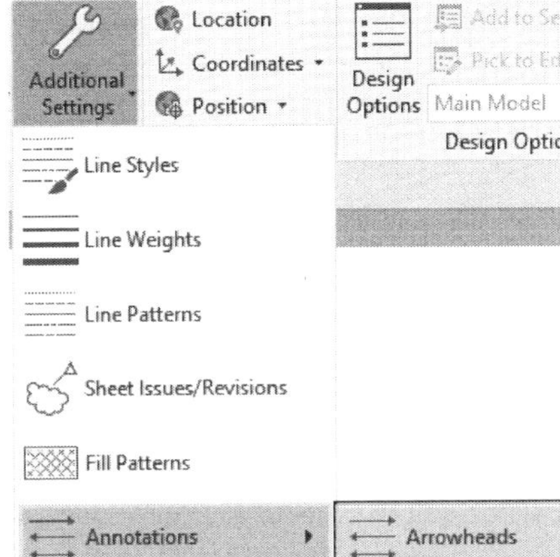

Switch to the Manage ribbon.

Select **Arrowheads** under Additional Settings.

44. 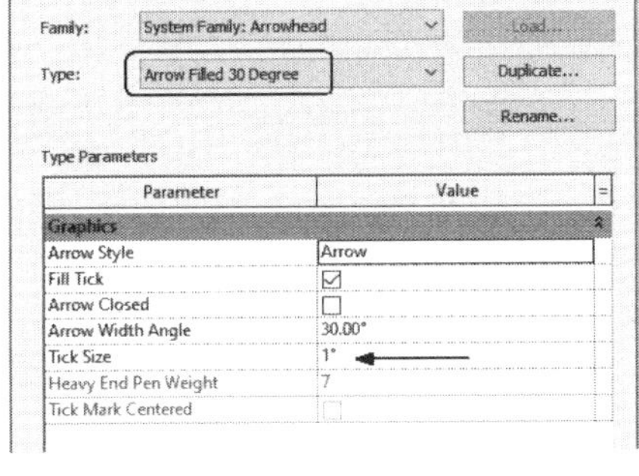

Select the **Arrow Filled 30 Degree** from the drop-down list.

Change the Tick Size to **1"**.

Click **OK**.

45. 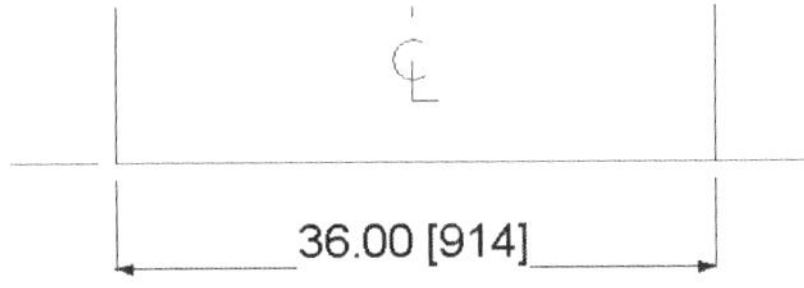

The new dimension family should look similar to the image.

46. 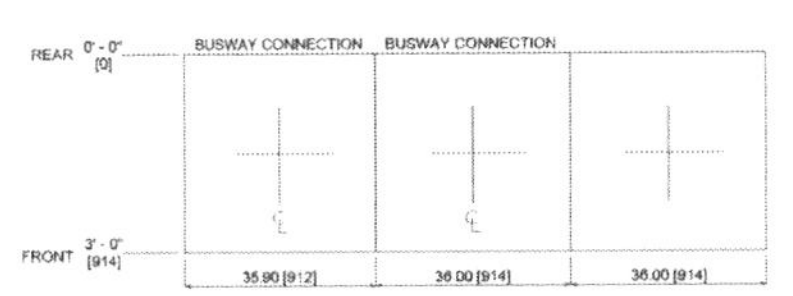

Place additional dimensions.

47.　Save as *ex9-4.rvt*.

Text Notes

Text notes can be added to a view with or without leaders. The appearance of text is controlled using Text Styles. Text is the information added to a view to label or provide a description about the building elements. It is view-specific and automatically updates when the view scale changes.

You can use the default test types which load with a template or create custom text types. Text can have leaders automatically added to designate specific elements in a view.

When you add text, the text and leaders will automatically snap into alignment with existing text and leaders. Text can be modified after it is placed to assign it to a new text style or to change the size, font, justification, width, leader, etc. You can import text notes from Word.

Guidelines for Working with Text and Tags

- Add text and tags after a view is created and the elements have been placed.
- Create copies of main model views and annotate the copied view. This way you have one view with annotations and one without. This makes it easier to make changes to the model in the non-annotated view.
- Plan and crop the documentation views to add text notes easily. Text notes and their associated leaders should not obscure the display of building elements.
- Align text notes to make it easier for reading.
- Create different text types for specific situations.

Exercise 9-5:
Adding a Text Note

Drawing Name: *text.rvt*
Estimated Time: 5 minutes

This exercise reinforces the following skills:

❑ Adding Text to a View

1. Open the **Main Floor – Power** floor plan.

2. 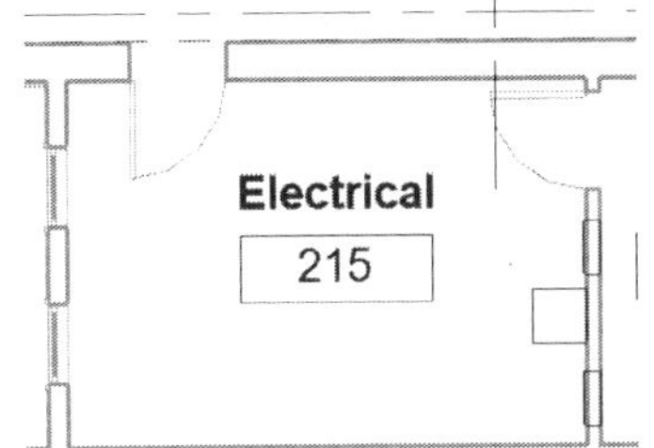   Zoom into **Room 215-Electrical**.

3.   Activate the **Annotate** ribbon.

Select the **Text** tool from the ribbon.

4.   Enable the two segment leader option on the ribbon.

5.   Verify that the **3/32" Arial** text style is selected on the Properties palette.

6.   Left click to start the leader at the transformer.

Place a second left click to the left to start the text.

Type **MTD 6" AFF**.

Click **Close** on the ribbon to complete the text.

7.   Save as *ex9-5.rvt*.

Exercise 9-6:

Create a Text Type

Drawing Name: *text type.rvt*
Estimated Time: 5 minutes

This exercise reinforces the following skills:

- Defining a new Text Type

1. 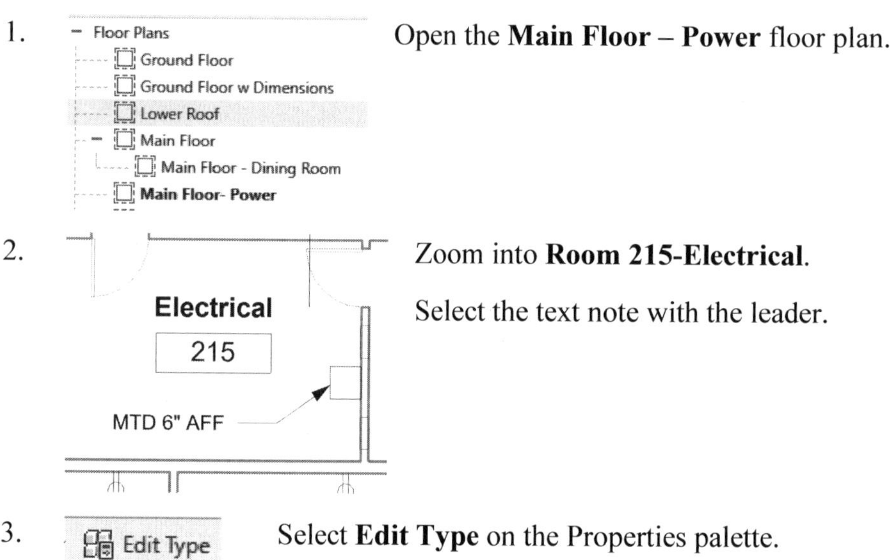

    Open the **Main Floor – Power** floor plan.

2. Zoom into **Room 215-Electrical**.

    Select the text note with the leader.

3. Edit Type   Select **Edit Type** on the Properties palette.

4. Duplicate...   Select **Duplicate**.

5. Name: 3/32" Romans

    Change the Name to **3/32" Romans**.

    Click **OK**.

6. 

    Change the Background to **Transparent**.

    Change the Leader Arrowhead to **Arrow Filled 15 Degree**.

    Change the Text Font to **RomanS**.

    Click **OK**.

Type Parameters	
Parameter	
Graphics	
Color	■ Black
Line Weight	1
Background	Transparent
Show Border	
Leader/Border Offset	5/64"
Leader Arrowhead	Arrow Filled 15 Degree
Text	
Text Font	RomanS
Text Size	3/32"
Tab Size	1/2"

7. 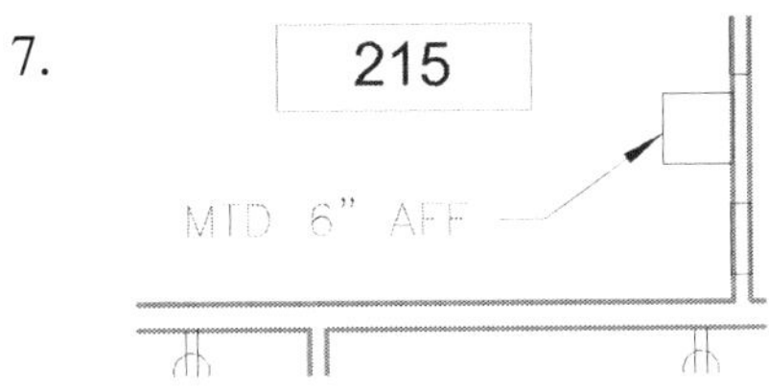 Left click anywhere in the display window to release the selection.

Review the changes to the text.

Save as *ex9-6.rvt*.

Keynotes

Keynotes are used to tag elements or materials with standard CSI keynotes or custom keynotes.

A keynote parameter is available for all model elements (including detail components) and materials. You can tag each of these elements using a keynote tag family. The keynote value is derived from a separate text file that contains a list of keynotes.

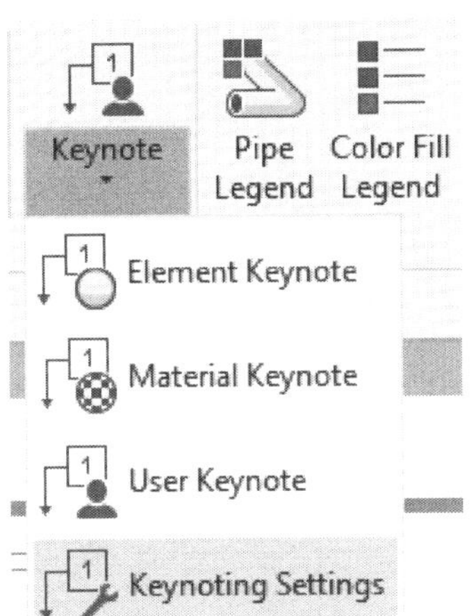

Many companies develop their own keynotes to be used on their projects.

To assign a custom keynote file or verify the location of the keynote file, go to the Annotate ribbon and access Keynoting Settings under the Keynote tool.

The keynote text file is located under the Libraries folder:

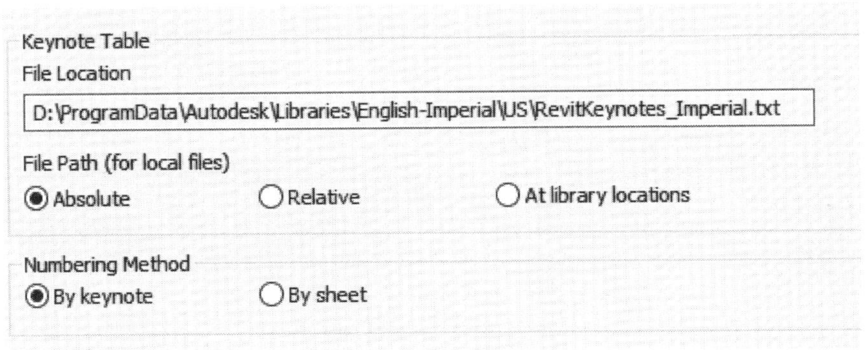

You will not be able to place a keynote unless you have the file location set correctly.

Exercise 9-7:
Using Keynotes

Drawing Name: *keynotes.rvt*
Estimated Time: 20 minutes

This exercise reinforces the following skills:

- Add tags to lighting fixtures using keynotes

1. Open the **Pendant Lighting** section under Lighting.

2. Activate the **Annotate** ribbon.

   Select **Element Keynote** under Keynote.

3. On the Type Selector:

   Select **Keynote Number**.

4. Enable **Leader** on the ribbon.

5. 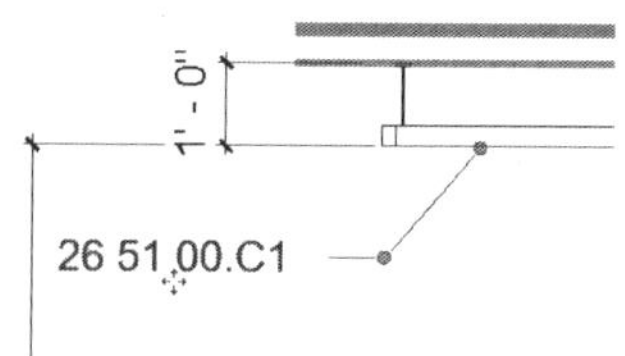

   Select the pendant light fixture and place the keynote text.

6. 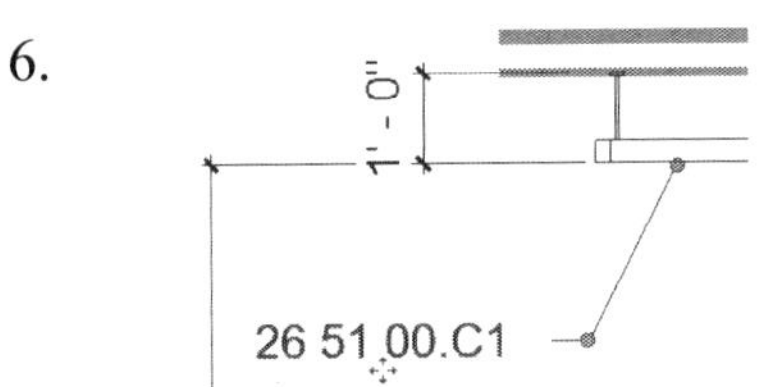 

Select **Edit Type** on the Properties palette with the keynote selected.

7. Set the Leader Arrowhead to **Arrow Filled 15 Degree**.

Click **OK**.

8. Open the **Recessed Lighting Fixture** section under Lighting.

9. Activate the **Annotate** ribbon.

Select **Element Keynote** under Keynote.

10. On the Type Selector:

Select **Keynote Number**.

11. Place the keynote.

12. Open the **Sconce Lighting Fixture – Callout 1** section under Lighting.

13. Activate the **Annotate** ribbon.

Select **Element Keynote** under Keynote.

14.
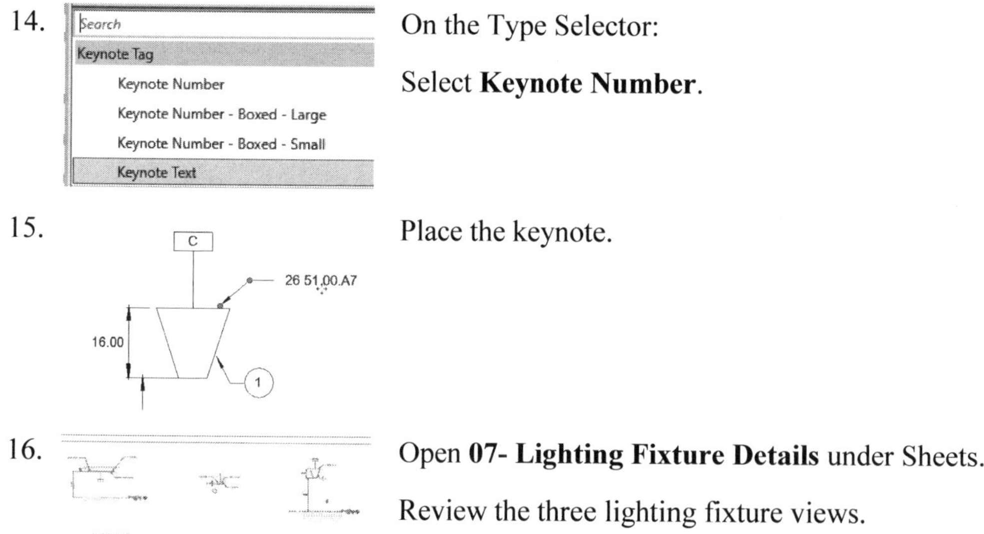

On the Type Selector:

Select **Keynote Number**.

15.

Place the keynote.

16.

Open **07- Lighting Fixture Details** under Sheets.

Review the three lighting fixture views.

17. Save as *ex9-7.rvt*.

Keynote Legends

Keynote Legends automatically create legends from the Keynotes that you have used in your project. By default, it only has two columns: the key number and the related key text. Place the legend on any sheet with views using keynote tags.

Exercise 9-8:

Create a Keynote Legend

Drawing Name: *keynote_legend.rvt*
Estimated Time: 10 minutes

This exercise reinforces the following skills:

- ❑ Legends
- ❑ Schedules
- ❑ Sheets
- ❑ Keynotes

1.  Activate the **View** ribbon.

    Select **Keynote Legend** under Legend.

2. Type **Keynotes** in the Name field.

    Click **OK**.

3. The available fields are already pre-selected.

4. 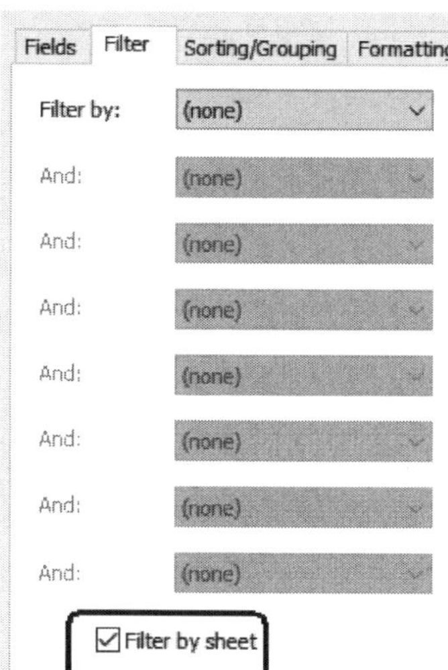   Activate the Filter tab.

Enable **Filter by sheet.**

This means that only keynotes appearing in views on the sheet will be listed in the legend.

5.   Activate the Appearance tab.

Enable **Grid lines**.

Enable **Outline**.

Set the Grid lines to use **Wide Lines**.

Set the Outline to use **Medium Lines**.

Disable **Show Title**.

Disable **Show Headers**.

Set the Body Text to **3/32" Arial**.

Click **OK**.

6. 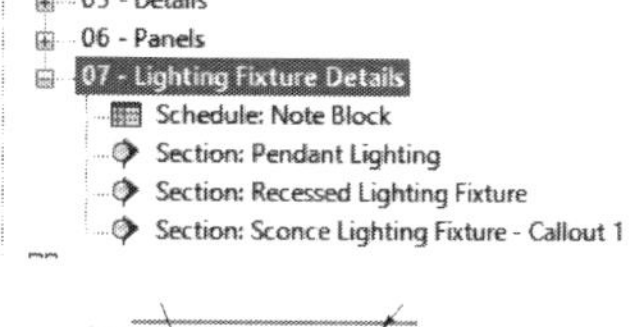   Open the **07-Lighting Fixture Details** sheet.

7. 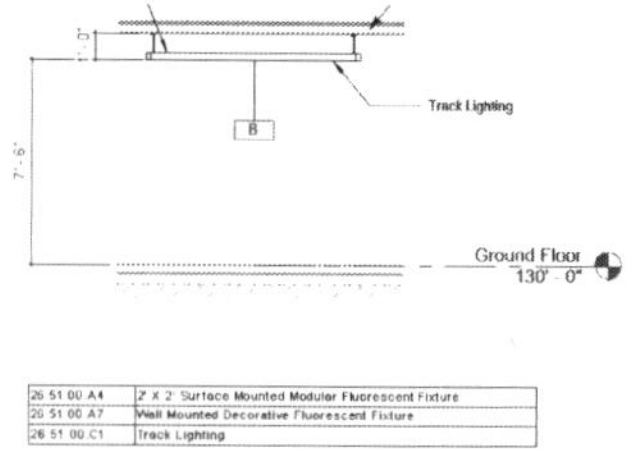   Drag and drop the keynotes legend onto the sheet.

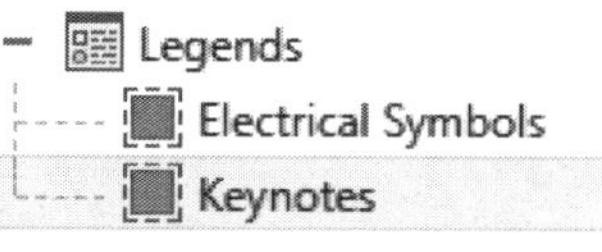

8. Save as *ex9-8.rvt*.

Tags

A tag is an annotation for identifying elements in a drawing.

Every category in the family library has a tag. Some tags automatically load with the default Revit template, while others you need to load. If desired, you can make your own tag in the Family Editor by creating an annotation symbol family. In addition, you can load multiple tags for a family.

You can tag elements in a view of a host model, linked model and nested model. Tags are view-specific. This means tags will only appear in the views where they are placed. Tags will automatically scale when the view scale is changed.

Tags display the parametric information about the associated/selected elements.

You can create custom tags by editing predefined tags and saving them with a new name.

Tags can be added with or without a leader. Tags can be oriented horizontally or vertically. Once tags are placed, they can be modified using the Type Selector or by changing their properties.

You can Tag by Category, Tag All, or do a Multi-Category Tag.

Tag by Category places tags based on family. For example, tagging all light fixtures or tagging all electrical panels. When you tag building elements by category, Revit identifies the element type and automatically provides the appropriate tag (if the tag has been loaded into the project).

Tag All places tags on any element where that tag has been loaded into the project. Tags are placed on any elements that don't have an existing tag. This function can be useful when you place and tag rooms in a floor plan view and you want to see the same tags in the reflected ceiling plan. Load all the desired tag families into the project prior to selecting Tag All. You can opt to tag all elements or selected elements only.

Tag Multiple allows you to tag all untagged elements in more than one category in one operation.

Guidelines for Using Tags

- Add tags after a view has been created and the model is fairly well along.
- Duplicate the view and place tags on one version of the view and no annotations on the other view. Use the non-annotated view to make changes to the model.
- Load more than one tag type for building elements so they can easily be tagged.

Exercise 9-9:

Tag Light Fixtures

Drawing Name: *tags_1.rvt*
Estimated Time: 5 minutes

This exercise reinforces the following skills:

❑ Add tags to lighting fixtures

1. 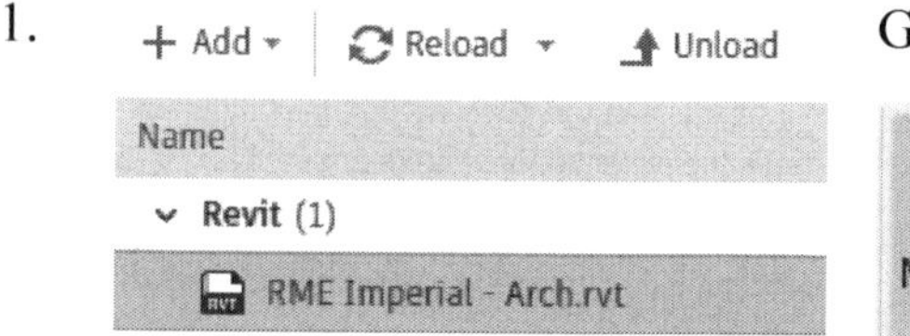

   Go to the Insert ribbon.

   Click **Manage Links**.

   Reload *RME Imperial- Arch.rvt*.

   Close the dialog.

2. Activate the **Annotate** ribbon.

   Select **Tag by Category** from the ribbon.

3. On the ribbon:

   Enable Horizontal.

   Disable Leader.

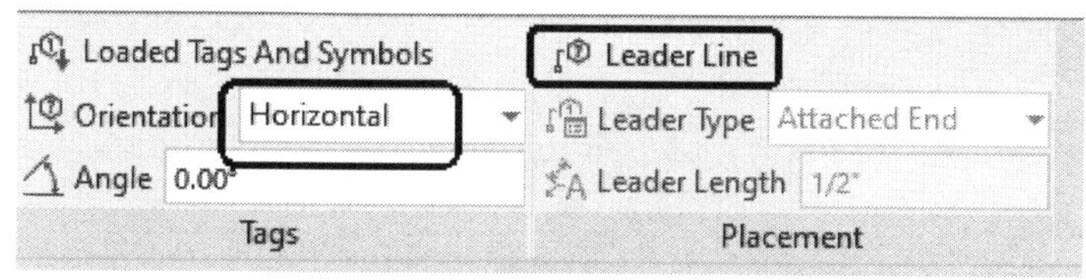

4. Left click on each lighting fixture in Classroom 5.

   Note that the tags are centered on each light fixture selected.

   Right click and Click **Cancel** or Click **ESC** to exit the command.

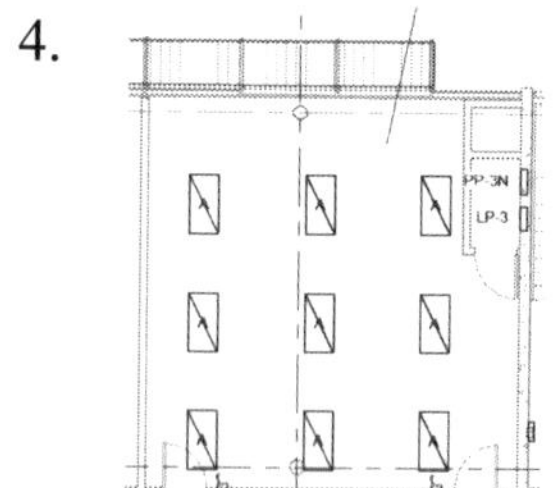

5. Save as *ex9-9.rvt*.

Exercise 9-10:

Tag Devices

Drawing Name: *tags_2.rvt*
Estimated Time: 5 minutes

This exercise reinforces the following skills:

- Add tags to electrical equipment
- Tag All

1. 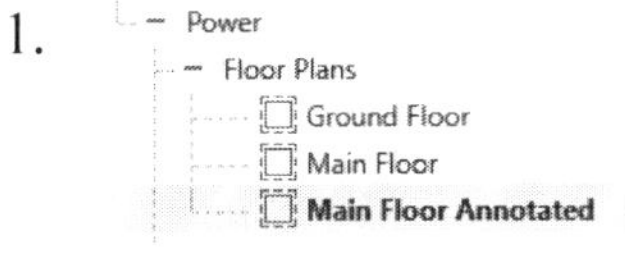

Open the **Main Floor Annotated Power** floor plan.

2. Zoom into the electrical equipment in the middle of the view.

3. 

Select the Switchboard on the left.

   Note that there is no Panel Name assigned in the Properties palette.

   Repeat for the two devices next to the switchboard. None of the devices have been assigned names.

4. Activate the **Annotate** ribbon.

   Select **Tag All** from the ribbon.

5. 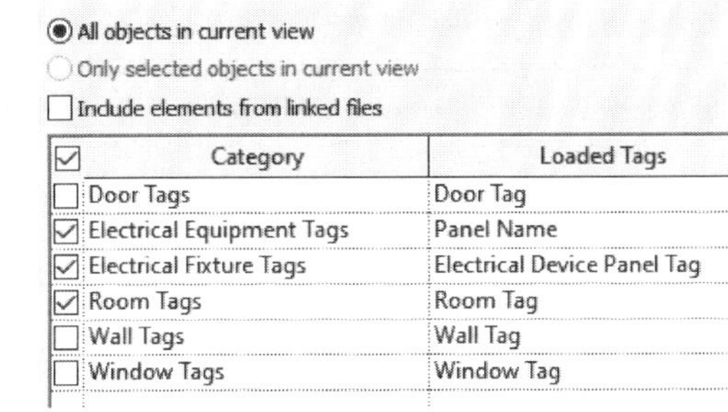
Enable

- Electrical Equipment Tags
- Electrical Fixture Tags
- Room Tags

Disable **Leader** at the bottom of the dialog.

Click **OK**.

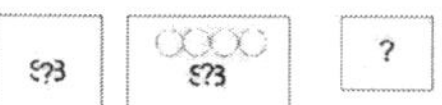

? symbols appear on all the unnamed devices.

6. 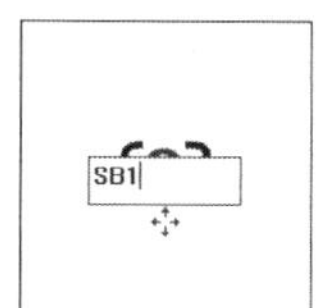

Select the Metering Switchboard tag on the left.

Type **SB1** for the panel name.

Click **ENTER**.

Click ESC to release the selection.

7.

General	
Enclosure	
Mounting	
Panel Name	SB1
Location	

Select the Metering Switchboard device.
In the Properties palette, note that the Panel Name has updated.

Click ESC to release the selection.

8.

Select the device tag in the middle.

You can use the TAB key to cycle through selections.

Type **SB2** for the panel name.

Click **ENTER**.

Click ESC to release the selection.

9.

Select the device tag on the right.

You can use the TAB key to cycle through selections.

Type **T1** for the panel name.

Click **ENTER**.

Click ESC to release the selection.

10. Save as *ex9-10.rvt.*

Global Parameters

Use global parameters to drive or report values.

You can use global parameters in a project to:

- drive the value of a dimension or constraint.

- associate to an element instance or type property to drive its value.

- associate to an instance or type project parameter.

- report the value of a dimension, so this value can be used in equations of other global parameters.

A global parameter is a parameter that you create inside a Project that can be used to assign or report a value across the entire project. Global parameters are useful to ensure your project meets local building codes. We can use global parameters to ensure that minimum clearance distances are met.

Exercise 9-11:

Using Global Parameters

Drawing Name: *global parameters.rvt*
Estimated Time: 10 minutes

This exercise reinforces the following skills:

- ❑ Global Parameters
- ❑ Dimensions
- ❑ Groups

The OSHA standard (29 CFR 1910.303 (g)) requires sufficient access and working space around all equipment serving 600 volts or less. For equipment serving between 120 volts and 250 volts, the regulations require a minimum of three feet of clearance. The width of the working space in front shall be 30 inches minimum or width of the equipment.

1.   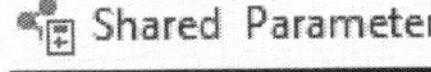   Switch to the Manage ribbon.

    Select **Global Parameters**.

2.    Select **New** (located at the bottom of the dialog).

3. 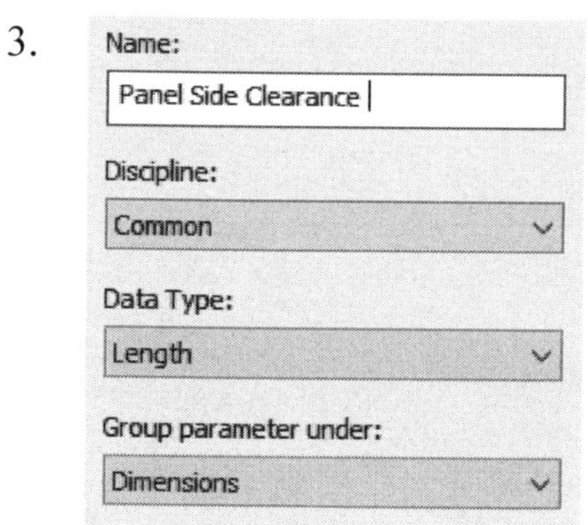

Type **Panel Side Clearance** in the Name field.

Set the Discipline to **Common**.

Set the Type of parameter to **Length**.

Group parameter under **Dimensions**.

Click **OK**.

4.

Parameter	Value
Text	
Panel Side Clearance	3 0

Set the Value to **3' 0"**.

5.    Select **New** (located at the bottom of the dialog).

6. 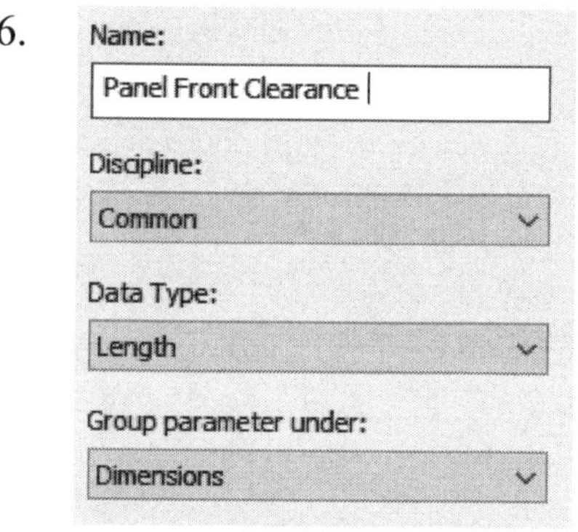

Type **Panel Front Clearance** in the Name field.

Set the Discipline to **Common**.

Set the Type of parameter to **Length**.

Group parameter under **Dimensions**.

Click **OK**.

7.

Dimensions	
Panel Front Clearance	2' 6"
Panel Side Clearance	3' 0"

Set the Value to **2' 6"**.

Click **OK**.

8.

Zoom into the area next to Storage Rm 215.

9. 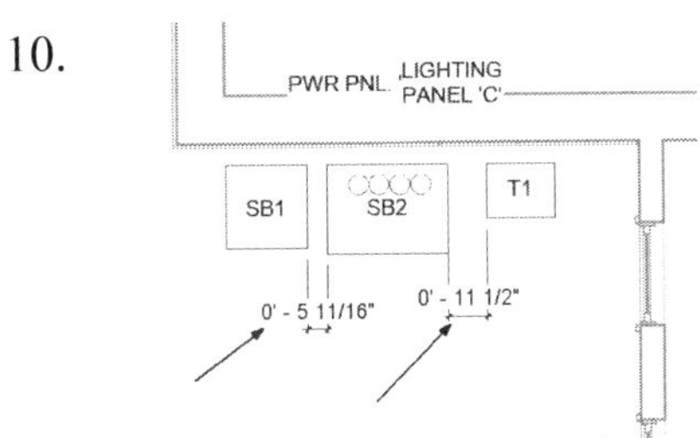 Select the **Aligned** tool from the Annotate ribbon.

10. 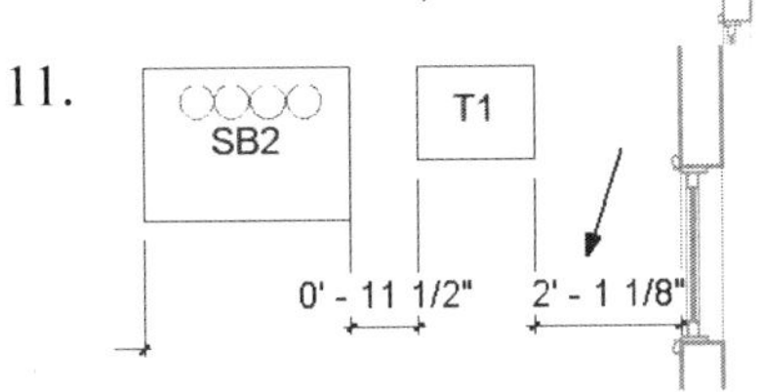 Place two dimensions between the panels.

11. 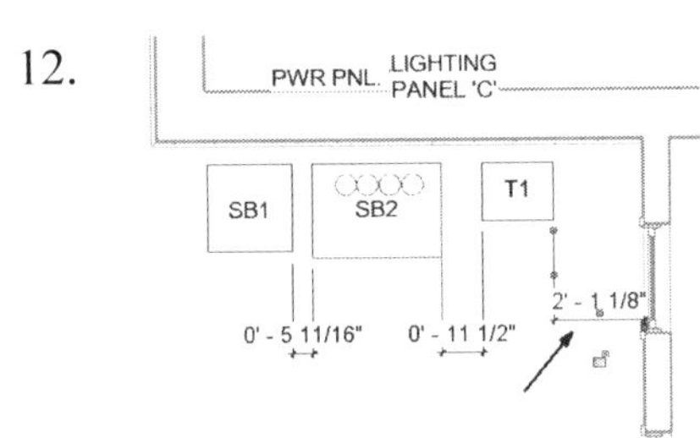 Place an aligned dimension between T1 and the wall face.

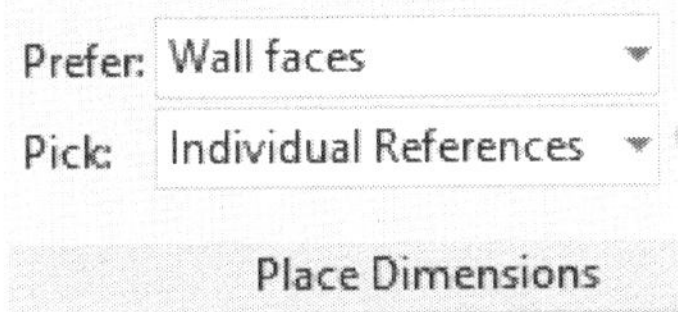

Hint: *Select Wall Faces on the ribbon.*

12. 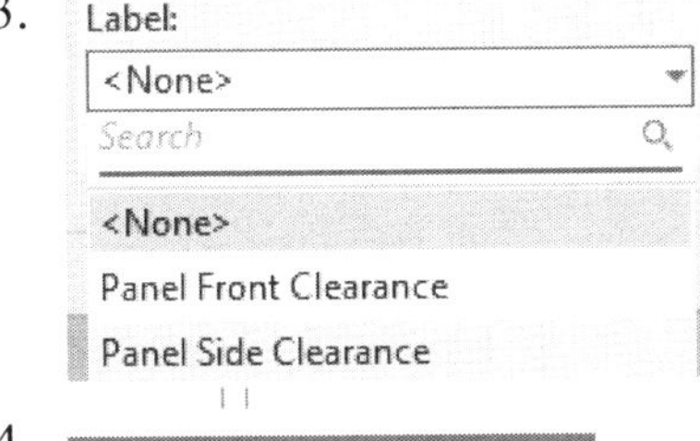 Select the dimension placed between the wall and T1.

13. On the ribbon, select **Panel Side Clearance** below the Label: drop-down list.

Left click in the window to release the selection.

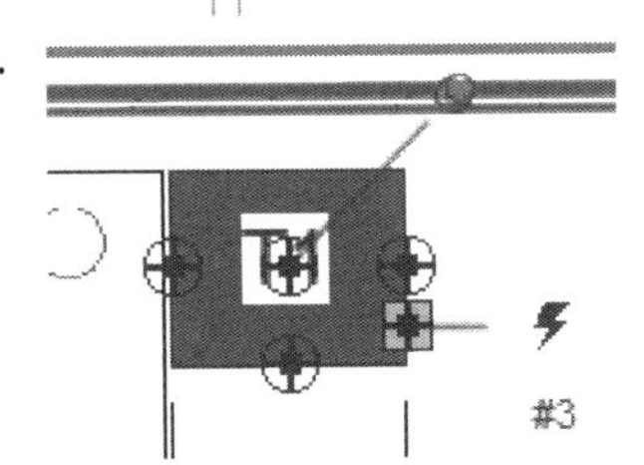

14. Select the T1 panel.

Select the **PIN** tool to lock it in place.

15.

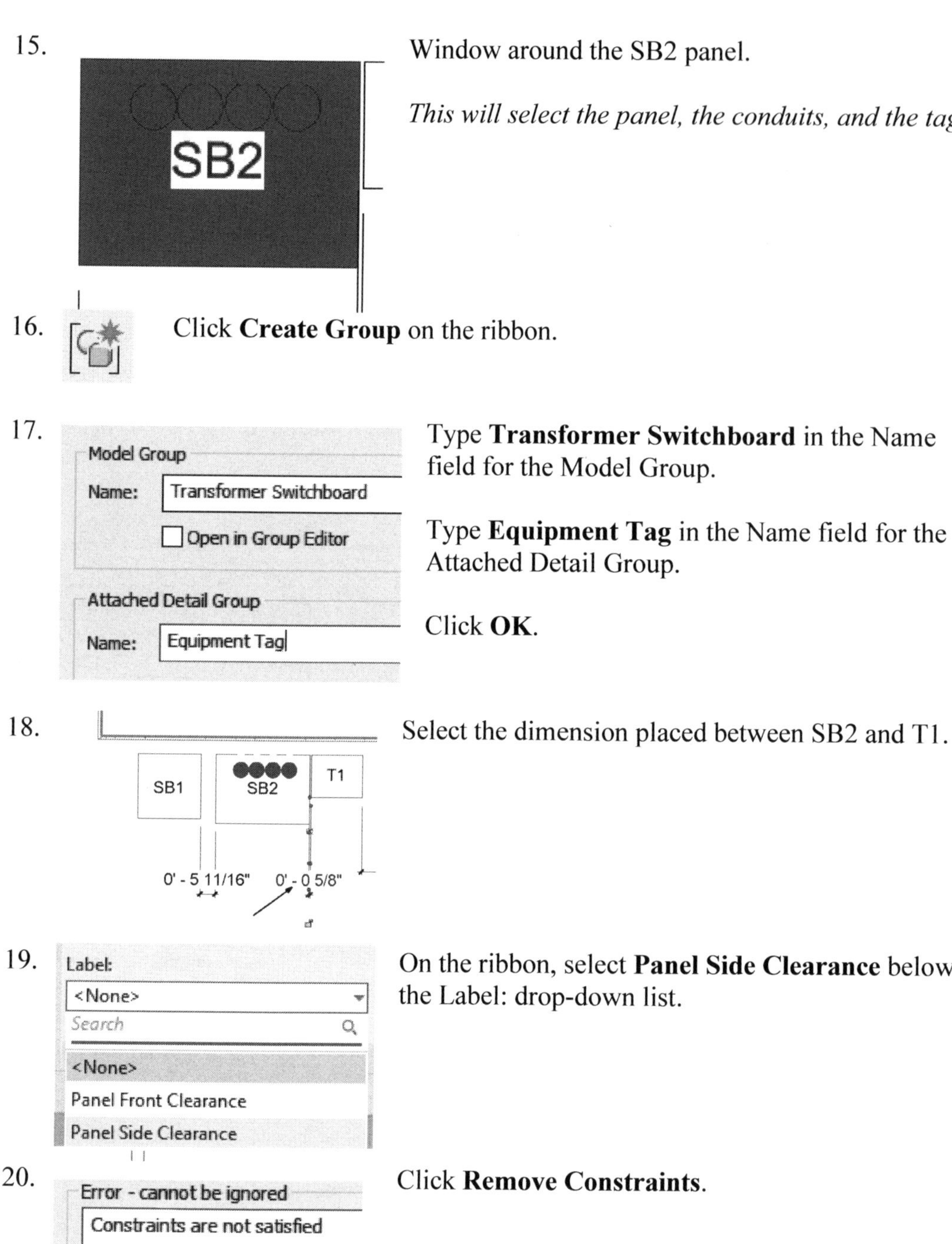

Window around the SB2 panel.

This will select the panel, the conduits, and the tag.

16. Click **Create Group** on the ribbon.

17. Type **Transformer Switchboard** in the Name field for the Model Group.

Type **Equipment Tag** in the Name field for the Attached Detail Group.

Click **OK**.

18. Select the dimension placed between SB2 and T1.

19. On the ribbon, select **Panel Side Clearance** below the Label: drop-down list.

20. Click **Remove Constraints**.

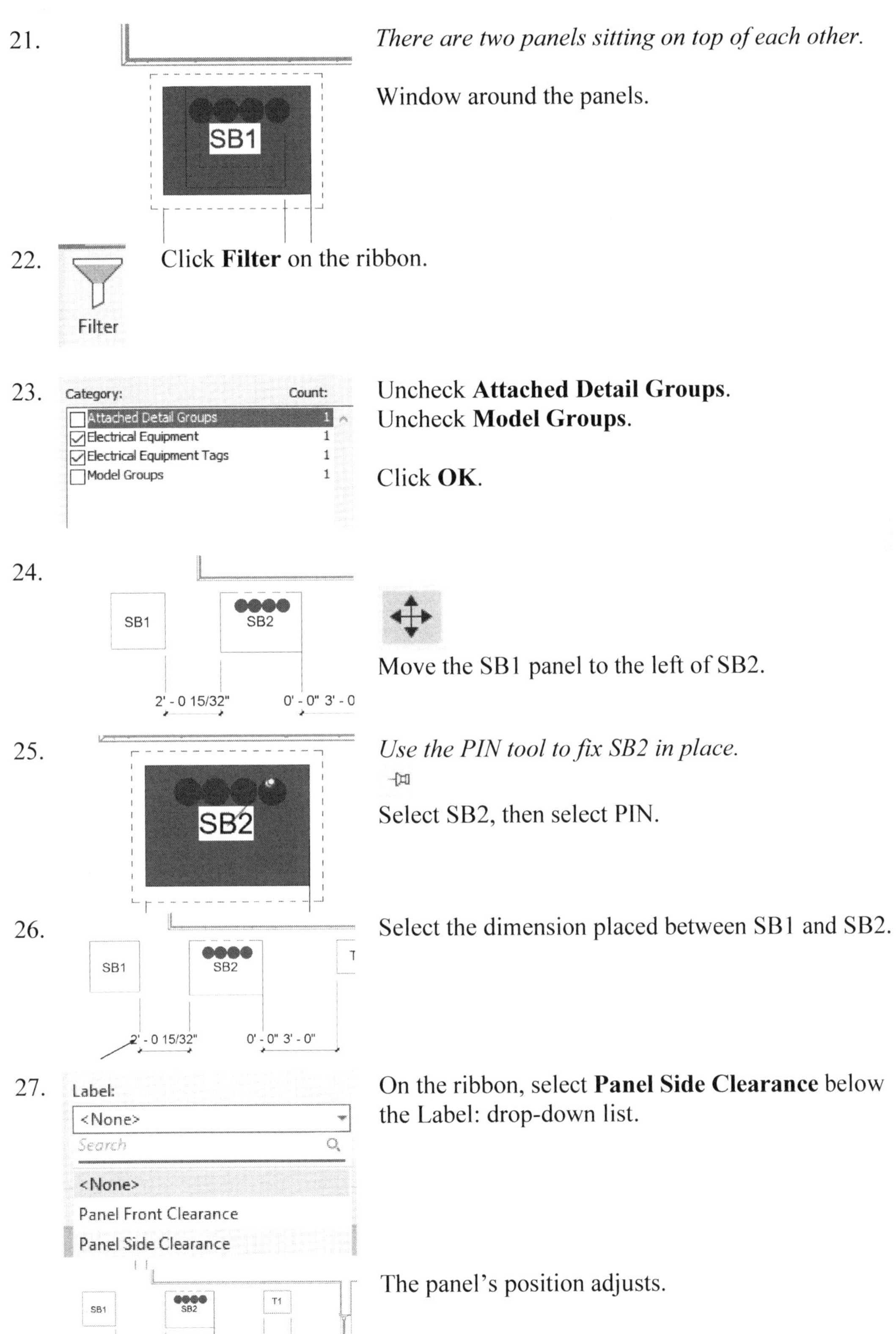

21. *There are two panels sitting on top of each other.*

Window around the panels.

22. Click **Filter** on the ribbon.

23. Uncheck **Attached Detail Groups**.
Uncheck **Model Groups**.

Click **OK**.

24. Move the SB1 panel to the left of SB2.

25. *Use the PIN tool to fix SB2 in place.*

Select SB2, then select PIN.

26. Select the dimension placed between SB1 and SB2.

27. On the ribbon, select **Panel Side Clearance** below
the Label: drop-down list.

The panel's position adjusts.

28.

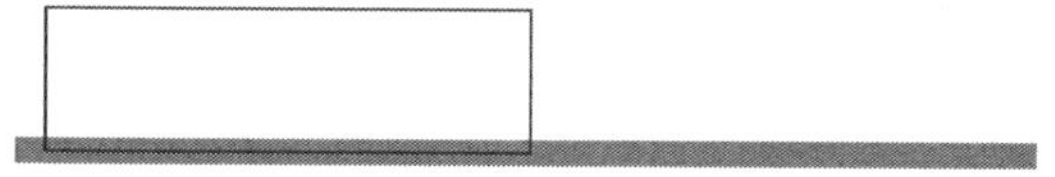

Locate the panels above the switchboards that were just positioned.

29.

LIGHTING PANEL 'C'

Hold down the CTL key.

Select the LIGHTING PANEL 'C' tag and the panel.

30.

Select **Group** on the ribbon.

31.

Model Group

Name: Lighting Panel C

☐ Open in Group Editor

Attached Detail Group

Name: Equipment Tag

Type **Lighting Panel C** in the Name field for the Model Group.

Type **Equipment Tag** in the Name field for the Attached Detail Group.

Click **OK**.

Left click to release the selection.

32.

PWR PNL. 'C'

Hold down the CTL key.

Select the PWR PANEL 'C' tag and the panel.

33. 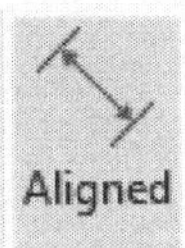 Select **Group** on the ribbon.

34. Type **PWR Panel C** in the Name field for the Model Group.

Type **Equipment Tag** in the Name field for the Attached Detail Group.

Click **OK**.

Left click to release the selection.

35. Select the **Aligned** tool from the Annotate ribbon.

36. 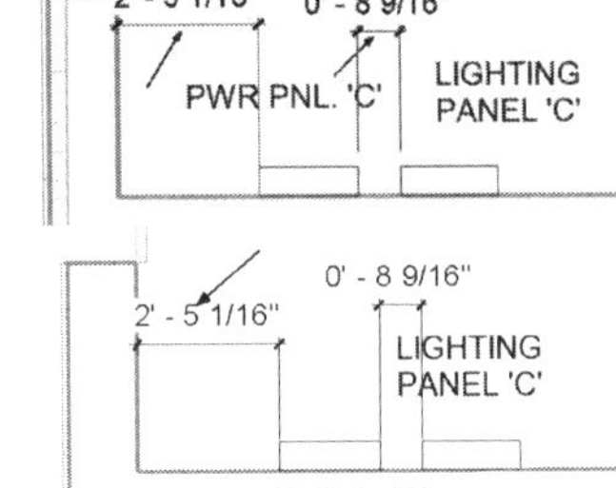

Place two dimensions between the panels and the power panel and the inside face of the wall.

37. Select the dimension between the wall face and PWR PNL "C".

38. Label:

On the ribbon, select **Panel Side Clearance** below the Label: drop-down list.

The panel's position adjusts.

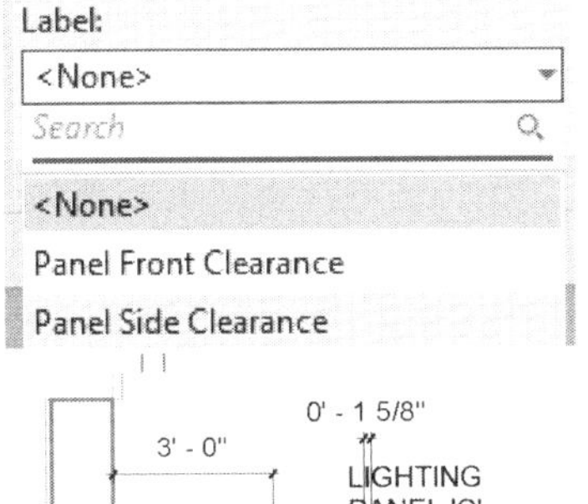

39.

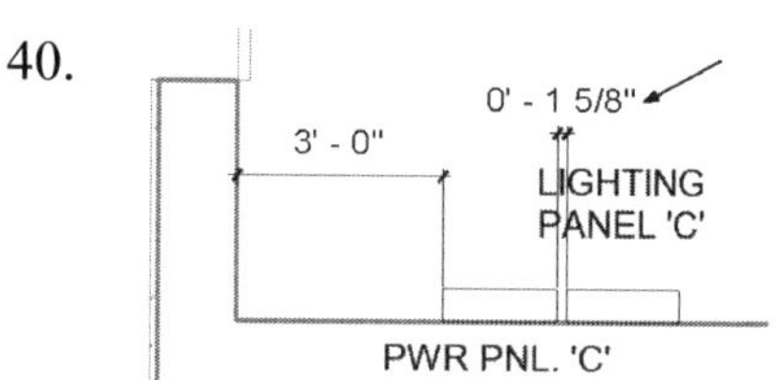

Use the PIN tool to fix the PWR panel in place.

Select PWR PNL C, then select PIN.

40.

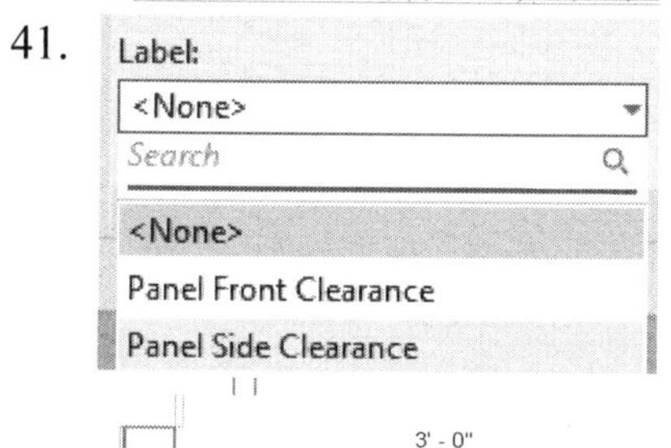

Select the dimension between the PWR PNL "C" and LIGHTING PANEL "C".

41.

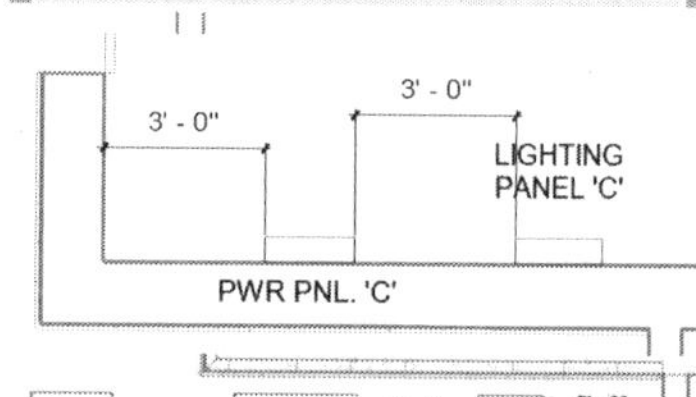

On the ribbon, select **Panel Side Clearance** below the Label: drop-down list.

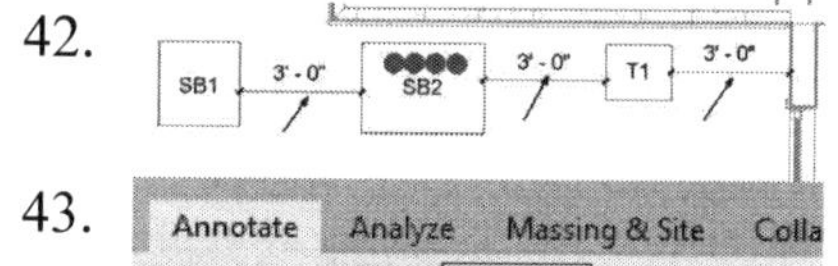

Lighting Panel C shifts to the right.

42.

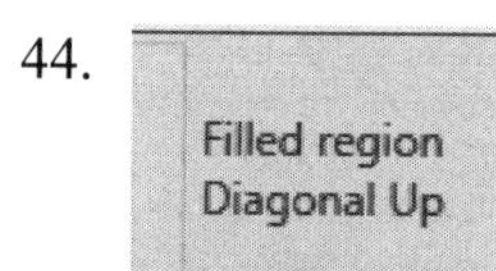

Reposition the dimensions so you have a clear space in front of the panels.

43.

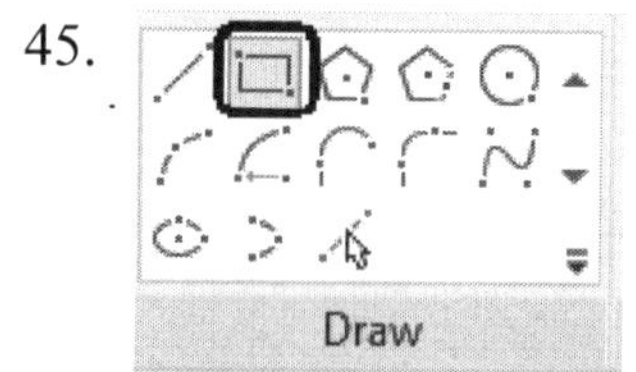

Switch to the Annotate ribbon.

Select **Filled Region**.

44.

Use the Type Selector to set the filled region type to **Diagonal Up** on the Properties panel.

45.

Select the **Rectangle** tool on the Draw panel.

46. Draw a rectangle in front of the panels.

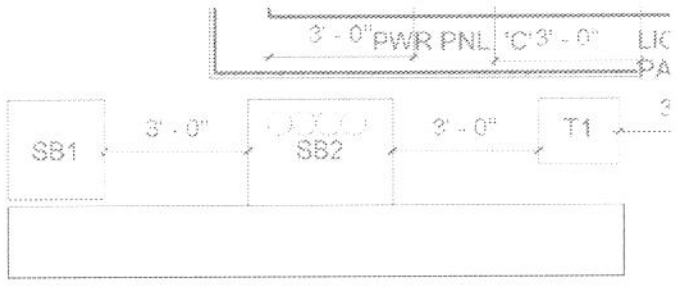

47. Place an aligned dimension to designate the width of the filled region.

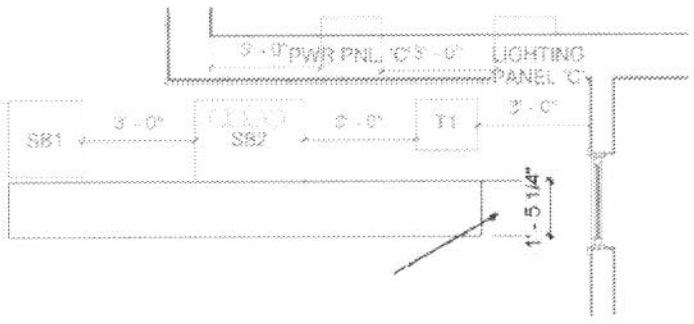

    Your dimension value may be different depending on how you drew the rectangle.

    ESC out of the dimension command.

48. Select the dimension so it highlights.

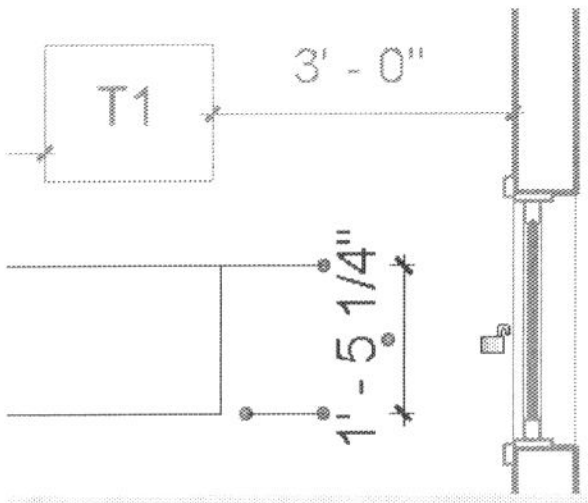

49. Select **Panel Front Clearance** from the ribbon.

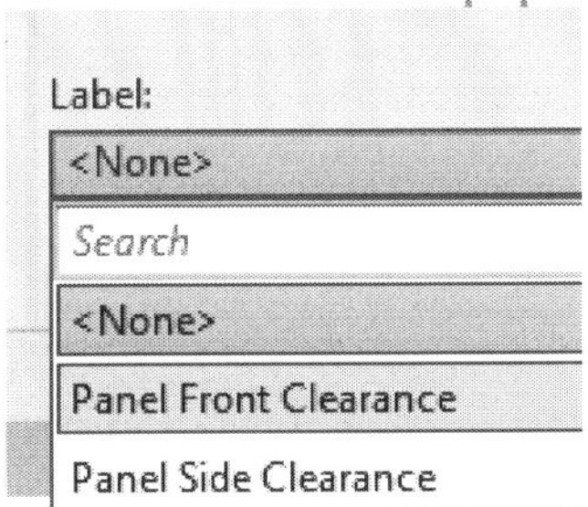

50. Select the ribbon tab labeled **Create Filled Region Boundary**.

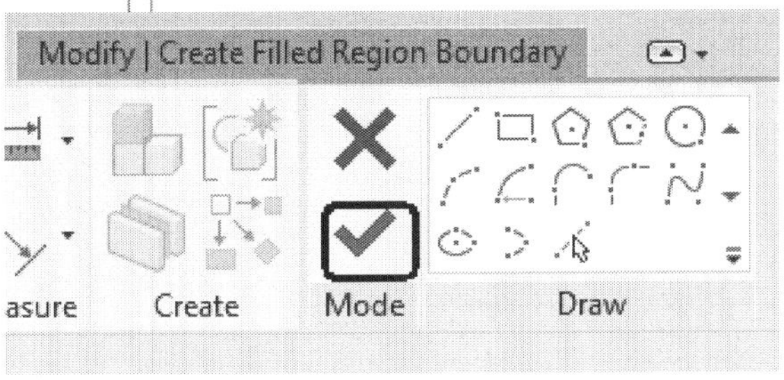

    Select **Green Check** to complete the filled region.

51. 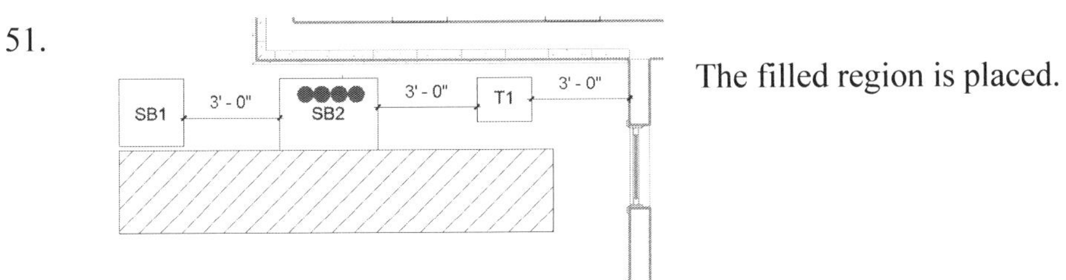
    The filled region is placed.

52. Save as *ex9-11.rvt*.

Extra: Place a filled region in front of PWR Panel C and Lighting Panel C and assign the front clearance global parameter to control the size of the region.

Adjust the location of the dimensions for the 'C' panels and use Edit Group to adjust the location of the equipment tags.

Add text to indicate the clearance areas.

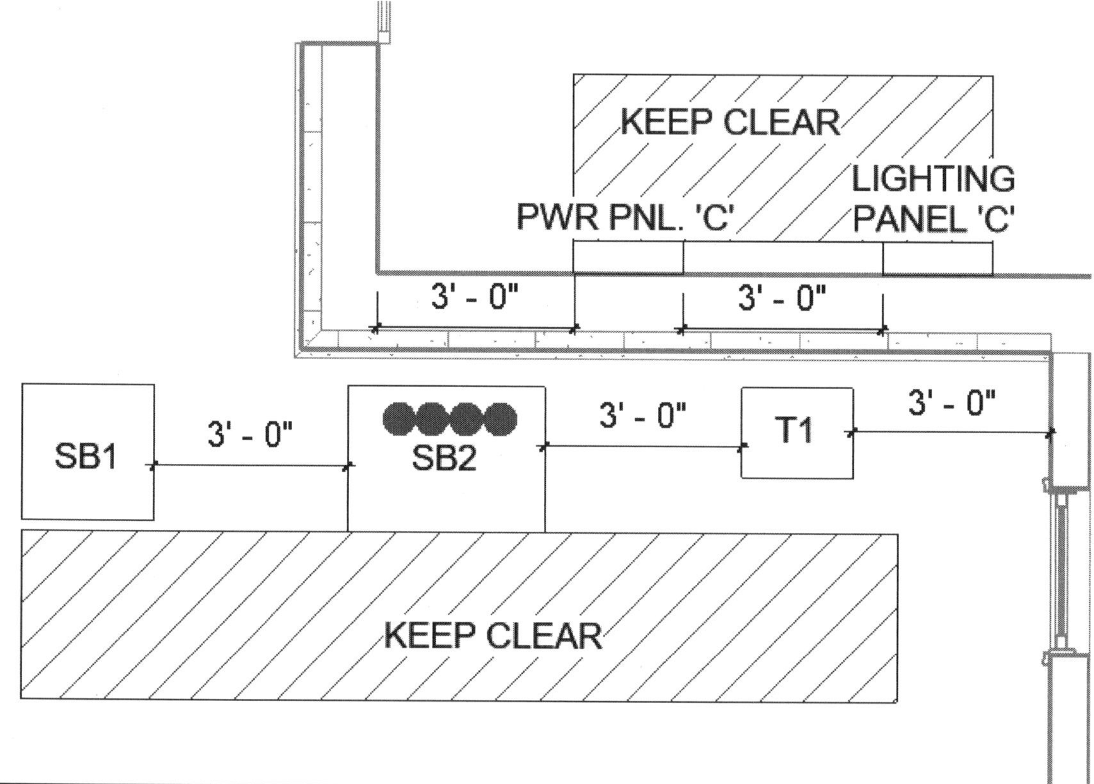

Lab Exercises

Open *lesson_9_lab.rvt*.

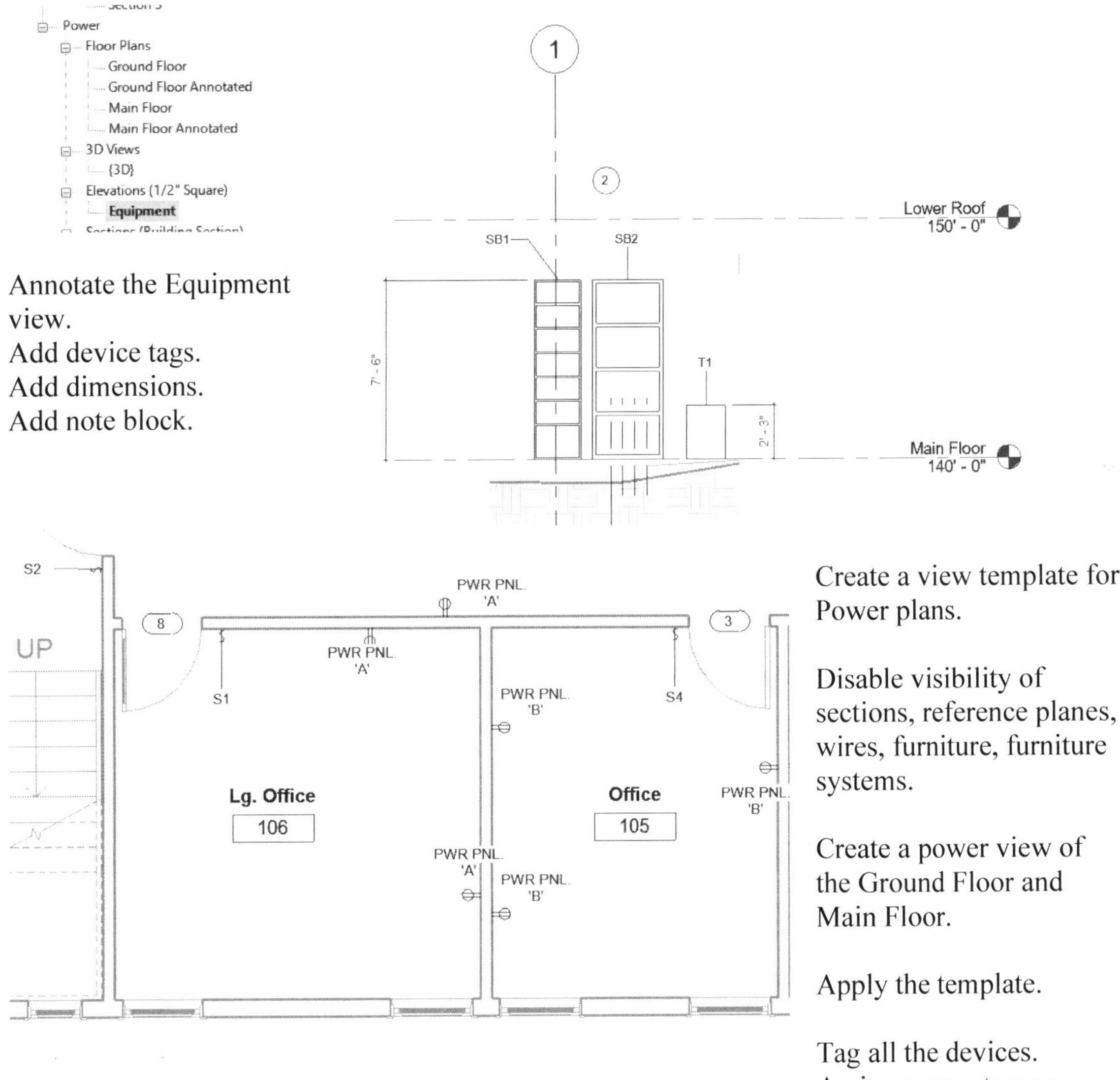

Annotate the Equipment view.
Add device tags.
Add dimensions.
Add note block.

Create a view template for Power plans.

Disable visibility of sections, reference planes, wires, furniture, furniture systems.

Create a power view of the Ground Floor and Main Floor.

Apply the template.

Tag all the devices. Assign names to any unnamed devices.

Verify that all the devices have been assigned a circuit.

Use the System Browser to verify that all the circuits have been defined.

Notes:

Sheets and Titleblocks

In Revit, sheets are included in the project file. You add sheets as needed, then place views on a sheet. Views can only be "consumed" once by placing on a sheet. If you need to use the same view on more than one sheet, you need to duplicate the view. Since schedules are also considered views, they also can only be placed once on a sheet. The only view that can be placed multiple times is a legend.

Sheets are the basis for construction documentation sets. A sheet allows you to place different views side by side on a page with titleblock information. You can print sheets to paper or save them to an electronic file, like a pdf.

You can activate a view on a sheet and modify the model elements. The building model will automatically update.

A viewport is a rectangular boundary around each view placed on a sheet. Each viewport has an identifying title below the boundary that displays the view name, view scale, and an identifier bubble. You can control the display of viewport titles and change the appearance of viewport titles. You can also create your own viewport title families.

Some architects use a cartoon set to plan the document requirements for a project. A cartoon set is a rough plan for the sheets that you want to include in the construction document set, and the drawings, schedules, or other information to show on each sheet.

By creating a cartoon set, you can ensure that the final construction document set includes all desired information. You can also use this method to ensure that the construction document set meets standards established by your organization.

With Revit, you can create a digital cartoon set. First add the required views (drawings and schedules) to the project and sketch the basic design of the building model. Add the desired sheets to the project and give them appropriate names and numbers. Then add the views to the appropriate sheets. If desired, you can set the view scales, titles, and other attributes now, so the resulting sheets use the desired settings.

Even though these views and sheets do not yet show the completed design, they provide an overall structure for the project. As you develop the building model in the project views, the schedules update accordingly, and the sheets display the desired information. This technique streamlines the project documentation process.

When you create a digital cartoon set that reflects corporate standards or a typical project setup, you can use the project to create a project template.

You can include information that is external to a project on the sheets that Revit generates. You can use external text, spreadsheets, and images on sheets.

Guidelines for Working with Sheets

- Create and name several copies of views for different design and documentation purposes.
- A viewport name on a sheet can be different from the view name in the Project Browser.
- Create viewport types that do not display the title or extension line.
- Create sheets using your organization's titleblocks and place views on the sheet at an early stage of your project. The views will update as the model progresses, and you can use the sheets to provide design reviews to team members during the design phase.
- Create and save different print setups as part of the project template. Name the print setups to coincide with different project stages, so it is easy for you to create documentation sets for design reviews at different points in the project.

Exercise 10-1:

Add a Sheet

Drawing Name: *sheets.rvt*
Estimated Time: 25 minutes

This exercise reinforces the following skills:

- Sheets
- Duplicate Views
- Add Views to a Sheet
- View Properties
- Activate View
- Deactivate View
- View Scale
- Visibility/Graphics Overrides
- Edit Crop

1. Activate the **View** ribbon.

   Select the **New Sheet** tool on the ribbon.

2. Highlight the E size titleblock.

   Click **OK**.

3. Locate the **Level 1 Lighting Plan** in the Project Browser.

   Right click and Select **Duplicate View→Duplicate with Detailing**.

4. Under Identity Data in the Properties palette:

   Change the View Name to **South Level 1 Lighting Plan**.

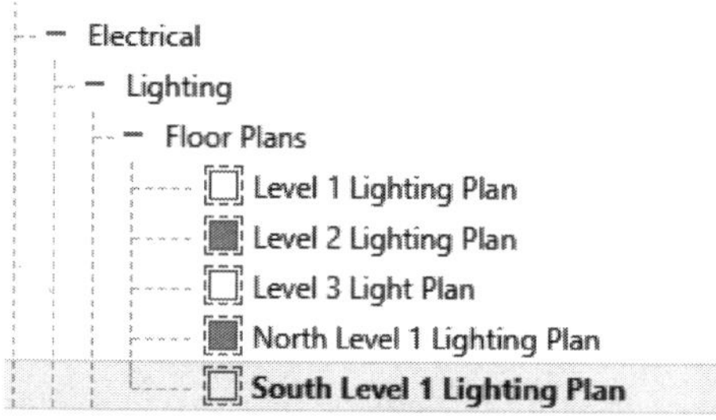

Notice that the name updates in the Project Browser.

5.

Under Extents in the Properties palette:

Enable **Crop View**.

Enable **Crop Region Visible**.

Enable **Annotation Crop.**

1/8" = 1'-0"

These can also be toggled in the Display bar at the bottom of the screen.

6.

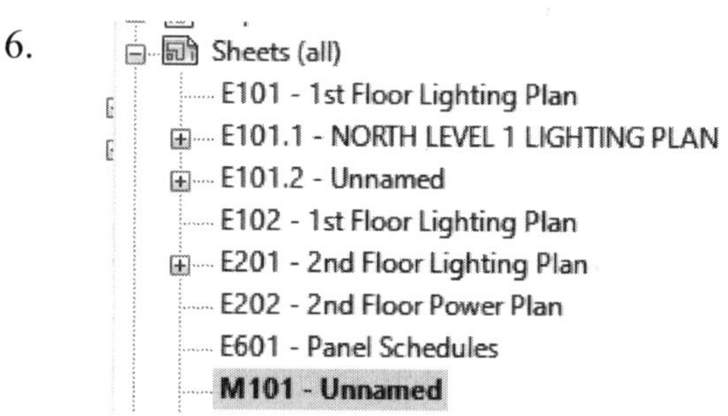

In the Project Browser under Sheets:

Open the **M101-Unnamed** sheet.

7.

Select the **View** tool on the ribbon to add a view to the sheet.

8.

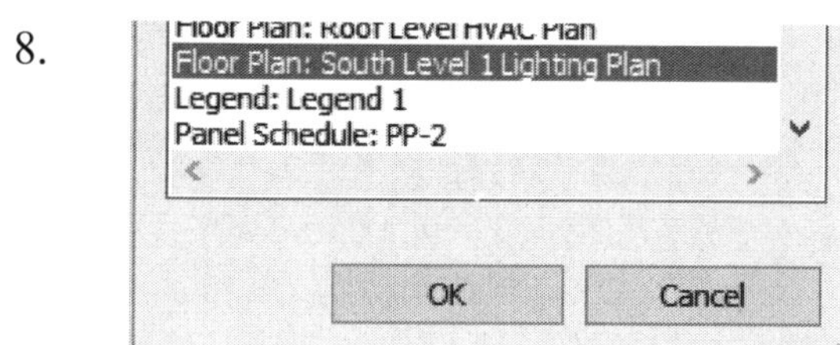

Locate the **South Level 1 Lighting Plan**.

Click OK.

9.

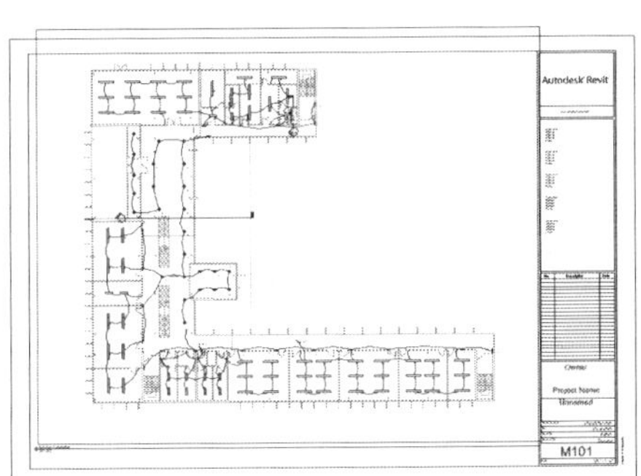

Left click to place the view on the sheet.

10.

Activate View

Select the view.

Select **Activate View** on the ribbon.

This allows you to modify the view and the elements in the view.

11.

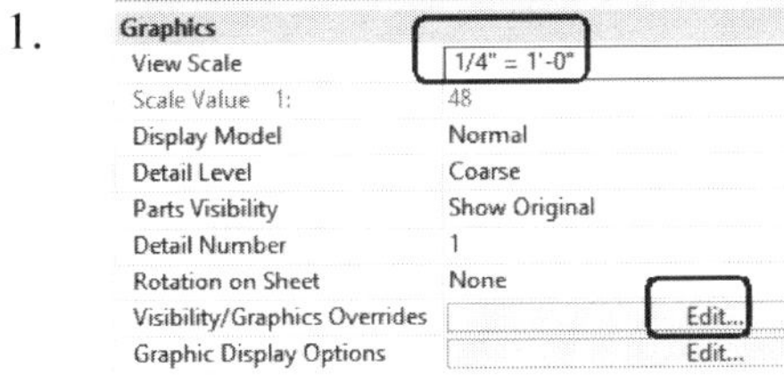

Under Graphics in the Properties palette:

Change the View Scale to **¼" = 1'-0"**.

Left click on **Edit** next to Visibility/Graphics Overrides.

12.

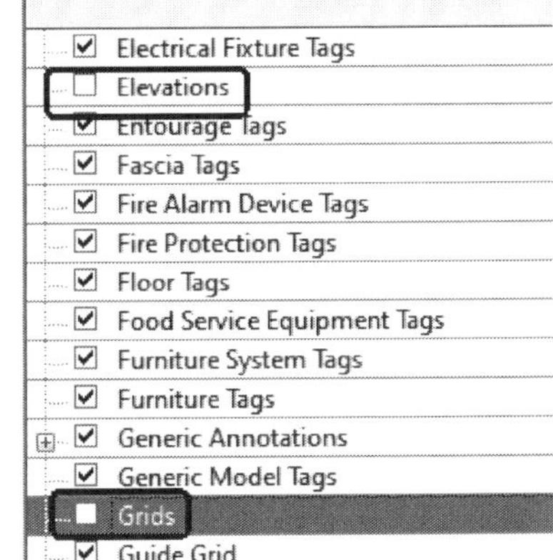

Activate the Annotation Categories tab.

Disable **Elevations** and **Grids** to hide those elements.

Click **OK** to close the dialog.

13.

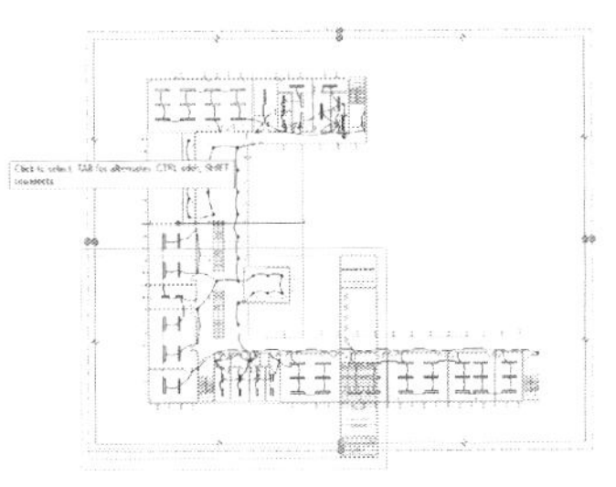

Click on the viewport to activate the grips.

14.  Select **Edit Crop** from the ribbon.

15. 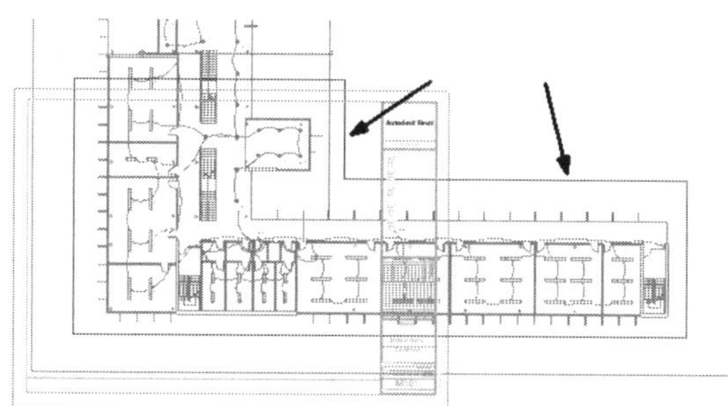 Add two lines.

Use the Trim tool to eliminate the extending lines.

Reposition the lines to enclose only the lower half of the floor plan.

Check to make sure you have created a closed polygon.

16.  Click **Green Check** to complete the Edit Crop operation.

17. 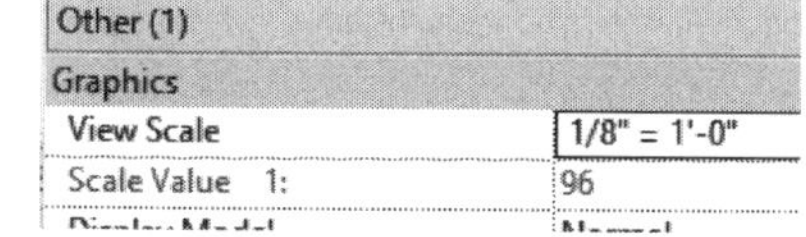 Change the View Scale back to **1/8" = 1'-0"**.

18.  Toggle **Hide Crop Region** on the Display bar to hide the crop region on the view.

19. 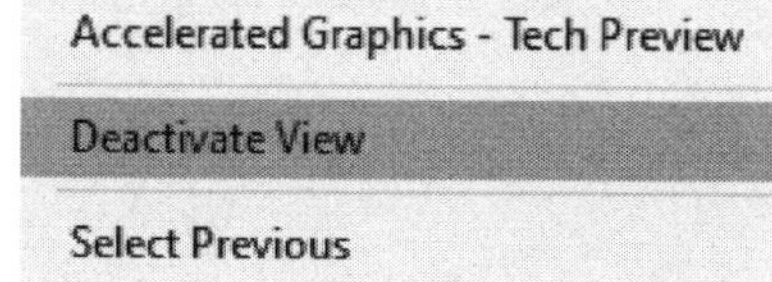 Right click on the view.

Select **Deactivate View.**

20. 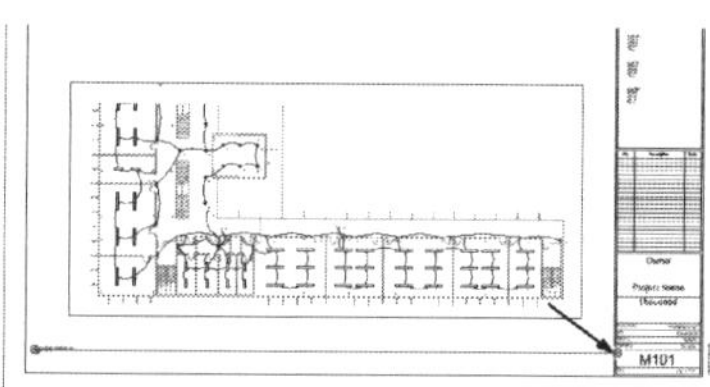 Select the view to activate the title line.

Use the grip to shorten the extension line on the title.

21. 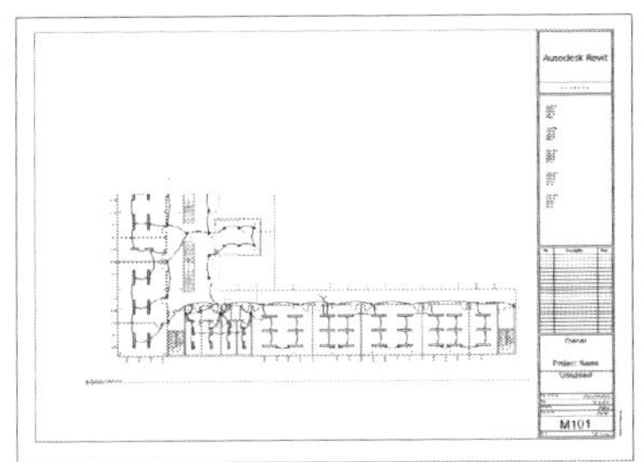   Click outside the view to be able to select the title line to reposition it.

22.   Save as *ex10-1.rvt*.

Exercise 10-2:

Add Views to a Sheet

Drawing Name: *views 2.rvt*
Estimated Time: 20 minutes

This exercise reinforces the following skills:
- Views
- Sheets

1.   – 🗎 Sheets (all)
       ╌╌╌ 00 - Sheet List
       ╌ + 01 - Main Floor Lighting
       ╌╌╌ **02 - Ground Floor Lighting**
       ╌╌╌ 03 - Main Floor Power
       ╌╌╌ 04 - Ground Floor Power
       ╌╌╌ 05 - Details
       ╌ + 06 - Panels
       ╌╌╌ 07 - Lighting Fixture Details

    Open the **Ground Floor Lighting** Sheet.

2.   
View

    Select the **Insert View** tool from the View ribbon.

3.   Type **swi** in the search field.

Select the **Reflected Ceiling Plan: Ground Floor Lighting Fixtures & Switches**.

Click **OK**.

Left click in the display window to place the view.

4.   Right click and select **Activate View**.

5.   Toggle on the Crop Region.

6.   Use the grips to crop the view.

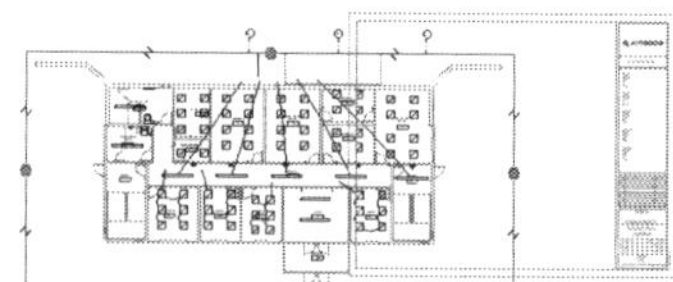

7.   Toggle off the Crop Region.

8.   Right click and select **Deactivate View**.

9.   Select the titleblock.

Use the Type Selector to change to an **E 30x42 Horizontal** size titleblock.

10. 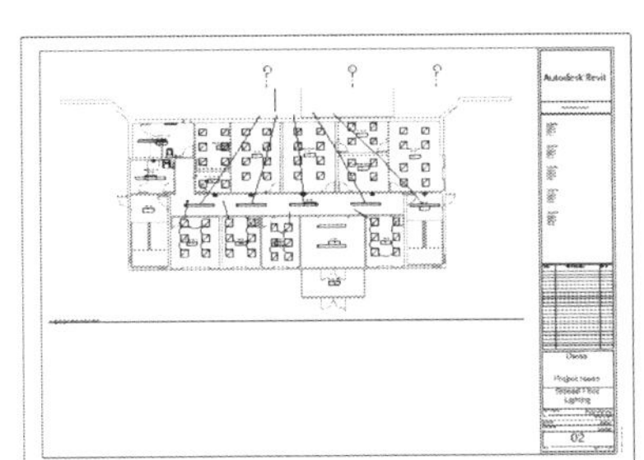

Reposition the view on the sheet.

You can't re-scale the view because a view template has been applied.

11.
 − Sheets (all)
  00 - Sheet List
  + 01 - Main Floor Lighting
  + 02 - Ground Floor Lighting
  03 - Main Floor Power
  04 - Ground Floor Power
  05 - Details
  + 06 - Panels
  07 - Lighting Fixture Details

Open the **Main Floor Power** Sheet.

12. 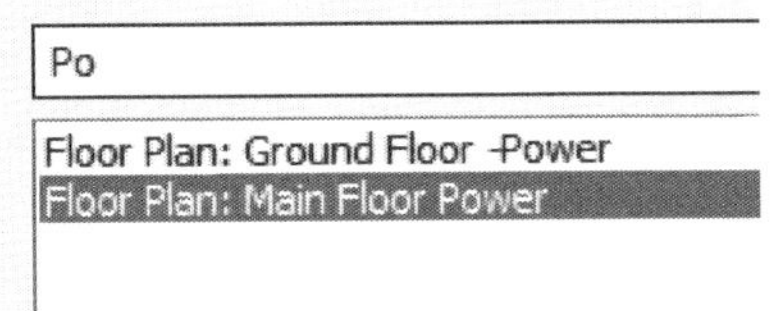
View

Select the **Insert View** tool from the View ribbon.

13.

Po

Floor Plan: Ground Floor -Power
Floor Plan: Main Floor Power

Select the **Floor Plan: Main Floor Power**.

Click **OK**.

Left click in the display window to place the view.

14.

E1 30 x 42 Horizontal
E1 30x42 Horizontal

Select the titleblock.

Use the Type Selector to change to an **E 30x42 Horizontal** size titleblock.

15. 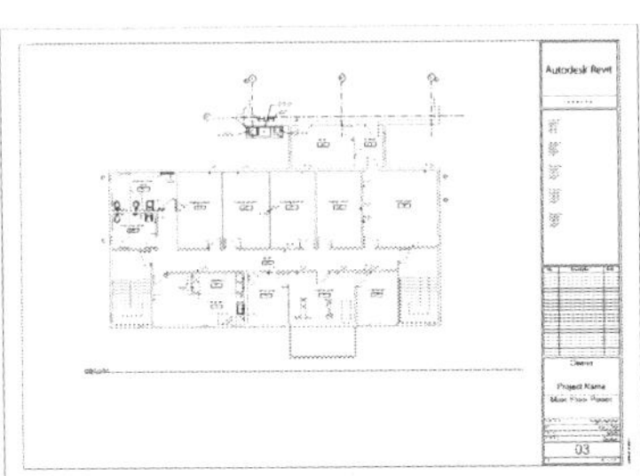

Reposition the view on the sheet.

You can't re-scale the view because a view template has been applied.

To turn off the visibility of the tag above the view, activate the view, window around the tag, right click and select Hide in View→Elements.

Deactivate the view when you are done.

16. 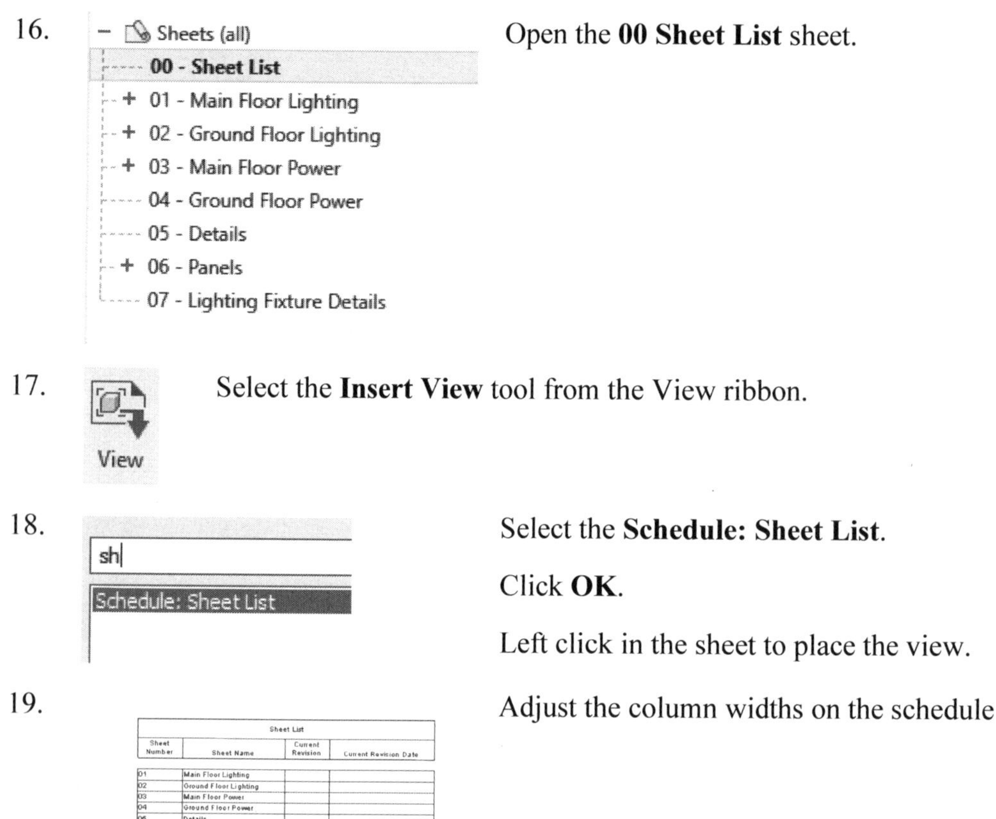 Open the **00 Sheet List** sheet.

17. Select the **Insert View** tool from the View ribbon.

18. Select the **Schedule: Sheet List**.

Click **OK**.

Left click in the sheet to place the view.

19. Adjust the column widths on the schedule

20. Save as *ex10-2.rvt*.

Guide Grid

Guide grids help arrange views so that they appear in the same location from sheet to sheet or align views on the same sheet.

You can display the same guide grid in different sheet views. Guide grids can be shared between sheets.

When new guide grids are created, they become available in the instance properties of sheets and can be applied to sheets. It is recommended to create only a few guide grids and then apply them to sheets. When you change the guide grid's properties/extents in one sheet, all the sheets which use that grid are updated accordingly.

You can change the appearance of Guide Grids using Object Styles on the Manage ribbon.

Exercise 10-3:

Align Views on a Sheet

Drawing Name: *align_views.rvt*
Estimated Time: 15 minutes

This exercise reinforces the following skills:
- Guide Grid
- Insert View
- Sheets
- Visibility/Graphics
- Move

1. 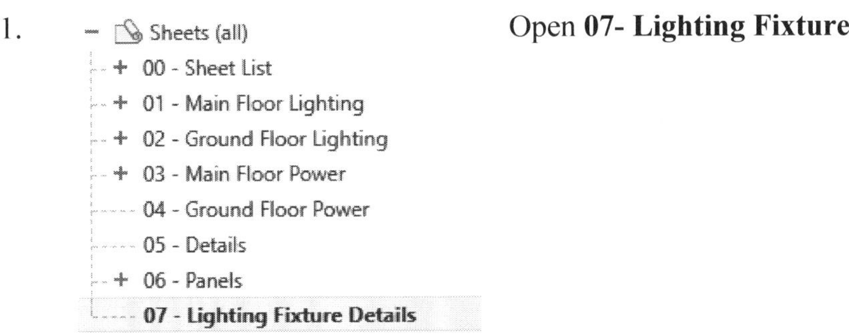 Open **07- Lighting Fixture Details** sheet.

2. 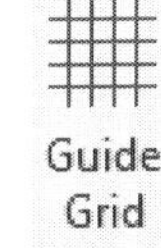 Select the **Guide Grid** tool from the View ribbon.

3. 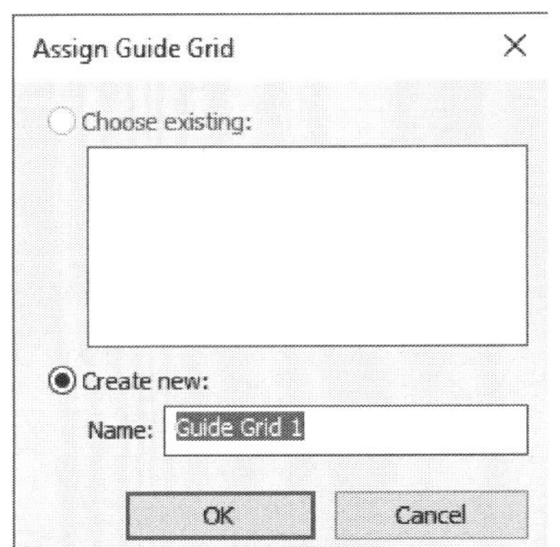 Enable **Create new**.

   Click **OK**.

4. Use the MOVE tool to adjust the position of the grid so it aligns with the titleblock outline. Use the grips to adjust the size of the grid.

Use the ALIGN tool to align the outside of the grid to the title block border.

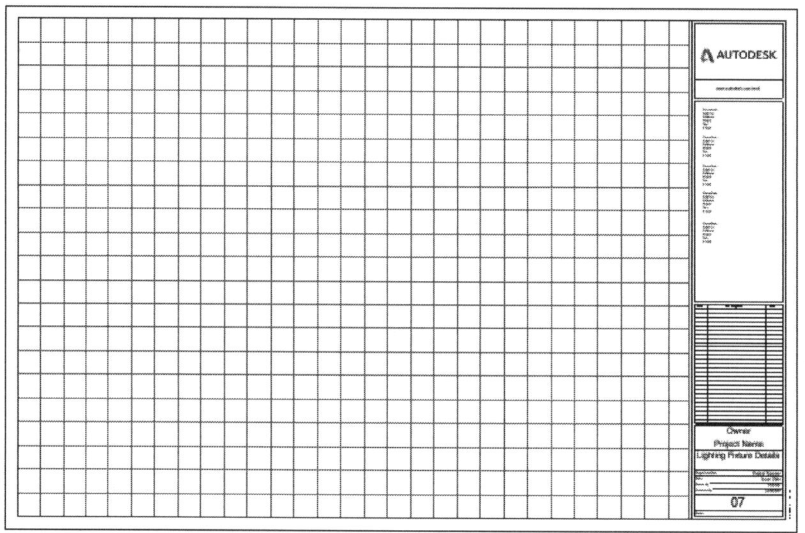

5. Select the **Insert View** tool from the View ribbon.

6. 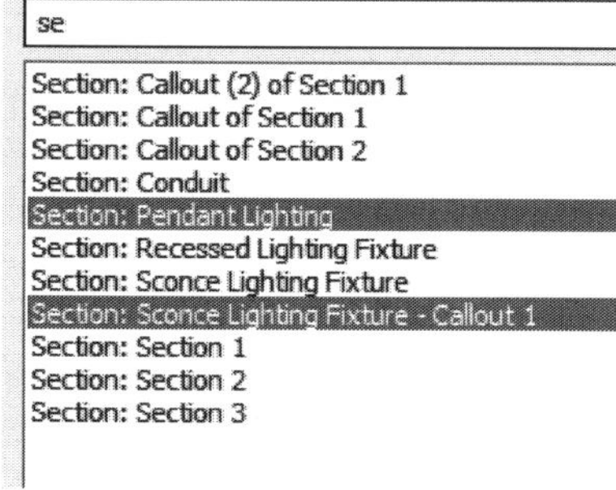

Hold down the CTL key.

Highlight **Section: Pendant Lighting** and **Sconce Lighting Fixture – Callout 1**.

Click **OK**.

Left click in the display window to place the views.

7. *One view is scaled at ¼"= 1'. The other view is scaled at ½" = 1'.*

Select the pendant light view.

Change the scale to **½" = 1'-0".**

8.

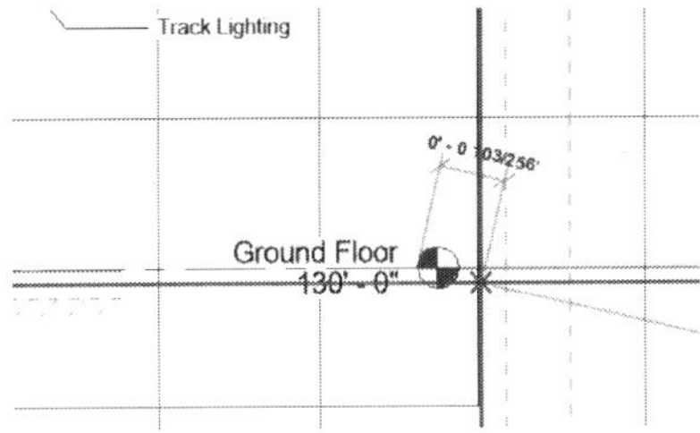

Use the MOVE tool to align the Ground Floor level of the pendant light view with the grid.

9.

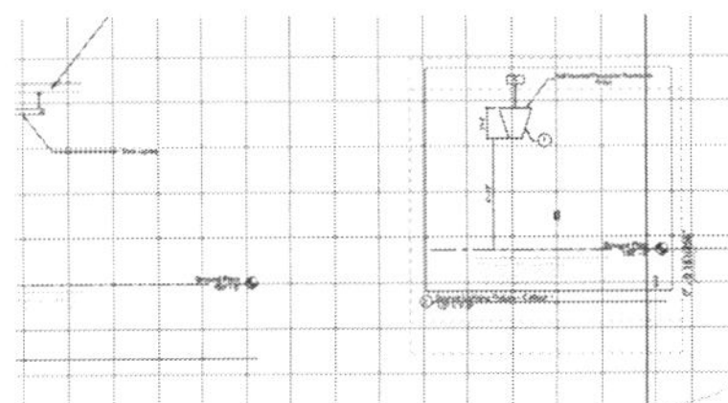

Use the MOVE tool to align the Ground Floor level of the sconce view with the grid. Select the same grid line used by the pendant light view.

Note that the views are aligned using the guide grid.

10.

Type **VV** to launch the Visibility/Graphics Overrides dialog.

On the Annotation Categories tab:

Disable **Guide Grid**.

Click **OK**.

11. Save as *ex10-3.rvt*.

Can you use the guide grid to align the two view titles?

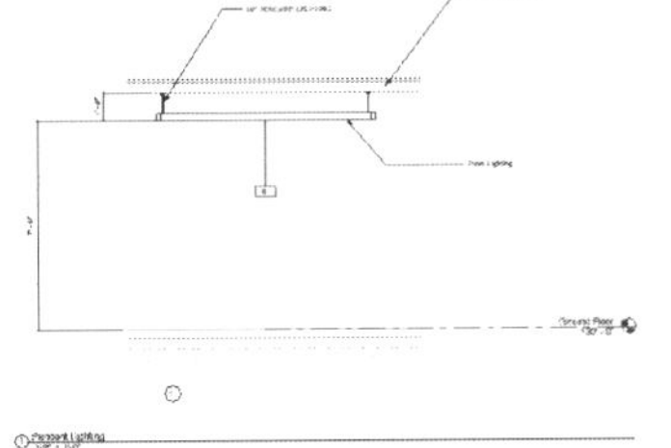

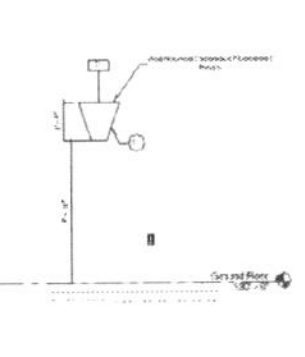

Titleblocks

Titleblocks are Revit families. You can load standard titleblocks into a project or create a custom titleblock using the Family Editor. Most companies have their own custom titleblock designed.

The title block you define includes the sheet size. If you delete the title block, the sheet of paper is also deleted. This means your title block is linked to the paper size you define.

You need to define a title block for each paper size you use.

Guidelines for Working with Titleblocks

- You should create a titleblock for each different sheet/paper size used when plotting. Keep in mind that the industry is moving more and more to pdf digital documents and less towards plotting.
- Create a titleblock to represent different phases of construction on a project.
- Load titleblocks into your project templates so they are easily accessible.
- Create custom labels to make it easier to fill in the data on titleblocks.

Exercise 10-4:

Update a Titleblock

Drawing Name: *titleblocks.rvt*
Estimated Time: 10 minutes

This exercise reinforces the following skills:
- ❏ Edit a Titleblock

1. 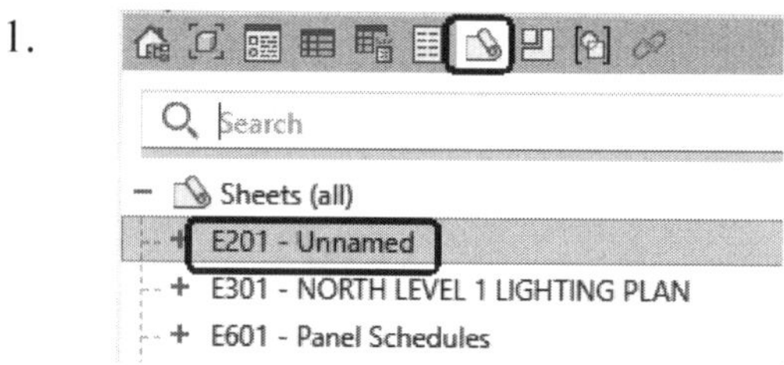

In the Project Browser:

Select the **Sheets** tab.

Double left click on **E201-Unnamed**.

This opens the view.

2. 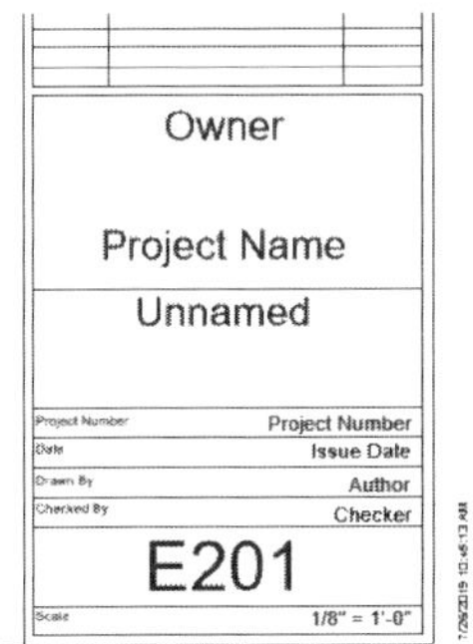 Zoom into the view title.

You see that Level 2 Lighting Plan has been placed on the sheet.

3. Zoom into the lower right corner of the titleblock.

4. 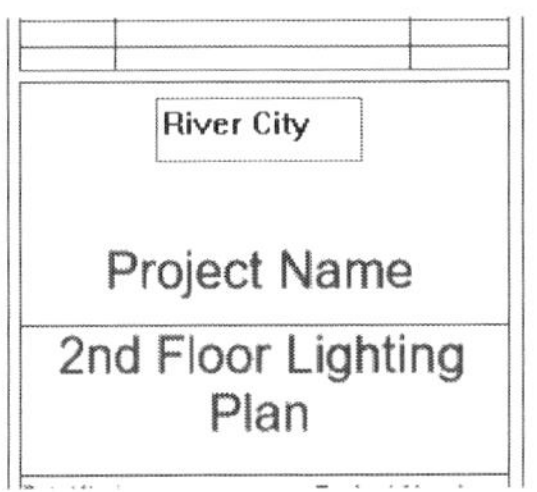 Left click on the text that reads **Unnamed**.

Modify the text to **2nd Floor Lighting Plan**.

5. Change Owner to **River City**.

6. 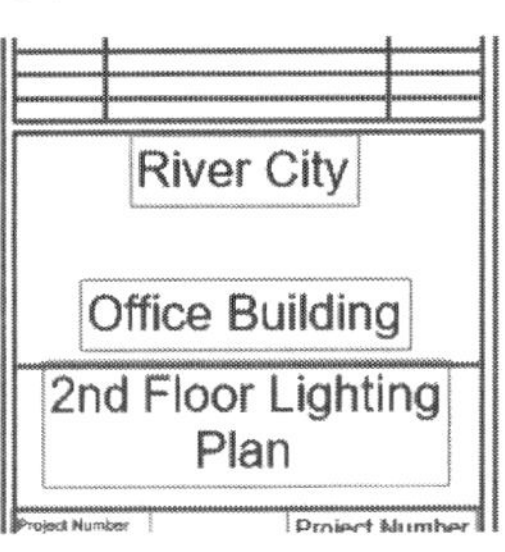 Change Project Name to **Office Building**.

7. 

Double left click on the **E301 – NORTH LEVEL 1 LIGHTING PLAN SHEET** in the Project Browser.

8.

Zoom into the lower right corner of the titleblock.

Note that the titleblock on this sheet has updated to the new owner and project names.

9. Save as *ex10-4.rvt*.

Exercise 10-5:

Load a Titleblock

Drawing Name: *load_titleblocks.rvt*
Estimated Time: 10 minutes

This exercise reinforces the following skills:
- ❑ Load a Titleblock
- ❑ Place a View
- ❑ Modify View Scale for a view
- ❑ Modify a title line
- ❑ Position a view on a sheet

1.

Right click on Sheets in the Project Browser.

Select **New Sheet**.

2. 

Select the **Load** button at the top of the dialog.

3. 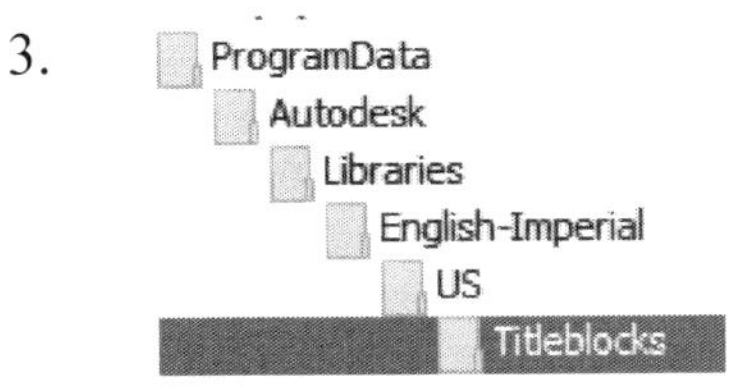   Browse to the Titleblocks folder under *Libraries\US Imperial.*

   *You have a shortcut for the Imperial Libraries folder on the left pane of the dialog.*

4.   Select the **C 17 x 22 Horizontal** titleblock.

Click **Open**.

5.   Highlight the **C 17 x 22 Horizontal** titleblock.

Click **OK**.

6.   Locate the **Level 1 Power Plan** in the Project Browser.

Hold down your left mouse button to drag and drop the view onto the sheet.

7.   The view is quite a bit bigger than the titleblock.

8.   On the Properties palette:

Change the View Scale to **1/16" = 1'-0"**.

9.   The view size adjusts.

Use the small grip at the end of the title line to adjust the title size.

10. 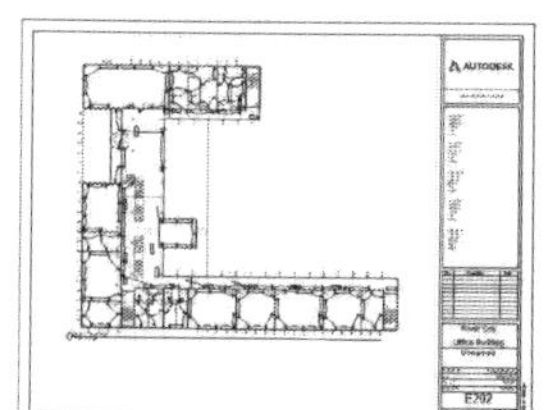

Reposition the view on the sheet.

Note that the project information is updated on the sheet to match the existing sheets.

Save as *ex10-5.rvt*.

Exercise 10-6:

Adding Project Information to a Titleblock

Drawing Name: *project_information.rvt*
Estimated Time: 10 minutes

This exercise reinforces the following skills:
- Project Information
- Titleblocks
- Titleblock properties

1. 

Select the **Manage** ribbon.

Select **Project Information** from the ribbon.

2. 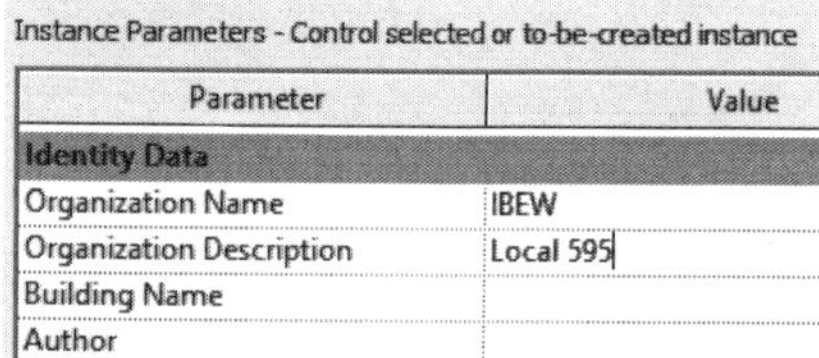

Type **IBEW** for Organization Name.

Type **Local 595** for Organization Description.

3. 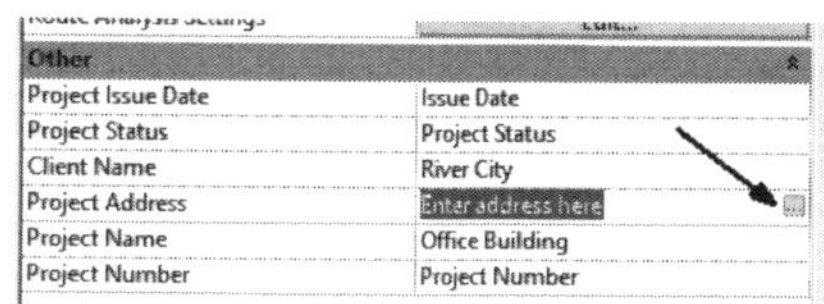

Scroll down to the Other category.

Left click in the **Project Address** field.

Select the … button located on the right.

4. 123 Main St
Any City, CA 10010

Type in an address.

Click **OK**.

5.

Other	
Project Issue Date	10/10/2026
Project Status	Client Review
Client Name	River City
Project Address	123 Main St
Project Name	Office Building
Project Number	20110-67

For Project Issue Date: Type today's date.

For Project Status: Type **Client Review**.

For Project Number: Type **20110-67**.

Click **OK**.

6.

Approved By	M. Teacher
Designed By	J. Student
Checked By	M. Teacher
Drawn By	J. Student
Sheet Issue Date	10/10/26

Identity Data	
Dependency	Independent
Sheet Collection	<None>
Sheet Number	E202
Sheet Name	1st Floor Power Plan

In the Properties palette:

In Checked By: Type M. Teacher.

In Drawn By: Type your first initial and last name.

In Sheet Name: Type 1st Floor Power Plan.

Update the Sheet Issue Date to today's date.

Note that the titleblock updates with the information entered in the Properties palette.

River City	
Office Building	
1st Floor Power Plan	
Project number	20110-67
Date	10/10/2026
Drawn by	J. Student
Checked by	M. Teacher
E202	
Scale	1/16" = 1'-0"

9/24/2025 12:56:36 PM

7. Save as *ex10-6.rvt*.

Exercise 10-7:

Creating a Custom Titleblock

Drawing Name: *none*
Estimated Time: 45 minutes

This exercise reinforces the following skills:

- ❑ Titleblock
- ❑ Import CAD
- ❑ Labels
- ❑ Text
- ❑ Family Properties

1. 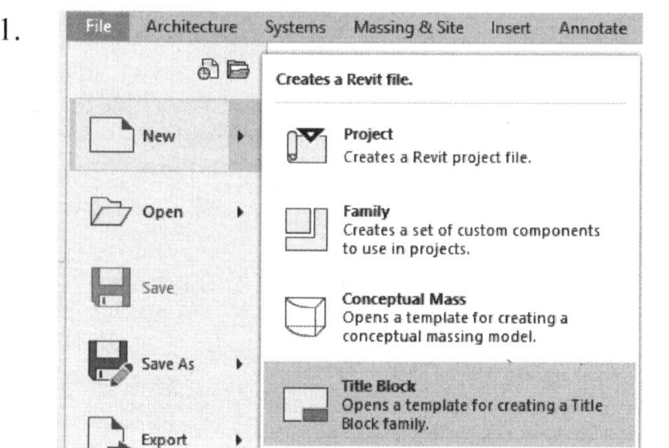 Go to **File → New → Titleblock**.

2. 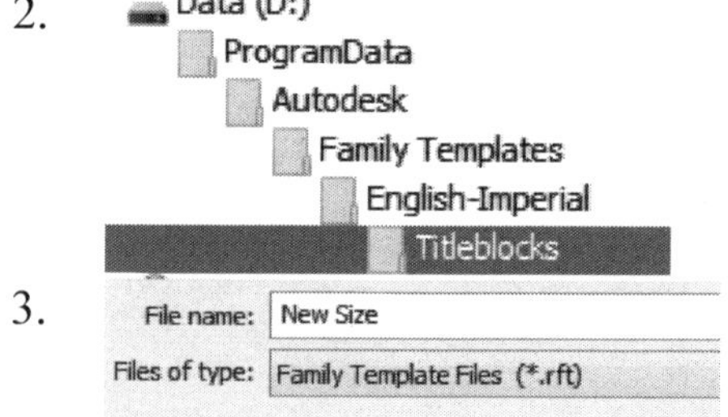 Browse to the *Titleblocks* folder under *ProgramData/Family Templates/English-Imperial.*

3. Select **New Size**.

   Click **Open**.

4. 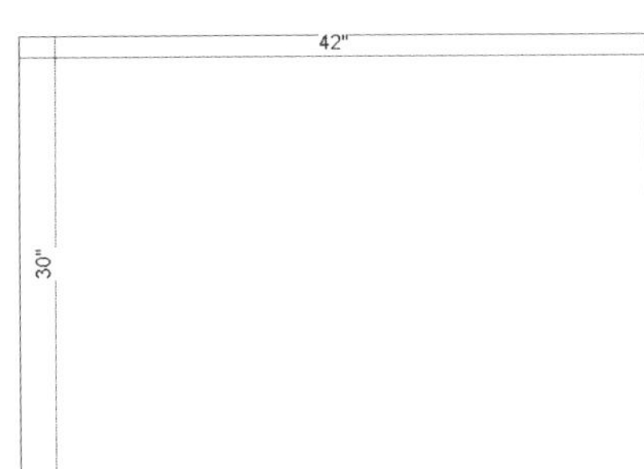 Pick the top horizontal line.

Select the dimension and change it to **30″**.

Pick the right vertical line.

Select the dimension and change it to **42″**.

5.  Right click in the graphics window and select **Zoom to Fit**.

You can also double click on the mouse wheel.

6. Activate the Insert ribbon.

Select **Import→Import CAD**.

7. Locate the *Architectural Title Block* in the downloaded exercise files.

8. 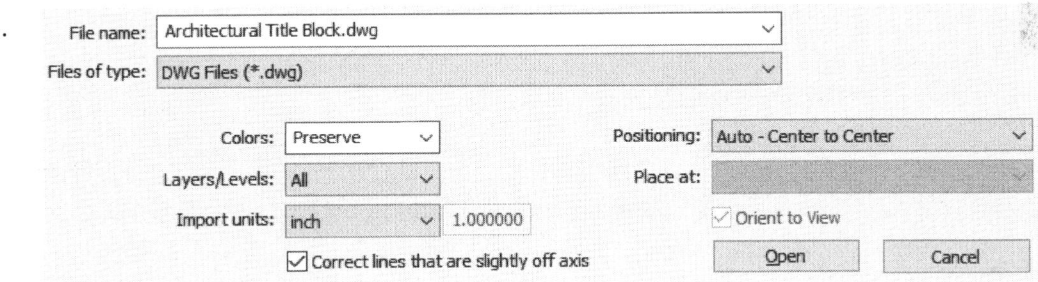

Set Colors to **Preserve**.
Set Layers to **All**.
Set Import Units to **Inch**.
Set Positioning to: **Auto - Center to Center**.
Click **Open**.

9. Import detected no valid elements in the file's Paper space. Do you want to import from the Model space?

Click **OK**.

10. Select the title block.

Use the **Move** tool on the Modify panel to reposition the titleblock so it is aligned with the existing Revit sheet.

11. Use the RESIZE tool to scale the title block to fit on the sheet.

12.  Select the imported title block so it is highlighted.

13. Select **Explode → Full Explode** from the Import Instance panel on the ribbon.

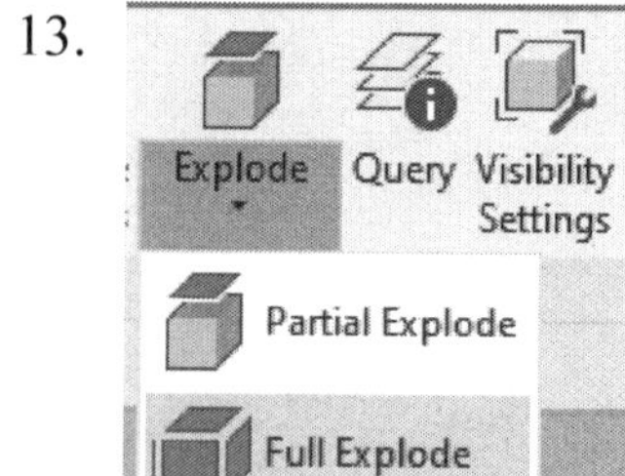

14. 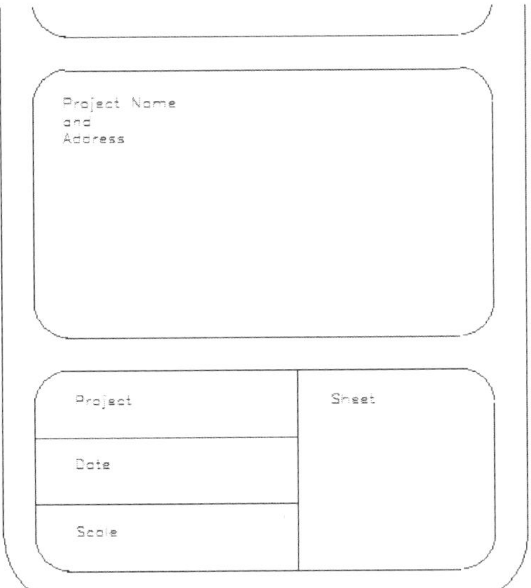 Move the text elements into the correct locations inside the title block.

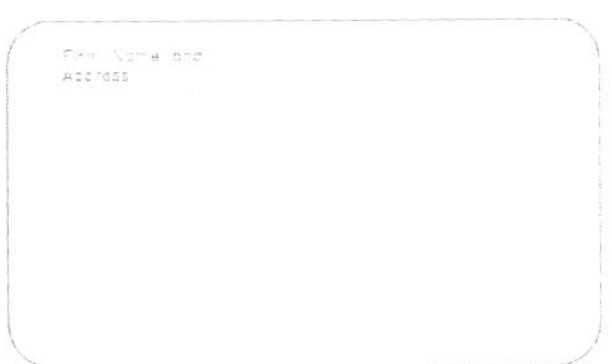

We will place an image in the rectangle labeled Firm Name and Address.

15.  Activate the **Insert** ribbon.

Select the **Import→Image** tool.

16. 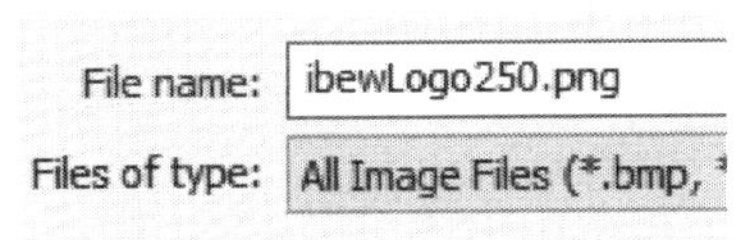 Open the *ibewLogo250.png* file from the downloaded Class Files.

17. 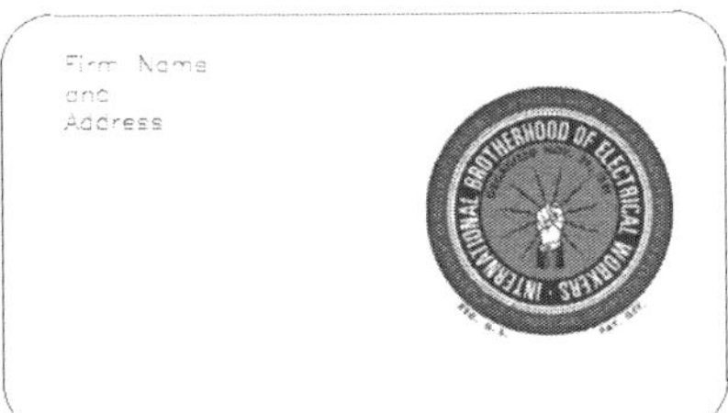 Place the logo on the right side of the Firm Name box.

Scale and move it into position.

To scale, just select one of the corners and drag it to the correct size.

18.  Select the **Text** tool from the **Create** Ribbon.

19. Select **Edit Type**.

20. 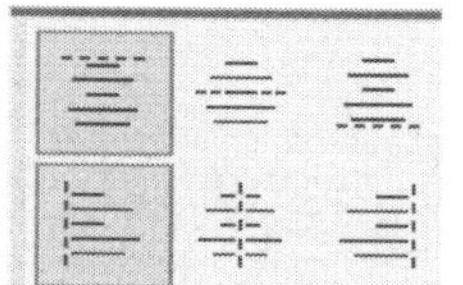 Change the Text Size to **1/8″**.

Click **OK**.

Revit can use any font that is available in your Windows font folder.

21. Select **Left** on the Alignment panel.

22. 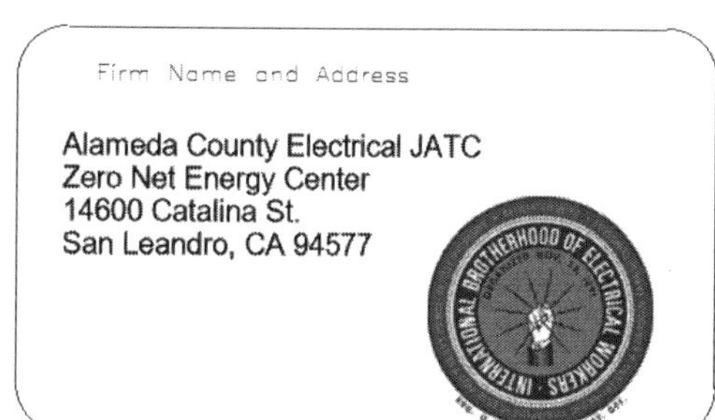

Type in the name of your school or company next to the logo.

Position the text and logo so they look correct in the rectangular outline.

23.  Select the **Label** tool from the Create ribbon.

Labels are similar to attributes. They are linked to project properties.

24. 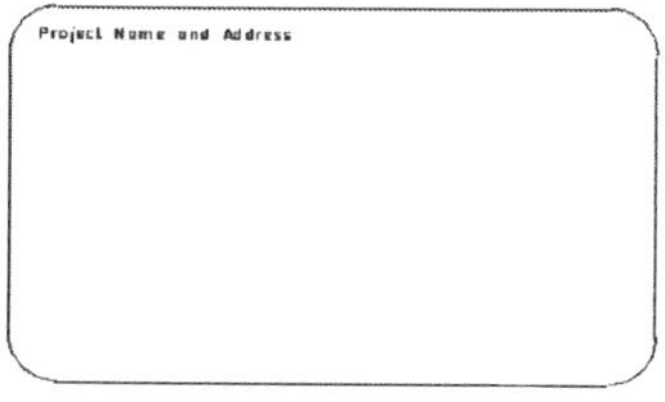

Left pick in the Project Name and Address box.

25. Click **OK**.
Left click to release the selection.
Pick to place when the dashed line appears.

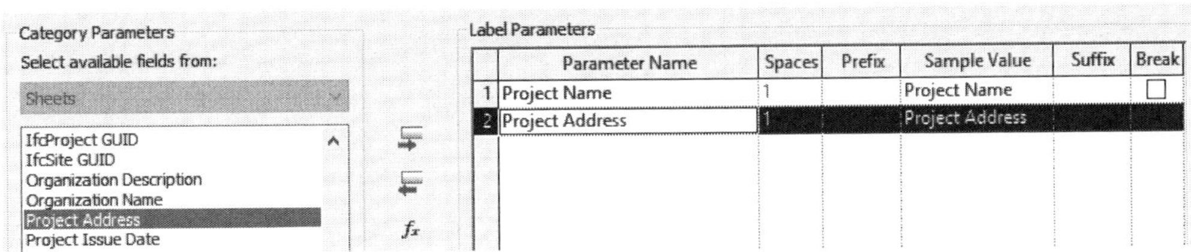

Select **Project Name**.
Use the **Add** button to move it into the Label Parameters list.
Add **Project Address**.
Click **OK**.

26. 

Cancel out of the Label command.

Position the label.
Use the grips to expand the label.

27.

Select the label.

In the Properties panel:

Enable **Wrap between parameters**.

Verify that the Horizontal Align is set to **Center**.

28.

Use Modify→Move to adjust the position of the project name and address label.

29. Edit Type

Select the label.

Select **Edit Type**.

30. Duplicate...

Select **Duplicate**.

31. Name: Tag 1/8" Arial

Change the Name to **Tag 1/8" Arial**.

Click **OK**.

32. 

Change the Text Size to **1/8"**.

Click **OK**.

33. 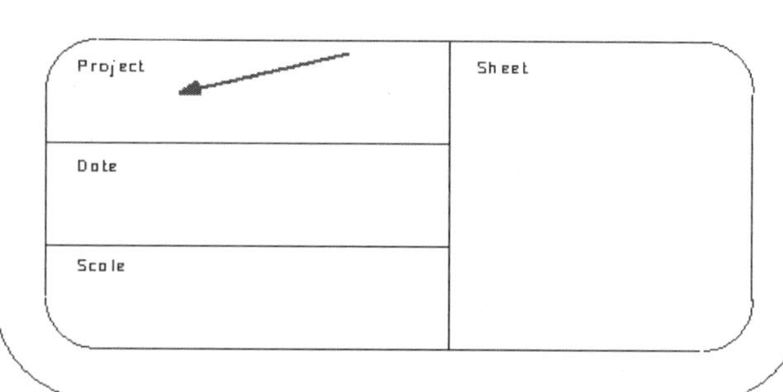

Adjust the size and position of the label.

34.

Select the **Label** tool from the Create ribbon.

Use the Type Selector to set the label type to **Tag 1/8" Arial**.

35. 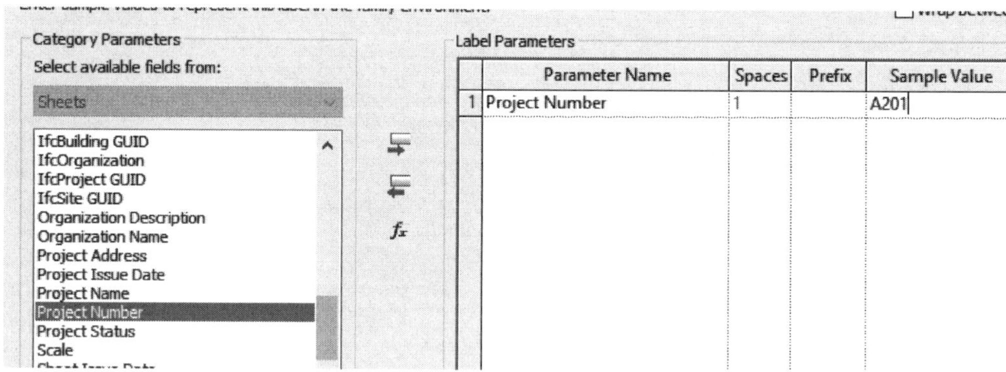

Left click in the Project box.

36. Locate **Project Number** in the Parameter list.

Move it to the right pane.

Add a sample value, if you like.

Click **OK**.

37.  Left click to complete placing the label.

Select and reposition as needed.

38.  Select the **Label** tool from the Create ribbon.

39. 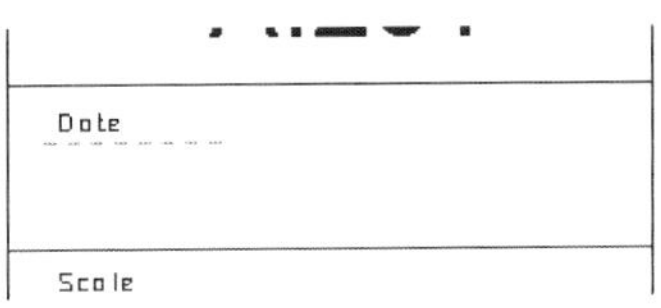 Left click in the Date box.

40.

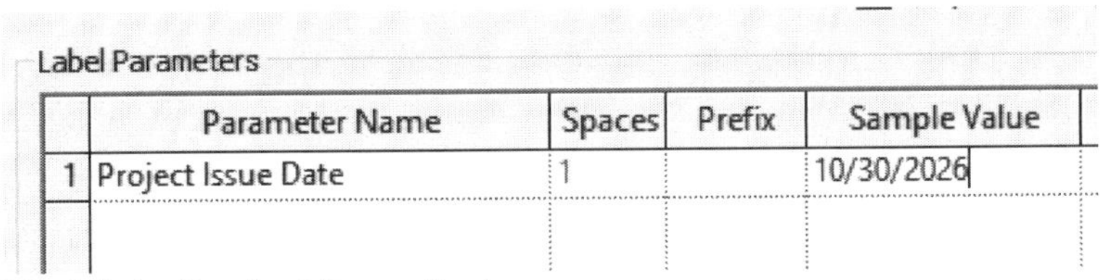

	Parameter Name	Spaces	Prefix	Sample Value
1	Project Issue Date	1		10/30/2026

Highlight **Project Issue Date**.
Click the **Add** button.
In the Sample Value field, enter the default date to use.
Click **OK**.

41. 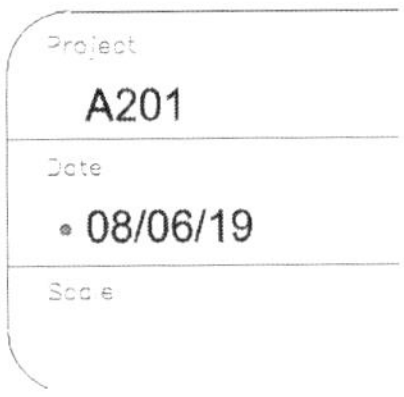 Position the date in the date field.

42. 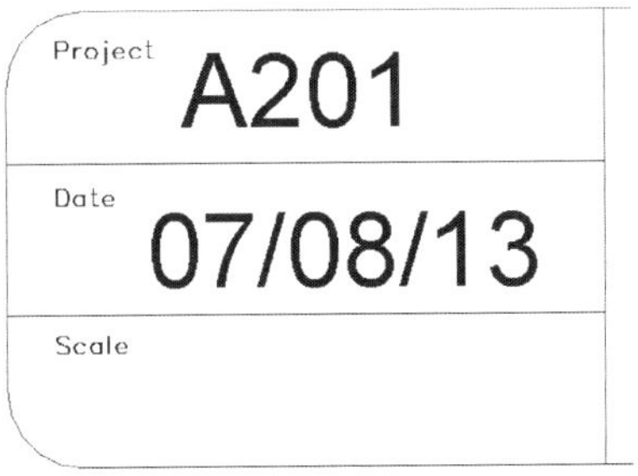 Left click in the Scale box.

43.

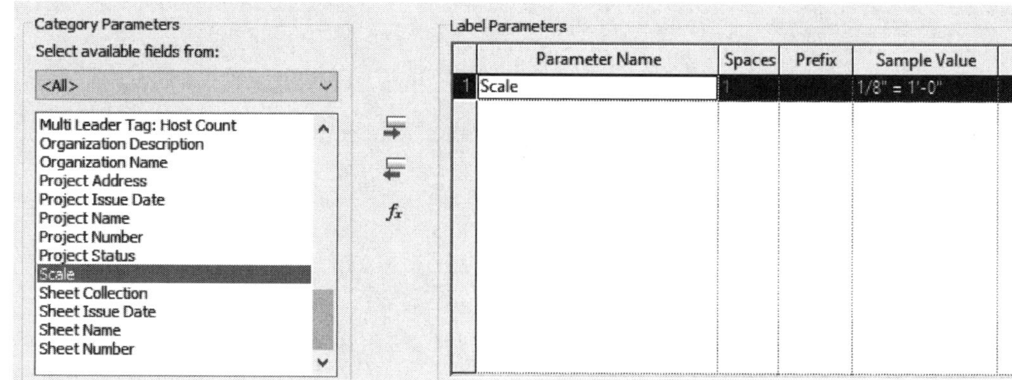

Highlight **Scale**.

Click the **Add** button.

Click **OK**.

44.

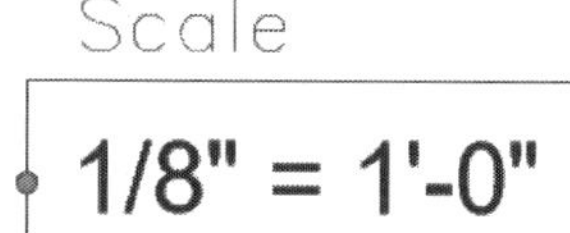

Highlight the scale label that was just placed and select **Edit Type** on the Properties panel.

45.

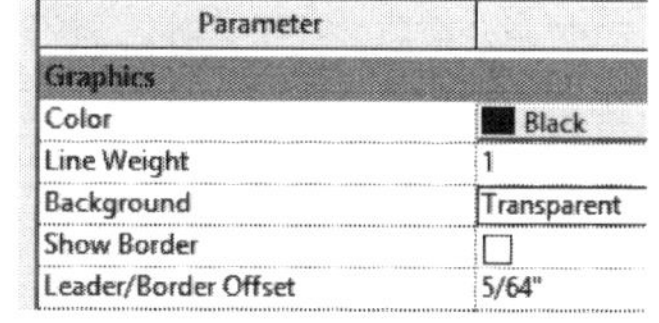

Set the Background to **Transparent**.

Click **OK**.

46.

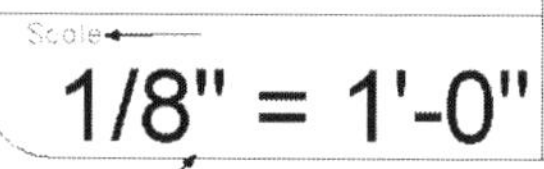

Cancel out of the label command.

Note that the border outline and the block text are no longer hidden by the label background.

47.

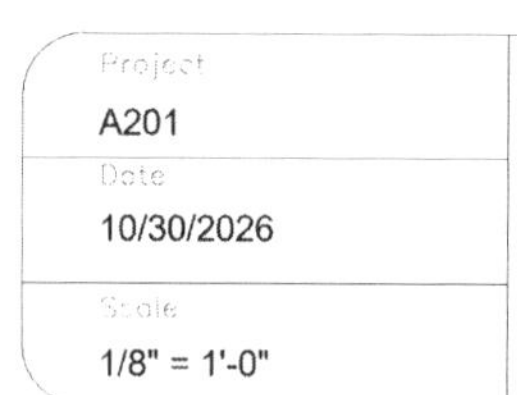

Adjust the lines, text and labels so that everything looks clean.

48. Select the **Label** tool.

49. 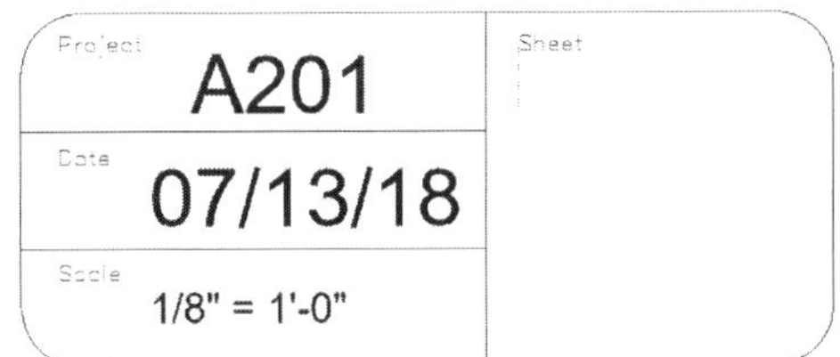

Left click in the Sheet box.

50. ...bined into a single label.

...nment.

☑ Wrap between parameters only

Label Parameters

	Parameter Name	Spaces	Prefix	Sample Value	Suffix	Break
1	Sheet Number	1		A101		☐
2	Sheet Name	1		Sheet Name		

Highlight **Sheet Number**.
Click the **Add** button.
Highlight **Sheet Name**.
Click the **Add** button.

Graphics

Sample Text	A101...
Label	
Wrap between parameters only	☑
Horizontal Align	Left
Vertical Align	Top
Keep Readable	☑
Visible	☑

Enable **Wrap between parameters only.**
Click **OK**.

51. 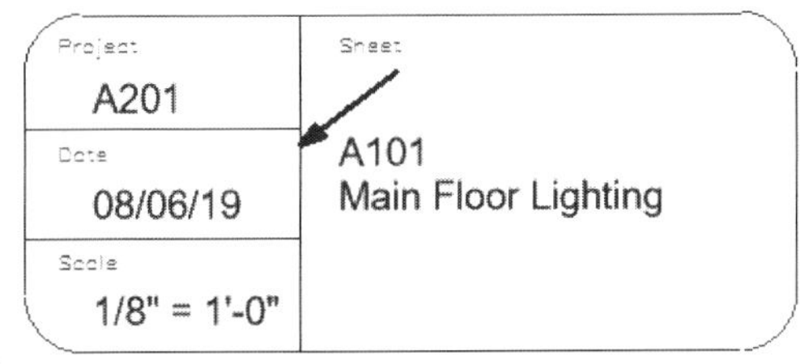

Shift the vertical divider line to the left to allow more space for the sheet name.

Position the Sheet label.

52. Save the file as *Titleblock 30 x 42.rfa.*

File name:	Titleblock 22 x 34
Files of type:	Family Files (*.rfa)

Exercise 10-8:

Using a Custom Title Block

Drawing Name: *titleblock.rvt*
Estimated Time: 10 minutes

This exercise reinforces the following skills:

- Title block
- Import CAD
- Labels
- Text
- Family Properties

1. Activate the Insert ribbon.

   Select **Load Family** in the Load from Library panel.

2.
File name:	Titleblock 30 x 42.rfa
Files of type:	All Supported Files (*.rfa, *.adsk)

   Browse to the exercise folder.

   Locate *Titleblock 30 x 42.rfa.*

   Select it and Click **Open**.

3. Activate the **01 -Main Floor lighting** sheet.

   - Sheets (all)
     - + 00 - Sheet List
     - + **01 - Main Floor Lighting**
     - + 02 - Ground Floor Lighting
     - + 03 - Main Floor Power
     - 04 - Ground Floor Power
     - 05 - Details
     - + 06 - Panels
     - + 07 - Lighting Fixture Details

4.

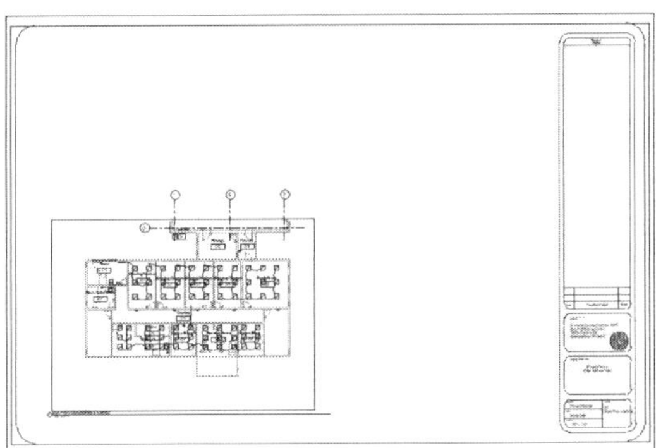

Select the title block so it is highlighted.

You will see the name of the title block in the Properties pane.

Select the **Title Block 30 x 42** using the Type Selector.

5.

You may need to reposition the view on the title block.

6. 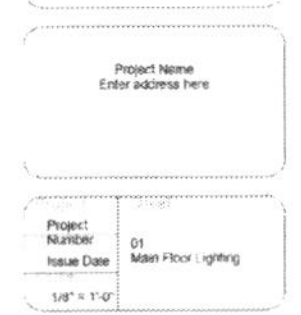

Zoom into the title block.

Note that the parameter values have all copied over.

7. 

Project
Information

Activate the Manage ribbon.

Select **Project Information**.

8.

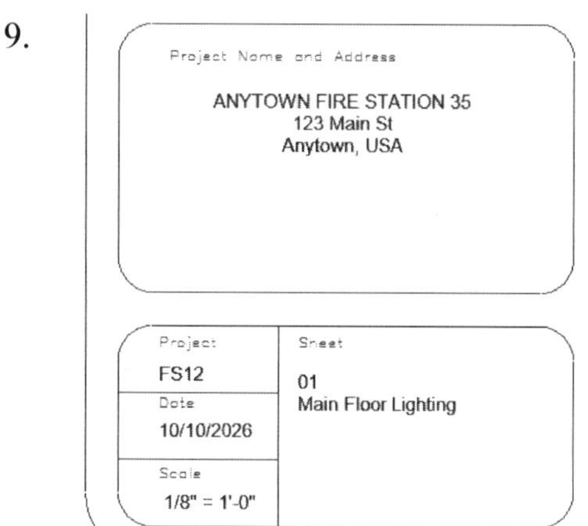

Fill in the dialog.

Organization Name: **IBEW**

Author: *Your initial and last name*

Project Issue Date: *Today's date*

Project Status: **In Design**

Client Name: **B. Brown**

Project Address: **123 Main St Anytown, USA**

Project Name: **ANYTOWN FIRE STATION 35**

Project Number **FS12**

Click **OK**.

9.

The titleblock updates with the project information.

10. Save the file as *ex10-8.rvt*.

Revisions

Every project requires revisions. Revisions are tracked using a revision schedule. The revision schedule is a "nested" family that is hosted by the titleblock. When you make a change to the model and you want to issue a revision, you can draw a revision cloud in the view, or the cloud can be drawn on the sheet displaying the view. Revision clouds are "view-specific". This means they are only visible in the view where they are placed. Revision clouds are "tagged" using a revision tag which is linked to the parameters in the revision schedule.

Exercise 10-9:

Defining a Revision Schedule

Drawing Name: *revisions.rvt*
Estimated Time: 10 minutes

This exercise reinforces the following skills:

- Setting up Revision Control in a project.

1. 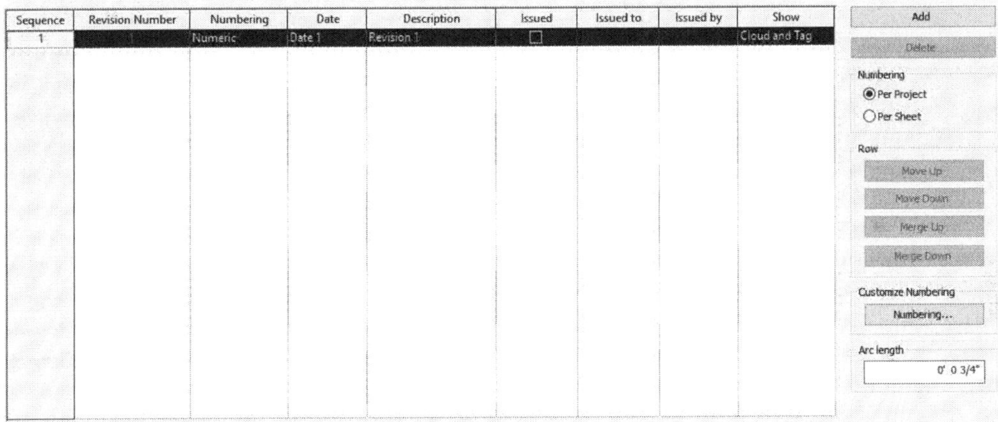 Activate the **View** ribbon. Select **Revisions** on the **Sheet Composition** panel.

   This dialog manages revision control settings and history.

Sequence	Revision Number	Numbering	Date	Description	Issued	Issued to	Issued by	Show
1	1	Numeric	Date 1	Revision 1	☐			Cloud and Tag

Numbering can be controlled per project or per sheet. The setting used depends on your company's standards.

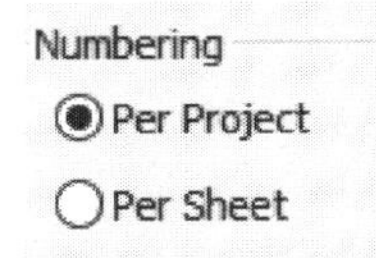

Enable **Per Project**.

One Revision is available by default. Additional revisions are added using the **Add** button.

2. The visibility of revisions can be set to **None**, **Tag** or **Cloud and Tag**. Use the **None** setting for older revisions which are no longer applicable so as not to confuse the contractors.

   Set the revision to show **Cloud and Tag**.

3.   Click **Numbering**.

4.   Highlight **Alphanumeric**.

5.   Click **Edit**.

6.   Change the Custom Sequence to remove the letters **I** and **O**.

A, B, C, D, E, F, G, H, J, K, L, M, N, P, Q, R, S, T, U, V, W, X, Y, Z

These get confused with the numbers 1 and 0.

Click **OK**.

7.   Highlight **Numeric.**

8.   Click **Edit**.

9.   Type **A** for the prefix.
This would allow revisions to be created using A1, A2, A3…

10. 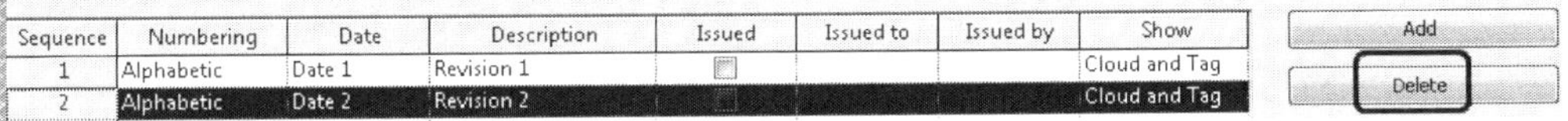

Click **OK to** close the dialog box.

11. Enter the two revision changes shown.

Sequence	Revision Number	Numbering	Date	Description	Issued	Issued to	Issued	Show
1	A1	Numeric	10.05	Change 96" Pendant Light to M125 Rcessed Flange	☐	Joe	Sam	Cloud and Tag
2	A2	Numeric	10.13	Change Sconce Model to Sconce Light Sphere	☐	Joe	Sam	Cloud and Tag

12. Click **OK** to close the dialog.
You can delete revisions if you make a mistake. Just highlight the row and Click **Delete**.

Sequence	Numbering	Date	Description	Issued	Issued to	Issued by	Show	
1	Alphabetic	Date 1	Revision 1	☐			Cloud and Tag	Add
2	Alphabetic	Date 2	Revision 2	☐			Cloud and Tag	Delete

13. Save the project as *ex10-9.rvt*.

Exercise 10-10:

Modify a Revision Schedule in a Title Block

Drawing Name: *revision_schedule.rvt*
Estimated Time: 20 minutes

This exercise reinforces the following skills:

- Titleblock
- Revision Schedules

1. 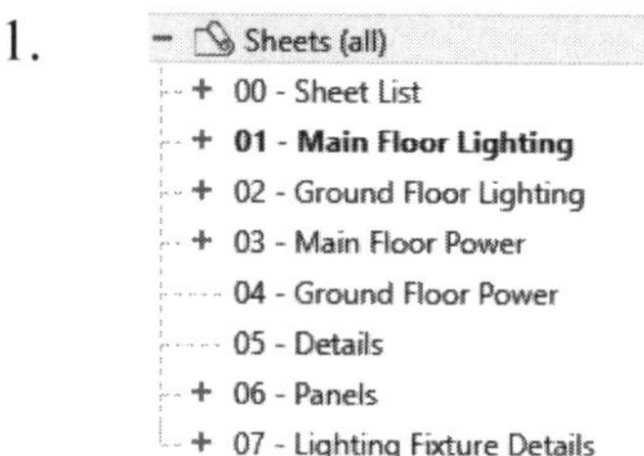 Open the **01 – Main Floor Lighting** sheet.

2. 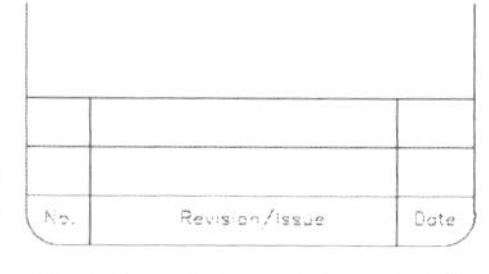 Zoom in to the **Revision Block** area on the sheet.

   Note that the title block includes a revision schedule by default.

3. 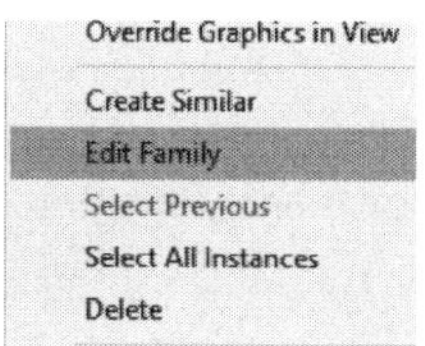 Select the titleblock.

   Right click and select **Edit Family**.

4. 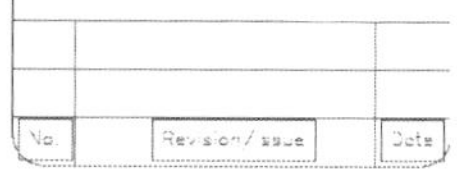 Window around the lines and text in the revision block to select.

   Right click and select **Delete**.

5. 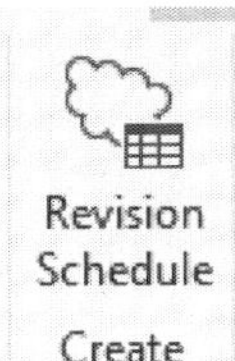 Go to the View ribbon.

Select **Revision Schedule**.

6. The Scheduled fields should be:

- Revision Sequence

- Revision Number

- Revision Description

- Revision Date

*Do **NOT** remove the Revision Sequence field. This is a hidden field.*

7. Select the Formatting tab.

Change the Revision Number Heading to **Rev**.

Change the Alignment to **Center**.

8. 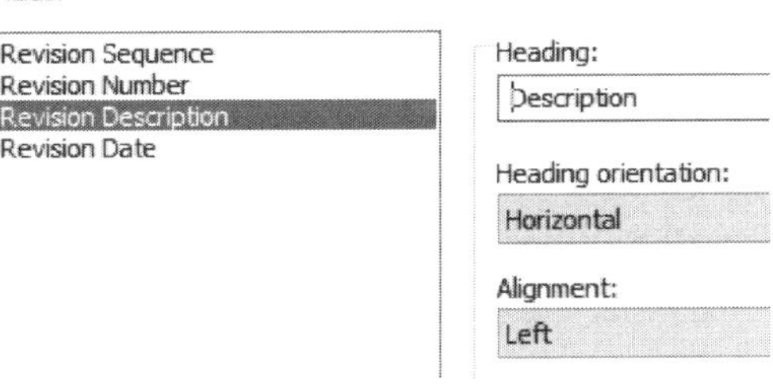 Change the Revision Description Heading to **Description**.

9. 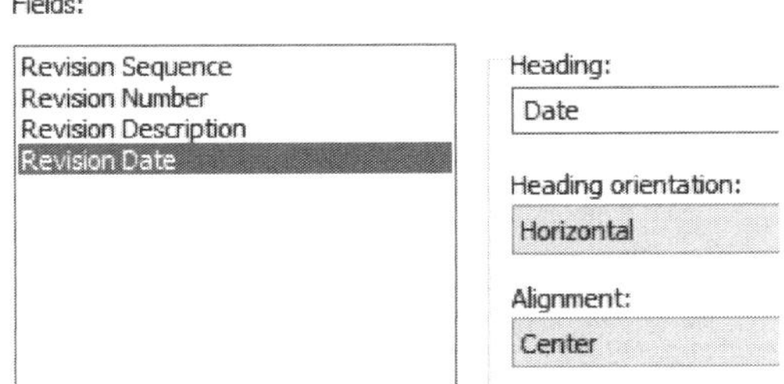 Change the Revision Date Heading to **Date**.

Change the Alignment to **Center**.

10. 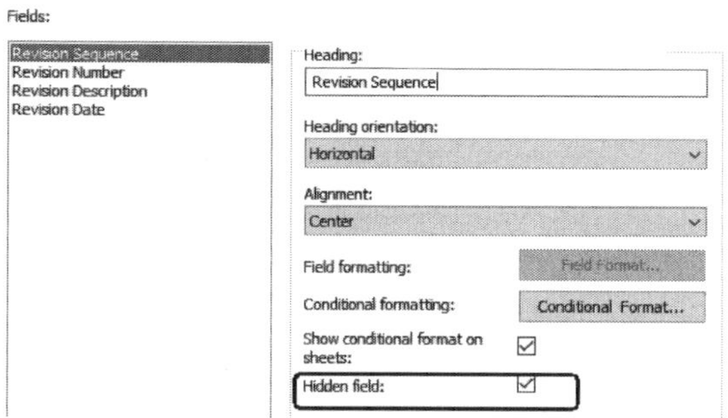 Highlight **Revision Sequence.**

Note that **Hidden Field** is enabled.

11. 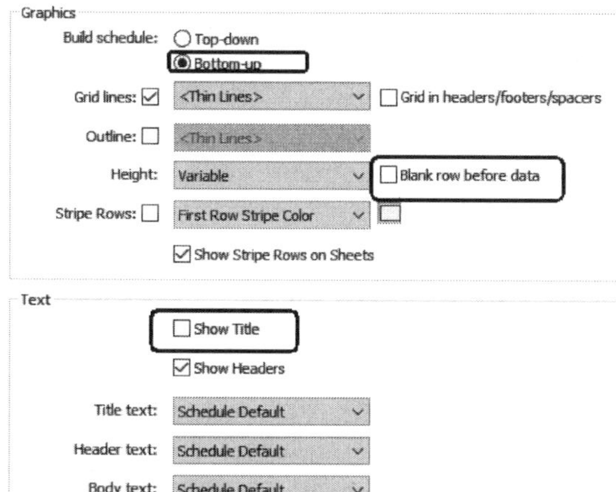 Activate the Appearance tab.

Enable **Bottom-Up**.

Disable **Blank row before data**.

Disable **Show Title**.

Click **OK.**

12. 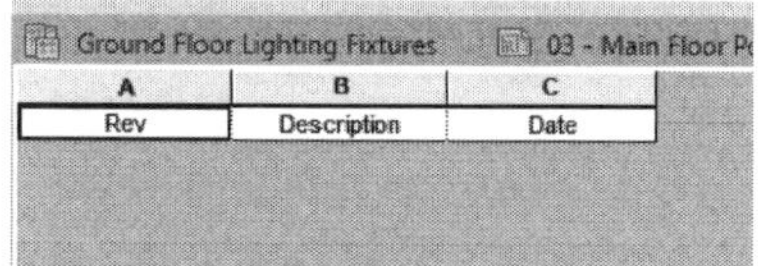 *The Schedule view opens.*

Return to the titleblock window.

13. 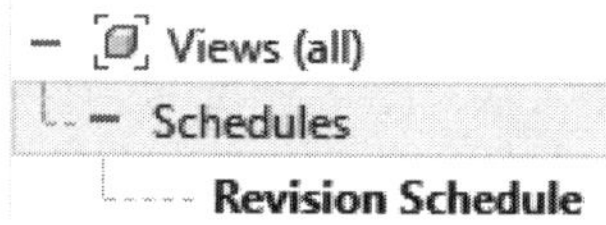 *The Revision Schedule is now listed in the browser.*

Drag and drop it into the correct location on the sheet above the firm name and address.

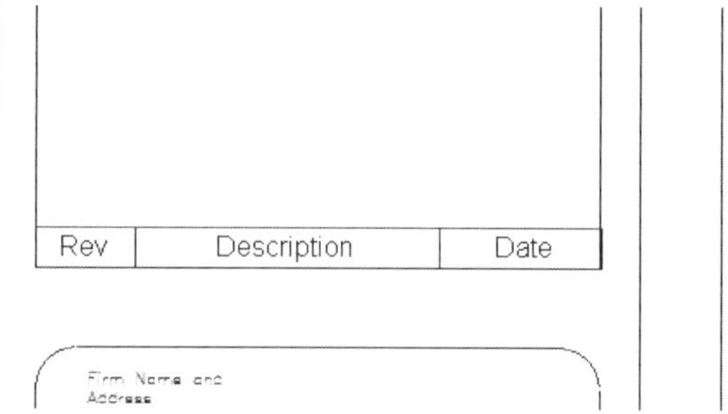

14. 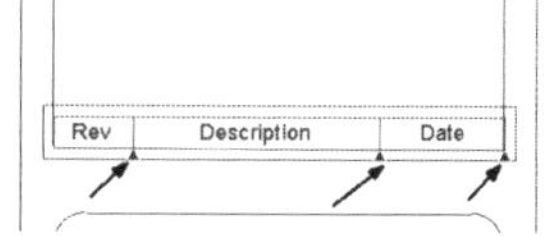 Adjust the column width of the schedule using the grips so it fits properly in the title block.

15. Save the file.

When prompted to replace the existing file, select **Yes**.

16. Select **Load into Project and Close** on the Family Editor panel on the ribbon.

17. If you have more than one project open:

Place a check next to *revision_schedule.rvt*.

Click **OK**.

18. Select **Overwrite the existing version** if this dialog appears.

You will only see this dialog if you have already loaded the new title block in the project.

19. Save as *ex10-10.rvt*.

Exercise 10-11:

Add Revisions in a Title Block

Drawing Name: *revisions_2.rvt*
Estimated Time to Completion: 30 Minutes
This exercise reinforces the following skills:

- Add revision clouds to a view.
- Tag revision clouds.

1. Open the **01-Main Floor Lighting** sheet.

2. Zoom into **Corridor 211**.

3. Activate the **Annotate** ribbon.

   Select **Revision Cloud** from the Detail panel.

4. 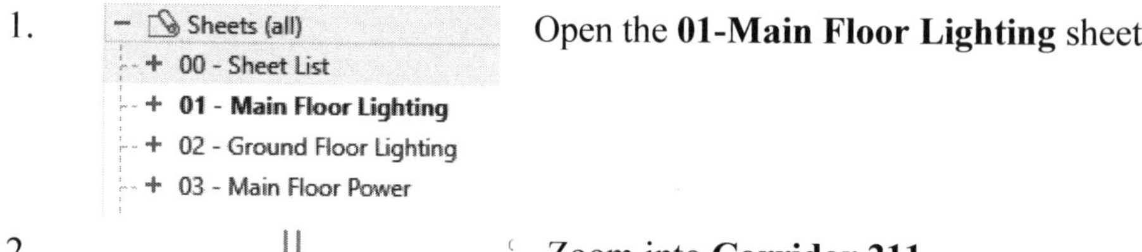
   On the Properties pane:

   Select the Revision that is tied to the revision cloud – **Seq 2 – Change Sconce.**

   Type **2** in the Mark field.

   Under Comments: Enter **Check with buyer on schedule**.

5. 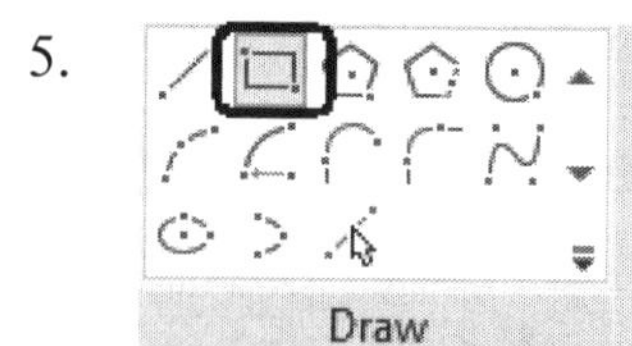
   You can use any of the available Draw tools to create your revision cloud.

   Select the **Rectangle** tool.

6. Draw the Revision Cloud on the sconce indicated.

Note that a cloud is placed even though you selected the rectangle tool.

7. Select the **Green Check** on the Mode panel to **Finish Cloud**.

8. Open the **02-Ground Floor Lighting** sheet.

- Sheets (all)
  - + 00 - Sheet List
  - + 01 - Main Floor Lighting
  - **+ 02 - Ground Floor Lighting**

9. Zoom into **Corridor 102**.

10. Activate the **Annotate** ribbon.

Select **Revision Cloud**.

11. Select the Revision that is tied to the revision cloud – **Seq 1 – Change 106" Pendant Light…**

Type **1** in the Mark field.

Under Comments: Enter **Check with buyer on schedule.**

Identity Data	
Revision	Seq. 1 - Change 96" Pendant Light to M125_Recessed Flange Lighting
Revision Number	A1
Revision Date	08.06
Issued to	Joe
Issued by	Sam
Mark	1
Comments	Check with buyer on schedule.

12. 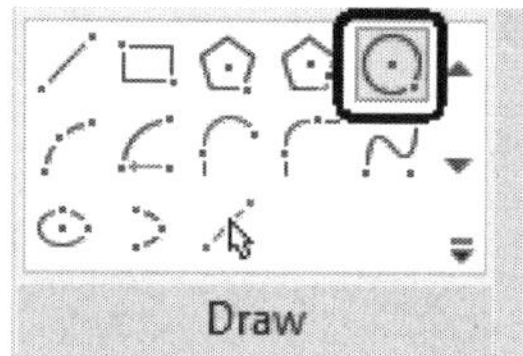 Select the **Circle** tool.

13. 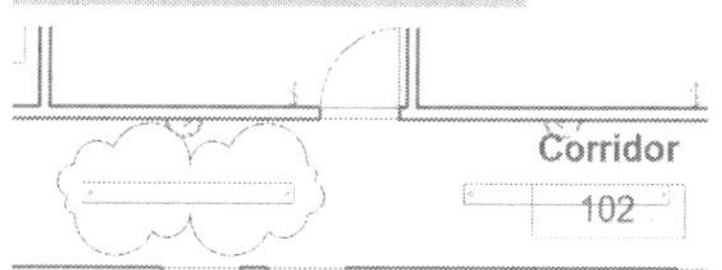 Draw the Revision Cloud on the lighting fixture to the left of the room tag.

    Note that a cloud is placed even though you selected the circle tool.

14.  Select the **Green Check** on the Mode panel to **Finish Cloud**.

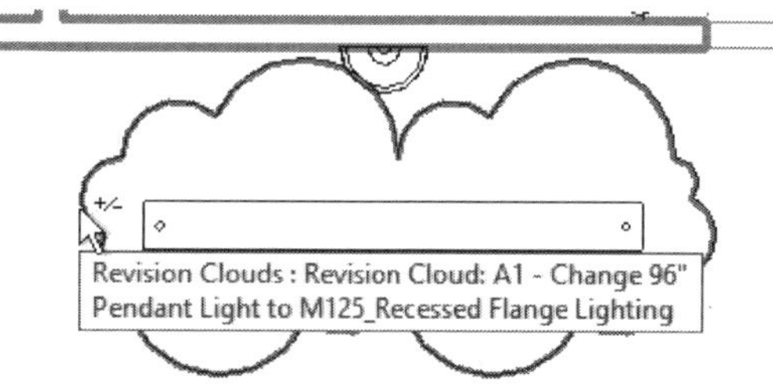

If you mouse over the revision cloud, you will see a tooltip to indicate what the revision is.

15.

No.	Description	Date
A1	Change 96" Pendant Light to M125_Recessed Flange Lighting	08.06

Zoom into the title block and note that the revision block has updated with the revision that is marked on the sheet.

16.

Rev	Description	Date
A2	Change Sconce Model to Sconce Light-Sphere	08.07

Open 01-Main Floor Lighting sheet.

Zoom into the title block and note that the revision block has updated with the revision that is marked on the sheet.

17. 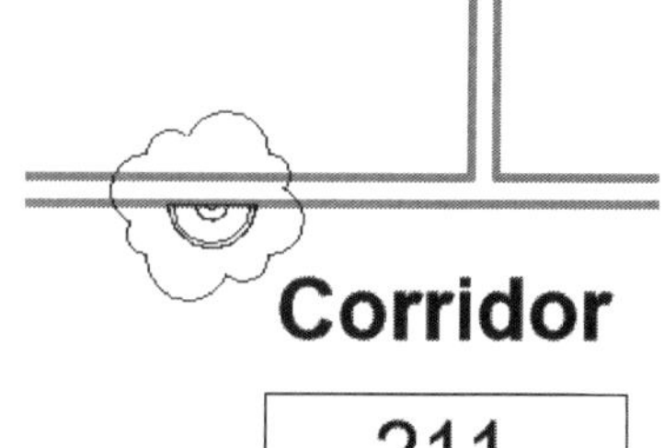 Zoom into **Corridor 211**.

18. 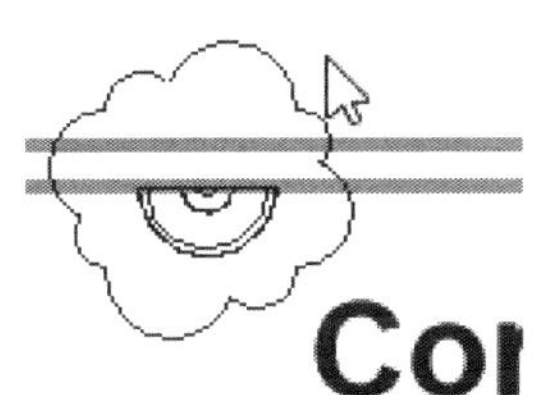 Select the **Tag by Category** tool from the Tag panel on the Annotate ribbon.

19. Left pick on the revision cloud to identify the category to be tagged.

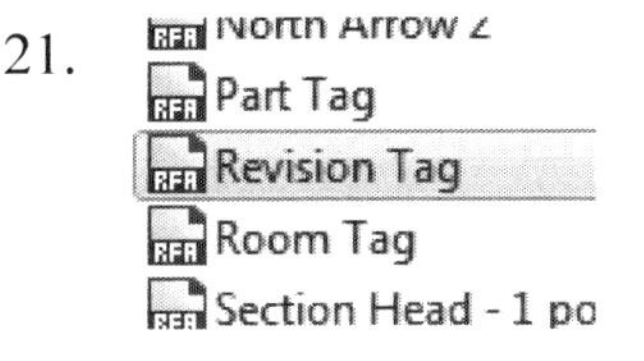

20. If you see this message:

There is no tag loaded for Revision Clouds. Do you want to load one now?

Click **Yes**.

21. 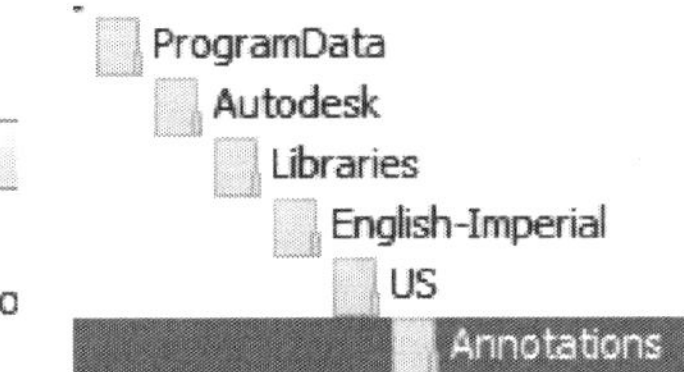

Select the *Annotations* folder.

Locate the **Revision Tag**.

Click **Open**.

22. Enable **Leader Line** on the ribbon.

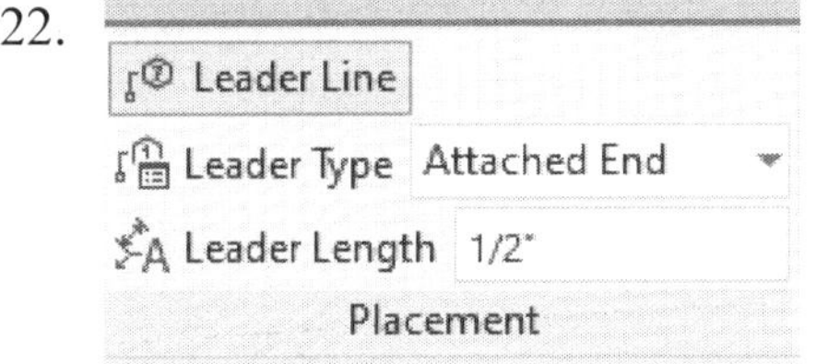

23. Select the revision cloud to add the tag.

The tag is placed.

Drag the cloud to a good location.

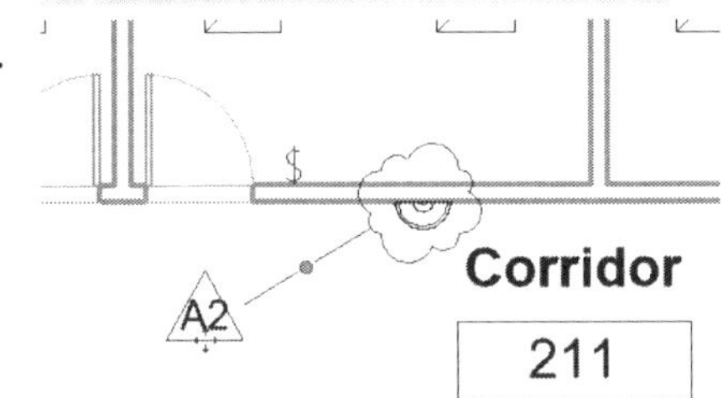

24. Repeat to add a tag to the other sheet.

Save as *ex10-11.rvt*.

Sheet Organization

Establish the organization of your drawing sheets in order to make sheet management consistent from project to project. Setting up sheet organization is similar to organizing the views in your Project Browser. You can set up the Browser – Sheets system family with different types to organize your sheets in the desired manner. To access the system family, right click on Sheets in the Project Browser and select Browser Organization.

Parameters can be applied to sheets, and those parameters can be used to filter and sort the sheets. The parameters can be included as project parameters in your template so that when a new sheet is created, the parameters are automatically added to the sheet. You can also use the parameters to organize your drawing views.

Exercise 10-12:

Defining Sheet Organization

Drawing Name: *sheet_organization.rvt*
Estimated Time: 20 minutes

This exercise reinforces the following skills:

- ❑ Project Browser
- ❑ Project Parameters

1.  Select the **Manage** ribbon.

   Select the **Project Parameters** tool.

2. Select **New Parameter**.

3. 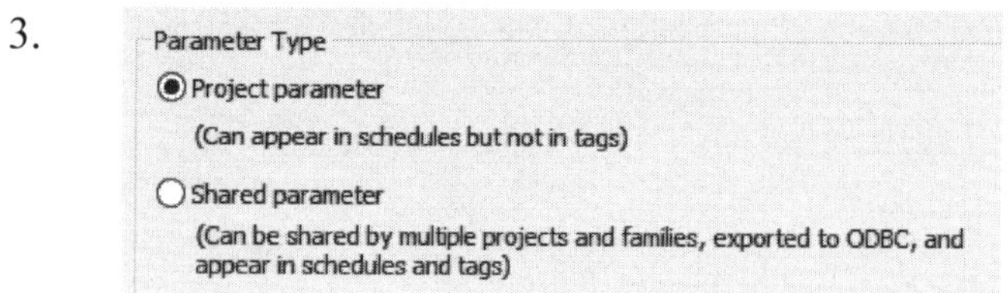 Enable **Project parameter**.

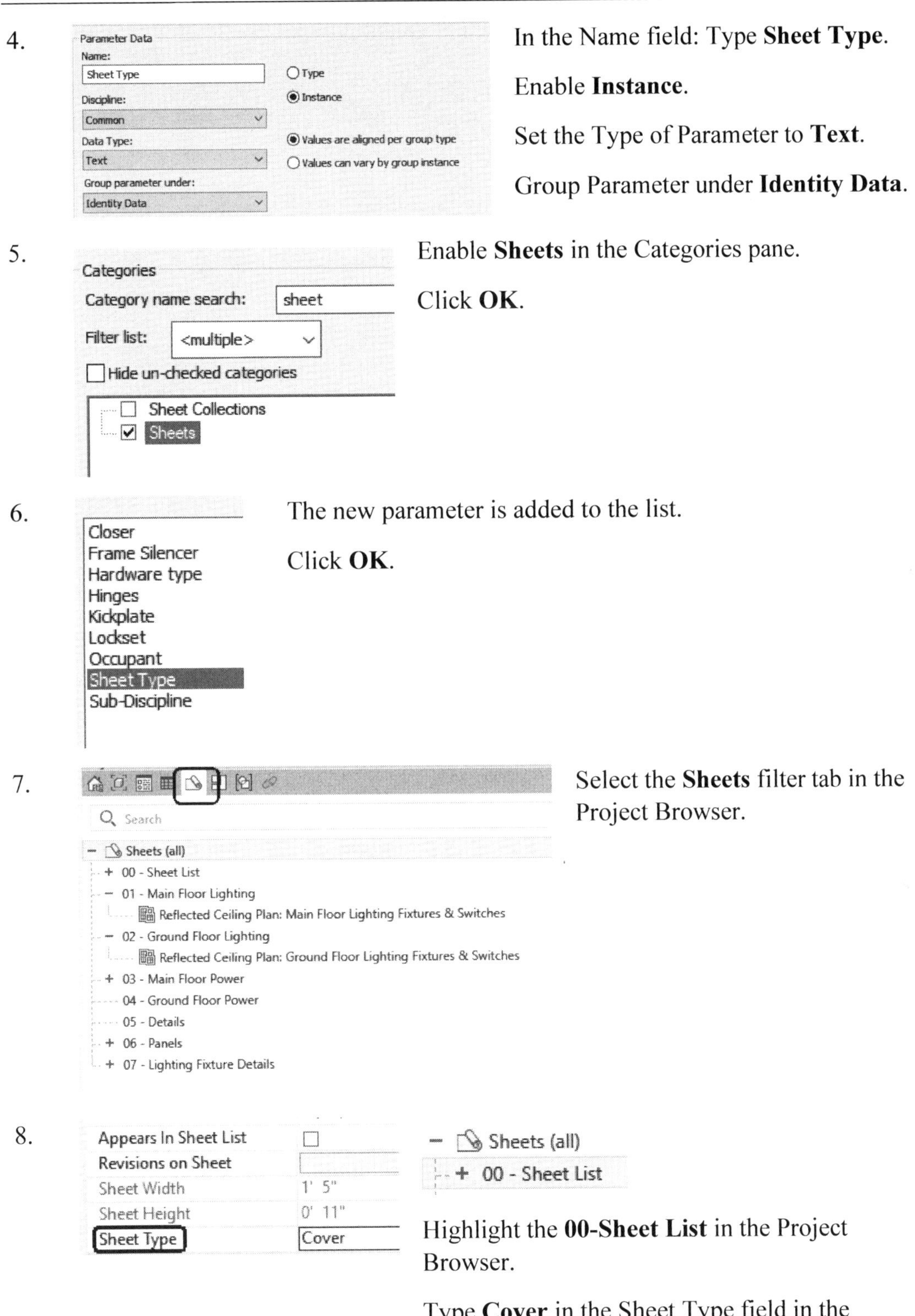

4. In the Name field: Type **Sheet Type**.

Enable **Instance**.

Set the Type of Parameter to **Text**.

Group Parameter under **Identity Data**.

5. Enable **Sheets** in the Categories pane.

Click **OK**.

6. The new parameter is added to the list.

Click **OK**.

7. Select the **Sheets** filter tab in the Project Browser.

8. Highlight the **00-Sheet List** in the Project Browser.

Type **Cover** in the Sheet Type field in the Properties palette.

9. 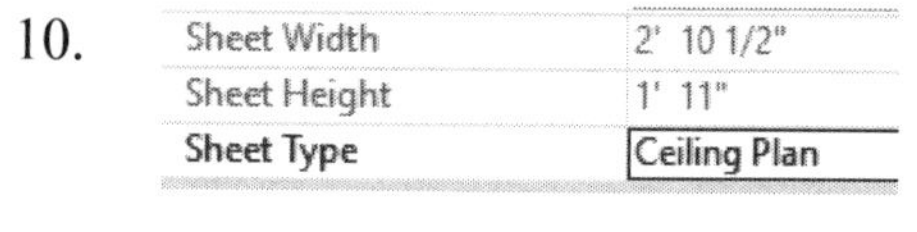

Highlight the **01-Main Floor Lighting** in the Project Browser.

Type **Ceiling Plan** in the Sheet Type field in the Properties palette.

10. 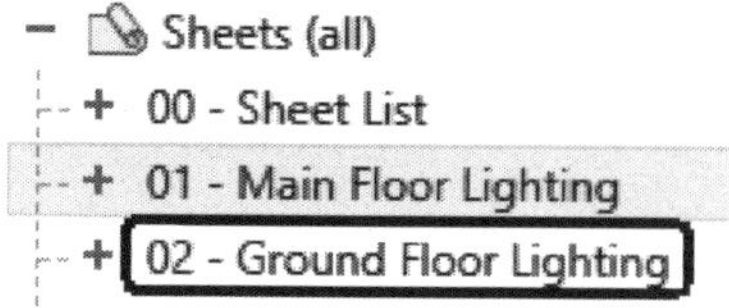

Highlight the **02-Ground Floor Lighting** in the Project Browser.

Select **Ceiling Plan** in the Sheet Type field in the Properties palette.

11. 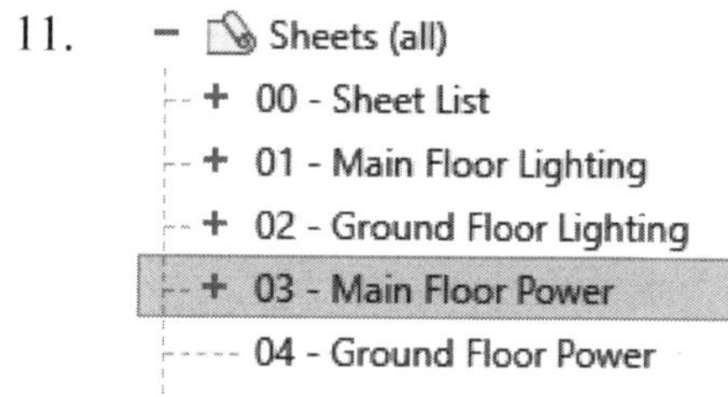

Highlight the **03-Main Floor Power** in the Project Browser.

Sheet Height	2' 6"
Sheet Type	Floor Plan

Type **Floor Plan** in the Sheet Type field in the Properties palette.

12.

Highlight the **04-Ground Floor Power** in the Project Browser.

Sheet Width	1' 10"
Sheet Height	1' 5"
Sheet Type	Floor Plan

Select **Floor Plan** in the Sheet Type field in the Properties palette.

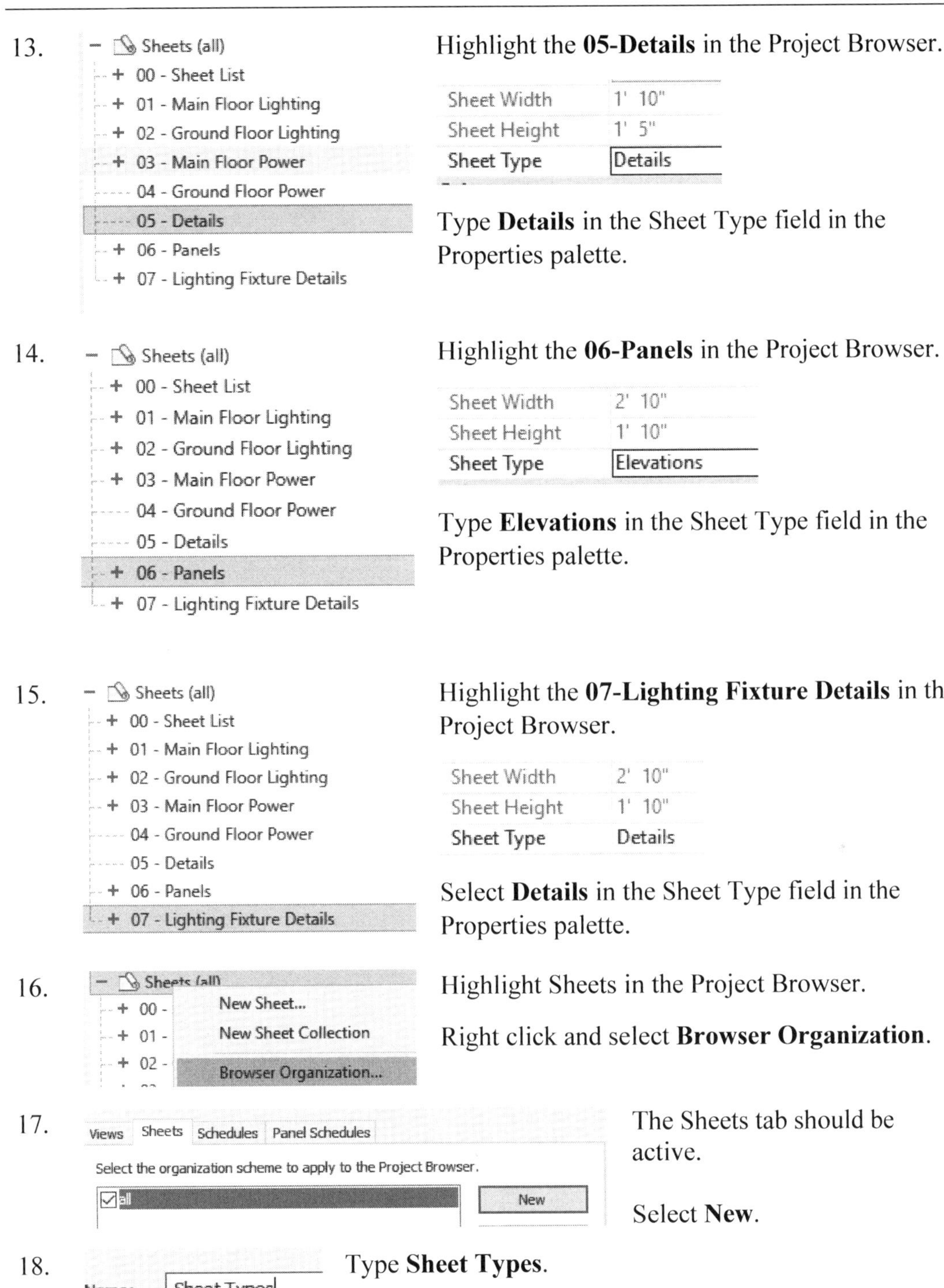

13. Highlight the **05-Details** in the Project Browser.

Type **Details** in the Sheet Type field in the Properties palette.

14. Highlight the **06-Panels** in the Project Browser.

Type **Elevations** in the Sheet Type field in the Properties palette.

15. Highlight the **07-Lighting Fixture Details** in the Project Browser.

Select **Details** in the Sheet Type field in the Properties palette.

16. Highlight Sheets in the Project Browser.

Right click and select **Browser Organization**.

17. The Sheets tab should be active.

Select **New**.

18. Type **Sheet Types**.

Click **OK**.

19. 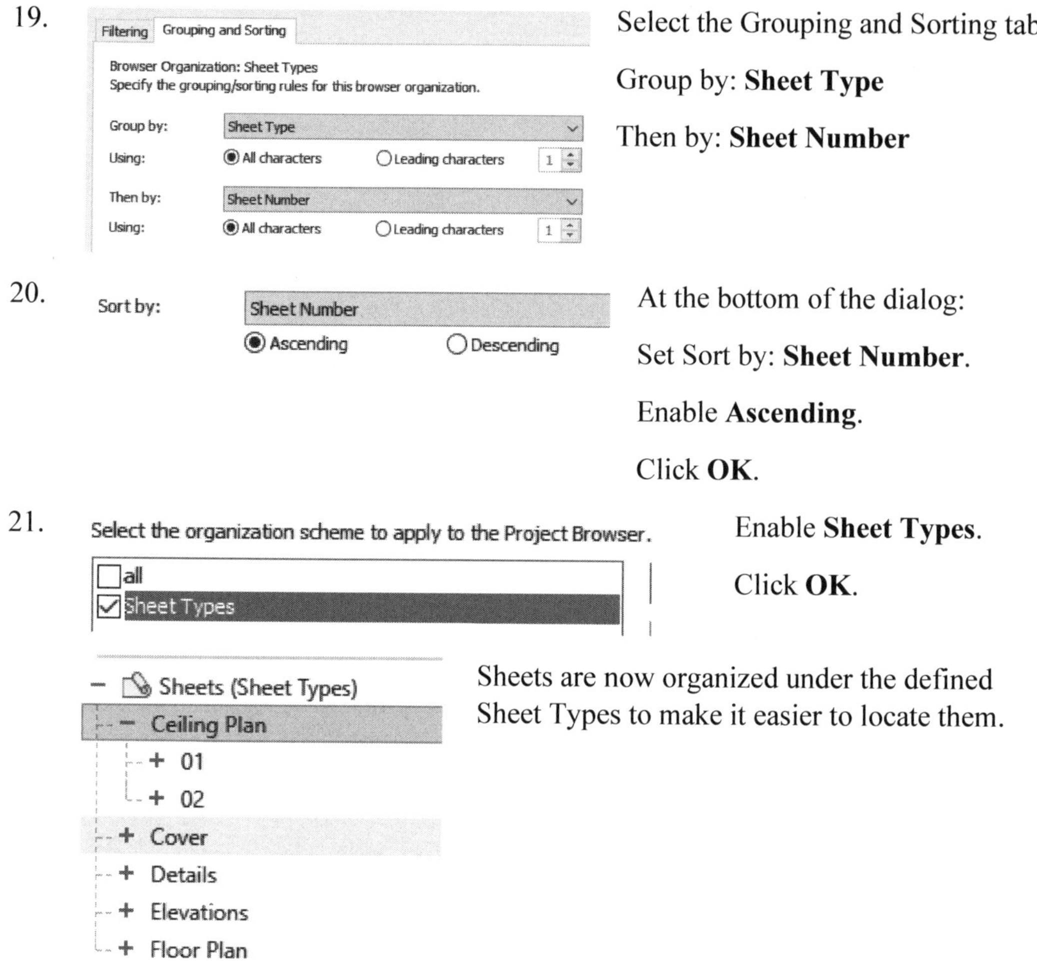   Select the Grouping and Sorting tab.

Group by: **Sheet Type**

Then by: **Sheet Number**

20.   At the bottom of the dialog:

Set Sort by: **Sheet Number**.

Enable **Ascending**.

Click **OK**.

21.   Enable **Sheet Types**.

Click **OK**.

Sheets are now organized under the defined Sheet Types to make it easier to locate them.

22. Save as *ex10-12.rvt*.

Sheet Collections

Sheet collections in electrical Revit projects are used to organize, manage, and publish all the electrical drawings (plans, diagrams, schedules, and details) in a systematic way, making documentation more efficient and consistent.

Sheet collections can be organized using different methodology.

Group Sheets by Discipline & Drawing Type

Most firms follow the National CAD Standard (NCS) or a similar convention. Electrical sheets usually start with **"E"** (e.g., E101, E201). Within that, you can break them down:

- **E100 Series – General / Legends / Notes**
    - E001: Electrical Symbols & Abbreviations
    - E002: General Electrical Notes
    - E003: Riser Diagrams / One-Line Diagrams
- **E200 Series – Lighting Plans**
    - E201: Lighting Plan – Level 1
    - E202: Lighting Plan – Level 2
    - E203: Exterior Lighting Plan
- **E300 Series – Power Plans**
    - E301: Power Plan – Level 1
    - E302: Power Plan – Level 2
    - E303: Equipment Power / Site Power
- **E400 Series – Special Systems (if applicable)**
    - E401: Fire Alarm Plan – Level 1
    - E402: Security / Data Layouts
- **E500 Series – Schedules**
    - E501: Panelboard Schedules
    - E502: Equipment Schedules
- **E600 Series – Details**
    - E601: Electrical Details (mounting, conduit, etc.)

You could also create collections into issue packages to be emailed or sent to other team members for review:

- **Permit Set** – All required sheets for permit submittal (might exclude details).
- **Bid Set** – All sheets needed for contractor pricing.
- **Construction Set (IFC)** – The full electrical package.
- **As-Builts / Record Set** – Final turnover documentation.

Best Practice Summary:
- Follow a logical numbering convention (E100s for general, E200s lighting, E300s power, etc.).
- Use Sheet Collections (Sets) to manage printing for different deliverables.
- Keep panel schedules & diagrams grouped separately so they don't get lost among plan sheets.
- Maintain a **Best Practice Summary:**
- Follow a logical numbering convention (E100s for general, E200s lighting, E300s power, etc.).
- Use Sheet Collections (Sets) to manage printing for different deliverables.
- Keep panel schedules & diagrams grouped separately so they don't get lost among plan sheets.
- Maintain a Sheet List Schedule for automatic indexing and coordination.

Exercise 10-13:

Sheet Collections

Drawing Name: *Elementary-School-Electrical.rvt*
Estimated Time: 10 minutes

This exercise reinforces the following skills:
- Collections
- Sheets
- Views Parameters
- Linked files
- Browser Organization

1. Open the Insert ribbon.

   Click **Manage Links**.

2. Use **Reload From** to locate and reload *Elementary-School-Architectural*. Close the dialog.

Name	Status
∨ **Revit** (1)	
Elementary-School-Architectural.rvt	✓

3. Go to the Project Browser.

   Activate the **Sheets** filter tab.

   The browser will display only sheets.

   Sheets (all)
   - + E201 - 01- Lighting Plan
   - + E202 - 02 Lighting Plan
   - + E203 - RCP - Level 1
   - + E204 - RCP - Level 2
   - + E301 - Power Plan - Level 1
   - + E302 - Power Plan - Level 2
   - + E303 - Electrical Room - First Floor
   - + E501 - Panel Schedule PP1
   - + E502 - Lighting Fixtures List - Level 1
   - + **E503 - Lighting Fixtures List - Level 2**

4. Right click on Sheets and select **Browser Organization.**

   Sheets
   - New Sheet...
   - New Sheet Collection
   - Browser Organization...

5. 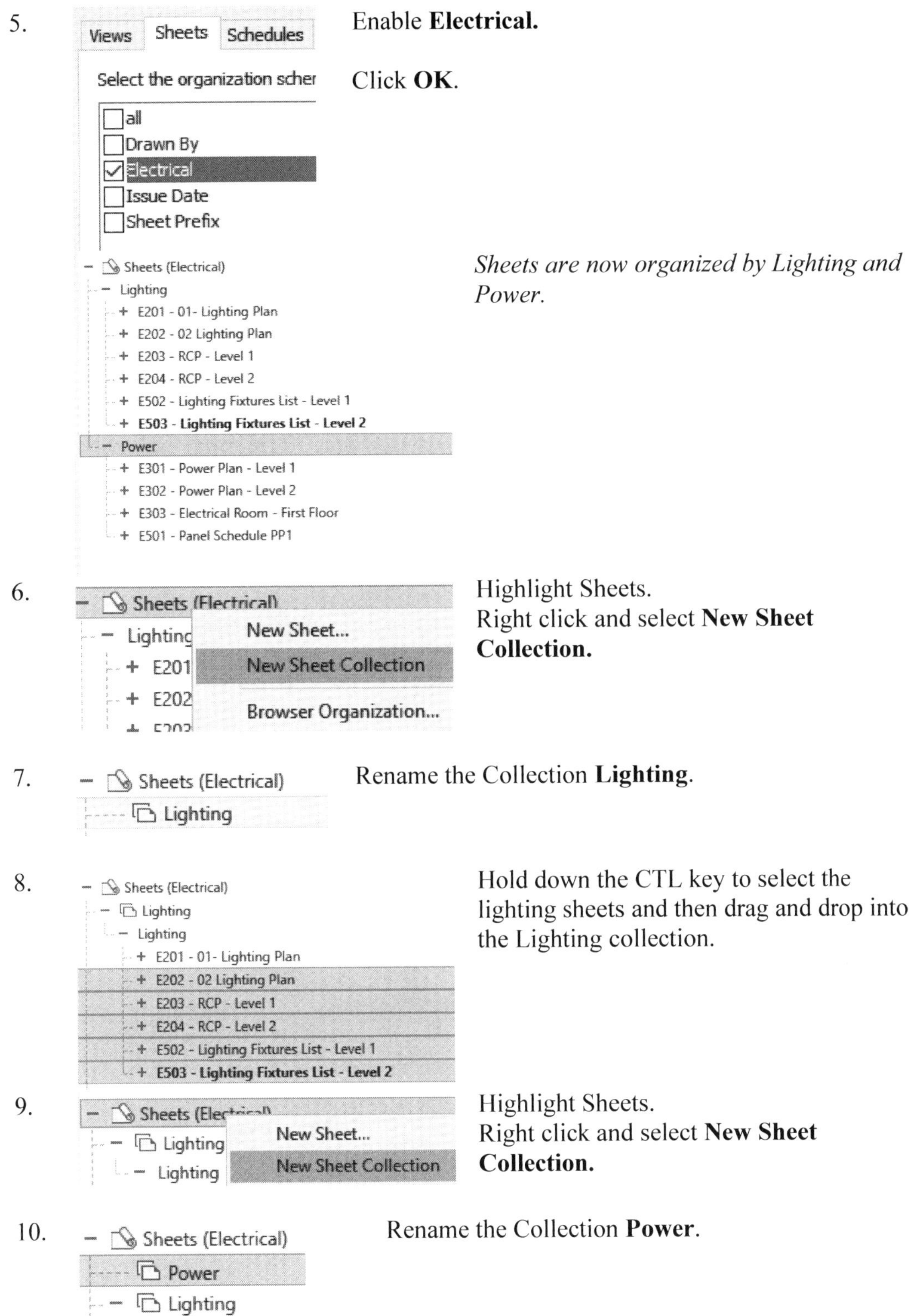

Enable **Electrical.**

Click **OK**.

Sheets are now organized by Lighting and Power.

6.

Highlight Sheets.
Right click and select **New Sheet Collection.**

7.

Rename the Collection **Lighting**.

8.

Hold down the CTL key to select the lighting sheets and then drag and drop into the Lighting collection.

9.

Highlight Sheets.
Right click and select **New Sheet Collection.**

10.

Rename the Collection **Power**.

11.

Hold down the CTL key to select the power sheets and then drag and drop into the Power collection.

You should have two sheet collections defined.

12.

Right click on **Sheets.**

Select **Browser Organization**.

13.

Enable **all.**

Click **OK.**

The two sheet collections are listed at the top of the sheets list.

Save as *ex10-13.rvt.*

Exercise 10-14:

Printing a Documentation Set to PDF

Drawing Name: *plotting.rvt*
Estimated Time: 30 minutes

This exercise reinforces the following skills:
- Plot
- Sheets
- Duplicate Views
- Schedules
- Sheet Collections

1. 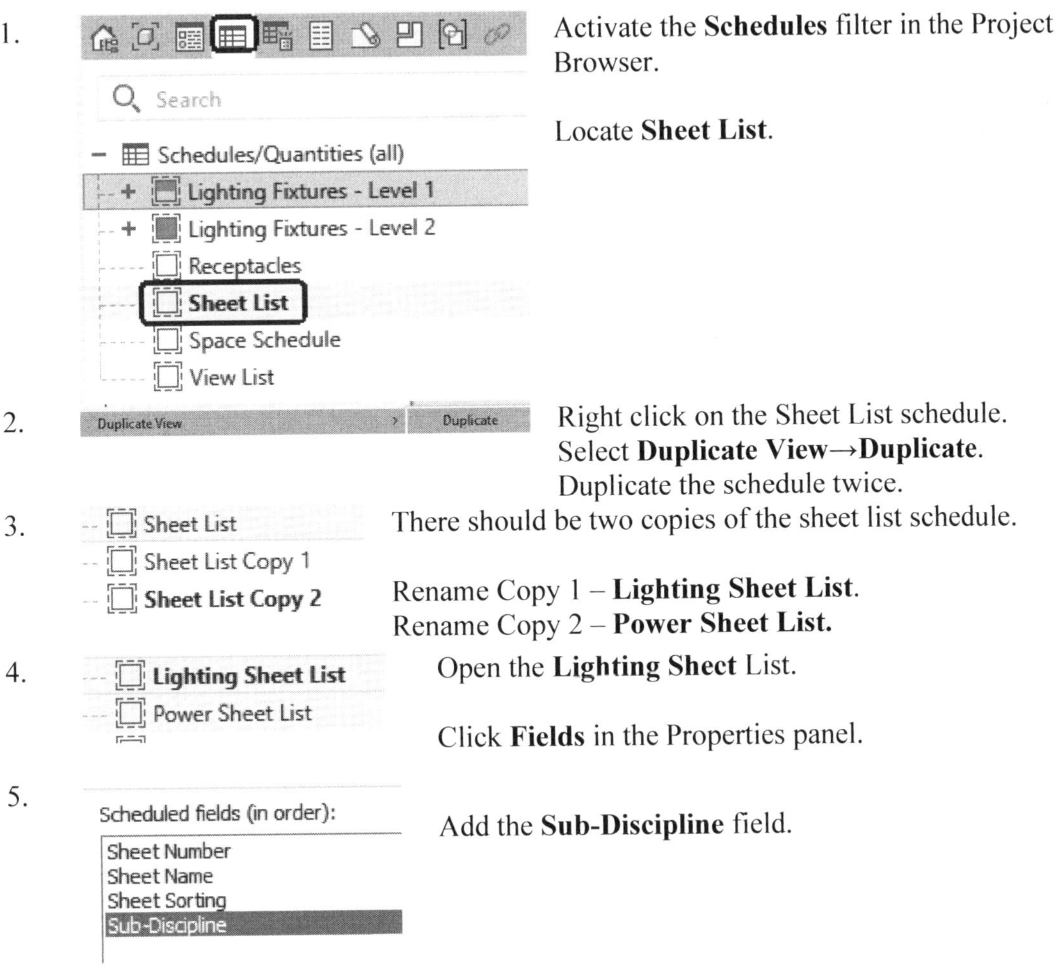 Activate the **Schedules** filter in the Project Browser.

    Locate **Sheet List**.

2. Right click on the Sheet List schedule.
   Select **Duplicate View→Duplicate**.
   Duplicate the schedule twice.

3. There should be two copies of the sheet list schedule.

    Rename Copy 1 – **Lighting Sheet List**.
    Rename Copy 2 – **Power Sheet List.**

4. Open the **Lighting Shect** List.

    Click **Fields** in the Properties panel.

5. Add the **Sub-Discipline** field.

6.

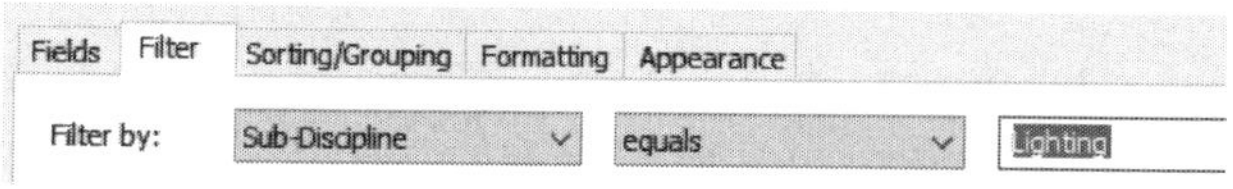

Select the Filter tab.

Filter by: **Sub-Discipline equals Lighting.**

7.

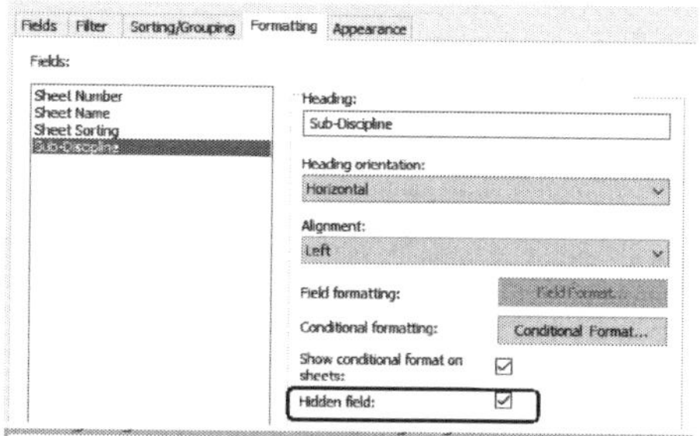

Select the Formatting tab.

Highlight **Sub-Discipline.**

Enable **Hidden Field.**

Click **OK.**

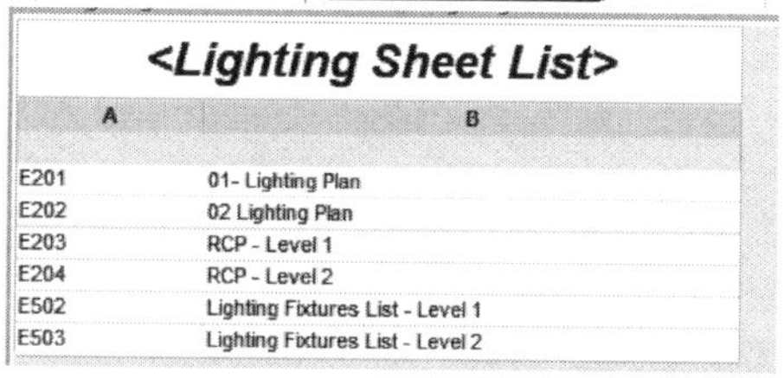

The schedule only lists the sheets used for lighting information.

8.

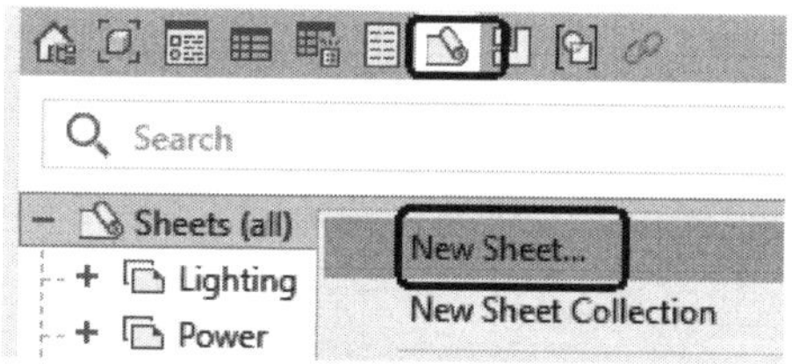

Activate the **Sheets** filter tab in the Project Browser.

Right click on **Sheets.**

Select **New Sheet.**

9.

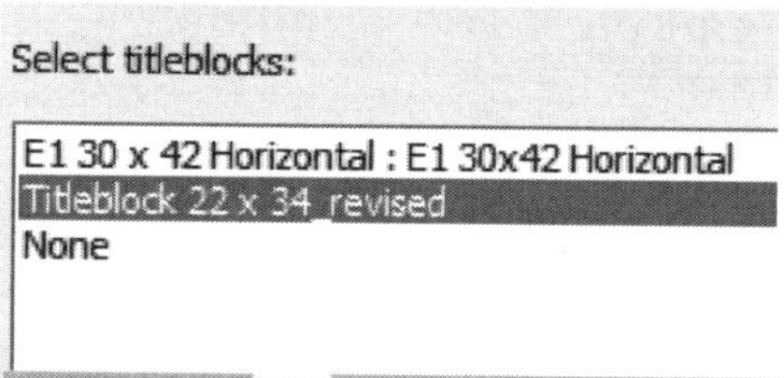

Select the **Titleblock 22x34_revised.**

Click **OK.**

10.

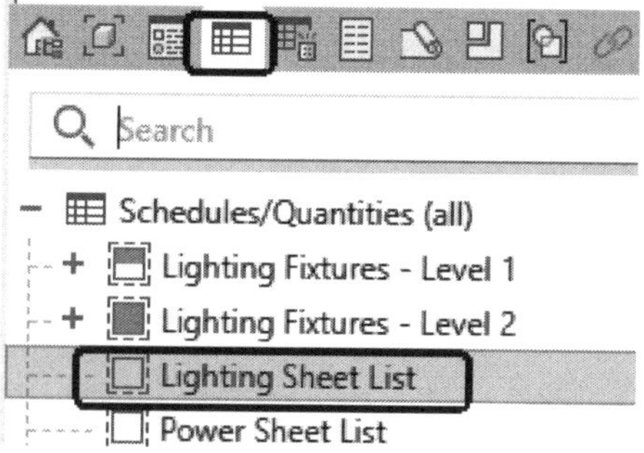

Activate the **Schedules** filter tab in the Project Browser.

Drag and drop the **Lighting Sheet List** onto the sheet.

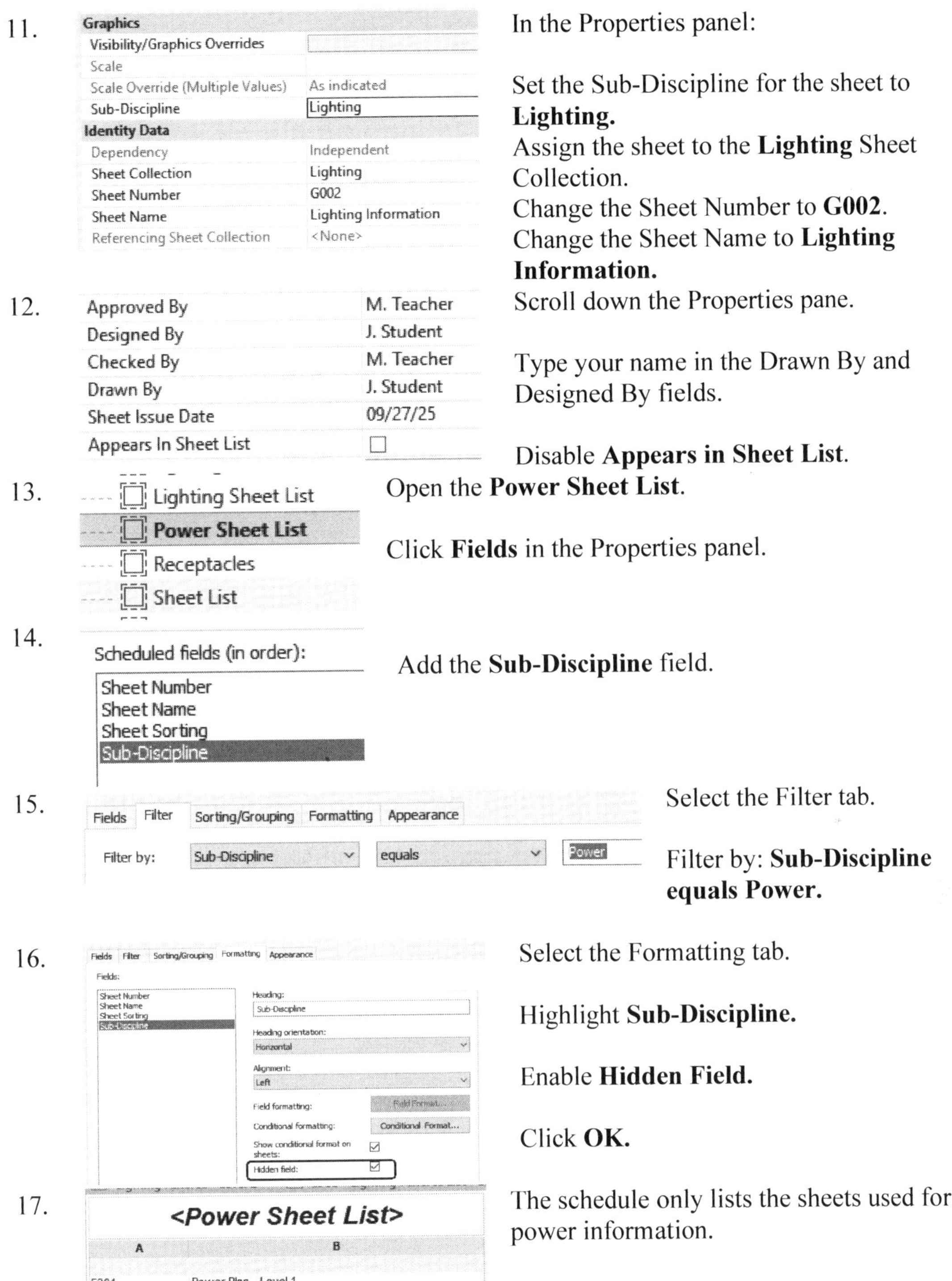

11. In the Properties panel:

Set the Sub-Discipline for the sheet to **Lighting.**
Assign the sheet to the **Lighting** Sheet Collection.
Change the Sheet Number to **G002**.
Change the Sheet Name to **Lighting Information.**

12. Scroll down the Properties pane.

Type your name in the Drawn By and Designed By fields.

Disable **Appears in Sheet List**.

13. Open the **Power Sheet List**.

Click **Fields** in the Properties panel.

14. Add the **Sub-Discipline** field.

15. Select the Filter tab.

Filter by: **Sub-Discipline equals Power.**

16. Select the Formatting tab.

Highlight **Sub-Discipline.**

Enable **Hidden Field.**

Click **OK.**

17. The schedule only lists the sheets used for power information.

18. 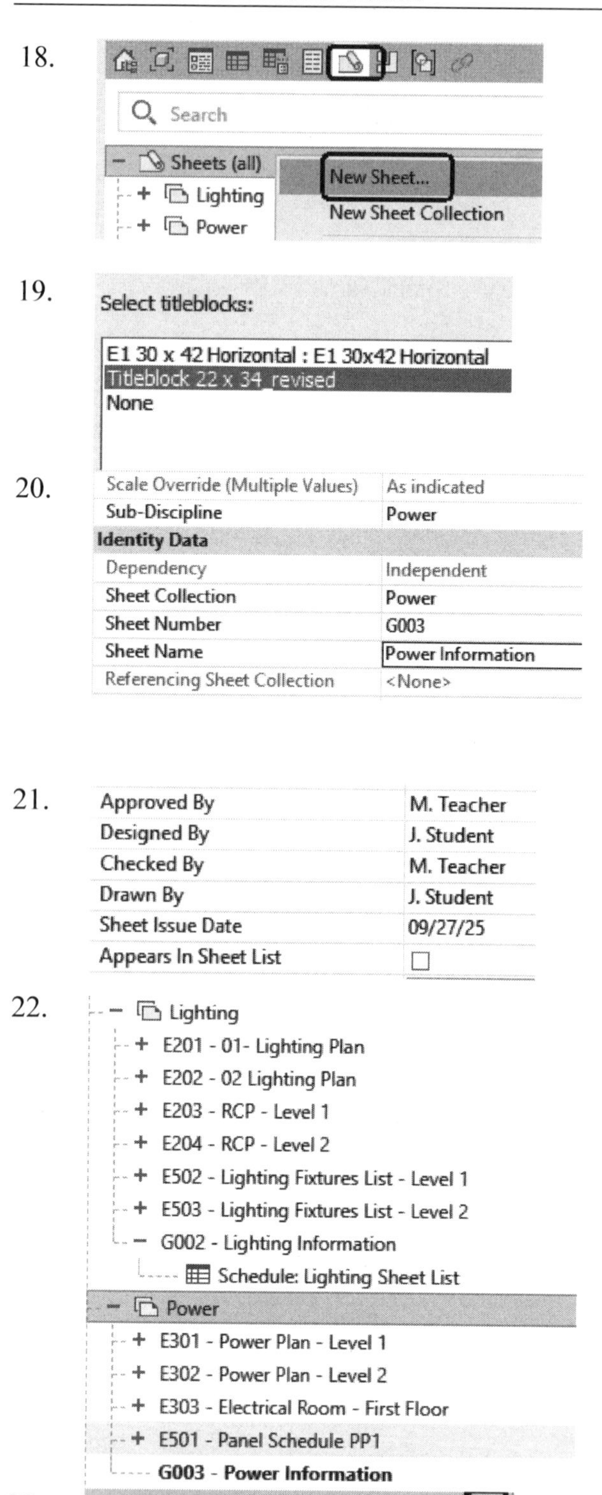

Activate the **Sheets** filter tab in the Project Browser.

Right click on **Sheets**.

Select **New Sheet**.

19. Select the **Titleblock 22x34_revised**.

Click **OK**.

20. In the Properties panel:

Set the Sub-Discipline for the sheet to **Power.**

Assign the sheet to the **Power** Sheet Collection.

Change the Sheet Number to **G003**.

Change the Sheet Name to **Power Information.**

21. Scroll down the Properties pane.

Type your name in the Drawn By and Designed By fields.

Disable **Appears in Sheet List**.

22. Expand the Sheet Collections in the Project Browser.

You see the sheet lists have been added to the collections.

23. Click the **Print to PDF** tool on the Quick Access Toolbar.

24.

Under Print Range:

Enable **Selected Views/Sheets**.

Click **Edit**.

25.

Enable **Sheets: Lighting** to select all the sheets listed in the Lighting Sheet Collection.

26.

Place a check next to all the sheets so they are included.

27.

Click the **Edit print order** button located at the bottom of the dialog.

28.

Drag and drop the sheet list so it is the first sheet to be printed.

Click **OK**.

29.

You can preview each sheet prior to printing to verify the sheets look correct.

Click **Select.**

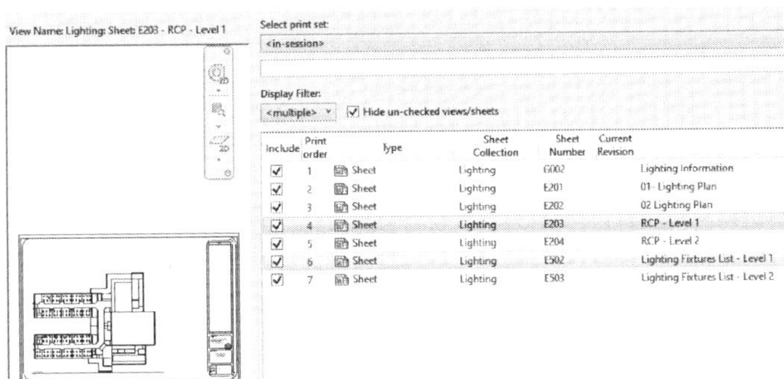

30.

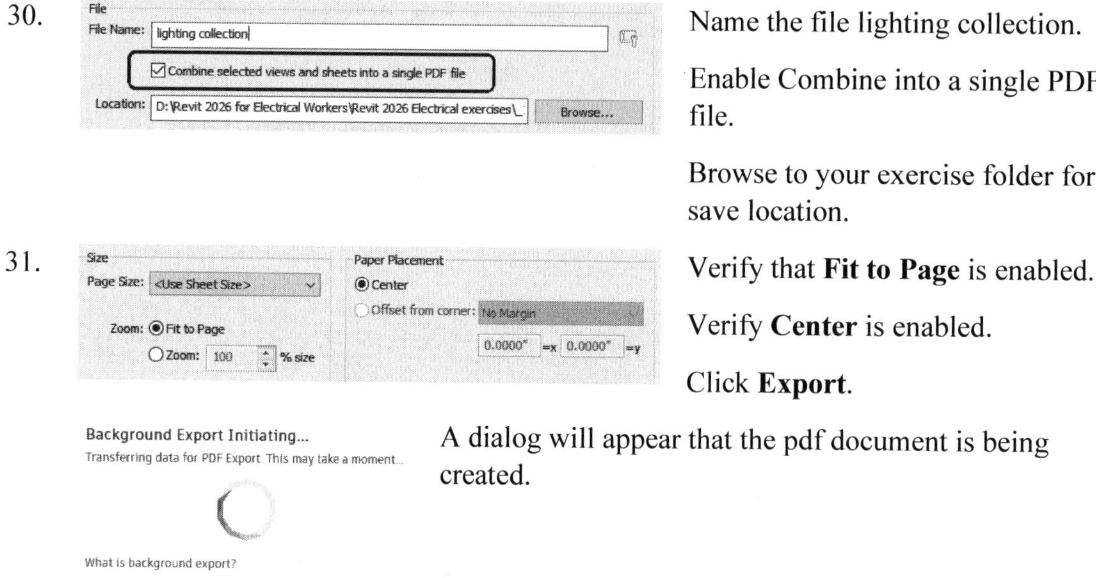

Name the file lighting collection.

Enable Combine into a single PDF file.

Browse to your exercise folder for the save location.

31. Verify that **Fit to Page** is enabled.

Verify **Center** is enabled.

Click **Export**.

A dialog will appear that the pdf document is being created.

32. Browse to the folder where the file is saved to review.

Close the project file without saving.

Lab Exercises

Open plotting.rvt.

Inspect the sheets, add missing views as needed, clean up the documentation by adding tags, dimensions, and assigning view templates.

About the Author

Elise Moss has worked for the past thirty years as a mechanical designer in Silicon Valley, primarily creating sheet metal designs. She has written articles for Autodesk's Toplines magazine, AUGI's PaperSpace, DigitalCAD.com, engineersrule.com, engineering.com, and Tenlinks.com. She is President of Moss Designs, creating custom applications and designs for corporate clients. She has taught CAD classes at Santa Clara University, Laney College, DeAnza College, Silicon Valley College, and for Autodesk resellers. Autodesk has named her as a Faculty of Distinction for the curriculum she has developed for Autodesk products, and she is a Certified Autodesk Instructor. She holds a baccalaureate degree in mechanical engineering from San Jose State.

She is married with two sons. Her older son, Benjamin, is an electrical engineer. Her middle son, Daniel, works with AutoCAD Architecture in the construction industry. Her husband, Ari, has a distinguished career in software development.

Elise is a third-generation engineer. Her father, Robert Moss, was a metallurgical engineer in the aerospace industry. Her grandfather, Solomon Kupperman, was a civil engineer for the City of Chicago.

She can be contacted via email at elise_moss@mossdesigns.com.

More information about the author and her work can be found on her website at www.mossdesigns.com.

Other books by Elise Moss

AutoCAD 2026 Fundamentals
Revit 2026 Basics
AutoCAD Architecture 2026 Fundamentals

Notes: